PHYSICAL ❖ SCIENCE

Fourth Edition

Leonard Bernstein ◆ Martin Schachter ◆ Alan Winkler ◆ Stanley Wolfe

Stanley Wolfe
Project Coordinator

About the Cover: Physical science is the study of both physics and chemistry. The roller coaster and the spaceship on the cover illustrate examples of these concepts. The roller coaster represents the study of forces and motion. The spaceship, as it is lifting off, represents the chemistry that goes into creating the right mix of fuels. These concepts are just a few of the many things you will be learning about in this book. What do you think are some other things that you will study in physical science?

Staff Credits: Amanda Aranowski, Doug Bauernschmidt, Melania Benzinger, Karen Blonigen, Sarah Brandel, Katie Colón, Barbara Drewlo, Daren Hastings, Helen Higgins, Mariann Johanneck, Becky Johnson, Mary Kaye Kuzma, Vivian Lemanowski, Charles Luey, Mary Lukkonen, Paul Ramos, Dan Ray, Marie Schaefle, Christopher Tures, Mike Vineski, Sue Will

ISBN-13: 978-0-7854-6767-0
ISBN-10:   0-7854-6767-X

1 2 3 4 5 6 7 8 9 10   12 11 10 09 08

1-800-321-3106
www.pearsonschool.com

Acknowledgments

Science Consultants

Jonathan Cohen
Science Teacher
Longfellow Arts and Technology
Magnet Middle School
Berkeley, California

Kenneth S. Fink
Liberty Science Center
Jersey City, New Jersey

Laboratory Consultants

Sean Devine
Science Teacher
Ridge High School
Basking Ridge, New Jersey

Vincent Dionisio
Science Teacher
Clifton High School
Clifton, New Jersey

Gregory Vogt, Ph.D.
Associate Professor, Civil Engineering
Colorado State University
Fort Collins, Colorado

Reading Consultant

Sharon Cook
Consultant
Leadership in Literacy

Internet Consultant

Janet M. Gaudino
Seventh Grade Science Teacher
Montgomery Middle School
Skillman, New Jersey

ESL/ELL Consultant

Elizabeth Jimenez
Consultant
Pomona, California

Content Reviewers

Dr. Vincent Adamo, M.D. (pp. 200, 201)
Parsippany, New Jersey

Ron Asteak (pp. 216, 217)
Bike King Manager
Clinton, New Jersey

Sharon Danielsen (pp. 352, 353)
Site Manager
Darrin Fresh Water Institute
Rensselaer Polytechnic Institute
Troy, New York

Scott Denny (pp. 138,139)
Food Service Manager
Denville, New Jersey

Ivan Dmochowski (Chs. 7–9)
Helen Hay Whitney Postdoctoral Scholar
California Institute of Technology
Pasadena, California

T. Ferbel (Ch. 20)
Professor of Physics
University of Rochester
Rochester, New York

Ernest Freund (Chs. 17–19)
Lecturer
University of California at Santa Barbara
Santa Barbara, California

Paul Heiney (Chs. 9, 12, and 13)
Professor of Physics
University of Pennsylvania
Philadelphia, Pennsylvania

Samuel P. Kounaves (Chs. 4–6)
Professor of Chemistry
Tufts University
Medford, Massachusetts

Dr. Charles Liu (pp. 236, 237, 250, 251)
Astrophysicist
Department of Astrophysics and Hayden
Planetarium
American Museum of Natural History
New York, New York

John Margrave (Chs. 10 and 11)
Department of Chemistry
Rice University
Houston, Texas

Terry Moran (pp. 46, 47, 324, 325)
Moran Research Service
Harvard, Massachusetts

George F. Palladino (Chs. 1 and 2)
Director, Master of Chemistry Education
Department of Chemistry
University of Pennsylvania
Philadelphia, Pennsylvania

Thomas Rauchfuss (Ch. 3)
School of Chemical Sciences
University of Illinois
Urbana, Illinois

Dr. Dirk Schulze-Makuch (pp. 24, 25, 98, 99)
Department of Geological Sciences
University of Texas at El Paso
El Paso, Texas

Dr. Raymond C. Turner (Chs. 14, 15, and 21)
Alumni Distinguished Professor Emeritus of Physics
Department of Physics and Astronomy
Clemson University
Clemson, South Carolina

Todd Woerner (Ch. 16 and pp. 66, 67, 162, 163, 184, 185, 278, 279,
298, 299)
Department of Chemistry
Duke University
Durham, North Carolina

Teacher Reviewers

Leonard GeRue
Hanshaw Middle School
Modesto, California

Charles Sehulster
Science Teacher
Horace Greeley High School
Chappaqua, New York

Contents

Scientific Skills and Investigations Handbooks

UNIT 1   INTRODUCTION TO MATTER

UNIT *4*   EXPLORING THE PERIODIC TABLE

Appendices

Physical Science Features

Hands-On Activities

How Do They Know That?

Integrating the Sciences

Real-Life Science

People in Science

Science and Technology

INVESTIGATE

Web InfoSearch

What are scientific skills?

People are naturally curious. They want to understand the world around them. The field of science would probably not exist if it were not for human curiosity about the natural world.

People also want to be able to make good guesses about the future. They want to know how to use alternative forms of energy. They want to improve technology and communications.

Scientists use many skills to explore the world and gather information about it. These skills are called science process skills. Another name for them is science inquiry skills.

Science process skills allow you to think like a scientist. They help you identify problems and answer questions. Sometimes they help you solve problems. More often, they provide some possible answers and lead to more questions. In this book, you will use a variety of science process skills to understand the facts and theories in physical science.

Science process skills are not only used in science. You compare prices when you shop and you observe what happens to foods when you cook them. You predict what the weather will be by looking at the sky. In fact, science process skills are really everyday life skills that have been adapted for problem solving in science.

▲ **Figure 1** Scientists use science process skills to understand what makes a nuclear power plant run safely, how robots work in spaces too small for humans, and why communications are better using fiber optics.

1 **NAME:** What is the name for the skills scientists use to solve problems?

Contents

1 Observing and Comparing
2 Classifying Data
3 Modeling and Simulating
4 Measuring
5 Analyzing Data and Communicating Results
6 Making Predictions

1 Observing and Comparing

Making Observations An important part of solving any problem is observing, or using your senses to find out what is going on around you. The five senses are sight, hearing, touch, smell, and taste. When you look at the properties of an ore or watch an ice cube melt, you are observing. When you observe, you pay close attention to everything that happens around you.

Scientists observe the world in ways that other scientists can repeat. This is a goal of scientific observation. It is expected that when a scientist has made an observation, other people will be able to make the same observation.

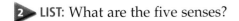 **LIST:** What are the five senses?

Comparing and Contrasting Part of observing is comparing and contrasting. When you compare data, you observe the characteristics of several things or events to see how they are alike. When you contrast data, you look for ways that similar things are different from one another.

▲ **Figure 2** Silver and aluminum are alike in many ways. They also have many differences.

▶ **COMPARE/CONTRAST:** How are a bar of aluminum and a bar of silver alike? How are they different?

Using Tools to Observe Sometimes an object is too small or too distant to see with your eyes alone. Often, special tools are needed for making observations. Sometimes scientists use tools to make observations of things like radio waves or X rays that are outside the range of our senses. Telescopes, spectrometers, microscopes, and magnifying glasses are all examples of tools that help with scientific observations.

▲ **Figure 3** Examining a slide with a magnifying glass

 INFER: What are some things that scientists might need a microscope to see?

Hands-On Activity
MAKING OBSERVATIONS

You and a partner will need 2 shoeboxes with lids, 2 rubber bands, and several small objects.

1. Place several small objects into the shoebox. Do not let your partner see what you put into the shoebox.
2. Cover the shoebox with the lid. Put a rubber band around the shoebox to keep the lid on.
3. Exchange shoeboxes with your partner.
4. Gently shake, turn, and rattle the shoebox.
5. Try to describe what is in the shoebox without opening it. Write your descriptions on a sheet of paper.

Practicing Your Skills

6. **IDENTIFY:** What science process skill did you use?
7. **IDENTIFY:** Which of your senses was most important to you?
8. **ANALYZE:** Direct observation is seeing something with your eyes or hearing it with your ears. Indirect observation involves using a model or past experience to make a guess about something. Which kind of observation did you use?

2 Classifying Data

Key Term

data: information you collect when you observe something

Collecting and Classifying Data The information you collect when you observe something is called **data.** The data from an experiment or from observations you have made are first recorded, or written down. Then, they are classified.

When you classify data, you group things together based on how they are alike. This information often comes from making comparisons as you observe. You may classify by size, shape, color, use, or any other important feature. Classifying data helps you recognize and understand the relationships between things. Classification makes studying large groups of things easier. For example, physical scientists use classification to organize different types of elements.

5▶ EXPLAIN: How can you classify data?

Hands-On Activity

ORGANIZING LIQUIDS

You will need 10 to 15 jars or bottles filled with a variety of liquids.

1. Carefully examine the liquids in the containers. Observe their color, thickness, and composition. Notice what happens when you gently shake the bottle. What happens when you let the liquid settle?
2. Make a system for classifying the liquids.
3. Categorize all the liquids.
4. Write a description of how you would use your classification system to classify a new liquid that you have never seen before.

Practicing Your Skills

5. ANALYZE: How did you classify the liquids?
6. EXPLAIN: Why is a classification system useful?

3 Modeling and Simulating

Key Terms

model: tool scientists use to represent an object or process

simulation: computer model that usually shows a process

Modeling Sometimes things are too small to see with your eyes alone. Other times, an object is too large to see. You may need a model to help you examine the object. A **model** is a good way to show what a very small or a very large object looks like. A model can have more details than what may be seen with just your eyes. It can be used to represent a process or an object that is hard to explain with words. A model can be a three-dimensional picture, a drawing, a computer image, or a diagram.

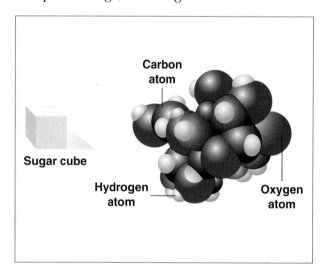

▲ **Figure 4** Some schools have molecule-building kits. Each atom is color-coded according to the element it represents.

6▶ DEFINE: What is a model?

Simulating A **simulation** is a kind of model that shows a process. It is often done using a computer. You can use a simulation to predict the outcome of an experiment. Scientists use simulations to study everything from chemical reactions to the global climate.

7▶ DEFINE: What is a simulation?

4 Measuring

Key Terms

unit: amount used to measure something

meter: basic unit of length or distance

mass: amount of matter in something

gram: basic unit of mass

volume: amount of space an object takes up

liter: basic unit of liquid volume

meniscus: curve at the surface of a liquid in a thin tube

temperature: measure of the amount of heat energy something contains

Two Systems of Measurement When you measure, you compare an unknown value with a known value using standard units. A **unit** is an amount used to measure something. The metric system is an international system of measurement. Examples of metric units are the gram, the kilometer, and the liter. In the United States, the English system and the metric system are both used. Examples of units in the English system are the pound, the foot, and the gallon.

There is also a more modern form of the metric system called SI. The letters *SI* stand for the French words *Système International*. Many of the units in the SI are the same as those in the metric system.

The metric and SI systems are both based on units of ten. This makes them easy to use. Each unit in these systems is ten times greater than the unit before it. To show a change in the size of a unit, you add a prefix to the unit. The prefix tells you whether the unit is larger or smaller. For example, a centimeter is ten times bigger than a millimeter.

PREFIXES AND THEIR MEANINGS	
kilo-	one thousand (1,000)
hecto-	one hundred (100)
deca-	ten (10)
deci-	one-tenth (1/10)
centi-	one-hundredth (1/100)
milli-	one-thousandth (1/1,000)

◄ Figure 5

8▶ IDENTIFY: What are two measurement systems?

Units of Length Length is the distance from one point to another. In the metric system, the basic unit of length or distance is the **meter.** A meter is about the length from a doorknob to the floor. Longer distances, such as the distances between cities, are measured in kilometers. A kilometer is 1,000 meters. Centimeters and millimeters measure shorter distances. A centimeter is 1/100 of a meter. A millimeter is 1/1,000 of a meter. Figure 6 compares common units of length. It also shows the abbreviation for each unit.

SI/METRIC UNITS OF LENGTH	
1,000 millimeters (mm)	1 meter (m)
100 centimeters (cm)	1 meter
10 decimeters (dm)	1 meter
10 millimeters	1 centimeter
1,000 meters	1 kilometer (km)

▲ Figure 6

Length can be measured with a meter stick. A meter stick is 1m long and is divided into 100 equal lengths by numbered lines. The distance between each of these lines is equal to 1 cm. Each centimeter is divided into ten equal parts. Each one of these parts is equal to 1 mm.

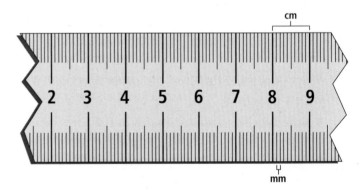
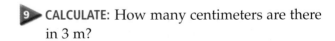

▲ Figure 7 A meter stick is divided into centimeters and millimeters.

9▶ CALCULATE: How many centimeters are there in 3 m?

4

Measuring Area Do you know how people find the area of the floor of a room? They measure the length and the width of the room. Then, they multiply the two numbers. You can find the area of any rectangle by multiplying its length by its width. Area is expressed in square units, such as square meters (m^2) or square centimeters (cm^2).

Area = length × width

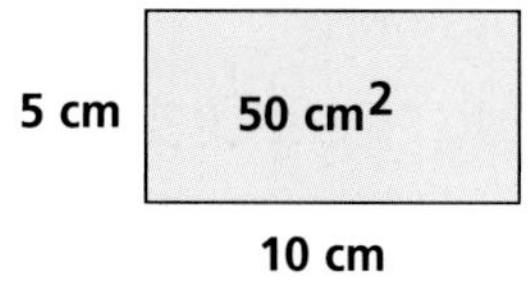

5 cm | 50 cm^2

10 cm

◀ **Figure 8** The area of a rectangle equals length times width.

10▶ CALCULATE: What is the area of a rectangle 12 cm by 6 cm?

Mass and Weight The amount of matter in something is its **mass.** The basic metric unit of mass is called a **gram (g).** A paper clip has about 1 g of mass. Mass is measured with an instrument called a balance. A balance works like a seesaw. It compares an unknown mass with a known mass.

One kind of balance that is commonly used to measure mass is a triple-beam balance. A triple-beam balance has a pan. The object being measured is placed on the pan. The balance also has three beams. Weights, called riders, are moved along each beam until the object on the pan is balanced. Each rider gives a reading in grams. The mass of the object is equal to the total readings of all three riders.

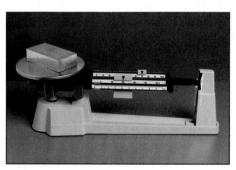

◀ **Figure 9** A triple-beam balance

Mass and *weight* are related; however, they are not the same. The weight of an object is a measure of Earth's pull of gravity between Earth and that object. Gravity is the force that pulls objects toward the center of Earth. The strength of the pull of gravity between two objects depends on the distance between the objects and how much mass they each contain. So, the weight of an object changes as its mass changes and as its distance from the center of Earth changes.

11▶ IDENTIFY: What instrument is used to measure mass?

Volume The amount of space an object takes up is its **volume.** You can measure the volume of liquids and solids. Liquid volume is usually measured in **liters.** Soft drinks in the United States often come in 2-liter bottles.

A graduated cylinder is used to measure liquid volume. Graduated cylinders are calibrated, or marked off, at regular intervals. Look at Figure 10. It shows a graduated cylinder. On this graduated cylinder, each small line is equal to 0.05 mL. The longer lines mark off every 0.25 mL up to 5.00 mL. However, every graduated cylinder is not marked in this manner. They come in different sizes up to 2,000 mL with different markings.

Always read the measurement at eye level. If you are using a glass graduated cylinder, you will need to read the mark on the graduated cylinder closest to the bottom of the meniscus. A **meniscus** is the curve at the surface of a liquid. A plastic graduated cylinder does not show a meniscus.

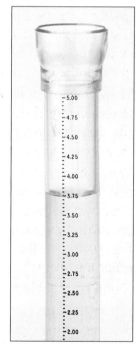

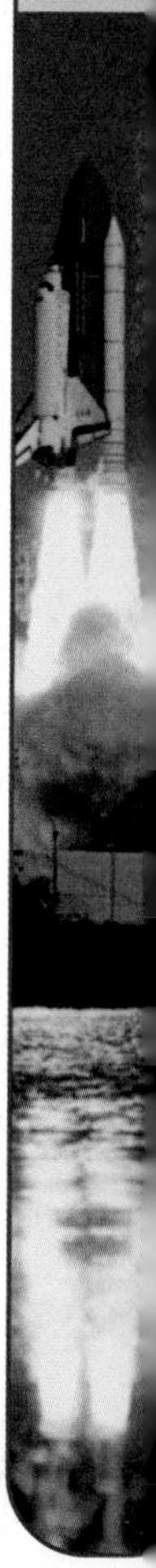

▲ **Figure 10** This glass graduated cylinder shows a meniscus.

The volume of solid objects is often measured in cubic centimeters. One cubic centimeter equals 1 mL.

Look at Figure 11. Each side of the cube is 1 cm long. The volume of the cube is 1 cubic centimeter (1 cm³). Now, look at the drawing of the box in Figure 12. Its length is 3 cm. Its width is 2 cm. Its height is 2 cm. The volume of the box can be found by multiplying length by width by height. In this case, volume equals 3 × 2 × 2. Therefore, the volume of the box is 12 cm³.

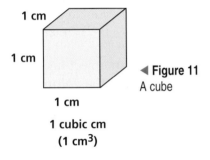

◄ **Figure 11**
A cube

1 cm
1 cm
1 cm
1 cubic cm
(1 cm³)

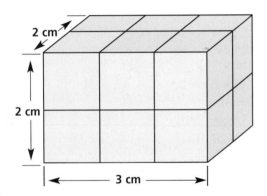

2 cm
2 cm
3 cm

▲ **Figure 12** The volume of a box equals length times width times height.

$$V = l \times w \times h$$

If you have a box that is 10 cm on each side, its volume would be 1,000 cm³. A liter is the same as 1,000 cm³. One liter of liquid will fill the box exactly.

12▶ CALCULATE: How many milliliters of water would fill a 12-cm³ box?

Hands-On Activity

CALCULATING AREA AND VOLUME

You will need 3 boxes of different sizes, paper, and a metric ruler.

1. Measure the length, width, and height of each box in centimeters. Record each measurement in your notes.
2. Calculate the volume of each box. Record each volume in your notes.
3. Find the surface area of each box. Record each area in your notes.

Practicing Your Skills

4. **ANALYZE:** Which of the three boxes has the largest volume?
5. **CALCULATE:** How many milliliters of liquid would fill each box?
6. **ANALYZE:** What is the surface area of the largest box?

Temperature **Temperature** is a measure of the amount of heat energy something contains. An instrument that measures temperature is called a thermometer.

Most thermometers are glass tubes. At the bottom of the tube is a wider part, called the bulb. The bulb is filled with liquid. Liquids that are often used include mercury, colored alcohol, or colored water. When heat is added, the liquid expands, or gets larger. It rises in the glass tube. When heat is taken away, the liquid contracts, or gets smaller. The liquid falls in the tube. On the side of the tube is a series of marks. You read the temperature by looking at the mark on the tube where the liquid stops.

Temperature can be measured on three different scales. These scales are the Fahrenheit (F) scale, the Celsius (C) scale, and the Kelvin (K) scale. The Fahrenheit scale is part of the English system of measurement. The Celsius scale is usually used in science. Almost all scientists, even in the United States, use the Celsius scale. Each unit on the Celsius scale is a **degree Celsius** (°C). The degree Celsius is the metric unit of temperature. Water freezes at 0°C. It boils at 100°C.

Scientists working with very low temperatures use the Kelvin scale. The Kelvin scale is part of the SI measurement system. It begins at **absolute zero**, or 0K. This number indicates, in theory at least, a total lack of heat.

COMPARING TEMPERATURE SCALES			
	Kelvin	Fahrenheit	Celsius
Boiling point of water	373K	212°F	100°C
Human body temperature	310K	98.6°F	37°C
Freezing point of water	273K	32°F	0°C
Absolute zero	0K	−459.67°F	−273.15°C

▲ Figure 13

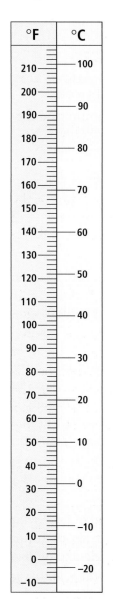

◄ **Figure 14** The Fahrenheit and Celsius scales

Hands-On Activity

READING A THERMOMETER

You will need safety goggles, lab apron, 2 beakers, a heat source, ice water, a wax pencil, a ruler, and a standard Celsius thermometer.

1. Boil some water in a beaker.
   ⚠CAUTION: Be very careful when working with heat. Place your thermometer in the beaker. Do not let the thermometer touch the sides or bottom of the beaker. Wait until the mercury rises as far as it will go. Record the temperature.

2. Fill a beaker with ice water. Place the unmarked thermometer into this beaker. Wait until the mercury goes as low as it will go. Record the temperature.

▲ **STEP 1** Record the temperature of the boiling water.

Practicing Your Skills

3. IDENTIFY: What is the temperature at which the mercury rose as high as it would go?

4. IDENTIFY: What is the temperature at which the mercury went as low as it would go?

13 ▶ NAME: What are the three scales used to measure temperature?

5 Analyzing Data and Communicating Results

Key Term
communication: sharing information

Analyzing Data When you organize information, you put it in a logical order. In scientific experiments, it is important to organize your data. Data collected during an experiment are not very useful unless they are organized and easy to read. It is also important to organize your data if you plan to share the results of your experiment.

Scientists often organize information visually by using data tables, charts, graphs, and diagrams. By using tables, charts, graphs, and diagrams, scientists can display a lot of information in a small space. They also make it easier to compare and interpret data.

Tables are made up of rows and columns. Columns run up and down. Rows run from left to right. Tables display data in an orderly arrangement, often numerically. For example, reading a table containing the uses of sulfuric acid shows that the largest use of sulfuric acid is in fertilizers. Figure 15 is a table that shows some uses of sulfuric acid.

USES OF SULFURIC ACID	
Product	**Percentage**
Dyes, batteries, paint, explosives	15
Raw materials	15
Fertilizers	60
Petroleum refining	5
Metal processing	5

▲ Figure 15

Graphs, such as bar graphs, line graphs, and circle graphs, often use special coloring, shading, or patterns to represent information. Keys indicate what the special markings represent. Line graphs have horizontal (*x*) and vertical (*y*) axes to indicate such things as time and quantities.

▶14 **EXPLAIN:** How do tables and graphs help you analyze data?

Sharing Results When you talk to a friend, you are communicating, or sharing information. If you write a letter or a report, you are also communicating but in a different way. Scientists communicate all the time. They communicate to share results, information, and opinions. They write books and magazine or newspaper articles. They may also create Web sites about their work. This is called written **communication.**

Graphs are a visual way to communicate. The circle graph in Figure 16 is showing the same information that is shown in Figure 15. The circle graph presents the information in a different way.

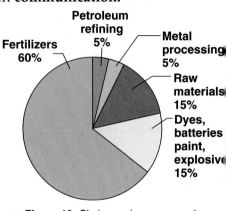

▲ **Figure 16** Circle graphs are a good way to show parts of a whole.

▶15 **LIST:** What are some ways to communicate the results of an experiment?

6 Making Predictions

Key Terms
infer: to form a conclusion

predict: to state ahead of time what you think is going to happen

Thinking of Possibilities When you **infer** something, you form a conclusion. This is called making an inference. Your conclusion will usually be based on observations or past experience. You may use logic to form your statement. Your statement might be supported by evidence and perhaps can be tested by an experiment. An inference is not a fact. It is only one possible explanation.

When you **predict,** you state ahead of time what you think will happen. Predictions about future events are based on inferences, evidence, or past experience. The two science process skills of inferring and predicting are very closely related.

▶16 **CONTRAST:** What is the difference between inferring and predicting?

How do you conduct a scientific investigation?

By now, you should have a good understanding of the science process skills. These skills are used to solve many science problems. There is also a basic procedure, or plan, that scientists usually follow when conducting investigations. Some people call this procedure the scientific method.

The scientific method is a series of steps that can serve as a guide to solving problems or answering questions. It uses many of the science process skills you know, such as observing and predicting.

Not all experiments use all of the steps in the scientific method. Some experiments follow all of them, but in a different order. In fact, there is no one right scientific method. Each problem is different. Some problems may require steps that another problem would not. However, most investigations will follow the same basic procedure.

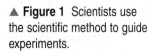 **DESCRIBE:** What is the scientific method?

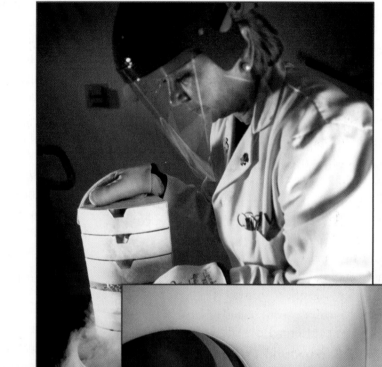

▲ **Figure 1** Scientists use the scientific method to guide experiments.

Contents

1 Identifying a Problem and Doing Research

Starting an Investigation Scientists often state a problem as a question. This is the first step in a scientific investigation. Most experiments begin by asking a scientific question. That is, they ask a question that can be answered by gathering evidence. This question is the reason for the scientific investigation. It also helps determine how the investigation will proceed.

Have you ever done background research for a science project? When you do this kind of research, you are looking for data that others have already obtained on the same subject. You can gather research by reading books, magazines, and newspapers, and by using the Internet to find out what other scientists have done. Doing research is the first step of gathering evidence for a scientific investigation.

 IDENTIFY: What is the first step of a scientific investigation?

BUILDING SCIENCE SKILLS

Researching Background Information Suppose you notice that the brown paper towels at school do not seem to soak up as much water as the paper towels used in your home. You wonder which kinds of paper towels absorb, or soak up, the most water. You wonder if there is a connection between the paper towels' thickness and absorbency.

To determine which paper towels are most absorbent, look for information on paper towels in magazines, in books, or on the Internet. Put your findings in a report.

▲ **Figure 2** Testing paper towels for absorbency

2 Forming a Hypothesis

Key Terms

hypothesis: suggested answer to a question or problem

theory: set of hypotheses that have been supported by testing over and over again

Focusing the Investigation Scientists usually state clearly what they expect to find out in an investigation. This is called stating a hypothesis. A **hypothesis** is a suggested answer to a question or a solution to a problem. Stating a hypothesis helps to keep you focused on the problem and helps you decide what to test.

To form their hypotheses, scientists must think of possible explanations for a set of observations or they must suggest possible answers to a scientific question. One of those explanations becomes the hypothesis. In science, a hypothesis must include something that can be tested.

A hypothesis is more than just a guess. It must consider observations, past experiences, and previous knowledge. It is an inference turned into a statement that can be tested. A set of hypotheses that have been supported by testing over and over again by many scientists is called a **theory.** An example is the theory that explains how living things have evolved, or changed, over time.

A hypothesis can take the form of an "if . . . then" statement. A well-worded hypothesis is a guide for how to set up and perform an experiment.

DESCRIBE: How does a scientist form a hypothesis?

BUILDING SCIENCE SKILLS

Developing a Hypothesis A hypothesis for an experiment about which paper towels absorb the most water might be stated as follows:

If thicker paper towels soak up more water than thin paper towels, then thickness is an important factor for paper towel absorbency.

However, what do you mean by thicker? Are the paper towels really different? Does color or design make a difference? You need to make your hypothesis specific. Revise the hypothesis above to make it more specific.

3 Designing and Carrying Out an Experiment

Key Terms

variable: anything that can affect the outcome of an experiment

constant: something that does not change

controlled experiment: experiment in which all the conditions except one are kept constant

Testing the Hypothesis Scientists need to plan how to test their hypotheses. This means they must design an experiment. The plan must be a step-by-step procedure. It should include a record of any observations made or measurements taken.

All experiments must take variables into account. A **variable** is anything that can affect the outcome of an experiment. Room temperature, amount of sunlight, and water vapor in the air are just some of the many variables that could affect the outcome of an experiment.

▶ **4 DEFINE:** What is a variable?

Controlling the Experiment One of the variables in an experiment should be what you are testing. This is what you will change during the experiment. All other variables need to remain the same. In this experiment, you will vary the type of paper towel.

A **constant** is something that does not change. If there are no constants in your experiment, you will not be sure why you got the results you did. An experiment in which all the conditions except one are kept constant is called a **controlled experiment.**

Some experiments have two setups. In one setup, called the control, nothing is changed. In the other setup, the variable being tested is changed. Later, the control group can be compared with the other group to provide useful data.

▶ **5 EXPLAIN:** Explain how a controlled experiment is set up.

Designing the Procedure Suppose you want to design an experiment to determine if a paper towel's thickness affects its absorbency. You decide to do a set of measurements to find out the absorbency of three kinds of paper towels in a controlled environment. You will measure the thickness of the paper towels and then determine how much water each paper towel soaks up to see if your hypothesis is correct.

In designing your experiment, you need to identify the variables. The three kinds of paper towels are all variables that could affect the outcome of your experiment. Everything about testing the effect of thickness on absorbency needs to be the same except the actual thickness of each paper towel.

Finally, you should decide on the data you will collect. How will you measure the thickness of the paper towels? In this case, you might want to record the thickness of each towel, its color, whether it absorbed water, and how much water was absorbed.

The hands-on activity on page 12 is one possible experiment you could have designed. It has one method for measuring the absorbency of the paper towels. Sometimes scientists try to measure the same thing two different ways to be sure the test is accurate. Can you think of another method to measure the absorbency of paper towels?

▶ **6 LIST:** How do constants and variables affect an experiment?

Hands-On Activity

CARRYING OUT AN EXPERIMENT

You will need 3 or more kinds of paper towels, a metric ruler, an eyedropper or pipette (preferably calibrated in millimeters), and water.

1. Get three different kinds of paper towels. To find the thickness of each kind of towel, measure the thickness of five towels and divide the result by five. Set up a data table for the information you gather.

2. Now you are ready to compare the absorbency of the paper towels. Cut the paper towels into squares of equal sizes. Squares that are 10 cm in size are good for testing.

3. Lay a square of paper towel on a tray or other nonabsorbent surface. Add drops of water one at a time until the paper towel has soaked up all the water it can. Record how much water was absorbed. If your eyedropper is not marked in milliliters, you can record your data in "drops." If it is marked, then you should record the milliliters.

4. Test all the paper towel samples the exact same way. Be sure that you only measure the water that is absorbed and that you let each paper towel sample soak up as much water as it will hold.

5. You are now ready to compare your data and see if they support your hypothesis.

Practicing Your Skills

6. **OBSERVE:** What happened in the experiment? How much water did each paper towel sample absorb?

7. **COMPARE:** Which paper towel absorbed the most?

8. **EXPLAIN:** What procedures did you follow to make sure the paper towels were all given a fair and equal test?

9. **IDENTIFY:** What is the variable being tested in this experiment?

4 Recording and Analyzing Data

Dealing With Data During an experiment, you must keep careful notes about what you observe. For example, you might need to note any special steps you took in setting up the experiment, exactly how you made the drops the same size each time, or the temperature of the water. This is important information that might affect your conclusion.

At the end of an experiment, you will need to study the data to find any patterns. Much of the data you will deal with is written text. You may read a report or a summary of an experiment. However, scientific information is often a set of numbers or facts presented in other, more visual ways. These visual presentations make the information more meaningful and easier to understand. Tables, charts, and graphs, for instance, help you understand a collection of facts on a topic.

After your data have been organized, you need to ask what the data show. Do they support your hypothesis? Do they show something wrong in your experiment? Do you need to gather more data by performing another experiment?

 LIST: What are some ways to display data?

BUILDING SCIENCE SKILLS

Analyzing Data You made the following notes during your experiment. How would you display this information?

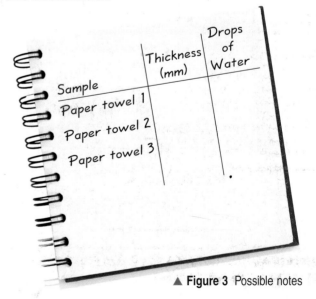

▲ **Figure 3** Possible notes

5 Stating a Conclusion

Drawing Conclusions A conclusion is a statement that sums up what you have learned from an experiment. When you draw a conclusion, you need to decide whether the data you collected supported your hypothesis. You may need to repeat an experiment several times before you can draw any conclusions from it. Conclusions often lead you to ask new questions and plan new experiments to answer them.

8 **EXPLAIN:** Why might it be necessary to repeat an experiment?

BUILDING SCIENCE SKILLS

Stating a Conclusion Review your hypothesis statement regarding the effect of the thickness of a paper towel on its absorbency. Then, review the data you obtained during your experiment.

- Was your hypothesis correct? Use your observations to support your answer.
- Which paper towel absorbed the most? Was it also the thickest?

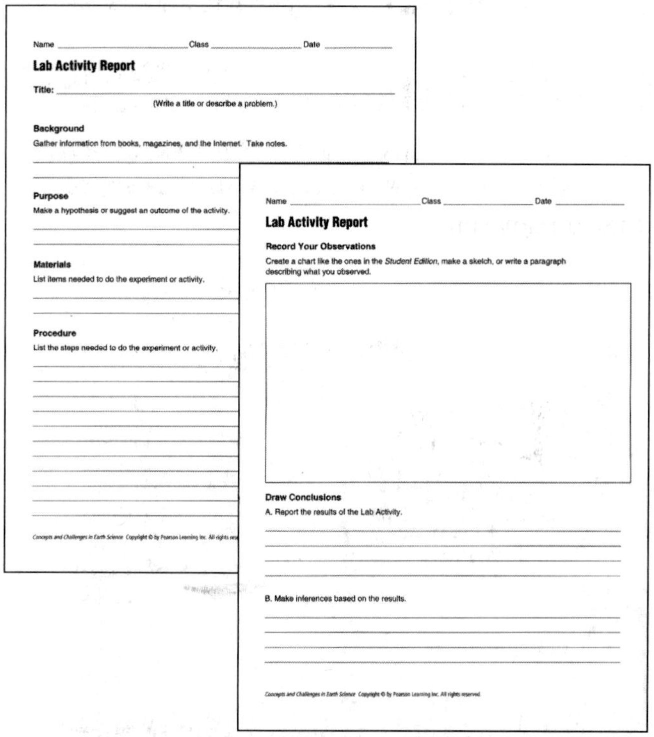

Name ______ Class ______ Date ______

Lab Activity Report

Title: ______

(Write a title or describe a problem.)

Background

Gather information from books, magazines, and the Internet. Take notes.

Purpose

Make a hypothesis or suggest an outcome of the activity.

Materials

List items needed to do the experiment or activity.

Procedure

List the steps needed to do the experiment or activity.

Concepts and Challenges in Earth Science Copyright © by Pearson Learning Inc. All rights res

Name ______ Class ______ Date ______

Lab Activity Report

Record Your Observations

Create a chart like the ones in the *Student Edition*, make a sketch, or write a paragraph describing what you observed.

Draw Conclusions

A. Report the results of the Lab Activity.

B. Make inferences based on the results.

Concepts and Challenges in Earth Science Copyright © by Pearson Learning Inc. All rights reserved.

▲ **Figure 4** Throughout this program, you may use forms like this one to organize your lab reports.

6 Writing a Report

Communicating Results Scientists keep careful written records of their observations and findings. These records are used to create a lab report. Lab reports are a form of written communication. They explain what happened in the experiment. A good lab report should be written so that anyone reading it can duplicate the experiment. It should contain the following information:

- A title
- A purpose
- Background information
- Your hypothesis
- Materials used
- Your step-by-step procedure
- Your observations
- Your recorded data
- Your analysis of the data
- Your conclusions

Your conclusions should relate back to the questions you asked in the "purpose" section of your report. Also, the report should not have any experimental errors that might have caused unexpected results. For example, did you follow the steps in the correct order? Did an unexpected variable interfere with your results? Was your equipment clean and in good working order? This explanation of possible errors should also be part of your conclusions.

9 **EXPLAIN:** Why is it important to explain possible errors in your lab report?

BUILDING SCIENCE SKILLS

Writing a Lab Report Write a lab report to communicate to other scientists your discoveries about the effect of a paper towel's thickness on its water absorbency. Your lab report should include a title, your hypothesis statement, a list of materials you used, the procedure, your observations, and your conclusions. Try to include one table of data in your report.

 LAB SAFETY

Working in a science laboratory can be both exciting and meaningful. However, you must always be aware of safety precautions when carrying out experiments. There are a few basic rules that should be followed in any science laboratory:

- Read all instructions carefully before the start of an experiment. Follow all instructions exactly and in the correct order.

- Check your equipment to make sure it is clean and working properly.

- Never taste, smell, or touch any substance in the lab that you are not told to do so. Never eat or drink anything in the lab. Do not chew gum.

- Never work alone. Tell a teacher at once if an accident occurs.

Experiments that use chemicals or heat can be dangerous. The following list of rules and symbols will help you avoid accidents. There are also rules about what to do if an accident does occur. Here are some rules to remember when working in a lab:

 1. Do not use glass that is chipped or metal objects with broken edges. Do not try to clean up broken glassware yourself. Notify your teacher if a piece of glassware is broken.

 2. Do not use electrical cords with loose plugs or frayed ends. Do not let electrical cords cross in front of working areas. Do not use electrical equipment near water.

 3. Be very careful when using sharp objects such as scissors, knives, or tweezers. Always cut in a direction away from your body.

 4. Be careful when you are using a heat source. Use proper equipment, such as tongs or a ringstand, when handling hot objects.

 5. Confine loose clothing and hair when working with an open flame. Be sure you know the location of the nearest fire extinguisher. Never reach across an open flame.

 6. Be careful when working with poisonous or toxic substances. Never mix chemicals without directions from your teacher. Remove any long jewelry that might hang down and end up in chemicals. Avoid touching your eyes or mouth when working with these chemicals.

 7. Use extreme care when working with acids and bases. Never mix acids and bases without direction from your teacher. Never smell anything directly. Use caution when handling chemicals that produce fumes.

 8. Wear safety goggles, especially when working with an open flame, chemicals, and any liquids.

 9. Wear lab aprons when working with substances of any sort, especially chemicals.

 10. Use caution when handling or collecting plants. Some plants can be harmful if they are touched or eaten.

 11. Use caution when handling live animals. Some animals can injure you or spread disease. Handle all live animals as humanely as possible.

 12. Dispose of all equipment and materials properly. Keep your work area clean at all times.

 13. Always wash your hands thoroughly with soap and water after handling chemicals or live organisms.

 14. Follow the ⚠ **CAUTION** and safety symbols you see used throughout this book when doing labs or other activities.

Chapter 1 Properties of Matter

▲ **Figure 1-1** Water can exist in any of three states on Earth.

All things are made of some kind of matter. On Earth, most matter exists in one of three states. Matter can change physically from one state to another or it can change chemically. Water is special. It can exist in all three states at the same time under ordinary conditions of temperature and pressure.

►Can you name the different states of matter by identifying them in Figure 1-1?

Contents

1-1 What is physical science?

Objective
Identify and describe the main branches of physical science.

Key Terms
chemistry: branch of science that deals with the interaction of atoms and molecules

physics: branch of science that deals with the interactions of energy, matter, space, and time

specialization (spehsh-uh-lih-ZAY-shuhn): studying or working in one area of a subject

Studying Physical Science Physical science is one of the major fields of science. It is the study of matter and energy. Everything around you is either matter or energy.

Two major brances of physical science are chemistry and physics. **Chemistry** deals with the study of the interaction of atoms and molecules. **Physics** deals with the interactions of energy, matter, space, and time.

1 NAME: What are the two main branches of physical science?

Specialization A specialist is a person who studies or works in one particular area of a subject. Working in one area of a subject is called **specialization**. Some of the specialized fields in physical science are listed in Figure 1-2.

2 DEFINE: What is a specialist?

Importance of Physical Science Why study physical science? Physical science is an important part of everyday life. It is difficult to think of anything that does not involve physical science and the discoveries of physical scientists. For example, each year seat belts save thousands of lives. Seat belt technology is based on the laws of motion.

Physical scientists have also discovered how to harness nuclear energy. Using nuclear energy has both problems and benefits. Physical scientists are constantly working to solve the problems related to nuclear energy. Their solutions may someday solve the world's energy problems. Physical scientists are also researching other forms of energy for power. Solar panels, wind farms, and fuel cells are some alternative sources of energy.

The discovery of new materials has resulted in the production of a variety of ceramic tiles, various glass products, and plastics. Our leisure time has benefited through cable and satellite dish TV, lasers,

---

SOME SPECIALIZED FIELDS IN PHYSICAL SCIENCE

Biochemistry
Biochemists study the chemical substances occurring in living things. Some careers in biochemistry include medical research, plant and animal genetics, and pharmaceuticals.

Thermodynamics
Thermodynamics deals with heat and its conversion to other forms of energy. Research and engineering are two careers to pursue if you are interested in the study of thermodynamics.

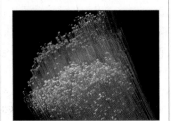

Optics
Optics is the science of light and vision. Some careers in the field of optics include optician and research scientist in such areas as lasers and optical fibers.

Nuclear Physics
Nuclear physicists study the characteristics, behavior, and structure of atomic nuclei. Careers include research, reactor manufacturing, and power plant operation.

▲ Figure 1-2

computers, holograms, and CD and DVD players. Cars and airplanes have been made safer and faster.

Studying matter and how it reacts with other substances has helped create all of these things. We will take a closer look at reactions and interactions of matter and energy as we progress through the book.

3 ▶ LIST: What are some of the products that have been created because of the work of physical scientists?

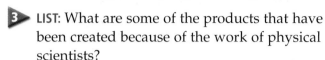

✔ CHECKING CONCEPTS

1. The two main branches of physical science are chemistry and _____.

2. Physical science is the study of matter and _____.

3. A person who works in only one area of a subject is a _____.

4. Physical scientists have helped develop ceramics, plastics, and _____.

5. The harnessing of _____ energy by physical scientists has helped reduce the world's energy problems.

THINKING CRITICALLY

6. **ANALYZE:** Why do you think the number of specialized fields in physical science has grown during the past few decades?

7. **LIST:** What are three ways in which physical science is important in your daily life?

Web InfoSearch

A Career in Physical Science If you like science, you may be interested in a career in physical science. Choose a career from Figure 1-2, or a field of science that interests you.

SEARCH: Use the Internet to find out what education is required, what you will do on the job, and what tools you might need to perform this job. Write a short report about your results. Start your search at www.conceptsandchallenges.com. Some key search words are **biochemist** and **nuclear physicist.**

 People in Science

SCIENTIFIC ILLUSTRATOR

Do you like to draw? If so, you may be interested in a career as a scientific illustrator. You can see the work of scientific illustrators on many pages in this book. Scientific illustrators make drawings, diagrams, and sketches to illustrate scientific processes, structures, cycles, or equations, helping people to understand scientific concepts.

Scientific illustrators are employed by publishers of science books and journals or by advertisers. The drawings of scientific illustrators are used in sales brochures, advertisements, and even in this book. In the catalogs of scientific supply houses and pharmaceutical companies, many drawings are used to demonstrate equipment and other supplies.

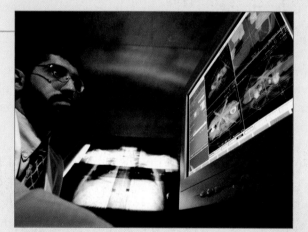

▲ **Figure 1-3** Scientific illustrators often use computers as tools.

If you are interested in becoming a scientific illustrator, you need a college degree in graphics or fine arts. Many scientific illustrators also find a background in the sciences helpful in their careers.

Thinking Critically How does the work of a scientific illustrator help people learn science?

1-2 What are the properties of matter?

INVESTIGATE

Air as Matter
HANDS-ON ACTIVITY

1. Stuff a tissue into the bottom of a glass. Fill a pail with water.

2. Turn the glass upside down; push it straight down into the water.

3. Pull the glass straight out of the water and feel the tissue.

4. Record your observations.

THINK ABOUT IT: Did water enter the glass? How do you know? What does this tell you about air?

STEP 2

Objective
Identify two basic properties of matter.

Key Terms
matter: anything that has mass and takes up space

properties (PRAHP-uhr-teez)**:** characteristics used to describe an object

Matter Look around you. What do all the objects you see around you have in common? They are all made up of matter. **Matter** is anything that has mass and takes up space. Mass is the amount of matter a sample of matter contains. The amount of space the sample takes up is its volume.

Water is matter. A glass filled with water is heavier than an empty glass. The water-filled glass is heavier because water has more mass than the air in the empty container. If you were to keep adding water to a filled glass, the water would overflow. It would overflow because water takes up space, leaving no room in the glass.

Air is matter, too. A balloon filled with air is heavier than a balloon that is not blown up because air has mass. When you blow air into a balloon, the balloon gets larger as air takes up space.

▶ **DEFINE:** What is matter?

Defining Properties How would you describe a hot-air balloon? You might say that it is rounded, blue, and striped. These are **properties** of that balloon. Properties are characteristics used to describe an object.

Not all hot-air balloons have the same properties. A different hot-air balloon may be rounded, green, and dotted. Some properties are not basic properties. They do not apply to all examples of the object. A basic property of all hot-air balloons is that they are balloons.

▲ **Figure 1-4** Hot-air balloons have properties that describe them.

▶ **DEFINE:** What is a property?

Properties of Matter Mass and volume are basic properties of all matter. Mass is a measure of the amount of matter in an object. Volume is a measure of how much space matter takes up. Mass is measured in kilograms. Volume is measured in cubic units, such as meters. A cubic meter is a cube that is one meter long on each side.

Weight and density are also properties that may be used to describe matter. Weight is a measure of the pull of gravity on a sample of matter. Density tells you how much is in a unit volume.

 LIST: What are two basic properties of matter?

 CHECKING CONCEPTS

1. All the objects you see around you are made up of _____.
2. Matter is anything that has mass and takes up _____.
3. Mass is a basic _____ of matter.

4. Weight is a measure of the pull of _____ on an object.
5. The amount of space taken up by matter is its _____.

THINKING CRITICALLY

6. **INFER:** What is the difference between mass and weight?
7. **EXPLAIN:** Why do you think scientists can use the basic properties of matter to help identify an unknown substance?

BUILDING SCIENCE SKILLS

Observing Choose three objects in your home or classroom. Examine each carefully. List four properties of each and the senses you used to help describe each.

How Do They Know That?

MASS IS A PROPERTY OF MATTER

Chemists are scientists who study matter. Antoine Lavoisier (1743–1794) was a French chemist. He was educated as a lawyer. However, he loved chemistry. Antoine was helped in his work by his wife Marie Anne. Unlike most women of the day, Marie Anne received an education in the arts and sciences. This enabled her to work side by side in the lab with her husband.

▲ **Figure 1-5** Marie Anne and Antoine Lavoisier working together

Before the work of the Lavoisiers, little was known about chemical reactions. For example, it was believed that there were only four elements. People also thought that chemical activities could create mass.

Marie Anne and Antoine showed that these ideas were not true. They explained that mass is not created or lost during a chemical reaction. Before an experiment, Antoine measured all of the materials going into the reaction. After the experiment, he measured the materials produced. He was the first scientist to realize that reactions began and ended with the same amount of mass. He wrote the Law of Conservation of Mass. It states that mass is neither created nor destroyed during a chemical change.

Thinking Critically The burning of wood is a chemical reaction. When wood burns, is mass destroyed?

1-3 What are the states of matter?

Objective
Identify and describe four states of matter.

Key Terms
state of matter: any of the four physical forms of matter

solid: state of matter with a definite shape and volume

liquid: state of matter with a definite volume but no definite shape

gas: state of matter that has no definite shape or volume

plasma (PLAZ-muh)**:** state of matter made up of electrically charged particles

States of Matter You cool drinks with solid ice cubes. You wash your hands in liquid water. Water that evaporates from puddles after a rainstorm has changed to a gas called water vapor. Ice, liquid water, and water vapor all are made up of particles of water. Different forms of the same substance are called states. A **state of matter** is any one of the four physical forms of matter. The three most familiar states of matter are solid, liquid, and gas. A fourth state, plasma, is found mainly in stars like our Sun.

▶ **1 IDENTIFY:** In how many states can matter exist?

Solids Most of the objects that surround you are made of solids. A **solid** is a state of matter that has a definite shape and volume. In a solid, particles of matter are tightly packed together. The particles cannot change position easily. They can only vibrate, or move back and forth in place.

▶ **2 DEFINE:** What is a solid?

Liquids Milk is a liquid. A **liquid** has a definite volume but no definite shape. Liquids are able to change shape because the particles of a liquid can change position. They can slide past one another. If you pour a liter of milk into different containers, the milk always takes the shape of the container. However, the volume of the milk stays the same. You cannot make a liter of milk fit into a half-liter bottle.

▶ **3 EXPLAIN:** Why can liquids change shape?

Gases A **gas** is a state of matter that has no definite shape or volume. A gas takes the shape of its container. For example, air can take the shape of a basketball, a football, or a bicycle tire. If you fill a balloon with air, the air completely fills the balloon. A container of gas is always completely full. The particles of a gas are in constant motion. They are much farther apart than the particles in solids or liquids. They can move freely to all parts of a container.

▶ **4 DEFINE:** What is a gas?

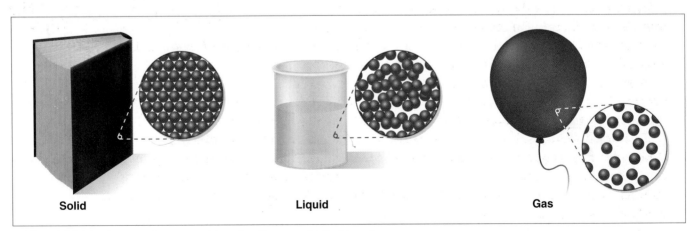

Solid   Liquid   Gas

▲ **Figure 1-6** The three most common states of matter are solid, liquid, and gas.

Another State of Matter Matter can exist in a fourth state called **plasma**. Plasma has been found in stars, where the temperatures and pressures are very high. Matter in the plasma state is made up of small, electrically charged particles. On Earth, plasma is found in lightning, auroras, and welding arcs.

Scientists have been able to create plasmas in the laboratory. Such plasmas are relatively cool compared with natural plasmas. This plasma technology has been applied to many things you see every day, such as flat-screen TVs, street lamps, and fluorescent tubes.

 DEFINE: What is plasma?

CHECKING CONCEPTS

1. Plasma exists where _____ and pressure are very high.

2. In what state of matter can particles only vibrate in place?

3. What happens to the shape of a liquid when you pour it into a container?

4. What determines the volume of a gas?

5. What state of matter is air?

THINKING CRITICALLY

6. **EXPLAIN:** What will happen to the particles of a gas if the gas is transferred from a small container to a much larger container?

7. **CLASSIFY:** Classify each of the following substances as a solid, a liquid, or a gas.

   a. Cotton cloth   f. Seltzer

   b. Rain   g. Hydrogen

   c. Carbon dioxide   h. Sugar

   d. Helium   i. Orange juice

   e. Salt   j. Bricks

Web InfoSearch

Plasma As rare as plasma is on Earth, scientists have found ways to make use of it in some interesting ways.

SEARCH: Use the Internet to find out what kinds of products contain plasma. Then, create a chart. Next to each item on your list, include a picture of it. Start your search at www.conceptsandchallenges.com. Some key search words are **plasma** and **digital TV**.

Integrating Earth Science

TOPIC: Earth's layers

EARTH'S MANTLE

The outer layer of Earth is called the crust. The crust is about 5 km to 40 km thick, with the thickest part under the mountains. Beneath the crust is the mantle. The mantle is about 2,900 km thick. The upper part of the mantle is solid rock. Below the solid rock, the mantle rock behaves like a very thick liquid, such as molasses. This is because of very high pressure and temperatures. Like all liquids, this rock can flow. The rock also has some properties of a solid. It is in an in-between state of matter called the plastic state. A plastic material is neither a solid nor a liquid; it has properties of both.

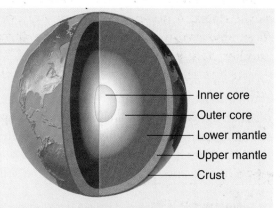
▲ **Figure 1-7** Earth's interior

Scientists would like to learn more about the plastic material in the mantle. However, they have not been able to drill that far into Earth. What they know has been learned by studying shock waves from earthquakes. Someday, scientists hope to find a way to drill deep enough to reach the mantle. Then, they will be able to study the properties of plastic rock directly.

Thinking Critically What might scientists do with the information they get from the plastic rock?

1-4 How does matter change state?

Objective
Identify ways in which matter can change from one state to another.

Key Terms
freezing: change from a liquid to a solid

melting: change from a solid to a liquid

evaporation (ee-vap-uh-RAY-shuhn)**:** change from a liquid to a gas at the surface of the liquid

condensation (kahn-dehn-SAY-shuhn)**:** change from a gas to a liquid

sublimation: change from a solid directly to a gas

State Changes Matter can change from one state to another. For example, water can change from a solid to a liquid. A change in matter from one state to another is called a change of state. There are five main kinds of changes of state. During a change of state, there is a change in heat energy. A substance either gains or loses heat as it changes from one state to another.

▶ **DESCRIBE:** What is a change of state?

Freezing and Melting If you fill an ice cube tray with water and place it in the freezer, the water will change to ice. Water changing into ice is an example of freezing. **Freezing** is a change from a liquid to a solid. Freezing occurs when the temperature of a liquid reaches its freezing point. At its freezing point, a liquid loses enough heat to change to a solid.

▼ **Figure 1-8** Part of this frozen iceberg is melting into the ocean.

When the temperature rises above the freezing point of water, ice changes to a liquid. A change from solid to liquid is called **melting**. Melting occurs when a solid gains enough heat to change into a liquid.

▶ **EXPLAIN:** What causes a liquid to freeze?

Evaporation and Condensation Before you go to bed tonight, fill an open plastic container with water. Mark the level of the water. Place the container in a warm, dry place. When you get up tomorrow, see what has happened to the water level. You will find that some of the water has "disappeared." Particles at the surface of the water gained enough heat energy to change into the gas state. **Evaporation** is a change from a liquid to a gas at the surface of the liquid.

You probably have noticed drops of water on your bathroom mirror after taking a hot shower. Hot water from the shower causes the temperature in the bathroom to rise. Some water particles gain enough heat energy to change to water vapor. Water vapor is the gas state of water. Water vapor is invisible. As particles of water vapor hit the cool surface of a mirror, they lose heat energy and change back into liquid water. This process is called condensation. **Condensation** is a change from a gas to a liquid.

▶ **EXPLAIN:** What causes condensation?

Sublimation When you fill an ice cube tray with water and place it in the freezer, you have ice cubes in a few hours. If you leave the tray untouched in the freezer for several days, the ice cubes get smaller. This is due to a process called sublimation. **Sublimation** is the changing of a solid directly to a gas, without passing through a liquid state. The temperature at which a solid changes to a gas is its sublimation point. Some other solids that sublime are moth balls (naphthalene), dry ice (CO_2), and iodine.

▶ **DEFINE:** What is sublimation?

✓ CHECKING CONCEPTS

1. Melting is a change from a solid to a
   _____.

2. Water changing into ice is an example of
   _____.

3. A change in matter from one state to another
   is called _____.

4. A change from a liquid to a gas at the surface
   of the liquid is _____.

5. Water vapor changing to liquid water is an
   example of _____.

6. Dry ice turning into gas is an example of
   _____.

THINKING CRITICALLY

7. **INFER:** What happens to the particles of a
   liquid as the liquid freezes?

8. **INFER:** What happens to the particles of a
   liquid as the liquid evaporates?

9. **CLASSIFY:** Identify the change of state taking
   place in each of the following situations.
   a. Water droplets form on the inside of your
      window on a chilly winter night.
   b. A full perfume bottle left open for several
      days is now half empty.
   c. A block of baking chocolate is heated until
      it can be poured into a measuring cup.

DESIGNING AN EXPERIMENT

*Design an experiment to solve the following problem.
Include a hypothesis, variables, a procedure, and a
type of data to study.*

PROBLEM: How can you identify an unknown
material?

 Real-Life Science

FOG MACHINES

Dry ice is frozen carbon dioxide, a gas found in the air around us. It looks like regular ice, but it is much colder. The temperature of dry ice is about −78.5°C or −109.3°F. If dry ice comes in contact with your skin, heat is removed from your body so fast that your skin seems to burn! For this reason, dry ice should only be handled with insulated gloves.

Frozen carbon dioxide is called dry ice because it does not melt. It changes directly from a solid to a gas. This process is called sublimation. If you watch a piece of dry ice, it seems to slowly disappear into thin air as it sublimes.

▲ **Figure 1-9** Dry ice subliming

When dry ice is placed in hot water, a fog made of tiny water droplets is produced. Such fogs, produced by a fog machine, can lend a dreamlike or eerie mood to the sets of stage plays, rock concerts, or movies. A dry ice fog machine is made up of a water barrel, a heater, and a fan. Dry ice is placed in a bucket with holes in it. When the bucket is lowered into the barrel of hot water, fog is produced. The fan then blows the fog through the air. The production of fog is stopped by removing the dry ice from the water barrel.

Thinking Critically Where does the water that makes up the fog come from?

THE Big IDEA

How are changes of state part of the water cycle?

The water cycle is Earth's water recycling program. The water inside your cells, in your bathtub, underground, and even in glaciers is all part of the water cycle. Water endlessly cycles all over Earth—from the oceans to the clouds; from rain or snow into the ground; from rivers and streams back to the sea.

Think about a molecule of water (H_2O) in a puddle. Light from the Sun hits the water molecule, giving it an energy boost. The water evaporates and the molecule joins other molecules as they move from the liquid state to the gas state. The molecules enter the atmosphere as water vapor. Soon the water vapor cools and loses energy, condensing back to the liquid state. The water molecule joins other water molecules to form tiny droplets or ice crystals that make up clouds. The droplets increase in size until they are pulled to Earth by gravity. That is when you see rain, snow, hail, or sleet. This is called precipitation. Precipitation takes many forms, depending on the weather conditions.

On Earth, about 97% of the water is in the oceans. So, most of the action in the water cycle is evaporation from and precipitation back into the oceans. Sometimes the water cycle carries water molecules on incredible journeys.

Look at the illustration on these two pages. Then, follow the directions in the Science Log to find out more about "the big idea." ✦

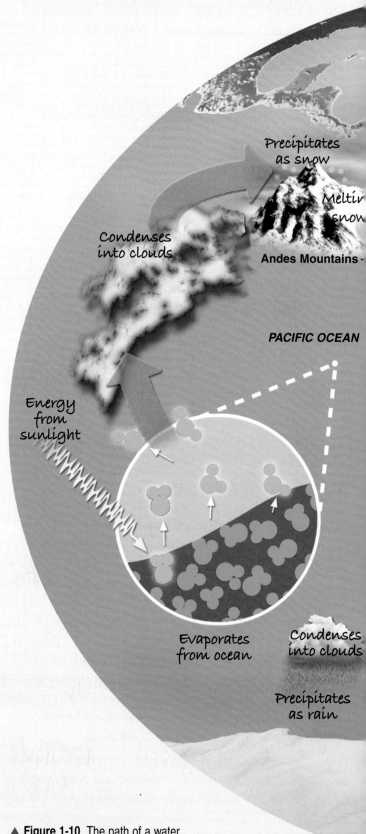

▲ **Figure 1-10** The path of a water molecule may be from ocean to ice cap and many places in between.

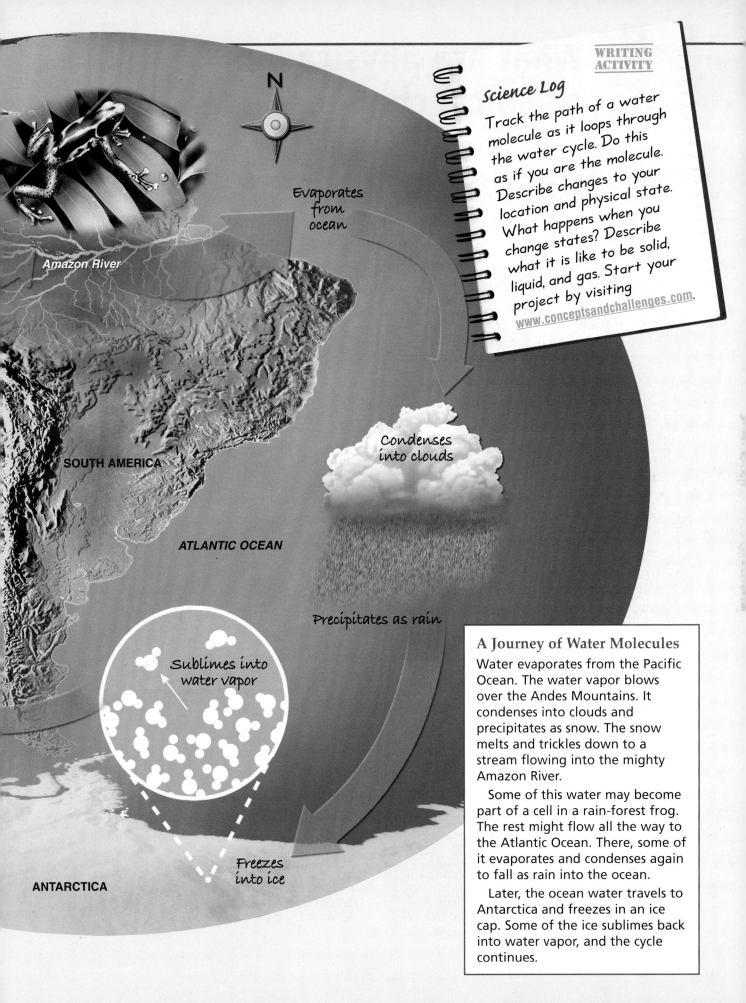

Amazon River

SOUTH AMERICA

ATLANTIC OCEAN

ANTARCTICA

Evaporates
from
ocean

Condenses
into clouds

Precipitates as rain

Sublimes into
water vapor

Freezes
into ice

WRITING
ACTIVITY

Science Log

Track the path of a water molecule as it loops through the water cycle. Do this as if you are the molecule. Describe changes to your location and physical state. What happens when you change states? Describe what it is like to be solid, liquid, and gas. Start your project by visiting www.conceptsandchallenges.com.

A Journey of Water Molecules

Water evaporates from the Pacific Ocean. The water vapor blows over the Andes Mountains. It condenses into clouds and precipitates as snow. The snow melts and trickles down to a stream flowing into the mighty Amazon River.

Some of this water may become part of a cell in a rain-forest frog. The rest might flow all the way to the Atlantic Ocean. There, some of it evaporates and condenses again to fall as rain into the ocean.

Later, the ocean water travels to Antarctica and freezes in an ice cap. Some of the ice sublimes back into water vapor, and the cycle continues.

1-5 What are physical and chemical changes?

Objective

Distinguish between physical and chemical changes in matter.

Key Terms

physical change: change that does not produce new substances

chemical change: change that produces new substances

Physical Properties The states of matter are physical properties. Some other physical properties of matter include shape, size, color, and texture. Physical properties are characteristics that can be observed or measured without changing the makeup of a substance.

▶ **1** LIST: What are some physical properties of matter?

Physical Changes If you cut an apple in half and share it with a friend, it is still an apple. If you change water to ice, it is still water. If you crumple a sheet of paper into a ball, it is still paper. All of these changes are examples of physical changes. A **physical change** does not produce new substances.

▲ **Figure 1-11** The sawing of wood is a physical change. The burning of wood is a chemical change.

A physical change involves the physical properties of a material. Cutting an apple in half changes its size. Freezing liquid water changes its state. Crumpling up a sheet of paper changes its size and shape.

▶ **2** DEFINE: What is a physical change?

Chemical Changes If you take a crumpled sheet of paper and smooth it out, you can still write on it. It is still paper. Now, suppose you burn a sheet of paper. When substances burn, they combine with oxygen. Burning is an example of a chemical change. A **chemical change** results in new kinds of matter being formed. When paper burns, ashes, soot, heat, light, and gases are produced. You no longer have paper. Some other examples of chemical changes include the rusting of iron, the digestion of food, and the burning of gasoline in a car engine.

▲ **Figure 1-12** Rusting is an example of a chemical change.

▶ **3** CONTRAST: How is a chemical change different from a physical change?

✓ CHECKING CONCEPTS

Complete each sentence with the word **physical** *or* **chemical**.

1. Volume and color are examples of _____ properties of matter.

2. State is a _____ property of matter.

3. Changing water to ice is an example of a _____ change.

4. New substances are produced by a _____ change.

5. Iron rusting is an example of a _____ change.

6. Color and shape are _____ properties.

THINKING CRITICALLY

7. **ANALYZE:** Describe the changes that take place when a match burns. Are these changes physical or chemical?

8. **INTERPRET:** Mixing vinegar with baking soda produces carbon dioxide and water. Is this a physical change or a chemical change? How do you know?

9. **HYPOTHESIZE:** You find small pieces of ice instead of ice cubes in the freezer. State how this is possible.

BUILDING SCIENCE SKILLS

Classifying Classify each of the following examples as a physical change or a chemical change. Explain your answers.

a. Match burns

b. Glass breaks

c. Rubber band is stretched

d. Iron rusts

e. Ice melts

f. Sugar cube is crushed

Hands-On Activity

OBSERVING PHYSICAL CHANGES

You will need a bottle or jar with a narrow neck, ice cubes, and hot water.

1. Put a small amount of hot water into a bottle or jar. Place an ice cube over the opening of the bottle so that the ice cube will not fall in.

2. Observe what you see coming from the surface of the hot water.

3. Observe the bottle for a few minutes and note what you see happening near the top of the bottle.

4. Watch for another minute or two. Note if you see anything fall from the top of the bottle.

▲ **STEP 2** Observe the inside of the bottle.

Practicing Your Skills

5. **OBSERVE: a.** What did you observe coming from the surface of the hot water in Step 2? **b.** What caused this to happen?

6. **OBSERVE: a.** What did you see near the top of the bottle in Step 3? **b.** What caused this to happen?

7. **HYPOTHESIZE: a.** Did you see anything fall inside the bottle in Step 4? **b.** If so, explain what you saw and how it was produced.

LAB ACTIVITY
Observing Physical and Chemical Changes

Materials
Safety goggles
Lab apron
Modeling clay
Wax paper
Plastic teaspoon
2 Plastic cups
1 Antacid tablet
Tape measure
Cold water
Triple-beam balance

▲ **STEP 2** Measure the block of clay.

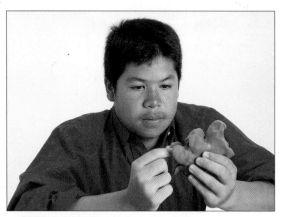

▲ **STEP 4** Mold the clay into any shape.

BACKGROUND

Physical and chemical changes occur everywhere around us. From a scientist's point of view, it is necessary to tell the difference between these two types of changes. A physical change involves a change in what you see but it does not change the identity of the substance. A chemical change alters the identity of a substance and may involve a change in the way a substance looks as well.

PURPOSE

In this activity, you will observe and record data to decide whether the activity involves a physical or a chemical change.

PROCEDURE

1. Copy the chart in Figure 1-13.

2. Take a block of modeling clay. Measure its dimensions using the tape measure. Record its mass using the triple-beam balance.

3. Shape the clay into a ball and record its mass. Measure the dimensions of the ball with the tape measure.

4. Mold the clay into a shape of your choice. Record its mass and try to measure its dimensions.

5. Put on safety goggles and apron. Take the antacid tablet and place it in a small plastic cup. Measure 2 mL of water into another small plastic cup. Place both cups on the balance and record their combined masses.

6. Crush the antacid tablet and place it back it in the plastic cup. Place the cup with the crushed tablet and the cup with the water on the balance. Record their masses.

7. Pour the water into the cup with the crushed tablet. Record your observations. Place the cup with the water-tablet mixture and the empty cup on the balance and record their masses.

8. Clean up your area and dispose of the substances as directed by your teacher.

▲ **STEP 7** Pour the water into the cup.

Clay			Antacid Tablet	
Shape	Dimensions	Mass	Materials	Mass
Block			Tablet in cup and water in cup	
Ball			Crushed tablet in cup and water in cup	
Choice			Water in cup and empty cup	

▲ **Figure 1-13** Copy this chart and use it to record your observations.

CONCLUSIONS

1. **OBSERVE:** How is shaping clay an example of a physical change?

2. **ANALYZE:** Describe the changes that take place with the antacid tablet. Why does the mixture of the antacid tablet and water have a different mass after the reaction?

3. **INFER:** Based on your observations of the antacid tablet, what kind of change takes place when it is placed in water? Explain your reasoning.

4. **CLASSIFY:** Classify each of the following examples as a physical change or a chemical change. Explain your answers.
   a. cutting wood
   b. burning gasoline
   c. crumpling a sheet of paper
   d. wine turning into vinegar over time
   e. milk turning sour

Chapter 1 Challenges

Chapter Summary

Lesson 1-1

- Physical science has two major branches. They are physics and chemistry. **Chemistry** is the branch of science that deals with the interaction of atoms and molecules. **Physics** is the branch of science that deals with the interaction of energy, matter, space, and time.

Lesson 1-2

- **Matter** is anything that has mass and takes up space.
- **Properties** are characteristics that describe an object. Mass, volume, weight, and density are four properties of matter.

Lesson 1-3

- A **state of matter** is a physical form of matter. A **solid** is a state of matter with a definite shape and volume.
- A **liquid** is a state of matter with a definite volume but no definite shape.
- A **gas** is a state of matter that has no definite shape or volume.
- **Plasma** is a fourth state of matter that is rare on Earth but plentiful in other parts of the universe.

Lesson 1-4

- Matter can change state.
- **Freezing** is a change from a liquid to a solid.
- **Melting** is a change from a solid to a liquid.
- **Evaporation** is a change from a liquid to a gas at the surface of the liquid.
- **Condensation** is a change from a gas to a liquid.
- **Sublimation** is a change from a solid to a gas.

Lesson 1-5

- Physical properties can be observed or measured without changing the makeup of a substance.
- A **physical change** does not produce any new substances. A **chemical change** produces new substances.

Key Term Challenges

chemical change (p. 26)
chemistry (p. 16)
condensation (p. 22)
evaporation (p. 22)
freezing (p. 22)
gas (p. 20)
liquid (p. 20)
matter (p. 18)
melting (p. 22)
physical change (p. 26)
physics (p. 16)
plasma (p. 20)
properties (p. 18)
solid (p. 20)
specialization (p. 16)
state of matter (p. 20)
sublimation (p. 22)

MATCHING Write the Key Term from above that best matches each description.

1. solid, liquid, or gas
2. branch of science that deals with the interaction of atoms and molecules
3. change from a gas to a liquid
4. change that does not produce a new substance
5. change from a solid to a liquid
6. state of matter that has no definite shape or volume
7. studying or working in only one area of a subject

FILL IN Write the Key Term from above that best completes each statement.

8. Water changing into ice is an example of _____.
9. During _____, liquids gain enough heat energy to change into the gas state.
10. A _____ is a state of matter with a definite shape and volume.
11. New substances are produced during a _____.
12. Anything that has mass and takes up space is _____.
13. Mass and volume are characteristics, or _____, of matter.
14. Milk is an example of a _____.
15. Two major branches of physical science are chemistry and _____.

Content Challenges TEST PREP

MULTIPLE CHOICE **Write the letter of the term or phrase that best completes each statement.**

1. Water vapor changes to liquid water in a process called
   a. condensation.
   b. evaporation.
   c. melting.
   d. freezing.

2. The four states of matter are solid, liquid, gas, and
   a. metals.
   b. nonmetals.
   c. plasma.
   d. air.

3. Burning is an example of a
   a. state change.
   b. chemical change.
   c. physical change.
   d. physical property.

4. Particles of matter are tightly packed together in
   a. a solid.
   b. a liquid.
   c. a gas.
   d. a vapor.

5. Four properties of matter are mass, volume, weight, and
   a. distance.
   b. pressure.
   c. density.
   d. size.

6. Sublimation is a process in which a solid changes directly to a
   a. gas.
   b. liquid.
   c. ice.
   d. plasma.

7. Matter is anything that has mass and
   a. changes state.
   b. has color.
   c. takes up space.
   d. energy.

8. Evaporation is an example of a
   a. change of state.
   b. chemical change.
   c. solid changing to a gas.
   d. property of matter.

9. Matter that has no definite shape or volume is
   a. in the nonmetal state.
   b. in the gas state.
   c. in the liquid state.
   d. in the solid state.

10. Freezing is the opposite of
    a. evaporating.
    b. melting.
    c. condensing.
    d. solidifying.

TRUE/FALSE **Write *true* if the statement is true. If the statement is false, change the underlined term to make the statement true.**

11. <u>Weight</u> is a measure of the pull of gravity on an object.

12. When a solid melts, its particles <u>lose</u> heat energy.

13. The particles of a <u>liquid</u> can only vibrate in place.

14. <u>Physical properties</u> can be observed without changing the makeup of a substance.

15. All matter takes up space and has <u>color</u>.

16. Iron rusting is an example of a <u>physical</u> change.

Concept Challenges TEST PREP

WRITTEN RESPONSE **Answer each of the following questions in complete sentences.**

1. **COMPARE:** What are the differences between physical change and chemical change?
2. **DESCRIBE:** What happens to the particles of a substance as it changes from a solid to a liquid to a gas?
3. **INFER:** Why does evaporation require that heat energy be added to a substance?
4. **RELATE:** What is the relationship between the mass and the volume of an object?
5. **ANALYZE:** Is tearing paper a physical change or a chemical change?

INTERPRETING A DIAGRAM **Match the picture of each object to the arrangement of its molecules.**

6.

Solid

A.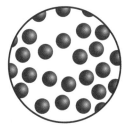

7.

Gas

B.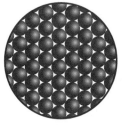

8.

Liquid

C.

Chapter 2 Density

▲ **Figure 2-1** A buoy floats in water.

What would happen if you were to drop an iron nail in the water next to the buoy in Figure 2-1? If you say that the nail would sink, you are correct. Yet, the buoy is also made of iron, and it is floating. Even the added mass of the animals on the buoy does not make it sink. It has to do with the density of the nail and the shape and density of the buoy. All matter has density. By making certain measurements, the density of any sample of matter can be calculated. Knowing the density of a substance can help us identify it.

▶How is knowing density helpful in the science lab?

Contents

2-1 What is density?

Objective
Define density.

Key Term
density (DEHN-suh-tee): mass per unit volume

Density Which do you think is heavier, a kilogram of cotton or a kilogram of iron? You may already know the answer to this riddle. They both weigh the same amount. However, a kilogram of cotton takes up a greater amount of space, or volume. A kilogram of iron is small enough to hold in your hand. A kilogram of iron takes up less space because iron has a much greater density than cotton does. **Density** is the mass per unit volume of a substance. In other words, density measures how much of a substance's mass fits in a given space.

▲ **Figure 2-2** The bale of cotton at the top has a mass of 1 kg. The iron frying pan below it also has a mass of 1 kg.

▶ DEFINE: What is density?

Units of Density You can find the density of a substance by finding the mass of a unit volume of the substance. Units of density include units of mass and volume. Mass is measured in grams. The volume of solids is measured in cubic centimeters. The volume of liquids can be measured in milliliters. One milliliter is equal to one cubic centimeter. Therefore, the density of any substance can be given in grams per cubic centimeter, or g/cm^3. For example, water has a density of 1 g/cm^3. One gram of water takes up one cubic centimeter of space. The densities of some common substances are listed in Figure 2-3.

DENSITIES OF SOME COMMON SUBSTANCES	
Substance	**Density (g/cm^3)**
Air	0.0013
Alcohol	0.8
Aluminum	2.7
Cork	0.2
Gold	19.3
Iron	7.8
Lead	11.3
Mercury	13.5
Silver	10.5
Steel	7.8
Water	1.0

▲ **Figure 2-3**

▶ IDENTIFY: In what units is density measured?

Using Density Density is a physical property of matter. Every kind of matter has a density that can be measured. The density of a pure substance is always the same. For example, the density of lead is always 11.3 g/cm^3. The density of mercury is always 13.6 g/cm^3. Density does not depend on the size or shape of the substance.

Density can be used to help identify different kinds of matter. Suppose two metals look similar. You know that one may be silver and the other aluminum. If you know the density of each sample, you can identify them. The sample with a density of 10.5 g/cm^3 is silver. The sample with a density of 2.7 g/cm^3 is aluminum.

▲ **Figure 2-4** Aluminum (left) and silver (right) look alike but have different densities.

3 ▶ **IDENTIFY:** What kind of property is density?

✓ CHECKING CONCEPTS

1. Density is the _____ per unit volume of a substance.
2. When a substance has a high density, a large mass fits into a _____ volume.
3. The units of _____ are grams per cubic centimeter.
4. Density is a physical _____ of all matter.
5. The density of silver is always _____.

💡 THINKING CRITICALLY

6. **CALCULATE:** What is the density of a metal block that has a mass of 525 g and a volume of 50 cm³?
7. **PREDICT:** How large a container would be needed to hold 800 g of water?
8. **SEQUENCE:** List the following substances in order from lowest density to highest density: iron, gold, steel, water, air, silver, and aluminum.

DESIGNING AN EXPERIMENT

Design an experiment to solve the following problem. Include a hypothesis, variables, a procedure, and a type of data to study.

PROBLEM: How can you determine the density of chalk?

Integrating Earth Science

TOPICS: neutron stars, black holes

THE DENSEST OBJECTS IN THE UNIVERSE

What are the densest objects thought to exist? The answer is neutron stars and black holes. Here is how they form. A new star is made mostly of hydrogen. As millions of years pass, the hydrogen fuses and changes into helium. When the hydrogen is used up, the star becomes a red giant or a supergiant.

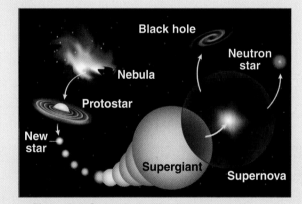

▲ **Figure 2-5** Stages in the life of a star

Supergiants start out with a much greater mass than the mass of our Sun. Such massive stars may blow up in a huge explosion called a supernova. After the explosion, some of the star's matter gets squeezed into a very dense object called a neutron star. The density of a neutron star is enormous. One teaspoon of matter from a neutron star would have a mass of 100 billion tons!

Some supergiants do not become neutron stars. The most massive stars collapse into black holes. A black hole has a density even greater than that of a neutron star. The density of a black hole behaves as if it is infinite. Not even light escapes the strong pull of gravity in a black hole.

Thinking Critically Explain the meaning of the name "black hole."

2-2 How is density measured?

Objective

Explain how to find the density of a solid or a liquid.

Finding Density To find the density of a material, you must measure both mass and volume. You can find density by dividing the mass by the volume. Remember that mass is measured in grams. Volume is measured in cubic centimeters or milliliters, so density is expressed in grams per cubic centimeter or grams per milliliter.

▶1 **IDENTIFY:** What measurements must you make before you can calculate the density of a material?

Density of a Liquid You can find the density of a liquid using a graduated cylinder and a balance.

- Find the mass of the graduated cylinder. Record your measurement.

- Pour some of the liquid you want to measure into the graduated cylinder. Write down the volume of the liquid.

- Place the graduated cylinder with the liquid on the balance. Record the mass.

- Find the mass of the liquid by subtracting the mass of the empty graduated cylinder from the mass of the graduated cylinder with the liquid.

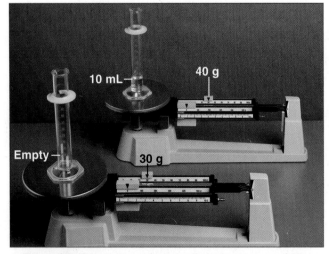

▲ **Figure 2-6** The empty graduated cylinder has a mass of 30 g. With the liquid the mass is 40 g, so the water has a mass of 10 g.

Now you are ready to calculate the density of the liquid. Look at the example shown. The mass of the liquid is 10 g. The volume is 10 mL. To find the liquid's density, divide its mass by its volume.

> density = mass ÷ volume
> density = 10 g ÷ 10 mL
> density = 1 g/mL

Notice that in this example, density is expressed in grams per milliliter. One milliliter is equal in volume to one cubic centimeter. The density of a liquid can be measured in grams per milliliter or grams per cubic centimeter.

▶2 **EXPLAIN:** Why can density be measured either in grams per cubic centimeter or in grams per milliliter?

Density of a Solid You can find the density of any solid if you know its mass and its volume. You can use a balance to find the mass of a solid. You can find the volume of a rectangular solid by multiplying its length by its width by its height. Look at the aluminum bar in Figure 2-7. Its mass is equal to 270 g. Its volume is equal to 10 cm × 5 cm × 2 cm, or 100 cm^3. To find the density of the aluminum bar, divide its mass by its volume.

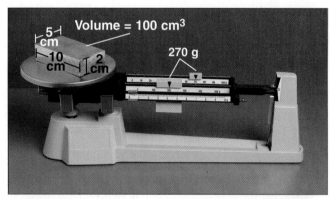

▲ **Figure 2-7** An aluminum bar of volume 100 cm^3 has a mass of 270 g.

> density = mass ÷ volume
> density = 270 g ÷ 100 cm^3
> density = 2.7 g/cm^3

▶3 **DESCRIBE:** How can you find the volume of a rectangular solid?

✓ CHECKING CONCEPTS

1. What measurements must be known in order to find the density of a substance?

2. What are the units of density for a liquid?

3. What equipment do you need to find the density of a liquid?

4. What three measurements must you make when finding the density of a liquid?

5. How can you find the density of a solid with a regular shape?

THINKING CRITICALLY

6. CALCULATE: If 5 mL of a liquid has a mass of 10 g, what is the density of the liquid?

7. EXPLAIN: When finding the density of a liquid, why must you first find the mass of the container holding the liquid?

BUILDING MATH SKILLS

Calculating Density Use Figure 2-8 to answer the following questions.

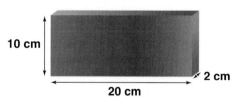

▲ Figure 2-8

8. What is the volume of the bar?

9. If the bar has a mass of 500 g, what is its density? Show your work.

10. How would the density of the bar be different if its mass was 4,520 g? What would the bar be made of?

Hands-On Activity

COMPARING DENSITIES OF LIQUIDS

You will need a graduated cylinder, food coloring, water, corn syrup, vegetable oil, and glycerine.

1. Color the water and glycerine differently, so you can tell them apart.

2. One at a time, slowly pour about 10 mL each of the water, corn syrup, vegetable oil, and glycerine into the graduated cylinder.

3. Observe the liquids as they form separate layers.

4. Make a sketch showing the order in which the liquids have settled in the graduated cylinder.

▲ STEP 3 Observe how the liquids separate.

Practicing Your Skills

5. HYPOTHESIZE: Why do you think the liquids separate into layers?

6. INFER: Which liquid is the most dense? Which liquid is the least dense?

7. SEQUENCE: List the four liquids in order from least to most dense.

2-3 What is specific gravity?

Objective
Explain what is meant by specific gravity.

Key Terms
specific (spuh-SIF-ik) **gravity:** density of a substance compared with the density of water

hydrometer (hy-DRAHM-uh-tuhr)**:** device used to measure specific gravity

Specific Gravity **Specific gravity** is the density of a substance compared with the density of water. It is often useful to compare the density of a substance with the density of water. Water is used as the standard for comparison because its density is 1 g/cm^3. You can find the specific gravity of a substance by dividing its density by the density of water.

Suppose you want to find the specific gravity of copper. The density of copper is 8.9 g/cm^3. The density of water is 1 g/cm^3. To find the specific gravity of copper, divide the density of copper by the density of water. The specific gravity of copper is 8.9. Notice that specific gravity has no units. When you divide like units, the units cancel each other out. The specific gravities of some common substances are listed in Figure 2-9.

| SPECIFIC GRAVITIES ||
Substance	Specific Gravity
Aluminum	2.64
Corn syrup	1.38
Diamond	3.5
Gasoline	0.7
Glycerine	1.26
Gold	19.3
Ice	0.92
Marble	2.56
Rubber	1.52
Water	1.00

▲ Figure 2-9

1 DEFINE: What is specific gravity?

Measuring Specific Gravity The specific gravity of a liquid can be measured with a device called a **hydrometer**. When a hydrometer is placed in a liquid, it floats. The higher the specific gravity of a liquid, the higher the hydrometer will float. You can tell the specific gravity of the liquid by reading the marking at the surface of the liquid.

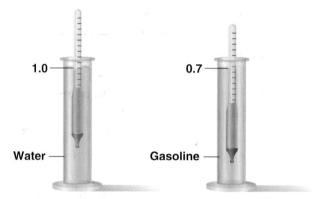

▲ **Figure 2-10** Water has a specific gravity of 1.00. Gasoline has a specific gravity of 0.7.

2 EXPLAIN: What determines the height at which a hydrometer floats in a liquid?

Uses of Specific Gravity Specific gravity has many practical uses. It can be used to identify pure substances, because each substance has a particular specific gravity. Hydrometers are used in clinical laboratory tests to find the specific gravity of blood and of urine. Lab technicians look for signs of increased glucose (sugar) or protein. Dehydration, a loss of fluid in the system, is also detected by specific gravity.

▲ **Figure 2-11** A hydrometer can test the specific gravity of any liquid.

Specific gravity can also be used to check the chemical purity of substances. Industries use specific gravity to check the quality of many of their products. For example, specific gravity is used to check the amount of cane sugar in a solution. It also is used to check the purity of milk.

 NAME: What are some uses of specific gravity?

✓ CHECKING CONCEPTS

1. Specific gravity compares the density of a substance with the density of _____.
2. Specific gravity has no _____ because the density units cancel each other out.
3. A hydrometer is a device that can be used to measure the specific gravity of a _____.
4. The _____ at which the hydrometer floats depends on the specific gravity of the liquid.
5. The purity of milk can be checked by using _____.

💡 THINKING CRITICALLY

6. **PREDICT:** In which liquid would a hydrometer float lower, gasoline or corn syrup? Explain.
7. **CALCULATE:** Silver has a density of 10.5 g/cm³. What is the specific gravity of silver?
8. **EXPLAIN:** Why does specific gravity have no units?

BUILDING SCIENCE SKILLS

Researching In a brief report, explain whether specific gravity could be useful in each of the following situations.

a. Determining the purity of vegetable oil
b. Determining whether a rock is real gold or fool's gold
c. Separating corn oil from corn syrup
d. Determining whether gasoline has been contaminated with water

 ## People in Science
MINERALOGIST

Minerals are natural substances found in soil and rock. Many products are made from minerals. For example, quartz is a mineral that is used to make timing devices in watches. Sulfur is a mineral that is used to make medicines.

Minerals must be mined, or taken from the earth. When a mineral deposit is found, a mining company needs to know how much of the mineral is present and what form the mineral is in. Mineralogists find answers to these questions. They take samples from a mineral deposit. They then study the specific gravity of the mineral to identify it and to determine its purity.

Mineralogists are employed by private industry, research laboratories, and the government. To be

▲ **Figure 2-12** This mineralogist is studying a limestone deposit.

a mineralogist, a person needs a college degree. Many mineralogists also have advanced degrees. If you are interested in this career, you should have a good background in science and mathematics.

Thinking Critically For what part of this job would you need math skills?

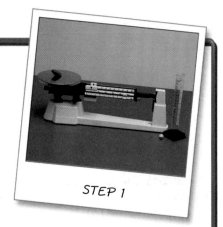

STEP 1

INVESTIGATE

Measuring Displacement
HANDS-ON ACTIVITY

1. Use a balance to find the masses of a small stone and a marble. Record your measurements in a data table.
2. Fill a 100-mL graduated cylinder with water to the 50-mL mark.
3. Gently place the stone in the water. Notice how much the water level rises. This increase is equal to the volume of water displaced. Record the change in volume of the water in your data table.
4. Repeat Step 3 with the marble.

THINK ABOUT IT: What is the volume of the stone? Of the marble? Does the amount of water displaced by an object depend on its mass? How do you know?

Objectives

Define displacement. Find the volume of an irregular solid.

Key Term

displacement (dihs-PLAYS-muhnt): the replacement, or pushing aside, of a volume of water, or any fluid, by an object

Displacement About 2,000 years ago, a Greek scientist named Archimedes (ahr-kuh-MEE-deez) made an interesting observation. As the story goes, he stepped into a bathtub full of water and noticed that the water level rose. When he sat down, some of the water spilled over the edge of the tub.

What Archimedes observed occurs whenever an object is placed in water. When objects are placed in water, they make the water level rise. The water level rises because water is pushed out of the way by the object. This replacement of a volume of water by an object is called **displacement**.

▲ Figure 2-13 Archimedes

▷ DEFINE: What is displacement?

Displacement and Volume When an object is placed completely under water, the volume of the water that the object displaces is equal to the volume of the object. Many objects, such as rocks, do not have a regular shape. You can use displacement to find the volume of an irregularly shaped object, as shown in Figure 2-14.

The stone displaces the water.

▲ **Figure 2-14** When a stone is lowered into a can of water, it displaces a volume of water equal to its own volume.

A simple way to find the volume of an irregularly shaped object is to pour some water into a graduated cylinder or a beaker that is marked to show volume. Record the volume of the water. Then, carefully place the object in the container of water. Record the new reading. The volume of the object is equal to the difference in the two volume readings.

For example, if a rock displaces 5 mL of water, the volume of the rock is 5 mL. This is shown in Figure 2-15.

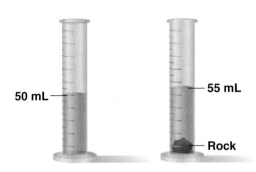

50 mL

55 mL

Rock

55 mL − 50 mL = 5 mL
Volume of rock = 5 mL

▲ **Figure 2-15** This rock displaced 5 mL of water.
It has a volume of 5 mL.

2 EXPLAIN: How can you find the volume of an irregularly shaped object?

 CHECKING CONCEPTS

1. If an object displaces 50 mL of water, the object's _____ is 50 mL.
2. When an object is placed in water, the water level _____.
3. The amount of water pushed aside by an object is called _____.

4. A rock is an _____ shaped object.
5. The _____ of an irregular object is equal to the volume of water it displaces.

THINKING CRITICALLY

6. ANALYZE: Does the amount of water displaced by an object depend on the object's mass? Explain your answer.
7. EXPLAIN: Why is displacement useful in finding the density of an irregularly shaped object?

BUILDING MATH SKILLS

Finding Volume Use displacement to find the volume of the following objects. Assume each has been placed in a graduated cylinder containing 50 mL of water.

a. A marble: new reading, 54 mL
b. A lead weight: new reading, 71 mL
c. A paper clip: new reading, 50.5 mL

Real-Life Science

PREVENTING SPILL-OVER

Have you ever made an ice cream soda? Did some, if not most, of the liquid wind up on the table after you put in the ice cream?

What happens when you fill a glass with a beverage, then try to put ice in the glass?

In order to prevent this displacement and the mess it causes, you must first place the ice in the glass, then add the liquid. This prevents spill-over.

In the bathroom, both the sink and tub have a feature built in to prevent accidental overflow. Do you know what that might be? If you fill the tub too high and then get into the water, you would cause a small flood without this feature. Pools and decorative fountains use the same principle to prevent overflow.

Thinking Critically How does placing the solid in the glass first prevent displacement?

▲ **Figure 2-16** Displacement can cause spill-over if you're not careful.

LAB ACTIVITY
Comparing Densities of Coins

Materials

Safety goggles, lab apron, triple-beam balance, 25-mL graduated cylinder, calculator, 10 pennies, 10 nickels, 10 dimes, water, eyedropper, plastic cup, paper towels

▲ **STEP 3** Fill the graduated cylinder to exactly 10 mL.

▲ **Figure 2-17** The water level should be at 10 mL.

BACKGROUND

You have just learned that matter has two basic properties. They are mass, which is the amount of material in an object, and volume, the amount of space that an object takes up. Dividing the mass of an object by its volume gives the density of the object, another property of matter. We will be finding the density of various coins using the displacement method.

PURPOSE

In this activity, you will observe and predict the density of the materials that make up pennies, nickels, and dimes using the displacement method. To do this, you will use 10 of each coin so that the measurements are easy to make.

PROCEDURE

1. Copy the chart in Figure 2-18.

2. Predict whether or not the densities of the coins will be different from each other. On what do you base your prediction?

3. Using the eyedropper, put exactly 10 mL of water into the 25-mL graduated cylinder as shown in Figure 2-17.

4. Find the mass of 10 pennies on the triple-beam balance and record it in the chart.

5. Carefully lower the pennies into the graduated cylinder. The water level should go up. Measure and record the new volume of the water.

6. Subtract 10 from the new volume of water to find the volume of the coins. Record this in the chart.

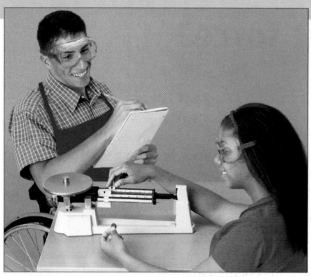

▲ **STEP 4** Find the mass of 10 pennies.

▲ **STEP 8** Record the volume of water when 10 dimes are added to 10 mL of water.

7. Now find the masses of 10 nickels and 10 dimes. Record the masses in the chart.

8. Repeat steps 4–6 for the 10 nickels and 10 dimes. Record the results in your chart.

Experiment	Mass (g)	Volume of Water (mL)	New Volume of Water (mL)	Volume of Coins (mL)	Density of Coins (g/mL)
10 pennies		10			
10 nickels		10			
10 dimes		10			

▲ **Figure 2-18** Copy this chart and use it to record your observations.

CONCLUSIONS

1. **CALCULATE:** Find the density of each coin. Divide the mass of coins by the volume of coins. Complete the chart.

2. **COMPARE:** How does your prediction compare with the actual results?

3. **INFER:** Which has a greater density, a penny or a nickel? Explain why.

4. **INFER:** Which has a greater density, a penny or a dime? Explain why.

5. **APPLY:** How would you find the density of a quarter? Explain your reasoning.

2-5 What is buoyant force?

Objective

Explain Archimedes' principle in terms of buoyant force and displacement.

Key Terms

buoyant force (BOI-unt-fors): the upward force that a fluid exerts on an object

newton: SI unit of force

What Makes Things Float? Have you ever tried to push a beach ball below the surface of the water? You can feel a force pushing up against the ball. If you let it go, the ball shoots right back up to the surface. The upward force that a fluid (liquid or gas) exerts on an object is called **buoyant force.**

Buoyant force acts in the direction opposite to the force of gravity. That's why you feel lighter in the pool than you do on land.

▶ **DEFINE:** What is buoyant force?

Archimedes' Principle In the last lesson, you read the story of Archimedes and the bathtub. When he stepped into the tub, he saw the water level rising. As he sat down, he also noticed that his body seemed to feel lighter in the water. He realized that the buoyant force on his body was equal to the weight of the water that his body displaced. This led to Archimedes' principle: the buoyant force on an object in a fluid equals the weight of the fluid that the object displaces.

▶ **STATE:** What does Archimedes' principle state?

Measuring Buoyant Force Look at Figure 2-19. The weight of the rock is shown in newtons (N). The **newton** is the SI unit of force. One kilogram equals 9.8N. If a rock weighing 4N displaces an amount of water weighing 1N, the buoyant force on the rock is 1N. If you take the weight of the rock and subtract the buoyant force, you can find the net force acting on the rock in water:

$$4N - 1N = 3N$$

The net force is the combination of the object's weight and the fluid's buoyant force. This makes the rock appear to weigh only 3N in the water.

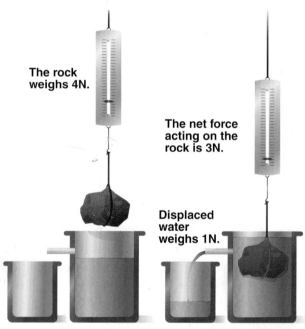

The rock weighs 4N.

The net force acting on the rock is 3N.

Displaced water weighs 1N.

▲ **Figure 2-19** The weight of the water that the rock displaces equals the buoyant force on the rock—1N.

▶ **APPLY:** If a buoyant force of 6N acts on a block placed in water, what is the weight of the water that the block displaces?

Buoyant Force and Floating Buoyant force explains why an object sinks or floats. The combination of the object's weight and the fluid's buoyant force is the net force acting on the object.

- If the buoyant force of a fluid is greater than the weight of the object, the net force is upward. The object will rise.
- If the buoyant force of a fluid is less than the weight of the object, the net force is downward. The object will sink.
- If the buoyant force equals the object's weight, there is no net force. The object will not rise or sink.

4 ▶ RECOGNIZE: When will an object float in water?

✓ CHECKING CONCEPTS

1. Buoyant force is the _____ force that a fluid exerts on an object..
2. The buoyant force on an object in a fluid equals the weight of the fluid it _____ .
3. When the buoyant force of a fluid is greater than the weight of an object, the object _____ .

4. Buoyant force decreases the downward pull of _____ on an object.
5. Archimedes' principle states the buoyant force on an object in a fluid equals the _____ of the fluid the object displaces.

THINKING CRITICALLY

6. **CALCULATE:** You submerge a metal block weighing 20N into a bucket of water. It displaces 6N of water. What is the net force acting on the block? How heavy does the block feel in water?
7. **EXPLAIN:** How are displacement and buoyant force related?

HEALTH AND SAFETY TIP

Always wear a life jacket if you go sailing or canoeing. If you fall into the water, the air in the jacket will decrease your overall density and help you to float, even if you cannot swim. Visit a local swimming pool. Ask the swimming instructor to describe how people are taught to float.

Science and Technology

SUBMARINE BALLAST

Submarines are specialized ships that travel on or under the surface of water. This is possible because the buoyancy of a submarine can be changed. Submarines have special containers called ballast tanks. Ballast tanks can be filled with either air or water, helping them float or sink.

Submarines are made of steel and other heavy materials. But, when a submarine's ballast tanks are full of air, the average density of the whole ship is less than the density of water. So, the buoyant force of water makes the submarine float.

To dive, the ballast tanks are flooded with water. This added weight makes the average density of the ship greater than the density of water. The buoyant force no longer supports the ship, and it sinks. To resurface, compressed air forces water out of the tanks. This action makes the submarine lighter again.

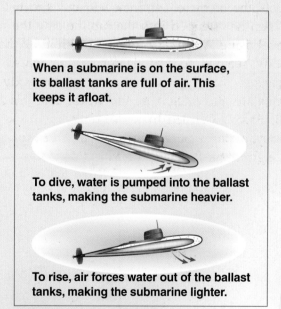

When a submarine is on the surface, its ballast tanks are full of air. This keeps it afloat.

To dive, water is pumped into the ballast tanks, making the submarine heavier.

To rise, air forces water out of the ballast tanks, making the submarine lighter.

▲ **Figure 2-20** How ballast tanks help submarines change their buoyancy

Thinking Critically What might happen if a ballast tank were to leak?

Integrating Social Studies

THE Big IDEA

How has shipbuilding changed throughout history?

How do you build a boat that will float? A boat floats when the weight of the water it displaces is equal to the weight of the boat itself. The more water the boat displaces, the greater the load it can carry.

Buoyancy is the tendency for an object to float in a fluid. Humans have made buoyant watercraft for ages. One ancient design is a raft built with a low-density material, like reeds or bamboo. A raft displaces water and remains buoyant, even though water may flow all around and through the raft. The first people of Australia probably arrived there from Asia

Bamboo Rafts, Circa 48,000 B.C.

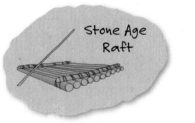

We can only guess what the boats looked like. However, there is strong evidence that the first people of New Guinea and Australia arrived in those countries on bamboo rafts 45,000 to 50,000 years ago.

Tree Trunk Canoes, Circa 1,500 B.C.

Around 1000 B.C., Polynesian sailors began to travel to the remote islands of the western Pacific. Their boats were made from hollowed tree trunks and planks lashed together with coconut fibers. The outrigger design gives stability. Double outrigger sailing canoes can make long ocean voyages.

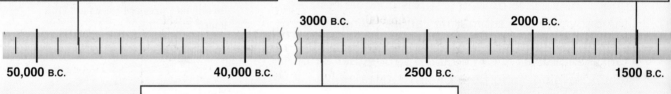

Reed Rafts, 3,000 B.C.

Pharaohs were buried with models of the boats that were used in Egypt in ancient times.

▲ **Figure 2-21** Shipbuilding throughout history

46

by floating on bamboo rafts. Ancient Egyptians used reed bundles to float on the Nile.

Another boat design is the watertight hull. A boat with a watertight hull encloses an air space that displaces water, giving buoyancy. The hull can be made of a material much more dense than water, like steel, iron, or even concrete. If the hull springs a leak, the air space in the boat fills with water and the boat begins to sink.

Look at the time line to compare boat designs throughout history. Then follow the directions in the Science Log to find out more about "the big idea."✦

WRITING ACTIVITY

Science Log

Plan a voyage on one of these crafts. How would you build your boat? Where would you go? What provisions would you bring? How would you navigate? Write a story about your voyage. To learn more about replicating ancient boats, start your project at www.conceptsandchallenges.com.

Oak Plank Long Ship, Circa A.D. 850

Viking Long Ship

The Vikings sailed around Europe in ships made of oak planks. Some carried dozens of oarsmen.

Steel Supertankers, A.D. 1980

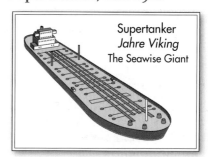

Supertanker *Jahre Viking* The Seawise Giant

One of the world's largest ships is an oil supertanker named *Jahre Viking*. It displaces 564,673 tons of water. It is 458 m long and 69 m wide.

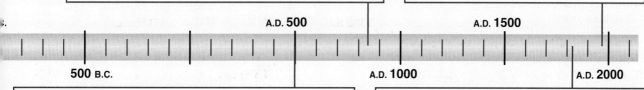

A.D. **500**   A.D. **1500**

500 B.C.   A.D. **1000**   A.D. **2000**

Wood and Leather Boats, A.D. **500**

The ancient "Voyage of Saint Brendan the Abbot" describes the crossing of the North Atlantic in a wood and leather boat in the sixth century. To see if this was possible, Tim Severin, a maritime historian, sailed from Ireland to Newfoundland on a replica of St. Brendan's boat.

St. Brendan's Curragh

Timber and Copper Barque, A.D. **1825**

First built as a warship, this ship changed to a survey ship in 1825. Her deck was raised and another mast was added. These changes helped in her new career as a scientific vessel. This small ship carried naturalist Charles Darwin around the world.

HMS *Beagle*

Chapter 2 Challenges

Chapter Summary

Lesson 2-1

- **Density** is the mass per unit volume of a substance.
- Density is measured in grams per cubic centimeter, or g/cm^3.
- Density is a basic property of all matter.
- Density can be used to identify different substances.

Lesson 2-2

- Density is equal to mass divided by volume.
- The density of a liquid can be measured in grams per milliliter or grams per cubic centimeter.
- To find the density of a solid with a regular shape, measure its mass and find its volume by multiplying its length by its width by its height.

Lesson 2-3

- **Specific gravity** is the density of a substance compared with the density of water. Specific gravity has no units.
- A **hydrometer** is a device used to measure the specific gravity of a liquid.

Lesson 2-4

- Archimedes observed that when an object is placed in water, it causes the water level to rise.
- The amount of water that an object replaces is called **displacement**.
- The volume of water that an object displaces is equal to the volume of the object.
- The volume of an irregularly shaped solid can be found by measuring how much water the object displaces.

Lesson 2-5

- **Buoyancy force** is the upward force that a fluid exert on an object.
- Archimedes' principle states that the buoyant force on an object in a fluid equals the weight of the fluid the object displaces.
- The buoyant force on an object is equal to the weight of the water that the object displaces.
- An object floats if the weight of the water it displaces is greater than its own weight.

Key Term Challenges

buoyant force (p. 44)
density (p. 34)
displacement (p. 40)
hydrometer (p. 38)
newton (p. 44)
specific gravity (p. 38)

MATCHING **Write the Key Term from above that best matches each description.**

1. device used to measure specific gravity
2. the upward force that a fluid exerts on an object.
3. density of a substance compared with the density of water
4. amount of water an object replaces
5. mass per unit volume

FILL IN **Write the Key Term from above that best completes each statement.**

6. To find the volume of an irregular solid, measure its _____.
7. A _____ floats high in a liquid with a high specific gravity.
8. The _____ of a substance tells the amount of mass in a certain volume.
9. A ship can float in water because of _____.
10. If the _____ of a substance is greater than 1.0, the substance is more dense than water.
11. The SI unit of force is _____.
12. If you know the density of a substance, you can easily find its _____.

Content Challenges TEST PREP

MULTIPLE CHOICE **Write the letter of the term or phrase that best completes each statement.**

1. Density is measured in
   a. milliliters per cubic centimeter.
   b. cubic centimeters per gram.
   c. grams per cubic centimeter.
   d. milliliters per gram.

2. Density is a basic physical property of
   a. gases.
   b. all matter.
   c. solids.
   d. liquids.

3. A hydrometer is used to measure
   a. mass.
   b. volume.
   c. length.
   d. specific gravity.

4. Archimedes discovered that objects weigh less when they
   a. have a larger volume.
   b. are placed in water.
   c. are suspended in air.
   d. are irregularly shaped.

5. The weight of the water that a floating object displaces is equal to the object's
   a. mass.
   b. weight.
   c. volume.
   d. density.

6. If the buoyant force on an object is equal to the object's weight, then the object will
   a. sink.
   b. float.
   c. become less dense.
   d. increase in mass.

7. If the buoyant force on an object is equal to the object's weight, then the weight of the object in water is
   a. 10.
   b. 100.
   c. zero.
   d. its own weight.

8. One milliliter is equal to one
   a. gram.
   b. cubic centimeter.
   c. meter.
   d. centimeter.

9. To find the density of a substance, you must measure
   a. mass and length.
   b. mass and weight.
   c. mass and volume.
   d. mass and buoyancy.

10. If a rock displaces 50 mL, the volume of the rock is
    a. 50 cm.
    b. 50 g/cm^3.
    c. 5 mL.
    d. 50 cm^3.

TRUE/FALSE **Write *true* if the statement is true. If the statement is false, change the underlined term to make the statement true.**

11. Specific gravity compares the density of a substance to the <u>weight</u> of water.

12. Units of <u>density</u> include units of mass and volume.

13. <u>Displacement</u> is the upward force a fluid exerts on an object.

14. When an object is placed in water, it will appear to lose all or some of its <u>mass</u>.

15. The buoyant force on an object is equal to the <u>volume</u> of the water it displaces.

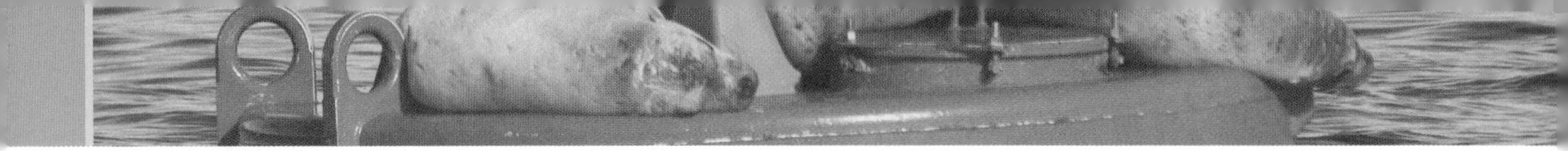

Concept Challenges TEST PREP

WRITTEN RESPONSE Answer each of the following questions in complete sentences.

1. **EXPLAIN:** Why is 1 cm^3 of wood lighter than 1 cm^3 of iron?

2. **ANALYZE:** Suppose two objects look alike, but one is made of marble and the other is made of plastic. How could you use specific gravity to identify the objects?

3. **EXPLAIN:** Why is it possible to measure the volume of a solid in milliliters?

4. **RELATE:** What is the relationship between the density of a substance and its specific gravity?

5. **RELATE:** What is the relationship between the buoyant force on an object and the amount of water that the object displaces?

6. **INFER:** What do you know about the density of an object that floats in water?

INTERPRETING A TABLE Use Figure 2-22 to answer the following questions.

7. **NAME:** What is the specific gravity of gold?

8. **INTERPRET:** Which substance has a higher specific gravity, diamond or glycerine?

9. **NAME:** What are two substances that will float in water?

10. **PREDICT:** What will happen if water and corn syrup are mixed together?

11. **ANALYZE:** Which will take up a greater volume, a kilogram of gold or a kilogram of rubber?

12. **ANALYZE:** Will a hydrometer float higher in glycerine or in gasoline? Explain.

SPECIFIC GRAVITIES	
Substance	**Specific Gravity**
Aluminum	2.64
Corn syrup	1.38
Diamond	3.5
Gasoline	0.7
Glycerine	1.26
Gold	19.3
Ice	0.92
Marble	2.56
Rubber	1.52
Water	1.00

▲ Figure 2-22

Chapter 3 Elements and Atoms

▲ **Figure 3-1** Bars of gold

Gold is one of the few things that can be found on Earth in pure form. If you could cut a bar of gold into smaller pieces, you would find that the smallest piece that could be identified as gold is one atom of gold. This atom is made up of even smaller parts. These very tiny parts are not gold. They can be found in all forms of matter. However, it is difficult to see them. Special tools are needed in order to study these small pieces of matter.

►Why is it difficult to study small pieces of matter?

Contents

3-1 What are elements?

INVESTIGATE

Observing Matter
HANDS-ON ACTIVITY

1. Copy the chart onto a sheet of paper. Your teacher will give you different models of matter. Examine each model. Notice how each one is made up of smaller, different-colored pieces.

2. Fill in the chart. The first line has been completed for you.

THINK ABOUT IT: How many models of matter are there? How many smaller pieces are there in each type of matter?

Observing Matter	
Model of Matter	What is it made of?
A	●●
B	
C	
D	

▲ **Figure 3-2** Model A is made up of two red circles.

Objective
Identify elements as substances that cannot be chemically broken down into simpler substances.

Key Term
element (EHL-uh-muhnt): substance that cannot be chemically broken down into simpler substances

Elements Most of the objects around you are made up of combinations of different kinds of matter. For example, the concrete in a sidewalk is made up of different types of matter—gravel, sand, cement, and water. However, even gravel, sand, cement, and water are made from other types of matter. But these types of matter, called elements, are different. **Elements** are substances that cannot be chemically broken down into simpler substances. All of the matter that you can observe on Earth is made up of elements or combinations of elements.

 DEFINE: What is an element?

The Known Elements There are more than 100 known elements. Most of the first ninety-two elements are found in nature. The rest of the elements have been made by scientists under special laboratory conditions.

Most elements are solids at room temperature. Some examples that you may be familiar with are iron, zinc, lead, silver, gold, calcium, sodium, nickel, and copper.

A few elements, such as mercury and bromine, are liquids at room temperature. Other elements, such as oxygen, hydrogen, helium, and neon, are gases at room temperature.

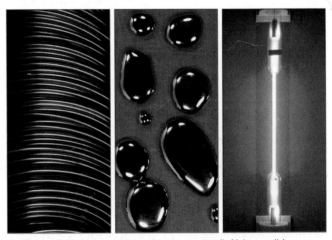

▲ **Figure 3-3** At room temperature, copper (left) is a solid, mercury (center) is a liquid, and neon (right) is a gas.

 IDENTIFY: How many elements are found in nature?

Elements and Matter All matter is made up of elements. Some types of matter are made up of only one element. An iron nail may contain only the element iron. Aluminum foil may be made up of only the element aluminum. Pure gold and pure silver are also made up of only one element.

There are some types of matter that are made up of more than one element. Water is made up of hydrogen and oxygen. Table salt is made up of sodium and chlorine.

In a laboratory, a chemist can break down this kind of matter. For example, sugar can be broken down into the elements that make it up—carbon, hydrogen, and oxygen. These elements cannot be chemically broken down into simpler substances.

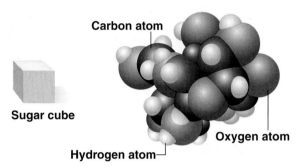

▲ Figure 3-4 Sugar can be broken down into the elements that make it up.

Carbon atom

Sugar cube

Oxygen atom

Hydrogen atom

3 NAME: What three elements make up sugar?

✓ CHECKING CONCEPTS

1. An _____ is a substance that cannot be chemically broken down into simpler substances.

2. Mercury is a _____ at room temperature.

3. There are more than _____ known elements.

4. Most of the known elements are _____ at room temperature.

5. An example of a substance made up of more than one element is _____.

THINKING CRITICALLY

6. **COMPARE:** Mercury and oxygen are elements. Explain one way in which they differ from each other.

7. **CLASSIFY:** Which of the following substances are elements?
   a. Gold   c. Mercury
   b. Hydrogen   d. Sugar

HEALTH AND SAFETY TIP

Many elements are dangerous to handle. The elements mercury and chlorine are poisonous. Sodium and potassium are explosive when exposed to water. Review the rules for chemical safety in the Handbook on page 14. Make a poster illustrating some chemical safety rules.

People in Science

MARIE CURIE (1867–1934)

Marie Sklodowska Curie was a Polish chemist. She worked and taught in Paris at the School of Physics and Chemistry and at the Sorbonne, the University of Paris. While teaching in Paris, she met the French scientist Pierre Curie, who became her husband.

Marie and Pierre Curie worked together. They became interested in radioactive (ray-dee-oh-AK-tihv) elements. Radioactive elements give off a form of energy known as radiation (ray-dee-AY-shuhn). Two years after radioactivity was first discovered in the element uranium, the Curies discovered the radioactive elements polonium and radium. In 1903, the Curies were awarded a Nobel Prize in physics.

▲ Figure 3-5 Marie Curie studied radioactive elements.

After the death of her husband in 1906, Marie Curie continued to study radioactive elements. In 1911, she was awarded a Nobel Prize in chemistry. Marie Curie is the only person ever to receive two Nobel Prizes in science.

Thinking Critically Why do you think Marie Curie was an important scientist?

3-2 What are atoms?

Atoms The element silicon cannot be broken down into a simpler type of matter. But what would happen if you took a piece of silicon and cut it into smaller and smaller pieces? There would be a piece of silicon so small that it could not be further divided. This smallest piece of the element silicon is called an atom. An **atom** is the smallest part of an element that can be identified as that element.

▶ **1** INFER: What would happen if you cut a piece of an element into smaller and smaller pieces?

Democritus The first person to suggest the idea of atoms was the Greek philosopher Democritus (dih-MAHK-ruh-tuhs). More than 2,400 years ago, Democritus asked whether it is possible to divide a sample of matter forever into smaller and smaller pieces. After much observation, he came to the conclusion that it is not possible to divide matter forever. At some point, a smallest piece of matter would be reached. Democritus named this smallest piece of matter an atom. The word *atom* comes from a Greek word that means "cannot be divided."

Democritus and his students did not know what atoms looked like. They did not know what scientists today know about atoms. However, they hypothesized that atoms were small, hard particles that were all made out of the same material but were of different shapes and sizes. They also thought that atoms were infinite in number, that they were always moving, and that they could be joined together.

▶ **2** STATE: What does the word *atom* mean?

Dalton's Atomic Theory In the early 1800s, an English chemist named John Dalton performed some experiments. He investigated properties of gases. His observations led him to believe that gases are made of individual particles. These individual particles are very similar to the idea of the atom proposed by Democritus. The results of his experiments and other observations about matter led Dalton to state an atomic theory of matter. The main parts of Dalton's atomic theory of matter are as follows:

- All elements are composed of atoms. Atoms cannot be divided or destroyed.

- Atoms of the same element are exactly alike.

- Atoms of different elements are different from each other.

- The atoms of two or more elements can join together to form types of matter called compounds.

Like Democritus, Dalton had some ideas about atoms that scientists no longer agree with. However, Dalton's atomic theory was the beginning of the modern theory of atoms.

▲ **Figure 3-6** John Dalton

▶ **3** LIST: What are the main parts of Dalton's atomic theory of matter?

Images of Atoms Atoms are extremely small. As small as they are, a special tool, called a scanning tunneling microscope (STM), can capture images of them. Figure 3-7 shows an image captured by an STM.

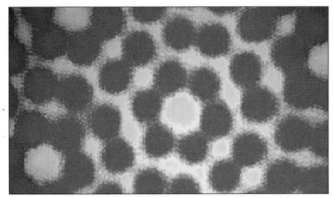

▲ **Figure 3-7** An image of silicon atoms produced by an STM

 NAME: What is an STM?

 CHECKING CONCEPTS

1. What is an atom?
2. Who was the first person to use the word *atom*?

3. Whose investigation on properties of gases led him to propose an atomic theory of matter?
4. What is the name of the tool that can capture images of an atom?

THINKING CRITICALLY

5. **COMPARE:** How are the ideas of Democritus and Dalton similar? How are they different?
6. **INFER:** How can an STM help prove Dalton's theory?

Web InfoSearch

Scanning Tunneling Microscopes STMs can take images of atoms.

SEARCH: Use the Internet to find out about the inventors of this type of microscope. Start your search at www.conceptsandchallenges.com. Some key search words are **Heinrich Rohrer** and **Gerd Karl Binnig**.

Science and Technology

PARTICLE ACCELERATORS

A particle accelerator is a device used to increase the energy of electrically charged particles. At very high speeds, these charged particles smash into atoms and break them apart. Then, scientists can study the pieces that are left after the collision.

▲ **Figure 3-8** In Batavia, Illinois, a particle accelerator lies under the circular outline.

Scientists use particle accelerators to study the forces that hold matter together. The machines speed up particles and race them around and around giant, usually circular, tracks. Many accelerators have one group of particles moving in one direction and another group moving in the other direction. When the particles are traveling fast enough, they are made to crash into each other. From their work with accelerators, scientists have been able to learn more about the parts that atoms are made of.

Particle accelerators are among the largest instruments ever built. In Batavia, Illinois, a particle accelerator is built around a 6.4-km circular track. A particle accelerator in Switzerland is build in a circular underground tunnel that is 27 km wide.

Thinking Critically Why do you think particle accelerators are so large?

3-3 What are the parts of an atom?

Objective
Identify the three basic parts of an atom.

Key Terms
nucleus: center, or core, of an atom
proton: particle that has a positive charge
neutron: particle that has no charge
electron: particle that has a negative charge

Structure of an Atom According to the modern atomic theory, an atom has a center, or core, called the **nucleus**. In the nucleus are protons and neutrons. A **proton** is a particle that has a positive charge (+). A **neutron** is a particle that does not have any charge. Surrounding the nucleus is a cloud of very tiny particles called electrons. An **electron** is a particle that has a negative charge (–). The negative charge on an electron is exactly equal to the positive charge on a proton.

▶ **STATE:** Where is the nucleus found?

Thomson's Model The first scientist to suggest that an atom contains smaller particles was J. J. Thomson of England. In 1897, Thomson passed an electric current through a gas. He found that the gas gave off rays made up of negatively charged particles. Today, these particles are known as electrons. Because atoms are neutral, Thomson reasoned that there must also be positively charged particles inside an atom. Thomson hypothesized that an atom was made up of a positively charged material with negatively charged particles scattered evenly throughout.

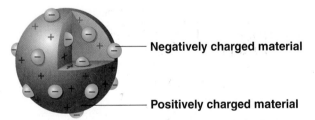

— Negatively charged material

— Positively charged material

▲ **Figure 3-9** Thomson's model of an atom

▶ **IDENTIFY:** What type of particle did Thomson discover in an atom?

Rutherford's Model
In 1911, a British scientist named Ernest Rutherford performed an experiment to test Thomson's atomic model. Rutherford discovered that an atom is mostly empty space. He concluded that the positively charged particles are contained in a small central core

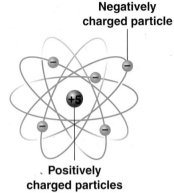

Negatively charged particle

Positively charged particles

▲ **Figure 3-10** Rutherford's model of an atom

called the nucleus. He also concluded that the negatively charged particles were attracted to the positively charged particles found in the nucleus. This attraction holds the negatively charged particles in the atom.

▶ **DESCRIBE:** What did Rutherford discover about an atom?

Bohr's Model
Rutherford's model of the atom was useful but it did not explain the arrangement of electrons. In 1913, Danish scientist Niels Bohr proposed that the electrons in an atom are found in

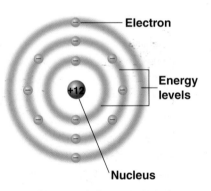

Electron

Energy levels

Nucleus

▲ **Figure 3-11** Bohr's model of an atom

different energy levels. Each energy level is at a certain distance from the nucleus. Electrons in different energy levels move around the nucleus in different orbits, much as the planets move in orbits around the Sun. Bohr's model explains simple atoms such as oxygen well, but it does not explain more complex atoms.

▶ **LOCATE:** Where did Bohr say that electrons are found in an atom?

Modern Model The modern atomic model is based on the works of Thomson, Rutherford, Bohr, and other scientists who have studied the nature of atoms. According to the modern model, the location of the electrons in an atom cannot be known. Therefore, the modern model of the atom does not show any paths that electrons could be found in. Instead, energy levels are used to predict the place where an electron is most likely to be found outside of the nucleus. This area is called the electron cloud. The modern model also identifies the nucleus as containing protons and neutrons.

◀ **Figure 3-12** Modern model of an atom

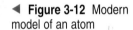

5 ▶ EXPLAIN: What is the electron cloud?

✓ **CHECKING CONCEPTS**

1. What are electrons?
2. Where are protons found in an atom?
3. What are the particles in an atom that do not have any charge called?
4. Who first suggested that atoms are made up of smaller particles?
5. Who discovered that an atom is mostly empty space?
6. Who proposed the idea that electrons are found in different energy levels around the nucleus?

💡 **THINKING CRITICALLY**

7. **CONTRAST:** How did Rutherford's model of the atom differ from Thomson's model?
8. **EXPLAIN:** According to the modern atomic model, where are protons, neutrons, and electrons found?

How Do They Know That?

QUARKS AND LEPTONS

In recent years, scientists have discovered that protons and neutrons are made up of even smaller particles. Based on experiments using particle accelerators, scientists have identified two groups of subatomic particles. All matter is made up of these particles. These groups of particles are known as quarks and leptons. The word *quark* was first used as the name of a subatomic particle by American physicist Murray Gell-Mann. The word *lepton* comes from a Greek word that means "small" or "thin."

Quarks make up protons, neutrons, and other particles found in the nucleus of an atom. There are six types of quarks and six types of leptons. Electrons are a type of lepton. Electrons are not believed to be made up of smaller particles. The basic particles in an atom are made up of combinations of two or three different quarks or one lepton.

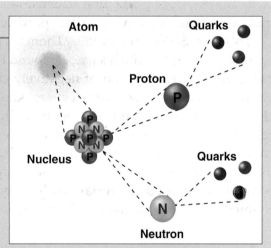

▲ **Figure 3-13** Protons and neutrons are made up of quarks.

Thinking Critically What is the relationship between an electron and a lepton?

3-4 What is an atomic number?

Objective

Explain what is meant by the atomic number of an element.

Key Term

atomic number: number of protons in the nucleus of an atom

Elements and Atomic Number The atoms of different elements have different numbers of protons. You have learned that protons are particles that have a positive charge (+) and are found within the nucleus of an atom. The number of protons found in the nucleus of an atom is called the **atomic number**. Each element has a different atomic number because the atoms of each element have a different number of protons in their nuclei.

The element with the smallest atomic number is hydrogen. Hydrogen has an atomic number of 1. This means that an atom of hydrogen has only one proton in its nucleus. Oxygen has an atomic number of 8 because there are 8 protons in the nucleus of an atom of oxygen. Gold has an atomic number of 79. There are 79 protons in an atom of gold. Figure 3-15 lists the atomic numbers of some common elements. Figure 3-14 shows the nuclei of the elements helium, beryllium, and neon. You can see that the number of protons in the nuclei of each element is the same as the atomic number of each element.

ATOMIC NUMBERS OF SOME ELEMENTS	
Element	Atomic number
Hydrogen	1
Helium	2
Carbon	6
Nitrogen	7
Oxygen	8
Sodium	11
Aluminum	13
Sulfur	16
Chlorine	17
Calcium	20
Iron	26
Copper	29
Silver	47
Gold	79
Lead	82

▲ Figure 3-15

1 DEFINE: What is an atomic number?

Importance of Atomic Number Your fingerprint is very important because it identifies you. No other person can have the same fingerprint as yours. The atomic number of an element is very important because it identifies that element. No two elements have the same atomic number. In fact, the number of protons in the nucleus of an atom tells you what that element is.

2 EXPLAIN: Why is the atomic number of an element important?

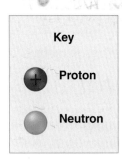

Key

 Proton

Neutron

Helium
Atomic number = 2

Beryllium
Atomic number = 4

Neon
Atomic number = 10

▲ **Figure 3-14** The nuclei of helium, beryllium, and neon

Atomic Number and Electrons If you know the atomic number of an element, you also know the number of electrons in an atom of that element. They are both the same number. They are the same because an atom has neither a positive nor a negative charge. It is neutral. In order for an atom to be neutral, the positive charges of the protons and the negative charges of the electrons must cancel each other out. So the number of electrons must be the same as the number of protons.

 CALCULATE: How many electrons are there in an atom of an element with an atomic number of 14?

✔ CHECKING CONCEPTS

1. The atomic number is the number of _____ in the nucleus of an atom.
2. Every _____ has its own atomic number.
3. The element with the smallest atomic number is _____.
4. No two elements have the same _____.
5. The number of protons in an atom is equal to the number of _____ in the atom.

💡 THINKING CRITICALLY

6. **ANALYZE:** If an atom has an atomic number of 12, how many electrons does the atom have?
7. **EXPLAIN:** How can knowing the atomic number of an atom help you to identify the element?

INTERPRETING VISUALS

Use Figure 3-15 to answer the following questions.

8. **IDENTIFY:** What is the atomic number of calcium?
9. **IDENTIFY:** How many protons are there in an atom of copper?
10. **NAME:** What element has an atomic number of 13?
11. **IDENTIFY:** How many electrons are there in an atom of aluminum?

People in Science

CHIEN-SHIUNG WU (1912–1997)

Chien-Shiung Wu was born in Liu Ho, China. She was a theoretical physicist. Chien-Shiung Wu came to America in 1936 to study for a doctorate in physics. She received her Ph.D. from the University of California at Berkeley. During World War II, she taught physics at Smith College and at Princeton University. After the war, she went to Columbia University to do research in nuclear physics. She became a professor of physics at Columbia in 1957.

▲ **Figure 3-16** Chien-Shiung Wu studied beta decay.

Chien-Shiung Wu's area of specialization was beta decay. In beta decay, the nucleus of an atom gives off electrons. This causes the atom to change into another element. Chien-Shiung Wu made many important contributions to scientists' present knowledge of the atom. Her experiments on beta decay confirmed a theory proposed by two other scientists. These scientists, Tsung Dao Lee and Chen Ning Yang, later won a Nobel Prize for their theory. Chien-Shiung Wu was the first woman to receive the Comstock Prize from the National Academy of Sciences.

Thinking Critically How did Chien-Shiung Wu's work contribute to the work of other scientists?

3-5 What is an atomic mass?

INVESTIGATE

Making a Model of a Nucleus
HANDS–ON ACTIVITY

1. Obtain colored disks, plastic wrap, and wire-ties from your teacher. Place two red disks and two blue disks in the center of a small piece of plastic wrap. Use a wire-tie to wrap the plastic around the disks.

2. Wrap and tie six red disks and six blue disks using another piece of plastic wrap.

3. Count the total number of disks inside each bag.

THINK ABOUT IT: If each "bundle" represents the nucleus of an atom, what does each colored disk represent? What does the total number of disks inside each bag represent?

STEP 1

Objective

Explain how to find the atomic mass and the mass number of an atom.

Key Terms

atomic mass: total mass of the protons and neutrons in an atom, measured in atomic mass units (amu)

mass number: number of protons and neutrons in the nucleus of an atom

Atomic Mass Unit Imagine trying to measure the mass of something so small that you cannot see it. Well, scientists do just that when they measure the mass of an atom. The mass of an atom is very small. It is not easy to measure the mass of an atom in grams. So, in order to measure the mass of an atom, scientists have developed a special unit. This unit is called the atomic mass unit, or amu.

One amu is equal to the mass of one proton. Neutrons and protons have almost the same mass. Therefore, one amu is also equal to the mass of one neutron. The mass of an electron is equal to 1/1,836 amu. Because electrons are so small, only the masses of protons and neutrons are used to find the mass of an atom.

▶ **1 INFER:** What is the mass, in amu, of an atom with one proton and two neutrons?

Atomic Mass The total mass of the protons and neutrons in an atom is called the **atomic mass**. Atomic mass is measured in atomic mass units (amu). Because the atoms of an element can have different numbers of neutrons, scientists often give the average atomic mass for an element.

▶ **2 DEFINE:** What is an atomic mass?

Mass Number The total number of protons and neutrons in an atom is called the **mass number**. You can find the mass number for any element. The mass number can be found by rounding the average atomic mass to the nearest whole number. For example, the average atomic mass of lithium is 6.941 amu. The mass number of lithium is 7 (6.941 rounds to 7).

AVERAGE ATOMIC MASS AND MASS NUMBER		
Element	Average atomic mass	Mass number
Hydrogen	1.008	1
Helium	4.003	4
Carbon	12.011	12
Oxygen	15.999	16

▲ **Figure 3-17** To find the mass number, round the average atomic mass to the nearest whole number.

▶ **3 DEFINE:** What is a mass number?

Finding Neutrons If you know the atomic number and the mass number of an element, then you can find the number of neutrons in an atom of the most common form of that element. You can use the following formula:

$$\text{mass number} - \text{atomic number} = \text{number of neutrons}$$

Look at Figure 3-18 to find the number of neutrons in an atom of lithium.

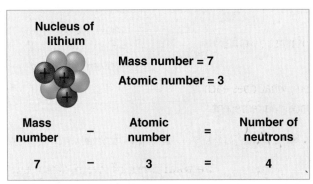

Nucleus of lithium

Mass number = 7
Atomic number = 3

Mass number	–	Atomic number	=	Number of neutrons
7	–	3	=	4

▲ **Figure 3-18** You can find the number of neutrons in an atom of the most common form of lithium.

 ANALYZE: How many neutrons are in the nucleus of an atom of carbon?

✓ CHECKING CONCEPTS

1. The mass of a neutron is the same as the mass of a _____.

2. Because they are so small, _____ are not counted when measuring the mass of an atom.

3. The _____ is the unit used by scientists to measure the mass of an atom.

4. The mass number tells the total number of _____ and neutrons in the nucleus of an atom.

💡 THINKING CRITICALLY

5. **ANALYZE:** Explain why the mass number of an element can never be less than the atomic number of that element.

6. **INFER:** Why is the mass of an electron not added to the atomic mass of an atom?

BUILDING MATH SKILLS

Calculating The atomic number of element *x* is 30 and the mass number is 65. Find the number of protons, neutrons, and electrons in an atom of element *x*.

 ## *People in Science*

DMITRI MENDELEEV (1834–1907)

Dmitri Mendeleev (men-duh-LAY-uhf) was a Russian chemist. He was a professor of chemistry at St. Petersburg University in Russia. He is best known for developing the first table of elements organized according to properties.

Mendeleev wrote a book called *Principles of Chemistry.* For this book, Mendeleev collected thousands of facts about the 60 elements that were known at that time. He tried to find a way to organize this information. He thought that a certain pattern, or order, of the elements must exist.

▲ **Figure 3-19** Dmitri Mendeleev

Mendeleev decided to test his hypothesis. He wrote the name of each element and the properties of that element on a card. Then, he tried different arrangements of the cards for the 60 elements. When he arranged the cards in order of increasing atomic mass, the elements fell into groups with similar properties.

Thinking Critically Why do you think it was important to Mendeleev to organize his information into a table?

3-6 How are electrons arranged in an atom?

Objective

Describe how the electrons in an atom are arranged in energy levels.

Key Term

energy level: place in an electron cloud where an electron is most likely to be found

The Electron Cloud For many years, scientists thought that electrons moved around the nucleus of an atom in much the same way as the planets orbit the Sun. Scientists now know that it is not possible to predict the exact path of an electron. You have learned that the area in an atom where electrons are likely to be found is called the electron cloud. Scientists use the word *cloud* because they know that they cannot predict the exact location of electrons nor the speed at which electrons move at any given time.

1 ▶ DESCRIBE: What is an electron cloud?

Energy Levels According to the modern atomic theory, electrons are arranged in energy levels around the nucleus of an atom. An **energy level** is the place in the electron cloud where an electron is most likely to be found. Each energy level is a different distance from the nucleus. The lowest, or first, energy level is closest to the nucleus. Electrons with more energy are found in energy levels farther away from the nucleus.

Each energy level can hold only a certain number of electrons. The first energy level can hold only two electrons. The second energy level can hold up to eight electrons. The third energy level can hold up to 18 electrons. The fourth energy level can hold up to 32 electrons. For the elements with atomic numbers between 1 and 20, the electrons in an atom of an element fill up the energy levels in order, beginning with the lowest.

An atom of helium has two electrons. These two electrons fill the first energy level. An atom of lithium has three electrons. Two of these electrons fill the first energy level. The third electron occupies the second energy level. An atom of chlorine has 17 electrons. Two electrons fill the first energy level, eight electrons fill the second level, and seven electrons occupy the third level.

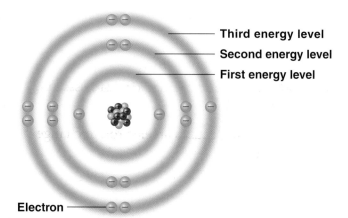

▲ **Figure 3-20** An atom of chlorine has three energy levels. The first two energy levels are completely filled. Seven electrons occupy the third energy level.

2 ▶ PREDICT: Where would you expect to find the six electrons in an atom of carbon?

Changing Energy Levels Adding energy to an atom or removing energy from an atom can cause the electrons in the atom to move from one energy level to another. If an electron gains enough energy, it jumps to a higher energy level. When this happens, the atom is in an "excited" state.

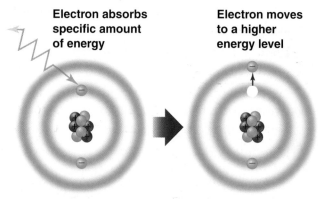

Electron absorbs specific amount of energy

Electron moves to a higher energy level

▲ **Figure 3-21** In an "excited" state, an electron jumps to a higher energy level.

If an electron in an excited atom loses enough energy, it drops back to a lower energy level. As it drops back, the electron gives off energy, often in the form of light.

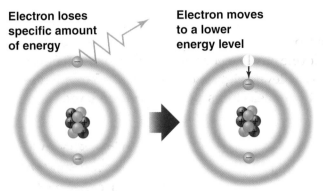

Electron loses specific amount of energy

Electron moves to a lower energy level

▲ **Figure 3-22** When an electron in an excited state loses energy, it drops to a lower energy level.

 ANALYZE: What causes an electron to change energy levels?

✔ **CHECKING CONCEPTS**

1. An energy level is the place in the electron cloud where an _____ is most likely to be found in an atom.

2. The _____ energy level is located closest to the nucleus of an atom.

3. The second energy level can hold up to _____ electrons.

4. An electron will drop to a lower energy level when it _____ energy.

 THINKING CRITICALLY

5. **ANALYZE:** The atoms of a certain element have the first and second energy levels completely filled with electrons. What is the atomic number of this element? Explain how you know this.

 Hands-On Activity

MAKING ELECTRON DOT DIAGRAMS

You will need element symbol cards, a periodic table, and a felt-tip marker.

1. An electron dot diagram is a simple way to show how the electrons in the outermost energy level of an atom are arranged. Look at the electron dot diagrams in Figure 3-23 for the elements carbon, atomic number 6, and nitrogen, atomic number 7.

2. Obtain three element symbol cards from your teacher. Notice how the element on each card has a symbol along with its atomic number.

3. Use the diagrams for carbon and nitrogen to help you make electron dot diagrams of each of your elements.

▲ **Figure 3-23** Electron dot diagrams for carbon and nitrogen

Practicing Your Skills

4. **EXPLAIN:** Why do you need to know the atomic number of an element to complete an electron dot diagram?

5. **OBSERVE:** What pattern do you notice in the way the electron dots are arranged around the symbol?

3-7 What is the periodic table?

Objective

Trace the development of the modern Periodic Table of Elements.

Key Terms

chemical symbol: shortened way of writing the name of an element

periodic (pihr-ee-AHD-ihk)**:** repeating pattern

group: vertical column of elements in the periodic table

period: horizontal row of elements in the periodic table

Shortened Names For many years, scientists had to spell out the names of all the known elements. However, in the early 1800s, a Swedish scientist named Jons Jakob Berzelius (buhr-ZEE-lee-uhs) created a new system of representing elements. This system uses letters called chemical symbols. **Chemical symbols** are a shortened way of writing the names of elements.

1▶ DEFINE: What is a chemical symbol?

Chemical Symbols Chemical symbols are created from the name of each element. There are usually one or two letters in a chemical symbol. The first letter of a chemical symbol is always capitalized. If there is a second letter, it is written using the lowercase. For example, Ne is the chemical symbol for neon. Some chemical symbols come from the Latin name for the element. The Latin name for lead is *plumbum*. The chemical symbol is Pb. Some elements have three letters in their chemical symbols. These chemical symbols are temporary until scientists come to an agreement on their permanent names.

2▶ EXPLAIN: How are chemical symbols written?

Arranging Elements By the 1800s, scientists had discovered many elements. They began to search for ways to organize these elements. In 1869, a Russian chemist named Dmitri Mendeleev listed the elements in order of increasing atomic mass.

Mendeleev noticed that elements with similar properties occurred periodically. The word **periodic** means "to repeat in a certain pattern." Based on the pattern he observed, Mendeleev arranged the elements in rows in a chart. Elements with similar properties were in the same column of his chart, one under the other. Mendeleev's chart was the first periodic table of elements. Figure 3-24 shows what Mendeleev's periodic table looked like.

			Ti = 50	Zr = 90	? = 180
			V = 51	Nb = 94	Ta = 182
			Cr = 52	Mo = 96	W = 186
			Mn = 55	Rh = 104, 4	Pt = 197
			Fe = 56	Rn = 104, 4	Ir = 198
			Ni = Co = 59	Pd = 106, 6	Os = 199
H = 1			Cu = 63, 4	Ag = 108	Hg = 200
	Be = 9,4	Mg = 24	Zn = 65, 2	Cd = 112	Au = 197
	B = 11	Al = 27, 4	? = 68	Ur = 116	Bi = 210
	C = 12	Si = 28	? = 70	Sn = 118	Ti = 204
	N = 14	P = 31	As = 75	Sb = 122	Pb = 207
	O = 16	S = 32	Se = 79, 4	Te = 128?	
	F = 19	Cl = 35, 5	Br = 80	J = 127	
Li = 7	Na = 23	K = 39	Rb = 85, 4	Cs = 133	
		Ca = 40	Sr = 87, 6	Ba = 137	
		? = 45	Ce = 92		
		?Er = 56	La = 94		
		?Yt = 60	Di = 95		
		?In = 75, 6	Th = 118?		

▲ **Figure 3-24** Mendeleev's periodic table

3▶ DESCRIBE: How were elements arranged in Mendeleev's periodic table?

The Modern Periodic Table Mendeleev's periodic table was useful, but it had some problems. Some elements did not have properties similar to the other elements in the same column. The discovery of atomic numbers, which occurred about 50 years after Mendeleev's table was developed, led to a new table. By arranging the elements in order of increasing atomic number instead of increasing atomic mass, all the elements in the same column had similar properties. This new arrangement is known as the modern Periodic Table of Elements.

4▶ COMPARE: How is the modern periodic table different from Mendeleev's periodic table?

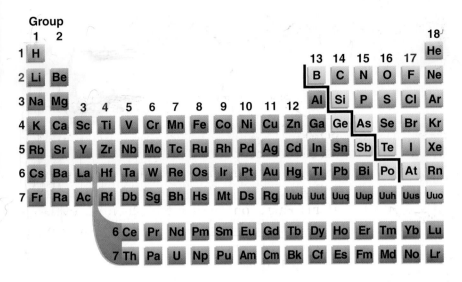

◀ **Figure 3-25** A simple version of the modern Periodic Table of Elements

Groups and Periods Look at the periodic table in Figure 3-25. Notice that there are 18 columns. These columns are called **groups**, or families. Elements that are in the same group have similar physical and chemical properties. For example, lithium (Li), sodium (Na), and potassium (K) are all solids that react explosively with water. Elements in the same group also have the same number of electrons in their outermost energy levels.

The table also has seven rows. Each row is called a **period**. You can see that Period 1 has only two elements, hydrogen and helium. The elements in a period do not have similar properties. In fact, the properties of each element in a period change greatly as you move from left to right. However, there is a pattern in a period. Part of the pattern is that each period starts with an element that is a solid and ends with an element that is a gas. The first period is the only exception. Elements in the same period also have the same number of energy levels.

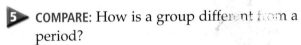 **COMPARE:** How is a group different from a period?

✓ CHECKING CONCEPTS

1. How is the first letter of a chemical symbol written?

2. How are the elements arranged in the modern periodic table?

3. What are the horizontal rows of the periodic table called?

4. How are elements in the same group similar?

5. Which scientist developed the first periodic table?

💡 THINKING CRITICALLY

6. **INFER:** Why would a scientist use Berzelius's system of representing elements?

7. **HYPOTHESIZE:** The symbol for carbon is C. The symbol for cobalt is Co. Why do you think a second letter was added to the chemical symbol of some elements? Why is the second letter written in the lowercase?

INTERPRETING VISUALS

Use Figure 3-25 to answer the following questions.

8. **IDENTIFY:** The first element in Group 17 is fluorine. What is its chemical symbol?

9. **IDENTIFY:** What group do boron (B) and thallium (Tl) belong to?

10. **NAME:** Name at least one element in Period 2.

11. **EXPLAIN:** Do you think calcium (Ca) and magnesium (Mg) have similar properties? Explain.

12. **IDENTIFY:** What group do copper (Cu) and gold (Au) belong to?

13. **IDENTIFY:** What period does iron (Fe) belong to?

BUILDING SOCIAL STUDIES SKILLS

Analyzing A few of the elements in the periodic table are named after countries, states, and planets. Use library resources, encyclopedias, or the Internet to find three of these elements. List their names and the name of the country, state, or planet for which they are named.

Integrating Physical, Earth, and Life Science

THE Big IDEA

What is the Periodic Table of Elements?

A great deal of information about the atoms that make up elements is presented in a chart called the Periodic Table of Elements. Every known element, including synthetic elements (elements made in a laboratory) is listed in the table. Information about each element, such as its name, chemical symbol, atomic number, and average atomic mass, is listed. Each element is arranged in the table in order of increasing atomic number.

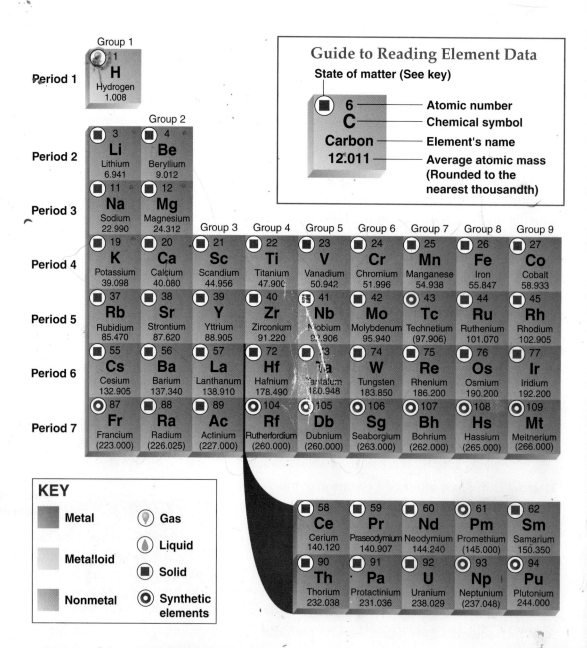

Guide to Reading Element Data

State of matter (See key)

6 — Atomic number
C — Chemical symbol
Carbon — Element's name
12.011 — Average atomic mass (Rounded to the nearest thousandth)

KEY

Metal | Gas
Metalloid | Liquid
Nonmetal | Solid | Synthetic elements

▲ **Figure 3-26** The Periodic Table of Elements

The elements that are arranged in vertical columns, called groups, have similar properties. The elements that are arranged in horizontal rows, called periods, have the same number of energy levels in each of their atoms. If more elements are discovered, they, too, will be listed in the table. The periodic table can also be used to help explain how elements combine to form every kind of matter in the universe. Elements are studied in all three major fields of science.

Look at the periodic table on these two pages. Then, follow the directions in the Science Log to find out more about "the big idea."✦

Science Log

Look at the periodic table. Which elements are you familiar with? In your science log, research and write about the kinds of elements that are in the objects that you use every day. Start your search at www.conceptsandchallenges.com.

Group 10	Group 11	Group 12	Group 13	Group 14	Group 15	Group 16	Group 17	Group 18
								2 **He** Helium 4.003
			5 **B** Boron 10.811	6 **C** Carbon 12.011	7 **N** Nitrogen 14.007	8 **O** Oxygen 15.999	9 **F** Fluorine 18.998	10 **Ne** Neon 20.183
			13 **Al** Aluminum 26.982	14 **Si** Silicon 28.086	15 **P** Phosphorus 30.974	16 **S** Sulfur 32.066	17 **Cl** Chlorine 35.453	18 **Ar** Argon 39.948
28 **Ni** Nickel 58.690	29 **Cu** Copper 63.546	30 **Zn** Zinc 65.370	31 **Ga** Gallium 69.720	32 **Ge** Germanium 72.590	33 **As** Arsenic 74.922	34 **Se** Selenium 78.960	35 **Br** Bromine 79.909	36 **Kr** Krypton 83.800
46 **Pd** Palladium 106.400	47 **Ag** Silver 107.870	48 **Cd** Cadmium 112.400	49 **In** Indium 114.820	50 **Sn** Tin 118.690	51 **Sb** Antimony 121.750	52 **Te** Tellurium 127.600	53 **I** Iodine 126.904	54 **Xe** Xenon 131.300
78 **Pt** Platinum 195.090	79 **Au** Gold 196.967	80 **Hg** Mercury 200.590	81 **Tl** Thallium 204.370	82 **Pb** Lead 207.200	83 **Bi** Bismuth 208.980	84 **Po** Polonium (209.000)	85 **At** Astatine (210.000)	86 **Rn** Radon (222.000)
110 **Ds** Ununnilium (269)	111 **Rg** Unununium (272)	112 **Uub** Ununbium (277)	113 **Uut** (284)	114 **Uuq** Ununquadium (296)	115 **Uup** (288)	116 **Uuh** (298)	117 **Uus** (Not yet recognized) (?)	118 **Uuo** (294)

63 **Eu** Europium 151.960	64 **Gd** Gadolinium 157.250	65 **Tb** Terbium 158.924	66 **Dy** Dysprosium 162.500	67 **Ho** Holmium 164.930	68 **Er** Erbium 167.260	69 **Tm** Thulium 168.934	70 **Yb** Ytterbium 173.040	71 **Lu** Lutetium 174.970
95 **Am** Americium (243.000)	96 **Cm** Curium (247.000)	97 **Bk** Berkelium (247.000)	98 **Cf** Californium (251.000)	99 **Es** Einsteinium (254.000)	100 **Fm** Fermium (257.000)	101 **Md** Mendelevium (258.000)	102 **No** Nobelium (259.000)	103 **Lr** Lawrencium (262.000)

Atomic masses in parentheses are of the most common form of the atom.

Go Online
active art
For: Periodic Table activity
Visit: PHSchool.com
Web Code: cgp-1032

3-8 What are metals and nonmetals?

Objective
Identify the properties of metals and nonmetals.

Key Terms
metal: element that has the property of shiny luster, ductility, and malleability

luster (LUHS-tuhr)**:** the way a material reflects light

malleable (MAL-ee-uh-buhl)**:** able to be hammered into different shapes

ductile (DUK-tuhl)**:** able to be drawn into thin wires

nonmetal: element that lacks most of the properties of a metal

Metals and Nonmetals If you look at the periodic table, you will see a dark zigzag line running from the top of Group 13 to the bottom of Group 16. This line separates two different types of elements. The elements to the left of the line, with the exception of hydrogen, are metals. The elements to the right of the line are nonmetals.

▶ **NAME:** What are two different types of elements?

Properties of Metals **Metals** are elements that have the properties of shiny luster, ductility, and malleability. All metals, except mercury, are solids at room temperature. Mercury is a liquid. The properties of metals are as follows:

- Some metals are shiny. A gold ring is shiny. The way a material reflects light is called its **luster**.

- Most metals are **malleable**. They can be hammered into thin sheets and different shapes. Aluminum can be hammered into a thin sheet and into the shape of a pot or pan.

- Metals are **ductile**. They can be made into thin wires. Most of the wires in electrical appliances are made of metals.

- Some metals allow electricity to flow through them easily. These metals are good conductors of electricity. Electricity flows easily through wires made of copper.

- Most metals are good conductors of heat. They allow heat to flow easily through them. This is the reason why radiators, pots, pans, and irons are made of metals.

◀ **Figure 3-27** Metals can be hammered into different shapes.

▶ **LIST:** What are three properties of metals?

Properties of Nonmetals Elements that lack most of the properties of a metal are called **nonmetals**, so they look dull. Most solid nonmetals are brittle. They are easily broken. They cannot be pounded into different shapes or pulled into thin wires. Nonmetals are poor conductors of electricity and heat. Nonmetallic elements may exist at room temperature as solids, liquids, or gases.

Nonmetals are very useful elements. For example, phosphorus is used in matches. Sulfur is used to make rubber. Nonmetals are also important to all living things in other ways. The nonmetals nitrogen and oxygen are found in the air that we breathe. Nitrogen helps organisms to make proteins. Most organisms need oxygen to breathe.

▲ **Figure 3-28** Matches and rubber are made from nonmetals.

▶ **RELATE:** Why do nonmetals look dull?

✓ CHECKING CONCEPTS

1. Elements to the right of the zigzag line in the periodic table are _____.
2. Metals can be hammered into thin sheets because they are _____.
3. It is possible to make copper wire because copper is _____.
4. Most _____ are good conductors of heat.
5. Nonmetals are _____ conductors of heat and electricity.
6. The nonmetal _____ is used in matches.

💡 THINKING CRITICALLY

7. **IDENTIFY:** What two properties of metals make them useful materials for the electrical wiring in your home?

8. **INFER:** What property of metals allows a jeweler to hammer a piece of silver to make jewelry?

9. **CLASSIFY:** Use the periodic table on pages 66 and 67 to identify the following elements as metals or nonmetals.

   a. Zinc
   b. Sulfur
   c. Xenon
   d. Potassium
   e. Selenium
   f. Magnesium
   g. Platinum
   h. Phosphorus

DESIGNING AN EXPERIMENT

Design an experiment to solve the following problem. Include a hypothesis, variables, a procedure, and a type of data to study.

PROBLEM: Element *x* is an unidentified element. Is it a metal or a nonmetal?

Hands-On Activity

COMPARING METALS AND NONMETALS

You will need safety goggles, an electrical conductivity tester, a 5- to 6-cm piece of uninsulated copper wire, graphite from a mechanical pencil, a paper clip, and a small block of wood.

1. Compare a piece of uninsulated copper wire to a piece of graphite from a mechanical pencil. Note the luster of both samples.

2. Put on safety goggles. Check for ductility. Bend the copper wire, the piece of graphite, a paper clip, and a block of wood as far as possible. Note changes in each of the samples.

3. Check for electrical conductivity. Touch the free ends of the wires in the electrical conductivity tester to each other. Make sure that the light bulb goes on. Next touch the ends of the wires to the ends of the uninsulated copper wire. Observe any changes to the light bulb. Do the same for the paper clip, the graphite, and the block of wood. Note any changes to the light bulb.

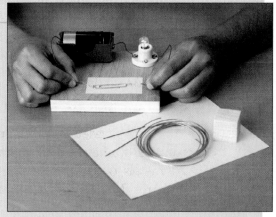

▲ **STEP 3** Observe any changes to the light bulb.

Practicing Your Skills

4. **COMPARE:** What are the properties of the copper wire compared to the properties of the graphite from the mechanical pencil?

5. **DESCRIBE:** Which of the four samples conducted electricity? How do you know?

3-9 What are the halogens and the noble gases?

Objectives

Locate the halogens and the noble gases on the periodic table. Identify the properties of the halogens and the noble gases.

Key Terms

halogens: elements that make up Group 17 in the periodic table

noble gases: elements that make up Group 18 in the periodic table

The Halogens Group 17 in the periodic table contains the five elements that make up the **halogens**. These elements—fluorine, chlorine, bromine, iodine, and astatine—have a similar atomic structure. The halogens can vary their physical states from solid to gas at room temperature. They can also change color when changing state. For example, bromine is a red-brown liquid that becomes a red gas at room temperature. Iodine is a gray-black solid that can become a blue-violet gas.

The halogens can also be quite dangerous. However, when they combine with other elements, they can form matter that is very useful. For example, chlorine combines with sodium to form table salt. Fluorine combines with other elements to form products that prevent tooth decay. Substances made with iodine can be used to help prevent infections. Figure 3-29 lists the halogens.

HALOGENS		
Element	**Symbol**	**Uses**
Fluorine	F	Prevents tooth decay
Chlorine	Cl	Purifies water
Bromine	Br	Used in photographic film
Iodine	I	Prevents infection
Astatine	At	Used in halogen lights

▲ **Figure 3-29** The halogens can be found in Group 17 in the periodic table.

▶ **LIST:** Name the five halogens.

The Noble Gases Look at Group 18 of the periodic table on page 67. What do the elements in Group 18 have in common? The six elements in the last group of the periodic table are gases. They are called the **noble gases**. All of these elements have similar properties and atomic structure.

In the past, these elements were also called inert gases. The word *inert* means "inactive." At one time, these elements were thought to occur naturally as pure substances. Pure substances that occur naturally do not interact with other substances. However, scientists have discovered that noble gases can be forced to combine with other elements, such as fluorine.

▶ **DEFINE:** What is a noble gas?

Familiar Noble Gases The six noble gases are helium, neon, argon, krypton, xenon, and radon. The names of some of the noble gases may be familiar to you. You have probably heard of helium and neon. If you have heard of kryptonite, krypton is not related to it. In fact, kryptonite, which is mentioned in fictional tales, is not a real substance. All the noble gases are found in small amounts in Earth's atmosphere. Of all the noble gases, helium is the most plentiful. It makes up about 23 percent of the mass of the universe. The names and chemical symbols of the six noble gases are listed in Figure 3-30.

NOBLE GASES		
Element	**Symbol**	**Uses**
Helium	He	Fills balloons
Neon	Ne	Lighting
Argon	Ar	Lighting
Krypton	Kr	Flash lamps
Xenon	Xe	Deep sea lamps
Radon	Rn	None

▲ **Figure 3-30** The noble gases can be found in Group 18 in the periodic table.

 LIST: Name the six noble gases.

Uses of Noble Gases Most of the noble gases have many important uses. Neon is used in lights because it gives off a bright red glow when electricity passes through it. By mixing neon with other gases, different colors can be produced. Helium is used to fill balloons and xenon is used in photographic lamps.

▲ **Figure 3-31** Neon is used in lights.

 EXPLAIN: What is helium used for?

 CHECKING CONCEPTS

1. Where are the halogens located in the periodic table?
2. Where are the noble gases located in the periodic table?
3. What is the meaning of inert?
4. Which noble gas makes up about 1 percent of Earth's atmosphere?

THINKING CRITICALLY

5. **STATE:** Why were noble gases once called inert gases?
6. **ANALYZE:** Why do you think neon is used in signs?

BUILDING LANGUAGE ARTS SKILLS

Researching Noble gases are so named because of nobles. Look up the word *noble* in a dictionary, an encyclopedia, or on the Internet. Find out how noble gases are related to nobles.

Real-Life Science

BLIMPS

Have you ever looked up into the sky and seen a blimp passing by? A blimp is a type of airship that is lifted into the air by the noble gas helium. Helium not only lifts a blimp high into the sky, it also gives a blimp its shape. The baglike body of a blimp, called the envelope, does not have structure unless helium fills it.

▲ **Figure 3-32** Blimps are airships that are filled with the noble gas helium.

Helium is used to lift blimps because helium is lighter than air and it will not burn in air. At one time, hydrogen gas was used to fill airships. Hydrogen is lighter than helium. However, on May 6, 1937, the largest airship ever built, the *Hindenburg*, burst into flames over Lakehurst, New Jersey. Since hydrogen was used to lift and fill the *Hindenburg*, it was no longer considered safe to use.

Today, blimps are used to advertise certain products, and to transport photographic equipment to film special events. In some countries, they are used in military operations.

Thinking Critically Hydrogen is lighter than helium. Why is hydrogen not used to lift blimps instead of helium?

3-10 What are isotopes?

Objectives

Explain what an isotope of an element is.
Compare the three isotopes of hydrogen.

Key Term

isotope (EYE-suh-tohp): atom of an element with the same number of protons as the other atoms but a different number of neutrons

Different Atomic Masses The atomic number of an element never changes. All atoms of the same element have the same number of protons in their nuclei. However, all atoms of the same element may not have the same number of neutrons in their nuclei. This means that atoms of the same element can have different atomic masses. The difference in atomic mass is caused by a different number of neutrons in the nuclei of the atoms of an element.

1 STATE: What causes atoms of the same element to have different atomic masses?

Isotopes Atoms of the same element that have different atomic masses are called isotopes. **Isotopes** are atoms of an element that have the same number of protons as the other atoms of the element but a different number of neutrons in their nuclei.

Although the number of neutrons in the atoms of an element may be different, atoms are always identified by the number of protons. For example, there are several isotopes of the element copper. One of the isotopes has 36 neutrons in the nuclei of its atoms. Another isotope has 34 neutrons in the nuclei of its atoms. Because both of these isotopes have 29 protons in the nuclei of their atoms, they are both atoms of the element copper.

2 DEFINE: What is an isotope?

Atomic Mass The atomic mass for each element can be found in the periodic table. The atomic mass given for each element is actually an average of the atomic masses of all the isotopes of that element. This explains why an element's atomic mass is not a whole number.

3 EXPLAIN: What does the atomic mass for each element actually represent?

Isotopes of Common Elements Hydrogen has three isotopes. The three isotopes of hydrogen are known as protium (PROHT-ee-uhm), deuterium (doo-TIR-ee-uhm), and tritium (TRIHT-ee-uhm). These isotopes of hydrogen are also called hydrogen-1 (H-1), hydrogen-2 (H-2), and hydrogen-3 (H-3). The numbers 1, 2, and 3 represent the mass numbers of each of the isotopes. An atom of protium (H-1) has only one proton and no neutrons in its nucleus. An atom of deuterium (H-2) has one proton and one neutron. An atom of tritium (H-3) has one proton and two neutrons.

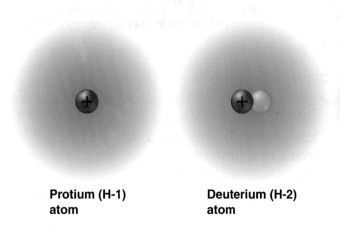

◀ **Figure 3-33**
The three isotopes of hydrogen

Protium (H-1) atom

Deuterium (H-2) atom

Tritium (H-3) atom

All elements have two or more isotopes. Carbon-12 and carbon-14 are two isotopes of the element carbon. These isotopes are also written as C-12 and C-14. Boron-10 (B-10) and boron-11 (B-11) are isotopes of the element boron. Two important isotopes of uranium are uranium-235 (U-235) and uranium-238 (U-238).

 LIST: What are the three isotopes of hydrogen called?

✓ CHECKING CONCEPTS

1. What causes some atoms of the same element to have different atomic masses?

2. In the periodic table, where can the atomic mass of an element be found?

3. What identifies an atom of an element?

4. How many neutrons are there in an atom of protium? Deuterium? Tritium?

💡 THINKING CRITICALLY

5. **EXPLAIN:** Why is the atomic mass of an element not a whole number?

6. **CALCULATE:** The atomic number of carbon is 6. How many protons and neutrons are there in an atom of carbon-12? Of carbon-14?

7. **ANALYZE:** The mass number of oxygen is 16. Its atomic mass is 15.999. The atomic number of oxygen is 8. Which of the following statements about the isotopes of oxygen are true? Why?

   a. All of the isotopes have eight neutrons.

   b. All of the isotopes have eight neutrons or more.

   c. Some of the isotopes have fewer than eight neutrons.

   d. All of the isotopes have fewer than eight neutrons.

INTERPRETING VISUALS

Use Figure 3-33 to answer the following questions.

8. **ANALYZE:** Which isotope contains two neutrons in its nucleus?

9. **IDENTIFY:** Which atom has the largest nucleus?

10. **INFER:** What is the atomic number of each isotope?

11. **INFER:** Which isotope has the smallest atomic mass?

 Integrating Life Science

TOPIC: cells

KILLING CANCER CELLS

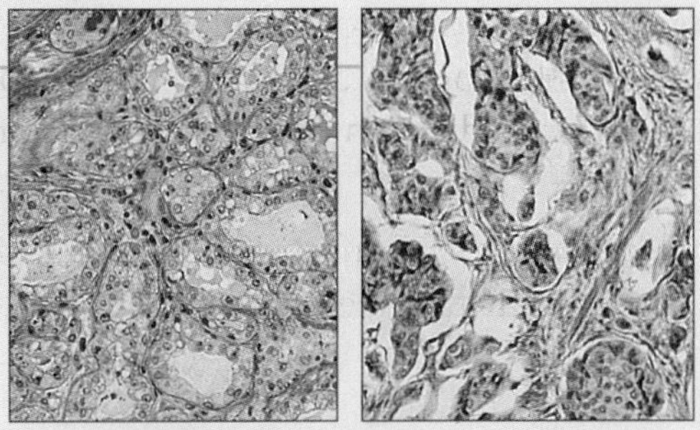

The human body is made up of trillions of cells. Cells divide and organize themselves to keep the body healthy. They can also replace themselves to promote repair. Cancer occurs when cells cannot control their growth and development. Cancer cells divide, multiply, and spread. These cells can also invade organs. As they invade organs, they damage healthy cells and send out substances that weaken the body.

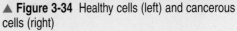
▲ **Figure 3-34** Healthy cells (left) and cancerous cells (right)

Research scientists have uncovered different ways to treat different types of cancer. Radiation therapy is one method. One type of radiation therapy uses radioactive isotopes to kill cancer cells. This type of treatment places radioactive isotopes close to the cancer cells. The high-energy rays from the isotopes attack the cancer cells. Some radioactive isotopes used in this type of therapy are cobalt-60 and cesium-137. Iodine-123, gallium-67, and fluorine-18 are used in diagnosis. Iodine-125, iodine-131, and strontium-89 are used to kill cancer cells.

Thinking Critically How are radioactive isotopes used to treat certain types of cancer?

LAB ACTIVITY
Investigating the Modern Model of the Atom

BACKGROUND

Over the past 100 years, the model of the atom has gone through several changes. Our current understanding is that protons and neutrons are found in the atom's center, the nucleus. The electrons are found in an electron cloud. An electron cloud shows the different locations in which an electron can be found. The cloud surrounds the nucleus of an atom.

PURPOSE

In this activity, you will use a target as a model to investigate the nucleus and the electron cloud of an atom according to the modern theory of the atom.

PROCEDURE

1. Copy the chart in Figure 3-36.

2. Work with a partner. Place 2 sheets of carbon paper side by side shiny-side up on a flat surface. Cover each sheet of carbon paper with a sheet of white paper.

3. Use a drawing compass to draw a circle with a diameter of 20 cm on each sheet of white paper. These circles will be your "targets."

4. Place one target with its sheet of carbon paper on a piece of cardboard. Insert a thumbtack or push pin into the center of the target.

Materials

2 Sheets of white paper
2 Sheets of carbon paper
Drawing compass
Cardboard
Thumbtack or push pin
Marble

▲ **Figure 3-35** Paper targets

Trial	Observations
#1	
#2	

▲ **Figure 3-36** Copy this chart and use it to record your observations.

▲ **STEP 4** Drop the marble on the target.

5. Carefully stand on a chair. While holding a marble in one hand, extend your arm so that it is about 2 m above the floor. Have your partner position the target directly below the marble.

6. Drop the marble on the target. Have your partner catch the marble on the first bounce and return it to you. Repeat this step 50 times.

7. Remove the target from the cardboard and turn over the sheet of white paper. Describe the pattern of dots for Trial #1 on your chart.

8. Switch roles with your partner for Trial #2. Using a new target, repeat steps 4 through 7.

▲ **STEP 5** Spots on the target show where the marble was dropped.

CONCLUSIONS

1. **MODEL:** What do the marks made by the marble-drops on the target represent?

2. **INFER:** What does the thumbtack in the center of the target represent? What is indicated by the fact that no marks were found in the center of the model?

3. **COMPARE:** Do you expect the other groups to get the same pattern? Explain your answer.

4. **INFER:** How might this experiment help to illustrate the modern theory of an atom?

5. **ANALYZE:** The atomic model proposed by Niels Bohr states that electrons are found in energy levels much like planets moving in orbits around the Sun. How is the electron cloud different from the orbits of planets moving around the Sun?

Chapter Summary

Lesson 3-1
• **Elements** are substances that cannot be chemically broken down into simpler substances.

Lesson 3-2
• An **atom** is the smallest part of an element that can be identified as that element.

Lesson 3-3
• Atoms are made up of **protons**, **neutrons**, and **electrons**.

Lesson 3-4
• The **atomic number** of an element is the number of protons in the nucleus of an atom of that element.

Lesson 3-5
• The total mass of the protons and neutrons in an atom is the **atomic mass** of that atom.
• The **mass number** of an element is equal to the number of protons and neutrons in the nucleus of an atom of that element.

Lesson 3-6
• Electrons are arranged in **energy levels** around the nucleus of an atom.

Lesson 3-7
• In the modern periodic table, elements are arranged in order of increasing atomic number.

Lesson 3-8
• A zigzag line on the periodic table separates the **metals** from the **nonmetals**.

Lesson 3-9
• The **halogens** are the five elements in Group 17 in the periodic table.
• The **noble gases** are the six elements in Group 18 in the periodic table.

Lesson 3-10
• Atoms of the same element that have different numbers of neutrons are called **isotopes**.

Key Term Challenges

atom (p. 54)
atomic mass (p. 60)
atomic number (p. 58)
chemical symbol (p. 64)
ductile (p. 68)
electron (p. 56)
element (p. 52)
energy level (p. 62)
group (p. 64)
halogens (p. 70)
isotope (p. 72)
luster (p. 68)
malleable (p. 68)
mass number (p. 60)
metal (p. 68)
neutron (p. 56)
noble gases (p. 70)
nonmetal (p. 68)
nucleus (p. 56)
period (p. 64)
periodic (p. 64)
proton (p. 56)

MATCHING **Write the Key Term from above that best matches each description.**

1. number of protons and neutrons in the nucleus of an atom
2. particle in an atom that has a negative charge
3. number of protons in the nucleus of an atom
4. smallest part of an element that can be identified as that element
5. particle in the nucleus of an atom that does not have any charge
6. has the same number of protons but a different number of neutrons

FILL IN **Write the Key Term from above that best completes each statement.**

7. The _____ are found in Group 18 of the periodic table.
8. A repeating pattern is _____.
9. The center, or core, of an atom is called the _____.
10. There are more than 100 known _____.
11. An _____ is the place in the electron cloud where electrons are most likely to be found.
12. There are 18 columns or _____ on the periodic table.

Content Challenges

MULTIPLE CHOICE **Write the letter of the term or phrase that best completes each statement.**

1. In the early 1800s, an atomic theory of matter was developed by
   a. Democritus.
   b. Dalton.
   c. Rutherford.
   d. Thomson.

2. The first scientist to suggest that atoms contain smaller particles was
   a. Thomson.
   b. Rutherford.
   c. Bohr.
   d. Dalton.

3. Rutherford pictured atoms as being made mostly of
   a. empty space.
   b. positively charged material.
   c. electrons.
   d. the nucleus.

4. Rutherford's model of the atom included
   a. a small central core.
   b. a positive material filled with electrons.
   c. energy levels for electrons.
   d. neutrons.

5. Niels Bohr proposed that electrons
   a. orbit the nucleus.
   b. are inside the nucleus.
   c. do not exist.
   d. cannot be located exactly in an atom.

6. If an electron gains enough energy,
   a. it jumps to a higher energy level.
   b. it falls to a lower energy level.
   c. it gives off light.
   d. it falls into the nucleus.

7. The atomic number of an atom is equal to
   a. the number of protons and neutrons.
   b. the number of electrons and neutrons.
   c. the number of protons.
   d. the number of protons and electrons.

8. The letters *amu* stand for
   a. atomic measuring unit.
   b. alternate mass unit.
   c. atomic mass unit.
   d. atomic matter unit.

9. Tritium is an
   a. electron energy level.
   b. isotope of hydrogen.
   c. element with atomic number 102.
   d. isotope of carbon.

10. Argon and krypton are
    a. metals.
    b. protons.
    c. neutrons.
    d. noble gases.

TRUE/FALSE **Write *true* if the statement is true. If the statement is false, change the underlined term to make the statement true.**

11. An isotope of an element has the same number of protons but a different number of <u>electrons</u>.

12. The second energy level can hold <u>eight</u> electrons.

13. Scientists <u>can</u> predict the exact location of an electron in an atom.

14. The number of protons and <u>electrons</u> in a neutral atom must be equal.

Concept Challenges TEST PREP

WRITTEN RESPONSE Answer each of the following questions in complete sentences.

1. **EXPLAIN:** How did Dalton come to the conclusion that matter is made up of atoms?

2. **COMPARE:** In what ways did Dalton, Thomson, and Rutherford have similar ideas about atoms? In what ways did their ideas differ?

3. **ANALYZE:** Why is the atomic mass of an element not a whole number, whereas the mass number is always a whole number?

4. **PREDICT:** How many electrons would be found in the second energy level of an atom of nitrogen, which has an atomic number of 7?

5. **COMPARE:** How are metals different from nonmetals?

INTERPRETING A DIAGRAM Use Figure 3-37 to answer the following questions.

6. How many electrons are in an atom of element *x*?

7. How many electrons are in the first energy level in an atom of element *x*?

8. How many protons are in an atom of element *x*?

9. If there are 18 neutrons in an atom of element *x*, what is the mass number of an atom of element *x*?

10. Use the periodic table on pages 66 and 67 to identify element *x*.

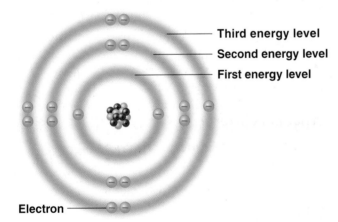

Third energy level

Second energy level

First energy level

Electron

▲ **Figure 3-37** Element *x*

Chapter 4
Compounds and Mixtures

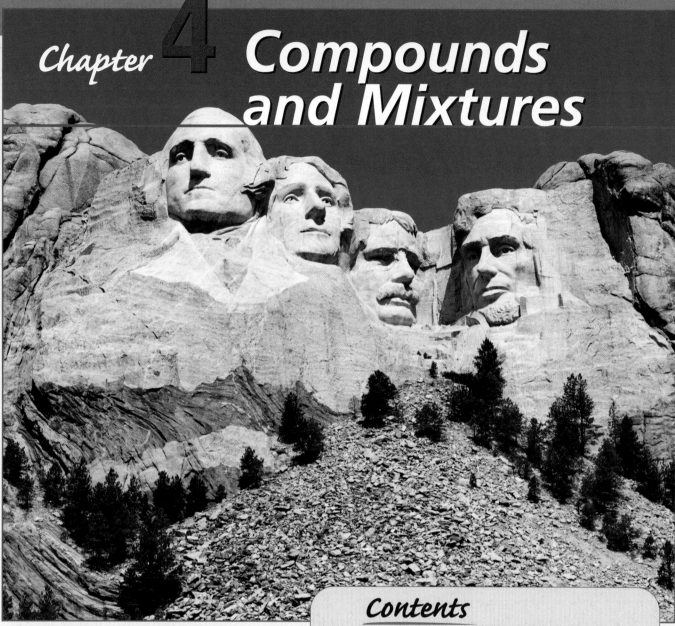

▲ **Figure 4-1** Mount Rushmore, South Dakota

Can you recognize the four faces carved in Figure 4-1? The faces are those of George Washington, Thomas Jefferson, Theodore Roosevelt, and Abraham Lincoln—four American presidents. The memorial is carved of granite. Granite is a hard rock that is actually made up of other types of matter. Granite keeps the properties of the different types of matter that it is made up of.

▶Why do you think the memorial is carved of granite?

Contents

4-1 What are three types of matter?

INVESTIGATE

Sorting Matter
HANDS-ON ACTIVITY

1. Prepare a chart divided into two columns. Label one column "Elements" and the other column "Not Elements."
2. Your teacher will give you samples of several different types of matter. Observe each type of matter.
3. Write the name of each type of matter in one of the two columns. Refer to the periodic table on pages 66 and 67 to help you identify which ones are elements.

THINK ABOUT IT: What do you think the objects that are not elements are made of?

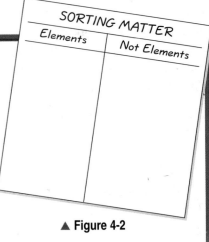

▲ Figure 4-2

Objective

Describe similarities and differences among elements, compounds, and mixtures.

Key Terms

element: substance that cannot be chemically broken down into simpler substances

compound: substance made up of two or more elements that are chemically combined

mixture: two or more substances that have been physically combined

substance: any element or compound

Organizing Matter You may have items that you like to collect, such as rocks, stamps, sea glass, or baseball cards. If you do, you may sort your collection based on different or similar characteristics, such as size, shape, date, or team. Kinds of matter can be sorted, too. Just like you might sort your collection based on one characteristic, matter can be organized, or classified, into three groups based on the makeup of the matter.

▶ **1** LIST: What are some of the ways to organize a collection?

Elements, Compounds, and Mixtures Matter can be classified into three main types—elements, compounds, and mixtures. You have learned that an **element** is made up of only one kind of atom. For example, pure gold is always made up of

atoms that contain 79 protons. A **compound** is made up of atoms of two or more elements that are chemically combined. The elements in a given compound are always combined in a fixed ratio. For example, every particle of the compound baking soda is made up of one atom of sodium, one atom of hydrogen, one atom of carbon, and three atoms of oxygen.

A **mixture** is made up of two or more kinds of matter that are physically combined, or mixed together. The kinds of matter in a mixture can be present in any amounts. A mixture of sugar and cinnamon can contain any amount of sugar and any amount of cinnamon.

▲ Figure 4-3 Examples of the three main types of matter

▶ IDENTIFY: What are the three main types of matter?

Substances Elements and compounds share a similar characteristic. Every sample of an element has the same exact properties as every other sample. Similarly, all samples of a given compound have the same exact properties as every other sample of that compound. For example, the copper used to make a teakettle will have the same properties as the copper used to make an electric wire. A sample of pure sugar, a compound used to sweeten coffee, will be identical to a sample of pure sugar used to make candy. Because they share this characteristic, elements and compounds are classified as substances. A **substance** is any element or compound.

 DEFINE: What is a substance?

☑ CHECKING CONCEPTS

1. Matter is classified into three groups based on the _____ of the matter.
2. An _____ is made up of only one kind of atom.
3. A _____ is made up of atoms of different elements that are chemically combined.
4. The elements in a given compound are always combined in a _____ ratio.
5. A _____ is made up of two or more different kinds of matter that are physically combined.
6. The amounts of the different kinds of matter in a _____ can vary.
7. A _____ is any element or compound.

 ## THINKING CRITICALLY

8. **ANALYZE:** A sample of matter is made up of three different atoms that are chemically combined. What type of matter is it? How do you know?
9. **HYPOTHESIZE:** A substance is made up of two atoms of oxygen. Is it an element or a compound? How do you know?

Web InfoSearch

Properties Substances can be recognized by their physical and chemical properties. These properties can be labeled as *extensive properties* and *intensive properties*. Extensive properties include weight and mass. Intensive properties include melting point and boiling point.

SEARCH: Use the Internet to find out more about these types of properties. List other intensive and extensive properties. Start your search at www.conceptsandchallenges.com. Some key search words are **intensive properties** and **extensive properties**.

 ## People in Science
ROBERT BOYLE (1627–1691)

The Irish-born scientist Robert Boyle is known as the Father of Chemistry. He used the scientific method of experimentation to test hypotheses. He questioned the early belief that materials were made up of four elements—earth, air, fire, and water. He believed that the basic elements of matter were "corpuscles." These corpuscles, or particles, could be found in various types and sizes, and could arrange themselves into groups called mixtures and compounds. Boyle also showed that the properties of a compound are different from those of the particles that it is made up of.

▲ **Figure 4-4** Robert Boyle

Boyle contributed a vast amount of knowledge to the scientific world. His work with gases and pressure led to Boyle's law. He is also credited with the invention of the match.

Thinking Critically Robert Boyle believed that the basic elements of matter were corpuscles. What would a modern scientist call these basic elements of matter?

4-2 What is a compound?

Objectives

Explain that a compound is made up of two or more elements. Describe how chemical bonds form new substances.

Key Terms

molecule: smallest part of a substance that has all the properties of that substance

chemical bond: force of attraction that holds atoms together

Combining Elements An element can combine with other elements to form a new substance called a compound. A compound is a substance made up of two or more elements that are chemically combined. For example, hydrogen and oxygen are elements. They are both gases with very different properties at room temperature. When these two elements chemically combine, they can form two different compounds that are liquids at room temperature. You are familiar with one of these compounds. It is water. The other compound is hydrogen peroxide, a substance used to clean cuts.

▶ **EXPLAIN:** What is a compound?

Common Compounds Sugar is a compound. It is made of carbon, hydrogen, and oxygen. Table salt is a compound, too. It is made of the elements sodium and chlorine. You may be familiar with some of the compounds listed in Figure 4-5.

SOME COMMON COMPOUNDS	
Compound	Elements
Sand	Silicon, oxygen
Hydrogen peroxide	Hydrogen, oxygen
Chalk	Calcium, carbon, oxygen
Rust	Iron, oxygen

▲ Figure 4-5

▶ **NAME:** What elements are in chalk?

Properties of Compounds The properties of a compound are very different from the properties of the elements that make it up. Some elements that make up a compound may be dangerous. But a compound formed from these elements may be relatively harmless. For example, sodium is a very active metal. Chlorine is a yellow, poisonous gas. When combined, these elements make up the compound sodium chloride, or table salt.

▲ **Figure 4-6** The active metal sodium (left) chemically combines with the poisonous gas chlorine (right) to form table salt.

▶ **CONTRAST:** What are the properties of sodium, chlorine, and sodium chloride?

Molecules Most compounds are made of molecules. A **molecule** is the smallest part of a substance that has all the properties of that substance. A molecule can be a single atom or may be made up of a great many atoms. For example, a molecule of iron is a single iron atom. A molecule of sucrose, a type of sugar, is made up of 45 atoms.

Silicon dioxide is a compound found in sand. It is made of the elements silicon and oxygen. One molecule of silicon dioxide is made from one atom of silicon and two atoms of oxygen. A single molecule of silicon dioxide has all the properties of silicon dioxide. Just as all the atoms of an element are alike, all the molecules of a compound are alike.

▶ **DEFINE:** What is a molecule?

Breaking Down Compounds A compound is formed as a result of a chemical change. The elements in a compound combine by forming chemical bonds between the atoms. A **chemical bond** is the force of attraction that holds atoms in a molecule together. Atoms bond together to form molecules. When bonding occurs, a new substance with its own properties is formed.

A chemical change can also cause the molecules that make up a compound to break down into simpler substances. To break the molecules down, the chemical bonds holding the atoms together have to be broken. Heating a compound is one way to break it down. When sugar is heated, it melts. If the melted sugar is heated long enough, hydrogen and oxygen enter the air in the form of water vapor. Finally, only a black solid remains. This solid is the element carbon. So, heating sugar can cause it to break down into water, containing hydrogen and oxygen, and carbon. These are the elements that make up sugar.

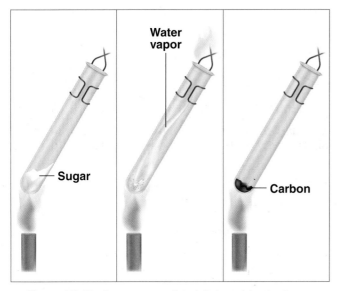

▲ **Figure 4-7** Heating sugar can break it down into simpler substances.

Another way to break down a compound is by using electricity. Scientists working in laboratories can obtain hydrogen gas and oxygen gas by passing electricity through a sample of slightly acidic water.

5 ▶ EXPLAIN: How can a compound be broken down into the elements that make it up?

✓ CHECKING CONCEPTS

1. A compound is made up of two or more _____.

2. The compound _____ is made up of the elements hydrogen, oxygen, and carbon.

3. The properties of a compound are _____ from the properties of the elements that form it.

4. A _____ is the smallest part of a substance that has all the properties of that substance.

5. A compound is formed as a result of a _____.

6. A _____ is the force of attraction that holds atoms together.

7. Using heat and electricity can _____ a compound into the elements that make up the compound.

💡 THINKING CRITICALLY

8. **INFER:** A recipe calls for a cup of sugar to be heated slowly over a low flame. What could happen if the sugar is heated over a high flame?

9. **HYPOTHESIZE:** When an unknown solid is heated, two different gases and a liquid are formed. Is the solid a compound or an element? How do you know?

10. **ANALYZE:** How is a molecule different from an atom?

HEALTH AND SAFETY TIP

The compound carbon monoxide is a deadly gas. It is difficult to detect because it is odorless and colorless. Carbon monoxide can be produced by the incomplete burning of fuels in cars and in heating furnaces. If it is inhaled in small amounts, it can cause people to feel sleepy. If it is inhaled in large amounts, it can cause death. Why do you think having a carbon monoxide detector in your home is a good idea?

4-3 What is a mixture?

INVESTIGATE

Separating a Mixture
HANDS-ON ACTIVITY

1. Place one-half cup of iron-fortified cereal into a plastic sandwich bag. Squeeze as much air out of the bag as you can. Seal the plastic bag.

2. Use your hands to crush the cereal into a fine powder. Then, pour the cereal into a bowl. Add enough water to the bowl to completely cover the cereal.

3. Cover one end of a magnet with plastic wrap and use it to stir the mixture for at least 10 minutes. Remove the magnet and let the liquid on the magnet drain back into the bowl.

4. Hold the magnet over a sheet of white paper. Use a hand lens to observe the particles on the end of the magnet.

THINK ABOUT IT: What did you observe on the end of the magnet? Where did the matter come from?

STEP 3

Objective

Describe the physical properties of a mixture.

Mixtures Cut up some tomatoes, lettuce, onions, and green peppers. Put the pieces in a bowl and stir them together. What do you have? Some people would say that you have a salad. A scientist might say that you have a mixture. You have learned that a mixture is made up of two or more substances that are physically combined. Each part of a mixture keeps its own properties.

Not all mixtures are as easy to identify. If you put some salt in a glass of water and stir, you would have a mixture of salt and water. But this mixture is different from the salad mixture. You cannot see the individual parts of salt or water.

1 **CONTRAST:** What is the difference between a salad mixture and a salt-water mixture?

Kinds of Mixtures The kinds of matter in a mixture can be present in varying amounts. The discussion above describes the two basic types of mixtures—evenly mixed and unevenly mixed. The mixture of salt and water is evenly mixed. You cannot see the individual particles of salt or water. The salt is still salt, and the water is still water. However, they are so evenly mixed that every part of this mixture is exactly the same as every other part. A drop taken from the top of the mixture will be identical to a drop taken from the bottom.

The salad is unevenly mixed. One part of the salad may have more tomato while another part has more green pepper. Each part of the mixture keeps its own properties. A tomato is still red and tastes like a tomato.

▲ **Figure 4-8** A salad is a mixture. Each part of the mixture keeps its own properties.

2 **INFER:** Why do the different kinds of matter in a mixture keep their own properties?

Separating a Mixture The properties of the different kinds of matter in a mixture can be used to separate the mixture. Because the parts of a mixture are not chemically combined, they can be separated by physical means. For example, each of the different vegetables could be picked out of the salad by hand.

A physical property of water is that it evaporates when it is heated. So, if you heat a mixture of salt and water, the water will evaporate and the salt will be left behind. The mixture will be separated. Some mixtures can be separated by filtering. If a mixture of sand and water is poured into a filter, the water will pass through. The sand will be trapped by the filter.

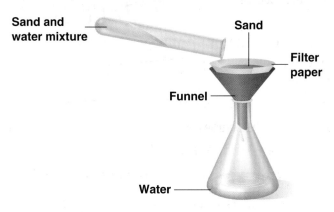

Sand and water mixture
Sand
Filter paper
Funnel
Water

▲ **Figure 4-9** Separating a mixture of sand and water

 EXPLAIN: How can you separate a mixture of sand and water?

☑ CHECKING CONCEPTS

1. Salt water is an example of a _____.
2. The substances in a mixture are _____ combined.
3. The substances in a mixture can be present in _____ amount.
4. The substances in a mixture always keep their own _____.
5. The substances in a mixture can be _____ by using the physical properties of the substances.
6. A mixture of _____ and water can be separated by filtering the mixture.

THINKING CRITICALLY

7. **HYPOTHESIZE:** Will freezing a mixture of salt and water separate the two substances? Explain your answer.
8. **CLASSIFY:** A teaspoon of instant coffee is placed in a cup of boiling water. Is this a mixture or a compound? Explain your answer.

DESIGNING AN EXPERIMENT

Design an experiment to solve the following problem. Include a hypothesis, variables, a procedure, and a type of data to study.

PROBLEM: You have a mixture of sand, water, and gravel. How can you separate this mixture into its different parts?

 Real-Life Science

MIXTURES THAT YOU CAN EAT

Have you ever gone camping or hiking and taken some trail mix with you? As the name of this snack tells you, trail mix is a mixture. You can see the individual bits of dried fruits and nuts. You could pick out the individual parts with your fingers if you wanted to.

Think about some of the other foods that you eat every day. Many of these foods are mixtures. Rice and beans, vegetable soup, ice cream—all are mixtures.

Thinking Critically If you were to make trail mix, do you have to follow the recipe exactly?

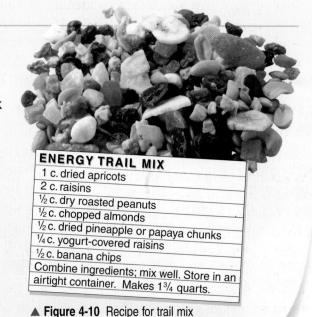

ENERGY TRAIL MIX
1 c. dried apricots
2 c. raisins
½ c. dry roasted peanuts
½ c. chopped almonds
½ c. dried pineapple or papaya chunks
¼ c. yogurt-covered raisins
½ c. banana chips
Combine ingredients; mix well. Store in an airtight container. Makes 1¾ quarts.

▲ **Figure 4-10** Recipe for trail mix

4-4 How are mixtures and compounds different?

Objective
Contrast the properties of mixtures with the properties of compounds.

Making a Mixture The different kinds of matter in a mixture are physically combined. A fruit salad is a mixture of different kinds of fruit. You can make a mixture of iron filings and sulfur by mixing the two substances together.

Iron filings are magnetic slivers of gray metal. Sulfur is a nonmetallic yellow powder. Just like each piece of fruit in a salad keeps its properties, each substance in the iron-sulfur mixture will keep its own properties. You would be able to see the grains of yellow powder and slivers of gray metal in a mixture of these two substances.

Sulfur

Iron filings

◀ **Figure 4-11**
Making a mixture
of sulfur and iron

**A mixture of
sulfur and
iron filings**

▶ **1** INFER: How can you make a mixture of iron filings and sulfur?

Making a Compound A compound is made up of two or more elements. It is formed as a result of a chemical change. The elements in a compound combine by forming chemical bonds between the atoms of the elements. For example, molecules of sugar are formed as a result of a chemical change. Atoms of hydrogen form chemical bonds with atoms of oxygen and atoms of carbon to produce molecules of sugar.

Not only can iron and sulfur be physically combined to make a mixture, they can also be chemically combined to form a compound. This compound is called iron sulfide. Iron sulfide forms when a mixture of iron filings and sulfur is heated. The atoms of the two elements will combine to form chemical bonds with each other. The compound iron sulfide will be produced. Like all compounds, the properties of iron sulfide are different from the properties of the elements that make it up.

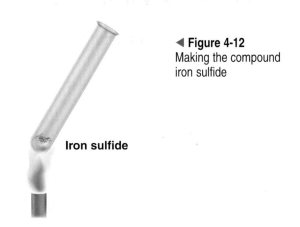

◀ **Figure 4-12**
Making the compound
iron sulfide

Iron sulfide

▶ **2** EXPLAIN: What happens when a mixture of iron filings and sulfur is heated?

Comparing Mixtures and Compounds Mixtures and compounds are different in several ways. A mixture of iron and sulfur does not have a definite chemical composition. The mixture might contain equal parts of each element. Or, it might have twice as much of one element as the other. Each substance in a mixture of iron and sulfur keeps its own properties. A mixture of iron and sulfur can be separated by physical means. For example, a magnet can be used to attract the iron.

The compound iron sulfide always has a definite chemical composition. Every molecule of iron sulfide contains one atom of iron and one atom of sulfur.

When elements combine chemically, each element loses its properties. The iron and sulfur in iron sulfide cannot be separated by physical means. Figure 4-13 lists some differences between mixtures and compounds.

COMPARING MIXTURES AND COMPOUNDS	
Mixtures	Compounds
Made of two or more substances physically combined	Made of two or more substances chemically combined
Substances keep their own properties	Substances lose their own properties
Can be separated by physical means	Can be separated only by chemical means
Have no definite chemical composition	Have a definite chemical composition

▲ **Figure 4-13** Differences between mixtures and compounds

▶3 **CONTRAST:** How are mixtures and compounds different?

✓ **CHECKING CONCEPTS**

1. The elements in a _____ are chemically combined.
2. Each kind of matter in a _____ keeps its own properties.
3. A _____ does not have a definite chemical composition.
4. A _____ cannot be separated by physical means.

💡 **THINKING CRITICALLY**

5. **INFER:** When a certain poisonous gas is combined with a chemically active metal, a fine white powdery substance results. The new substance is neither poisonous nor chemically active. Is the powder a mixture or a compound? How do you know?
6. **COMPARE:** Water is a compound. Salt water is a mixture. List the differences between water and salt water.

Integrating Earth Science

TOPICS: rocks, minerals

CLASSIFYING ROCKS

Like other types of matter, rocks can be classified as elements, compounds, or mixtures. Some rocks are actually made of pure elements. For example, copper and gold are elements that can be found in nearly pure form. However, rocks that are mixtures of different compounds are more common than are rocks made of pure elements.

Some compounds that can be found in certain rocks include quartz, mica, and feldspar. Quartz is a hard, cloudy-looking rock that is actually a compound made up of silicon and oxygen. One form of mica is a black compound made up of the elements potassium, aluminum, silicon, oxygen, and hydrogen. Feldspar is a milky-white or pink compound that can be made up of aluminum, silicon, sodium, potassium or calcium, and oxygen. A mixture of these three compounds can be found in a type of rock called granite. Granite is a hard rock with big grains of quartz, mica, and feldspar.

Thinking Critically How would you classify granite?

▲ **Figure 4-14** Granite is a mixture.

▲ **Figure 4-15** Mica can be found in granite.

LAB ACTIVITY
Separating Mixtures

Materials
Safety goggles,
lab apron, plastic gloves,
sand,
epsom salts,
sawdust, iron filings,
2 clear plastic cups,
teaspoons, stirrers,
water,
magnet,
plastic wrap,
paper towels,
2 beakers,
fine sieve, filter paper

BACKGROUND

Mixtures surround you—Everything from salt water in the ocean to your bowl of morning cereal. Mixtures are part of our everyday lives. Salt water and cereal are mixtures because both contain two or more kinds of matter that are mixed together physically but not chemically. Because the kinds of matter in a mixture are not chemically combined, it is possible to separate the parts based on their physical properties.

PURPOSE

In this activity, you will observe and analyze the separation of mixtures based on four physical properties of matter—the ability to dissolve in water, the ability to float in water, magnetism, and size.

PROCEDURE

1. Copy the chart in Figure 4-17. Put on safety goggles, a lab apron, and plastic gloves.

2. Spread two or three sheets of paper towels on your work area.

3. Obtain a clear plastic cup and put in one teaspoon of sand and one teaspoon of Epsom salts. Record your observations of the two substances on the chart. With a stirrer, mix the two substances together.

4. Cover one end of a bar magnet with plastic wrap and insert it into the cup with the mixture. Use the magnet to stir the mixture. Take the magnet out and examine it closely. Record your observations.

5. Obtain a cup of water and pour it into the cup with the mixture. Stir the mixture with the stirrer. Record your observations.

6. Line a sieve with filter paper. Place the sieve over the mouth of a beaker. Pour the mixture into the sieve. Record your observations.

▲ **STEP 3** Make a sand and Epsom salts mixture.

▲ **STEP 5** Obtain a cup of water to pour into the mixture.

7. Dispose of the mixture in a waste beaker. Rinse and dry out the plastic cup, the sieve, and the first beaker.

8. Repeat Steps 2 through 6 using sand, sawdust, and iron filings to make another mixture. Follow your teacher's directions on how to add iron filings to the mixture.

▲ **STEP 6** Pour the mixture into the sieve.

◀ **Figure 4-16** Iron filings, sand, and sawdust mixture

Separating Mixtures				
Substance	Dissolves in Water	Floats in Water	Magnetic	Filtered by Sieve
Epsom salt				
Iron				
Sand				
Sawdust				

▲ **Figure 4-17** Copy this chart and use it to record your observations.

CONCLUSIONS

1. **INFER:** Describe how each substance was able to keep its own physical properties when it was mixed with another substance.

2. **INFER:** How do you know that each combination was not a chemical combination?

3. **ANALYZE:** Design procedures to separate each mixture into its parts.

4-5 What is an ionic bond?

Objective

Describe how atoms form ionic bonds.

Key Terms

valence electron: electron in the outermost energy level of an atom

ion: atom with an electrical charge

ionic bond: bond formed between atoms that have gained or lost electrons

Valence Electrons The formation of chemical bonds is a process involving valence electrons. A **valence electron** is an electron in the outermost energy level of an atom. Except for the elements hydrogen and helium, the outermost energy level of an atom can hold a maximum of eight electrons. An atom with eight electrons in its outermost energy level is very stable.

Atoms of all elements have valence electrons. Atoms with fewer than eight valence electrons tend to form bonds with other atoms. Atoms can give electrons, receive electrons, or share electrons with other atoms to reach the stable number of eight valence electrons.

▶ **DEFINE:** What are valence electrons?

Neutral Atoms All matter is made up of atoms. Every atom is made up of smaller particles called protons, neutrons, and electrons. A proton has a positive charge. An electron has a negative charge. A neutron has no charge.

In an atom, the number of protons and the number of electrons are the same. Because the charges are balanced, all atoms are neutral.

▶ **EXPLAIN:** Why are atoms neutral?

Charged Atoms When forming chemical bonds, the atoms of nonmetals tend to gain electrons while the atoms of metals tend to lose electrons. When the number of electrons in an atom is different from the number of protons, the atom becomes electrically charged. An atom with an electrical charge is called an **ion.**

If a neutral atom gains electrons, it becomes a negative ion. It is a negative ion because there are now more electrons than there are protons. Electrons have a negative charge. If a neutral atom loses electrons, it becomes a positive ion. There are more protons than there are electrons.

▶ **COMPARE:** Does a negative ion have more protons or more electrons?

Ionic Bonds In compounds, particles of matter are held together by chemical bonds. A bond that forms when one atom gains one or more electrons from another atom is called an **ionic bond.** The atom that gains electrons becomes a negative ion. The atom that loses electrons becomes a positive ion. The two ions have opposite electrical charges. As a result, they are attracted to each other. This force of attraction holds atoms together in an ionic bond.

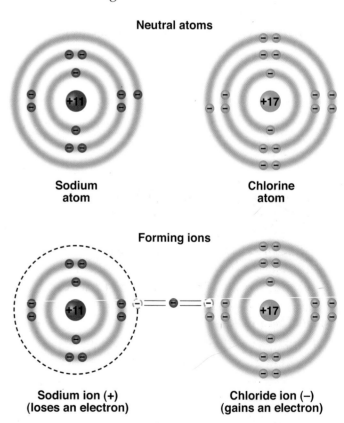

Neutral atoms

Sodium atom   Chlorine atom

Forming ions

Sodium ion (+) (loses an electron)   Chloride ion (−) (gains an electron)

▲ **Figure 4-18** Atoms of sodium and chlorine form ionic bonds.

▶ **EXPLAIN:** How does an ionic bond form?

Ionic Compounds Compounds whose atoms are held together by ionic bonds are called ionic compounds. Ionic compounds are not made up of molecules. Instead, they are made up of one or more positive ions and one or more negative ions. Because the atoms are held together by ionic bonds, ionic compounds have similar properties. One of these properties is crystal shape. A crystal is a solid that contains atoms arranged in a regular pattern. Many ionic compounds, such as sodium chloride, form crystals. Ionic compounds also have high melting points, and they are conductors of electricity when they are melted.

 IDENTIFY: What is a crystal?

CHECKING CONCEPTS

1. Electrons have a _____ electrical charge.

2. When an atom loses electrons, it becomes a _____ ion.

3. An _____ forms when one atom takes an electron from another atom.

4. Particles with opposite electrical charges _____ each other.

5. An ionic compound is not made up of _____.

6. A _____ is a solid that contains atoms arranged in a regular pattern.

THINKING CRITICALLY

7. **INFER:** Could an atom ever lose an electron without another atom gaining the electron? Explain.

8. **ANALYZE:** Why are ionic compounds not made of molecules?

BUILDING SCIENCE SKILLS

Modeling Crystal A crystal is a solid that contains atoms arranged in a regular pattern. The pattern of atoms forms a crystal lattice. The shape of a crystal is determined by its crystal lattice. Table salt, or sodium chloride, is an example of a crystal. Research the type of crystal lattice found in table salt. Draw a diagram of the crystal lattice of sodium chloride and display it to the class. Label the sodium ions and chloride ions in the lattice.

How Do They Know That?
CRYSTALLOGRAPHY

Crystals have been the object of scientific study for hundreds of years. Early mineralogists classified crystals according to observable properties such as shape and color. Around 1800, mineralogists began measuring the angles found on a crystal's surface. The mineralogists thought that the size of a crystal's

▲ **Figure 4-19** Scientists use X rays to determine the structure of crystals.

angles was related to the type of substances that make up the crystal. However, they had no way of looking at the internal structure of a crystal.

In 1895, X rays were discovered. Using X rays, scientists could examine the structure of crystals. They discovered that crystal angles are caused by common structural patterns inside the crystal. As a result of X-ray crystallography, scientists were able to identify six basic crystal systems. The names of these crystal systems are cubic, tetragonal, orthorhombic, monoclinic, hexagonal/trigonal, and triclinic.

Thinking Critically How do you think the names of the crystal systems are related to their shapes? Use a reference to find out.

4-6 What is a covalent bond?

Objective
Describe how atoms combine in covalent bonds.

Key Term
covalent bond: bond formed when atoms share electrons

Outermost Energy Levels In most atoms, the outermost energy level is not completely filled. The outermost energy level does not contain the maximum number of valence electrons that it can hold. In order to complete their outermost energy levels, atoms gain, lose, or share electrons. These electrons come from other atoms that also have incomplete outermost energy levels.

Ionic bonds form when one atom gains one or more electrons from another atom. The result is an ionic compound. Elements can also form compounds when their atoms share electrons to form a molecule. This type of bonding is called a **covalent bond.**

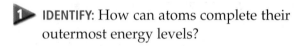

▶ **IDENTIFY:** How can atoms complete their outermost energy levels?

Covalent Compounds Compounds whose atoms share electrons in covalent bonds are called covalent compounds. The shared electrons are in the outermost energy levels of all the atoms in a molecule of the covalent compound.

Water is an example of a covalent compound. A water molecule has covalent bonds between an atom of oxygen and two atoms of hydrogen. The oxygen atom has six electrons in its outermost energy level. It needs two more electrons to completely fill this energy level. A hydrogen atom has one electron in its one and only energy level. This energy level is complete when it has two electrons. So, a hydrogen atom needs only one more electron to fill its outermost energy level. Figure 4-20 shows the covalent bonds in a molecule of water. Notice how two atoms of hydrogen form covalent bonds with one atom of oxygen to form the water molecule.

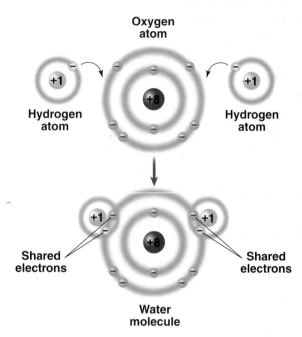

▲ **Figure 4-20** A molecule of water has covalent bonds between the atoms of hydrogen and the atom of oxygen.

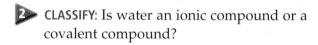

▶ **CLASSIFY:** Is water an ionic compound or a covalent compound?

Comparing Ionic and Covalent Compounds Covalent compounds are formed differently from ionic compounds. Atoms joined by a covalent bond do not lose or gain electrons. So, they do not become positively or negatively charged. They do not become ions. The atoms remain neutral. Figure 4-21 lists the main points to know about ionic compounds and covalent compounds.

COMPARING IONIC AND COVALENT COMPOUNDS	
Ionic Compounds	**Covalent Compounds**
Atoms complete their outermost energy levels.	Atoms complete their outermost energy levels.
Electrons are lost and gained.	Electrons are shared.
Atoms form ions.	Atoms remain neutral.

▲ **Figure 4-21** Ionic compounds and covalent compounds act differently.

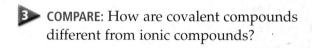

▶ **COMPARE:** How are covalent compounds different from ionic compounds?

Electron Dot Diagrams Electron dot diagrams include the symbols of the elements in a compound and the arrangement of the valence electrons for each element. These diagrams can be used to show the positive and negative ions in an ionic compound. They can also be used to show a molecule of a covalent compound. Figure 4-22 shows the electron dot diagrams for sodium chloride and water.

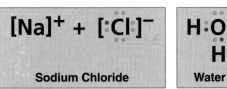

Sodium Chloride   **Water**

▲ **Figure 4-22** Electron dot diagrams for an ionic compound (left) and a covalent compound (right)

 INFER: What do electron dot diagrams show?

✓ CHECKING CONCEPTS

1. In most atoms, the _____ energy level is not completely filled.
2. In a covalent bond, electrons are _____.

3. Water is an example of a _____ compound.
4. In a covalent compound, the atoms join together to form a _____.
5. In a covalent compound, the atoms remain _____.
6. Diagrams that show the symbol of the elements in a compound and the arrangement of the electrons for each element are called _____.

THINKING CRITICALLY

7. **HYPOTHESIZE:** A carbon atom has four valence electrons in its outermost energy level. An oxygen atom has six valence electrons. Hypothesize about the type of bonding that will take place between carbon and oxygen.

 ## Hands-On Activity

MAKING A MOLECULAR MODEL

You will need white and red modeling clay and toothpicks.

1. Using the red clay, make four round balls that are the same size.
2. Make one round ball of white clay that is the same size as the red balls.
3. Use toothpicks to connect each of the four red balls to the white ball. Space the red balls equally around the white ball. You have just made a model of a methane molecule. A molecule of methane contains four hydrogen atoms joined to one carbon atom.

▲ **STEP 3** Make a model of a methane molecule.

Practicing Your Skills

4. **OBSERVE:** What element is represented by the red balls?
5. **OBSERVE:** What element is represented by the white ball?
6. **ANALYZE:** What type of bond joins the atoms?
7. **ANALYZE:** Do the atoms in a methane molecule have an electrical charge? Why or why not?

Objective

Identify some organic compounds.

Key Terms

organic compound: compound containing carbon

organic chemistry: study of organic compounds

structural formula: molecular model that uses straight lines to indicate bonds

polymers: large molecules that are formed by many smaller, simpler molecules

Classifying Compounds Scientists classify compounds based on which ones contain the element carbon and which ones do not. The compounds that contain carbon are called **organic compounds.** The compounds that do not usually contain carbon are called inorganic compounds. An example of an organic compound is sugar, which is made up of carbon, hydrogen, and oxygen. An example of an inorganic compound is water. Water is made up of oxygen and hydrogen.

At one time, scientists thought that only living things contained organic compounds. Today, scientists know that some nonliving substances, such as plastics, contain organic compounds. Also, the compounds carbon dioxide and carbon monoxide are classified as inorganic compounds even though they do contain carbon.

▶ **DEFINE:** What is an organic compound?

Organic Chemistry About 95 percent of all known substances are organic compounds. Because so many of the compounds around us are organic compounds, the study of these substances has been given its own special branch of science called **organic chemistry.**

Scientists studying organic chemistry have learned that a molecule of an organic compound can contain large numbers of atoms. This can happen because a carbon atom has four electrons in its outermost energy level. As a result, a carbon atom can form covalent bonds with up to four other atoms. A carbon atom can form three

different kinds of covalent bonds—a single bond, a double bond, and a triple bond.

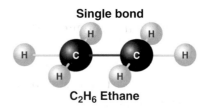

Single bond

C₂H₆ Ethane

In a single bond, a carbon atom shares one pair of electrons with another atom.

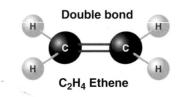

Double bond

C₂H₄ Ethene

In a double bond, two pairs of electrons are shared between atoms.

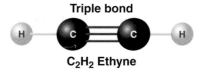

Triple bond

C₂H₂ Ethyne

In a triple bond, three pairs of electrons are shared between atoms.

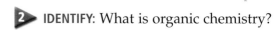

▲ **Figure 4-23** Three types of covalent bonds allow many different organic compounds to be formed.

▶ **IDENTIFY:** What is organic chemistry?

Structural Formulas When carbon atoms join together, they can form many different atomic structures. The atoms can join in a straight chain or a branched chain, or curve around in a ring. These arrangements of atoms can be shown in a structural formula. A **structural formula** is a molecular model that uses straight lines to show bonds. Structural formulas are frequently used to represent organic compounds. Figure 4-24 shows the structural formulas of some organic compounds.

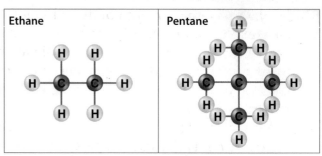

Ethane | Pentane

▲ **Figure 4-24** Structural formulas

▶ **IDENTIFY:** What is a structural formula?

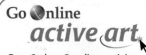

Go Online
active art

For: Carbon Bonding activity
Visit: PHSchool.com
Web Code: cgp-2041

Polymers Organic compounds can join together to form very large molecules. These molecules can contain thousands or even millions of atoms. Very large molecules that are formed by many smaller molecules are called **polymers.** The smaller, simpler molecules that make up polymers are called monomers.

You may be familiar with some polymers, such as silk, nylon, and wool. Many kinds of polymers are used to make materials that we use every day. Some products made from polymers include foam drinking cups, garden hoses, milk containers, and automobile parts.

 LIST: Name some products made from polymers.

 CHECKING CONCEPTS

1. All organic compounds contain the element _____.

2. A carbon atom can form covalent bonds with up to _____ other atoms.

3. In a _____ bond, two pairs of electrons are shared between atoms.

4. The study of organic compounds is called _____.

5. A _____ shows the arrangement of atoms in a molecule of an organic compound.

6. Very large molecules made up of many smaller molecules are called _____.

THINKING CRITICALLY

7. **INFER:** An atom of hydrogen contains one electron in its one energy level. Could a hydrogen atom form a triple bond with another atom? Explain your answer.

8. **EXPLAIN:** Why are there more organic compounds than inorganic compounds?

INTERPRETING VISUALS

Use Figure 4-24 to help you answer the following questions.

9. What is the chemical formula of ethane?

10. What is the chemical formula of pentane?

Science and Technology

ISOMERS

A structural formula can show you that a certain kind of organic compound can have different arrangements. Two or more compounds that have the same chemical makeup but different structures are called **isomers.** For example, Figure 4-25 shows the two structural formulas for the compound butane. Each isomer has four carbon atoms and ten hydrogen atoms in each of its molecules. However, the atoms of each isomer are arranged differently. One isomer is a straight chain and the other isomer is a branched chain. Because each molecule has a different arrangement, each compound has different physical and chemical properties.

Organic compounds that have a large number of carbon atoms may have many isomers. In general, as the number of carbon atoms increases, the number of isomers will also increase.

Thinking Critically Why do you think the number of isomers increases when the number of carbon atoms increases?

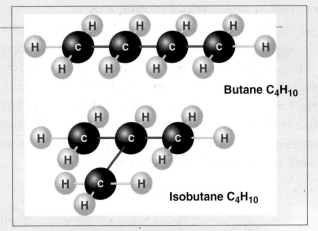

▲ **Figure 4-25** Butane (top) and isobutane (bottom) are isomers.

4-8 What organic compounds are needed by living things?

Objective

Identify organic compounds needed by living things.

Key Terms

carbohydrates (kahr-boh-HY-drayts)**:** sugars and starches

lipids: fats and oils

proteins: compounds used to build and repair body tissues

amino acids: building blocks of proteins

nucleic acids: compounds made up of carbon, oxygen, hydrogen, nitrogen, and phosphorus

Needs of Living Things All living things need certain organic compounds to stay alive. An organism gets the organic compounds it needs from its food. Most foods are made up of carbohydrates, lipids, and proteins.

1 ▶ IDENTIFY: How do organisms obtain the organic compounds they need?

Carbohydrates The organic compounds that are made up of carbon, hydrogen, and oxygen are called carbohydrates. Sugars and starches are **carbohydrates**. These organic compounds are the body's main source of energy. Foods such as cereals, grains, pasta, vegetables, and fruits are good sources of carbohydrates.

2 ▶ EXPLAIN: Why do all living things need carbohydrates?

Lipids The organic compounds that are made up mostly of carbon and hydrogen are called lipids. Fats and oils are **lipids**. These compounds are another energy source for the body. Lipids can be stored in the body for use at a later time. For this reason, lipids are often called the body's stored energy supply. Foods such as butter, meat, cheese, and nuts are good sources of lipids.

Cholesterol is a kind of lipid. Animal fat contains cholesterol. Eating too many foods high

▲ Figure 4-26 Sources of lipids

in certain kinds of cholesterol can be harmful to the body. Excess amounts of cholesterol may form fatty deposits on the inner walls of blood vessels. These fatty deposits can interfere with the flow of blood through the body.

3 ▶ DESCRIBE: Why do living things need lipids?

Proteins Organic compounds that are used to build and repair the body are called **proteins**. Proteins are made up of substances called **amino acids**. Amino acids contain carbon, hydrogen, oxygen, and nitrogen. Amino acids join together in long chains to form proteins. For this reason, amino acids are called the building blocks of proteins. Meat, milk, fish, eggs, and beans are good sources of protein. Foods such as fish and soybeans provide the body with most of the amino acids it needs.

▲ Figure 4-27 Sources of amino acids and proteins

4 ▶ RELATE: What is the relationship between amino acids and proteins?

Nucleic Acids Other organic compounds that your body needs are called nucleic acids. **Nucleic acids** are made up of carbon, oxygen, hydrogen, nitrogen, and phosphorus. There are two types of nucleic acids, deoxyribonucleic acid (DNA) and ribonucleic acid (RNA). These organic compounds are made up of very large molecules. Each molecule is a type of polymer made up of chains of smaller molecules joined together. You have probably heard of DNA. It contains the information about the characteristics that you have inherited and it also controls the activities of the cells in your body.

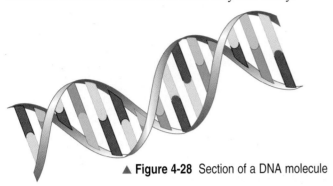

▲ **Figure 4-28** Section of a DNA molecule

5 **DESCRIBE:** What elements are nucleic acids made up of?

☑ CHECKING CONCEPTS

1. An organism gets the organic compounds it needs from its _____.

2. Organic compounds made up of carbon, hydrogen, and oxygen are called _____.

3. Sugars and starches are _____.

4. Fats and oils are _____.

5. Organic compounds used to build and repair body parts are called _____.

6. The organic compounds that control the activities in body cells are called _____.

💡 THINKING CRITICALLY

7. **INFER:** Why do many long-distance runners eat a meal of pasta before running a race?

BUILDING SCIENCE SKILLS

Organizing Information Make a table with the following headings: *Carbohydrates*, *Lipids*, and *Proteins*. Under each heading, identify five types of foods that you enjoy eating that contain that type of organic compound.

 Real-Life Science

MY PYRAMID

To keep your body healthy you should eat a balanced diet. For many years, people followed a standard Food Pyramid as a guide to nutrition. Recently, the United States Department of Agriculture (USDA) recognized that different ages, sexes, and body types need different diets to stay healthy. The My Pyramid Web site (mypyramid.gov) helps people find the best pyramid for their body types.

▲ **Figure 4-29** The My Pyramid guide

The pyramid shows six major food groups that provide important organic compounds. It also tells how much food you should eat from each group every day. The orange portion of the pyramid is the grains group. It includes foods like bread, cereal, rice, wheat, and pasta. These foods contain carbohydrates. The green portion is the vegetable group. The red portion is the fruit group. The foods in these groups contain carbohydrates and other substances your body needs. The blue portion is the milk group. This group contains foods made from milk that are full of calcium like low-fat milk, yogurt, and many cheeses. The purple portion is the meat and beans group. This high-protein group contains lean meats, poultry, eggs, beans, and many nuts. The yellow portion is the oils group. It contains oils like butter, olive oil, and avocados that are healthy when eaten in small amounts. Watching your total calorie intake and regular activity are also important parts of My Pyramid.

Thinking Critically How does the food pyramid tell you how much food you should eat from each group?

THE Big IDEA

What organisms produce poisonous compounds?

Your bones and your organs are very different in chemical structure. Yet, they are all made up of molecules. It takes thousands of different molecules to make up one cell and even more to make up a whole human. Many molecules in living things are complex. We can learn a lot by studying the variety of molecules in Earth's living things.

The cells in all organisms can make different kinds of molecules. Some of these molecules make compounds that help organisms to grow, to fight germs, and to make new cells when old cells die. Some organisms can even make molecules that form poisonous substances.

Poisons from living things are called toxins. Animals and plants that produce toxins are very successful at defending themselves against predators. These organisms can also pass on their ability to make the toxic substances to future generations. Over millions of years, some organisms have evolved to produce very strong toxins.

Some organisms that can produce toxins include the strychnos (STRIHK-nohs) vine, the cinchona (sihn-KOH-nuh) plant, many kinds of snakes, and some tropical frogs.

Look at the photographs of the organisms that appear on these two pages. Read about the poisons that they produce. Find out how some of their poisons can be used in medicines that help treat certain diseases. Then, follow the directions in the Science Log. Go on your own adventure to find other organisms that produce special molecules. ✦

Cinchona Plant

The cinchona plant is grown in countries in South America, India, and parts of Africa. The bark of this poisonous tree is used to make a medicine for the fever caused by the disease malaria. Taking too much of the medicine may, however, lead to coma and death.

Poison Dart Frog

The poison dart frog is a colorful rain forest frog. It produces strong toxins in its skin. These toxins can cause paralysis and eventually death if absorbed into the bloodstream of other animals. The frog's bright color warns predators not to eat it.

Science Log

Sometimes biochemists travel the world looking for useful molecules in exotic organisms. In your science log, plan a research trip. In what part of the world would you look for useful molecules in plants and animals? What are some uses of these molecules? Start your search at www.conceptsandchallenges.com.

Saw Scaled Viper

The saw scaled viper is usually found in very dry desert regions. It makes a highly poisonous toxin. A bite from this snake causes its victim to bleed to death. Medical researchers have studied this toxin to help them make a drug that prevents blood clots in patients at risk for heart attacks.

Strychnos Vine

The strychnos vine makes toxic molecules in its bark. Native peoples of South America use it to make a poison used in hunting called curare. A medicine that helps treat rabies has been made from this poison.

Chapter Summary

Lesson 4-1
- The three types of matter are **elements**, **compounds**, and **mixtures**.

Lesson 4-2
- A **compound** is a substance made up of two or more elements that are chemically combined.
- Compounds are formed as a result of a chemical change.

Lesson 4-3
- A **mixture** contains two or more substances that have been physically combined.
- The substances in a mixture keep their original properties.

Lesson 4-4
- Mixtures differ from compounds in several ways.

Lesson 4-5
- When an atom gains or loses electrons, it becomes an **ion**.
- An **ionic bond** forms between atoms that gain or lose electrons.

Lesson 4-6
- A **covalent bond** forms when atoms share electrons.

Lesson 4-7
- **Organic compounds** contain the element carbon and can form many different structures.

Lesson 4-8
- Organic compounds needed by living things include **carbohydrates**, **lipids**, **proteins**, and **nucleic acids**.

Key Term Challenges

amino acids (p. 96)
carbohydrates (p. 96)
chemical bond (p. 82)
compound (p. 80)
covalent bond (p. 92)
element (p. 80)
ion (p. 90)
ionic bond (p. 90)
lipids (p. 96)
mixture (p. 80)
molecule (p. 82)
nucleic acids (p. 96)
organic chemistry (p. 94)
organic compound (p. 94)
polymers (p. 94)
proteins (p. 96)
structural formula (p. 94)
substance (p. 80)
valence electron (p. 90)

MATCHING Write the Key Term from above that best matches each description.

1. any element or compound
2. study of organic compounds
3. compounds containing carbon
4. bond formed when atoms share electrons
5. fats and oils
6. sugars and starches

FILL IN Write the Key Term from above that best completes each statement.

7. Salt water is an example of a _____.
8. An atom with an electrical charge is called an _____.
9. The force of attraction that holds atoms together is a _____.
10. Very large molecules that are made of a chain of many smaller molecules are called _____.

Content Challenges

MULTIPLE CHOICE **Write the letter of the term or phrase that best completes each statement.**

1. The compound formed when hydrogen and oxygen combine chemically is
   a. salt.
   b. water.
   c. sugar.
   d. sand.

2. Compounds are formed as a result of
   a. evaporation.
   b. filtration.
   c. a physical change.
   d. a chemical change.

3. A molecule is the smallest part of
   a. a crystal.
   b. a substance.
   c. an atom.
   d. compounds.

4. A salt and water mixture can be separated by
   a. hand.
   b. filtering.
   c. melting.
   d. evaporating.

5. The compound iron sulfide can be formed by
   a. heating.
   b. filtering.
   c. evaporating.
   d. mixing.

6. A molecular model of an organic compound is called a
   a. molecular formula.
   b. compound structure.
   c. structural formula.
   d. compound formula.

7. A covalent bond is formed when atoms
   a. trade electrons.
   b. gain electrons.
   c. lose electrons.
   d. share electrons.

8. In an ionic bond, two atoms form
   a. ions.
   b. protons.
   c. neutrons.
   d. electrons.

9. All organic compounds contain
   a. hydrogen.
   b. oxygen.
   c. nitrogen.
   d. carbon.

10. The building blocks of protein are
    a. carbohydrates.
    b. molecules.
    c. ions.
    d. amino acids.

TRUE/FALSE **Write *true* if the statement is true. If the statement is false, change the underlined term to make the statement true.**

11. The three main groups of <u>substances</u> are elements, compounds, and mixtures.

12. The substances in a mixture have not been <u>chemically</u> combined.

13. You can <u>physically</u> separate a mixture of sand and water.

14. A <u>compound</u> is made up of two or more elements.

15. An <u>ionic</u> bond is formed between two atoms that have gained or lost electrons.

16. <u>Nucleic acids</u> control the activities of a cell.

Concept Challenges TEST PREP

WRITTEN RESPONSE **Answer each of the following questions in complete sentences.**

1. **DESCRIBE:** Describe a method of separating each of the following mixtures:
   a. sand and sugar
   b. sugar and water
   c. sawdust and iron filings
   d. nickels and dimes

2. **COMPARE:** How are ionic and covalent compounds the same? How are they different?

3. **EXPLAIN:** How are the properties of table salt different from the properties of the elements that make it up?

4. **PREDICT:** What might happen if you did not get enough carbohydrates in your diet? Explain your answer.

5. **ANALYZE:** Why can carbon form so many different kinds of compounds?

INTERPRETING A DIAGRAM **Use Figure 4-30 to answer the following questions.**

6. What kind of compound is formed in Diagram B?

7. How many electrons are there in the outermost energy level of a neutral oxygen atom?

8. How many protons are there in a neutral oxygen atom? In a neutral hydrogen atom?

9. How many electrons does an atom of oxygen need in order to complete its outermost energy level?

10. What kind of bonds are being formed?

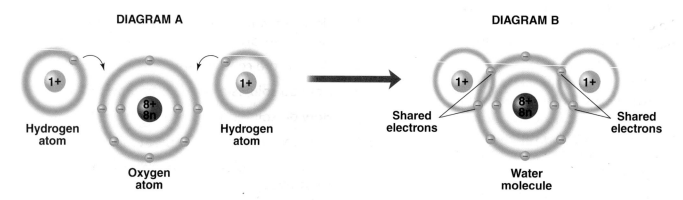

DIAGRAM A

Hydrogen atom
Oxygen atom
Hydrogen atom

DIAGRAM B

Shared electrons
Shared electrons
Water molecule

▲ **Figure 4-30** Forming a water molecule

Chapter 5 Solutions

▲ **Figure 5-1** A surfer is riding the "saltwater solution."

Surfers travel the world looking for the "perfect wave." In our culture, the ocean is important to us for many things. It supplies us with entertainment, food, travel, and shipping. More than 70 percent of Earth is covered by water. About 97 percent of that is ocean. Ocean water is the largest solution we know of. It contains many salts and minerals.

▶What makes the ocean's water so important to us?

Contents

5-1 What is a solution?

INVESTIGATE

Identifying a Solution
HANDS-ON ACTIVITY

1. Put 50 mL of water into a clear plastic cup. Add 1 tsp of pepper and stir.
2. Put the same amount of water in a second cup, and add 1 tsp of salt. Stir.
3. Compare the two mixtures.

THINK ABOUT IT: What differences do you observe? Can you infer which mixture is a solution? On what do you base your inference?

STEP 1

Objective

Describe the characteristics of a solution.

Key Terms

dissolve (dih-ZAHLV): go into solution

solution: mixture in which the particles of one substance are evenly mixed with the particles of another substance

Salt and Water What would happen if you added some sand to a test tube of water? The sand would settle to the bottom of the test tube. Suppose you then added some salt to another test tube of water. The salt seems to disappear in the water. The salt is still in the water, but you cannot see it. The salt has dissolved in the water. When a substance **dissolves,** it goes into solution. The sand did not dissolve in the water.

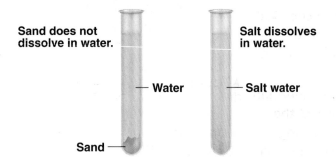

Sand does not
dissolve in water.

Salt dissolves
in water.

— Water

— Salt water

Sand —

▲ **Figure 5-2** One test tube holds a solution. The other does not.

▶ **EXPLAIN:** Why does salt seem to disappear in water?

Solutions A mixture of salt and water is an example of a solution. A **solution** is a mixture in which the particles (molecules or ions) of one substance are evenly mixed with the particles of another substance. In a saltwater solution, sodium ions and chlorine ions are evenly mixed with molecules of water.

 DEFINE: What is a solution?

Types of Solutions Liquid solutions are formed when solids, liquids, or gases dissolve in liquids. Salt water is a liquid solution. A liquid solution may also be formed when a gas dissolves in a liquid. Club soda is a solution of the gas carbon dioxide dissolved in water. Liquids may dissolve in other liquids.

Solutions can also be formed when different substances dissolve in solids and gases. Figure 5-3 shows some examples of different kinds of solutions.

TYPES OF SOLUTIONS		
Substance	**Dissolved in**	**Examples**
Liquid	Liquid	Antifreeze (ethylene glycol) in water
	Gas	Water droplets in air (fog)
	Solid	Sulfur in rubber
Gas	Liquid	Club soda (CO_2 in water)
	Gas	Air (O_2 and other gases in N_2)
	Solid	Hydrogen in palladium
Solid	Liquid	Salt in water (ocean)
	Gas	Iodine vapor in air
	Solid	Brass (zinc in copper)

▲ **Figure 5-3**

▶ **LIST:** What are the different types of solutions?

Other Solutions Tap water, the water you use every day, is not pure water. It is a solution. Most tap water contains dissolved compounds of iron and compounds of calcium. Tap water may also contain dissolved chemicals, such as chlorine, that have been added to make the water safe to drink. Air is a solution of gases, mainly nitrogen and oxygen, evenly mixed together.

 ANALYZE: Why is air called a solution?

✔ CHECKING CONCEPTS

1. Solutions are formed when substances _____ in other substances.
2. Salt water is a solution formed when a _____ dissolves in a liquid.
3. A mixture in which one substance is evenly mixed with another substance is called a _____.
4. Club soda is an example of a solution formed when a _____ dissolves in a liquid.
5. Air is a solution of gases, such as _____ and _____.

💡 THINKING CRITICALLY

6. **CLASSIFY:** Which of the following mixtures are solutions?
   a. sugar and water   e. sea water
   b. brass   f. salt and pepper
   c. club soda   g. sand and water
   d. flour and salt   h. air

7. **ANALYZE:** For each of the mixtures you classified as solutions in question 6, identify the type of solution formed.

Web InfoSearch

Hard Water Because tap water is not pure water, it does not freeze at exactly 0°C. Instead, it freezes at a lower temperature. Tap water containing high concentrations of dissolved salts of calcium, iron, and magnesium is called hard water. This is because the salts make it hard for soap to form a lather with the water.

SEARCH: Find out how these solutes are added to your tap water. Start your search at www.conceptsandchallenges.com. Some key search words are **tap water**, **hard water**, and **water solutes**.

 People in Science

ANALYTICAL CHEMIST

Do you enjoy studying science and mathematics? Can you make careful, precise measurements? Are you determined to find the answer to a problem? If so, you may enjoy a career as an analytical chemist. Analytical chemists analyze the chemical composition of substances. They perform experiments to identify characteristics of the substances and to find out what will happen when different substances are combined.

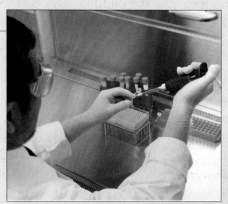

▲ **Figure 5-4** Analytical chemists study the chemical composition of substances.

Most analytical chemists work in laboratories. Dr. Sherman K. W. Fung is such a chemist. He founded and directed the Bio-Sciences Division of SGS Hong Kong Limited, a testing, inspection, and verification organization. Currently, Dr. Fung has served as chief operating officer of the Institute of Chinese Medicine in Hong Kong, China.

To become an analytical chemist, you need a college degree in chemistry. Dr. Fung studied at the University of London and Oxford University.

Thinking Critically Why is it important to be precise and detailed in this line of work?

5-2 What are the parts of a solution?

Objective

Identify the parts of a solution.

Key Terms

solute (SAHL-yoot): substance that is dissolved in a solvent

solvent: substance in which a solute dissolves

soluble (SAHL-yoo-buhl): able to dissolve

solubility: maximum amount of a substance that will dissolve in a given quantity of a solvent at a given temperature

insoluble (in-SAHL-yoo-buhl): not able to dissolve

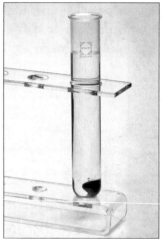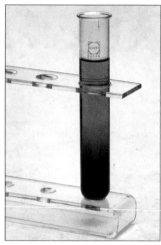

▲ **Figure 5-5** Potassium permanganate dissolves slowly in water. After a few minutes, the solution becomes purple.

Parts of a Solution All solutions are made when one substance dissolves in another substance. A solution of salt and water forms when salt dissolves in water. The part of a solution that dissolves is called the **solute.** Salt is the solute in a solution of salt and water. The part of the solution in which a solute dissolves is called the **solvent.** This substance is usually present in the greater amount, so water is the solvent in a saltwater solution. In pure air, nitrogen is present in the greatest amount of three gases; it is the solvent. Oxygen and argon are the solutes.

▶ CONTRAST: What is the difference between a solute and a solvent?

Soluble Substances In many solutions, the solute becomes invisible. For example, when sugar dissolves in water, the solution looks like plain water. When some substances dissolve, they produce a colored solution. Look at Figure 5-5 at the top of the next column. The picture on the left shows a crystal of potassium permanganate just after it has been placed in a test tube containing water. The picture on the right shows the same test tube a few minutes later. The crystal has begun to dissolve. If the test tube is allowed to sit long enough, or if the mixture is stirred, the entire solution will be a uniform purple color.

Some substances are more **soluble**, able to dissolve, than other substances. The **solubility** of a substance tells you how much of that substance will dissolve in 100 g of solvent at a given temperature. For example, about 33 g of sodium chloride will dissolve in 100 g of water at 20°C. If you add more than 33 g of sodium chloride to this solution, the excess will not dissolve. It will sink to the bottom of the solution.

▶ PREDICT: What will happen when a substance that is soluble in water is mixed with water?

Insoluble Substances Many substances do not dissolve in water. A granite statue does not dissolve in rainwater. Sand does not dissolve in ocean water. A drinking glass does not dissolve when you pour water into it. All of these materials are said to be **insoluble,** or not able to dissolve, in water. A substance that will not dissolve in a given solvent, such as water, is said to be insoluble in that solvent.

You may have heard the saying "water and oil don't mix." This saying means that oil is not soluble in water. If you add oil to a glass of water, the oil will float in a separate layer on top of the water. Even if you stir or shake the mixture, no dissolving will take place. Instead, you will get a mixture like the one shown in Figure 5-6 on the next page. In a short time, this mixture will again separate into its two layers.

▲ Figure 5-6 Oil droplets do not dissolve in water.

A substance may dissolve in one solvent but not in another solvent. For example, sugar will dissolve in water but will not dissolve in vegetable oil. So, sugar can be described as being soluble in water and insoluble in vegetable oil. The chemical makeup of a solvent determines whether another substance is soluble or insoluble in that solvent.

 ANALYZE: How can a substance be both soluble and insoluble?

 CHECKING CONCEPTS

1. Salt is the _____ in a saltwater solution.
2. In air, _____ is the solvent.
3. The substance in which a solute dissolves is called a _____.
4. Sugar is _____ in water.
5. In a solution of sugar and water, water is the _____.

THINKING CRITICALLY

6. **CLASSIFY:** Instant coffee is a solution formed from powdered coffee and hot water. Identify the solute and the solvent in this solution.
7. **INFER:** Is wood soluble in water? How do you know?

DESIGNING AN EXPERIMENT

Design an experiment to solve the following problem. Include a hypothesis, variables, a procedure, and a type of data to study.

PROBLEM: Identify the solute and solvent in iced tea.

Integrating Earth Science

TOPIC: chemical weathering

AN ACIDIC SOLUTION

Weathering is the breaking down of rocks and minerals by natural forces, such as wind and water. In mechanical weathering, rocks are broken down by the action of wind, water, or ice. In chemical weathering, substances in water cause substances in the rock to dissolve. This action weakens the structure of the rock. The rock is then more easily broken apart by mechanical weathering.

A common type of chemical weathering takes place when carbon dioxide from the air dissolves in rainwater. A solution called carbonic acid forms. When this weak acid seeps into rocks, it

▲ Figure 5-7 Carbonic acid has dissolved the features of this limestone face.

dissolves the limestone in the rocks. The dissolved limestone is carried away by the rainwater. As a result, cracks are left in the rocks. Over time, as the rocks are struck by wind or moving water, they will easily crumble.

Thinking Critically What is the difference between chemical and mechanical weathering?

5-3 Why is water a good solvent?

Objective

Explain why water is sometimes called the universal solvent.

Key Term

polar molecule: molecule in which one end has a positive charge and the other end has a negative charge

Water Molecules Water molecules are polar. A **polar molecule** is a molecule in which one end has a positive charge and the other end has a negative charge. A water molecule is made up of two atoms of hydrogen joined to one atom of oxygen. The hydrogen end of a water molecule has a positive charge. The oxygen end of a water molecule has a negative charge.

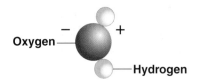

Oxygen — Hydrogen

◀ **Figure 5-8** The two ends of a water molecule carry opposite charges.

Water is sometimes called the universal solvent. This is because many types of substances dissolve in water. The electrical charges associated with the polar molecules of water help to dissolve different kinds of substances.

 EXPLAIN: Why is a water molecule called a polar molecule?

Molecular Solutions The charged ends of a water molecule help separate particles of a solute and spread them throughout the water. Figure 5-9 shows what happens when you place a sugar cube in a glass of water. The ends of the polar water molecules attract the molecules in the sugar cube. Each sugar molecule is pulled to a water molecule. As the sugar dissolves, sugar molecules are evenly mixed throughout the water. This is a molecular solution.

2 **DESCRIBE:** What happens to the sugar molecules when sugar is placed in water?

Force of Attraction Molecular solutions form when the force of attraction between the solute molecules and the solvent molecules is greater than the forces of attraction holding the molecules of the solute together. A sugar crystal gets its shape from the force of attraction between sugar molecules. The sugar molecules will break away from the sugar crystal only if they are pulled by a greater force of attraction. This is also true of other types of solutes.

3 **PREDICT:** What will happen if the force of attraction holding solute particles together is greater than the force of attraction between solute and solvent?

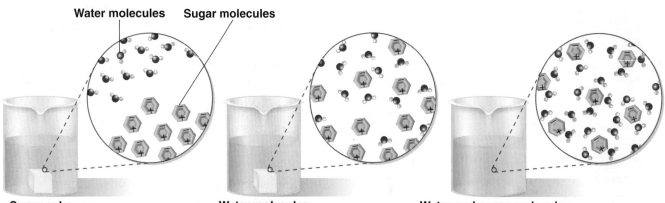

Water molecules   Sugar molecules

Sugar cube in water

Water molecules attract sugar molecules.

Water and sugar molecules spread evenly throughout the solution.

▲ **Figure 5-9** Sugar dissolves in water to form a molecular solution.

Ionic Solutions Ionic compounds are made up of charged particles—positive ions and negative ions. These particles are held together by the force of attraction created by their opposite charges.

When an ionic compound such as sodium chloride—table salt—is added to water, these ions are attracted by the charged ends of the polar molecules of water. In time, the water molecules surround the ions and separate them, as shown in Figure 5-9. The salt dissolves completely, forming an ionic solution.

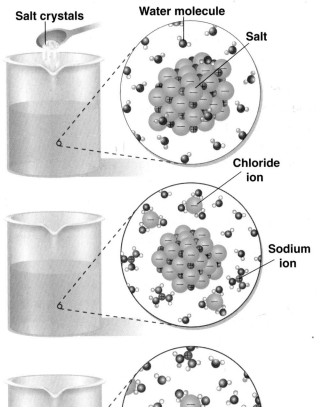

▲ **Figure 5-10** Salt water is an ionic solution.

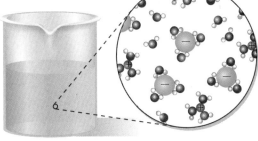

Go **O**nline
active art

For: Salt Dissolving in Water activity
Visit: PHSchool.com
Web Code: cgp-2031

▶ COMPARE: How are molecular solutions similar to ionic solutions? How are they different?

☑ CHECKING CONCEPTS

1. Water is a _____ molecule.

2. Water is sometimes called the _____ solvent.

3. The hydrogen end of a water molecule has a _____ electrical charge.

4. The force of attraction between water molecules and sugar molecules is _____ than the force of attraction between the sugar molecules.

5. Solutions form when the force of attraction between the solute and the solvent is greater than the force of attraction between the particles of the _____.

💡 THINKING CRITICALLY

6. INFER: A substance put in a glass of water does not dissolve. What does this tell you about the force of attraction between the particles of this substance?

7. HYPOTHESIZE: Will a teaspoon of water dissolve in a glass of water? Explain. (Hint: Review the definitions of *dissolve* and *solution* from Lesson 5-1.)

Web InfoSearch

Water Purification Chemist Drinking water has to be treated before it reaches your home. A water purification process begins after the water is analyzed. Various tests are performed on the water to find out what chemicals it contains. Based on the results of the tests, chemicals that should be removed from or added to the water to make it suitable for drinking are identified. Most of this work is done in the laboratories of purification plants.

SEARCH: Use the Internet to find out more about water purification chemists. Then create a poster. Start your search at www.conceptsandchallenges.com. Some key search words are **water purification, chemist,** and **purification chemistry.**

5-4 How can you change the rate at which substances dissolve?

Objective
Describe four ways to speed up the rate of dissolving.

Stirring Solutions form when a solute dissolves in a solvent. The rate at which a solid solute dissolves can be changed. Certain factors can speed up the rate at which a solute dissolves. Stirring a solution will make the solute dissolve faster. If you put a cube of sugar into a glass of water, it will eventually dissolve. However, stirring the water will cause the sugar to dissolve faster. Stirring the water causes the sugar molecules to leave the crystals more rapidly.

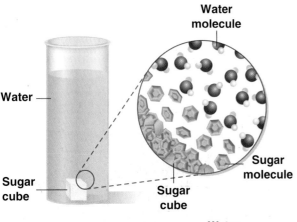

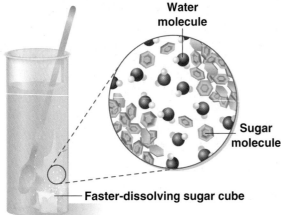

▲ **Figure 5-11** Stirring (bottom) causes sugar to dissolve faster.

▶ **INFER:** Why does stirring make a sugar cube dissolve faster in water?

Temperature The temperature of a liquid solvent affects the rate at which a solid solute dissolves. A cube of sugar dissolves faster in hot water than in an equal amount of cold water. Heat increases the motion of water molecules. This increased energy helps separate sugar molecules more quickly. As the temperature of a liquid solvent increases, the rate at which a solid solute dissolves also increases.

Some gases, such as oxygen and carbon dioxide, are soluble in water. Increasing the temperature of a liquid solvent has the opposite effect on gaseous solutes than it does on solid solutes. As the temperature of the solvent increases, the dissolving rate of a gaseous solute decreases.

▶ **2 RELATE:** What is the relationship between the temperature of a liquid solvent and the rate at which a solid dissolves in it?

Surface Area The size of the particles of a solid solute also affects the rate at which it dissolves. The smaller the size of the solute particles, the faster the solute dissolves. A crushed sugar cube dissolves faster in water than does a solid sugar cube placed in an equal amount of water at the same temperature. As the size of the solute particles decreases, the rate at which the solute dissolves increases.

▶ **3 PREDICT:** Which would dissolve faster in the same amount of water at the same temperature, a sugar cube or powdered sugar?

Pressure The solubility of most gases is affected by pressure. When pressure is increased, more gas can dissolve. For example, when you open a bottle or can containing a carbonated soft drink, you hear the gas escaping. This is because carbon dioxide is added under high pressure. However, pressure has little effect on the dissolving of solids or liquids.

▶ **4 HYPOTHESIZE:** Why do you think more gas can dissolve when pressure is increased?

Types of Solvents You have learned that water molecules are polar. Water, then, is a polar solvent. Polar solvents such as water will dissolve compounds made up of polar molecules and compounds that separate into ions. However, polar solvents will not dissolve compounds made up of nonpolar molecules, such as oils and fats. These substances will, however, dissolve in nonpolar solvents, such as benzene. A good way to remember this "rule" is "like dissolves like."

 RELATE: What type of compounds will water dissolve?

✔ CHECKING CONCEPTS

1. Stirring a solvent _____ the rate at which a solute dissolves in it.
2. Sugar dissolves more slowly in _____ water than in hot water.
3. The smaller the size of the solute particles, the _____ the rate of dissolving.
4. As the _____ of a solvent increases, the rate at which a solid solute dissolves also increases.

THINKING CRITICALLY

5. **INFER:** Why are most types of instant coffee made in powdered form?
6. **ANALYZE:** Explain how each of the following will make a solid solute dissolve faster.
   a. Grind the solute into small pieces.
   b. Place the solvent in a blender.
   c. Heat the solvent.

DESIGNING AN EXPERIMENT

Design an experiment to solve the following problem. Include a hypothesis, variables, a procedure, and a type of data to study.

PROBLEM: How does changing each of these factors affect the rate at which 5 g of sugar will dissolve in 100 mL of water?

a. stirring
b. temperature
c. surface area

Hands-On Activity

CHANGING THE RATE AT WHICH A SUBSTANCE DISSOLVES

You will need four beakers, a graduated cylinder, water, a spoon, and four sugar cubes.

1. Put 100 mL of water in each beaker.
2. Place one sugar cube in each of the first two beakers. Stir the water in the first beaker with a spoon. Leave the second beaker untouched. Compare the results.
3. Use a spoon to crush a sugar cube. Carefully drop the crushed sugar into the third beaker. Place one uncrushed sugar cube in the fourth beaker. Stir both mixtures and compare the results.

▲ **STEP 2** See what happens to the sugar cube when the water is stirred.

Practicing Your Skills

4. **OBSERVE:** What effect did stirring have on the dissolving rate of the sugar cube?
5. **OBSERVE:** What effect did crushing the sugar cube have on the rate of dissolving?
6. **HYPOTHESIZE:** How could you find the fastest way to dissolve a sugar cube in 100 mL of water?

5-5 What is the concentration of a solution?

Objective

Differentiate between saturated and unsaturated solutions.

Key Terms

dilute solution: solution containing a small amount of solute compared with the amount of solvent present

concentrated solution: solution containing a large amount of solute compared with the amount of solvent present

unsaturated solution: solution containing less solute than it can hold at a given temperature

saturated solution: solution containing all the solute it can hold at a given temperature

supersaturated solution: solution containing more solute than it can normally hold at a given temperature

Dilute and Concentrated Solutions The terms *dilute* and *concentrated* are used to describe the relative amounts of solute and solvent present in a solution. Figure 5-12 shows the appearance of three different concentrations of copper sulfate in 100 mL of water at the same temperature.

As the illustration shows, a **dilute solution** is one containing a small amount of solute compared with the amount of solvent present. Dilute solutions are weak. A **concentrated solution** is one containing a large amount of solute compared with the amount of solvent present. Concentrated solutions are strong.

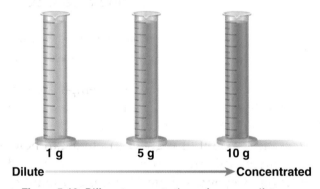

| 1 g | 5 g | 10 g |

Dilute ──────────────────────▶ Concentrated

▲ **Figure 5-12** Different concentrations of copper sulfate

1 COMPARE: What is the difference between a dilute solution and a concentrated solution?

Unsaturated Solutions If you were to add 1 g of the compound copper sulfate to 100 mL of water at 20°C, the copper sulfate would quickly dissolve. In fact, quite a bit more copper sulfate could dissolve in that much water at that temperature. This copper sulfate solution is unsaturated. An **unsaturated solution** contains less dissolved solute than it can hold at a given temperature.

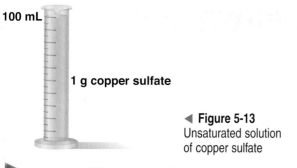
100 mL

1 g copper sulfate

◀ Figure 5-13
Unsaturated solution
of copper sulfate

▶2 **ANALYZE:** When is a solution unsaturated?

Saturated Solutions There is a limit to the amount of solute a given amount of solvent can hold at a specific temperature. If you continued to add copper sulfate to the solution described above, the solution would become saturated. A **saturated solution** contains all the solute it can hold at a given temperature. If you added more copper sulfate to the saturated solution, it would not dissolve. It would settle out of the solution.

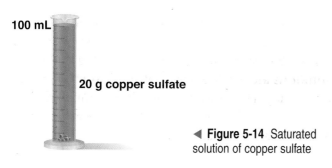
100 mL

20 g copper sulfate

◀ **Figure 5-14** Saturated
solution of copper sulfate

▶3 **HYPOTHESIZE:** If you were preparing a solution, how could you tell when it became saturated?

Supersaturated Solutions The temperature of a solvent determines the amount of solute it can dissolve. As the temperature of a solvent increases, so does the amount of a given solute it can hold. For example, 100 mL of water at 20°C can hold about 14 g of copper sulfate. The same amount of water at 100°C can hold about five times as much copper sulfate.

Suppose you have a saturated solution of copper sulfate at 50°C. The solution contains as much solute as it can hold at that temperature. What will happen if the solution is allowed to cool? At the lower temperature, the solution will be holding *more* solute than it could normally hold at that temperature. Such a solution is said to be **supersaturated**.

▶4 **INFER:** What happens to a solution that enables it to hold more solute than it normally would?

☑ **CHECKING CONCEPTS**

1. A _____ solution contains a small amount of dissolved solute.

2. A _____ solution contains a large amount of dissolved solute.

3. An unsaturated solution contains less _____ than it can hold at a given temperature.

4. A solution that contains all the solute it can hold at a given temperature is called a _____ solution.

5. When saturated solutions are _____, they usually become unsaturated.

💡 **THINKING CRITICALLY**

6. **HYPOTHESIZE:** Is a can of frozen juice a concentrated or a dilute solution? Explain.

7. **PREDICT:** Suppose the directions on a can of frozen juice state that it should be mixed with three cans of water. What type of solution would you make if you added five cans of water? Explain.

INTERPRETING VISUALS

The graph in Figure 5-15 shows the solubility of ammonia, NH₃, and potassium chloride, KCl, at different temperatures. Use the graph to answer the questions.

8. **ANALYZE:** How much more KCl will dissolve in 100 mL of water at 100°C than at 0°C?

9. **INFER:** Is NH_3 a gas or a solid? How do you know?

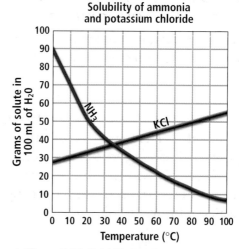
Solubility of ammonia
and potassium chloride

▲ **Figure 5-15** Solubility graph

5-6 How do solutes affect freezing point?

Objective

Describe how the presence of a solute affects the freezing point of a liquid solvent.

Key Terms

freezing point: temperature at which a liquid changes to a solid

freezing point depression: decrease in the freezing point of a liquid solvent because of the addition of a solute

Freezing Point of Water The temperature at which a liquid changes to a solid is called its **freezing point.** The freezing point of pure water is 0°C. When pure liquid water reaches this temperature, it begins changing to solid ice. When water freezes, its molecules become arranged in a crystal pattern called a lattice.

Salt water does not freeze at 0°C. The particles of salt dissolved in the water interfere with the change from a liquid to a solid. Because salt water contains dissolved salt and other minerals, its freezing point is lower than that of pure water.

Fresh water   **Salt water**

Ice   **Liquid**

▲ **Figure 5-16** Sodium and chloride ions in salt water lower the freezing point of the water. Crystals cannot form unless the temperature is below 0°C.

 DESCRIBE: What happens to liquid water at its freezing point?

Freezing Point Depression The amount of solute dissolved in a solvent affects the freezing point of the solvent. This special property of solutions is called **freezing point depression.** Adding solute lowers the freezing point of the solvent. The greater the amount of dissolved solute, the lower the freezing point of the solvent.

 PREDICT: What will happen to the freezing point of water as you add solute to the water?

Melting Danger Away Have you ever sprinkled rock salt or calcium chloride pellets on an icy sidewalk? Ice melters like these lower the freezing point of water. When the ice begins to melt, the chemical compounds dissolve in the water, forming solutions that freeze at a lower temperature than pure water.

Unfortunately, the use of salts for deicing can be hazardous to us and harmful to the environment. The salt residue that remains after the ice has melted can weaken pavement, forming potholes. In addition, chemicals wash off paved surfaces into storm drains, increasing the salinity, or salt content, of nearby streams and lakes. Look at the differences among ice melters in the table in Figure 5-17.

ICE MELTERS		
Compound	Practical Melting Temperature	Advantages/Disadvantages
Rock salt (NaCl) Sodium chloride	−9° C	Abundant resource; pollutes streams and lakes; corrodes metal
Calcium chloride ($CaCl_2$)	−32° C	Abundant resource; may cause skin irritation; attacks concrete
Magnesium chloride ($MgCl_2$)	−15° C	Less toxic to plants and concrete surfaces than rock salts; leaves no powder residue
Calcium magnesium acetate (CMA)	−7° C	Less corrosive to automobiles and roads and less toxic to plants than other salts
Potassium chloride (KCl)	−7° C	Less toxic to plants and surfaces than rock salt; used in fertilizer so overuse may cause plants and grass to burn

▲ **Figure 5-17** The practical melting temperature is the lowest outdoor temperature for which each compound is effective. Below that temperature, the solution will start to freeze.

 PREDICT: What effects do you think the use of salts would have on plants and animals in the environment?

✓ CHECKING CONCEPTS

1. The _____ of pure water is 0°C.

2. The greater the amount of dissolved solute in a solvent, the _____ the freezing point of the solvent.

3. The freezing point of salt water is _____ than the freezing point of pure water.

4. Lowering the freezing point of a liquid solvent by adding solute is a property called _____.

5. Putting salt on icy roads _____ the freezing point of the melted ice.

THINKING CRITICALLY

6. **ANALYZE:** Beaker A contains 2 g of sugar dissolved in 100 mL of water. Beaker B contains 10 g of sugar dissolved in 100 mL of water. Which beaker contains the solution with the lower freezing point? Explain your answer.

7. **ANALYZE:** Beaker C and Beaker D each contain 5 g of dissolved copper sulfate. Beaker C contains 100 mL of water while Beaker D contains 250 mL of water. Which beaker contains the solution with the lower freezing point? Explain your answer.

Web InfoSearch

Salt and Ice Cream "I scream, you scream, we all scream for…" Rock salt is not only for deicing sidewalks. It can also be used to reduce the temperature of a container of juice, milk, or cream to make frozen desserts.

SEARCH: Use the Internet to find out about the history of the hand-cranked ice cream freezer. In a short report, describe its parts and how it can be used to make ice cream. Start your search at www.conceptsandchallenges.com. Some key search words are **Nancy Johnson** and **ice cream**.

Integrating Life Science

TOPICS: cold-blooded animals, circulation

FISH WITH ANTIFREEZE

Fish that live in the Arctic and Antarctic Oceans must survive freezing and near-freezing water temperatures. Scientists wondered why these fish did not freeze in such an environment.

By studying fish in the Arctic region of northern Labrador, in Canada, scientists discovered that the blood of the Arctic fish contained a high concentration of a certain protein. This antifreeze protein (AFP) acts like a solute in a solution. The greater the amount of protein in the blood of the fish, the lower the freezing point of the blood.

As a result of this freezing point depression, the fish can survive in the cold Arctic environment. Should the water temperature reach 0°C, the blood of the fish would still be a liquid.

▲ **Figure 5-18** These fish can survive in subfreezing conditions.

Thinking Critically What helps fish live in such frigid water?

5-7 How do solutes affect boiling point?

Objective

Describe how a solute affects the boiling point of a solution.

Key Terms

boiling point: temperature at which a liquid changes to a gas

boiling point elevation: increase in the boiling point of a liquid solvent because of the addition of a solute

Boiling Point of Water When water is heated, its temperature rises. The temperature at which a liquid changes to a gas is called its **boiling point.** The boiling point of pure water at sea level is 100°C, at which point water changes to steam. Adding heat to boiling water does not raise its temperature.

Salt water does not boil at 100°C. This is because salt water contains dissolved salt particles. The particles of salt dissolved in the water interfere with the change from a liquid to a gas. The temperature of salt water must be higher than 100°C before the water will boil.

▶ **DESCRIBE:** What happens when the temperature of pure water reaches 100°C?

Boiling Point Elevation The boiling point of a liquid solvent is increased by adding a solute. This property of all solutions is called **boiling point elevation**. As the amount of solute in the solvent increases, the boiling point of the solvent also increases. For example, a solution of sugar and water does not boil at the same temperature as pure water because of boiling point elevation. Figure 5-20 lists some normal boiling points.

BOILING POINTS OF DIFFERENT SOLUTIONS	
Substance	**Normal Boiling Point**
Distilled water (at sea level)	100°C
Sea water	103°C
Vinegar	118°C
Ethyl alcohol	78.5°C
Acetone	56°C

▲ Figure 5-20

 DEFINE: What is boiling point elevation?

Keep That Engine Running Whenever the engine of a car is running, large amounts of heat are produced. A coolant is used to protect the engine from this heat. A coolant must also be able to remain liquid at low temperatures. The most common coolant is a solution of water and another liquid, usually ethylene glycol.

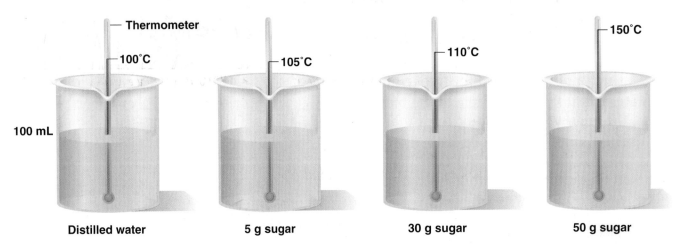

▲ **Figure 5-19** The boiling point of a solution increases as more solute is added.

Ethylene glycol freezes at –13°C and boils at 197°C. Although it is commonly called antifreeze, this compound could also be called antiboil because it lowers the freezing point of water and elevates its boiling point. In recent years, new antifreeze products have been developed. These products contain materials that are less toxic and safer for the environment than is ethylene glycol.

 DESCRIBE: What two important functions does an engine coolant have?

✔ CHECKING CONCEPTS

1. The _____ of pure water is 100°C.
2. The boiling point of salt water is _____ than the boiling point of pure water.
3. As the amount of solute in a solution increases, the boiling point of the solution _____.
4. Raising the boiling point of a liquid solvent by adding solute is called _____.

THINKING CRITICALLY

5. **ANALYZE:** Solution A contains 5 g of sugar dissolved in 100 mL of water. Solution B contains 20 g of sugar dissolved in 100 mL of water. Which solution has the higher boiling point? Explain your answer.
6. **ANALYZE:** Two beakers each contain 12 g of salt dissolved in water. Beaker A contains 200 mL of water and Beaker B contains 100 mL of water. Which solution has the higher boiling point? Explain your answer.

DESIGNING AN EXPERIMENT

Design an experiment to solve the following problem. Include a hypothesis, variables, a procedure, and a type of data to study.

PROBLEM: How does the addition of salt to water affect the time it takes to boil an egg?

 Hands-On Activity

OBSERVING BOILING POINT ELEVATION

You will need three beakers, a thermometer, safety goggles, a heat source, a spoon, distilled water, and salt.

1. Put on safety goggles. Put 100 mL of water in each beaker.
2. Add 5 g of salt to the first beaker and stir.
3. Heat the water in the beaker until it begins to boil. Record the temperature.
4. Add 10 g of salt to the second beaker and stir. Repeat Step 3.
5. Add 20 g of salt to the third beaker and stir. Repeat Step 3.

▲ **STEP 3** Heat the water until it begins to boil.

Practicing Your Skills

6. **OBSERVE:** What was the boiling point of the first solution?
7. **OBSERVE:** What was the boiling point of the second solution?
8. **OBSERVE:** What was the boiling point of the third solution?
9. **ANALYZE:** What is the relationship between the amount of salt (a solute) and the boiling point of water (a solution)?

Objective

Describe two methods for separating the solute from the solvent in a solution.

Key Terms

evaporation (ee-vap-uh-RAY-shuhn): change from a liquid to a gas at the surface of the liquid

condensation (kahn-duhn-SAY-shuhn): change from a gas to a liquid

distillation (dihs-tuh-LAY-shuhn): process of evaporating a liquid and then condensing the gas back into a liquid

Evaporation A solute can be separated from a solution by evaporation. **Evaporation** is the change of a liquid to a gas at the surface of the liquid. The molecules at the surface of the liquid gain enough energy to break free of the liquid and move into the air as a gas.

You can separate copper sulfate crystals from a solution of copper sulfate and water. Place the solution in a shallow dish and let it stand. After a few days, all the water will have evaporated. Crystals of copper sulfate remain in the bottom of the dish.

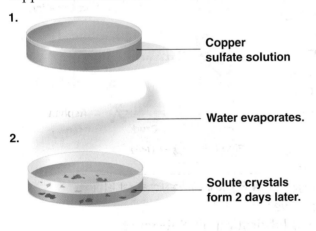

1.
— Copper sulfate solution

— Water evaporates.

2.
— Solute crystals form 2 days later.

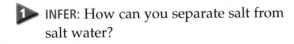

3.
— Dish contains only crystals 4 days later.

▲ **Figure 5-21** The evaporation of a solvent leaves the solute.

 INFER: How can you separate salt from salt water?

Condensation Have you ever come out of a hot shower to find drops of water on your bathroom mirror? The drops of water are the result of condensation. **Condensation** is the change of a gas to a liquid. Some of the shower water evaporates to form water vapor, an invisible gas. When the water vapor strikes the mirror, the water is cooled. This causes the water vapor to change back to liquid water.

2 **DEFINE:** What is condensation?

Distillation A liquid solution can be separated into its separate parts by the process of distillation. In the process of **distillation**, a liquid is heated until it evaporates. The gas is then cooled until it condenses back into a liquid.

When a solution is distilled, both the solvent and the solute can be recovered. The solution to be separated is heated. The solvent evaporates and forms a gas. The gas moves through a tube called a condenser. The condenser cools the gas, which changes back to a liquid. The liquid drips into a container. The solute remains in the original container. Both the solute and the solvent are

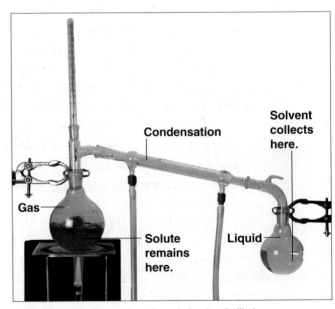

Condensation

Solvent collects here.

Gas

Solute remains here.

Liquid

▲ **Figure 5-22** Separation of a solution by distillation

recovered.

3 **IDENTIFY:** What two processes are involved in distillation?

✓ CHECKING CONCEPTS

1. Evaporation changes a liquid to a _____.

2. Condensation changes a gas to a _____.

3. A solution can be separated into its solute and solvent by _____.

4. As a liquid is heated, the molecules at the liquid's _____ evaporate first.

5. A solvent can be evaporated from a solution to recover the _____.

6. Evaporation takes place at the _____ of a liquid.

7. During distillation, cooling the evaporated solute causes _____ to occur.

💡 THINKING CRITICALLY

8. **INFER:** What causes steam to escape from the spout of a teakettle?

9. **HYPOTHESIZE:** Why do droplets of water form on the underside of the lid of a pot of boiling water?

BUILDING SCIENCE SKILLS

Researching Distillation can be used to purify water. Chemists and pharmacists use distilled water to make solutions. Distilled water is also used in car batteries. Use library references to find out how distilled water is prepared. Why is it sometimes important to use distilled water instead of ordinary tap water? Write a brief report of your findings.

Science and Technology

FRACTIONAL DISTILLATION OF PETROLEUM

Petroleum is a mixture of different substances. Gasoline, kerosene, and heating oil are just some of the products obtained from petroleum. Petroleum is separated by the process of fractional distillation. In this process, petroleum is heated in a fractionating (FRAK-shuhn-ayt-ing) tower. The different substances in petroleum have different boiling points. Each substance, or fraction, changes to a vapor at a different temperature. The process of fractional distillation depends on each substance's boiling point.

As the temperature in the fractionating tower increases, each substance changes to a vapor. The vapors pass through pipes where they cool and condense. Then, they collect separately. The substances with the highest boiling points cool and condense and drain from the lower part of the tower. These substances include asphalt and lubricating oil. Substances that boil at a lower temperature rise higher in the tower before they cool and condense. Fuel oil and kerosene drain off in the middle of the tower. Gasoline, with the lowest boiling point, rises to the top of the tower and drains off. Once the petroleum is separated into liquid fractions, each liquid drains into its storage tank.

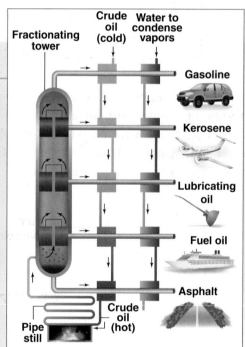

▲ **Figure 5-23** Fractional distillation

Thinking Critically Why do the substances with lower boiling points drain from the top of the tower, whereas those with higher boiling points drain from the bottom?

LAB ACTIVITY
Making Supersaturated Solutions

Materials

Safety goggles,
lab apron, heat source,
marking pen,
3 250-mL beakers,
100-mL graduated
cylinder,
glass stirrers,
3 plastic teaspoons,
water, sugar,
Epsom salts, table salt

BACKGROUND

The solubility of a solute is the amount of solute that will dissolve in a given amount of a certain solvent. This will produce a saturated solution. Increasing the temperature usually increases the solubility of a solute. To make a supersaturated solution, heat the solution, add more solute to it, and then cool it.

PURPOSE

In this activity, you will observe the solubility of different substances in solutions. Also, you will observe the relationship among solutes, solvents, and heat.

PROCEDURE

1. Copy the chart in Figure 5-24. Put on safety goggles and a lab apron.

2. Label each beaker with the following: 1 (table salt), 2 (Epsom salts), and 3 (sugar).

3. Add 100 mL of water to each beaker.

▲ **STEP 2** Label each beaker.

Observing the Effects of Heat on a Solute and a Solvent			
Beaker	Solute	Number of Teaspoons to Make Saturated Solution	Number of Teaspoons After Heating
1	Table salt		
2	Epsom salts		
3	Sugar		

▲ **Figure 5-24** Copy this chart and use it to record your observations.

▲ **STEP 4** Make saturated solutions of each substance.

▲ **STEP 5** Place the beaker on the heat source and stir the contents.

4. Make saturated solutions of each substance. For each solution, add a teaspoonful of table salt, Epsom salts, or sugar to the corresponding beaker. Stir for one minute. Continue adding the solute and stirring until some does not dissolve. Record how many teaspoonfuls you add to make each saturated solution.

5. Place the beaker that contains table salt on a heat source. Stir the mixture with a glass stirrer as it is heating. As soon as the solid particles dissolve, add another teaspoon of table salt and stir. Add more table salt until some table salt is left behind. Record the number of teaspoons you add.
⚠ CAUTION: Be extremely careful when handling anything on a hot plate.

6. Allow the solution to cool. As it cools, record your observations.

7. Repeat Step 4 with the beakers that contain the Epsom salts and the sugar. Record your observations.

CONCLUSIONS

1. **OBSERVE:** Describe the appearance of the solutions at room temperature.

2. **OBSERVE:** Describe what happened to the solutions upon heating.

3. **INFER:** Which part of the activity represents a supersaturated solution? How do you know?

4. **ANALYZE:** How is the knowledge of solubility useful for people who make drink mixes or instant soups?

5-9 How are crystals formed?

Objective
Explain how crystals are formed from solutions.

Crystal Chemistry The particles that make up a crystal are arranged in a pattern. This pattern gives the crystal a definite shape. All crystals of the same substance have the same shape. Figure 5-25 shows how crystals of copper sulfate can "grow" from a saturated solution of this compound. As the saturated solution sits, water will evaporate. Copper sulfate crystals will appear in the bottom of the solution. These crystals will increase in size as more and more water evaporates.

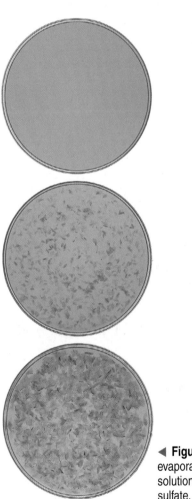

◀ **Figure 5-25** Over time, water evaporates from the copper sulfate solution, leaving crystals of copper sulfate.

▶ **1** INFER: Why are all salt crystals shaped like a cube?

Seeding Another way to grow crystals is to use a supersaturated solution. Figure 5-26 shows how to grow crystals from a supersaturated solution of sodium acetate. After a saturated solution is prepared at a high temperature, let it cool to room temperature. Then add a small sodium acetate crystal to the solution. This sodium acetate "seed" causes the excess crystals of sodium acetate to come out of solution and settle quickly to the bottom of the container.

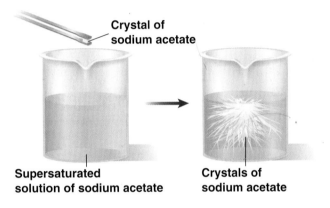

Crystal of sodium acetate

Supersaturated solution of sodium acetate

Crystals of sodium acetate

▲ **Figure 5-26** Growing sodium acetate crystals

▶ **2** DEFINE: How does a supersaturated solution allow you to grow crystals?

Synthetic Crystals Natural crystals may contain flaws or impurities, but synthetic, or human-made, crystals can be made flawless. They can be made to grow in a particular shape or size to suit specific needs. Synthetic crystals are crucial to the development of new technology.

Optical crystals made of sodium chloride, potassium chloride, and many other crystalline compounds can be used in the development of laser and fiber-optic communication. Silicon chips are very thin slices of artificially grown silicon crystals. They are used in many electronic devices, such as the circuit boards of computers, to hold information and control mechanical functions. "Smart cards" are credit or debit cards that have a microprocessor built into the silicon chip on the card. These cards may be used in the future to store and update personal bank or credit account information.

Synthetic gems such as diamonds are used in industry primarily because of their strength and durability. Saws set with diamonds and diamond-tipped drill bits are

▲ **Figure 5-27**
A synthetic gem

used to cut and drill through glass, ceramics, and rocks. Because they do not corrode, diamonds are also used in medical instruments like diamond-bladed scalpels for eye surgery. Other types of gems can also be made with synthetic crystals.

 LIST: What are some uses of synthetic crystals?

CHECKING CONCEPTS

1. When water is evaporated from a copper sulfate solution, copper sulfate _____ remain.

2. All crystals of the same substance have the same _____.

3. A supersaturated solution contains more _____ than it would normally hold at a given temperature.

4. Crystals form when extra _____ is added to a supersaturated solution.

THINKING CRITICALLY

5. **PREDICT:** What will happen when sugar is added to a supersaturated solution of sugar and water?

BUILDING SCIENCE SKILLS

Organizing Information When you organize information, you put the information in some kind of order. Draw a chart showing the six basic crystal shapes. Use library references to identify a substance whose crystals have each type of shape.

Hands-On Activity

MAKING ROCK CANDY

You will need a sugar crystal, sugar-water solution prepared ahead of time, pencil, thread, large drinking glass, and paper towels.

1. From the container your teacher will supply, select a large sugar crystal. Remove it with tongs and dry it with a paper towel.

2. Pour some of the sugar-water solution from the container into a glass. Be careful not to pour any other crystals into the glass.

3. Tie one end of the thread to a pencil and the other end of the thread gently around the sugar crystal.

4. Balance the pencil over the opening of the glass so that the crystal is suspended in the solution. Do not let the crystal touch the bottom of the glass.

5. Let the glass sit undisturbed for several days to a week. Observe what grew on the string.

▲ **STEP 5** Observe the thread after a few days.

Practicing Your Skills

6. **OBSERVE:** What formed on the string after several days?

7. **HYPOTHESIZE:** What caused the result you observed?

THE Big IDEA

How are crystals formed on Earth?

Gases and liquids are disordered. The molecules in a liquid or a gas bounce off each other and flow. Think about some perfume evaporating from a liquid into a gas. The perfume vapor spreads out. Your nose can easily prove that molecules of perfume in a gas state have flowed all around the room.

Solids, however, do not flow. If you put a solid into an empty jar, it just sits at the bottom of the jar. It does not spread out or flow. The solid stays together because its molecules are often ordered in regular geometric patterns called crystals.

How do crystals form? When a substance cools from liquid to solid, its flowing molecules slow down. The molecules begin to line up, forming rows and layers. They pack together tightly to form a crystal.

Crystals can be found in many places. You can find crystals in a kitchen in the form of sugar and salt. Rock candy is a giant sugar crystal. Diamonds are very hard crystals of carbon. In the heart of a battery-powered watch is a quartz crystal, which vibrates when electricity flows through it. Crystals can form in volcanoes, teakettles, caves, and candy shops. Crystals form anywhere molecules line up in geometric rows and layers.

Look at the photos that appear on these two pages. Then, follow the directions in the Science Log to find out more about "the big idea." ✦

The Caverns of Sonora
These crystalline structures (above) form in caves over thousands of years. They are deposits of minerals called calcite and aragonite, which come from water dripping into the cave. This close-up (right) shows calcite crystals.

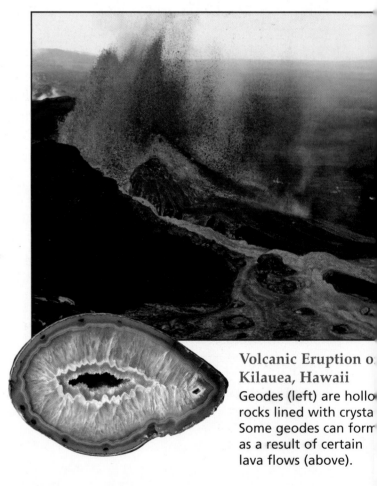

Volcanic Eruption o Kilauea, Hawaii
Geodes (left) are hollo rocks lined with crysta Some geodes can form as a result of certain lava flows (above).

WRITING ACTIVITY

Science Log

Some crystals are as ordinary as table salt; others are as rare as priceless gems. Find out more about crystals. Then, in your science log, write an extraordinary story about a crystal. Start your search at www.conceptsandchallenges.com.

Kitchen Crystals
Sometime crystals form in teakettles. Minerals dissolved in water crystallize when the water boils and evaporates. This close-up (right) shows these crystals.

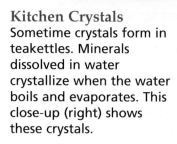

Tufa Towers at Mono Lake, California
The formations you see above are made as salt water evaporates, leaving the salty towers. This close-up (right) shows salt crystals.

Chapter 5 *Challenges*

Chapter Summary

Lesson 5-1
- When a substance dissolves, it goes into **solution**, a mixture in which one substance is evenly mixed with another substance.

Lesson 5-2
- The substance that dissolves in a solution is called the **solute**. The **solvent** is the substance in which a solute dissolves.
- A substance that dissolves in another substance is **soluble** in that substance.

Lesson 5-3
- A molecule is polar if one end has a positive charge and the other end has a negative charge.
- Water is called the universal solvent because it can dissolve many different substances.

Lesson 5-4
- Stirring, crushing, or heating a solvent increases the rate at which a solute dissolves.

Lesson 5-5
- An **unsaturated solution** contains less solute than it can hold at a given temperature.
- A **saturated solution** contains all the solute it can hold at a given temperature.

Lesson 5-6
- Lowering the **freezing point** of a liquid solvent by adding solute is called **freezing point depression**.

Lesson 5-7
- The temperature at which a liquid changes to a gas is called its **boiling point**. Raising the boiling point of a liquid solvent by adding solute is called **boiling point elevation.**

Lesson 5-8
- **Evaporation** is the process by which a liquid changes to a gas at the surface of the liquid.
- **Condensation** is the process by which a gas changes to a liquid.

Lesson 5-9
- Crystals form when extra solute is added to a supersaturated solution.

Key Term Challenges

boiling point (p. 116)
boiling point
    elevation (p. 116)
concentrated solution
    (p. 112)
condensation (p. 118)
dilute solution (p. 112)
dissolve (p. 104)
distillation (p. 118)
evaporation (p. 118)
freezing point (p. 114)
freezing point
    depression (p. 114)

insoluble (p. 106)
polar molecule (p. 108)
saturated solution (p. 112)
solubility (p. 106)
soluble (p. 106)
solute (p. 106)
solution (p. 104)
solvent (p. 106)
supersaturated
    solution (p. 112)
unsaturated solution
    (p. 112)

MATCHING Write the Key Term from above that best matches each description.

1. temperature at which a liquid changes to a solid

2. solution containing more solute than it can normally hold at a given temperature

3. change of a gas to a liquid

4. temperature at which a liquid changes to a gas

5. lowering the freezing point of a liquid solvent by adding solute

6. solution containing less solute than it can hold at a given temperature

FILL IN Write the Key Term from above that best completes each statement.

7. Extra solute sitting at the bottom of a solution indicates the solution is a _____.

8. Increasing the amount of solute in a solution can make a _____.

9. In distillation of a liquid, _____ occurs first and then condensation.

10. For a solution to form, a _____ must dissolve in a solvent.

11. Powdered sugar _____ faster than a sugar cube.

12. The _____ of pure water is 0°C.

Content Challenges TEST PREP

MULTIPLE CHOICE **Write the letter of the term or phrase that best completes each statement.**

1. Extra solute sitting at the bottom of a solution indicates the solution is
   a. dilute.
   b. unsaturated.
   c. saturated.
   d. supersaturated.

2. As the amount of solute in a solution increases, the _____ of the solution also increases.
   a. boiling point
   b. temperature
   c. freezing point
   d. solubility

3. In distillation, a liquid _____ and then condenses.
   a. sublimes
   b. freezes
   c. boils
   d. evaporates

4. For a solution to form, a _____ must dissolve in a solvent.
   a. chemical
   b. solute
   c. soda
   d. salt

5. Crystals of the same substance have the same
   a. shape.
   b. size.
   c. faces.
   d. irregularities.

6. Powdered sugar dissolves _____ a sugar cube.
   a. more slowly than
   b. at the same rate as
   c. faster than
   d. the same way as

7. The _____ of pure water is 0°C.
   a. boiling point
   b. freezing point
   c. room temperature
   d. solubility

8. Adding antifreeze to a car's cooling system raises the _____ of the water it contains.
   a. amount
   b. freezing point
   c. concentration
   d. boiling point

9. Placing rock salt on an icy sidewalk lowers the _____ of melted ice.
   a. evaporation
   b. freezing point
   c. boiling point
   d. condensation

10. A _____ solution contains more solute than it can normally hold at a given temperature.
    a. dilute
    b. supersaturated
    c. unsaturated
    d. saturated

TRUE/FALSE **Write *true* if the statement is true. If the statement is false, change the underlined term to make the statement true.**

11. Stirring a solution <u>speeds up</u> the rate at which a solute dissolves.

12. The freezing point of salt water is <u>higher</u> than that of pure water.

13. Crystals form when extra solute is added to <u>an unsaturated</u> solution.

14. The ends of a water molecule are <u>electrically charged</u>.

15. As the amount of solute in a solution increases, the boiling point of the solution <u>decreases</u>.

Concept Challenges TEST PREP

WRITTEN RESPONSE Complete the exercises and answer each of the following questions in complete sentences.

1. **ANALYZE:** The law of conservation of matter states that matter cannot be created or destroyed but only changed from one form to another. How does the evaporation of water support this law?

2. **COMPARE:** Compare the effect of an increased amount of solute on both the boiling point and the freezing point of a solution.

3. **INFER:** How could information about crystal shape be used to identify an unknown substance?

4. **HYPOTHESIZE:** What effect does evaporation have on Earth's oceans?

5. **EXPLAIN:** Club soda contains carbon dioxide gas dissolved in liquid water. Explain why a bottle of club soda goes "flat" when it is left open at room temperature.

INTERPRETING A GRAPH Use Figure 5-28 to answer the following questions. Round your numbers to the nearest tenth.

6. About how many grams of sodium nitrate can be dissolved in 100 g of water at a temperature of 50°C?

7. At what temperature will 100 g of water dissolve 160 g of sodium nitrate?

8. About how much sodium nitrate can be dissolved in 100 g of water at a temperature equal to the boiling point of pure water?

9. About how much sodium nitrate can be dissolved in 100 g of water at a temperature equal to the freezing point of pure water?

10. What is the relationship between the temperature of a solvent and the amount of solute it can dissolve?

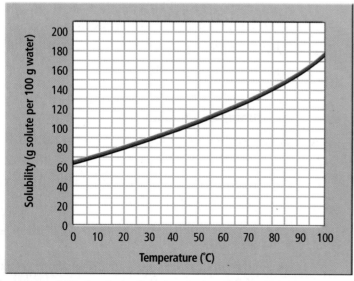

▲ **Figure 5-28** Graph showing the solubility of sodium nitrate

Chapter **6** **Suspensions**

▲ **Figure 6-1** A decorative stained-glass window

Stained glass is used to decorate because light shines through certain types, making colors look as if they are glowing. It is used in windows, lamp shades, and sculptures.

Clear glass is an unusual solution in which particles of sand and other substances are evenly mixed. Stained glass is different. It is actually a mixture in which color particles are suspended within the clear glass. The color particles are minerals. Cobalt makes blues. Copper makes reds. Iron makes greens.

▶What is the difference between the particles in two different colors?

Contents

6-1 What is a suspension?

Objective

Describe the characteristics of a suspension.

Key Term

suspension (suh-SPEHN-shuhn): mixture of two materials or more that separate on standing

Suspensions If you add some soil to a jar of water, the water will become cloudy. If you let the mixture stand, you will notice that the soil particles settle to the bottom of the jar. A mixture of soil and water is an example of a suspension. A **suspension** is a mixture of two or more materials that separate on standing. An important thing to remember about suspensions is that most types of suspensions are temporary. The materials in an ordinary suspension may appear to be well mixed at first, but in time they will separate.

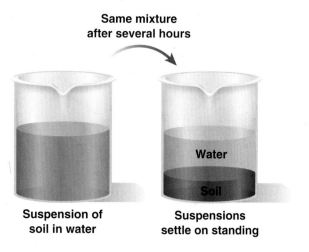

Same mixture after several hours

Water

Soil

Suspension of soil in water

Suspensions settle on standing

▲ **Figure 6-2** Soil and water make a temporary suspension.

In many cases the particles of a suspension will separate into layers. Think about a suspension of soil and water. If you were to examine this mixture after it has separated, you would notice that the soil has formed definite layers. Soil is made up of particles of different sizes and weights. As the particles settle, they form layers, with the heaviest particles on the bottom and the lightest particles on top.

▶ **DEFINE:** What is a suspension?

Particles in Suspensions The particles in a solution are much too small to be seen, even with the aid of a microscope. That is because the particles in a solution are mixed at the smallest level possible—as atoms or molecules. However, the particles in a suspension are much larger. You can see the particles in some suspensions without a microscope. In other suspensions, the particles are visible with a microscope.

2 **COMPARE:** How does the size of the particles in a suspension compare with the size of the particles in a solution?

Properties of Suspensions An important property of suspensions is that the particles of a suspension scatter light. You can observe this property by darkening a room and shining a flashlight through a mixture of soil and water. The beam of light will be visible as it passes through the cloudy water. One way you can tell the difference between a solution and a suspension is that the particles of a solution do not scatter light. Figure 6-3 compares some properties of solutions and suspensions.

PROPERTIES OF SOLUTIONS AND SUSPENSIONS	
Solution	**Suspension**
Mixture	Mixture
Clear	Cloudy
Particles evenly mixed	Particles settle on standing
Particles too small to be seen	Particles can be seen

▲ **Figure 6-3** Compare the properties of solutions and suspensions.

3 **OBSERVE:** What property do suspensions and solutions have in common?

Examples of Suspensions A familiar example of a suspension is an oil and vinegar salad dressing. If you shake a bottle of salad dressing, the contents mix together. Once you put the bottle down, however, the ingredients separate. That is why the labels on bottles of salad dressing often state "Shake well before using."

Not all suspensions involve liquids. A common suspension of a solid in a gas is dust or smoke particles suspended in the air. Smog, a suspension of smoke, fog, and chemicals in air, is a common pollutant. Clouds, another suspension, are made up of tiny particles of water or ice suspended in air.

▲ Figure 6-4 A dust storm is a suspension of a solid in a gas.

 LIST: What are two common examples of suspensions?

 CHECKING CONCEPTS

1. If a suspension is allowed to stand, the substances will _____.

2. The appearance of a _____ is cloudy.

3. The _____ in a suspension are larger than atoms or molecules.

4. An example of a suspension of a solid in a gas is _____ suspended in air.

5. Solutions and suspensions are similar in that both are _____.

THINKING CRITICALLY

6. CONTRAST: How are the particles in a suspension different from those in a solution?

7. CLASSIFY: Look at Figure 6-3. Are the properties listed physical or chemical properties?

BUILDING SCIENCE SKILLS

Analyzing Prepare mixtures of each of the following in water: salt, sand, pepper, and sugar. Stir each mixture and use what you have learned to decide whether each mixture is a solution or a suspension. Record all your observations and tell how you reached your conclusions.

Hands-On Activity

MAKING A SUSPENSION

You will need safety goggles, water, vegetable oil, starch, a spoon, and two small jars with lids.

1. Put on the goggles. Half-fill each jar with water.
2. To one jar, add two spoonfuls of starch.
3. Add vegetable oil to the other jar until it is about two-thirds full.
4. Put the lids tightly on both jars.
5. Shake each jar for about 30 seconds.
6. Allow the jars to remain still for five minutes.

▲ STEP 5 Shake each jar.

Practicing Your Skills

7. EXPLAIN: Why did you shake the jars?

8. OBSERVE: What happened when you allowed the jars to sit?

9. ANALYZE: Are both of the mixtures you made suspensions? How do you know?

6-2 How can a suspension be separated?

Separating a Suspension
HANDS-ON ACTIVITY

STEP 4

1. Half-fill two clear plastic glasses with water. Add a teaspoon each of sand, clay, and pebbles to each glass and stir.
2. Allow one glass to stand undisturbed.
3. Place a piece of paper towel over a third plastic glass and hold it in place with a rubber band. Allow the paper towel to sag into the glass slightly.
4. Stir the mixture in the second glass and carefully pour the suspension through the paper towel into the third glass.

THINK ABOUT IT: Which method of separating the suspension was faster? Which separated better? Explain.

Objective
Describe some ways to separate a suspension.

Key Terms

filtration: separation of particles in a suspension by passing the suspension through filter paper or some other porous material

coagulation (koh-ag-yoo-LAY-shuhn)**:** use of chemicals to make the particles in a suspension clump together

Settling   Particles in a suspension settle on standing. Large particles settle out quickly. Smaller particles take a longer time to settle. You can see how this works in Figure 6-5.

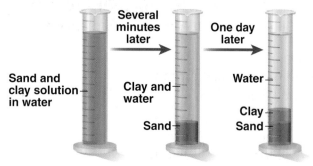

Several minutes later

One day later

Sand and clay solution in water

Clay and water

Sand

Water

Clay

Sand

▲ Figure 6-5 Suspensions separate on standing.

▶ **EXPLAIN:** When sand and clay are mixed with water, which settles faster? Explain.

Filtration   **Filtration** is the removal of particles in a suspension by passing the suspension through a filter. Filters can be made of paper, charcoal, or other materials. Filters are porous. They have tiny openings, or pores, through which some materials can pass and some cannot. Materials that cannot pass through the filter have particles that are larger than the pores in the filter.

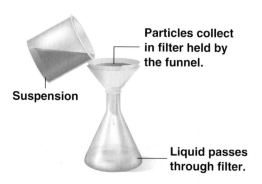

Particles collect in filter held by the funnel.

Suspension

Liquid passes through filter.

▲ Figure 6-6 Suspensions can be separated by filtration.

▶ **2** **PREDICT:** What happens to particles in a suspension that are larger than the pores in a filter?

Coagulation   Another way to separate a suspension is to add chemicals that make the particles of the suspension stick together. The particles form clumps that are larger and heavier than the original particles. As a result, the particles settle out more quickly. This process is called **coagulation.** Alum is a common coagulant. Coagulation takes place when you cut your finger. Chemicals in your blood cause the blood to coagulate and form a clot.

 DEFINE: What is coagulation?

Spinning A fourth way to separate a suspension is to spin a mixture at high speeds. The device used to spin a mixture is called a centrifuge (SEN-truh-fyooj). As the suspension is spun around, the particles in the suspension are pulled to the bottom of the container. Use of a centrifuge greatly increases the rate at which a suspension separates. The solid materials in blood cells are separated from the liquid materials, the plasma, by centrifugation.

 IDENTIFY: What is a centrifuge?

 CHECKING CONCEPTS

1. What happens when a suspension is left to stand overnight?
2. What is filtration?

3. What is coagulation?
4. How is a centrifuge used to separate the particles in a suspension?

 THINKING CRITICALLY

5. **ANALYZE:** Which method of separating a suspension is described? **a.** A solution of ammonium hydroxide and alum is added to a clay-and-water suspension. **b.** A suspension is passed through a piece of linen cloth.

BUILDING SCIENCE SKILLS

Modeling Make a model to show how coagulation works. Half-fill two test tubes with water. Add a small amount of clay to each. To one of the test tubes, add several drops of alum solution. Then, add several drops of ammonium hydroxide to the same test tube. Observe both test tubes for several minutes. In the test tube to which you added the alum solution and the ammonium hydroxide, you should see a jellylike material form. This causes the clay particles to clump together. In which test tube do the clay particles settle faster? Why?

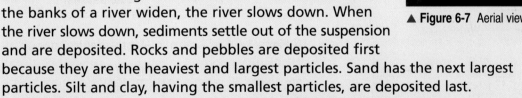

Integrating Earth Science

TOPICS: sediments, rivers, erosion

THE MISSISSIPPI DELTA

As a river flows, it carries particles of clay, sand, and gravel. These particles are called sediments. The sediments are suspended in the water.

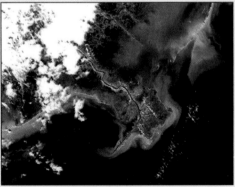

▲ **Figure 6-7** Aerial view of Mississippi delta

A river picks up sediments as it floods and erodes its banks. A fast-moving river carries the most sediments. As the banks of a river widen, the river slows down. When the river slows down, sediments settle out of the suspension and are deposited. Rocks and pebbles are deposited first because they are the heaviest and largest particles. Sand has the next largest particles. Silt and clay, having the smallest particles, are deposited last.

The widest part of a river is usually its mouth, where it empties into a larger body of water. The Mississippi River's mouth is located at the Gulf of Mexico. Here, the Mississippi moves so slowly that sediments from the river are deposited. Gradually, the sediments form new land called a delta. The land of the Mississippi delta is good for farming because new topsoil is always being deposited.

Thinking Critically Why do you think materials are deposited in the order given above?

6-3 What is an emulsion?

Objective
Describe and give examples of an emulsion.

Key Terms
emulsion (ee-MUL-shuhn): suspension of two liquids

homogenization (huh-mahj-uh-nih-ZAY-shuhn): formation of a permanent emulsion

Emulsions When a liquid is suspended in another liquid, the result is an **emulsion.** Milk, paint, and many medicines are examples of emulsions.

You can make an emulsion by mixing some cooking oil with water and then shaking the mixture. This emulsion will not stay mixed for long. If you let the mixture stand, the oil and water will soon separate. An emulsion that does not stay mixed is called a temporary emulsion.

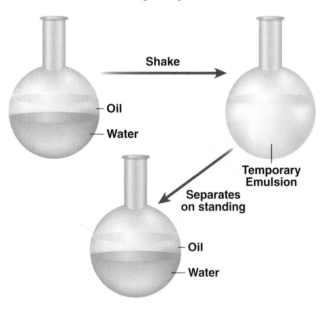

▲ **Figure 6-8** A temporary emulsion separates on standing.

▶ **PREDICT:** What will happen to a temporary emulsion?

Permanent Emulsions Many types of commercial products that are emulsions do not separate on standing. These emulsions are called permanent emulsions. The particles in a permanent emulsion are much smaller than the particles in a temporary emulsion. The particles in a permanent emulsion are small enough to stay in suspension.

A familiar example of a permanent emulsion is homogenized milk. **Homogenization** is the formation of a permanent emulsion. Fresh milk is a temporary emulsion that quickly separates into milk and cream. Fresh milk is homogenized in a machine that breaks down the cream into very small particles. The small particles of cream remain permanently suspended in the milk.

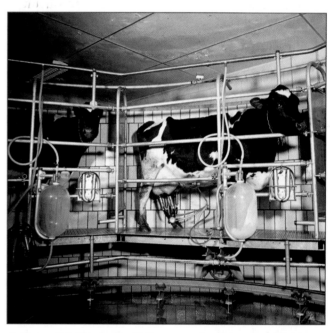

▲ **Figure 6-9** The fresh milk from cows is a temporary emulsion.

▶ **CONTRAST:** What is the difference between a temporary emulsion and a permanent emulsion?

Emulsifying Agents Many detergents or other cleaning products contain substances called emulsifying agents. An emulsifying agent keeps an emulsion from separating. The soap in cleaning products is an emulsifying agent. Soap breaks apart grease or dirt into smaller particles. These particles are small enough to form a permanent emulsion with water. The dirt or grease is washed away in the water.

134

Other emulsifying agents include gelatin and egg yolk. These substances are often used in food to keep ingredients from separating.

3 IDENTIFY: What is an emulsifying agent?

✓ CHECKING CONCEPTS

1. An emulsion is a suspension of a _____ in a liquid.
2. Oil and water separate on standing because they form a _____ emulsion.
3. The particles in a _____ emulsion are small enough to stay in suspension.
4. Soap is an example of an _____ agent.
5. Milk and cream form a permanent emulsion through the process of _____.

💡 THINKING CRITICALLY

6. HYPOTHESIZE: Bile is produced by the liver. It emulsifies the fats a person eats. Why is this process important to the digestive process?

7. INFER: When you buy a can of paint, you usually have to stir the paint before you can use it. Why do you think it is necessary to stir the paint?

Web InfoSearch

Homogenization Fresh milk right from a cow is a temporary emulsion. It separates on standing into cream and milk. Before it is sold in stores, the milk is homogenized, making it a permanent emulsion.

SEARCH: Use the Internet to find out how milk is homogenized. Create a poster to show the steps. Start your search at www.conceptsandchallenges.com. Some key search words are **milk** and **homogenize.**

Hands-On Activity

MAKING AN EMULSION

You will need safety goggles, vinegar, vegetable oil, an egg, a bowl, a measuring cup, and an eggbeater.

1. Separate the yolk from the white of the egg. Put the yolk in the bowl.
2. Beat the egg yolk until it looks foamy.
3. Add 1/4 cup of vinegar to the egg yolk. Beat the mixture of vinegar and egg yolk.
4. Add 1/8 cup of oil to the mixture one tablespoon at a tme. Beat the mixture thoroughly each time you add a tablespoon of oil.

▲ **STEP 2** Beat the egg yolk.

Practicing Your Skills

5. OBSERVE: When did the mixture begin to thicken?
6. PREDICT: If the mixture is allowed to stand, will it separate?
7. ANALYZE: What is the emulsifying agent in the mixture?
8. PREDICT: What would happen if you did not add the egg yolk to the mixture?

6-4 What is a colloid?

Objective

Describe and give examples of a colloid.

Key Term

colloid (KAHL-oid): suspension in which the particles are permanently suspended

Colloids What do whipped cream, fog, mayonnaise, and smoke have in common? All of these substances are colloids. A **colloid** is a suspension in which the particles are permanently suspended. Colloids can be mixtures of different phases of matter. Figure 6-10 shows some common types of colloids and examples of each type.

1▶ DEFINE: What is a colloid?

Colloid Particle Size The particles in a colloid are not as small as the particles in a solution. However, they are much smaller than the particles in an ordinary suspension. They cannot be seen with an ordinary microscope. Because the particles are so small, a colloid cannot be separated by normal means of filtration. A colloid such as homogenized milk passes right through filter paper. The particles in milk are smaller than the pores in the filter.

2▶ EXPLAIN: Why can a colloid not be separated by filtration?

Movement of Colloid Particles Have you ever traveled in a car on a foggy night? If so, you probably know that the car's headlight beams do not penetrate very far into the fog. Fog is a colloid made up of tiny water droplets suspended in air. When light passes through fog, the light strikes these droplets and is scattered, or spreads out. This scattering of light by the particles of a colloid is known as the Tyndall effect.

◀ **Figure 6-11** Light is scattered by a colloid.

Why do the particles of a colloid not settle out, much like the particles do in an ordinary suspension? After all, there is no emulsifying agent keeping them in suspension. The answer is that the very tiny particles of a colloid are constantly bumping into molecules of the surrounding material. For example, the water droplets in fog keep colliding with air molecules. These collisions keep the droplets from settling out of the colloid.

TYPES OF COLLOIDS

Solid in Solid
Glass

Solid in Liquid
Paint

Solid in Gas
Smoke

Liquid in Liquid
Homogenized milk

Liquid in Gas
Fog

Gas in Solid
Seafoam

▲ Figure 6-10

Instead, the droplets move rapidly through the air with a ramdon zigzag-like motion. When light passes through a colloid, it strikes the moving particles and is scattered, or spreads out. The cloudy appearance of a colloid is caused by the scattering of light.

 EXPLAIN: Why does a colloid appear cloudy?

✔ CHECKING CONCEPTS

1. How do the particles in a colloid compare in size with those in a solution?

2. Are colloids permanent or temporary suspensions?

3. What happens if a colloid is passed through a filter?

4. What happens to light that passes through a colloid?

5. Give an example of a colloid consisting of a solid in a liquid.

💡 THINKING CRITICALLY

6. **INFER:** Why can the beam of a flashlight be seen as it passes through a bowl of gelatin?

7. **COMPARE:** In what ways are colloids like solutions? In what ways are they different?

8. **EXPLAIN:** How is paint made that it can be classified as a colloid?

Web InfoSearch

Brownian Motion If you look at a colloid through a very powerful microscope, you will see that the particles of a colloid are in continuous random motion. This motion is called Brownian motion. Brownian motion is named for the biologist Robert Brown. Brown first noticed this motion while observing the motion of particles in a suspension of pollen grains in water.

SEARCH: Use the Internet to find out more about Brownian motion and the scientist who first noticed it. Write a short report. Start your search at www.conceptsandchallenges.com. Some key search words are **Robert Brown, biologist,** and **Brownian motion.**

 ## Science and Technology
USE OF COLLOIDS TO PURIFY WATER

Do you know where your household water comes from? In many cases, the water you use in your home comes from wells or reservoirs some distance from your house. Before this water reaches your house, it goes to a treatment plant. At the treatment plant, the water passes through several stages before it is clean enough for people to use.

Water from wells or reservoirs is passed through screens, which remove debris. Then, the water is sent to tanks or ponds where suspended materials are allowed to settle. Even after settling has taken place, some fine particles still remain suspended. At one time, these fine particles were allowed to remain in the water. Today, colloids are used to trap and remove these undesirable materials from our drinking water. Next, the water is filtered through sand or charcoal. Then it is pumped to sprinklers that spray the water into the air. This aerated water is then treated with chemicals to purify it before it is sent to our homes.

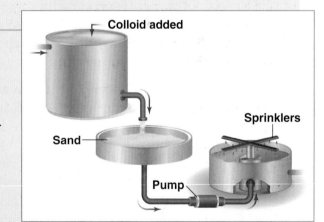
▲ **Figure 6-12** Colloids are used to help purify water.

Thinking Critically Which stage in water treatment removes the largest particles?

THE Big IDEA

What suspensions, emulsions, or colloids do you eat?

You have learned that a solution is a mixture in which substances are evenly mixed. The dissolved particles in a solution are about the size of molecules. If a solution of salt water sits for 100 years without evaporating, the salt stays dissolved. Not all mixtures are solutions. A suspension is a cloudy mixture of different substances.

My Pyramid (www.mypyramid.gov) is a guide to good nutrition. It reflects the findings of research on nutrition. The right amount of foods from each group is recommended for a balanced, healthy diet on a daily basis. Many of the foods we eat are suspensions, emulsions, or colloids. They are from different parts of the Pyramid.

Salad dressing and split pea soup are suspensions. In a suspension, the particles in the mixture are big enough to be separated by gravity or by filtering. An emulsion is a special kind of suspension made from two liquids that are permanently mixed. Ever had an emulsion for breakfast? Milk is a delicious and nutritious emulsion. Eggs are the emulsifiers in some products, such as mayonnaise.

Permanent suspensions are called colloids. In a colloid, the particles are so tiny that they stay mixed. Flavored gelatin and whipped cream are tasty colloids.

Look at the illustrations, photographs, and text that appear on these two pages. Then, follow the directions in the Science Log to learn more about "the big idea." ✦

MyPyramid.gov
STEPS TO A HEALTHIER YOU

▮ Grain Group		▮ Milk Group	
▮ Vegetable Group		▮ Meat & Beans Group	
▮ Fruit Group		▮ Fats & Oils Group	

▲ **Figure 6-13** The My Pyramid Plan shows what you should eat every day for a healthy diet. Go to mypyramid.gov to determine yours.

Temporary Suspension

A soup, such as this one, is a mixture of many ingredients. A serving of soup contains several food groups, such as vegetables, proteins, and grains.

Emulsion

The egg yolks in mayonnaise keep the molecules of oil mixed with molecules of water. The egg yolks in mayonnaise function as emulsifiers. Because of its fat content, you should not eat too much mayonnaise.

Emulsion

Milk, fresh from a cow, separates into cream and milk. Milk that you buy in a store does not separate because it has been homogenized. The cream and the milk are permanently mixed. This emulsion is an important part of a healthy diet. three servings a day are needed for active 12–14 year-olds.

Colloid

Whipped cream is a colloid made by mixing gas into liquid cream. Cream is part of the milk group. Because it is high in fat, cream should be eaten sparingly. If you eat a small amount of it with a cup of strawberries, you have a nutritious colloid-topped snack.

Temporary Suspension

A salad dressing with vinegar and oil is a suspension that will separate quickly. The harder it is shaken, the smaller the particles become, and the longer it remains mixed. A small amount of this suspension on a salad is part of a healthy diet.

WRITING ACTIVITY

Science Log

Many foods are suspensions. Pick a suspension you enjoy eating and research how to make it. Describe other foods you like to eat with the suspension. Here are some examples of foods that are suspensions: split pea soup, tomato sauce, applesauce, salad dressing, mayonnaise, whipped cream, butter, and jelly. Start your search at www.conceptsandchallenges.com.

Objective
Describe some causes of air and water pollution.

Key Terms
pollution (puh-LOO-shuhn): release of harmful substances into the environment

potable (POHT-uh-buhl) **water:** water that is safe to drink

Pollution What would happen if you did not have clean air to breathe or clean water to drink? One thing that would happen is that your health would be harmed. Every day our air and water resources are being threatened by pollution. **Pollution** is the adding of harmful substances, called pollutants, to the environment. Pollutants may be solids, liquids, or gases.

▶ 1 **DEFINE:** What are pollutants?

Causes of Pollution Most pollution is caused by human activities. Exhaust from cars, trucks, and buses is a major source of air pollution. Waste products from factories pollute air, land, and water. Burning fossil fuels releases harmful gases into the atmosphere.

▶ 2 **LIST:** What are three sources of pollution?

Safe Water There are many sources of water pollution. Agricultural use of pesticides and fertilizers is one major source. Another is the release of sewage and chemical wastes into rivers and lakes by cities and towns, factories, and even individuals. Nuclear power plants release very hot water into nearby sources of water. This heats a river or stream to higher than normal temperatures. These pollutants harm fish and other organisms that live in the water. They also make the water unsafe to drink.

Water that is safe to drink is called **potable water.** Water can be made potable when it is passed through a series of steps in a process called purification (pyoor-uh-fih-KAY-shuhn). One of the steps is to add chemicals, such as chlorine, to kill germs. Other steps include settling, coagulation, and filtration. These steps remove solid particles that are suspended in water.

▶ 3 **IDENTIFY:** What is potable water?

Reducing Air Pollution Air pollution can be harmful to people in many ways. Gases and solid particles in the air can cause irritation of the eyes, nose, and throat. They can cause breathing problems and respiratory illness.

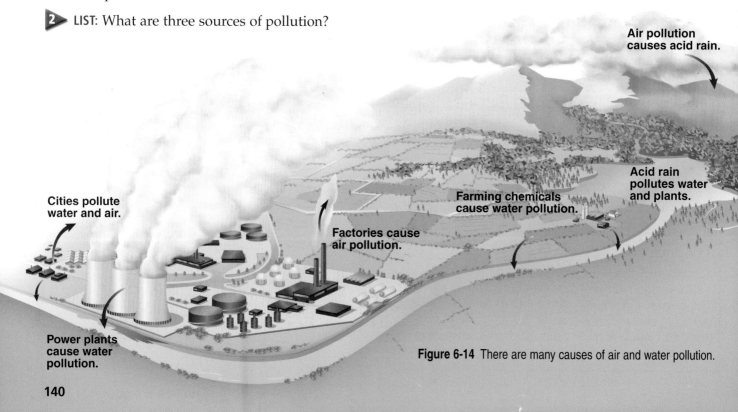

Air pollution causes acid rain.

Acid rain pollutes water and plants.

Cities pollute water and air.

Factories cause air pollution.

Farming chemicals cause water pollution.

Power plants cause water pollution.

Figure 6-14 There are many causes of air and water pollution.

▲ **Figure 6-15** Air pollution over Montreal, Canada

Everyone can help reduce air pollution. You can ride a bike or walk short distances instead of using a car or a bus. You might join a car pool with friends to help reduce the number of cars on the road. By lowering the temperature in your home, your family can use less heating oil. Find out what else you can do to help reduce air pollution.

 INFER: How would fewer cars on the road help reduce air pollution?

 ✓ CHECKING CONCEPTS

1. Substances that are harmful to the environment are _____.
2. Using less fuel to heat your home helps reduce _____ pollution.
3. Water that is safe to drink is called _____.
4. Chemical wastes and sewage are major causes of _____ pollution.

💡 THINKING CRITICALLY

5. HYPOTHESIZE: Often trees that are planted along city streets do not grow well. What is a possible reason for this?

HEALTH AND SAFETY TIP

Never drink the water in a stream or brook. It may be polluted with chemicals or bacteria. Use library references to find out how you can purify water to make it safe for you to drink.

 Hands-On Activity

OBSERVING POLLUTANTS IN AIR

You will need glass slides, petroleum jelly, and a hand lens.

1. Coat one side of several glass slides with a thin layer of petroleum jelly.
2. Choose several indoor and outdoor spots for testing the air quality.
3. At each spot, place a slide with the coated side up.
4. Record the location and the time when you placed each slide. Leave the slides overnight.
5. Collect the slides the next day. Record the time of collection.
6. Using the hand lens, examine each slide. Record your observations.

▲ **STEP 6** Examine each slide with a hand lens.

Practicing Your Skills

7. OBSERVE: What kinds of particles did you see on the slides?
8. OBSERVE: Which slide had the most particles?
9. OBSERVE: Which slide had the fewest particles?
10. HYPOTHESIZE: How can you explain your results?

LAB ACTIVITY
Testing for the Tyndall Effect—
Solution or Nonsolution?

Materials List

Goggles, apron,
6 jars with lids,
flashlight, funnel,
rubbing alcohol,
black construction paper,
sharpened pencil,
powdered juice mix,
sugar, sand, whole milk,
vegetable oil, water,
10 mL and 100 mL
graduated cylinders,
teaspoon, eyedropper

BACKGROUND

Some mixtures that may appear to look like a solution may not be one after all. Some of these "nonsolutions" may be suspensions or colloids. If a path of light can be seen easily through a mixture, then the mixture is not a solution. This happens because the particles are large enough to scatter or reflect the light. This light scattering is called the Tyndall effect.

PURPOSE

In this activity, you will make various mixtures and observe the difference between solutions and nonsolutions using the Tyndall effect.

PROCEDURE

1. Copy the chart in Figure 6-16. Put on safety goggles, plastic gloves, and a lab apron.

2. Label the jars A through F for the following mixtures to be tested:

   A. 1 teaspoon of powdered juice mix to 100 mL of water

   B. 10 mL of rubbing alcohol to 100 mL of water

   C. 5 drops of whole milk to 100 mL of water

   D. 1 teaspoon of sugar to 100 mL of water

   E. 10 mL of vegetable oil to 100 mL of water

   F. 1 teaspoon of sand to 100 mL of water

3. Shake each jar and observe the mixtures. Predict which mixtures will be solutions or nonsolutions.

▲ **STEP 2** Add mixtures to the jars labeled A–F.

▲ **STEP 3** Shake the jars with the mixtures.

4. Make a solution tester. First cut out a small circle from a piece of black construction paper. The circle should just cover the lens of the flashlight. Use a sharpened pencil to punch a small hole in the center of the circle. Then, tape the paper circle over the flashlight lens.

5. In a darkened area of the room, press the solution tester very close to the jar holding mixture A. Record what you see. If you can see the path of light through the mixture, it is not a true solution.

6. Repeat Step 5 for mixtures B–F. Record your results.

▲ **STEP 5** Shine the solution tester into the jar.

Testing for the Tyndall Effect–Solution or Nonsolution?

Beaker	Mixture	Observations Upon Mixing	Observations When Testing With Solution Tester
A	Powdered juice mix and water		
B	Rubbing alcohol and water		
C	Whole milk and water		
D	Sugar and water		
E	Vegetable oil and water		
F	Sand and water		

▲ **Figure 6-16** Copy this chart and use it to record your observations.

CONCLUSIONS

1. **OBSERVE:** Describe what you observed with each mixture.

2. **MODEL:** Which mixtures represented solutions? How do you know?

3. **MODEL:** Which mixtures represented nonsolutions?

4. **INFER:** Explain how the nonsolutions show the Tyndall effect.

5. **ANALYZE:** How might you be able to determine if the nonsolutions are suspensions or colloids?

Chapter Summary

Lesson 6-1

- A **suspension** is a mixture of two or more substances that settle out over time.
- The particles in a suspension are larger than the particles in a solution.
- The particles in a suspension scatter light.
- Some familiar examples of suspensions include salad dressing and dust in the air.

Lesson 6-2

- The particles in a suspension settle out.
- **Filtration** is a method of separating a suspension by passing it through a filter.
- **Coagulation** is a process in which chemicals are used to make the particles in a suspension clump together.
- A centrifuge is a device that separates a suspension by spinning it at high speeds.

Lesson 6-3

- An **emulsion** is a suspension of two liquids.
- Temporary emulsions separate on standing, whereas permanent emulsions do not.
- **Homogenization** is the formation of a permanent emulsion.
- Emulsifying agents are substances that prevent an emulsion from separating.

Lesson 6-4

- A **colloid** is a suspension in which the particles are permanently suspended.
- The particles of a colloid are larger than the particles of a solution but smaller than those of an ordinary suspension.
- The particles of a colloid are kept in suspension because they are always colliding with the molecules around them.

Lesson 6-5

- **Pollution** is the release of harmful substances into the environment.
- Most pollution is caused by human activities.
- Air pollution is harmful to people.
- Everyone can help reduce air pollution.
- **Potable water** is safe to drink.

Key Term Challenges

- coagulation (p. 132)
- colloid (p. 136)
- emulsion (p. 134)
- filtration (p. 132)
- homogenization (p. 134)
- pollution (p. 140)
- potable water (p. 140)
- suspension (p. 130)

MATCHING Write the Key Term from above that best matches each description.

1. water that is safe to drink
2. making the particles in a suspension clump together
3. formation of a permanent emulsion
4. suspension in which particles are permanently suspended
5. release of harmful substances into the environment
6. suspension of two liquids

FILL IN Write the Key Term from above that best completes each statement.

7. A _____ is a cloudy mixture of two or more substances that settles on standing.
8. Passing a suspension through paper or other substances is called _____.
9. A suspension of two liquids is called an _____.
10. Particles in a suspension are clumped together by the process of _____.

Content Challenges TEST PREP

MULTIPLE CHOICE Write the letter of the term or phrase that best completes each statement.

1. If a suspension of clay, sand, and gravel is allowed to stand, the particles that settle out first would be
   a. clay.
   b. sand.
   c. gravel.
   d. water.

2. Colloids cannot be separated by filtration because colloid particles are
   a. round.
   b. too large.
   c. too small.
   d. clumped together.

3. A process that speeds up the separation of a suspension is
   a. homogenization.
   b. pollution.
   c. emulsification.
   d. coagulation.

4. An example of an emulsifying agent is
   a. milk.
   b. egg yolk.
   c. fog.
   d. oil and water.

5. A device that separates a suspension by spinning is called a
   a. centrifuge.
   b. homogenizer.
   c. filter.
   d. coagulator.

6. Both colloids and suspensions
   a. have large particles.
   b. are clear.
   c. scatter light.
   d. settle on standing.

7. The particles in a colloid are
   a. smaller than in a solution.
   b. smaller than in a suspension.
   c. smaller than molecules.
   d. larger than in a suspension.

8. An emulsifying agent makes an emulsion that is
   a. temporary.
   b. liquid.
   c. permanent.
   d. soapy.

9. All the following are colloids except
   a. fog.
   b. salad dressing.
   c. smoke.
   d. whipped cream.

10. Settling, coagulation, and filtration are examples of
   a. suspensions.
   b. emulsifying agents.
   c. homogenization.
   d. separation methods.

TRUE/FALSE Write *true* if the statement is true. If the statement is false, change the underlined term to make the statement true.

11. Light is scattered by particles in a <u>suspension</u>.

12. Unhomogenized milk is a <u>temporary</u> suspension.

13. When a suspension is left standing, the <u>larger</u> particles are the last to settle.

14. Solutions, colloids, and suspensions are all <u>mixtures</u>.

15. An emulsion is a suspension of two <u>gases</u>.

Concept Challenges *TEST PREP*

WRITTEN RESPONSE Complete the exercises and answer each of the following questions in complete sentences.

1. **EXPLAIN:** How does an emulsifying agent work?

2. **CONTRAST:** In what ways do colloids differ from ordinary suspensions?

3. **EXPLAIN:** How does the constant motion of colloid particles affect the properties of a colloid?

4. **EXPLAIN:** How could you test a mixture to find out if it is a solution, a suspension, or a colloid?

INTERPRETING A VISUAL Use Figure 6-17 to answer the following questions.

5. What sources of air pollution are shown in the picture?

6. What sources of water pollution are shown?

7. Which pollutants are gases? Which are liquids? Which are solids?

8. How could each source of air pollution be reduced?

9. Would you expect to find healthy fish and plants in the lake? Why or why not?

10. A rural area 20 km from the area shown in this picture has no factories or other industry. However, the town's water supply is polluted with chemical wastes. How might this be explained?

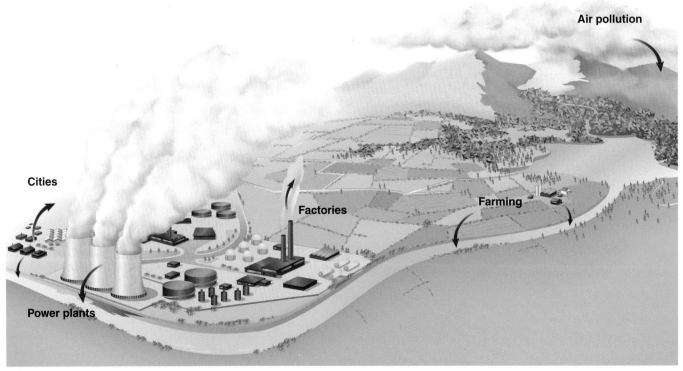

▲ Figure 6-17

Chapter 7 Chemical Formulas

▲ **Figure 7-1** Smog forms over a city.

Oxygen is an important part of the air we breathe. Each molecule of the substance air is made up of two oxygen atoms. Smog contains a different form of oxygen called ozone. A molecule of ozone is made up of three oxygen atoms. Ozone can make breathing very difficult. As you can see in Figure 7-1, the ozone in smog is very different from the oxygen in clean air. Yet, the two gases are made up of the same element.

▶How do the properties of oxygen found in clean air compare with those found in ozone?

Contents

7-1 What is a chemical formula?

Objective

Write chemical formulas.

Key Terms

chemical formula: way of writing the name of a compound using chemical symbols

subscript: number written to the lower right of a chemical symbol in a chemical formula

Chemical Symbols Chemical symbols are used to represent elements. Each element has its own symbol. Symbols for all the known elements are made up of one or two letters. For example, C is the chemical symbol for carbon. Fe is the symbol for iron. Permanent names for some synthetic elements, elements made in a laboratory, have not yet been agreed on. For these elements, temporary names and three-letter symbols have been assigned. For example, Uun is the temporary symbol for ununnilium.

1 ▶ STATE: What is the chemical symbol for iron?

Chemical Formulas Compounds are made up of two or more elements that are chemically combined. Scientists use a chemical formula to show the elements that make up a compound. A **chemical formula** is a way of writing the name of a compound using chemical symbols. The compound water contains the elements hydrogen and oxygen. Each molecule of water contains two atoms of hydrogen and one atom of oxygen.

The chemical symbol for hydrogen is H. The chemical symbol for oxygen is O. The chemical formula for water is H_2O. The chemical formula includes the symbols for each element in the compound. Figure 7-2 shows the chemical formulas of some common compounds.

2 ▶ DESCRIBE: What is a chemical formula?

Subscripts Chemical formulas also indicate how many atoms of each element are in a molecule or an ion of a compound. The number of atoms of each element is indicated by a subscript. A **subscript** is a number written to the lower right of a chemical symbol. The 2 in the chemical formula H_2O is a subscript. It indicates that there are two atoms of hydrogen in a molecule of water. There is one atom of oxygen in a molecule of water, however, there is no subscript written after the O in H_2O. This is because the number 1 is never written in a chemical formula. When there is no subscript after a symbol in a formula, you know there is only one atom of that element.

3 ▶ INFER: How many atoms of hydrogen are in a molecule of table sugar with the chemical formula $C_{12}H_{22}O_{11}$?

Writing Chemical Formulas In some compounds, a metal is chemically combined with a nonmetal. For example, sodium chloride is made up of the metal sodium and the nonmetal chlorine. In a chemical formula, the symbol for the metallic element is always written first. The chemical formula for the compound sodium chloride is

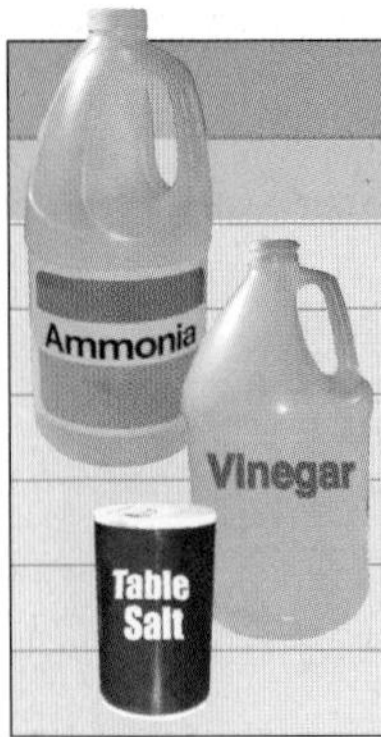

CHEMICAL FORMULAS OF SOME COMMON COMPOUNDS				
	Common name	Chemical name	Chemical formula	Elements
	Table salt	Sodium chloride	NaCl	Sodium, chlorine
	Stomach acid	Hydrochloric acid	HCl	Hydrogen, chlorine
	Lye	Sodium hydroxide	NaOH	Sodium, oxygen, hydrogen
	Ammonia	Ammonia	NH_3	Nitrogen, hydrogen
	Laughing gas	Nitrous oxide	N_2O	Nitrogen, oxygen
	Vinegar	Acetic acid	CH_3COOH	Hydrogen, carbon, oxygen

▲ Figure 7-2

NaCl. Figure 7-3 shows some compounds and the metals and nonmetals that make them up.

SOME COMPOUNDS MADE OF METALS AND NONMETALS

Compound	Chemical formula	Metallic element	Nonmetallic element
Sodium chloride	NaCl	Na (Sodium)	Cl (Chlorine)
Aluminum chloride	$AlCl_3$	Al (Aluminum)	Cl (Chlorine)
Silver sulfide	Ag_2S	Ag (Silver)	S (Sulfur)

▲ Figure 7-3

 **STATE:** What is the chemical formula for aluminum chloride?

✓ CHECKING CONCEPTS

1. The chemical symbol for hydrogen is _____.

2. The chemical formula for acetic acid is _____.

3. The nonmetal in sodium chloride is _____.

4. In a chemical formula, the symbol for a _____ element is always written first.

 ## THINKING CRITICALLY

5. **CONTRAST:** The chemical formula for water is H_2O. The chemical formula for hydrogen peroxide is H_2O_2. How does a molecule of water differ from a molecule of hydrogen peroxide?

BUILDING SCIENCE SKILLS

Identifying Elements List the names of the elements that make up each of the following compounds.

   a. carbon dioxide (CO_2)

   b. ammonia (NH_3)

   c. calcite ($CaCO_3$)

 ## *Real-Life Science*

PLASTICS

Plastics are long-chain polymer molecules made up of carbon, hydrogen, nitrogen, chlorine, and sulfur. Plastics can be molded, stretched, bent, and drawn into fibers. It all begins by heating hydrocarbons (compounds containing hydrogen and carbon). This process leads to a series of small molecules called monomers. One type of monomer is vinyl chloride. Its chemical formula is C_2H_3Cl. Monomers can be recombined into different long-chain polymers. These polymers make up plastics that have a variety of properties and characteristics.

▲ **Figure 7-4** Products made of plastics

   Today's world is filled with plastics. From medicine bottles, food containers, computer parts, and toys to carpet and clothing fibers, plastics are used every day. Scientists have discovered many specialized plastics and are looking to develop new polymer chains that can be used to make other useful products. The many different ways in which plastics can be used make them very important compounds.

Thinking Critically Why do you think plastics can be considered one of the most important inventions?

7-2 What is an oxidation number?

Modeling Valence Electrons
HANDS-ON ACTIVITY

1. Obtain a Valence Electrons Chart (Figure 7-5), counters, and an element card from your teacher. Look up the atomic number of the element on the periodic table. The atomic number is the number of counters you will place on the chart.

2. Place the counters on top of the small circles in the order in which the circles are numbered. Observe how many counters are in the last energy level you filled.

THINK ABOUT IT: The chart represents how electrons are arranged around the nucleus of an atom. What do you think the counters represent?

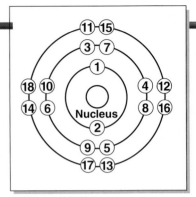

▲ **Figure 7-5** Valence Electrons Chart

Objective
Describe how to use oxidation numbers to write the chemical formula of a compound.

Key Terms
valence electron: electron in the outermost energy level of an atom

oxidation number: number of electrons an atom gains, loses, or shares when it forms a chemical bond

Valence Electrons You have learned that electrons move around the nucleus of an atom in energy levels. The lowest or first energy level of an atom can hold up to two electrons. For energy levels beyond the first level, eight is a very important number. Whenever the outermost energy level of an atom contains eight electrons, the atom is very stable, or complete. Atoms tend to gain, lose, or share electrons by bonding with other atoms in order to reach this stable arrangement. The electrons in an atom's outermost energy level are called **valence electrons**.

 IDENTIFY: How many electrons are in the outermost energy level of a stable atom?

Oxidation Number An **oxidation number** shows how many electrons an atom gains, loses, or shares when it forms a chemical bond. In general, atoms of nonmetals tend to gain electrons, and atoms of metals tend to lose electrons. For example, a chlorine

atom has seven valence electrons. To complete its outermost energy level, the atom must gain one electron from another atom. An atom that gains electrons has a negative oxidation number. When it gains an electron, it gains a negatively charged particle. Thus, the chlorine atom becomes an ion with a negative charge. Therefore, the oxidation number of chlorine is 1–.

An atom that loses electrons has a positive oxidation number. The outermost energy level of a sodium atom contains one electron. If the sodium atom loses its one valence electron, then the next lower energy level becomes its outermost energy level. This level has eight electrons, so it is complete. When a sodium atom loses its one valence electron, it becomes an ion with a positive charge. Therefore, the oxidation number of sodium is 1+.

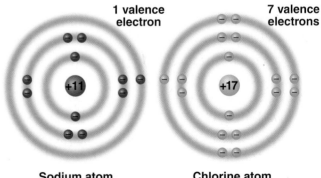

Sodium atom
Oxidation number = 1+

Chlorine atom
Oxidation number = 1–

▲ **Figure 7-6** The number of valence electrons in an atom determines the atom's oxidation number.

 INFER: If an atom loses an electron, what kind of oxidation number will it have?

Determining the Signs of Oxidation Numbers

In general, the location of an element on the periodic table can tell you whether its oxidation number will be positive or negative. Look back at the periodic table on pages 66 and 67. The elements to the left of the dark zigzag line, with the exception of hydrogen, are metals. Metals tend to lose electrons during a chemical reaction. Therefore, metals have positive oxidation numbers.

Elements to the right of the dark zigzag line on the periodic table are nonmetals. Nonmetals tend to gain electrons. So, nonmetals usually have negative oxidation numbers. Knowing the signs of the oxidation number of elements can help you write the chemical formulas for different compounds.

 INFER: What kind of oxidation numbers do nonmetals usually have?

Writing Chemical Formulas The oxidation number of an element tells you if it tends to lose (+) or gain (−) electrons when forming a chemical bond. When writing a chemical formula, remember that the oxidation numbers of the elements in a compound must add up to zero. For example, sodium chloride is a compound made up of sodium and chlorine. The oxidation number of sodium is 1+. The oxidation number of chlorine is 1−. The oxidation numbers of the elements add up to zero:

(1+) positive charge + (1−) negative charge = 0

In the compound sodium chloride, one atom of sodium forms an ionic bond with one atom of chlorine. The chemical formula for sodium chloride is NaCl.

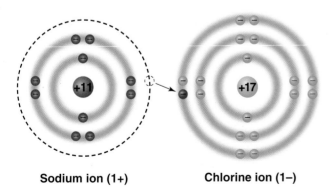

Sodium ion (1+)   **Chlorine ion (1−)**

▲ **Figure 7-7** An ionic bond forms between an atom of sodium and an atom of chlorine.

 STATE: What is the sum of the oxidation numbers of the elements in a compound?

✔ CHECKING CONCEPTS

1. What is the number of electrons that an atom gains, loses, or shares when it forms a chemical bond called?

2. What determines how many electrons an atom will gain, lose, or share when it forms a chemical bond?

3. Is the oxidation number of an atom that gains electrons positive or negative?

4. How many valence electrons does an atom of chlorine have?

5. In general, does a metal tend to gain electrons or lose electrons?

6. What kind of elements are to the right of the dark zigzag line on the periodic table?

💡 THINKING CRITICALLY

7. **EXPLAIN:** What is true about the oxidation numbers of the elements in a chemical formula?

8. **ANALYZE:** What is the oxidation number of aluminum in $AlCl_3$? What is the oxidation number of chlorine? Explain how you arrived at your answers.

9. **PREDICT:** The oxidation number of magnesium is 2+ and of sulfur is 2−. What is the formula for magnesium sulfide?

10. **CALCULATE:** The chemical formula for calcium oxide is CaO. If the oxidation number for calcium is 2+, what is the oxidation number for oxygen?

INTERPRETING VISUALS

Explain how the electron dot diagram shows how an atom of sodium and an atom of chlorine combine to make sodium chloride.

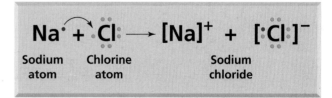

▲ **Figure 7-8** An electron dot diagram for the formation of sodium chloride

7-3 How are chemical compounds named?

Identifying Elements in Compounds
HANDS-ON ACTIVITY

1. Copy Figure 7-9 onto a sheet of notebook paper.
2. Look at the list of compounds. Each compound is made up of only two elements.
3. Fill in the chart.

THINK ABOUT IT: In each compound, which element has a positive oxidation number? When writing the name of a compound with only two elements, which one do you write first?

IDENTIFYING ELEMENTS IN COMPOUNDS		
Compound	Element with positive oxidation number	Element with negative oxidation number
Sodium chloride		
Iron oxide		
Copper oxide		

▲ Figure 7-9

Objective
Explain how chemical compounds are named.

Key Term
binary (BY-nuh-ree) **compound:** compound containing two elements

Binary Compounds Two different elements that are chemically combined form a **binary compound**. The name of a binary compound tells which two elements are found in the compound. Sodium chloride is an example of a binary compound. It is formed from the elements sodium and chlorine. The name of the element with a positive oxidation number is written first. Sodium has a positive oxidation number, 1+. If the second element only has one oxidation number, the name of that element is changed to end in *-ide* and is written last. For example, chlorine is changed to chloride when naming sodium chloride.

▶ **PREDICT:** What elements would you expect to find in the compound hydrogen chloride?

Different Oxidation Numbers Many elements have more than one oxidation number. For example, the oxidation number of iron can be either 2+ or 3+. Scientists indicate different oxidation numbers of an element by including a Roman numeral in parentheses after the name of the

element. Iron (II) shows that an atom of iron has an oxidation number of 2+. Iron (III) shows that an atom of iron has an oxidation number of 3+.

Iron and chlorine can combine to form the compound $FeCl_2$. Iron and chlorine can also combine to form the compound $FeCl_3$. $FeCl_2$ and $FeCl_3$ are two different compounds with different properties. These compounds are identified as iron (II) chloride and iron (III) chloride. In both cases, chlorine has an oxidation number of 1−.

▲ **Figure 7-10** Iron and chlorine can combine to form iron (II) chloride (left) and iron (III) chloride (right).

▶ **INFER:** What is the oxidation number of an atom of gold (III)?

Other Elements Most elements that have more than one oxidation number are usually metals. For example, tin can have an oxidation number of 4+ or 2+. Copper can have an oxidation number of 2+ or 1+. The Roman numeral in the name of a compound shows the oxidation number of the element in the compound. Figure 7-11 lists some metals that have more than one oxidation number.

OXIDATION NUMBERS OF SOME METALS		
Metal	Higher oxidation number	Lower oxidation number
Iron	3+, iron (III)	2+, iron (II)
Mercury	2+, mercury (II)	1+, mercury (I)
Copper	2+, copper (II)	1+, copper (I)
Tin	4+, tin (IV)	2+, tin (II)
Nickel	3+, nickel (III)	2+, nickel (II)
Gold	3+, gold (III)	1+, gold (I)

▲ Figure 7-11

 IDENTIFY: What is the oxidation number of copper in the compound copper (II) chloride?

✓ CHECKING CONCEPTS

1. The oxidation number of iron (III) is _____.

2. Iron (II) chloride and iron (III) chloride are different _____.

3. In the compound hydrogen chloride (HCl), _____ has a positive oxidation number.

4. Because the compound water contains the elements hydrogen and oxygen, it is a _____ compound.

5. The name mercury (II) bromide indicates that the oxidation number of _____ is 2+.

 ## THINKING CRITICALLY

6. **INFER:** The chemical formula for oxygen gas is O_2. Is this a binary compound?

Web InfoSearch

Prefixes In naming compounds made up of two nonmetals, prefixes are used. For example, the compound carbon monoxide contains one atom of oxygen. The prefix *mono-* means "one."

SEARCH: Use the Internet to find other compounds whose names start with prefixes. List the elements and the number of each kind of atom that make up each compound. Start your search at www.conceptsandchallenges.com. Some key search words are **compound**, **chemical formula**, and **prefixes**.

 ## *People in Science*

NIELS BOHR (1885–1962)

To write chemical formulas, the atomic structure of an atom has to be known. Much of our present knowledge of atomic structure is based on the work of the Danish physicist Niels Bohr.

Bohr proposed that the electrons in an atom travel in fixed energy levels around the nucleus, like planets orbiting the Sun. He also continued to explain that atoms could absorb an amount, or quantum, of energy that allows the electrons to jump to higher energy levels. When the atoms

▲ Figure 7-12 Niels Bohr studied the structure of atoms.

lose the energy, the electrons fall back to their original energy levels. When this happens, the atoms release the same quantum of energy that they absorbed. The released energy is often in the form of light. This work earned Bohr the Nobel Prize in physics in 1922. Bohr's work with electrons also led to the understanding of valence electrons.

Thinking Critically How does the work of Niels Bohr relate to writing chemical formulas?

7-4 What is a polyatomic ion?

Objective

Identify the chemical formula for polyatomic ions.

Key Term

polyatomic (pahl-ee-uh-TAHM-ihk) **ion:** group of atoms that acts as a charged atom, or ion, when combining with other atoms

Polyatomic Ions Sometimes a group of atoms stays together when chemically combining with other atoms. The atoms in this group are bound very tightly to each other. Thus, the group acts as a single atom with an electrical charge. A group of atoms that acts as a single charged atom, or ion, when combining with other atoms is called a **polyatomic ion.** The prefix *poly-* means "more than one." The group of atoms is called an ion because it has an overall electrical charge. The atoms in a polyatomic ion are held together by covalent bonds. Figure 7-13 shows some polyatomic ions. Notice how the electrical charge for each atom is written to the upper right of the chemical formula and the molecular model.

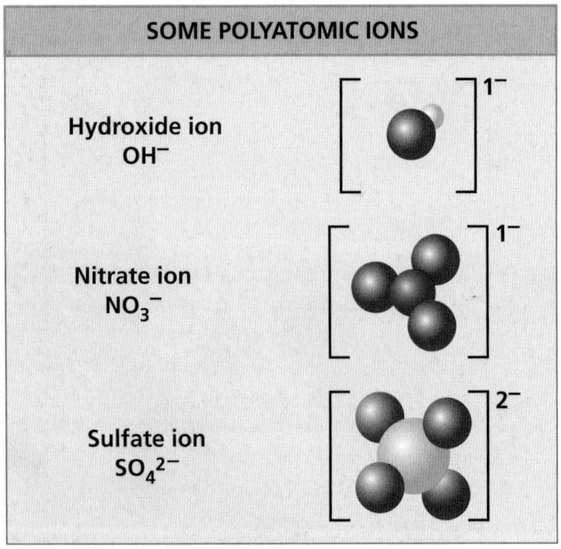

SOME POLYATOMIC IONS

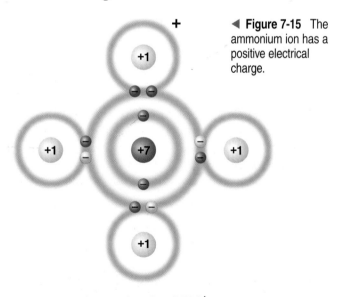

Hydroxide ion OH$^-$

Nitrate ion NO$_3^-$

Sulfate ion SO$_4^{2-}$

▲ **Figure 7-13** The chemical formulas and molecular models of some polyatomic ions

▶ **1** DEFINE: What is a polyatomic ion?

Hydroxide Ions An example of a polyatomic ion is the hydroxide ion. The hydroxide ion is made up of one oxygen atom and one hydrogen atom. The oxygen atom and the hydrogen atom are joined together by a covalent bond. The hydroxide ion has a negative electrical charge. The chemical formula for the hydroxide ion is OH$^-$.

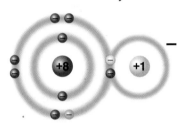

◀ **Figure 7-14** The hydroxide ion has a negative electrical charge.

Hydroxide ion (OH$^-$)

▶ **2** IDENTIFY: What is the formula for the hydroxide ion?

Ammonium Ions The ammonium ion is made up of one nitrogen atom, three hydrogen atoms, and one hydrogen ion. The chemical formula for the ammonium ion is NH$_4^+$. The ammonium ion is a common polyatomic ion with a positive electrical charge.

◀ **Figure 7-15** The ammonium ion has a positive electrical charge.

Ammonium ion (NH$_4$)$^+$

▶ **3** ANALYZE: What is the charge on an ammonium ion?

154

Writing Chemical Formulas To write the formula for a polyatomic ion, you follow the same rules for writing other chemical formulas. However, if there is more than one polyatomic ion in a compound, you would write the chemical formula for the polyatomic ion in parentheses. The number of polyatomic ions would be written as a subscript after the parentheses. For example, in $Ba(OH)_2$, two hydroxide ions chemically combine with a barium atom to form barium hydroxide.

 IDENTIFY: How many hydroxide ions are there in $Al(OH)_3$?

✔ CHECKING CONCEPTS

1. A polyatomic ion contains _____ one atom.

2. The polyatomic ion made up of an oxygen and hydrogen atom is the _____ ion.

3. The hydroxide ion has a _____ electrical charge.

4. The nitrate ion contains one nitrogen atom and _____ oxygen atoms.

THINKING CRITICALLY

5. **CLASSIFY:** Look at the following chemical compounds. Which ones contain hydroxide ions? Which do not? Explain your answers.
   a. Limewater, $Ca(OH)_2$
   b. Milk of magnesia, $Mg(OH)_2$
   c. Table salt, NaCl
   d. Water, H_2O
   e. Lye, NaOH

6. **INFER:** When atoms of different elements combine to form polyatomic ions, what holds these atoms together?

7. **INFER:** How many sulfate ions are there in a molecule of potassium sulfate, K_2SO_4?

BUILDING LANGUAGE ARTS SKILLS

Building Vocabulary The prefix *poly-* means "more than one." Use a dictionary to find the definitions of the words *polygon*, *polymer*, and *polysyllabic*. Write the definitions on a sheet of paper.

Science and Technology
NITRATES IN FERTILIZERS

The nitrate polyatomic ion plays a major role in fertilizers and plant life. It is made up of one nitrogen atom and three oxygen atoms. Plants need nitrogen to make proteins. Plants can obtain the needed nitrogen from the nitrates that are naturally found in soil and in both organic and commercial fertilizers. Nitrogen fertilizers include ammonium nitrate, NH_4NO_3, and calcium nitrate, $Ca(NO_3)_2$. The presence of nitrates in soil can improve plant growth.

▲ **Figure 7-16** Spreading nitrogen-rich fertilizer

People have used fertilizers for thousands of years. Before their benefits were known scientifically, people observed that animal droppings, ashes, and certain minerals helped plants thrive. All these substances contain nitrates. Today, farmers spend thousands of dollars on commercial fertilizers each year. Farmers add a certain amount of fertilizers to soil to ensure that plants will have the nitrogen needed to grow healthy and plentiful.

Thinking Critically Why does adding fertilizers to soil help plants grow?

LAB ACTIVITY
Constructing Chemical Formulas

Materials

Graph paper

Ruler

Marker

Construction paper

Scissors

Glue or tape

▲ **STEP 1** Make 3 cm × 3 cm boxes.

▲ **STEP 3** Prepare a list of chemical formulas.

BACKGROUND

In order to write the chemical formula of a compound, you must know the oxidation numbers of the elements or the charges of the polyatomic ions of that particular compound. The oxidation numbers of the elements or the charges of the polyatomic ions in a compound must add up to zero.

PURPOSE

In this activity, you will model various examples of elements and polyatomic ions with their oxidation numbers and charges. Also, you will construct various chemical formulas of common substances.

PROCEDURE

1. On graph paper, make about 60 3 cm × 3 cm boxes.

2. In each box, write the following chemical symbols and chemical formulas with their oxidation numbers. The number in the parentheses to the left of the chemical symbol tells you how many of each element or polyatomic ion you should make.

(8) H^{1+}	(6) Cl^{1-}
(4) Na^{1+}	(6) OH^{1-}
(4) Ca^{2+}	(4) O^{2-}
(4) Mg^{2+}	(4) S^{2-}
(4) Al^{3+}	(4) SO_4^{2-}
(4) CO_3^{2-}	

▲ **Figure 7-17** Chemical symbols with the oxidation numbers for certain elements and with the charges for certain polyatomic ions

3. Cut out all your boxes. On a sheet of construction paper, label the top *Constructing Chemical Formulas*. Using your boxes, construct the chemical formulas listed in Figure 7-18 on construction paper.

4. Glue or tape your chemical formulas onto the paper. Label each chemical formula.

5. With the leftover boxes, try to construct other possible chemical formulas. (REMEMBER: oxidation numbers must equal zero.) Glue or tape them to your construction paper.

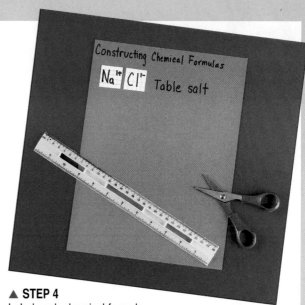

▲ **STEP 4**
Label each chemical formula.

Some Chemical Formulas			
table salt	NaCl	sulfuric acid	H_2SO_4
water	H_2O	"rotten egg" smell	H_2S
lye	NaOH	lime water	$Ca(OH)_2$
marble chips	$CaCO_3$	bauxite	Al_2O_3
Epsom salt	$MgSO_4$	milk of magnesia	$Mg(OH)_2$

▲ **Figure 7-18**

CONCLUSIONS

1. **CALCULATE:** What do you notice about the sum of the oxidation numbers and charges of all the chemical formulas you have constructed?

2. **MODEL:** Use an example from the list to explain how the boxes help in writing a chemical formula.

3. **CALCULATE:** List the chemical formulas you constructed on your own. Do the oxidation numbers and charges of all the elements in each formula add up to zero?

7-5 What is a diatomic molecule?

Objective

Identify a diatomic molecule.

Key Term

diatomic molecule: molecule made up of only two atoms

Hydrogen Molecules An atom of hydrogen has one electron in its first energy level. A hydrogen atom needs another electron in order to complete this energy level. It can receive that extra electron from another hydrogen atom. By sharing two electrons, the two hydrogen atoms complete their first energy levels. The two hydrogen atoms combine to form a hydrogen molecule, H_2. Hydrogen gas is always made up of pairs of hydrogen atoms.

 INFER: How many electrons does an atom of hydrogen need to complete its energy level?

Diatomic Molecules The molecule formed by the covalent bonding between two hydrogen atoms is called a diatomic molecule. A **diatomic molecule** is made up of only two atoms. Most elements that are gases form diatomic molecules. For example, carbon monoxide (CO) is a diatomic molecule. Atoms in a diatomic molecule are usually held together by a covalent bond.

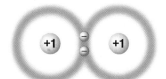

Molecular model   **Electron dot diagram**

▲ **Figure 7-19** Diatomic hydrogen (H_2)

 DEFINE: What is a diatomic molecule?

Oxygen Molecules Oxygen is another element that can form a diatomic molecule. Oxygen gas (O_2) in the air is formed when two oxygen atoms share two pairs of electrons. However, oxygen can also form molecules made up of three oxygen atoms. This substance is called ozone (O_3). Ozone is a triatomic molecule. A layer of ozone is found

in Earth's atmosphere from about 10 km to about 45 km above Earth's surface.

Molecular model   **Electron dot diagram**

▲ **Figure 7-20** Diatomic oxygen (O_2)

Molecular model   **Electron dot diagram**

▲ **Figure 7-21** Triatomic oxygen (O_3), also called ozone

3 **CONTRAST:** How do oxygen gas and ozone differ?

Other Diatomic Molecules Other elements can be found as diatomic molecules, too. For example, an atom of chlorine has seven valence electrons. It can complete its outermost energy level by forming a covalent bond with another chlorine atom. By sharing a pair of electrons, both chlorine atoms can complete their outermost energy levels. Figure 7-22 lists other elements that can form diatomic molecules.

SOME DIATOMIC MOLECULES		
Molecule	**Chemical formula**	**Physical state**
Iodine	I_2	Solid
Nitrogen	N_2	Gas
Chlorine	Cl_2	Gas
Fluorine	F_2	Gas
Bromine	Br_2	Liquid

▲ **Figure 7-22**

4 **LIST:** Name some elements that form diatomic molecules.

✔ CHECKING CONCEPTS

1. A hydrogen atom needs _____ electrons to complete its first energy level.

2. A molecule that contains only two atoms is called a _____ molecule.

3. Most elements that are _____ form diatomic molecules.

4. A molecule of _____ contains three atoms of oxygen.

5. The atoms in a diatomic molecule are held together by a _____ bond.

6. Diatomic molecules of _____ can form a liquid.

💡 THINKING CRITICALLY

7. **CLASSIFY:** Which of the following molecules are diatomic molecules?

   a. Br_2

   b. CO_2

   c. H_2O

   d. Cl_2

8. **APPLY:** The elements fluorine (F), chlorine (Cl), bromine (Br), iodine (I), and astatine (At) are called halogens. As gases, the halogens exist as diatomic molecules. Write the formula for one molecule of each of these elements.

9. **ANALYZE:** In a diatomic molecule of hydrogen, how many valence electrons does each atom of hydrogen have?

Integrating Environmental Science

TOPIC: the atmosphere

DESTRUCTION OF THE OZONE LAYER

Ozone is a triatomic molecule. It forms in the atmosphere when ultraviolet rays from the Sun strike oxygen molecules in the air. A layer of ozone in the atmosphere absorbs most of the Sun's harmful ultraviolet radiation.

Certain chemicals called chlorofluorocarbons, or CFCs, destroy ozone molecules. CFCs are compounds that contain carbon, fluorine, and chlorine. In many countries, CFCs were used in spray cans, air conditioners, refrigerators, and aircraft engines. However, it has been found that when CFCs are released into the atmosphere, they break down ozone molecules. As a result of the use of CFCs, the ozone layer has thinned. The thinning of the ozone layer is especially noticeable in the section over Antarctica.

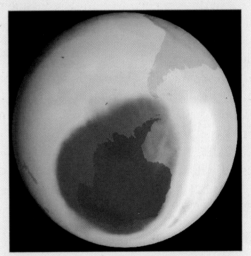

▲ **Figure 7-23** The dark blue ring in the photograph shows the size of the hole in the ozone layer above Antarctica.

In 1987, the United States government and other industrialized nations agreed to reduce the use of CFCs. Then, after further destruction of the ozone layer, another agreement was signed by most industrialized nations to stop using CFCs by 2000. However, some countries still use CFCs. Because CFC molecules can last a long time, they can still be found in the atmosphere.

Thinking Critically Why have some countries banned the use of CFCs?

7-6 What is formula mass?

Objective
Explain how to find formula mass.

Key Term
formula mass: sum of the mass numbers of all the atoms in a molecule or ions in an ionic compound

Formula Mass A molecule contains atoms chemically joined together. Each atom in a molecule has its own mass number. Remember that the mass number of an atom is the number of protons and neutrons in the nucleus. It is equal to the atomic mass rounded to the nearest whole number. The sum of the mass numbers of all the atoms in a molecule is called the **formula mass** of the molecule. Formula mass is also the sum of the mass numbers of all the ions in an ionic compound.

▲ **Figure 7-24** If you could put a molecule of water on a scale, you would find its formula mass.

 DEFINE: What is formula mass?

Finding Formula Mass Neon is an element that can exist as a molecule with only one atom. Therefore, a molecule of neon contains one atom of neon. The mass number of neon is 20. Because there is only one atom in a molecule of neon, the formula mass of neon is also 20. However, most molecules and ionic compounds contain more than one atom. To find the formula mass of molecules or ions in ionic compounds that contain more than one atom, use the following steps.

Step 1 Write the chemical formula of the compound.

Step 2 Use the periodic table on pages 66 and 67 to find the atomic mass of each element in the compound. Round the atomic mass to find the mass number.

Step 3 Multiply the mass number of each element by its subscript. If there is no subscript, multiply the mass number by 1.

Step 4 Add the total masses of all the atoms in the compound. The total is the formula mass of the compound.

2 **INFER:** If there is no subscript for an element, what do you multiply the mass number by?

Formula Mass of Ethyl Chloride You can find the formula mass of the compound ethyl chloride by following the steps listed above.

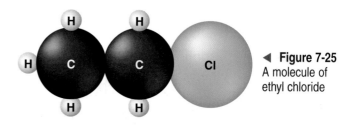

◀ **Figure 7-25** A molecule of ethyl chloride

- Write the chemical formula for ethyl chloride. The formula for ethyl chloride is C_2H_5Cl.

- Find the mass number of each element in the compound. The mass number of C = 12, H = 1, and Cl = 35. Then, multiply the mass number of each element by its subscript: $12 \times 2 = 24$; $1 \times 5 = 5$; $35 \times 1 = 35$.

- Add the total masses of all the elements in the compound: $24 + 5 + 35 = 64$. The formula mass of ethyl chloride is 64.

3 **CALCULATE:** If the mass number of hydrogen is 1 and the mass number of oxygen is 16, what is the formula mass of water (H_2O)?

✓ CHECKING CONCEPTS

1. Each type of atom in a molecule has its own _____.

2. The mass number of an atom is the number of protons and _____ in the nucleus.

3. The mass number of an atom of neon is the same as the _____ of a molecule of neon.

4. The first step in finding the formula mass of a molecule is to write the _____ of the compound.

5. The formula mass is the sum of the _____ of all the atoms in a molecule or ionic compound.

6. When finding formula mass, multiply the mass number of each element by its _____.

7. The final step in finding the formula mass of a molecule is to _____ the total masses of all the atoms in the molecule.

THINKING CRITICALLY

8. **INFER:** The mass number of a certain element is the same as the formula mass of the element. What does this tell you about a molecule of that element?

9. **HYPOTHESIZE:** Could the formula mass of an element ever be less than the mass number of the element?

10. **CALCULATE:** What is the formula mass of a molecule of sugar, $C_{12}H_{22}O_{11}$?

11. **ANALYZE:** Could the formula mass of a compound ever contain a decimal point?

BUILDING MATH SKILLS

Predicting Formula Mass The chemical formula of the compound carbon monoxide is CO. The chemical formula of the compound carbon dioxide is CO_2. Predict how the formula masses of both molecules differ. Check the accuracy of your prediction by calculating the formula mass of each molecule.

Hands-On Activity

HOW TO FIND FORMULA MASS

You will need a pencil and a sheet of paper.

1. Review the steps to follow when calculating formula mass.

2. Copy the table in Figure 7-26 onto a sheet of paper. Use the periodic table on pages 66 and 67 to fill in the table.

Practicing Your Skills

3. **CALCULATE:** What is the atomic mass of sodium? What is its mass number?

4. **EXPLAIN:** What is the difference between the atomic mass and the mass number of an element? Which is used to calculate formula mass?

CALCULATING FORMULA MASS

Compound	Elements	Mass number	Sub-script	Mass of each element	Formula mass
NO_2 Nitrogen dioxide	Nitrogen	14	1	14	46
	Oxygen	16	2	32	
H_2O_2 Hydrogen peroxide					
$CaCO_3$ Calcium carbonate					
Na_3PO_4 Sodium phosphate					

▲ Figure 7-26

Integrating Mathematics

THE Big IDEA

How is a chemical formula written?

The formation of a chemical bond involves the transfer or sharing of valence electrons between atoms. An oxidation number tells how many electrons an atom can give, receive, or share when forming chemical bonds.

Water is a compound made up of hydrogen and oxygen. Hydrogen has an oxidation number of 1^+ because it tends to give up its one electron when forming chemical bonds. Oxygen has six valence electrons. It needs two electrons to complete its outermost energy level, so its oxidation number is 2^-.

The oxidation numbers of all the atoms in one molecule of water must add up to zero. So, for every oxygen atom (oxidation number 2^-), there must be two hydrogen atoms ($1^+ + 1^+ = 2^+$).

Water (H_2O)
Three-fourths of Earth is covered by water. Hydrogen and oxygen combine to form the compound water.

STEP 1 Write the chemical formula.

H_2O

STEP 2 Write each atom and its oxidation number as an equation that equals zero.

$H^{1+} + H^{1+} + O^{2-} = 0$

STEP 3 Write the oxidation numbers of each atom as an equation that equals zero.

$1 + 1 + (-2) = 0$

STEP 4 Make sure that the left side of the equation adds up to zero.

$2 + (-2) = 0$

Iron (III) Oxide (Fe_2O_3)
Tapes in audio cassettes are often coated with iron oxide. Iron combines with oxygen forming ferric oxide, also called iron (III) oxide or rust.

STEP 1 Write the chemical formula.

Fe_2O_3

STEP 2 Write each atom and its oxidation number as an equation that equals zero.

$Fe^{3+} + Fe^{3+} + O^{2-} + O^{2-} + O^{2-} = 0$

STEP 3 Write the oxidation numbers of each atom as an equation that equals zero.

$3 + 3 + (-2) + (-2) + (-2) = 0$

STEP 4 Make sure that the left side of the equation adds up to zero.

$6 + (-6) = 0$

162

The formula for one molecule of water is H_2O. The element that gives electrons, hydrogen, is written first in the chemical formula. The subscript "2" written to the right of the hydrogen symbol indicates there are two atoms of hydrogen in a molecule of water. If there is no number after a chemical symbol in a formula, it means there is only one atom of that element. Because there is no number written to the right of the oxygen symbol, that means there is only one atom of oxygen in a molecule of water.

Study the steps on checking chemical formulas in the examples below. Then, follow the directions in the Science Log to learn more about "the big idea."✦

WRITING ACTIVITY

Science Log

Look at the periodic table on pages 66 and 67. Group 2 elements have oxidation numbers of 2+. Group 16 elements have oxidation numbers of 2−. In your science log, write chemical formulas using an element from each group. Search the Internet to see if any of your chemical formulas are used to make products. Start your search at www.conceptsandchallenges.com.

Magnesium Nitride (Mg_3N_2)

Early photographers used magnesium flash powder to take pictures in low light before flashbulbs were invented. When magnesium and nitrogen combine, the compound magnesium nitride is formed.

STEP 1 Write the chemical formula.

Mg_3N_2

STEP 2 Write each atom and its oxidation number as an equation that equals zero.

$Mg^{2+} + Mg^{2+} + Mg^{2+} + N^{3-} + N^{3-} = 0$

STEP 3 Write the oxidation numbers of each atom as an equation that equals zero.

$2 + 2 + 2 + (-3) + (-3) = 0$

STEP 4 Make sure that the left side of the equation adds up to zero.

$6 + (-6) = 0$

Sulfur Dioxide (SO_2)

Sulfur dioxide is produced when coal containing sulfur is burned, such as in these coal-burning stacks. Sulfur burns in air, forming sulfur dioxide.

STEP 1 Write the chemical formula.

SO_2

STEP 2 Write each atom and its oxidation number as an equation that equals zero.

$S^{4+} + O^{2-} + O^{2-} = 0$

STEP 3 Write the oxidation numbers of each atom as an equation that equals zero.

$4 + (-2) + (-2) = 0$

STEP 4 Make sure that the left side of the equation adds up to zero.

$4 + (-4) = 0$

Chapter Summary

Lesson 7-1

- Every element has its own chemical symbol.
- A **chemical formula** identifies the elements in a compound.
- The symbol for a metallic element is always written first in a chemical formula.

Lesson 7-2

- **Valence electrons** are the number of electrons in an atom's outermost energy level.
- Atoms that lose electrons have positive **oxidation numbers**.
- Atoms that gain electrons have negative oxidation numbers.

Lesson 7-3

- A **binary compound** contains atoms of two elements.
- An element can have more than one oxidation number.

Lesson 7-4

- A group of atoms that acts as a charged atom, or ion, when combining with other atoms is called a **polyatomic ion**.
- The atoms in a polyatomic ion are held together by covalent bonds.

Lesson 7-5

- A **diatomic molecule** contains only two atoms.
- Atoms in a diatomic molecule are usually held together by a covalent bond.

Lesson 7-6

- Each atom in a molecule or ion of an ionic compound has its own mass number.
- The sum of the mass numbers of all the atoms in a molecule or ion of an ionic compound is equal to the **formula mass** of the molecule.

Key Term Challenges

binary compound (p. 152)
chemical formula (p. 148)
diatomic molecule (p. 158)
formula mass (p. 160)
oxidation number (p. 150)
polyatomic ion (p. 154)
subscript (p. 148)
valence electron (p. 150)

MATCHING Write the Key Term from above that best matches each description.

1. number written to the lower right of a chemical symbol
2. electron in an atom's outermost energy level
3. compound containing two elements
4. molecule made up of only two atoms
5. sum of the mass numbers of all the atoms in a molecule
6. chemical symbols that identify the elements that make up a compound
7. group of atoms that acts as a charged atom, or ion, when combining with other atoms
8. $1-$ for an atom of chlorine

FILL IN Write the Key Term from above that best completes each statement.

9. The "2" in the formula H_2O is a _____.
10. A molecule of hydrogen gas is an example of a _____.
11. Chlorine has seven _____s in its outermost energy level.
12. Sodium chloride is an example of a _____.
13. The _____ of ethyl chloride is 64.
14. The ammonium ion is an example of a _____.

Content Challenges TEST PREP

MULTIPLE CHOICE **Write the letter of the term or phrase that best completes each statement.**

1. Scientists represent elements by using
   a. atomic numbers.
   b. subscripts.
   c. chemical symbols.
   d. words.

2. The compound NaOH contains the elements
   a. sodium and hydrogen.
   b. sodium and oxygen.
   c. oxygen and hydrogen.
   d. sodium, oxygen, and hydrogen.

3. The formula mass of neon is equal to its
   a. mass number.
   b. atomic number.
   c. atomic mass.
   d. oxidation number.

4. The oxidation numbers of the elements in a compound must add up to
   a. 8.
   b. 0.
   c. 1.
   d. 7.

5. The oxidation number of iron in iron (II) chloride is
   a. 2+.
   b. 2–.
   c. 3+.
   d. 0.

6. An example of a binary compound is
   a. NaOH.
   b. O_2.
   c. NaCl.
   d. Na.

7. A polyatomic ion always has
   a. no electrical charge.
   b. a positive charge.
   c. a negative charge.
   d. an electrical charge.

8. A common polyatomic ion with a positive charge is the
   a. nitrate ion.
   b. ammonium ion.
   c. sulfate ion.
   d. phosphate ion.

9. Of the following molecules, the one that is <u>not</u> a diatomic molecule is
   a. ozone.
   b. oxygen.
   c. hydrogen.
   d. iodine.

10. Diatomic molecules of nitrogen and oxygen are
    a. solids.
    b. liquids.
    c. gases.
    d. crystals.

TRUE/FALSE **Write *true* if the statement is true. If the statement is false, change the underlined term to make the statement true.**

11. A binary compound contains atoms of <u>two</u> elements.

12. The mass number of an atom is equal to the <u>atomic mass</u> rounded to the nearest whole number.

13. Chemical symbols are made up of one or two <u>numbers</u>.

14. The chemical formula of a compound tells you what <u>valences</u> the compound contains.

Concept Challenges TEST PREP

WRITTEN RESPONSE Complete the exercises and answer each of the following questions in complete sentences.

1. **HYPOTHESIZE:** Why do you think chemical symbols and chemical formulas are an important part of communication among scientists?

2. **CALCULATE:** Find the formula mass for each of the following compounds.
   a. $NaOH$ **b.** HCl **c.** $AgCl$ **d.** Al_2O_3 **e.** $NaHCO_3$

3. **EXPLAIN:** What is the relationship between an atom's oxidation number and the number of valence electrons the atom has?

4. **HYPOTHESIZE:** Why do you think carbon can have an oxidation number of 4+ or 4–? (Hint: Carbon has four valence electrons.)

INTERPRETING A TABLE Use Figure 7-27 to answer each of the following questions.

5. What are the metallic elements listed in this table? What are the nonmetallic elements?

6. What kind of element is written first in the chemical formulas of the compounds?

7. What is the oxidation number of aluminum in aluminum chloride?

8. Which compound is made up of three atoms? Four atoms?

SOME COMPOUNDS MADE OF METALS AND NONMETALS			
Compound	Chemical formula	Metallic element	Nonmetallic element
Sodium chloride	NaCl	Na (Sodium)	Cl (Chlorine)
Aluminum chloride	$AlCl_3$	Al (Aluminum)	Cl (Chlorine)
Silver sulfide	Ag_2S	Ag (Silver)	S (Sulfur)

▲ Figure 7-27

Chapter 8

Chemical Reactions

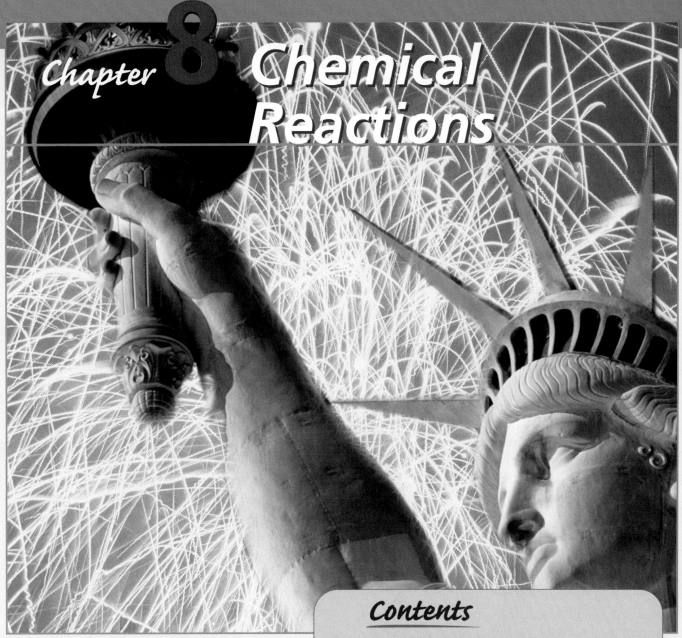

▲ **Figure 8-1** Fireworks over the Statue of Liberty at night

The sky lights up in brilliant colors over the Statue of Liberty. Not only is this a celebration, it is also an example of how chemical reactions can produce new substances. The colors produced by the burning of fireworks are evidence that new substances are forming. The color of the Statue of Liberty in daylight also indicates that a chemical reaction has taken place. The statue used to look like a shiny new penny. Now, after many years of exposure to gases in air and water, it has become a bluish green.

▶ What do the fireworks and the Statue of Liberty have in common?

Contents

8-1 What is a chemical reaction?

Objective
Describe what happens in a chemical reaction.

Key Terms
chemical reaction: process in which new substances with new chemical and physical properties are formed

reactant: substance that is changed in a chemical reaction

product: substance that is formed in a chemical reaction

law of conservation of matter: law that states that matter cannot be created or destroyed by a chemical change

Chemical Reactions   New substances are formed as a result of a chemical change. During a chemical change, chemical bonds are formed or broken. The process by which a chemical change takes place is called a chemical reaction. In a **chemical reaction,** new substances with new chemical and physical properties are formed.

Chemical reactions are taking place around you all the time. If you have noticed rust that has formed on an iron fence, then you have seen the results of a chemical reaction. The iron in the fence has combined with the oxygen in air to form a new substance—rust. Figure 8-2 lists some signs that a chemical reaction has taken place.

SOME SIGNS OF A CHEMICAL REACTION	
Evidence	**Example**
Production of a gas	Carbon dioxide is produced when a log burns.
A change in color	When iron combines with oxygen, it changes to a reddish color.
A change in energy	When fuel burns, a large amount of energy is released.

▲ Figure 8-2

 DESCRIBE: What always happens in a chemical reaction?

Reactants and Products   In any chemical reaction, certain substances are present at the start of the reaction and different substances are present at the end of the reaction. A substance that is present at the start of a chemical reaction is called a reactant. A **reactant** is a substance that is changed in a chemical reaction. A substance that is present at the end of a chemical reaction is called a product. A **product** is a substance that is formed as a result of a chemical reaction.

DEFINE: What is a reactant?

Conservation of Matter   When a log burns, a chemical reaction takes place. The wood burns away and ashes are left. What has happened? Has matter really disappeared? Can matter be lost during a chemical reaction? The answer is no. In addition to ashes, water vapor and carbon dioxide are also produced when a log burns. If you could add the masses of each of these products, you would find that their total mass equals the mass of the original log. This example illustrates an important scientific law called the **law of conservation of matter.** This law states that matter cannot be created or destroyed by a chemical change. In a chemical reaction, the amount of matter present in the products must always equal the amount of matter present in the reactants.

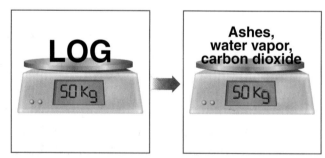

▲ **Figure 8-3** In a chemical reaction, the amount of mass never changes.

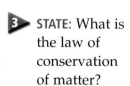 **STATE:** What is the law of conservation of matter?

Changing the Speed of a Chemical Reaction

Some chemical reactions occur very fast and some chemical reactions occur very slowly. A dynamite explosion takes place very quickly. The formation of rust takes place more slowly. By changing certain factors, the speed of some chemical reactions can also be changed.

To speed up a chemical reaction, the particles of the reactants need to come together more often. Increasing the temperature, increasing the surface area of the reactants, and adding certain kinds of catalysts (KAT-uh-lihsts) are ways to speed up some reactions. A catalyst is a chemical that changes the rate of a reaction without itself being changed.

To slow down chemical reactions, the particles of the reactants need to be brought together less often. Lowering the temperature, decreasing the surface area, and adding catalysts that slow down a reaction are some ways to decrease the speed of some chemical reactions.

 DEFINE: What is a catalyst?

 CHECKING CONCEPTS

1. A substance that is changed during a chemical reaction is called a _____.
2. Matter cannot be created or _____ in a chemical reaction.
3. A _____ takes place during the formation of rust.
4. Increasing the surface area of a reactant can _____ the speed of the reaction.

THINKING CRITICALLY

5. **EXPLAIN:** When rust forms on a piece of iron, what evidence do you have that a chemical reaction has taken place?

BUILDING MATH SKILLS

Calculating How many kilograms of water form when 48 kg of oxygen gas chemically combine with 6 kg of hydrogen gas?

 ## Hands-On Activity

OBSERVING A CHEMICAL REACTION

You will need safety goggles, an apron, plastic gloves, a balloon, a funnel, water, paper towels, a narrow-necked bottle, vinegar, baking soda, and a teaspoon.

1. Put on an apron, safety goggles, and plastic gloves. Stretch out the balloon by inflating and deflating it a few times.
2. Insert the narrow end of a funnel into the opening of the deflated balloon. Pour two teaspoonfuls of baking soda into the funnel so that the baking soda settles to the bottom of the balloon. Remove the funnel from the balloon.
3. Rinse the funnel with water and dry it with a paper towel. Insert the narrow end into the narrow-necked bottle. Pour six spoonfuls of vinegar into the funnel.
4. Carefully stretch the opening of the balloon over the neck of the bottle, making sure that the baking soda does not fall out of the balloon.
5. Lift the balloon so that the baking soda falls into the bottle. Observe what happens as the baking soda combines with the vinegar.

▲ **STEP 4** Stretch the balloon over the neck of the bottle.

Practicing Your Skills

6. **DESCRIBE:** What signs are there that a chemical change has taken place?
7. **HYPOTHESIZE:** What happened inside the bottle?

LAB ACTIVITY
Changing the Speed of a Chemical Reaction

Materials
Safety goggles, apron, plastic gloves, 6 plastic foam cups, 6 antacid tablets, room-temperature water, ice water, hot water, thermometer, stopwatch, 3 small plastic bags, marking pen

BACKGROUND

All chemical reactions are affected by the physical conditions and the environment in which they occur. For example, a campfire is easier to start with small twigs and branches rather than with a large log. Also, food lasts longer in warm weather if it is stored in an ice-cold cooler. Surface area, in the case of the wood for the fire, and temperature, in the case of the food, play a role in the speed of a chemical reaction.

PURPOSE

In this activity, you will be comparing the speed of chemical reactions by changing the surface area and the temperature of the reactants.

PROCEDURE

1. Copy the chart shown in Figure 8-4.

2. Put on safety goggles and an apron.

3. With a marking pen, label two plastic foam cups *Ice*, two plastic foam cups *Room*, and two plastic foam cups *Hot*.

4. Put on plastic gloves. Place one antacid tablet into each of the three small plastic bags. Carefully break each tablet into three or four pieces.

5. Measure the temperature of the ice water. Record the temperature on your chart.

▲ **STEP 3** Label the plastic foam cups.

▲ **STEP 4** Carefully break each antacid tablet.

6. Half-fill both cups labeled *Ice* with the ice water. At the same time, drop one whole antacid tablet into one of the cups and in the other cup, empty one of the plastic bags containing broken pieces of an antacid tablet. Record the time it takes for each tablet to completely dissolve.

7. Repeat Steps 5 and 6 using hot water and room-temperature water.
   ⚠ CAUTION: Hot water can burn. Allow your teacher to pour the water into your cup.

▲ **STEP 6** Drop a whole antacid tablet into one cup and pieces of a broken antacid tablet into the other cup.

Changing the Speed of a Chemical Reaction

	Temperature	Time of Reaction with Whole Tablet	Time of Reaction with Tablet Pieces
Cups marked Ice			
Cups marked Hot			
Cups marked Room			

▲ **Figure 8-4** Copy this chart onto a sheet of paper. Enter your observations from your experiment.

CONCLUSIONS

1. **OBSERVE:** In which cup did the chemical reaction take place the fastest? In which cup did the chemical reaction take place the slowest?

2. **HYPOTHESIZE:** What does the effect of surface area have on the speed of a chemical reaction? What does the effect of temperature have on the speed of a chemical reaction? Explain your hypothesis using the results of your experiment.

3. **ANALYZE:** Which do you think will mix faster in a cup of hot tea, a lump of sugar or a teaspoon of sugar?

8-2 What is a chemical equation?

INVESTIGATE

Modeling Conservation of Mass
HANDS-ON ACTIVITY

1. Obtain connecting cubes from your teacher. Connect the cubes to form models of two "molecules." Make a drawing of your models on a sheet of paper.

2. Take apart your models and create two new ones. Next to your first drawing, make a drawing of the new models.

THINK ABOUT IT: Look at your drawings. What do you notice is similar about all your models? How do your models illustrate the law of conservation of mass?

STEP 1

Objectives

Explain how a chemical equation describes a chemical reaction. Write balanced chemical equations.

Key Terms

chemical equation: statement in which chemical formulas are used to describe a chemical reaction

coefficient (koh-uh-FIHSH-uhnt)**:** number that shows how many molecules of a substance are involved in a chemical reaction

Chemical Equations Scientists use a special "language" to describe chemical reactions. They use chemical equations. A **chemical equation** is a statement in which chemical symbols and chemical formulas are used to describe a chemical reaction. It tells you what substances are the reactants and what substances are the products in a chemical reaction.

▶ **DEFINE**: What is a chemical equation?

Writing Chemical Equations To write a chemical equation, first write the correct symbols or formulas for the reactants and the products. The chemical formulas for the reactants are always written on the left side of a chemical equation followed by an arrow. The arrow indicates what substances are formed. It is like an equal sign and is read as "yields." The chemical formulas for the

products are written to the right of the arrow. When there are two or more reactants or two or more products, a plus sign (+) is placed between the chemical formulas of the different substances.

The following chemical equation shows the reaction between two reactants that produce one product.

$$2Na + Cl_2 \rightarrow 2NaCl$$
reactant reactant product

Read the equation as the reaction of "sodium and chlorine yields sodium chloride."

The production of water and oxygen from hydrogen peroxide (H_2O_2) is an example of a reaction in which one reactant yields two products.

$$2H_2O_2 \rightarrow 2H_2O + O_2$$
reactant product product

The formation of tarnish (Ag_2S) on silver is an example of a chemical reaction in which three reactants yield two products.

$$4Ag + 2H_2S + O_2 \rightarrow 2Ag_2S + 2H_2O$$

▶ **EXPLAIN**: In a chemical equation, where are the chemical formulas for the products written?

Balanced Chemical Equations A chemical equation shows the atoms and molecules that are involved in a chemical reaction. Recall that matter cannot be created or destroyed during a chemical reaction. So, in a chemical equation the total number of atoms of each element must be the same on both sides of the equation. When the number of atoms of each element is the same on both sides of the equation, the equation is said to be balanced.

To balance a chemical equation, you place numbers called coefficients in front of chemical formulas. A **coefficient** is a number that shows how many molecules or atoms of a substance are involved in a chemical reaction. Look at the reaction between sodium (Na) and chlorine (Cl_2). If the equation were written with just the formulas for the reactants and the products, it would read as follows:

$$Na + Cl_2 \longrightarrow NaCl$$

There are two chlorine atoms on the left side of the equation and only one chlorine atom on the right side. Write a 2 before the product:

$$Na + Cl_2 \longrightarrow 2NaCl$$

Now the chlorine atoms are balanced, but the sodium atoms are not. Write another 2 on the left side of the equation before the Na:

$$2Na + Cl_2 \longrightarrow 2NaCl$$

Now the equation is balanced.

▶3 **DEFINE:** What is a coefficient?

Go **Online**
active art

For: Balancing Equations activity
Visit: PHSchool.com
Web Code: cgp-2022

✓ CHECKING CONCEPTS

1. A chemical equation describes a _____.
2. The arrow in a chemical equation means _____.
3. A plus sign (+) in a chemical equation means _____.
4. The reactants in a chemical equation are written on the _____ side of the equation.
5. A balanced chemical equation must show the same number of _____ of each element on both sides of the equation.
6. The reaction of hydrogen peroxide is an example of a reaction in which one reactant yields _____.
7. A _____ shows how many molecules or atoms of a substance are involved in a chemical reaction.

💡 THINKING CRITICALLY

8. **ANALYZE:** Count the atoms. Which of the following equations are balanced?
   a. $H_2O_2 \rightarrow H_2O + O_2$
   b. $CO + O_2 \rightarrow CO_2$
   c. $Si + O_2 \rightarrow SiO_2$
   d. $2KClO_3 \rightarrow 2KCl + 3O_2$
   e. $N_2 + H_2 \rightarrow NH_3$
9. **CALCULATE:** Write balanced equations for the unbalanced equations in exercise 8.
10. **INFER:** When there is no number in front of a chemical formula in a chemical equation, what number is understood?
11. **EXPLAIN:** How do you read the following equation?
   $$Fe + 2S \rightarrow FeS_2$$

BUILDING SCIENCE SKILLS

Stating the Problem The following equations are not balanced correctly. What errors were made?
   a. $Cl_2 + NaBr \rightarrow Br_2 + NaCl$
      $2Cl + 2NaBr \rightarrow 2Br + 2NaCl$
   b. $Mg + O_2 \rightarrow MgO$
      $Mg + O \rightarrow MgO$
   c. $Na + O_2 \rightarrow Na_2O$
      $2Na + 2O_2 \rightarrow 2Na_2O$

8-3 What are oxidation and reduction?

Objective

Compare oxidation and reduction reactions.

Key Terms

oxidation (ahk-sih-DAY-shuhn): chemical change in which electrons are lost

reduction (rih-DUK-shuhn): chemical change in which electrons are gained

Oxidation and Reduction When different substances (elements and compounds) react chemically, electrons are transferred or shared among the atoms that make up those substances. Some atoms gain electrons in the reaction. Other atoms lose electrons. When the atoms of an element lose electrons, the reaction is called oxidation. **Oxidation** is any chemical change in which electrons are lost. When the atoms of an element gain electrons, the reaction is called reduction. **Reduction** is any chemical change in which electrons are gained.

▶ **CONTRAST:** What is the difference between oxidation and reduction?

Redox Reactions Oxidation and reduction always take place together. The electrons lost by one element are gained by another element. Reactions involving oxidation and reduction are often referred to as "redox" reactions. In redox reactions, some elements are oxidized (lose electrons), and other elements are reduced (gain electrons).

The chemical reaction between sodium and chlorine is an example of an oxidation and reduction reaction. The chemical equation for this reaction is as follows:

$$2Na + Cl_2 \rightarrow 2NaCl$$

Each sodium atom loses an electron and is oxidized. Each chlorine atom gains an electron and is reduced.

The combination of hydrogen and chlorine forms a strong substance called hydrochloric acid. This is another example of a reaction involving oxidation and reduction. Each hydrogen atom loses an electron and is oxidized. Each chlorine atom gains an electron and is reduced.

$$H_2 + Cl_2 \rightarrow 2HCl$$

▶ **ANALYZE:** What are reactions that involve oxidation and reduction often called?

Combining with Oxygen The most familiar kind of oxidation and reduction reactions involve oxygen. The formation of rust is an example of a reaction in which an element combines with oxygen. The chemical equation for the production of iron oxide (rust) is as follows:

$$4Fe + 3O_2 \rightarrow 2Fe_2O_3$$

Each iron atom loses three electrons and is oxidized. Each oxygen atom gains two electrons and is reduced. When a substance combines chemically with oxygen, the chemical reaction is also called oxidation. Other examples of this type of oxidation reaction include the burning of a match and the burning of fireworks.

▲ **Figure 8-5** The burning of fireworks is an example of oxidation.

▶ **DEFINE:** What is oxidation?

☑ CHECKING CONCEPTS

1. When rust forms, iron chemically combines with _____.

2. In an oxidation reaction, electrons are _____.

3. In a reduction reaction, electrons are _____.

4. Oxidation and _____ reactions always occur together.

5. When a substance combines chemically with oxygen, the chemical reaction is also called _____.

6. The burning of a match and the burning of fireworks are examples of _____.

THINKING CRITICALLY

7. **ANALYZE:** Why must oxidation and reduction always happen together in a chemical reaction?

8. **HYPOTHESIZE:** Is oxygen always needed in order for an oxidation reaction to occur? Explain your answer.

Web InfoSearch

Reactions and Energy Some chemical reactions give off energy. This energy may be in the form of heat, light, or mechanical energy. Reactions that give off energy are called exothermic (ehk-soh-THUR-mihk) reactions. Other chemical reactions absorb energy. They need a steady supply of energy in order to take place. Reactions that absorb energy are called endothermic (ehn-doh-THUR-mihk) reactions.

SEARCH: What kinds of chemical reactions are endothermic or exothermic? Use the Internet to find out. Start your search at www.conceptsandchallenges.com. Some key search words are **chemical reaction, exothermic,** and **endothermic.**

Science and Technology

COPPER OXIDATION

Copper is used for pipes, electrical wires, and other building materials. You may have seen buildings with copper roofs. When they are first built, these roofs look like shiny new pennies. As the roofs are exposed to gases in air and water, an oxidation reaction takes place that changes the color of the copper. First, the copper changes from pink to brown, then to black. Finally, the copper is coated with a blue-green material called a patina (puh-TEE-nuh). The patina is made of copper sulfate, a compound of copper and sulfur. Once copper has a patina, air cannot touch the surface and corrosion stops. The copper may last for hundreds of years.

Because it resists corrosion, copper was used as the covering, or skin, on the Statue of Liberty. The Statue of Liberty has been exposed to air, water, and other forms of weathering for more than one hundred years. In 1986, the Statue of Liberty was restored. Because of its patina, very little of the statue's skin needed to be replaced. This copper skin will continue to protect the Statue of Liberty for another hundred years.

▲ **Figure 8-6** Statue of Liberty

Thinking Critically Why do you think copper is a good material to use to make pipes?

What is a synthesis reaction?

Objective
Describe what happens in a synthesis reaction.

Key Term
synthesis (SIHN-thuh-sihs) **reaction:** reaction in which substances combine to form a more complex substance

Synthesis Reactions There are many types of chemical reactions. One type of chemical reaction is called a **synthesis reaction.** To *synthesize* means "to put together." In a synthesis reaction, two or more substances combine to form a more complex substance. The reactants in a synthesis reaction can be elements, compounds, or both. The product of a synthesis reaction is always a compound.

▶ **DEFINE:** What is a synthesis reaction?

Examples of Synthesis Reactions The formation of iron sulfide (FeS_2), also known as pyrite or fool's gold, is an example of a synthesis reaction. The formation of table salt (NaCl) is also a synthesis reaction.

$$Fe + S_2 \rightarrow FeS_2$$
$$2Na + Cl_2 \rightarrow 2NaCl$$

▶ **INFER:** What elements form iron sulfide?

Oxidation Reactions Many oxidation reactions are synthesis reactions. The burning of carbon to form carbon dioxide (CO_2) and the oxidation of magnesium to form magnesium oxide (MgO) are also synthesis reactions.

$$C + O_2 \rightarrow CO_2$$
$$2Mg + O_2 \rightarrow 2MgO$$

▶ **EXPLAIN:** How are the formation of carbon dioxide and magnesium oxide examples of synthesis reactions?

Synthesis Reactions Involving Compounds Some synthesis reactions involve the combination of a compound and an element. When the compound carbon monoxide (CO) burns, it combines with an element, oxygen, to produce a more complex compound, carbon dioxide.

$$2CO + O_2 \rightarrow 2CO_2$$

Two compounds react when calcium oxide (CaO) combines with water to produce calcium hydroxide.

$$CaO + H_2O \rightarrow Ca(OH)_2$$

▶ **IDENTIFY:** Give an example of a compound that combines with an element to form a more complex compound.

SOME SYNTHESIS REACTIONS

Forming iron sulfide
$Fe + S_2 \longrightarrow FeS_2$

Forming carbon dioxide
$2CO + O_2 \longrightarrow 2CO_2$

Forming calcium hydroxide
$CaO + H_2O \longrightarrow Ca(OH)_2$

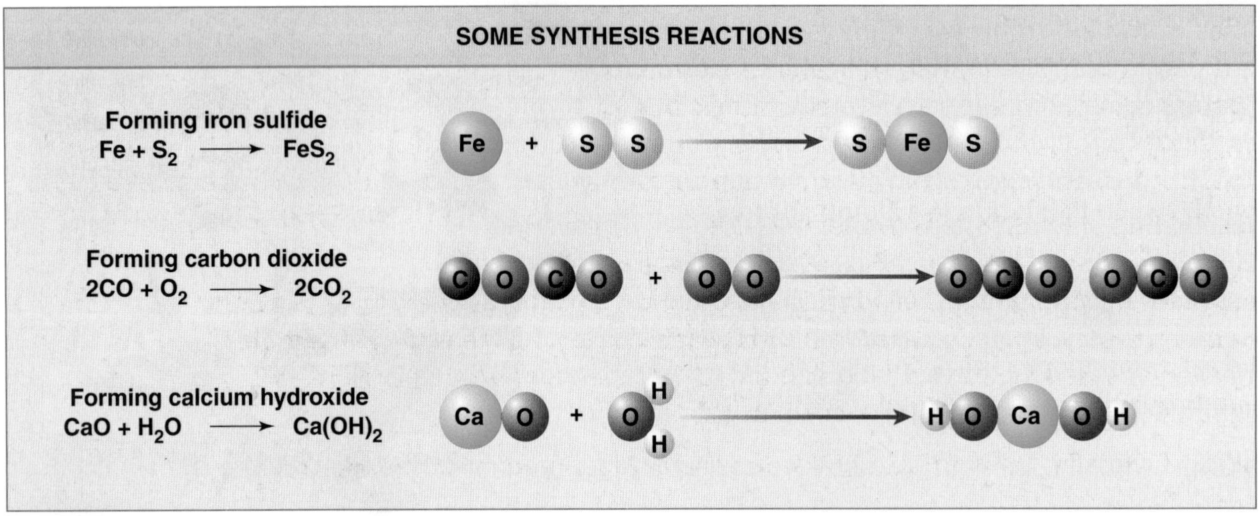

▲ Figure 8-7

Synthesis Reactions with More than Two Reactants Some synthesis reactions can involve the combination of more than two reactants. Sulfuric acid (H_2SO_4), a substance found in acid rain, is formed when sulfur dioxide gas (SO_2) and oxygen in the air combine with water.

$$2SO_2 + O_2 + 2H_2O \rightarrow 2H_2SO_4$$

5 IDENTIFY: What three reactants combine to form sulfuric acid?

✓ CHECKING CONCEPTS

1. To synthesize means "_____."
2. In a synthesis reaction, the product formed is always a _____.
3. In a synthesis reaction, two or more substances produce a _____ substance.
4. When carbon monoxide combines with oxygen, _____ is produced.
5. Three _____ combine in a synthesis reaction to form sulfuric acid.

THINKING CRITICALLY

6. **ANALYZE:** Which of the following reactions are synthesis reactions?
   a. $2H_2O \rightarrow 2H_2 + O_2$
   b. $N_2 + 2O_2 \rightarrow 2NO_2$
   c. $4Al + 3O_2 \rightarrow 2Al_2O_3$
   d. $Zn + 2HCl \rightarrow ZnCl_2 + H_2$
   e. $CaO + H_2O \rightarrow Ca(OH)_2$

7. **APPLY:** Explain why the following general equation describes a synthesis reaction.
   $A + B \rightarrow C$

INTERPRETING VISUALS

Look at the diagram of a synthesis reaction in Figure 8-8. Write the balanced equation for the synthesis reaction.

▲ **Figure 8-8** The formation of water

Real-Life Science

DEVELOPMENT OF SYNTHETIC FABRICS

Do you own a rayon blouse or a polyester shirt? Can some of your clothes be washed and then worn with little or no ironing? Are your bathing suits or exercise clothes made of a special material that stretches for a good fit? If you answered yes to any of these questions, then you are familiar with synthetic (sihn-THEHT-ihk) fabrics.

Synthetic fabrics are materials that were invented by chemists to take the place of natural fibers such as silk, cotton, and wool. Synthetic fabrics are made from very large molecules called polymers. Polymers are made up of many smaller molecules joined together in long chains.

▲ **Figure 8-9** Making synthetic fabric

The first synthetic fiber to be developed was rayon. Rayon was invented at the end of the 19th century. Rayon is manufactured from cellulose. Cellulose comes from wood pulp. This synthetic fiber can be treated to resemble wool, cotton, linen, or silk. Nylon was introduced in 1938 as a substitute for silk. It soon replaced silk in the manufacture of stockings.

Thinking Critically Why do you think people would buy materials made from synthetic fabrics?

8-5 What is a decomposition reaction?

Objective
Describe what happens in a decomposition reaction.

Key Terms
decomposition (dee-kahm-puh-ZISH-uhn) **reaction:** reaction in which a complex substance is broken down into two or more simpler substances

electrolysis (ee-lehk-TRAHL-uh-suhs)**:** process by which a substance is decomposed using an electric current

Decomposition Reactions When a substance breaks down into simpler substances, the reaction is called a **decomposition reaction.** Decomposition reactions are the opposite of synthesis reactions. In a decomposition reaction, a single complex substance is broken down into two or more simpler substances. The products of a decomposition reaction can be elements, compounds, or both.

▶ **DEFINE:** What is a decomposition reaction?

The Need for Energy Most decomposition reactions need energy from an outside source in order to take place. The energy is usually in the form of heat or electricity. Chemists often show the type of energy that is needed for a decomposition reaction by writing a symbol above the arrow in the chemical equation. A triangle drawn above the arrow means that heat needs to be added. You can see how this symbol is used in the following equation. This equation shows the decomposition of mercuric oxide.

$$2HgO \xrightarrow{\triangle} 2Hg + O_2$$

▶ **EXPLAIN:** What does a triangle drawn above an arrow in a chemical equation mean?

Electrolysis of Water An example of a decomposition reaction is the electrolysis of water. In **electrolysis,** a substance is decomposed using an electric current. The energy from the electric current causes a chemical reaction to take place.

When an electric current is passed through water, the water breaks down, or decomposes, into oxygen and hydrogen.

$$2H_2O \rightarrow 2H_2 + O_2$$

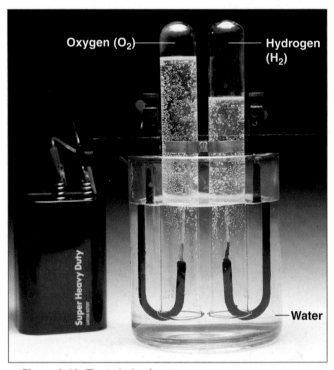
Oxygen (O$_2$) Hydrogen (H$_2$)

Water

▲ **Figure 8-10** Electrolysis of water

Electrolysis can be used to break down other substances as well. Although difficult to do, sodium chloride can be melted. Once melted, it can be decomposed by an electric current.

$$2NaCl \rightarrow 2Na + Cl_2$$

▶ **DESCRIBE:** What happens during the electrolysis of water?

Decomposition Reactions Without Added Energy Some decomposition reactions do not require added energy. Hydrogen peroxide (H_2O_2) is a substance used to clean skin wounds. Over time, hydrogen peroxide will decompose into water and oxygen.

$$2H_2O_2 \rightarrow 2H_2O + O_2$$

▶ **STATE:** Give an example of a decomposition reaction that does not require added energy.

✔ CHECKING CONCEPTS

1. What are the kinds of products formed in decomposition reactions?

2. What is the opposite of a decomposition reaction called?

3. How many reactants are there in a decomposition reaction?

4. What are the products when water decomposes?

5. What forms of energy are usually needed in decomposition reactions?

6. What is used to decompose water in an electrolysis reaction?

7. What are the products in a decomposition reaction of table salt?

8. What kind of symbol is used to show that heat is needed in a decomposition reaction?

THINKING CRITICALLY

9. ANALYZE: If substance AB is broken down into simpler substances in a decomposition reaction, how would you represent the products?

10. INFER: Why can the reactant in a decomposition reaction never be an element?

11. INFER: Over time, what does hydrogen peroxide decompose into?

DESIGNING AN EXPERIMENT

Design an experiment to solve the following problem. Include a hypothesis, variables, a procedure, and a type of data to study.

PROBLEM: The sugar glucose ($C_6H_{12}O_6$) can be broken down into simpler substances. What products are formed when glucose is decomposed by heating?

Science and Technology

AIR BAGS

▲ **Figure 8-11** Air bags can protect passengers during an auto crash.

Chemistry provides a way of inflating a pillow to help cushion passengers during an automobile crash. The pillow is called an air bag.

Air bags are made of nylon. They can be located inside steering wheels, dashboards, and door mounts. A chemical decomposition reaction puts the air in air bags. If a crash occurs, a sensor device installed in the car activates the inflation system. Decomposition reactions take place and produce nitrogen gas, N_2. The nitrogen gas comes from the decomposition of sodium azide, NaN_3. Air bags can inflate at rates close to 200 miles per hour.

Studies show that air bags can reduce the risk of fatal injuries by more than 46 percent during frontal automobile crashes. Most new vehicles are built with air bags in the steering wheel and in the dashboard in front of the passenger seat. New designs of vehicles may contain as many as eight air bags for overall protection.

Thinking Critically What do you think will be the effect of increasing the number of air bags in automobiles?

8-6 What is a single-replacement reaction?

Objective

Describe what happens in a single-replacement reaction.

Key Term

single-replacement reaction: reaction in which one element replaces another element in a compound

Single-Replacement Reactions In certain types of chemical reactions, one element replaces another element in a compound. This type of chemical reaction is called a **single-replacement reaction.** All single-replacement reactions begin with a compound and a free element. When the element and the compound react, the free element replaces one of the elements in the compound. The element that is replaced then becomes a free element. The reactants in a single-replacement reaction are always a compound and a free element. The products are always a new compound and a new free element. This general equation will help you remember what happens in a single-replacement reaction.

$$A + BC \rightarrow AC + B$$

▶ **DEFINE:** What is a single-replacement reaction?

Single-Replacement Reactions with Metals Three common groups of substances are acids, bases, and salts. A salt is an ionic compound made up of a positive metallic ion and a negative nonmetallic ion, such as sodium chloride. Many metals react with acids to produce hydrogen gas and a salt. In this type of reaction, the metal is the free element and the acid is the compound. When the metal and the acid react, the metal replaces hydrogen in the acid. When the reaction is over, hydrogen is the free element, which escapes as a gas. A salt is the new compound.

You can see how this works by looking at the equation below for the reaction between zinc and hydrochloric acid (HCl).

$$\underset{\text{metal}}{Zn} + \underset{\text{acid}}{2HCl} \rightarrow \underset{\text{salt}}{ZnCl_2} + \underset{\text{hydrogen}}{H_2}$$

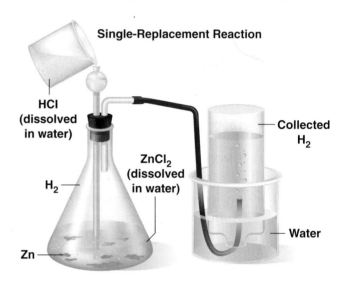

▲ **Figure 8-12** The reaction between zinc and hydrochloric acid is a single-replacement reaction.

▶ **INFER:** What is produced when a metal reacts with an acid?

Other Examples Some other types of single-replacement reactions include the reaction between sodium and water and the reaction between chlorine and sodium bromide (NaBr).

$$2Na + 2H_2O \rightarrow 2NaOH + H_2$$
$$Cl_2 + 2NaBr \rightarrow 2NaCl + Br_2$$

One way in which the element copper (Cu) can be obtained from a rock containing copper oxide (CuO) is in a single-replacement reaction. If carbon can be made to react with copper oxide, carbon dioxide will form and copper will become the free element.

$$\underset{\substack{\text{copper} \\ \text{oxide}}}{2CuO} + \underset{\text{carbon}}{C} \rightarrow \underset{\substack{\text{carbon} \\ \text{dioxide}}}{CO_2} + \underset{\text{copper}}{2Cu}$$

◀ **Figure 8-13** The element copper can be obtained in a single-replacement reaction.

 INFER: What is the compound produced in the reaction between chlorine and sodium bromide?

✓ CHECKING CONCEPTS

1. A single-replacement reaction always takes place between an element and a _____.

2. In a single-replacement reaction, one element _____ another element.

3. The products of a single-replacement reaction are always a compound and an _____.

4. When zinc reacts with hydrochloric acid, hydrogen is replaced by _____.

5. When the reaction between zinc and hydrochloric acid is complete, _____ is the free element.

💡 THINKING CRITICALLY

6. **ANALYZE:** Tell what is happening in the following reaction.

$$Cu + AgNO_3 \rightarrow CuNO_3 + Ag$$

HEALTH AND SAFETY TIP

The element sodium is dangerous to handle. Sodium reacts explosively with water. As a result, sodium must be stored in oil. What safety precautions do you think scientists must use when handling sodium?

⚛ *Hands-On Activity*

REPLACING METALS

You will need safety goggles, copper sulfate, silver nitrate, water, two ungalvanized nails, two copper strips, two 100-mL beakers, four test tubes, a graduated cylinder, a clock or timer, and a balance.

1. Prepare a copper sulfate solution in a 100-mL beaker by adding 2 g of copper sulfate to 100 mL of water.

2. Half-fill two test tubes with the solution.

3. Place a nail in one test tube and a copper strip in the other. Wait 5 minutes.

4. Pour the copper sulfate solution out of both test tubes. Remove the nail and the copper strip. Observe any changes.

5. Repeat steps 1 to 3 substituting silver nitrate for the copper sulfate.

Practicing Your Skills

6. **OBSERVE:** What happened to the iron nail?

7. **OBSERVE:** What happened to the copper strip?

8. **ANALYZE:** Which element is replaced?

▲ **Figure 8-14** A nail in copper sulfate (left) and a strip of copper in copper sulfate (right)

8-7 What is a double-replacement reaction?

Objective

Describe what happens in a double-replacement reaction.

Key Terms

double-replacement reaction: reaction in which elements from two different compounds replace each other, forming two new compounds

precipitate (pree-SIHP-uh-tayt)**:** solid that settles to the bottom of a mixture

Double-Replacement Reactions   In certain types of chemical reactions, the elements from two different compounds replace each other, forming two new compounds. This type of reaction is called a **double-replacement reaction.** A double-replacement reaction can be shown by the following general equation.

$$AB + CD \rightarrow AD + CB$$

Have you ever taken medicine to relieve an upset stomach? If you have, the medicine may have contained magnesium carbonate ($MgCO_3$). This substance can cause a double-replacement reaction to take place. Magnesium carbonate can help break down the substance hydrochloric acid (HCl), which is produced in your stomach. In this reaction, the magnesium and the hydrogen replace each other. Magnesium chloride ($MgCl_2$) and carbonic acid (H_2CO_3) are produced.

$$MgCO_3 + 2HCl \rightarrow MgCl_2 + H_2CO_3$$

The carbonic acid produced in the double-replacement reaction then goes through a decomposition reaction that produces water and carbon dioxide. Your upset stomach is relieved.

▶ **1** DEFINE: What is a double-replacement reaction?

Formation of a Precipitate Double-replacement reactions take place in solutions. Although water does not take part in these reactions, it does help to speed them up. In many double-replacement reactions, a substance called a precipitate is formed. A **precipitate** is a solid that settles to the bottom of a mixture. For example, in the double-replacement reaction between lead nitrate and potassium iodide, lead iodide is one of the products. As it forms, this compound settles out as a yellow precipitate.

$$\underset{\substack{\text{lead} \\ \text{nitrate}}}{Pb(NO_3)_2} + \underset{\substack{\text{potassium} \\ \text{iodide}}}{2KI} \rightarrow \underset{\substack{\text{potassium} \\ \text{nitrate}}}{2KNO_3} + \underset{\substack{\text{lead} \\ \text{iodide}}}{PbI_2}$$

▲ **Figure 8-15** When potassium iodide is poured into lead nitrate, lead iodide is the precipitate that forms.

In the double-replacement reaction between silver nitrate and sodium chloride, silver chloride is the precipitate.

$$\underset{\substack{\text{silver} \\ \text{nitrate}}}{AgNO_3} + \underset{\substack{\text{sodium} \\ \text{chloride}}}{NaCl} \rightarrow \underset{\substack{\text{sodium} \\ \text{nitrate}}}{NaNO_3} + \underset{\substack{\text{silver} \\ \text{chloride}}}{AgCl}$$

In the double-replacement reaction between aluminum sulfate and barium chloride, aluminum chloride is the precipitate.

$$\underset{\substack{\text{aluminum} \\ \text{sulfate}}}{Al_2(SO_4)_3} + \underset{\substack{\text{barium} \\ \text{chloride}}}{3BaCl_2} \rightarrow \underset{\substack{\text{barium} \\ \text{sulfate}}}{3BaSO_4} + \underset{\substack{\text{aluminum} \\ \text{chloride}}}{2AlCl_3}$$

▶ **2** DEFINE: What is a precipitate?

Acid-Base Reactions Another common type of double-replacement reaction is the reaction that takes place between an acid and a base. This type of reaction produces a salt and water. It is called a neutralization (noo-truh-lih-ZAY-shuhn) reaction. In a neutralization reaction, an acid and a base combine to form a salt and water. The following equation describes the reaction between the base sodium hydroxide (NaOH) and hydrochloric acid (HCl).

$$NaOH + HCl \rightarrow NaCl + H_2O$$

 DESCRIBE: What happens in a neutralization reaction?

CHECKING CONCEPTS

1. In a double-replacement reaction, two new _____ are formed.

2. A precipitate is a _____ that settles to the bottom of a mixture.

3. When lead nitrate and potassium iodide react, the precipitate formed is _____.

4. Double-replacement reactions take place in _____.

5. When a _____ and an acid react, water and a salt are formed.

THINKING CRITICALLY

6. **PREDICT:** What products are formed in the following reaction?

   $KOH + HCl \rightarrow ? + ?$

7. **ANALYZE:** Which of the following reactions are double-replacement reactions?

   a. $2Al_2O_3 \rightarrow 4Al + 3O_2$

   b. $Ca + 2H_2O \rightarrow Ca(OH)_2 + H_2$

   c. $AgNO_3 + NaBr \rightarrow AgBr + NaNO_3$

   d. $2Na + Br_2 \rightarrow 2NaBr$

   e. $2NaOH + H_2SO_4 \rightarrow Na_2SO_4 + 2H_2O$

Integrating Life Science

TOPIC: digestive system

RELIEVING INDIGESTION

Your stomach produces a strong substance called gastric juice. Gastric juice contains hydrochloric acid (HCl) and other molecules that help you digest food. Special cells found inside the lining of your stomach produce hydrochloric acid by taking H^+ ions and Cl^- ions from substances in your blood.

Sometimes your stomach produces too much hydrochloric acid. This can cause a condition called acid indigestion to occur. Antacids are medicines that can relieve the pain of acid indigestion by breaking down hydrochloric acid. Calcium carbonate, sodium bicarbonate, and magnesium hydroxide are common ingredients in antacids. All these compounds can react with H^+ ions to break down the acid in a double-replacement reaction.

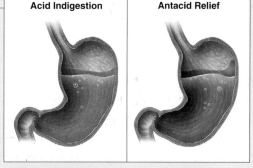

▲ **Figure 8-16** In the stomach, antacids can relieve indigestion (left) by breaking down hydrochloric acid (right).

For example:

$NaHCO_3$	+	HCl	$\rightarrow$	$NaCl$	+	H_2O	+	CO_2
sodium bicarbonate		hydrochloric acid		salt		water		carbon dioxide

The salt and water produced pass through your digestive system. Carbon dioxide may be released as a burp.

Thinking Critically Why are these medicines called antacids?

Integrating Earth Science

THE Big IDEA

What are deep-sea vents?

Chemical reactions occur deep on the ocean floor. One particular set of chemical reactions affects the shape of the ocean floor. Another set of chemical reactions helps a community of bacteria live there.

Deep in the Atlantic and Pacific Oceans, researchers have found formations called black smokers. These tall structures are made up of certain minerals. These minerals are the result of chemical reactions that take place when hot fluids come in contact with the cold ocean floor.

In Earth's crust, these chemical reactions cause the formation of sulfur compounds. The black color of these compounds gives black smokers their name.

Black smokers look like tall chimneys with black smoke blowing out of them into the water. These structures can be as tall as a 15-story building.

These underwater formations are actually vents or cracks in the ocean floor. Hot water pours out of them. The water is heated by magma, which is hot, melted rock found deep in the ocean's crust. The heat of the water in the vents causes the minerals in the crust to become dissolved in the water. As the water rises out through the vents, it is cooled by the surrounding ocean water. The sulfur compounds precipitate out of the rising water and add to the tops of the chimneys.

Certain types of bacteria can live off the sulfur compounds. These bacteria go through chemical reactions in a process called chemosynthesis. During this process, bacteria use the sulfur in a similar way to which plants use the Sun for photosynthesis. The energy released by the chemical reaction is used by the bacteria to make food. Larger organisms then eat the bacteria, and a food chain is established. This deep-sea vent community is home to giant clams, tube worms, and other creatures found nowhere else on Earth.

Study the black smoker on these two pages. Then follow the directions in the Science Log to learn more about "the big idea." ✦

Bacteria
Certain bacteria live in deep-sea vents. These bacteria form the basis of food chains.

2°C

Crust

400°C

1,200°C

▲ **Figure 8-17** A deep-sea vent

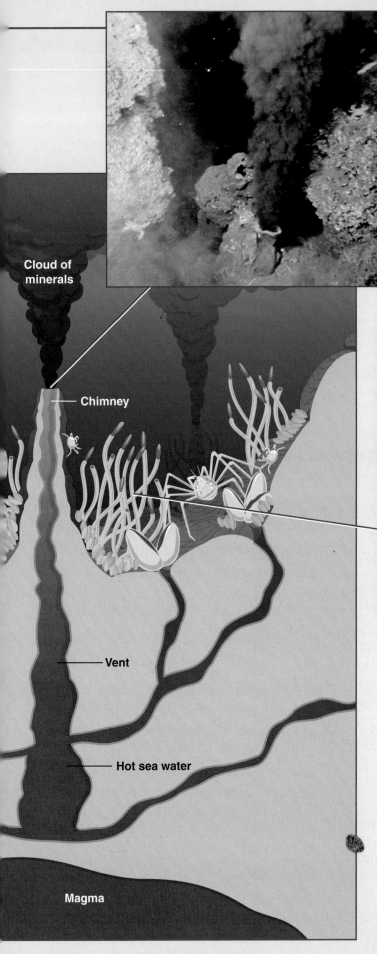

Cloud of minerals

Chimney

Vent

Hot sea water

Magma

Black Smoker

Black "smoke" erupts from a chimney on the ocean floor. This "smoke" is filled with minerals.

Deep-Sea Vent Community

Deep-sea vents are home to many creatures, such as giant tube worms and clams.

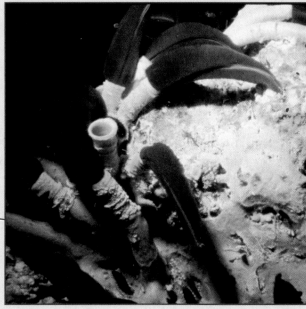

WRITING ACTIVITY

Science Log

Black smokers are found in very deep water. Light from the Sun does not reach such far depths. Research what the conditions are like around a black smoker. In your science log, describe the kinds of life forms that can be found around them. Start your search at www.conceptsandchallenges.com.

Chapter Summary

Lesson 8-1

- A **chemical reaction** is a process in which new substances with new physical and chemical properties are formed.
- The **law of conservation of matter** states that matter cannot be created or destroyed by a chemical change.

Lesson 8-2

- A **chemical equation** is a statement in which chemical formulas are used to describe a chemical reaction.
- To balance chemical equations, numbers called **coefficients** are placed in front of chemical formulas.

Lesson 8-3

- **Reduction** is any chemical change in which electrons are gained.
- **Oxidation** is any chemical change in which electrons are lost.
- When a substance chemically combines with oxygen, the reaction is called **oxidation.**

Lesson 8-4

- In a **synthesis reaction,** two or more substances chemically combine to form a more complex substance.

Lesson 8-5

- In a **decomposition reaction,** a complex substance is broken down into two or more simpler substances.

Lesson 8-6

- In a **single-replacement reaction,** one element replaces another element in a compound.

Lesson 8-7

- In a **double-replacement reaction,** elements from two different compounds replace each other, forming two new compounds.

Key Term Challenges

chemical equation (p. 172)
chemical reaction (p. 168)
coefficient (p. 172)
decomposition reaction (p. 178)
double-replacement reaction (p. 182)
electrolysis (p. 178)
law of conservation of matter (p. 168)
oxidation (p. 174)
precipitate (p. 182)
product (p. 168)
reactant (p. 168)
reduction (p. 174)
single-replacement reaction (p. 180)
synthesis reaction (p. 176)

MATCHING Write the Key Term from above that best matches each description.

1. substance formed in a chemical reaction
2. chemical reaction in which electrons are gained
3. decomposition using an electric current
4. chemical reaction in which electrons are lost
5. substance changed in a chemical reaction
6. chemical reaction in which one element replaces another element in a compound
7. solid that settles out of a mixture

FILL IN Write the Key Term from above that best completes each statement.

8. In a _____, two new compounds are formed.
9. A _____ describes a chemical reaction.
10. The _____ states that matter cannot be created or destroyed by a chemical change.
11. The opposite of a synthesis reaction is a _____.
12. A more complex substance is formed from two simpler substances in a _____.
13. During _____, water is broken down into hydrogen and oxygen.
14. To balance a chemical equation, you would use a _____.

Content Challenges TEST PREP

MULTIPLE CHOICE **Write the letter of the term or phrase that best completes each statement.**

1. The substance produced when iron is oxidized is
   a. water.
   b. oxygen.
   c. iron precipitate.
   d. rust.

2. The reactants in the equation $2H_2 + O_2 \rightarrow 2H_2O$ are
   a. hydrogen and energy.
   b. hydrogen and oxygen.
   c. water and energy.
   d. oxygen and water.

3. In a chemical reaction, matter cannot be
   a. created or destroyed.
   b. conserved.
   c. seen.
   d. measured.

4. The arrow in a chemical equation means
   a. "yields."
   b. "and."
   c. "balances."
   d. "changes."

5. The number of atoms of each element on both sides of a chemical equation must always be
   a. greater than one.
   b. less than two.
   c. different.
   d. equal.

6. The chemical formula $3H_2O$ means
   a. three atoms of hydrogen and three atoms of oxygen.
   b. six atoms of hydrogen and three atoms of oxygen.
   c. three atoms of water.
   d. three atoms of hydrogen and two atoms of oxygen.

7. The burning of a match is an example of
   a. rusting.
   b. oxidation.
   c. synthesis.
   d. respiration.

8. In a chemical reaction, atoms gain and lose
   a. oxygen.
   b. protons.
   c. electrons.
   d. matter.

9. The product of a synthesis reaction is always
   a. an element.
   b. a solid.
   c. a precipitate.
   d. a compound.

10. In electrolysis, an electric current produces a chemical reaction by providing
    a. reactants.
    b. energy.
    c. oxygen.
    d. water.

TRUE/FALSE **Write *true* if the statement is true. If the statement is false, change the underlined term to make the statement true.**

11. In a synthesis reaction, the product is always an <u>element</u>.

12. The electrolysis of water is a <u>single-replacement</u> reaction.

13. Many metals replace hydrogen when they react with <u>acids</u>.

14. A double-replacement reaction involves the reaction of <u>two elements</u>.

15. A <u>neutralization</u> reaction involves an acid and a base.

16. You can recognize a precipitate because it settles at the <u>surface</u> of a mixture.

Concept Challenges

WRITTEN RESPONSES Complete the exercises and answer each of the following questions in complete sentences.

1. **EXPLAIN:** How do balanced chemical equations illustrate the law of conservation of matter?

2. **ANALYZE:** How can you tell from a chemical equation that a chemical change is taking place?

3. **COMPARE:** Discuss the two different meanings of the term *oxidation*.

4. **CONTRAST:** Explain the difference between a single-replacement reaction and a double-replacement reaction.

5. **APPLY:** Describe the physical and chemical changes that take place when silver nitrate reacts with sodium chloride.

6. **CLASSIFY:** Identify each of the following reactions as synthesis, decomposition, single-replacement, or double-replacement.

   a. $2Mg + O_2 \rightarrow 2MgO$

   b. $BaCl_2 + H_2SO_4 \rightarrow BaSO_4 + 2HCl$

   c. $Si + O_2 \rightarrow SiO_2$

   d. $Zn + 2HCl \rightarrow ZnCl_2 + H_2$

   e. $H_2CO_3 \rightarrow CO_2 + H_2O$

   f. $NaOH + HBr \rightarrow NaBr + H_2O$

   g. $2CO + O_2 \rightarrow 2CO_2$

   h. $Ca + 2H_2O \rightarrow Ca(OH)_2 + H_2$

   i. $2H_2O_2 \rightarrow 2H_2O + O_2$

   j. $BaCl_2 + Na_2SO_4 \rightarrow BaSO_4 + 2NaCl$

INTERPRETING A DIAGRAM Use Figure 8-18 to answer the following questions.

7. What kind of a reaction is shown?

8. What is this reaction called?

9. What is the reactant in this reaction?

10. What are the products?

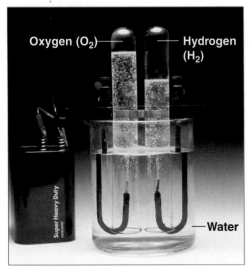

Oxygen (O_2)
Hydrogen (H_2)
Super Heavy Duty
Water

◄Figure 8-18

Chapter 9 Acids and Bases

▲ **Figure 9-1** This pattern is etched on glass.

Patterns can be produced on glass by etching it with hydrofluoric acid. Hydrofluoric acid is a very strong acid that can cause severe burns if not used correctly. The first step in glass etching is the preparation of the glass. The surface to be etched is covered with a protective layer called a resist. This layer is usually made of vinyl. The desired pattern is then cut from the resist. Next, the glass is placed in an acid bath, and the exposed parts of the glass are eaten away, or etched. After removing the glass from the bath, the artist grinds the etched portions to give them an opaque finish.

▶Why is it important to be careful when using acids?

Contents

9-1 What is an acid?

Objective

Define and give some examples of acids.

Key Term

acid: substance that releases hydrogen ions (H^+) when dissolved in water

Acids What do vinegar, lemons, and sour milk have in common? They all taste sour. This is true because they all contain acids. An **acid** is a substance that releases hydrogen ions (H^+) when dissolved in water. It is the presence of these H^+ ions that give an acid its sour taste.

▲ **Figure 9-2** Citrus fruits have a sour taste.

Acids are found in many common materials. Figure 9-3 lists the names and chemical formulas of some common acids and where they can be found.

COMMON ACIDS		
Acid	**Chemical Formula**	**Found In**
Acetic acid	$HC_2H_3O_2$	Vinegar
Boric acid	H_3BO_3	Insecticide
Carbonic acid	H_2CO_3	Club soda
Citric acid	$H_3C_6H_5O_7$	Citrus fruit flavors
Hydrochloric acid	HCl	Digestive juices
Nitric acid	HNO_3	Fertilizers
Sulfuric acid	H_2SO_4	Fertilizers, batteries

▲ **Figure 9-3**

Notice that the symbol for hydrogen appears first in the chemical formula for an acid. All acids contain hydrogen.

1 IDENTIFY: What is it that gives lemons their sour taste?

Properties of Acids All acid solutions have the following properties in common.

- Acids taste sour. Remember that you should never taste or touch a substance to find out what it is.
- Acids conduct electricity.
- Acids are corrosive. Some acids can cause painful burns to the skin.
- Acids react with certain chemicals to produce predictable color changes.

Some acids react with some metals to release hydrogen gas. Figure 9-4 shows what happens when hydrochloric acid is added to zinc metal.

$$2HCl + Zn \rightarrow ZnCl_2 + H_2$$

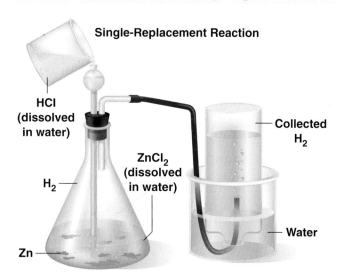

▲ **Figure 9-4** Hydrogen is released when an acid reacts with some metals.

When an acid is dissolved in water, the acid forms positive ions (H^+) and negative ions. For example, hydrochloric acid (HCl) forms positive hydrogen ions and negative chloride ions. The chemical equation for this reaction is shown here.

$$HCl \rightarrow H^+ + Cl^-$$
hydrochloric acid → hydrogen ions + chloride ions

A hydrogen atom is made up of one proton and one electron. A hydrogen ion is simply a hydrogen atom that has lost its single electron. In other words, a hydrogen ion is the same as a proton. For this reason, acids are sometimes called proton donors. A strong acid is one that has a strong tendency to release its hydrogen ion.

 NAME: What is another name for an acid?

✓ CHECKING CONCEPTS

1. Club soda contains _____ acid.
2. The stomach produces _____ acid to aid in digestion.
3. Acids release _____ ions when placed in water.
4. Acids are _____ donors
5. Vinegar contains _____ acid.
6. Some acids react with some _____ to release hydrogen gas.

💡 THINKING CRITICALLY

7. **INFER:** Why are acids called proton donors?
8. **CLASSIFY:** Which of the following chemical formulas are not acids? How do you know?
   a. HCl   e. $HC_2H_3O_2$
   b. NaCl   f. KBr
   c. H_3PO_4 g. CO_2
   d. $CaSO_4$ h. H_2CO_3

HEALTH AND SAFETY TIP

Strong acids, such as sulfuric acid, can be very dangerous if they come in contact with your skin. They also are poisonous. Use library references to find out how to handle acids safely in a science laboratory. Draw a poster to show what you learned about laboratory safety.

 ## Science and Technology

SULFURIC ACID

One of the most important chemical compounds in the world is sulfuric acid (H_2SO_4). Each year, the United States uses more than 80 billion pounds of it, more than 325 pounds per person. Most of the sulfur mined around the world is used to make sulfuric acid.

Sulfuric acid has many uses. Much of it goes into the production of fertilizer. Batteries, paints, dyes, and paper all contain some sulfuric acid. Petroleum refining and metal processing also make use of sulfuric acid. It is also the raw material used to make other chemicals.

You can tell how well our country's economy is doing by looking at the production of sulfuric acid. During periods of economic growth, industries are busy and need a lot of sulfuric acid. During difficult times, its production is very low.

Thinking Critically Why is sulfuric acid so important?

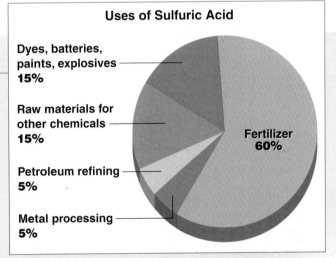

Uses of Sulfuric Acid

Dyes, batteries, paints, explosives 15%
Raw materials for other chemicals 15%
Petroleum refining 5%
Metal processing 5%
Fertilizer 60%

▲ **Figure 9-5** The breakdown of the major uses of sulfuric acid

9-2 What is a base?

INVESTIGATE

Comparing Cleaning Agents
HANDS-ON ACTIVITY

1. Rub some butter or margarine on three plates.
2. Try to clean the first plate with a sponge soaked in plain water.
3. Use a sponge soaked in ammonia water on the second plate, and a sponge soaked in water and liquid soap on the third plate.

THINK ABOUT IT: Which cleaning agent removed the grease most easily? Why?

STEP 2

Objective
Define and give some examples of a base.

Key Terms

base: substance that releases hydroxyl ions (OH⁻) when dissolved in water

hydroxyl (hy-DRAHK-sihl) **ion:** negative ion made up of one atom of hydrogen and one atom of oxygen

Bases Early settlers in the United States made their own soap from animal fat and ashes. Today, soaps are made by chemically combining fats or oils with a type of chemical compound called a base. A **base** is a substance that releases hydroxyl ions (OH^-) when dissolved in water. Ashes contain the bases sodium hydroxide (NaOH) and potash (KOH).

▲ **Figure 9-6** Early settlers made their own soap.

Like acids, bases are found in many common materials. Figure 9-7 lists the names and chemical formulas of some common bases and where they can be found.

1 ▶ DESCRIBE: How are soaps made?

Properties of Bases All base solutions have the following properties in common. You will find that some of these properties are very similar to the properties of acids.

- Bases taste bitter and feel slippery. Never taste or touch a substance to find out what it is.
- Bases conduct electricity.
- Bases can be corrosive and may cause painful burns to the skin.
- Bases react with certain chemicals to produce predictable color changes.

2 ▶ IDENTIFY: What are two properties of bases?

Composition of Bases When some active metals are placed in water, a chemical reaction takes place. The reaction produces a base plus hydrogen gas. For example, sodium, a very active metal, reacts with water to produce sodium hydroxide, a strong base, and hydrogen gas.

$$Na + H_2O \rightarrow NaOH + H$$
sodium + water → sodium hydroxide + hydrogen

COMMON BASES		
Base	**Chemical Formula**	**Found In**
Calcium hydroxide	$Ca(OH)_2$	Plaster, cement, mortar
Magnesium hydroxide	$Mg(OH)_2$	Laxatives, antacids
Potassium hydroxide	KOH	Soap, bleach, drain cleaners
Sodium hydroxide	NaOH	Soap, paper, textiles, some drain cleaners

▲ **Figure 9-7**

Look at the chemical formulas of the bases listed in Figure 9-7. They all contain a group called a **hydroxyl ion.** The hydroxyl ion, OH⁻, is a negative ion made up of one atom of hydrogen and one atom of oxygen. All bases release hydroxyl ions when dissolved in water.

$$NaOH \rightarrow Na^+ + OH^-$$

Hydroxyl ions can combine with hydrogen ions to form water. A hydrogen ion is a proton. Therefore, bases are also known as proton acceptors. The more hydroxyl ions a base releases in water, the stronger the base.

 EXPLAIN: Why are bases often called proton acceptors?

✔ CHECKING CONCEPTS

1. Soaps are made by chemically combining _____ with fats or oils.

2. Strong bases are dangerous to handle because they can _____.

3. Bases form when some active _____ react with water.

4. The negative ion found in all bases is called the _____ ion.

5. Bases are proton _____.

💡 THINKING CRITICALLY

6. **HYPOTHESIZE:** How does the concentration of hydroxyl ions affect the strength of a base?

7. **APPLY:** Match the chemical formulas to each base.

   a. calcium hydroxide   1. NaOH
   b. potassium hydroxide   2. Ca(OH)₂
   c. sodium hydroxide   3. NH₄OH
   d. ammonium hydroxide   4. KOH

HEALTH AND SAFETY TIP

Strong bases, such as sodium hydroxide, can be dangerous if they come in contact with your skin. They also are poisonous. Use library references to find out how to handle bases safely in a science laboratory.

 Real-Life Science

SOAP

Soaps are made up of large molecules whose ends have different properties. One end of a soap molecule is soluble in water. This end has a negative charge, so it is attracted to the positive ends of water molecules. The other end has no charge, so it is soluble in oil. This is why soap can remove grease and oil from clothes or from your skin.

What happens when you wash dirty clothes in soapy water? Soap molecules gather around a grease spot with their oil-soluble ends pointing in. The water-soluble ends of the molecules point out into the water. The grease then forms little drops covered by soap. These drops can then easily mix with the water and be washed away.

Soap is made by boiling fats with lye. Lye contains either sodium hydroxide or potassium hydroxide. Soaps can be made with either one.

| fat | + | lye | → | soap | + | glycerin |

Sometimes the glycerin is left in the soap. Glycerin can also be used to make cellophane, printer's ink, cosmetics, and medicines.

Thinking Critically Explain how soap can remove grease and oil from your skin.

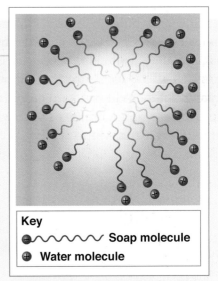

Key
〰 Soap molecule
⊕ Water molecule

▲ **Figure 9-8** Soap molecules surround an oil drop in water.

9-3 What are indicators?

Objective

Describe how indicators are used to identify acids and bases.

Key Term

indicator: (IHN-dih-kay-tuhr): substance that changes color in an acid or a base

Color Change Suppose you have an unknown solution and you want to know if it is an acid or a base. How might you find out? Remember—you should never taste or touch anything to find out what it is. So, how can you identify your unknown solution? You can test it with an indicator. An **indicator** is a chemical that changes color in an acid or a base.

 DESCRIBE: What are indicators used for?

Indicators Litmus is an indicator that turns red in acids and blue in bases. Paper treated with litmus can be used to test acids and bases. For example, vinegar is acidic and soap is basic. If you dip one end of a strip of blue litmus paper into vinegar, the blue litmus turns red. If you dip one end of a strip of red litmus paper into soapy water, the red litmus turns blue.

Vinegar　　　**Soapy water**

▲ **Figure 9-9** Litmus paper is an indicator.

Phenolphthalein (fee-nohl-THA-lee-uhn) is another indicator. Phenolphthalein is colorless in acids and ranges from pink to red in bases.

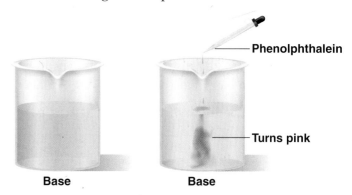

Phenolphthalein

Turns pink

Base　　　**Base**

▲ **Figure 9-10** Phenolphthalein changes color in bases.

The indicator methyl red is red in acids and yellow in bases. The indicator bromthymol blue will turn blue in a base. Figure 9-11 shows some common indicators and the colors they turn in acids and bases.

INDICATORS		
Indicator	**Color in Acids**	**Color in Bases**
Litmus	Red or pink	Blue
Phenolphthalein	Colorless	Pink or red
Methyl red	Red	Yellow
Congo red	Blue	Red
Bromthymol blue	Yellow	Blue

▲ **Figure 9-11**

 NAME: What are three common indicators?

Everyday Indicators Many common, everyday substances are indicators. Grape juice is a good indicator. It will change color depending on how much acid or how much base is present. Red cabbage, beets, rhubarb, cherries, blueberries, and blackberries all can be used as indicators.

Hydrangeas (hy-DRAYN-juhz) are a special kind of flower that act as indicators. They have pink flowers in basic soil and blue flowers in acidic soil.

▲ Figure 9-12 These hydrangeas are growing in soil that is acidic in some places and basic in others.

3 ▶ EXPLAIN: How do hydrangeas act as acid-base indicators?

✓ CHECKING CONCEPTS

1. Blue litmus paper turns red in _____.
2. Phenolphthalein turns _____ in bases.
3. Methyl red turns yellow in _____.
4. Congo red turns _____ in acids.
5. Hydrangeas have _____ flowers in basic soil.

💡 THINKING CRITICALLY

6. **ANALYZE:** An unknown solution turns bromthymol blue from yellow to blue. Is the solution an acid or a base? How do you know?

7. **CLASSIFY:** Identify each of the following properties as belonging to an acid or a base.
   a. tastes bitter
   b. reacts with metals to produce hydrogen
   c. turns methyl red from red to yellow
   d. feels slippery
   e. tastes sour
   f. turns phenolphthalein from colorless to pink

DESIGNING AN EXPERIMENT

Design an experiment to solve the following problem. Include a hypothesis, variables, a procedure, and a type of data to study.

PROBLEM: If you plant hydrangeas in your garden, will the flowers be pink or blue?

 Hands-On Activity

MAKING AN INDICATOR

You will need red cabbage leaves, a heat source, water, a beaker, a strainer, samples to be tested, and a graduated cylinder.

1. Boil several red cabbage leaves in water until the mixture turns dark red. ⚠CAUTION: Be careful when boiling liquids.
2. Let the mixture cool. Pour the liquid through a strainer into a beaker. This is the indicator.
3. Choose several samples to be tested, for example, milk, fruit juice, shampoo, household cleaner, soda, liquid soap. Pour a small amount of each sample into a separate container.
4. Add 2 mL of red cabbage indicator to each of your samples. Observe what happens.

▲ **STEP 4** Add 2 mL of the indicator to each sample.

Practicing Your Skills

5. **OBSERVE:** What color did the indicator turn in each sample?
6. **OBSERVE:** What is the color of the indicator in acids?
7. **OBSERVE:** What is the color of the indicator in bases?

9-4 What is the pH scale?

Objective

Describe how the pH scale is used to measure the strength of acids and bases.

Key Terms

pH scale: measure of the concentration of hydrogen ions in a solution

neutral: neither acidic nor basic

Strength of Acids and Bases Acids and bases can be strong or weak. Sulfuric acid and nitric acid are strong acids that can burn the skin. Carbonic acid and boric acid are weak acids. Boric acid is even used as an antiseptic to kill germs. Sodium hydroxide and potassium hydroxide are strong bases. Ammonium hydroxide is a weak base that is used as a household cleaner. Aluminum hydroxide is a weak base that is used as an antacid.

The strength of acids or bases depends on their tendency to release ions when dissolved in water. A strong acid, such as hydrochloric acid (HCl) releases many hydrogen ions when dissolved in water. A weak acid, such as carbonic acid (H_2CO_3) releases only a few hydrogen ions in a solution. Strong bases, such as sodium hydroxide (NaOH) release many hydroxyl ions, whereas weak bases, such as ammonium hydroxide (NH_3OH) release few hydroxyl ions.

▶ **IDENTIFY:** What determines the strength of an acid or a base?

Concentration of Acids and Bases The terms *concentrated* and *dilute* are often used to describe acids and bases. A concentrated solution contains a large amount of acid or base compared with the amount of water in which it is dissolved. A dilute solution contains a small amount of acid or base compared with the amount of water present.

The amount of water present in a solution does not change the strength of an acid or a base. Hydrochloric acid is a strong acid, regardless of whether it is in a concentrated solution or a dilute solution. However, adding water to an acidic or a basic solution makes the solution safer to use. The addition of water tends to spread out the ions that make the acid or base so reactive.

▶ **EXPLAIN:** How is it possible for a strong acid to be dilute?

The pH Scale Scientists have developed a scale to measure how acidic or basic a solution is. This scale is called the pH scale. The **pH scale** indicates the concentration of hydrogen ions in a solution.

The pH scale is a series of numbers from 0 to 14. A neutral solution has a pH of 7. A **neutral** solution is neither acidic nor basic. Acids have a pH below 7. Strong acidic solutions have a low pH. Bases have a pH that ranges from 7 to 14. Strong basic solutions have a high pH.

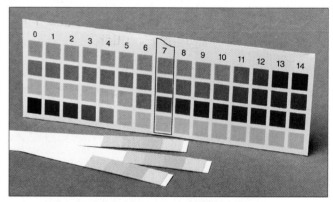

▲ **Figure 9-13** The pH of items can be tested using pH paper. The pH paper uses a range of colors to help make the test more accurate.

▶ **DEFINE:** What is a neutral solution?

Indicators and pH Indicators can be used to help find the pH of an acid or a base. pH paper is an indicator that changes color depending on the pH of the solution. In strong acids, pH paper is red. It is yellow in weak acids and green in weak bases. In strong bases, pH paper is blue.

▶ **PREDICT:** What color will concentrated sulfuric acid turn pH paper?

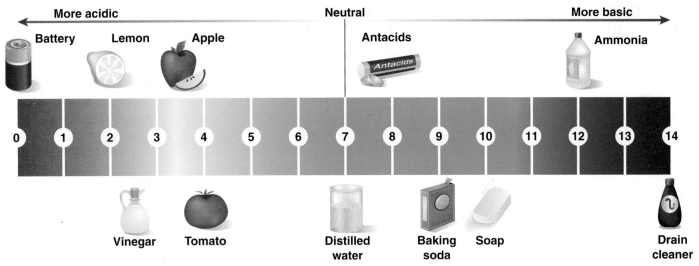

▲ **Figure 9-14** A sample pH scale

✓ CHECKING CONCEPTS

1. Sulfuric acid is a _____ acid.

2. Nitric acid is a _____ acid.

3. Ammonium hydroxide is a _____ base.

4. Sodium hydroxide is a _____ base.

5. The strength of a base depends on the number of _____ ions in a solution.

6. Acids have a pH _____ 7.

7. A solution with a pH of 12 is _____.

💡 THINKING CRITICALLY

Use the pH scale in Figure 9-14 to answer the following questions.

8. **ANALYZE:** What is the pH of the following substances?

   a. baking soda

   b. distilled water

   c. soap

   d. drain cleaner

   e. lemon

   f. antacids

   g. apple

9. **IDENTIFY:** Which of the substances shown on the pH scale are acids?

10. **IDENTIFY:** Which of the substances shown on the pH scale are bases?

11. **IDENTIFY:** Which of the substances shown on the pH scale are neutral?

BUILDING MATHEMATICS SKILLS

Graphing Many common household products are acids or bases. Make a list of products around your house that are acids and a list of those that are bases. Use library references to identify the acid or base present in each product. Then, find out the pH.

Create a bar graph such as the one in Figure 9-15. Compare the different pH levels. Label the *y* axis from 0 to 14. Label the *x* axis with each product you found.

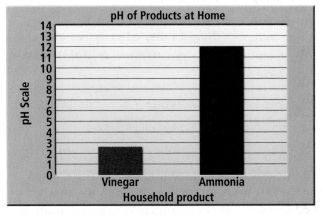

▲ **Figure 9-15** Make a bar graph like this one.

LAB ACTIVITY
Classifying Household Materials as Acids or Bases

Materials
Safety goggles,
lab apron, gloves,
12 stirring rods,
12 small test tubes
   and test tube rack,
eyedroppers,
pH paper and pH chart,
various household liquids:
wax pencil and markers,
paper towels

▲ **STEP 4** Clearly label the paper towels.

▲ **STEP 6** Test each liquid with pH paper.

BACKGROUND

Many times, we think of acids and bases as dangerous substances. However, your home is filled with many useful acids and bases. Many of these materials are part of your everyday life.

PURPOSE

In this activity, you will predict and classify various household materials as acids or bases. Then, you will determine the pH level of each item.

PROCEDURE

1. Copy the chart in Figure 9-16 onto a sheet of paper. Make your predictions as to which materials will be acids and which will be bases.

2. Put on your safety goggles, lab apron, and plastic gloves. Place a few sheets of paper towel on your area.

3. Obtain 12 small test tubes and a test-tube rack. Using a wax pencil, label the test tubes with the corresponding numbers from the chart.

4. Label areas on the paper towels with the same numbers. You will leave the pH paper to dry on the paper towels.

5. Add ten drops of each household liquid into its corresponding numbered test tube.

6. Dip a clean stirring rod into the test tube. Place a drop of the material onto the pH paper. Place the pH paper on the paper towel under the correct number.

7. Allow the pH paper to dry for 1 to 2 minutes. Compare the color change to the pH chart. Record your results.

8. Repeat Steps 6 and 7 for each material. Use a new stirring rod for each material tested. Otherwise, thoroughly clean the one you have after each test.

9. Dispose of the household materials properly. Wash your hands thoroughly after all work is finished.

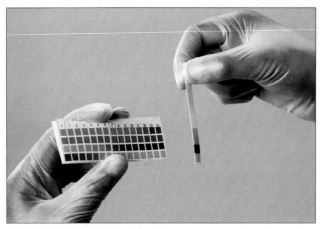

▲ **STEP 7** Compare the color change to the pH chart.

Classifying Household Materials as Acids or Bases

Material	Prediction	Observation of pH Paper	pH According to Chart
1. Ammonia			
2. Apple cider			
3. Distilled water			
4. Ginger ale			
5. Liquid soap			
6. Milk			
7. Milk of magnesia			
8. Mineral water			
9. Orange juice			
10. Salt water			
11. Tap water			
12. Tomato juice			

▲ **Figure 9-16** Copy this chart and use it to record your observations.

CONCLUSIONS

1. **OBSERVE:** Which household materials were acids? Which were bases? Which were neutral?

2. **ANALYZE:** Which household materials did not match your prediction? Explain the reason behind your prediction.

3. **ANALYZE:** Which household item was the strongest acid? The strongest base?

4. **HYPOTHESIZE:** The pH of cow's milk is about 6.5. When milk spoils, we say that it has gone sour because of the lemonlike taste. What has happened to the milk's pH?

THE Big IDEA

How does pH affect the blood?

Our bodies need a balance of acid and base. Some organs, such as the stomach, need to be acidic. On the other hand, blood fluid, called plasma, needs to be slightly basic. A drastic change in the pH of blood plasma can be deadly. Blood pH affects many chemical reactions in the human body, including the way oxygen gets from our lungs to our cells.

Getting oxygen to all the body cells is the job of hemoglobin, a protein in red blood cells that contains iron. Hemoglobin changes its chemical characteristics depending on pH.

When muscle cells turn sugar into energy for movement, they take up oxygen and release carbon dioxide. When you exercise, you use more energy and need more oxygen. You breathe faster and more deeply. Oxygen carried by hemoglobin flows through the bloodstream to your muscle cells. Carbon dioxide is carried back to the lungs. The more oxygen you need in your cells, the better hemoglobin gets at doing its job.

Here is how it works: In the lungs, carbon dioxide is released. This causes the pH of the blood to increase, becoming more basic. This makes hemoglobin better at grabbing oxygen molecules. In the tiny blood vessels that supply the muscles, the pH is lower. This makes the hemoglobin molecule lose its chemical grip on the oxygen that it is carrying. Hemoglobin unloads oxygen right where the muscle cells need it.

Look at the illustrations and text boxes that appear on these two pages. Then, follow the directions in the Science Log to find out more about "the big idea."✦

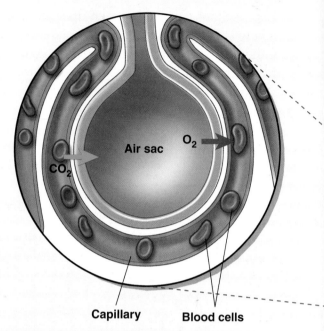

CO$_2$ Air sac O$_2$

Capillary **Blood cells**

pH is Higher in Lungs

In the lungs, the pH of the blood is higher. This increases the attraction of oxygen to hemoglobin. Oxygen in the air sacs moves across the capillary membranes. The red blood cells easily pick up the needed oxygen.

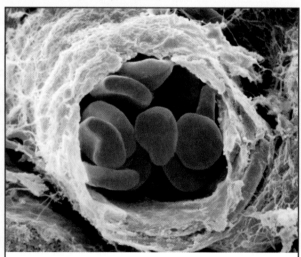

Red Blood Cells

Red blood cells travel through blood vessels. Oxygen is carried throughout the body by hemoglobin in the red blood cells.

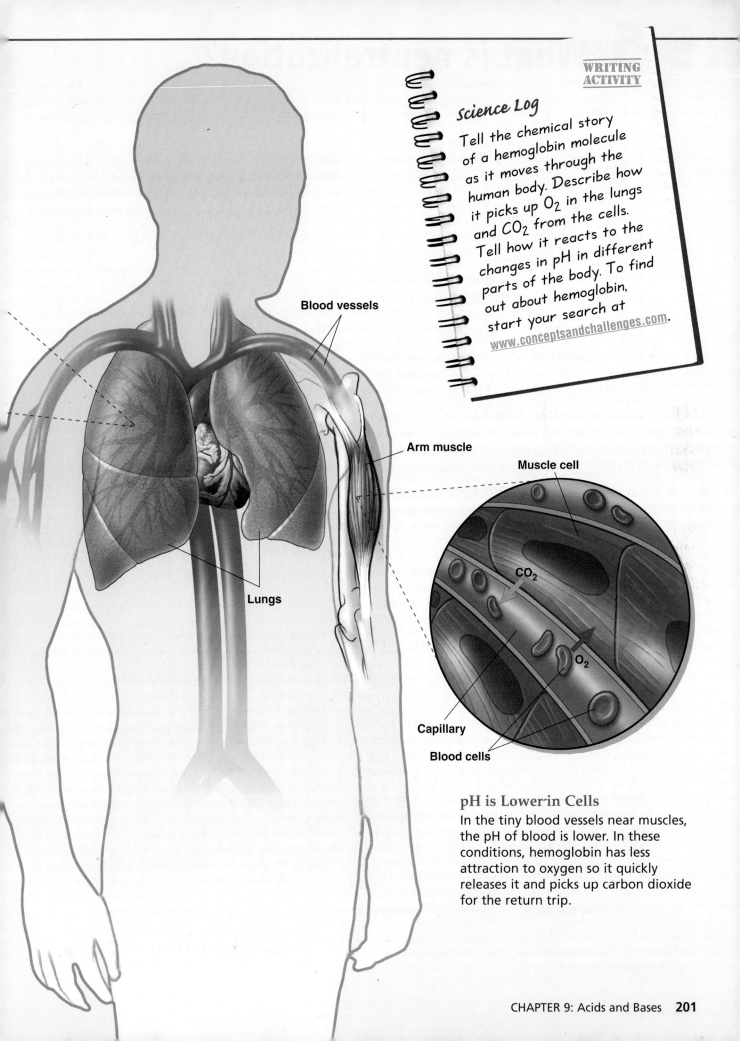

Blood vessels

Arm muscle

Lungs

Muscle cell

CO_2

O_2

Capillary

Blood cells

WRITING ACTIVITY

Science Log

Tell the chemical story of a hemoglobin molecule as it moves through the human body. Describe how it picks up O_2 in the lungs and CO_2 from the cells. Tell how it reacts to the changes in pH in different parts of the body. To find out about hemoglobin, start your search at www.conceptsandchallenges.com.

pH is Lower in Cells

In the tiny blood vessels near muscles, the pH of blood is lower. In these conditions, hemoglobin has less attraction to oxygen so it quickly releases it and picks up carbon dioxide for the return trip.

9-5 What is neutralization?

Objective

Describe what happens when an acid reacts with a base.

Key Terms

neutralization (noo-truh-lih-ZAY-shuhn): reaction between an acid and a base to produce a salt and water

salt: substance formed from the negative ion of an acid and the positive ion of a base

Mixing Acids and Bases Some acids and bases are dangerous, corrosive compounds. However, different compounds are formed when acids and bases are mixed together. Hydrochloric acid and sodium hydroxide can cause burns if they are spilled on the skin. When they are mixed together, they form sodium chloride and water. Sodium chloride is a common substance known as table salt. The chemical reaction between hydrochloric acid and sodium hydroxide produces two new compounds with different properties.

▶ **1** DESCRIBE: What happens when hydrochloric acid is mixed with sodium hydroxide?

Neutralization The reaction between an acid and a base forms a neutral substance. When red litmus paper is placed in a solution of table salt and water, the paper does not change color. When blue litmus paper is placed in a solution of table salt and water, the paper does not change color. Salt water is neither acidic nor basic. It is a neutral substance.

When acids and bases are mixed, a **neutralization** reaction takes place. Neutralization reactions are double-replacement reactions. Water and a salt are always formed in a neutralization reaction.

▶ **2** DEFINE: What is a neutralization reaction?

Salts Sodium chloride is common table salt. It is just one of many different salts. A **salt** is a substance produced when an acid reacts with a base. A salt is made up of the negative ion from the acid and the positive ion from the base. Mixing sulfuric acid with sodium hydroxide produces the salt sodium sulfate and water.

▶ **3** IDENTIFY: When is a salt produced?

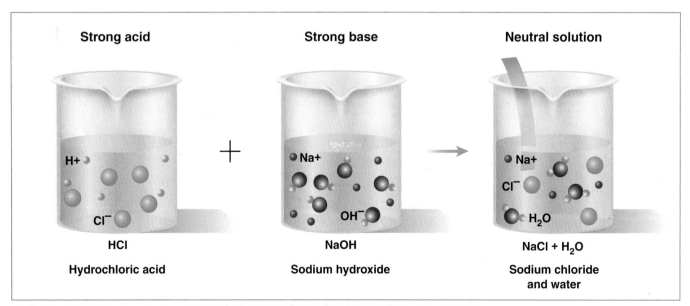

Strong acid	Strong base	Neutral solution
H+ Cl⁻	Na+ OH⁻	Na+ Cl⁻ H₂O
HCl	NaOH	NaCl + H₂O
Hydrochloric acid	Sodium hydroxide	Sodium chloride and water

▲ **Figure 9-17** These two dangerous compounds react to form safe salt water. If the water evaporates, crystals of sodium chloride will be left.

1. What is a neutral substance?
2. Why is sodium hydroxide dangerous?
3. What happens when hydrochloric acid and sodium hydroxide are mixed together?
4. What is sodium chloride?
5. What is a neutralization reaction?
6. What is a salt?
7. What happens when red litmus paper and blue litmus paper are placed in a solution of salt and water?

 THINKING CRITICALLY

8. Match the salts in the second column with the acids and bases in the first column from which they were formed.

Acid + Base → Salt

a. $HCl + NaOH$ 1. $CaSO_4$
b. $H_2SO_4 + Ca(OH)_2$ 2. $NaCl$
c. $HNO_3 + HN_4OH$ 3. K_3PO_4
d. $H_3PO_4 + KOH$ 4. NH_4NO_3

BUILDING SCIENCE SKILLS

Experimenting You can compare the strengths of acids by neutralizing them with a base. Try this experiment. Place 10 mL of an acid into a beaker. Add a few drops of phenolphthalein. Add a base one drop at a time to the acid and indicator. Stop when the phenolphthalein turns light pink. How many drops of base did you add? Repeat this experiment with a different acid. The stronger the acid, the more base you will have to add to neutralize it. Make a table like the one in Figure 9-18. List each acid you are testing. Record the number of drops of base needed for each.

Acid	Name and Number of Drops of Base

▲ **Figure 9-18** Copy this table. Use it to record your observations.

Real-Life Science

HISTORY OF SALT

The saying that people are "worth their salt" comes from a time when salt had great value. Being described as the salt of the earth was a great compliment. In many places, spilling salt was considered bad luck because it was too valuable to be wasted. Salt was so valuable in ancient Rome that soldiers were paid so they could buy it. This part of their wages was called their salary.

▲ **Figure 9-19** Lake Grassmere Salt Works

When table salt (NaCl) is added to water, a substance called brine is produced. Brine is used to pickle and preserve many different types of foods. Before canning and refrigeration were available, pickling was used to keep meat and vegetables from spoiling.

Today, salt is used to make ice cream, dyes, rubber, soap, leather, and many other items. Salt can be readily obtained by the evaporation of seawater, but it is usually mined like other minerals. Deposits of salt are found where prehistoric inland seas have dried up.

Thinking Critically Why do we find salt where dried-up seas used to be?

9-6 What is an electrolyte?

Objective

Explain how ions in a solution conduct electricity.

Key Terms

electrolyte (ee-LEHK-troh-lyt): substance that conducts an electric current when it is dissolved in water

ionization (eye-uh-nih-ZAY-shuhn): formation of ions

nonelectrolyte: substance that will not conduct an electric current when it is dissolved in water

Electrolytes   A substance that conducts an electric current when it is dissolved in water is called an **electrolyte.** Pure distilled water is not a good conductor of electricity. Figure 9-20 shows what happens when electrodes connected to a battery are placed in pure water. The bulb does not light. This indicates that electricity does not flow through the circuit.

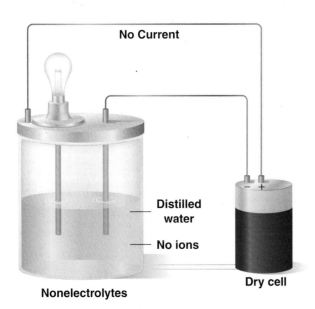

No Current

Distilled water

No ions

Dry cell

Nonelectrolytes

▲ **Figure 9-20** Distilled water is not a good conductor.

Figure 9-21 shows what happens when a small amount of hydrochloric acid is added to the water. The bulb lights. A slightly acidic solution of water is a good conductor of electricity.

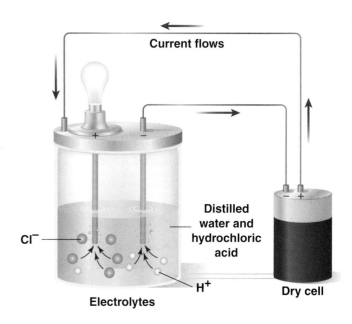

Current flows

Distilled water and hydrochloric acid

Cl^-

H^+

Dry cell

Electrolytes

▲ **Figure 9-21** A slightly acidic solution is a good conductor.

1 ▶ **INFER:** Is hydrochloric acid an electrolyte? Why or why not?

Ionization   Electrolytes can conduct electricity because they form ions when they dissolve in water. A solution that contains ions can conduct an electric current. The ions move and carry the current through the solution.

The formation of ions is called **ionization.** When sodium chloride dissolves in water, it forms sodium (Na^+) ions and chloride (Cl^-) ions. When hydrochloric acid is added to water, it separates into hydrogen (H^+) ions and chloride (Cl^-) ions. The base potassium hydroxide forms potassium (K^+) ions and hydroxide (OH^-) ions in solution.

2 ▶ **DEFINE:** What is ionization?

Nonelectrolytes A substance that does not conduct an electric current when it is dissolved in water is called a **nonelectrolyte**. A sugar solution does not conduct electricity. Sugar is a nonelectrolyte. Nonelectrolytes do not conduct an electric current because they do not form ions in a solution.

 CLASSIFY: Is sugar an example of an electrolyte or a nonelectrolyte?

✓ CHECKING CONCEPTS

1. Pure water _____ conduct electricity.
2. A solution of hydrochloric acid and water is an example of an _____.
3. Acids, bases, and salts are all good _____.
4. A substance that forms _____ in a solution is a good electrolyte.
5. Sugar is an example of a _____.
6. The separation of a salt into ions is called _____.

THINKING CRITICALLY

7. What ions will be formed in solutions of the following acids, bases, and salts?
   a. KCl
   b. NH_4OH
   c. $CaCl_2$
   d. HI
   e. $Ca(OH)_2$
   f. HNO_3
   g. NaBr
   h. $MgSO_4$

DESIGNING AN EXPERIMENT

Design an experiment to solve the following problem. Include a hypothesis, variables, a procedure, and a type of data to study.

PROBLEM: How can you identify a substance as an electrolyte or a nonelectrolyte?

 Hands-On Activity

TESTING HOUSEHOLD MATERIALS FOR ELECTRICAL CONDUCTIVITY

You will need safety goggles, apron, distilled water, several plastic cups, a conductivity tester provided by your teacher, wet paper towels, and several different samples to be tested.

1. Choose several samples to be tested, such as table salt, sugar, vinegar, ammonia, lemon juice, and baking soda. Put on apron and goggles.

▲ **STEP 3** Place the electrodes into the sample to test it.

2. Pour about 50 mL of distilled water in a clean plastic cup. Add a small amount of the sample to be tested and stir.
3. Test the sample with your conductivity tester.
4. Record your observations. Clean the electrodes (wires) one at a time with a wet paper towel.
5. Repeat Steps 2, 3, and 4 for each material to be tested.

Practicing Your Skills

6. ANALYZE: Which of your samples are electrolytes? How do you know?
7. ANALYZE: Which of your samples are nonelectrolytes? How do you know?

Chapter 9 Challenges

Chapter Summary

Lesson 9-1
- **Acids** are chemical compounds that produce hydrogen ions (H^+) when dissolved in water. They are called proton donors.

Lesson 9-2
- **Bases** are chemical compounds that produce **hydroxyl ions** (OH^-) when dissolved in water. They are called proton acceptors.

Lesson 9-3
- Litmus paper can be used to identify both acids and bases.
- **Indicators** are chemical substances that change color in acids and bases.

Lesson 9-4
- The strength of an acid or a base depends on the number of hydrogen or hydroxyl ions in the solution.
- The **pH scale** is a measure of the concentration of H^+ ions in a solution.

Lesson 9-5
- When acids and bases are mixed, new compounds with different properties are formed.
- The reaction between an acid and a base forms a neutral substance.
- Water and a salt are always formed in a **neutralization** reaction.
- A **salt** is made up of the negative ion from an acid and the positive ion from a base.

Lesson 9-6
- An **electrolyte** is a substance that conducts electricity when it is dissolved in water.
- Electrolytes conduct electricity because they form ions when they dissolve in water.
- The formation of ions is called **ionization**.
- **Nonelectrolytes** do not conduct electricity because they do not form ions when they dissolve in water.

Key Term Challenges

acid (p. 190)
base (p. 192)
electrolyte (p. 204)
hydroxyl ion (p. 192)
indicator (p. 194)
ionization (p. 204)
neutral (p. 196)
neutralization (p. 202)
nonelectrolyte (p. 204)
pH scale (p. 196)
salt (p. 202)

MATCHING Write the Key Term from above that best matches each description.

1. formed when metals react with water
2. neither acidic nor basic
3. changes color in acids and bases
4. reaction between an acid and a base
5. formation of ions
6. conducts an electric current in water
7. negative ion made up of a hydrogen atom and an oxygen atom

FILL IN Write the Key Term from above that best completes each statement.

8. A _____ is always formed in a neutralization reaction.
9. Sugar is a _____ because it does not conduct an electric current when it is dissolved in water.
10. Scientists use an _____ to measure the strengths of acids and bases.
11. Vinegar is an example of an _____.
12. On the _____, a neutral solution has a pH of 7.

Content Challenges TEST PREP

MULTIPLE CHOICE **Write the letter of the term or phrase that best completes each statement.**

1. Acids are sometimes called
   a. proton donors.
   b. proton acceptors.
   c. electron donors.
   d. electron acceptors.

2. When they are placed in water, all bases release
   a. chloride ions.
   b. ammonium ions.
   c. hydrogen ions.
   d. hydroxyl ions.

3. Phenolphthalein and bromthymol blue are
   a. acids.
   b. bases.
   c. electrolytes.
   d. indicators.

4. If you put a strip of blue litmus paper into a cup of vinegar, the litmus paper will turn
   a. red.
   b. yellow.
   c. green.
   d. colorless.

5. The pH of a neutral solution is
   a. 0.
   b. 7.
   c. 10.
   d. 14.

6. A solution with a pH of 2 is
   a. strongly basic.
   b. weakly basic.
   c. strongly acidic.
   d. weakly acidic.

7. A neutralization reaction is a reaction between
   a. an acid and a base.
   b. a salt and water.
   c. an acid and water.
   d. a base and water.

8. A reaction between hydrochloric acid and sodium hydroxide produces water and
   a. sodium chloride.
   b. sulfur hydroxide.
   c. hydrochloric acid.
   d. sodium sulfate.

9. Electrolytes can conduct electricity when they are dissolved in water because they form
   a. molecules.
   b. compounds.
   c. ions.
   d. salts.

10. Of the following substances, the one that is a nonelectrolyte is
    a. sodium chloride.
    b. acetic acid.
    c. potassium hydroxide.
    d. sugar.

TRUE/FALSE **Write *true* if the statement is true. If the statement is false, change the underlined term to make the statement true.**

11. Acids react with metals to release <u>oxygen</u> gas.

12. All bases release <u>hydrogen</u> ions in water.

13. Chemicals, such as phenolphthalein, that change color in acids and bases are called <u>indicators</u>.

14. A neutral solution has a pH of <u>4</u>.

15. A salt contains <u>positive</u> ions from an acid.

16. A neutralization reaction is a <u>double</u>-replacement reaction.

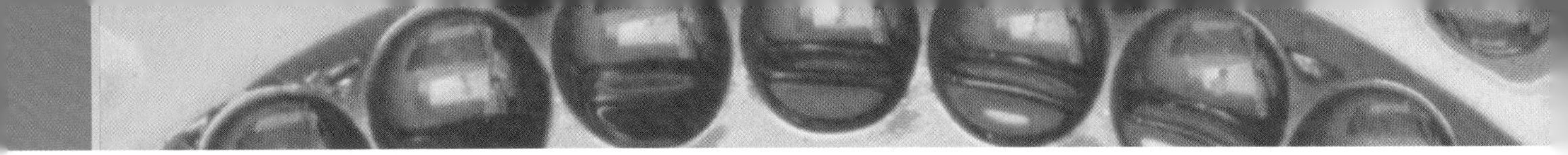

Concept Challenges TEST PREP

WRITTEN RESPONSE **Answer each of the following questions in complete sentences.**

1. **ANALYZE:** Why should you never taste an unknown substance to identify it as an acid or a base?

2. **CLASSIFY:** An unknown solution is found to have a pH of 3. Congo red turns blue in this solution, and bromthymol blue turns yellow. Is the unknown solution an acid or a base?

3. **PREDICT:** Will the unknown solution in exercise 2 conduct an electric current? How do you know?

4. **EXPLAIN:** What is the difference between an acid and a base? Use specific examples to explain.

INTERPRETING A TABLE **Use Figure 9-22 to answer each of the following questions.**

5. What element do all of the acids listed have in common?

6. What is the chemical formula for acetic acid?

7. Which acids are used to make fertilizers?

8. What is the chemical formula of the acid found in citrus fruits? What is the name of this acid?

COMMON ACIDS		
Acid	**Chemical Formula**	**Found In**
Acetic acid	$HC_2H_3O_2$	Vinegar
Boric acid	H_3BO_3	Insecticide
Carbonic acid	H_2CO_3	Club soda
Citric acid	$H_3C_6H_5O_7$	Citrus fruit flavors
Hydrochloric acid	HCl	Digestive juices
Nitric acid	HNO_3	Fertilizers
Sulfuric acid	H_2SO_4	Fertilizers, batteries

▲ Figure 9-22

Chapter 10 Metals

▲ **Figure 10-1** Copper mine at Bingham Canyon, Utah

All minerals are elements or compounds with definite chemical compositions. Minerals form by natural processes. People must mine minerals to get them from Earth. Once mined, ores must undergo a process to separate the pure metals from the rest of the ore. Metals have properties that make them very useful. Most metals are strong and conduct heat and electricity. Metals can also be mixed with other metals to form alloys such as brass, bronze, and sterling silver.

▶Why do you think raw ores must be processed?

Contents

10-1 What is an ore?

Objective
Name some common ores and the metals that are obtained from them.

Key Term
ore: rock or mineral from which a useful metal or element can be removed economically

Ores Metals are found in nature, usually in Earth's crust. They are often combined with other elements. The metals have to be removed from their compounds before they can be used. An **ore** is a rock or mineral from which an element, often a metal, can be removed. Many types of ores are found in nature.

Metals are a useful part of your life. Some of the most common metals are iron, copper, aluminum, and lead. These metals are used to make cars, appliances, electrical wires, jewelry, and many other objects. Metals are shiny and are usually good conductors of both heat and electricity. Other useful properties of most metals are their abilities to be stretched into thin wires and pounded into thin sheets.

▶ 1 **DEFINE:** What is an ore?

Common Ores All rock contains minerals. Rock often contains small quantities of a metal or valuable mineral. However, if the metal or mineral is not present in great enough amounts, the rock is not an ore. It is not mined. Pyrite is a good example of such a rock.

Pyrite, also called fool's gold, is yellow and has a shiny surface. Its chemical name is iron sulfide. As its name implies, pyrite contains iron. However, it does not contain enough iron to make it worthwhile to mine.

Hematite is an ore that is mined because iron is present in greater quantities. Pure iron can be removed from hematite by heating the ore. Figure 10-2 shows some other common ores and the metals that can be removed from them.

▶ 2 **ANALYZE:** What metal is obtained from the ore hematite?

Types of Ores The metals in an ore are usually combined with oxygen, sulfur, or carbon. A metal combined with oxygen is called an oxide. A metal combined with sulfur is called a sulfide. A metal combined with carbon and oxygen is called a carbonate.

▶ 3 **IDENTIFY:** Which of the ores in Figure 10-2 is a carbonate?

METALLIC ORES		
Hematite Iron Fe_2O_3	Bauxite Aluminum Al_2O_3	Galena Lead PbS
Cuprite Copper Cu_2O	Sphalerite Zinc ZnS	Magnesite Magnesium $MgCO_3$

▲ **Figure 10-2** This chart shows some ores, their formulas, and the metal obtained from that ore.

✓ CHECKING CONCEPTS

1. An ore is made of a _____ and other elements.

2. Three types of ores are sulfides, oxides, and _____.

3. Pyrite is a combination of sulfur and _____.

4. Useful _____ can be removed from rocks and minerals.

THINKING CRITICALLY

5. **INFER:** What element must be removed from an oxide ore to obtain the useful metal?

6. **INFER:** What element must be removed from sphalerite to obtain zinc?

7. **ANALYZE:** Gold and silver are not found combined with other elements. Are gold and silver examples of oxides, sulfides, or carbonates? How do you know?

8. Write the chemical formula for each of the following ores.
   a. sphalerite
   b. magnesite
   c. hematite
   d. bauxite
   e. cuprite
   f. galena

BUILDING SCIENCE SKILLS

Observing Metals are a useful part of your life. Look at the objects you use around the house. Make a list of all the objects that are made of metal. How many objects have metal parts? Do most of the objects have some parts that are metal? What kinds of metals are used?

Real-Life Science

DESIGNING AND MAKING JEWELRY

Even before Columbus arrived in the Americas, the Incas of South America crafted jewelry of gold and silver. There is evidence in both South America and Central America that jewelry making was widespread. Metal articles that have been discovered are the forerunners of southwestern-style jewelry.

During the mid 1800s, Mexican silversmiths introduced the art of designing silver jewelry to the Navajo. Because silver was in short supply, early Navajo silversmiths used Mexican and U.S. coins as their source of this metal. Sometimes they melted down silver candlesticks and teapots. By the 1920s, silver could be purchased in the form of sheet metal and wire.

▲ **Figure 10-3** A silversmith makes turquoise and silver jewelry.

The Navajo incorporated local minerals, such as turquoise, in their jewelry designs. Turquoise, a blue compound, contains copper and aluminum phosphate. Deposits of iron in the mineral cause it to have a greener color. Most of the turquoise used by the Navajo and other Native Americans comes from Mexico, Arizona, New Mexico, Nevada, and Colorado.

Thinking Critically Why do you think the Navajo used coins and other objects for their supply of silver?

Objective

Describe how some metals are removed from their ores.

Key Terms

reduction: process of removing oxygen from an ore

roasting: process in which an ore is heated in air to produce an oxide

Removing Metals from Oxide Ores Metals are removed from their ores through chemical processes. The three common types of ores are oxides, sulfides, and carbonates. The different types of ores require different processes to remove the metals they contain. Metals are usually removed from oxides.

Suppose you want to separate copper from cuprite (Cu_2O). You could combine two parts of cuprite to one part of carbon and heat the mixture. This process is shown in the following chemical equation.

$$2Cu_2O \ + \ C \ \rightarrow \ 4Cu \ + \ CO_2 \uparrow$$
cuprite   carbon   copper   carbon dioxide

One atom of carbon and two atoms of oxygen combined to form one molecule of carbon dioxide. The CO_2 escaped as a gas, as shown by the arrow pointing upward. The oxygen was separated from the copper. When the carbon dioxide was formed, four atoms of copper were left over.

▼ **Figure 10-4** When ore is processed, the resulting metals are in liquid form until they cool.

For any oxide ore, the metal is obtained by removing the oxygen. The process of removing oxygen from an ore is called **reduction**.

1 ▶ **DESCRIBE:** How is a metal removed from an oxide?

Metals from Sulfide Ores Two steps are needed to remove the metal from a sulfide ore. The first step is called roasting. In **roasting**, an ore is heated in air to produce an oxide. For example, suppose galena (PbS) is roasted. Galena is a sulfide. After roasting, it forms an oxide called litharge. This process is shown in the following chemical equation.

$$2PbS \ + \ 3O_2 \ \rightarrow \ 2PbO \ + \ 2SO_2$$
galena   oxygen   litharge   sulfur dioxide

Once the ore has been changed into an oxide, the oxygen can be removed by reduction.

$$2PbO \ + \ C \ \rightarrow \ 2Pb \ + \ CO_2 \uparrow$$
litharge   carbon   lead   carbon dioxide

2 ▶ **IDENTIFY:** How is a metal removed from a sulfide?

Metals from Carbonate Ores A two-step process is also used to separate metals from carbonate ores. For example, the first step in removing calcium from limestone, $CaCO_3$, is to heat the limestone in the absence of air. This process drives off carbon dioxide gas as shown in the following equation.

$$CaCO_3 \ + \ heat \ \rightarrow \ CaO \ + \ CO_2 \uparrow$$
calcium   calcium   carbon dioxide
carbonate   oxide

The second step in the process is to pass an electric current through melted calcium oxide. The passage of the electric current causes the compound to decompose, or break down, into its elements, calcium and oxygen.

$$2CaO \ + \ electricity \ \rightarrow \ 2Ca \ + \ O_2 \uparrow$$

3 ▶ **EXPLAIN:** What is the purpose of heating a carbonate ore?

1. Obtaining metals from both _____ ores is usually a two-step process.

2. Metals are usually removed from _____ ores.

3. In the process of _____, a sulfide or carbonate is made into an oxide.

4. Both roasting and reduction require energy in the form of _____.

5. In the process of _____, oxygen is removed from the ore.

THINKING CRITICALLY

6. ANALYZE: Look at the chemical equations for removing magnesium from magnesite ($MgCO_3$). What is missing from each equation?

$$MgCO_3 + heat \rightarrow \underline{\hspace{2cm}} + CO_2$$

$$2 \underline{\hspace{2cm}} + electricity \rightarrow 2Mg + O_2$$

7. SEQUENCE: The following two equations show the two steps involved in removing zinc from the ore sphalerite. Which equation shows Step 1? Which equation shows Step 2?

$$2ZnO + C \rightarrow 2Zn + CO_2$$

$$2ZnS + 3O_2 \rightarrow 2ZnO + 2SO_2$$

8. ANALYZE: In exercise 7, how many molecules of sphalerite were used in Step 1? How many molecules of zinc were produced in Step 2?

BUILDING SCIENCE SKILLS

Balancing Equations Write balanced equations for the following reduction reactions.

$$C + CuO \rightarrow Cu + CO_2$$

$$C + PbO \rightarrow Pb + CO_2$$

$$C + ZnO \rightarrow Zn + CO_2$$

▲ **Figure 10-5** Open-pit iron mines near Lake Superior

Integrating Environmental Science

TOPICS: mining, the environment

METALLURGY

Metallurgy (MEHT-uhl-uhr-jee) is the science and art of separating metals from their ores. Metallurgy began in about 4000 B.C. in the Middle East. Copper was the first metal to be used. The remains of copper mines have been found throughout parts of the Middle East. Over the centuries, ores containing tin, iron, silver, and gold were successfully mined and the metals separated from their ores.

Ores must be removed from Earth by mining before the metals can be obtained. For example, at one time an important source of the iron ore called hematite was in Minnesota. This mine was near Lake Superior. Open-pit mining was the process used. It has damaged the environment.

A two-step process is used to separate a metal from its ore. First, the ore is broken up and crushed. The smaller particles are then separated either by hand or by using machines. Next, the metal is removed from the remaining bits of ore. This process can involve roasting and reduction, or simply heating the ore in a furnace. The metal that results from the second step is almost, but not quite, pure. Further refining of the metal is necessary to obtain a completely pure metal. Once the needed purity is reached, the metal can be worked. This means the metal can be used for the purpose intended.

Thinking Critically How might mining damage the environment?

INVESTIGATE

Comparing Alloys
HANDS-ON ACTIVITY

1. Take an empty soda can and an empty vegetable can.

2. Find the mass of each can.

3. With a magnet, try to pick up each type of can.

4. Placing the cans on the floor, attempt to crush each one.

5. Record your results.

THINK ABOUT IT: What differences did you notice between the two cans? Explain why these differences occur.

STEP 2

Objective
Identify some alloys and their uses.

Key Term
alloy: material made of a mixture of two or more metals

Pure Metals Through roasting and reduction, a metal can be separated from its ore. Pure metals have certain properties.

- They are solids at room temperature (21°C). The only exception is mercury, which is a liquid.

- They are malleable. They can be hammered into different shapes.

- They are ductile. They can be made into wires.

- Most are good conductors of both heat and electricity.

▶ **LIST:** What are the properties of pure metals?

Alloys Two pure metals or more can be mixed to form a material called an **alloy**. The properties of an alloy differ from the properties of the original metals. They may form a solid solution or they may just be a mixture of the metals. For example, brass is an alloy of copper and zinc. Brass is harder than either copper or zinc. Brass is used in water pipes because it lasts longer than either copper or zinc. Many things you use are made of an alloy instead of pure metal. This is because most alloys are

stronger than pure metals. Figure 10-6 shows some alloys, the metals that make them up, and some uses for the different alloys.

ALLOYS		
Alloy	**Elements**	**Uses**
Steel	Iron, chromium, nickel, carbon	Bridges, buildings, tools
Brass	Copper, zinc	Plumbing
Bronze	Copper, tin	Machine parts
Pewter	Tin, copper, antimony	Dishes, cups
Sterling silver	Silver, copper	Jewelry
Alnico	Iron, aluminum, nickel, cobalt	Magnets
Nichrome	Nickel, iron, chromium, manganese	Electrical wires

▲ **Figure 10-6**

▶ **DEFINE:** What is an alloy?

Alloys of Steel Steel is one of the most useful alloys ever developed. Iron is the main element used to make steel. By combining iron with different amounts of chromium, nickel, and carbon, different alloys of steel can be made. One alloy of steel used today is called low-alloy steel. Low-alloy steel contains small amounts of nickel, chromium, molybdenum, tungsten, titanium, niobium, and vanadium. Low-alloy steel is very strong and sturdy. It is used to make machine parts and the metal supports on bridges and buildings. Stainless steel is a type of low-alloy steel.

▲ **Figure 10-7** A turbofan engine on a KC-135 Strato tanker contains high-alloy steel.

Another alloy of steel is called high-alloy steel. High-alloy steel contains larger amounts of nickel, chromium, and the other metals found in low-alloy steel. High-alloy steel is very shiny. It is used to make cooking utensils, cutting tools, and jet-engine parts.

3 ▶ **IDENTIFY:** What is the main element in any steel alloy?

Ancient to Modern Uses of Bronze The Bronze Age was a period in history that existed for nearly 2,000 years. More than 4,000 years ago, people discovered that combining copper with tin produced a very strong alloy called bronze. Pots, bowls, weapons, and other utensils were made from bronze. With the discovery of iron, the Bronze Age ended.

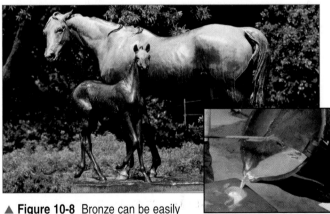

▲ **Figure 10-8** Bronze can be easily cast into many useful and beautiful objects, including sculptures.

Today, bronze is still used, although it is more expensive than brass. It can often be found in plumbing fixtures. Bronze is also used when there will be exposure to salt water, because it does not react with the minerals in salt water.

4 ▶ **EXPLAIN:** What makes bronze such a useful alloy?

✔ CHECKING CONCEPTS

1. _____ is an alloy of iron, carbon, and other elements such as nickel or chromium.

2. Most metals are _____ at room temperature.

3. Pewter is a combination of tin, _____, and antimony.

4. _____ is harder than the metals that are used to make it.

5. All _____ are malleable.

6. _____ is the only metal that is liquid at room temperature (21°C).

7. Pure metals _____ good conductors of heat and electricity.

8. Because metals are _____, they can be made into wires.

9. _____ is made of silver and copper.

💡 THINKING CRITICALLY

10. **INFER:** Electrical wires are usually made of copper. Why is a pure metal better than an alloy for electrical wires?

11. **ANALYZE:** Why do you think there are different types of alloys of steel?

Web InfoSearch

Amalgam An alloy of mercury is called an amalgam (uh-MAL-guhm). One of the most used amalgams is made up of mercury, silver, tin, copper, and zinc. This amalgam is sometimes used by dentists for filling teeth. The advantage of this alloy is that it will fill a cavity completely. It becomes rigid and can withstand the temperature changes in the mouth from hot and cold foods.

SEARCH: Use the Internet to find out more about amalgam. Start your search at www. conceptsandchallenges.com. Some key search words are **amalgam**, **amalgam mercury**, and **amalgam harmful**.

THE Big IDEA

What is the importance of alloys in bike design?

Bikes are great machines. They are fun, durable, and pollution-free. They are better at turning energy from our muscles into motion than any other machine. The first step in building a great bicycle is determining its purpose. Bikes for different purposes are designed differently and built with different alloys.

The main part of a bike is the frame. It should be strong, lightweight, and a bit flexible. The metal frame comes from ores that have been mined, refined, and formed into tubes. Frame tubes are formed by rolling narrow sheets of metal into tubes and then joining the seam, or by drilling out a solid rod to form a seamless hollow tube.

The rest of the bike is made of components such as a seat, pedals, wheels, brakes, a drive train, and shocks. The components are what make the bike go. They are attached to the frame.

Steel, an alloy of iron and carbon, is strong, durable, and easy to weld. Steel alloys can be made containing chromium, vanadium, molybdenum, manganese, nickel, and titanium. Adding chromium, for example, helps steel resist corrosion. Chromium molybdenum steel (called chro-moly) is popular for bikes. It is twice as strong as carbon steel.

Aluminum comes from bauxite ore. It is strong and light and much stiffer than steel. To improve its performance, aluminum is alloyed with copper, silicon, zinc, and sometimes scandium.

Some people consider titanium excellent for building bikes. It is used for racing bikes, where every ounce counts. The latest in bike design, though, is an alloy made with zirconium. Bikes made with this are 15 percent stronger than steel and 15 percent lighter than titanium.

Look at the photo and text that appear on these two pages. Then, follow the directions in the Science Log to find out more about "the big idea."✦

Wheels

In bike racing, any rotating mass need to save weight. Weight is focused in the hub, so the wheel rims are made from aluminum. This makes them lightweight and stiff. The spokes contain combinations of aluminum, steel, or even titanium to keep them stiff and lightweight.

▲ **Figure 10-9** Professional racing mountain bikes like this one need to be strong, stiff, and light. The combination of components and frame is important in making the entire racing bike.

Frame

Titanium, also called Ti, is popular in bike building. It is 45 percent lighter than steel and stronger than aluminum. Do not park this bike on the street! A custom-made titanium bike frame might cost $1,500–$6,000, or more!

Shocks

Some shocks are made of magnesium alloys that are even lighter than titanium. Shocks need to be strong and light.

Drivetrain

The drivetrain contains many parts, including the pedals and crank, front chain ring, derailleur, chain, cassette, and pulleys. Wherever the chain touches other metal parts, these parts need to be very durable. They might contain a steel alloy hardened with nickel.

WRITING ACTIVITY

Science Log

Design a bike. Draw a picture of a unique bicycle. Describe what it will be used for and the special features that help the bike do its job. Describe the alloys you will choose for the frame and the components. To help you research your bike, visit www.conceptsandchallenges.com.

10-4 Why are some metals more active than others?

Objective

List the most active metals in the periodic table.

Key Terms

alkali metals: metals in Group 1 of the periodic table

alkaline earth metals: metals in Group 2 of the periodic table

Group 1 Metals Some metals are chemically active. These metals readily combine with certain nonmetals. One group of very active metals is called the **alkali metals**. The alkali metals include lithium, sodium, potassium, rubidium, cesium, and francium. The most common alkali metals are lithium, sodium, and potassium.

Found in Group 1 of the periodic table, atoms of these metals have one electron in their outermost energy level. Each alkali metal has one valence electron. Figure 10-10 shows the Group 1 metals as they appear in the periodic table. The alkali metals are so chemically active that they are always found combined with other elements. These metals are not found as pure metals in nature. The structure of each Group 1 metal is similar to the others.

 IDENTIFY: What are the six Group 1 metals?

Group 2 Metals The metals next to the alkali metals in the periodic table are the **alkaline earth metals.** These metals include beryllium, magnesium, calcium, strontium, barium, and radium. Found in Group 2 of the periodic table, atoms of these metals have two electrons in their outer shell. Figure 10-10 shows the Group 2 metals as they appear in the periodic table. These metals are also chemically active. They readily combine with other elements. Although less active than the Group 1 metals, the extra valence electron makes the Group 2 metals harder and stronger than the Group 1 metals. The most active Group 2 metals are beryllium, magnesium, and barium.

 IDENTIFY: What are the six Group 2 metals?

Group 1	Group 2
3 **Li** Lithium 6.941	4 **Be** Beryllium 9.012 182
11 **Na** Sodium 22.989 768	12 **Mg** Magnesium 24.3050
19 **K** Potassium 39.0983	20 **Ca** Calcium 40.078
37 **Rb** Rubidium 85.4678	38 **Sr** Strontium 87.62
55 **Cs** Cesium 132.905.43	56 **Ba** Barium 137.327
87 **Fr** Francium (223.0197)	88 **Ra** Radium (226.0254)

◄ **Figure 10-10** Group 1 and 2 metals

Electromotive Series

Some metals are more active than others. In a chemical reaction, some metals will replace other metals in a compound. For example, when iron is placed in a copper sulfate solution, the iron will replace the copper to form iron sulfate.

Figure 10-11 shows the electromotive series of metals. The most active metals are at the top of the table. The least active metals are at the bottom of the table. A metal will replace those metals below it on the list. For example, lithium will replace sodium, but sodium will not replace calcium.

 ANALYZE: Which metals will replace magnesium in a chemical reaction?

ELECTROMOTIVE SERIES OF METALS
Most active
Lithium (Li)
Potassium (K)
Barium (Ba)
Calcium (Ca)
Sodium (Na)
Magnesium (Mg)
Aluminum (Al)
Zinc (Zn)
Iron (Fe)
Tin (Se)
Lead (Pb)
Copper (Cu)
Silver (Ag)
Platinum (Pt)
Gold (Au)
Least active

▲ **Figure 10-11**

1. Another name for the Group 1 metals is the _____ metals.

2. Another name for the Group 2 metals is the _____ metals.

3. In the electromotive series, a metal can be replaced by a metal _____ it on the list.

4. The alkali metals are found in _____ of the periodic table.

5. The alkaline earth metals are found in _____ of the periodic table.

6. The most active metal in the electromotive series is _____.

7. The least active metal in the electromotive series is _____.

8. **EXPLAIN:** Look at the following chemical equation.

$$Fe + CuSO_4 \rightarrow Cu + FeSO_4$$

Why was iron able to replace copper in copper sulfate? Is the copper oxidized or reduced?

9. **INFER:** Why is gold usually found as a pure metal in nature, unlike most of the other metals?

DESIGNING AN EXPERIMENT

Design an experiment to solve the following problem. Include a hypothesis, variables, a procedure, and a type of data to study.

PROBLEM: How can you compare the chemical activity of two metals or more?

People in Science

WELDER

Welding is a process used to join two pieces of metal. The process usually involves heating a metal and hammering it into shape. Several layers of metals can be heated and hammered together. This process is known as forge welding. A forge is a furnace in which the metal is heated for welding.

Today, most welders use a technique known as arc welding. In arc welding, heat from an electric current is used to weld together two pieces of metal. Another type of welding uses lasers. The intense light from a laser heats and melts the metals, welding them together. High-frequency, or ultrasonic, sounds can also be used in welding. The vibrations from the sound waves are transferred to the metals where they are changed to heat energy. The heat is used to weld the metals.

▲ **Figure 10-12** Welders use a heat source to join two metals together.

Welders need to take many safety precautions. The woman in Figure 10-12 is looking through a special mask to protect her eyes from the bright light. Special equipment is also needed to protect the welders from the intense heat produced. Welders may work for automobile manufacturers, for construction companies, or in other industries.

Thinking Critically What are four different types of welding? How do they differ from one another?

10-5 What is corrosion?

Objective

Explain what causes corrosion.

Key Term

corrosion: chemical change in a metal

Corrosion Metals are chemically active. One result of this chemical activity is corrosion. **Corrosion** is a chemical change on the surface of metals. It results from the reaction of metals with chemicals in the environment. When a metal becomes corroded, its properties change. The metal changes color and loses its shine.

▶ **1** DESCRIBE: What happens when a metal becomes corroded?

Types of Corrosion The most common example of corrosion is rust. Iron that is exposed to air and moisture will become rusted. The rusted iron has a reddish brown color and no shine. Rust, or iron oxide, is much weaker than iron. Tarnish is another example of corrosion. A tarnished metal loses its shine and has a dull color. For example, tarnished silver looks dark and dull because of a coating of silver sulfide.

▲ **Figure 10-13** Iron rusts when exposed to air and moisture.

Corrosion forms layers on the surface of a metal. When you polish silver, you remove the layers of tarnish. Once the corrosion is removed, the surface of the metal is exposed again with its usual color and shine.

▶ **2** IDENTIFY: Name two types of corrosion.

Cause of Corrosion Corrosion is often caused by oxidation. Remember that oxidation is a loss of electrons. Rust forms when iron combines with oxygen in the air to form iron oxide. The chemical equation for this is as follows.

$$4Fe + 3O_2 \rightarrow 2Fe_2O_3$$

An atom of iron has three valence electrons to "give away." An oxygen atom needs to gain two electrons. In this reaction, the four atoms of iron will lose 12 electrons. The six atoms of oxygen will gain the 12 electrons. Water also helps facilitate this process.

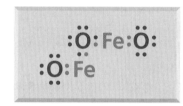

◀ **Figure 10-14** An electron dot diagram of one molecule of iron oxide

▶ **3** DESCRIBE: What happens to a metal during oxidation?

Preventing Corrosion Corrosion may wear away and weaken metals. Therefore, it is important to prevent metals from corroding. There are several ways to prevent corrosion.

▲ **Figure 10-15** Coating metals with paint helps prevent corrosion.

Painting is an effective way to prevent rust. A layer of paint over a piece of iron will keep air and moisture away from the surface of the metal. Coating the surface of a metal with oil also protects the metal from corrosion.

Using alloys is a way of avoiding rust. For example, stainless steel is an alloy of iron. Unlike iron, stainless steel will not rust. Even though an alloy is usually more expensive than the pure metal, it is often less expensive in the long run to use the alloy.

 LIST: What are three ways to prevent corrosion in metals?

CHECKING CONCEPTS

1. What is corrosion?
2. What is the chemical formula for rust?
3. What causes corrosion?
4. Why is it important to prevent metals from corroding?
5. How does painting a metal prevent corrosion?
6. What happens when iron combines with oxygen in the air?

THINKING CRITICALLY

7. **PREDICT:** Can corrosion take place if a metal is kept in a vacuum? Why or why not?
8. **INFER:** Why do ships always have more rust along their bottoms than on any other part of the ship?

HEALTH AND SAFETY TIP

Corrosion wears away metal, and it can also be harmful to people. Rust tends to chip and peel, and can leave sharp, jagged edges that can harbor germs and that cause serious injury. If you accidentally cut yourself with a rusted object, you should see a doctor right away. Use first aid books or other reference materials to find out why cuts from rusty objects are dangerous. Find out what treatment you must receive to prevent further problems. Show on a poster what you learned.

 Hands-On Activity

OBSERVING THE TARNISHING OF SILVER

You will need a silver spoon and a hard-boiled egg.

1. Peel the hard-boiled egg and remove the yolk.
2. Place the silver spoon into the egg yolk. Leave it in the yolk for 10 to 20 minutes.
3. Remove the spoon from the yolk. Observe the appearance of the spoon.

Practicing Your Skills

4. **OBSERVE:** What did the spoon look like when you removed it from the egg yolk?
5. **INFER:** Egg yolk contains sulfur. What do you think happened when you placed the silver spoon into the egg yolk?
6. **PREDICT:** How could you remove tarnish from the silver spoon?

▲ **STEP 2** Place the spoon in the yolk for 10 to 20 minutes.

LAB ACTIVITY
Testing Activity and Corrosion of Metals

Materials
Safety goggles,
lab apron, gloves,
3 plastic cups,
100-mL graduated cylinder,
forceps,
plastic wrap,
paper towels,
wax pencil,
water, salt,
white vinegar,
3 ungalvanized nails,
3 galvanized nails,
3 metal paper clips,
3 plastic-coated paper clips,
3 pennies,
3 quarters

▲ STEP 4 Organize the metals to be tested.

▲ STEP 6 Carefully place the samples in each cup.

BACKGROUND

We use many types of metals in our daily lives. Metals are used in things such as cars, bicycles, cans for food, and coins. Since metals are reactive, one problem is corrosion. People need to understand how to prevent metals from becoming corroded.

PURPOSE

In this activity, you will observe and compare the rates of corrosion of various samples of metals in different liquids.

PROCEDURE

1. Copy the chart in Figure 10-16.

2. Put on your safety goggles, lab apron, and gloves. Using a wax pencil or labeling marker, label three plastic cups *Water*, *Vinegar,* and *Salt water*. Also, write your initials on each cup.

3. Using a graduated cylinder, pour 100 mL of water into the cup labeled *Water*. Measure 100 mL of vinegar into the next cup. Measure 100 mL of salt water into the last cup.

4. Place these items on a paper towel: three ungalvanized nails, three galvanized nails, three metal paper clips, three plastic-coated paper clips, three pennies, and three quarters.

5. Use a paper towel to wipe off the nails, paper clips, and coins. Record the appearance—shine and color—of the samples in the section of the chart area labeled *Before*.

6. Using forceps, place one of each item into the liquids in the plastic cups. Cover each cup with a piece of plastic wrap. Place the cups in a separate area of the classroom. Let them stand undisturbed for four to five days.

7. After four to five days, bring the cups back to your work area. Lay down a few paper towels and label them *Water*, *Salt Water*, and *Vinegar*. Use the forceps to carefully remove the samples from the cups. Place the samples on the corresponding labeled sheets of paper towel.

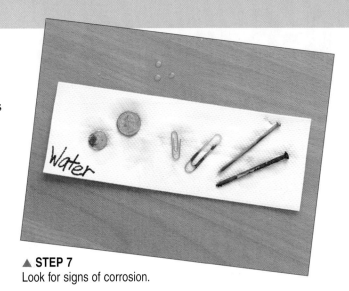

▲ **STEP 7**
Look for signs of corrosion.

8. Observe the items carefully for any signs of metal corrosion. This can include loss of shine, change in color, and rusting. Record your observations in the section of the chart labeled *After*.

Testing Activity and Corrosion of Metals

Samples	Before	After Water	After Salt Water	After Vinegar
Ungalvanized nail				
Galvanized nail				
Metal paper clip				
Plastic-coated paper clip				
Penny				
Quarter				

▲ **Figure 10-16** Copy this chart and use it to record your observations.

CONCLUSIONS

1. **OBSERVE:** According to your observation, which objects changed most? Which objects changed least?

2. **OBSERVE:** Which solution caused the most corrosion?

3. **INFER:** Why did the galvanized nail and plastic-coated paper clip not change much?

4. **INFER:** According to your observations, which metallic sample is the most active and why?

5. **ANALYZE:** A builder uses galvanized nails to build a wooden deck. With what you know about the activity and corrosion of metals, explain why galvanized nails are a better choice than ungalvanized nails.

10-6 How are metals plated?

Objective
Explain how metals are plated.

Key Terms
plating: coating one metal with another metal
electroplating (ee-LEHK-troh-playt-ing): use of an electric current to plate one metal with another metal

Protecting Metals

▲ Figure 10-17
Galvanized bolts

One way to protect metals from corrosion is through the process of **plating**. In this process, a metal is coated with another metal. For example, a plating of zinc on the surface of iron will prevent the iron from rusting. Iron coated with zinc is called galvanized (GAL-vuh-nyzed) iron. When the zinc corrodes, it forms zinc oxide. The layer of zinc oxide prevents any further corrosion. Garbage cans, nails, and snow shovels often are made of galvanized iron.

Aluminum is "self-plating." When aluminum is exposed to air, a thin coating of aluminum oxide forms on the surface of the metal. This compound forms a protective coating for the aluminum beneath and keeps it from corroding further. The aluminum oxide gives the metal a dull appearance.

▶ **DEFINE:** What is the process of plating?

Electrolysis

Electrolysis is a process used to separate a compound into the elements it contains. It requires a chemical change in which atoms of an element are separated from other atoms in the compound. The process is used to remove pure metals from its ore or to plate a surface with a metal.

Figure 10-18 shows a setup for electrolysis. Two carbon rods are placed into a solution of copper sulfate. The copper sulfate is the electrolyte. The carbon rods are attached to the terminals of a battery. The carbon rod attached to the positive terminal becomes the positive electrode. The rod attached to the negative terminal becomes the negative electrode.

Positively charged copper ions move to the negative electrode. At the negative electrode, each ion gains two electrons and becomes a copper atom.

$$Cu^{2+} + 2 \text{ electrons} \rightarrow Cu$$

The pure copper is seen plated onto the carbon rod.

▶ **ANALYZE:** What ion moves to the negative electrode in the electrolysis of copper nitrate?

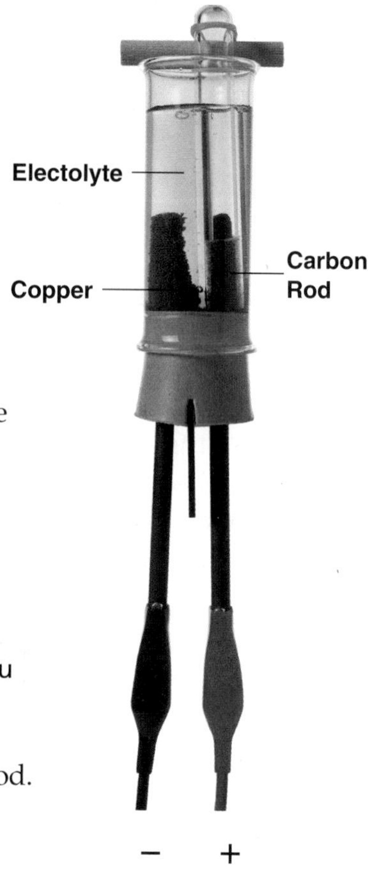

Electolyte —

Copper — | — Carbon Rod

−   +

▲ **Figure 10-18** In this setup, electrolysis is used to plate copper onto the negative carbon electrode.

Electroplating

Electricity is often used to plate metals onto other surfaces. This process is called **electroplating**. Nickel, silver, copper, and zinc can be used in electroplating. Brass is an alloy of copper and zinc. Copper and zinc can be used to electroplate a metal surface with brass.

▼ **Figure 10-19** Electroplating with brass

To plate an object with brass, the object is placed in a solution of copper and zinc, as shown in Figure 10-19. The copper and zinc in this solution are positively charged. When the current flows, these positive ions are attracted to the negative electrode, or the object to be plated.

 HYPOTHESIZE: Why are ions of metals attracted to negative electrodes?

✔ CHECKING CONCEPTS

1. Iron that has a coating of zinc is called _____ iron.

2. A layer of zinc will prevent iron from _____.

3. When a protective layer of zinc corrodes, it forms _____.

4. Plating a metal by using an electric current is _____.

5. When electroplating with copper, the copper ions will be attracted to the _____ electrode.

THINKING CRITICALLY

6. **PREDICT:** A solution of zinc sulfate ($ZnSO_4$) is used as an electrolyte for electroplating. Which electrode will the zinc ions, Zn^{2+}, be attracted to?

7. **HYPOTHESIZE:** Galvanized iron is used to make garbage cans and snow shovels. What is the advantage of using galvanized iron for these objects?

8. **ANALYZE:** Suppose you want to electroplate an object with silver. To which electrode would you attach the object? Explain. Is the silver being oxidized or reduced?

DESIGNING AN EXPERIMENT

Design an experiment to solve the following problem. Include a hypothesis, variables, a procedure, and type of data to collect and study.

PROBLEM: How can you determine if an object is silver-plated or is made of pure silver?

 Hands-On Activity

PROTECTING METALS FROM CORROSION

You will need three ungalvanized nails, three cups of water, vinegar, clear nail polish, and oil or petroleum jelly.

1. Cover one ungalvanized nail with clear nail polish. Let the nail polish dry completely.

2. Coat a second nail with oil or petroleum jelly.

3. Do not put anything on the third nail.

4. Label each cup. Put each nail into a beaker of water. Add a little vinegar to the water to speed up the rusting process.

5. Remove the nails from the water and vinegar after several days. Record your observations.

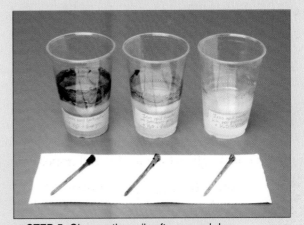
▲ **STEP 5** Observe the nails after several days.

Practicing Your Skills

6. **OBSERVE:** Which nail shows signs of rust?

7. **ANALYZE:** How do the nail polish and oil or petroleum jelly affect the corrosion of the ungalvanized nails?

8. **INFER:** Can you think of other substances that would keep the nails from rusting? What are they?

Chapter 10 Challenges

Chapter Summary

Lesson 10-1
- Metals are usually found combined with other elements.
- An **ore** is a rock or mineral from which a useful metal can be removed.
- Three types of ores are oxides, sulfides, and carbonates.

Lesson 10-2
- Metals are removed from their ores through chemical processes.
- For oxides, the metal is removed through the process of **reduction**.
- For sulfides and carbonates, the metal is removed by first **roasting** and then reducing the ore.

Lesson 10-3
- The metals removed from ores are pure metals.
- An **alloy** is a mixture of two pure metals or more.
- Alloys have different properties from the metals that make them up.

Lesson 10-4
- The Group 1 metals, or **alkali metals**, are chemically active. They include lithium, sodium, potassium, rubidium, cesium, and francium. The alkali metals have one valence electron.
- The Group 2 metals, or **alkaline earth metals**, are also chemically active. They include beryllium, magnesium, calcium, strontium, barium, and radium. The alkaline earth metals have two valence electrons.
- Some metals can replace others in a chemical reaction.

Lesson 10-5
- **Corrosion** is a chemical change on the surface of metals.
- Two examples of corrosion are rust and tarnish.
- Corrosion is usually caused by oxidation.
- Two ways to prevent corrosion are sealing a surface with paint or oil and by using alloys.

Lesson 10-6
- In **plating**, a protective layer of one metal is placed over another metal.
- A type of plating called **electroplating** uses an electric current.

Key Term Challenges

alkali metals (p. 218)
alkaline earth metals (p. 218)
alloy (p. 214)
corrosion (p. 220)
electroplating (p. 224)
ore (p. 210)
plating (p. 224)
reduction (p. 212)
roasting (p. 212)

MATCHING Write the Key Term from above that best matches each description.

1. rock or mineral from which a useful metal can be removed
2. coating of one metal on another metal
3. heating an ore in air
4. Group 1 metals
5. Group 2 metals
6. substance made up of two metals or more
7. process that changes the surface of metals
8. electrically coating one metal with another metal
9. removing oxygen from an ore

FILL IN Write the Key Term from above that best completes each statement.

10. Steel is an _____ of iron, carbon, and other elements, such as chromium or nickel.
11. In _____, a copper rod is sometimes used as an electrode.
12. Sodium is an _____.
13. Another name for the Group 2 metals is _____.
14. Sulfides and carbonates are converted to oxides by the process of _____.
15. One of the best examples of _____ is rust.
16. A layer of zinc placed over iron is an example of _____.
17. Litharge is an _____ of lead.
18. The process of _____ is used to separate a metal from an oxide ore.

226

Content Challenges TEST PREP

MULTIPLE CHOICE Write the letter of the term or phrase that best completes each statement.

1. Corroded metals are
   a. smooth and shiny.
   b. dull and discolored.
   c. silvery.
   d. reddish brown.

2. Most metals are not found in their pure form in nature because they are
   a. chemically active.
   b. rusted.
   c. tarnished.
   d. corroded.

3. The ores from which we usually remove metals are
   a. sulfides.
   b. carbonates.
   c. oxides.
   d. alloys.

4. Brass is an alloy of
   a. copper and tin.
   b. iron and gold.
   c. copper and zinc.
   d. copper and chromium.

5. Corrosion should be prevented because corrosion
   a. causes surfaces to react.
   b. discolors metal.
   c. makes the metal shiny.
   d. plates metal.

6. All of the following are ways to reduce corrosion except
   a. painting.
   b. electroplating.
   c. exposing to air.
   d. using alloys.

7. Silver is more active than
   a. lithium.
   b. copper.
   c. calcium.
   d. gold.

8. The ore from which aluminum is removed is
   a. cuprite.
   b. bauxite.
   c. galena.
   d. hematite.

9. Each of the following is a property of pure metals except being
   a. ductile.
   b. malleable.
   c. solid.
   d. a poor conductor of heat.

10. The two steps in removing a metal from a sulfide ore are
    a. roasting followed by reduction.
    b. reduction followed by roasting.
    c. reduction followed by oxidation.
    d. oxidation followed by roasting.

TRUE/FALSE Write *true* if the statement is true. If the statement is false, change the underlined term to make the statement true.

11. An ore is a combination of a <u>metal</u> and another element.

12. <u>Lead</u> can be removed from bauxite.

13. When iron rusts, it forms <u>iron oxide</u>.

14. Electroplating is one way to prevent <u>corrosion</u>.

15. When a metal is oxidized, it <u>gains</u> electrons.

16. Two examples of corrosion are rust and <u>tarnish</u>.

17. Bronze is a combination of copper and <u>iron</u>.

18. To remove a metal from a <u>sulfide</u> ore, the ore must first be roasted.

Concept Challenges TEST PREP

WRITTEN RESPONSE Answer each of the following questions in complete sentences.

1. **EXPLAIN:** What part of a metal's atomic structure makes it a good conductor of electricity?

2. **HYPOTHESIZE:** Some periods of human history are known by the metals that were used during that time. The Bronze Age was about 6,000 years ago. The Iron Age was about 3,000 years ago. What does this tell you about the technology needed to produce bronze and iron?

3. **INFER:** The Statue of Liberty in New York Harbor is made of copper. Why do you think the statue has a green color? (Hint: You may have seen a similar green coating on old copper pennies.)

4. **EXPLAIN:** Lithium is the most active metal in the electromotive series of metals. It is an alkali metal. Why is lithium so active?

INTERPRETING A DIAGRAM Use Figure 10-20 to answer each of the following questions.

5. What process does the figure show?

6. What is the positive electrode made of?

7. What is the electrolyte?

8. What has happened at the negative electrode?

Copper sulfate solution

− +

◀ Figure 10-20

Chapter 11

Nonmetals, Metalloids, and Radioactive Elements

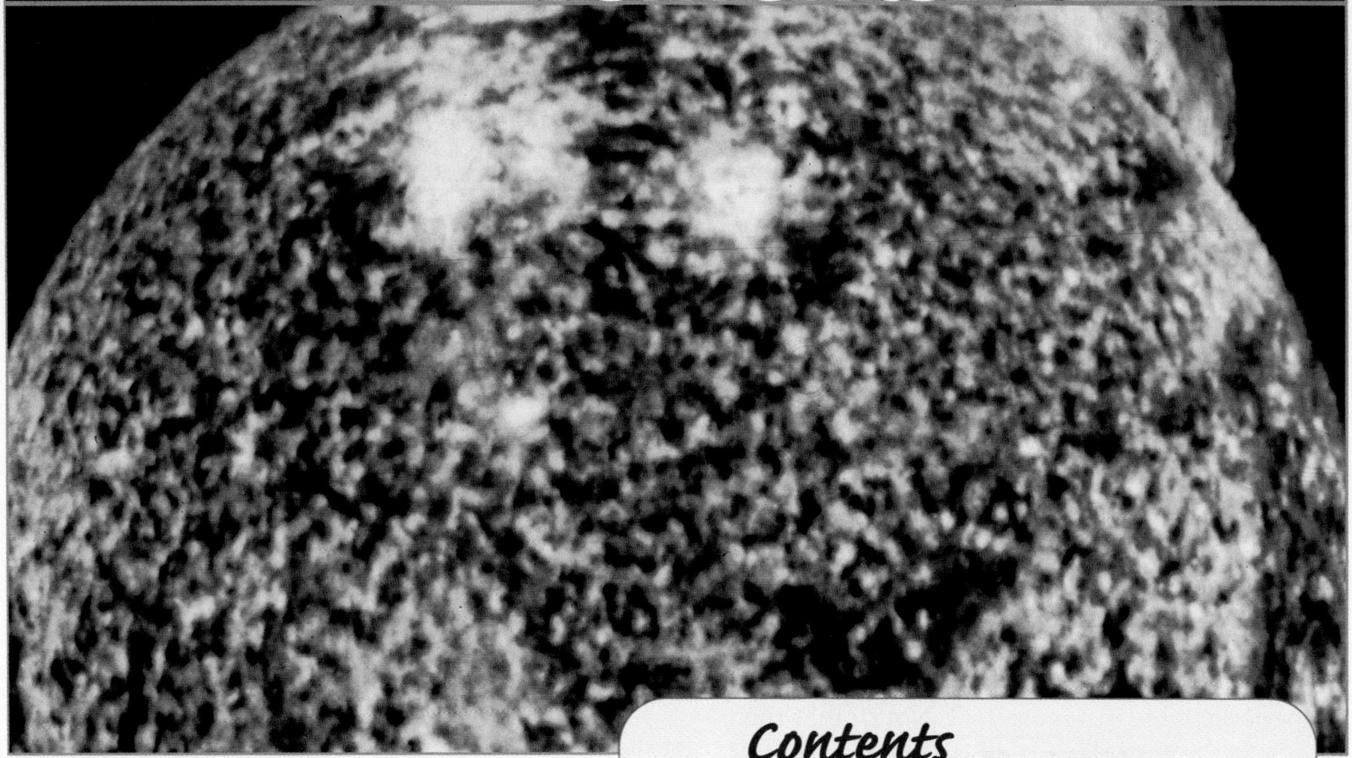

▲ **Figure 11-1** Scientists hope to someday reproduce the nuclear reactions of the Sun.

The Sun's energy is produced by nuclear fusion reactions that take place deep inside the Sun. A fusion reaction occurs when nuclei of lighter elements combine to form nuclei of heavier elements. Such reactions release great amounts of energy. Scientists are trying to produce fusion reactions that they can control. Hopefully, controlled fusion reactions will someday be used to meet many of our energy needs.

►Why is it important for scientists to find new sources of energy?

Contents

11-1 What elements are not metals?

STEP 1

INVESTIGATE

Identifying Metals and Nonmetals
HANDS-ON ACTIVITY

1. Look carefully at some of the different objects in your classroom.
2. Make a two-column chart in your notebook. Label one column "Metal" and the other column "Not a Metal."
3. Walk around the room and list as many objects as you can under the appropriate heading on your chart.
4. Read over your list. Compare the number of items you listed in each column.

THINK ABOUT IT: Which column has more items listed? Do you think there will always be more of one type of material than the other? Explain.

Objectives

Describe some of the properties of nonmetals. List the families of nonmetals and describe their features.

Key Terms

nonmetals: elements that have different properties from metals

luster: the way a material reflects light

Metals, Nonmetals, and Metalloids Look at the periodic table in Figure 11-2. Notice that there are three main classes of elements: metals, nonmetals, and metalloids. The heavy zigzag line separates elements that are metals from those that are not metals. Elements that are metals make up the largest class by far. Nonmetals are located at the right side of the table. In between the metals and the nonmetals is a small class of elements known as metalloids. These elements have some properties of metals and some properties of nonmetals.

 OBSERVE: How many groups of the periodic table have one or more elements that are nonmetals?

Properties of Nonmetals **Nonmetals** are elements that have different properties from metals. The way a material reflects light is called **luster**. Solid nonmetals have a dull luster and tend to be brittle, or easily broken. These properties are different from the properties of metals. Most metals are good conductors of heat and electricity. Nonmetals are generally poor conductors of heat and electricity.

Nonmetals exist in all three states of matter: solid, liquid, and gas. Only one nonmetal, bromine, is found in nature as a liquid. The rest are either solids or gases. Carbon, sulfur, and iodine are examples of solid nonmetals. Helium, oxygen, and radon are gaseous nonmetals.

 NAME: What are three properties of nonmetals?

Families of Nonmetals Look at the simplified Periodic Table of Elements in Figure 11-2. Notice that most nonmetals are found in Groups 14, 15, 16, 17, and 18. Although most of the nonmetals are contained in these five groups, each group is unique.

The nonmetals in a group have some properties similar to the other nonmetals in that group. The first three groups, or families, are named by the element in the top row of the group.

- **The Carbon Family** Group 14 is called the carbon family. In fact, carbon is the only nonmetal in the group. Carbon is a very important element found in all living things and in many nonliving things.

- **The Nitrogen Family** Group 15 is called the nitrogen family. Nitrogen and phosphorus are

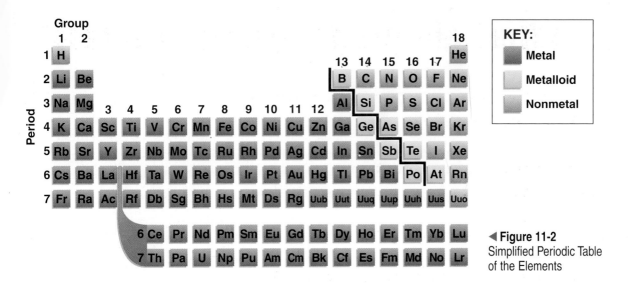

Group

	1	2											13	14	15	16	17	18

KEY:
- Metal
- Metalloid
- Nonmetal

◀ **Figure 11-2**
Simplified Periodic Table of the Elements

the two nonmetals in this family. Nitrogen gas makes up most of Earth's atmosphere and is an important nutrient in soil. Phosphorus is used to make fertilizers, pesticides, matches, and fireworks.

- **The Oxygen Family** Group 16 is called the oxygen family. Oxygen, sulfur, and selenium are the three nonmetals in this family. Oxygen is an important part of our atmosphere. We must breathe in oxygen to survive. Oxygen also makes up ozone, a protective layer of gas in the upper atmosphere. Sulfur is used to make batteries, fertilizers, tires, and some medicines. Selenium is used in photographic equipment and photocopy machines.

- **The Halogen Family** Group 17 is called the halogens. The halogens are chemically very active. They combine with other elements to make very useful compounds. There are four nonmetals in this family: fluorine, chlorine, bromine, and iodine. Fluorine occurs in many minerals and is added to toothpaste. It is also found in most of the coolants used in air conditioners and refrigerators. Chlorine is found in many salts, including table salt. It is also used to purify drinking water. Bromine is used in dyes. Iodine is found in products used to prevent infections.

- **The Noble Gases** Group 18 is called the noble gases. Unlike the elements of the halogen family, the noble gases are chemically inactive. They do not easily take part in chemical reactions. All six elements in this family are nonmetals. These elements are helium, neon,

argon, krypton, xenon, and radon. Helium is used to inflate balloons. Neon, argon, krypton, and xenon are all used for lighting. Radon is used for radiotherapy and radiography.

▶ **3** LIST: Name the five families of nonmetals.

☑ CHECKING CONCEPTS

1. There are fewer _____ than metals in the periodic table.
2. Nonmetals exist in all three states of _____.
3. Nonmetals have few of the properties of _____.
4. Elements in Group 17 are called _____.
5. Group 18 is called the _____.

💡 THINKING CRITICALLY

6. **CONTRAST:** How do nonmetals differ from metals?
7. **INFER:** How might the properties of neon compare with those of argon? Explain.

INTERPRETING VISUALS

Use Figure 11-2 to answer the following questions.

8. **OBSERVE:** Which group includes two nonmetals, two metalloids, and one metal?
9. **OBSERVE:** Which group contains no metals or metalloids?
10. **INFER:** Which nonmetal probably has properties similar to the properties of nitrogen?

11-2   What are metalloids?

Objective
Describe the properties of metalloids.

Key Term
metalloid: element that has properties of both metals and nonmetals

Locating the Metalloids on the Periodic Table A zigzag line separates the metals from the nonmetals on the periodic table. The elements along this line are called metalloids. The section of the periodic table containing the metalloids is shown in Figure 11-3.

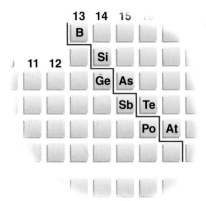

◀ **Figure 11-3**
Eight elements are metalloids.

1 CONTRAST: How do metals and nonmetals differ in their location on the periodic table?

Properties of Metalloids **Metalloids** are elements that have properties of both metals and nonmetals. You have learned that metals are usually hard, shiny, and good conductors of heat and electricity. Nonmetals are usually softer than metals, dull, and poor conductors of heat and electricity.

Because a metalloid may have properties of both metals and nonmetals, it may conduct heat and electricity better than a nonmetal but not as well as a metal. All metalloids on the periodic table are solids.

2 DESCRIBE: How would you describe the properties of metalloids?

Examples of Metalloids The eight metalloids are arranged along the zigzag line of the periodic table. Except for aluminum, each element that touches the zigzag line is a metalloid. Figure 11-4 lists the names and symbols of the eight metalloids.

METALLOIDS		
Element Name	Symbol	Atomic Number
Boron	B	5
Silicon	Si	14
Germanium	Ge	32
Arsenic	As	33
Antimony	Sb	51
Tellurium	Te	52
Polonium	Po	84
Astatine	At	85

▲ **Figure 11-4**

3 OBSERVE: What element located next to the zigzag line of the periodic table is not a metalloid?

Uses for Some Metalloids

- **Boron (B)** Boron is used to make insect poisons and to provide the bright green color in fireworks. Boron is also used in the production of boric acid. Many cleaning products contain compounds of boron.

- **Silicon (Si)** Silicon is the second most common element in Earth's crust after oxygen. It combines with oxygen to produce silicon dioxide, the main mineral in sand. Silicon has many uses. Perhaps its most familiar uses are in the production of glass and computer chips.

- **Germanium (Ge)** Germanium is very important in the production of transistors. It is also used in some alloys, in fluorescent lights, and in lenses and other optical equipment.

- **Arsenic (As)** Arsenic and its compounds are poisonous. The compounds are used in farming to fight insects. An arsenic compound is also used in lasers to convert electricity directly to light.

- **Antimony (Sb)** Oxides of antimony are used in the production of paints, glass, and pottery.

4 **DESCRIBE:** What makes silicon unusual among the metalloids?

✔ CHECKING CONCEPTS

1. The elements along the zigzag line on the periodic table are called _____.
2. There are _____ elements that are metalloids.
3. All metalloids are found in the _____ state of matter.
4. The only element along the zigzag line that is not a metalloid is _____.
5. The metalloid _____ is used in the production of glass and computer chips.

THINKING CRITICALLY

6. **INFER:** Which is a better conductor of electricity, germanium or copper? Explain.
7. **EXPLAIN:** Why is it possible for the metalloid silicon to conduct heat better than the nonmetal oxygen?
8. **ANALYZE:** What property of arsenic and arsenic compounds make these substances both useful and dangerous?

DESIGNING AN EXPERIMENT

Design an experiment to solve the problem below. Include a hypothesis, variables, a procedure, and a type of data to study.

PROBLEM: Which metalloid is the best conductor of electricity?

Science and Technology
COMPUTER CHIPS

The metalloid silicon is an important part of today's fastest computers. Silicon makes up the computer's microprocessor, also called a computer chip. The invention of the silicon chip helped make computers much faster, more powerful, and much more compact.

Silicon is a perfect choice for making computer chips because it is a semiconductor. A semiconductor is a material that conducts electricity only under certain conditions. Electronic devices such as computers need the flow of electricity to be controlled by semiconductors like silicon.

▲ **Figure 11-5** A silicon chip, which is smaller than your fingernail, can hold millions of circuits.

How are silicon chips made? Silicon comes from one of the most common substances on Earth—sand. Silicon compounds are mined and shipped to companies that specialize in converting the compounds into purified silicon. Eventually, the silicon is made into very thin pieces to be used for computer chips. Then, thousands of electrical devices are built onto the silicon chip.

Scientists keep trying to improve the silicon chip by putting even more electrical devices on the chip. By improving the chip, they hope to make computers even faster and more powerful. What will future computers be like? Although we will have to wait and see, we expect that silicon will continue to play a major part in chip production.

Thinking Critically How have faster computer chips changed the way we use computers?

Objectives

Locate radioactive elements on the periodic table and describe their properties.

Key Terms

radioactive element: unstable element whose nucleus breaks down

radiation: energy and particles released from the nucleus of a radioactive element

radioisotope: isotope that releases radiation

Radioactive Elements Some elements are unstable. These elements are unstable because the nuclei of their atoms break down, or decay. When the nuclei of these atoms break down, energy and particles are released. Elements with unstable nuclei are called **radioactive elements.**

▶ **1** EXPLAIN: What makes an element unstable?

Radiation When the nuclei of radioactive elements break down, the energy released is called **radiation.** The release of radiation is called radioactivity. You cannot see, smell, taste, touch, or hear radioactivity. There are small amounts of radiation all around you. There is even some radioactivity occurring within your body.

▶ **2** CLASSIFY: What is radiation?

Radioactive Isotopes The individual atoms of an element have the same atomic number. However, these atoms may have different atomic weights. Most elements are found in several forms, called isotopes. Isotopes are atoms of an element with the same number of protons but a different number of neutrons. Hydrogen is an example of an element with three isotopes. All three isotopes have a single proton but different numbers of neutrons. The three isotopes of hydrogen are hydrogen-1, hydrogen-2, and hydrogen-3. The numbers 1, 2, and 3 represent the mass numbers of the isotopes.

A number of elements have some isotopes that are stable and others that are unstable. The unstable isotopes release radiation. Such isotopes are called radioactive isotopes, or **radioisotopes.**

Consider the element carbon, for example. The nuclei of most carbon atoms contain six protons and six neutrons. This isotope, called carbon-12 (C-12), is stable. C-13 is also a stable isotope of carbon. However, some carbon isotopes contain six protons and eight neutrons. This isotope, called carbon-14, is unstable. It is radioactive. Carbon-14 isotopes are used to determine the age of certain rocks and fossils.

Many radioactive isotopes are important in our lives. Americium-241, an isotope of americium (Am), is used in smoke detectors and to measure lead amounts in paint. Californium-252 (Cf-252) is used by airlines in the detectors that check luggage

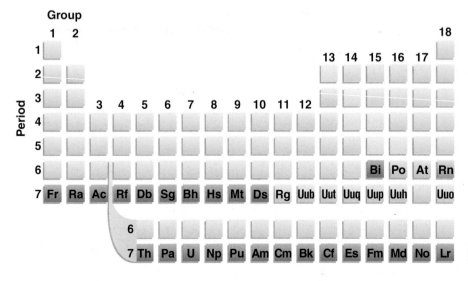

Go **O**nline
active art

For: Radioactive Tracers activity
Visit: PHSchool.com
Web Code: cgp-1044

◀ **Figure 11-6** The most common isotopes of these elements are naturally radioactive.

for hidden explosives. Cesium-137 (Cs-137) is used to treat cancer cells. Cobalt-60 (Co-60) is used to sterilize medical equipment used in surgery.

 DEFINE: What are radioisotopes?

Large Nuclei The larger the nucleus of an atom is, the more unstable it tends to be. In this case, the forces binding the protons and neutrons in the nuclei of these atoms become unbalanced. This causes the atom to split or give off energy. This is called nuclear decay. Large atomic nuclei tend to break down to produce radiation. During the process of decay, elements may change into different elements. When Uranium-238 decays, it changes into Thorium-234 and Helium-4. This is called alpha decay. There are several ways in which atoms decay.

 EXPLAIN: What happens when atomic nuclei decay?

✔ CHECKING CONCEPTS

1. What happens when the nuclei of radioactive elements break down, or decay?

2. What is a radioactive element?

3. Name four elements on the periodic table that are naturally radioactive.

4. How are radioisotopes different from stable isotopes?

THINKING CRITICALLY

5. **CONCLUDE:** What is released from a nucleus that breaks down?

6. **INFER:** What can you infer about the element radon, which has an atomic number of 86? Explain.

HEALTH AND SAFETY TIP

Exposure to radiation can be dangerous to living things. Find out what kind of protective clothing scientists, doctors, and other workers wear when dealing with radioactive elements. Find out what to do if you are exposed to some radioactive source.

 People in Science

RADIATION THERAPIST

Radiation therapy is an important method of cancer treatment. People who give radiation therapy to cancer patients are called radiation therapists. Radiation therapists work to help patients by reducing or eliminating cancer cells in their bodies. In some treatments, drugs containing radioactive elements are given to patients to destroy cancer cells. Another method of treatment is to radiate cancerous tumors. Radiation can often destroy the cancer cells.

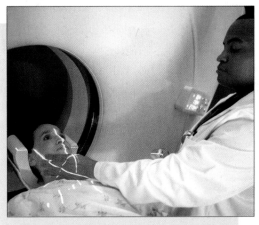
▲ **Figure 11-7** Radiation therapist at work

A radiation therapist has many different tasks. Radiation therapists work closely with oncologists, doctors who specialize in cancer treatment. Radiation therapists use computers to help them do their job. Computers help therapists find the best way to give the radiation treatment, to know how much radiation to give, and to decide how long the treatment will take.

Most radiation therapists work in hospitals. Others work in doctors' offices, clinics, and laboratories. To become a radiation therapist, a person must graduate from high school and complete a training program in radiation therapy. Most training programs last two years. Many hospitals, vocational or technical schools, and colleges and universities offer training programs.

Thinking Critically Why is a radiation therapist's job challenging?

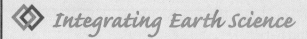
THE Big IDEA

How is half-life used to date fossils and rocks?

Scientists who specialize in the study of Earth's history often rely on radioactive isotopes to help them find out how old something is.

Radioactive isotopes do not stay radioactive forever. Over time, the nuclei of a radioactive element decay. When this happens, energy is released and a different element is formed. For example, when an atom of uranium-238 decays, it eventually forms an atom of lead-206, which is not radioactive.

Different radioactive elements decay at different rates. The half-life of an element is the time it takes for half the atoms in a sample of the element to decay. Scientists can use the half-life of certain radioactive isotopes to determine the ages of rocks, fossils, and other materials. This process is called radiometric dating.

Uranium-238 has a half-life of 4.5 billion years. That is the estimated age of Earth. Figure 11-8 below shows a simplified example of how the age of a very old rock containing uranium-238 can be found.

A different radioactive isotope, carbon-14, is used to calculate the age of things that were once living. All living things contain carbon-12, which is not radioactive. They also contain much smaller amounts of carbon-14, which is formed in the atmosphere. Carbon-14 has a half-life of 5,730 years. As soon as something dies, the carbon-14 atoms decay and are not replaced. These atoms change to atoms of nitrogen-14, which are released into the environment. Scientists can date fossils and artifacts by comparing the amount of carbon-14 to the total amount of carbon in them.

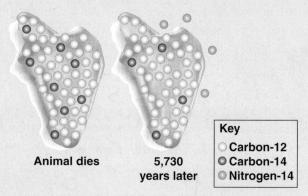

Animal dies   **5,730 years later**

Key
○ Carbon-12
● Carbon-14
◎ Nitrogen-14

▲ **Figure 11-9** Carbon-14 dating

Look at the photos and illustrations on these two pages. Then, follow the directions in the Science Log to find out more about "the big idea."◆

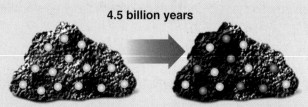

4.5 billion years

This rock sample contains 6 kg of uranium.   **About 4.5 billion years later, it has 3 kg of uranium left.**

Key
○ Uranium-238
● Lead-206

▲ **Figure 11-8** Uranium-238 dating

Archaeopteryx Fossil
Radioactive isotopes that have very long half-lives, such as U-238, can only be used to date very old rocks and fossils. The rock containing this fossil of the first known bird, called the archaeopteryx, is more than 100 million years old.

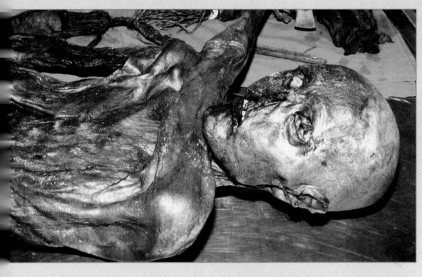

The Iceman

In 1991, the body of a man was found frozen in ice high in the Alps. He was nicknamed the Iceman. Scientists found the Iceman's age by measuring tiny amounts of carbon-14 in his remains and in tools found with him. The Iceman was found to be 5,300 years old!

WRITING ACTIVITY

Science Log

Find examples of fossils and artifacts that were dated using radioisotopes of uranium-238 or carbon-14. Draw sketches of the fossils and artifacts and write descriptions of them. Why is it important to know the age of fossils and ancient artifacts? Start your search at www.conceptsandchallenges.com.

Living Fossils

Bristlecone pine trees can live for more than 4,000 years. Scientists count the tree rings of dead bristlecone pines. Then, they measure their carbon-14 content. In this way, researchers have been able to make carbon-14 dating more accurate.

11-4 What are nuclear reactions?

Objective
Explain the processes of nuclear fission and nuclear fusion.

Key Terms:
nuclear energy: energy stored in the nucleus of the atom and released during a nuclear reaction

nuclear fission: reaction in which a large nucleus is split into smaller nuclei and energy is released

chain reaction: uncontrolled series of fission reactions

nuclear fusion: reaction in which two smaller nuclei are joined to form a larger nucleus

Nuclear Reactions There is tremendous energy stored in the nucleus of an atom. This energy, called **nuclear energy**, is released during a nuclear reaction. The breakdown of nuclei of radioactive elements is a natural process. For example, suppose you had a sample of pure uranium-238, a naturally radioactive element. It would take more than four billion years for all the nuclei to decay and form more stable nuclei of other elements.

If something happens to cause the nuclei of all the atoms of a radioactive element to change suddenly, the energy stored in the nuclei may be released all at once. Nuclear energy can be released in two types of nuclear reactions. These reactions are called nuclear fission and nuclear fusion.

1 LIST: Name the two types of nuclear reactions.

Nuclear Fission Nuclear energy has been an important energy source for more than a half century. The type of reaction that produces this energy is nuclear fission. **Nuclear fission** is a reaction in which a large nucleus is split into two smaller nuclei. Figure 11-10 shows what happens when the nucleus of an atom of uranium-235 (U-235) is split. Radiation and neutrons are released.

A fission reaction does not have to stop there, however. If the neutrons released are free to crash into other nuclei, those nuclei can also split. This

will release more energy and more neutrons. The fission process can go on and on, producing a chain reaction. A **chain reaction** is a continuing, uncontrolled series of fission reactions.

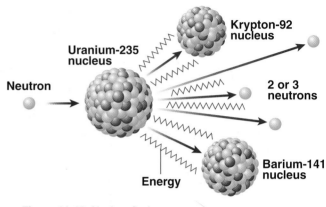

▲ Figure 11-10 Nuclear fission

2 ANALYZE: How is a chain reaction started?

Nuclear Reactors A nuclear reactor is a device used to control fission reactions and to make use of the energy they release. Control rods absorb neutrons to keep the chain reaction under control. A nuclear reactor is located in a nuclear power plant. The fuel used in most nuclear reactors is uranium. Carefully controlled uranium fission reactions are used to release large amounts of heat energy. This heat energy is then used to boil water and make steam. The steam leaves the reactor and is used to turn turbines and generate electricity. Figure 11-11 shows how fission reactions can be used to produce steam.

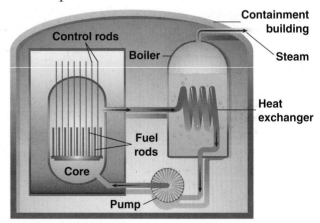

▲ Figure 11-11 In a nuclear reactor, fission reactions are used to generate steam.

3 INFER: What is the purpose of the control rods in a nuclear reactor?

Nuclear Fusion Another type of nuclear reaction is called nuclear fusion. **Nuclear fusion** is a reaction in which two smaller nuclei are joined together, or fused, to form a larger, more stable nucleus. A great amount of energy is released from a fusion reaction. Fusion reactions produce the energy released by our Sun and other stars.

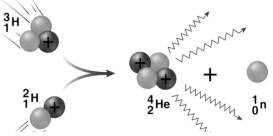

▲ **Figure 11-12** In a nuclear fusion reaction, nuclei of two different hydrogen isotopes can be joined to form a helium nucleus.

At present, scientists are trying to develop a method of starting and controlling fusion reactions. If a practical fusion reactor can be made, fusion will be the major energy source of the future. The problem is that fusion reactions take place only at very high temperatures and pressures. Such conditions exist in stars, but are difficult to control here on Earth.

 CONTRAST: How does nuclear fusion differ from nuclear fission?

✔ **CHECKING CONCEPTS**

1. The two types of nuclear reactions are _____ and fusion.
2. Fusion reactions take place in the _____.
3. In nuclear _____, a large nucleus is split into smaller, more stable nuclei.
4. An uncontrolled series of fission reactions is called a _____.

💡 **THINKING CRITICALLY**

5. **PREDICT:** Will there be more hydrogen atoms or helium atoms in our Sun in 4 billion years?

Web InfoSearch

Nuclear Waste Waste from nuclear fission reactors remains radioactive for tens of thousands of years. It must be carefully stored to protect the environment.
SEARCH: Use the Internet to find out how the government is dealing with this problem. Go to www.conceptsandchallenges.com. Some key search words are **nuclear waste disposal** and **nuclear reactor management.**

 Hands-On Activity

MODELING NUCLEAR FUSION IN THE SUN

You will need two colors of modeling clay.

1. Using modeling clay, make several small spheres of equal size. Make two spheres one color. These will represent protons. Then, make three spheres of a second color to represent neutrons.

2. Combine one proton and one neutron to make a nucleus of hydrogen-2 (H-2). Combine one proton and two neutrons to make a nucleus of hydrogen-3 (H-3).

3. On a flat surface, move the two nuclei toward each other until they collide and stick together. Then, remove one neutron and set it to one side. You have just completed the type of fusion reaction that takes place in the Sun.

PRACTICING YOUR SKILLS

4. **ANALYZE:** What is the atomic number of the element formed when two nuclei collide in Step 3?

5. **IDENTIFY:** Use the periodic table to identify this element.

▲ **Step 1** Make several small spheres of equal size.

LAB ACTIVITY
Modeling Half-Life

Materials
200 small cardboard squares with an X marked on one side

Shoebox with lid

Pencil and paper

Graph paper

BACKGROUND

When the nuclei of a radioactive element decay, energy is released and nuclei of a different element are produced. The nuclei of a radioactive element decay at a constant rate. The rate of decay is based on the element's half-life. The half-life of an element is the length of time it takes for one-half of its nuclei to decay.

PURPOSE

In this activity, you will model the half-life of an element by causing "nuclei" to decay.

PROCEDURE

1. Copy the data table shown in Figure 11-13.

2. The cardboard squares represent atomic nuclei. A square with the X facing up represents a nucleus that is radioactive. A square with the X facing down represents a nucleus that has decayed and is no longer radioactive. Place each of the 200 squares in the lid of a shoebox. Arrange the squares so that all of the Xs are facing up. All of these "nuclei" are radioactive.

3. Place the bottom of the box over the lid. Hold the box securely, and shake it to mix the squares thoroughly. Then, set the box, lid down, on your work surface and open it. Take out all the squares that do not have the X facing up. These nuclei have decayed.

4. Count the number of nuclei that decayed and the number that did not decay. Record this data in your table.

5. Repeat Steps 3 and 4 three more times, each time leaving the undecayed nuclei in the box lid.

▲ **STEP 2** Place all of the cardboard squares in the box with the Xs facing up.

▲ **STEP 3** Shake the box to mix the squares.

6. For each trial, calculate the percentage that decayed using this formula:

% decayed = number removed ÷ number before shaking × 100

7. On a sheet of graph paper, copy the axes shown in Figure 11-14. Then, prepare a graph of your results.

▲ **STEP 4** Count and record the data.

Trial Number	Number of Objects Before Shaking	Number of Objects "Decayed"	% of Decaying
1			
2			
3			
4			

▲ **Figure 11-13** Copy this chart and use it to record your observations.

CONCLUSIONS

1. **ANALYZE:** What fraction of the nuclei in the box would you expect to decay each time you shake the box?

2. **COMPARE:** How did your results compare to the prediction above?

3. **INFER:** If you were to shake the box for a fifth trial, about how many nuclei would you expect to decay? Explain.

4. **OBSERVE:** What is the shape of the line on your graph?

5. **ANALYZE:** If each trial represents 1,000 years, what is the half-life of substance X in years?

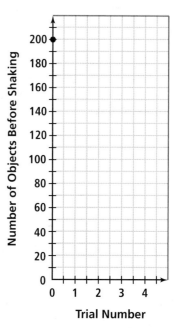

▲ **Figure 11-14** Make a graph using this figure as a guide.

Chapter 11 Challenges

Chapter Summary

Lesson 11-1
- **Nonmetals** are elements that lack most of the properties of metals.
- Solid nonmetals have a dull **luster** and are brittle. Most nonmetals do not conduct heat and electricity well.
- The families of nonmetals are the carbon family, the oxygen family, the nitrogen family, the halogens, and the noble gases.

Lesson 11-2
- **Metalloids** are elements that have properties of both metals and nonmetals.
- Metalloids are located along the zigzag line of the periodic table.

Lesson 11-3
- **Radioactive elements** are unstable elements whose nuclei decay. When this happens, **radiation** is released.
- Elements with an atomic number higher than 83 are radioactive.
- Elements of any size may have a radioactive isotope, which is called a **radioisotope.**

Lesson 11-4
- **Nuclear fission** is a reaction in which a large nucleus is split into smaller nuclei.
- An uncontrolled series of fission reactions produce a **chain reaction.**
- **Nuclear fusion** is a reaction in which two smaller nuclei are joined to form a larger nucleus.

Key Term Challenges

chain reaction (p. 238)
luster (p. 230)
nonmetals (p. 230)
metalloid (p. 232)
nuclear energy (p. 238)
nuclear fission (p. 238)
nuclear fusion (p. 238)
radiation (p. 234)
radioactive element (p. 234)
radioisotope (p. 234)

MATCHING Write the Key Term from above that best matches each description.

1. element that has properties of both metals and nonmetals
2. reaction in which a large nucleus is split into smaller nuclei
3. unstable element whose nucleus breaks down
4. isotopes that release radiation
5. energy stored in the nucleus of the atom that can be released during a nuclear reaction

FILL IN Write the Key Term from above that best completes each statement.

6. Energy released from a radioactive element is called _____.
7. Elements that have a dull luster and are brittle are _____.
8. An uncontrolled fission reaction that goes on and on is a _____.
9. The type of reaction that takes place in the Sun is called _____.
10. The way the surface of a material reflects light is called _____.

Content Challenges TEST PREP

MULTIPLE CHOICE **Write the letter of the term or phrase that best completes each statement.**

1. Radiation is the energy released from a
   a. metallic element.
   b. radioactive element.
   c. nonmetallic element.
   d. metalloid.

2. On the periodic table, the number of groups that contain nonmetals is
   a. two.
   b. three.
   c. four.
   d. five.

3. A group that is not one of the families of nonmetals is
   a. the halogens.
   b. the noble gases.
   c. the boron family.
   d. the oxygen family.

4. Metalloids are located
   a. in Group 7.
   b. in Group 10.
   c. to the left of the zigzag line.
   d. along the zigzag line.

5. One element that is a metalloid is
   a. boron.
   b. neon.
   c. oxygen.
   d. aluminum.

6. Isotopes are elements with
   a. the same number of neutrons but a different number of protons.
   b. the same number of protons but a different number of neutrons.
   c. the same number of protons but a different number of electrons.
   d. the same number of electrons but a different number of protons.

7. Radioactive elements have atomic numbers greater than
   a. 13.
   b. 43.
   c. 73.
   d. 83.

8. Fusion reactions are difficult to control because they
   a. use highly radioactive materials.
   b. take place so slowly.
   c. take place at very high temperatures.
   d. involve helium.

9. Fusion reactions in the Sun change
   a. helium to hydrogen.
   b. helium to oxygen.
   c. hydrogen to helium.
   d. oxygen to helium.

10. To determine if radiation is around you, you can
    a. see it.
    b. smell it.
    c. feel it.
    d. none of the above

TRUE/FALSE **Write _true_ if the statement is true. If the statement is false, change the underlined term to make the statement true.**

11. Elements with the properties of both metals and nonmetals are <u>gases</u>.

12. <u>Radioactive</u> elements are elements whose nuclei break down.

13. A reaction in which a large nucleus is split into smaller nuclei is called <u>fission</u>.

14. Group 15 is called the <u>carbon</u> family.

15. Isotopes that release radiation are called <u>radioisotopes</u>.

Concept Challenges TEST PREP

WRITTEN RESPONSE Answer each of the following questions in complete sentences.

1. **CONTRAST:** What are two ways that fusion is different from fission?

2. **EXPLAIN:** Where are metals, nonmetals, and metalloids located on the periodic table?

3. **EXPLAIN:** Why do fusion reactions take place in stars but not in Earth's interior?

4. **ANALYZE:** Why would the element bromine not be used to make pots and pans?

5. **EXPLAIN:** When is an isotope of an element radioactive?

INTERPRETING VISUALS Use the simplified periodic table in Figure 11-15 to complete the following questions.

6. On which side of the zigzag line are more elements?

7. On which side of the periodic table do you find the elements that are good conductors of heat and electricity? Explain.

8. How many groups contain only nonmetals?

9. How many elements in the carbon family are metals?

10. Which noble gas is most likely to be more radioactive? Explain.

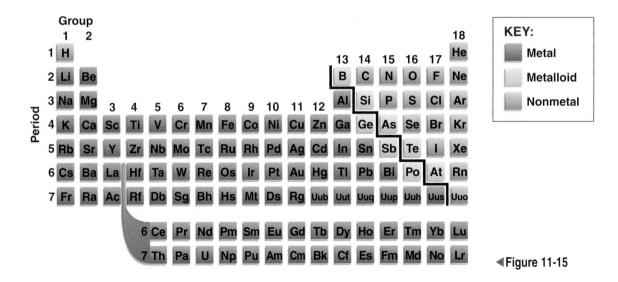

◀Figure 11-15

244

Chapter 12 Force

▲ **Figure 12-1** An electromagnet at work

The machine shown in Figure 12-1 uses magnetic force to lift and move car bodies and other large metal objects. If you have ever had to push a car, you know how much force is needed to move the car. Now think about the amount of force the machine can exert. The best part is that, unlike a permanent magnet, the magnetic force applied by the machine is supplied by electricity and can be turned on and off.

►Can you name other machines that use force to move things?

Contents

12-1 What is a force?

Objectives

Define force and give some examples of forces in nature. Identify balanced and unbalanced forces and describe their effects.

Key Terms

force: a push or a pull

balanced forces: forces that are equal in size but opposite in direction

unbalanced forces: forces that cause a change in the motion of an object

Force A **force** is a push or a pull. To open a door, you have to push or pull the door. In other words, you have to exert a force on the door. A force always acts in some direction. When you push on a door, the force is in the direction of the push. When you pull on a doorknob, the force is in the direction of the pull. If the force is strong enough, the door will move in the direction of the force.

1▶ DEFINE: What is force?

Balanced Forces To describe a force, you must know two things—the size of the force and the direction of the force. For example, think about two teams in a tug of war. Each team pulls with equal force in opposite directions, as shown in Figure 12-2. Neither team can make the other move.

Forces that are equal in size and opposite in direction are called **balanced forces.** As the name suggests, balanced forces acting on an object do not cause a change in the motion of the object.

2▶ PREDICT: What effect will balanced forces have on a book?

Unbalanced Forces Look at Figure 12-3. A member of one team has fallen and let go of the rope. One team now pulls harder than the other, and the rope moves. The forces acting on the rope are no longer balanced. **Unbalanced forces** cause a change in the motion of an object.

▲ **Figure 12-3** Unbalanced forces

3▶ IDENTIFY: What kinds of forces cause an object to move?

Forces and Motion Unbalanced forces can change the motion of an object in two ways.

- When unbalanced forces act on an object at rest, the object will move.

- When unbalanced forces act on a moving object, the motion of the object will change. The object may speed up, slow down, stop moving, or change direction.

4▶ PREDICT: What might happen when unbalanced forces act on a moving car?

▲ **Figure 12-2** Balanced forces

Forces in Nature You experience many different kinds of forces every day. A few examples of these forces are described here.

- How much do you weigh? The weight of an object is a measure of the force of gravity acting between Earth and the object.

- The attraction of a magnet for a paper clip is an example of a magnetic force.

- A kite flies in the air as a result of wind pushing against it. The force of the wind results from the moving air pushing against the kite.

- The force of falling water in a waterfall is caused by Earth's gravity acting on the water.

5 IDENTIFY: What force causes a rock to roll down the side of a mountain?

 CHECKING CONCEPTS

1. A _____ is a push or a pull.

2. To describe a force, you must know the size and _____ of the force.

3. Balanced forces are equal in size and _____ in direction.

4. Unbalanced forces cause a change in the _____ of an object.

5. The weight of an object is a measure of the force of _____ acting on it.

6. The force of the _____ is produced by moving air.

THINKING CRITICALLY

7. INFER: Describe the two forces that act on a flying kite.

 Hands-On Activity

INTERPRETING FORCE DIAGRAMS

You will need a metric ruler.

1. Look at Figure 12-4. The arrow represents the force used to push a desk across the floor. Use a metric ruler to measure the length of the arrow.

2. Look at Figure 12-5. It shows a second force helping to push the desk. Measure the total length of the two arrows.

3. Look at Figure 12-6. It shows a force pushing in the opposite direction. Measure the length of the arrow pointing in the opposite direction.

Practicing Your Skills

4. CALCULATE: Force is measured in newtons (N). If 1 cm = 1 N, what force was used to push the desk in Figure 12-4?

5. CALCULATE: What was the total force used to push the desk in Figure 12-5?

6. CALCULATE: Look at Figure 12-6. **a.** What force was used to push the desk in the opposite direction? **b.** Subtract that force from the result in question 5 to find the total force acting on the desk.

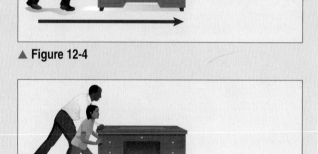
▲ Figure 12-4

▲ Figure 12-5

▲ Figure 12-6

12-2 What is gravity?

Objective

Explain Newton's law of gravity.

Key Term

gravity: force of attraction between all objects in the universe

Sir Isaac Newton Isaac Newton was a famous scientist. He was born in England over 350 years ago. Newton wondered why all objects fall to the ground. He hypothesized that there is a force that makes all objects move toward each other. This force is gravity. All objects in the universe are attracted to one another because of the force of gravity between them. This idea is now known as Newton's law of gravity, or universal gravitation.

▲ **Figure 12-7** A falling apple provided Newton's "inspiration."

▶ **1** NAME: What scientific law explains why objects fall?

Gravity Gravity is a force of attraction between all objects in the universe. On Earth, all objects fall toward the center of Earth's mass. An apple falls to the ground because it is pulled by Earth's gravity. In fact, every object near Earth's surface is pulled toward Earth's center.

▶ **2** DESCRIBE: In which direction does an object fall on Earth?

Gravity and Mass The amount of gravitational force between two objects depends on the mass of each object. Earth's mass appears to be concentrated in Earth's center. When an apple falls from a tree, the gravitational force between Earth and the apple tends to pull them toward each other. However, because Earth has much more mass than the apple, Earth does not seem to move at all.

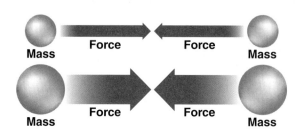

▲ **Figure 12-8** Larger masses exert greater gravitational force.

▶ **3** EXPLAIN: Why is the force of Earth's gravity so strong?

Gravity and Distance The force of gravity between two objects decreases as the distance between them increases. When you stand on Earth at sea level, the amount of gravitational force you feel is your weight. If you were far away from Earth, the gravitational force between you and Earth would be less. The force of gravity decreases by an amount equal to 1 divided by the distance (d) squared, or $1/d^2$. For example, if the moon were twice as far from Earth, the force of gravity between Earth and the Moon would be $1/2^2$ or 1/4 of its present value.

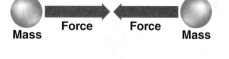

▲ **Figure 12-9** Gravitational force decreases as distance increases.

▶ **4** CALCULATE: If you were twice as far from Earth's center as you are now, how much would you weigh?

1. The idea of universal gravitation was suggested by _____.

2. All objects in the universe are attracted to each other because of the force of _____.

3. Near Earth's surface, all objects fall in the direction of Earth's _____.

4. The farther away you are from Earth, the _____ you weigh.

5. Gravity between two objects decreases as the distance between the objects _____.

THINKING CRITICALLY

6. **ANALYZE:** Why does an apple fall toward Earth, instead of Earth moving toward the apple?

7. **INFER:** The Moon travels in an orbit around Earth. What force keeps the Moon from flying off into space?

INTERPRETING VISUALS

Look at the three pairs of masses labeled a, b, and c shown in Figure 12-10.

8. Compare the forces of gravity acting between each pair of spheres and tell how you reached your conclusion.

a.

b.

c.

▲ **Figure 12-10** Compare mass, distance, and gravitational force.

Science and Technology

G FORCES

Gravity pulls your body toward Earth's center. You feel that pull as your weight. Pilots and astronauts refer to this force as 1 G. Sometimes you may have the sensation of having more or less than 1 G of force on your body. For example, as you plunge down the first hill of a roller coaster, your body lifts up off the seat. This action is caused by the fact that the seat is moving down away from you. When you reach the bottom and start up the next hill, your seat pushes up against you. This action makes it feel as if you are being pushed down into your seat. These sensations are due to changing forces on your body.

▲ **Figure 12-11** As this pilot turns, he feels increased G forces.

During flight, test pilots experience much greater changes in forces. The human body cannot withstand more than 9 Gs of force. As forces increase, blood is forced from the brain and the heart cannot pump it back quickly enough. After a short time, a person loses consciousness.

To deal with increased forces, pilots wear special suits. Tubes along the sides of these suits inflate, preventing the blood from rushing from the brain.

Thinking Critically What might happen to a pilot who experienced more than 9 Gs of force during a flight maneuver?

THE Big IDEA

What keeps planets and satellites in their orbits?

The great physicist Albert Einstein liked to do something he called thinking physics. He performed thought experiments to try out new ideas in his imagination. Sometimes he did this before doing mathematical proofs or calculations. Let's try a thought experiment to visualize the forces keeping planets and satellites in orbit.

Imagine that Earth has no atmosphere, so there will be no air resistance to slow the ball down in this experiment. You are standing on top of a very tall mountain as shown in the figure on the right. You throw a ball straight out, parallel to the ground. The harder you throw the ball, the farther the ball travels before hitting the ground. The falling ball traces a curved path as it is pulled by Earth's gravity. The more force you use to throw the ball, the longer the curve.

Because there is no air resistance, if the ball is thrown hard enough, its curved falling-path matches the curve of Earth's surface. So the ball will fall continuously without hitting Earth. It will be in orbit. It is falling without reaching the ground.

Orbit happens when the velocity of an object is such that the forward motion of the object keeps the object from falling directly toward a surface. The object travels in a circular or elliptical path. When a planet orbits the Sun, it is pulled toward the Sun's surface by the powerful force of gravity between the planet and the Sun. However, the forward motion of the planet is great enough to keep the planet from falling straight to the Sun's surface. Instead, the planet goes around the Sun.

Look at the illustrations that appear on these two pages. Then, follow the directions in the Science Log to find out more about "the big idea." ✦

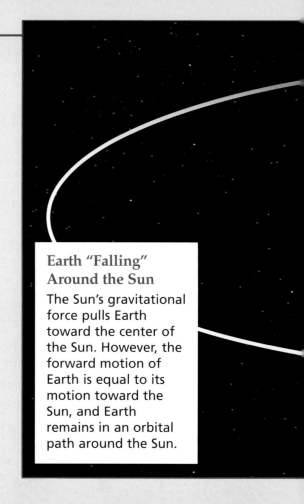

Earth "Falling" Around the Sun
The Sun's gravitational force pulls Earth toward the center of the Sun. However, the forward motion of Earth is equal to its motion toward the Sun, and Earth remains in an orbital path around the Sun.

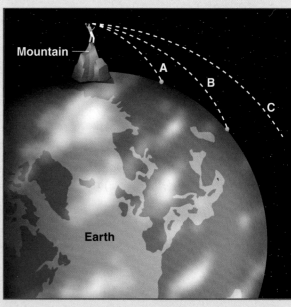

Throwing a Ball into Orbit
A ball thrown straight out from a very high mountain peak would follow a curved path (A and B) as it fell to Earth's surface. If it were thrown hard enough, its forward motion would be equal to its downward motion. This ball (C) would go into orbit around Earth.

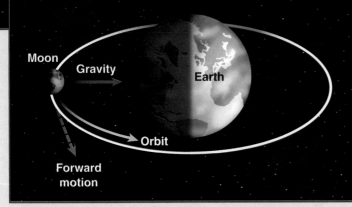

Satellites in Balance with Earth's Gravity

The forward motions of the Moon (above) and the artificial satellite (below) keep these bodies in orbit around Earth.

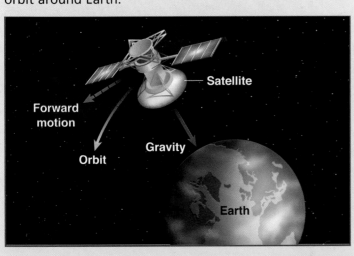

WRITING ACTIVITY

Science Log

Describe a thought experiment involving balanced and unbalanced forces. You can use any kind of force you can imagine, such as tug-of-war teams, a rocket launch, parts of an atom, or a large kite flying in a breeze. Describe how you could test your ideas in real life to see if your hypotheses about your thought experiment were accurate. For more help visit www.conceptsandchallenges.com.

How does a spring scale work?

Objective

Describe how a spring scale is used to measure weight.

Key Term

newton: SI unit of force

The SI Unit of Force There are different SI units for different types of measurements. For example, the basic unit of distance is the meter (m). The basic unit of mass is the kilogram (kg). The **newton** (N) is the basic SI unit of force. The unit is named in honor of Sir Isaac Newton. On Earth, it takes a force equal to 9.8 N to lift a 1-kg mass.

Weight is a familiar example of force. An object's weight is a measure of the force of gravity acting on the object. When you weigh an object, you measure the pull of gravity on the object. Because weight is a force, an object's weight is measured in newtons. For example, an object that weighs 15 N is heavier than an object that weighs 10 N when weighed at the same location.

▶ **IDENTIFY:** What are you measuring when you weigh an object?

Using a Spring Scale A spring scale is used to measure weight. A spring scale measures the force of gravity on an object. Figure 12-12 shows the main parts of a spring scale.

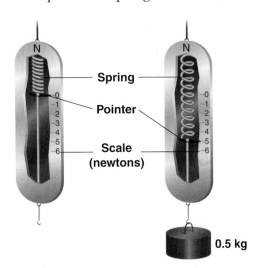

Spring

Pointer

Scale (newtons)

0.5 kg

▲ **Figure 12-12** Parts of a spring scale

To use the scale, attach a mass to the hook. The weight of the mass stretches the spring. The pointer moves down along the scale. The number at which the pointer stops is the object's weight. For example, suppose one mass moves the pointer to 5, and another mass moves the pointer to 1. The first mass weighs five times as much as the other mass.

▶ **IDENTIFY:** What does a spring scale measure?

Types of Spring Scales There are many types of spring scales. The scale shown in Figure 12-12 is similar to the type of spring scale used in a science lab. Many bathroom scales are also spring scales. When you stand on the scale, your weight pushes on a spring. The spring causes a circular scale to turn until the number on the scale lines up with the pointer. This number shows your weight.

Another type of spring scale is the one you see in the fruit and vegetable section of a market. If you place some grapes or apples on the scale, the weight of the fruit pulls a spring. The spring turns the pointer to show the weight of the fruit.

▲ **Figure 12-13** A grocer's scale can weigh fruits and vegetables.

▶ **LIST:** What are three types of spring scales?

1. The SI unit of force is the _____.
2. Weight is a _____ measured in newtons.
3. The greater the mass of an object the _____ its weight will be.
4. A spring scale is used to measure _____.
5. A bathroom scale is a kind of _____.

THINKING CRITICALLY

6. **INFER:** It takes 10 N to lift an object. What is the object's weight? How do you know?
7. **IDENTIFY:** What force is being measured when you use a spring scale to measure weight?
8. **CALCULATE:** One object causes the spring of a scale to stretch four times farther than a second object. If the second object weighs 3 N, what is the weight of the first object?

Web InfoSearch

Bathroom Scale Have you ever wondered how your bathroom scale is able to measure over 200 pounds while being so thin and small? Most bathroom scales use spring scales like those found in supermarkets. However, bathroom scales use ratios to allow smaller, less powerful springs to accurately measure heavier weights.

SEARCH: Use the Internet to find out how a bathroom scale works. What is a ratio? How is a bathroom scale able to use a small spring to measure heavy weights? Start your search at www.conceptsandchallenges.com. Some key search words are **how bathroom scale works, inside bathroom scale,** and **bathroom spring scale.**

Hands-On Activity

USING A SPRING SCALE

You will need a spring scale, a small mass, and several small objects.

1. Be sure that the pointer of the spring scale is at zero when nothing is hanging from it.
2. Carefully place a mass on the hook of the spring scale. Do not let the mass drop. This might damage the spring scale.
3. Observe where the pointer stops on the scale. If the pointer stops between two numbers, round the number to the nearest half. Record your measurement.
4. Use the spring scale to weigh several small objects. Record and compare your measurements.

▲ **STEP 2** Place a mass on the hook.

Practicing Your Skills

5. **ANALYZE:** What force are you measuring when you weigh an object?
6. **COMPARE:** How much does a 1-kg mass weigh in newtons?
7. **OBSERVE:** In newtons, what are the weights of the masses measured in the activity?

12-4 What is friction?

Objective
Identify examples of friction.

Key Term
friction: force that opposes the motion of an object

Forces and Motion To stop a moving object, a force must act in the direction opposite to the direction of motion. If you give your book a push across your desk, the book will move. The force of the push moves the book. As the book slides across the desk, it slows down and stops moving.

1 OBSERVE: Give your textbook a slight push across your desk. What must you do to keep the book moving?

Friction A force that opposes the motion of an object is called **friction.** Look at Figure 12-14. At first, the book is at rest. A push (F) causes the book to start sliding across the desk. As the book slides across the desk, a force of friction (f) acts in the opposite direction. The friction slows the motion of the book. Finally, the book is once again at rest.

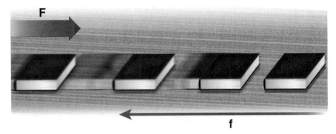

F

f

▲ **Figure 12-14** What force slows the moving book?

2 DEFINE: What is friction?

Types of Friction There are different types of friction. A book sitting on a desk has static friction. This is the force that must be overcome to start the book moving. A book moving across the desk is an example of sliding friction. As the book slides across the desk, the bottom of the book is touching the desk. The source of the friction is the contact between the surface of the book and the desk. Air

resistance is a type of friction. As an object falls, air resistance pushes up on the object. When you ride a bicycle, the contact between the tires and the road is an example of rolling friction.

3 STATE: When does friction occur?

Useful Friction On Earth, friction makes motion possible. When you ride a bicycle, the friction between the road and the bicycle wheels is necessary to keep the bicycle in motion. Without friction, you would not be able to stop the bicycle. You would not be able to climb a rope, throw a ball, or even walk down the street. Pencils would not work, and kites, birds, and airplanes would not be able to fly. As you can see, life without friction would be very different and very difficult.

▲ **Figure 12-15** Drag racers depend on friction between their tires and the track.

4 LIST: Name several activities that would not be possible without friction.

Harmful Friction Sometimes friction is not helpful. For example, think about trying to ski down a hill covered with grass instead of snow. You might be able to do it, but friction between the grass and the skis would make it a slow, bumpy ride.

Unwanted friction can also be found in machines and engines. Many machines have moving metal parts that touch. The rubbing together of these parts produces heat and can cause parts to wear out.

5 EXPLAIN: Why is it sometimes useful to reduce friction?

✔ CHECKING CONCEPTS

1. A book sliding across a desk will come to a stop because of the force of _____.

2. A book sliding across a desk is an example of _____ friction.

3. The type of friction that acts on an object falling through the atmosphere is called _____.

4. Friction makes _____ possible.

THINKING CRITICALLY

5. **INFER:** When a car's tires are stuck in snow or mud, is it better to have more or less friction? Why?

6. **HYPOTHESIZE:** Sand is often placed on top of ice on roads and highways. Why do you think the sand is used?

7. **CLASSIFY:** Decide which of the following is an example of sliding friction, rolling friction, or air resistance. **a.** an airplane descending **b.** a person roller-skating **c.** a person ice skating **d.** a falling leaf

8. **CALCULATE:** Copy the diagram in Figure 12-16 onto a sheet of paper. A force of 10 N is causing the object to slide across a tabletop from left to right. There is a 3-N force of friction opposing that motion. Complete the diagram, using arrows to show all the forces acting on the object.

▲ **Figure 12-16** Complete the diagram.

⚛ *Hands-On Activity*

MEASURING FRICTION

You will need a spring scale, a small object, a long sheet of sandpaper, and tape.

1. Place the small object on a tabletop. Attach the spring scale to the object. Pull the object across the table at a constant speed. Record the amount of force shown on the spring scale.

2. The force measured in Step 1 is the force of friction on the object from the tabletop.

3. Repeat Steps 1 to 3. This time use the sheet of sandpaper. Tape the sandpaper to the tabletop. Use the spring scale to pull the object across the sandpaper at the same speed as before.

Practicing Your Skills

4. **OBSERVE:** What was the force of friction on the object from the tabletop?

5. **OBSERVE:** What was the force of friction on the object from the sandpaper?

6. **INFER:** Does a smooth surface offer less friction or more friction than a rough surface?

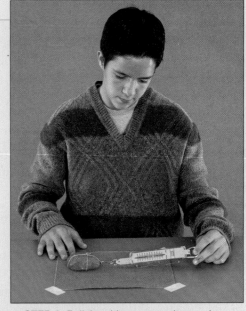

▲ **STEP 3** Pull the object across the sandpaper with the spring scale.

12-5 How can friction be changed?

Objective

Describe some ways to change friction.

Key Term

lubricants (LOO-brih-kuhnts): materials that reduce friction

Moving Against Friction Friction makes it hard to move objects. Force is needed to overcome the force of friction. Suppose you wanted to push a heavy wooden box across the floor. As you push against the box, sliding friction equal to a force of 5 N pushes in the opposite direction. This means that it will take a total force greater than 5 N to push the box.

▲ **Figure 12-17** Overcoming sliding friction

▶ **1** CALCULATE: If the force of friction is 16 N, how much force is needed to move the object?

Using Rolling Friction Reducing friction makes it easier to move an object. One way to reduce friction is to change sliding friction to rolling friction. When you try to push a wooden box across a floor, you have to overcome sliding friction. The size of this frictional force depends on the types of surfaces in contact with each other. In this case, the bottom of the box is in contact with the floor. If you put the box on a wheeled cart, there will be much less friction. Rolling friction is always less than sliding friction. With the box on wheels, you use less force to push the box.

▲ **Figure 12-18** Using rolling friction

▶ **2** EXPLAIN: Why must you reduce friction in order to move certain objects?

Using Lubricants You can also reduce friction by using lubricants. **Lubricants** are materials that reduce friction. For example, in a car's engine, metal parts called pistons are in contact with other metal parts. When two pieces of metal touch, there is a lot of friction. Oil is used to reduce the friction between the metal parts. Oil is a lubricant. It separates the metal parts from one another. Without the oil, the metal parts would scrape against one another. This would make the engine overheat and wear out more quickly.

▶ **3** IDENTIFY: When would it be helpful to use a lubricant?

Not Enough Friction Have you ever slipped on an icy sidewalk or seen a car skid out of control? These things happen when there is not enough friction between surfaces such as your feet and the ice or the tires and the road. In such cases, it is necessary to increase friction. This can be done by spreading sand on an icy surface or using tires with a deeper tread.

Athletes often wear special footwear to increase friction between their feet and the surfaces over which they move. Basketball players wear shoes with soles designed not to slip on a hardwood floor. In several sports, players wear shoes with spiked soles to give their feet a better grip on the ground.

▲ **Figure 12-19** Starting blocks provide runners helpful friction.

4 ▶ HYPOTHESIZE: Why do staircases often have rubber mats on the steps?

✓ CHECKING CONCEPTS

1. Because of friction, it takes _____ force to move an object.

2. When friction is _____ , it is easier to move an object.

3. Waxing a floor makes the floor slippery because wax is a _____.

4. If you wear roller skates instead of shoes, you _____ the friction between your feet and the floor.

💡 THINKING CRITICALLY

5. ANALYZE: Is it easier to push a heavy object across a carpeted floor or across a polished wooden floor? Why?

6. CALCULATE: Find the amount of force in each example. **a.** If it takes 20 N to slide a wooden crate across the floor, what is the force of friction? **b.** By putting wheels on the crate, the force of friction is reduced to 2 N. How much force is now needed to push the crate?

7. HYPOTHESIZE: On rainy days, the amount of friction between the road and the wheels of a car can sometimes be reduced by half. Why would reducing friction not be helpful in this case?

DESIGNING AN EXPERIMENT

Design an experiment to solve the following problem. Include a hypothesis, variables, a procedure, and a data table to be completed.

PROBLEM: Which is more effective in reducing friction between a block of steel and a smooth, flat surface, rollers or a lubricant?

 Real-Life Science

FRICTION AND SKIING

Friction is one of the major forces that affects the movement of skis across a snow-covered surface. Friction can slow the speed of a downhill racer. That same friction makes it possible for another skier to make sharp turns while maneuvering through a slalom course.

A good ski run can be affected by the type of snow on the course. In some cases, the snow might be icy or crusty. At other times, it may be soft and sticky. Skiers often apply wax to the bottom of their skis in order to adapt to the snow conditions, especially when the snow is soft or wet.

▲ **Figure 12-20** Waxing skis reduces friction and helps to increase speed.

The type of equipment a skier uses is also important. The skis used for cross-country skiing are longer and narrower than those used for downhill skiing.

Thinking Critically What things can a skier do to adapt to varying snow conditions?

12-6 What is air resistance?

INVESTIGATE

Observing Air Resistance
HANDS-ON ACTIVITY

STEP 2

1. Obtain two identical sheets of paper. Crumple one sheet into a ball.
2. Hold the crumpled sheet of paper in one hand and the uncrumpled sheet in the other hand. Extend your arms straight out in front of you at shoulder height.
3. Release both sheets of paper at the same time and observe them fall.

THINK ABOUT IT: Both sheets of paper are identical, yet one fell faster than the other. Why do you think this happened?

Objective

Explain how air resistance affects moving objects.

Key Terms

air resistance: force that opposes the movement of an object in air

terminal velocity: speed at which air resistance and gravity acting on a falling object are equal

vacuum: empty space

Falling Objects The force that opposes the downward motion of objects falling through Earth's atmosphere is called **air resistance.** Air resistance is not the same for all objects. The greater the surface area of an object, the greater the air resistance. Suppose, for example, an oak leaf and an acorn fall from a tree. The leaf flutters slowly to the ground, whereas the acorn drops straight down. As each object falls, air pushes up against the surfaces of the objects. The leaf has a greater surface area than the acorn. As a result, air pushes with more force against the leaf than it does against the acorn. The leaf is slowed more than the acorn, so the acorn hits the ground first.

▶ **PREDICT:** Which falling object will hit the ground first, a marble or a feather?

Terminal Velocity When an object is dropped from a high place, gravity pulls the object toward Earth. As it falls, gravity causes the object to accelerate. Its velocity and air resistance increase at steady rates. At some point, the upward force of air resistance becomes equal to the downward pull of gravity. At this point, the object reaches its **terminal velocity.** It stops accelerating and its velocity remains the same for the rest of its downward trip.

▶ **DESCRIBE:** What happens to an object's velocity as it falls?

Free Fall A **vacuum** is empty space. If a bowling ball and a sheet of paper were dropped from the same height in a vacuum, they would hit the ground at the same time. Because there is no air in a vacuum, there is no air resistance to slow the objects as they fall.

▲ **Figure 12-21** When on the Moon's surface, an astronaut dropped a hammer and a feather to test the idea of free fall.

All objects fall at the same speed in a vacuum. When the Apollo astronauts landed on the moon, they tested this idea. There is no air on the moon. One of the astronauts dropped a feather and a hammer at the same time and from the same height. Look at Figure 12-21. What do you think happened? The hammer and the feather hit the ground at the same time!

 DEFINE: What is a vacuum?

✓ CHECKING CONCEPTS

1. When an object is first dropped, its speed _____.

2. As an object falls, it will reach _____ because of air resistance.

3. When you drop an object, _____ slows it down.

4. There is no _____ in a vacuum.

5. All objects accelerate at the same rate in a _____.

💡 THINKING CRITICALLY

6. **HYPOTHESIZE:** Certain birds spread their wings before they land. Why do they do this? Explain.

Web InfoSearch

Effects of Streamlining A large truck and a sports car traveling at the same speed both have to overcome air resistance. Because of its size and shape, the truck has more air resistance acting on it than does the sports car. The sports car has less surface area. Also, the sports car is streamlined. Its shape has been designed to help reduce air resistance.

SEARCH: Cars, airplanes, and other vehicles all have to overcome air resistance as they move. Use the Internet to find out how engineers design shapes to reduce air resistance. Start your search at www.conceptsandchallenges.com. Some key search words are **streamlining air resistance, wind tunnel streamlining,** and **streamlining airplanes.**

 How Do They Know That?

WEIGHT DOESN'T MATTER

All falling objects speed up as they fall. Until Galileo, everyone believed that if two objects of different weight were dropped from some height at the same time, the heavier object would reach the ground first. It is said that during a storm, Galileo watched hailstones of different size and weight fall. Based on what he saw, Galileo hypothesized that weight had little or no effect on the change in speed of a falling object.

Legend has it that, to test his idea, Galileo climbed to the top of the Leaning Tower of Pisa. He dropped two rocks of different weight from the tower at the same time. People at the base of the tower saw the two rocks hit the ground at the same time. It is not clear whether Galileo actually did this experiment. But he did test and prove his hypothesis.

▲ **Figure 12-22** Galileo may have tested his hypothesis at the Leaning Tower of Pisa.

Perhaps Galileo's most important contribution to science was his use of the scientific method. Galileo served as a model for all later scientists.

Thinking Critically If a 10-N stone and a 2-N stone are dropped from a tall building at the same time, which will hit the ground first? Explain.

12-7 What is pressure?

Objective

Identify pressure as a force acting on a unit area.

Key Term

pressure: force per unit area

Force and Area The amount of force acting on a unit of area is called pressure. **Pressure** is equal to force divided by area. Suppose you hold a can as shown in Figure 12-23. If the can weighs 10 N, it presses down on your hand with a force of 10 N. Now suppose the bottom of the can has an area of 100 cm². The pressure caused by the weight of the can on your hand can be found by using the equation:

pressure = force ÷ area

pressure = 10 N ÷ 100 cm²

pressure = 0.1 N/cm²

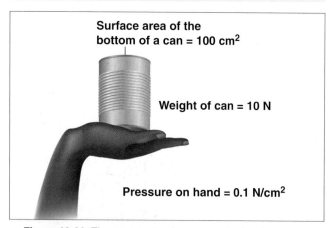

Surface area of the bottom of a can = 100 cm²

Weight of can = 10 N

Pressure on hand = 0.1 N/cm²

▲ Figure 12-23 The can exerts pressure on the hand.

1 ▶ CALCULATE: How much pressure is produced by a 30-N force acting on an area of 10 m²?

Changing Pressure Pressure can be changed by changing the force. When the area stays the same, increasing the amount of force increases the pressure. Think of a pencil point. Press the point gently against a piece of modeling clay. The point of the pencil will make a small dent in the clay. If you press a little harder, you increase the force and the pressure. The pencil point will sink deeper into the clay.

Pressure can also be changed by changing the area on which the force is pushing. If you apply the same amount of force to a larger area, the pressure is decreased. Think of the same pencil. Turn it around and gently press the eraser against the clay with the same force you used before. The pencil will barely make a mark on the clay. If you increase the force, the eraser will dent the clay but will not sink into the clay as far as the pencil point did. This shows that the pressure applied with the eraser is less than the pressure applied with the point of the pencil.

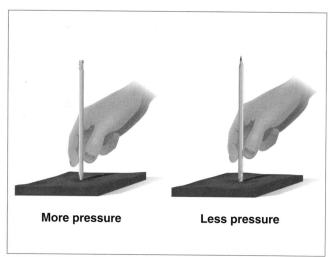

More pressure   **Less pressure**

▲ Figure 12-24 The pencil point exerts more pressure than the eraser.

2 ▶ LIST: What are two ways to change the amount of pressure being exerted?

Pressure in Nature Pressure can also be found and felt in nature. When pumped into a tire or a balloon, air exerts pressure to keep the item inflated. The air pressure in a tire can be great enough to support the weight of a truck. The pressure exerted by moving air, or wind, can turn the vanes of a windmill or keep a kite flying.

Deep below Earth's surface, pressure is very great. The weight of rocks and soil above can cause dramatic changes in rocks at great depths. Pressures build up to cause volcanoes to erupt and earthquakes to occur.

3 ▶ LIST: Name some examples of pressure in nature.

✓ CHECKING CONCEPTS

1. Pressure is equal to force divided by _____.

2. Pressure can be measured in _____ /cm².

3. You can decrease pressure by _____ the amount of force on the same area.

4. If you increase the area on which a force acts, you will _____ the pressure.

💡 THINKING CRITICALLY

5. CALCULATE: Find the amount of pressure for each of the following examples. **a.** How much pressure is applied when a 50-N force acts over an area of 10 m²? **b.** What will happen to the pressure if the force is increased to 60 N? **c.** How could you decrease the pressure from 6 N/m² to 3 N/m²?

6. ANALYZE: A rectangular building brick rests on a tabletop. How can you change the amount of pressure the brick exerts on the tabletop?

7. ANALYZE: You can get a stronger spray of water from a garden hose if you make the opening of the hose smaller. Explain why.

BUILDING MATH SKILLS

Calculating When you measure, you compare an unknown quantity with a known quantity. You can use the equation pressure = force ÷ area to find the force. To find force, rearrange the equation as follows:

$$force = pressure \times area$$

Use the equation above to find the force for each of the following examples:

8. A pressure of 12 N/m² is applied over an area of 10 m².

9. The contents of a spray can are at a pressure of 1,500 N/mm². The opening of the spray nozzle has an area of 0.2 mm².

10. A pressure of 250 N/cm² is applied to a nail. The point of the nail has an area of 0.25 cm².

Hands-On Activity

OBSERVING AIR PRESSURE

You will need a 2-L plastic bottle with cap, hot water, and cold water.

1. Half-fill a 2-L plastic bottle with hot tap water and screw the cap on tightly.

2. Swirl the hot water around in the bottle for a few seconds.

3. Remove the cap, pour the water out, and quickly replace the cap.

4. Hold the bottle under the cold-water tap for several seconds. Then stand the bottle on a flat surface and observe what happens.

Practicing Your Skills

5. DESCRIBE: What happened to the bottle? What caused this to happen?

6. INFER: What effect did filling the bottle with hot water have?

▲ **STEP 2** Swirl the water in the bottle.

Go **O**nline
active art

For: Gas Laws activity
Visit: PHSchool.com
Web Code: cgp-1023

12-8 What is air pressure?

Objective

Explain what causes air pressure and how it is measured.

Key Terms

air pressure: pressure caused by the force exerted by Earth's atmosphere

barometer (buh-RAHM-uh-tuhr)**:** instrument used to measure air pressure

Bernoulli's principle: as the speed of a fluid increases, its pressure decreases

---

Air Pressure Earth's atmosphere is made up of a mixture of gases. This mixture is called air. Air molecules are in constant motion and are pulled toward Earth's center by gravity. The force of all these moving air molecules causes **air pressure.** Most of the air in Earth's atmosphere is concentrated near Earth's surface. So air pressure is greatest near Earth's surface and decreases as altitude increases.

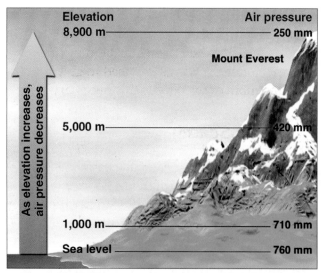

▲ **Figure 12-25** Air pressure decreases as altitude increases.

▶ **INFER:** How does air pressure at the top of a mountain compare with the air pressure at sea level?

Measuring Air Pressure Air pressure is measured with an instrument called a **barometer.**

Figure 12-26 shows how a barometer works. The open container and the glass tube contain mercury, a very heavy liquid. The space above the mercury in the tube is a vacuum. As air presses down on the surface of the mercury in the container, the air pressure holds the column of mercury in the glass tube. The greater the air pressure, the higher the mercury will rise in the tube. Normal air pressure at sea level will support a column of mercury 760 mm high in the glass tube. Air pressure decreases with altitude. So, if you carried the barometer up a mountain, the level of the mercury in the tube would move down.

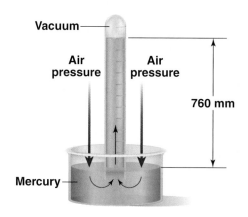

▲ **Figure 12-26** A mercury barometer

▶ **IDENTIFY:** What does a barometer measure?

Bernoulli's Principle Air, moving or still, exerts pressure on the Earth's surface. **Bernoulli's principle** tells us that moving air exerts less pressure than still air. As the speed of a gas or liquid increases, the pressure it exerts decreases. You can try a simple experiment to show this principle: Hold a sheet of paper in front of you like you are going to read from it. Place your fingers about two inches from the bottom. Let the top of the paper fall away from you. Blow straight ahead over the highest point of the paper. The sheet of paper will rise. This shows that the air pressure above the paper has decreased. As you blow, the pressure is lower on top of the paper than below it. The high pressure below pushes the paper up.

▶ **DEFINE:** What is Bernoulli's principle?

Air Pressure and Wing Shape Airplane wings are designed to make use of Bernoulli's principle. Look at the shape of the wing in Figure 12-27. Notice that the top of the wing is more curved than the bottom. As the airplane moves through the air, the shape of the wing causes air pressure on top of the wing to be reduced. So the pressure of the air pushing up on the wing is greater than the pressure of the air pushing down. This unbalanced force, called lift, helps push the wing up.

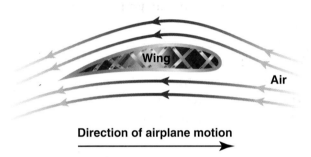

Direction of airplane motion

▲ **Figure 12-27** The shape of an airplane wing helps create unbalanced forces on the wing.

 IDENTIFY: What force pushes up on an airplane wing?

Flight Four forces act on an airplane in flight. Figure 12-28 shows a view of an airplane. The arrows show the directions of the four forces.

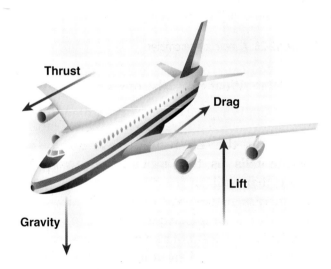

▲ **Figure 12-28** Four forces act on an airplane in flight.

- The weight of the airplane is due to gravity. This force pulls the plane toward the ground.

- The upward force on the bottom of the airplane's wings is called lift. This force pushes the wings up. In normal flight, the lift is equal to the weight of the airplane.

- The forward force on the plane is called thrust. The plane's engines provide the force, or thrust, needed to move the plane forward.

- The flow of air over the wings is a form of air resistance. This frictional force is called drag. Drag slows an airplane down. Too much drag causes the plane to use too much fuel. Engineers design planes that will reduce drag. The process of reducing drag is called streamlining.

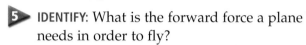 **IDENTIFY:** What is the forward force a plane needs in order to fly?

☑ CHECKING CONCEPTS

1. Air pressure is caused by the force of moving _____.

2. A barometer measures _____.

3. Air pressure _____ as altitude increases.

4. As the speed of a fluid increases, the pressure it exerts _____.

5. The force that tends to slow a moving airplane is called _____.

💡 THINKING CRITICALLY

6. **HYPOTHESIZE:** A plane flying into a strong wind feels more drag than in calm air. Explain.

7. **HYPOTHESIZE:** When a plane is landing, the flaps under the wings are used to give the plane more drag. Why is this necessary?

Web InfoSearch

Aneroid Barometers Mercury barometers are not always practical to use because they take up so much space. Another type of barometer, called an aneroid barometer, is widely used for its convenience.

SEARCH: Use the Internet to find out how aneroid barometers work and how they can be used to measure altitude. What does *aneroid* mean? Start your search at www.conceptsandchallenges.com. Some key search words are **aneroid barometer, how aneroid barometer works,** and **how barometer works.**

12-9 What is water pressure?

Objective

Identify water pressure as the pressure caused by the weight and movement of water molecules.

Water Pressure Like air, water is a fluid. However, water is a liquid. Water molecules are more tightly packed than the molecules that make up air. Water exerts pressure because of the weight and movement of the water molecules. If you place an object in a container of water, the water applies pressure to the object in all directions.

Water pressure changes with depth. There is more pressure on a submarine the deeper it goes underwater. Below certain depths, the pressure from the water is so great that it can crush an object. Submarines are built to withstand a great deal of force from water pressure.

When you dive to the bottom of a swimming pool, you can feel the water pressure, especially against your ears. The pressure of the water is greater than that of the air that normally presses against your body.

▲ **Figure 12-29** How does water pressure at depth *y* compare with that at depth *x*?

▶ DESCRIBE: How does water pressure change with depth?

Water Pressure at Home What happens when you open a faucet at home? Hopefully, water comes flowing out in a steady stream. This shows that you have good water pressure in your home. Where does this pressure come from? Some force must be pushing the water out of the faucet.

If your family has its own well, you probably have a system for pumping water up from the well and through the water pipes of your house. The pump provides your water pressure. Chances are your water comes from some central source, such as a town or city water system. In such systems, water is obtained from wells, lakes, or rivers. After being cleaned and purified, the water is pumped into large tanks. The tanks may be on a hill or some location higher than that of the homes they will supply with water. Gravity supplies the force that provides water pressure in such systems.

▲ **Figure 12-30** Gravity provides the force that creates pressure for the water coming from water tanks.

▶ EXPLAIN: Why are water tanks located in high places?

Hydraulics Fluids, especially liquids, can transfer pressure. This is the idea behind hydraulic (hy-DRAW-lihk) systems. Look at the hydraulic system shown in Figure 12-31.

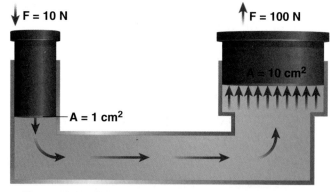

▲ **Figure 12-31** Fluid transfers pressure in this hydraulic system.

This system is filled with a liquid and has two movable pistons. The smaller piston has an area of 1 cm². If you push down on this piston with a force of 10 N, you will apply a pressure of 10 N/cm². This pressure will travel throughout the fluid. When it reaches the larger piston, this pressure will be applied over the entire area of that piston, which is 10 cm². So, a downward force of 10 N on the small piston will produce an upward force of 100 N on the large piston.

3 ▶ DESCRIBE: What happens when pressure is applied to an enclosed fluid?

✓ CHECKING CONCEPTS

1. Water pressure is caused by the weight and _____ of water molecules.

2. Water pressure is _____ than air pressure.

3. _____ provides the force for the water pressure in most homes and offices.

4. Water pressure at a depth of 1 m will be _____ than the pressure at a depth of 5 m.

5. _____ can transfer pressure.

THINKING CRITICALLY

6. HYPOTHESIZE: Why does water pressure increase as you move deeper into the water?

HEALTH AND SAFETY TIP

Snorkeling and scuba diving can be educational and great fun. However, these activities can be dangerous. You should always swim and dive with a partner. Don't snorkel or dive in unfamiliar waters. Learn as much as you can about the area you plan to investigate. Be sure to follow all safety precautions. Before diving, take a course and get a dive license.

Hands-On Activity

RELATING PRESSURE AND DEPTH

You will need a milk carton or plastic soda bottle, pencil, paper, metric ruler, modeling clay, basin, apron and safety goggles.

1. Use a pencil to make a hole in a milk carton about 5 cm from the bottom. Plug the hole with modeling clay.

2. Repeat Step 1, making two more holes at distances of 10 cm and 15 cm from the bottom.

3. Put on safety goggles and fill the milk carton with water.

4. Place the carton in a basin or sink and remove the clay plug at the 15-cm hole. Measure and record how far the water squirts.

5. Replug the hole and refill the milk carton with water. Repeat Step 4 for the 10-cm hole and the 5-cm hole.

Practicing Your Skills

6. DESCRIBE: From which hole did water squirt the greatest distance? The least distance?

7. INFER: From your observations, how does pressure change with depth?

▲ **STEP 2** Make small holes in the carton.

Go **O**nline
active art
For: Hydraulic Systems activity
Visit: PHSchool.com
Web Code: cgp-3033

LAB ACTIVITY
Making a Cartesian Diver

Materials

Safety goggles

2-L plastic bottle with cap

Plastic pipette

Insulated bell wire

Water

Permanent marker

Metric ruler

BACKGROUND

Pressure affects water and air differently. A plastic bottle filled with air can easily be squeezed with your fingers so that it dents. The pressure applied to the outside of the bottle is transferred to the air inside, squeezing it into a smaller space. However, the same bottle filled with water cannot be squeezed so that it dents. The water inside is not as compressible as air.

What will happen if a bottle that has both air and water inside is squeezed? You can find out by constructing and testing a Cartesian (kahr-TEE-zhuhn) diver.

PURPOSE

In this activity, you will construct a Cartesian diver and experiment with the effects of changing water pressure.

PROCEDURE

1. Copy the chart in Figure 12-32 on a sheet of paper.

2. Use a ruler and marking pen to place marks 5 mm apart on the bulb of the pipette. Then, wrap 10 to 12 coils of insulated bell wire around the pipette. The pipette will be your model diver.

▲ **STEP 2** Prepare the pipette for diving.

3. Put on safety goggles. Fill a 2-L plastic bottle almost to the top with water.

4. Squeeze the bulb of the pipette and insert the tip into the water. Relax the bulb to draw water into the pipette. Fill the pipette with water.

5. Squeeze the pipette bulb to empty out a small amount of water. Shake it gently to move the air bubble into the bulb.

6. Place the pipette into the bottle and cap it. In your chart, record the level of the water in the pipette.

▲ **STEP 5** Remove some water from the pipette bulb.

▲ **STEP 7** Squeeze the bottle containing the diver.

▲ **STEP 9** Try to control the depth of the diver.

7. Squeeze the bottle with your hands. If the pipette dives to the bottom, go to Step 8. If the pipette does not dive to the bottom, remove it and squeeze a bit more water out of it. Place it back in the bottle and see if it will dive.

8. Observe and record the water level inside the pipette. Squeeze the bottle to make the diver go to the bottom. Does the water level inside the diver change? If so, how much does it change? Record your observations in the table.

9. Try to make the diver stop halfway to the bottom. Observe and record the water level again.

Comparison of Cartesian Diver Depth with Air Chamber Volume

Depth	Air Chamber Mark	Change (mm)
Surface		
Middle		
Bottom		

▲ **Figure 12-32** Copy this chart and use it to record your observations.

CONCLUSIONS

1. **OBSERVE:** What happened to the Cartesian diver when you squeezed the bottle?

2. **INFER:** What happens to the pressure created by squeezing the bottle?

3. **ANALYZE:** What caused the diver to dive?

4. **HYPOTHESIZE:** Based on your observations, how does a submarine stay underwater?

5. **HYPOTHESIZE:** Why does a diver's ears hurt when he or she descends underwater?

Chapter Summary

Lesson 12-1

- A **force** is a push or a pull.
- A force always acts in a certain direction.
- Weight is a force.

Lesson 12-2

- All objects are attracted to each other because of the force of **gravity** between them.
- The gravitational force between two objects depends on their masses and the distance between them.

Lesson 12-3

- The **newton** (N) is the metric unit of force.
- Weight is a force that is measured in newtons.

Lesson 12-4

- **Friction** is a force that opposes the motion of an object. There are different types of friction.

Lesson 12-5

- Friction can be reduced by changing sliding friction to rolling friction and by using a **lubricant.**

Lesson 12-6

- **Air resistance** is the force that opposes objects moving through air.

Lesson 12-7

- **Pressure** is the amount of force acting on a unit area of a surface.
- Pressure can be changed by changing the amount of force acting on an area or by changing the area on which a force acts.

Lesson 12-8

- **Air pressure** is caused by the weight and movement of air molecules.
- Air pressure is measured with a **barometer.**
- **Bernoulli's principle** says that as the speed of a fluid increases, its pressure decreases.

Lesson 12-9

- Water pressure is caused by the weight and movement of water molecules.
- Water pressure increases with depth.

Key Term Challenges

air pressure (p. 262)
air resistance (p. 258)
balanced forces (p. 246)
barometer (p. 262)
Bernoulli's principle (p. 262)
force (p. 246)
friction (p. 254)
gravity (p. 248)
lubricants (p. 256)
newton (p. 252)
pressure (p. 260)
terminal velocity (p. 258)
unbalanced forces (p. 246)
vacuum (p. 258)

MATCHING Write the Key Term from above that best matches each description.

1. metric unit of force
2. substances used to reduce friction
3. empty space
4. force divided by area
5. instrument for measuring air pressure
6. push or pull
7. deals with the pressure of moving fluids
8. force opposing motion
9. maximum velocity for a falling object
10. force of attraction between all objects

FILL IN Write the Key Term from above that best completes each statement.

11. When you walk across the floor, there is _____ between your shoes and the floor.
12. As water flows faster through pipes, the pressure on the pipes from the water is decreased. This is an example of _____.
13. When skydivers jump from an airplane, they will reach _____ before landing.
14. Objects fall to the ground because of the force of _____.
15. Earth's force of _____ pulls objects in the direction of Earth's center.
16. The wheels on a skateboard help to reduce _____.

Content Challenges TEST PREP

MULTIPLE CHOICE Write the letter of the term or phrase that best completes each statement.

1. As the wheels of a bicycle move over the surface of the road, they must overcome
   a. sliding friction.
   b. gravity.
   c. rolling friction.
   d. air resistance.

2. An apple falls to the ground because of
   a. a magnetic force.
   b. an electric force.
   c. a gravitational force.
   d. a force of friction.

3. If it takes 25 N to push a car at a constant speed, the friction between the road and the car's tires is
   a. 20 N.
   b. 25 N.
   c. 15 N.
   d. 5 N.

4. A hydraulic lift uses force from
   a. weight.
   b. fluid pressure.
   c. air pressure.
   d. friction.

5. A submarine rising to the surface of the water from deep in the ocean is going from
   a. low pressure to high pressure.
   b. high pressure to low pressure.
   c. zero pressure to high pressure.
   d. high pressure to zero pressure.

6. A ball rolls off a table and hits the floor. The force that causes the ball to hit the floor is
   a. gravity.
   b. friction.
   c. air pressure.
   d. a magnetic force.

7. As an airplane lands, it lowers the flaps under the wings in order to
   a. increase air resistance.
   b. decrease air resistance.
   c. increase the plane's weight.
   d. decrease the plane's weight.

8. A barometer is used to measure
   a. friction.
   b. air pressure.
   c. gravity.
   d. water pressure.

9. An airplane can fly because the pressure on the plane's wings is
   a. greater on the top of the wings.
   b. zero.
   c. greater on the bottom of the wings.
   d. equal on both sides of the wings.

TRUE/FALSE Write *true* if the statement is true. If the statement is false, change the underlined term to make the statement true.

10. Weight is a <u>force</u>.

11. Pressure is equal to force <u>times</u> area.

12. Near Earth's surface, all objects fall in the direction of Earth's <u>center</u>.

13. Air pressure <u>decreases</u> as altitude increases.

14. Moving a box across the floor is an example of <u>rolling</u> friction.

15. A spring scale measures <u>weight</u>.

16. Air resistance <u>slows</u> the speed of a falling object.

17. A lubricant reduces <u>pressure</u>.

18. <u>Friction</u> slows down the motion of objects.

19. The upward force acting on an airplane's wing is called <u>drag</u>.

20. At Earth's surface, a feather falls more slowly than a rock because of <u>air resistance</u>.

Concept Challenges TEST PREP

WRITTEN RESPONSE Complete the exercises and answer each of the following questions in complete sentences.

1. **DESCRIBE:** What effect does altitude have on air pressure? Explain.

2. **HYPOTHESIZE:** How would the world be different if there were no friction?

3. **PREDICT:** Will you exert more pressure when you stand on your toes or when you stand flat-footed? Explain.

4. **EXPLAIN:** Why does an astronaut need to learn about apparent weightlessness?

5. **EXPLAIN:** Use the principle of hydraulics to explain how some car jacks work.

INTERPRETING A DIAGRAM Use Figure 12-33 to answer the following questions.

6. What force tends to slow the airplane's forward motion?

7. What force opposes the force of gravity?

8. What force is provided by the airplane's engines?

9. Bernoulli's principle helps to explain what force acting on the airplane?

10. What two forces tend to take over when the airplane prepares to land?

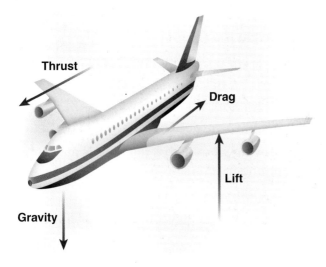

▲ **Figure 12-33** Forces acting on an airplane in flight

Chapter 13 Motion

▲ **Figure 13-1** Motion makes a roller coaster fun.

A roller coaster can be a lesson in motion. Imagine that everywhere you look, things are moving. Standing on the ground, you see that the roller coaster is moving. If you were in one of the cars, you would feel the motion and see things move past at very fast speeds. Now, suppose you were sitting next to a friend. Throughout the ride, your friend stays beside you. Has your friend moved? Have you?

▶ How can you tell when you or something around you is moving?

Contents

What are motion and speed?

Objective

Explain that an object is moving if it changes position relative to some object that is not moving.

Key Terms

motion: change in position relative to some fixed object or place

speed: distance traveled per unit of time

average speed: total distance traveled divided by the time it takes to travel that distance

Motion Has anything like this ever happened to you? You see a mail truck parked in front of your house. You run upstairs to get a letter you want to mail. When you come out, the truck is no longer in front of your house. It is now in front of the house next door.

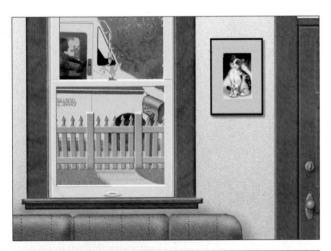

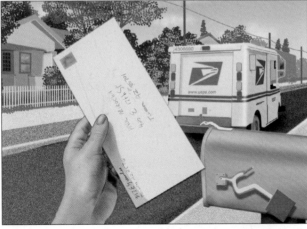

▲ **Figure 13-2** (Top) The position of the mail truck is in front of the house. (Bottom) How do you know the truck has moved?

This example shows that you do not have to see something move to know that motion has taken place. **Motion** is a change in position relative to some fixed object or place. Because you know that your house did not move, the mail truck must have changed position relative to your house.

▶ **EXPLAIN:** How do you know something moved?

Motion and Speed When dealing with moving objects, you often want to know how fast something moves. In other words, you want to know how far something travels and how long it takes to make the trip. **Speed** is the distance traveled per unit of time. The SI unit for distance is the meter. Kilometer is often used to measure long distances. The equation for finding speed is shown below.

$$\text{speed} = \text{distance} \div \text{time}$$

▶ **CALCULATE:** Which is moving faster, a car traveling 150 km in 3 hours or one traveling 100 km in 2 hours?

Average Speed When traveling in a car, you can tell how fast you are moving at any given instant by looking at the speedometer. This tells your instantaneous speed. You might travel at the same speed for some time. During this time, you would be traveling at a constant speed.

▲ **Figure 13-3**
An automobile speedometer

However, you seldom travel at the same speed for an entire trip. You probably speed up, slow down, and stop many times. When you finally get to your destination, you can find your average speed for the trip. **Average speed** is the total distance traveled divided by the time it takes to travel that distance.

$$\text{average speed} = \text{total distance} \div \text{time}$$

▶ **CALCULATE:** If you traveled 360 km in 4 hours, what was your average speed?

✓ CHECKING CONCEPTS

1. A change in position relative to some fixed object or place is called _____ .
2. The equation for calculating speed is _____ divided by time.
3. The speedometer of a car tells you your _____ speed.
4. Speed that does not change is called _____ speed.
5. The total distance traveled divided by the time it takes to travel that distance gives you the _____ .

💡 THINKING CRITICALLY

6. COMPARE: Explain the difference between instantaneous speed and average speed.
7. CALCULATE: If a car travels at an average speed of 90 km/h, how long will it take the car to travel 360 km?
8. INFER: A car makes a trip of 400 km in 4 hours. The return trip takes 3 1/2 hours. What can you infer about the average speed of the car on two trips?

BUILDING MATH SKILLS

Analyzing a Graph The distance an object travels in a certain amount of time can be shown on a graph. Figure 13-4 shows distance and time for a car trip. How far does the car travel in 5 hours? What was the average speed of the car during that time? What was the speed of the car between the second and third hours? What was the car's average speed during the first 2 hours? The last 2 hours?

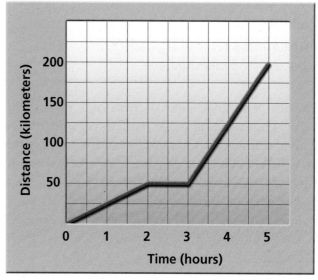

▲ Figure 13-4

Hands-On Activity

MEASURING AVERAGE SPEED

You will need a book, a piece of cardboard, a metric ruler, a watch or clock with a second hand, and a marble.

1. You will need about 1.5 m of floor space. Fold the piece of cardboard lengthwise. Place one end of the cardboard on a book so that the end of the cardboard is raised 1.5 cm off the floor.
2. Hold the marble at the raised end of the cardboard. Release the marble and let it roll down the center of the cardboard and across the floor.
3. Measure the distance in centimeters the marble rolls from the end of the cardboard in 2 seconds. Record your measurement in a table.
4. Repeat Steps 2 and 3 three more times. Record your measurements.

▲ STEP 2 Allow the marble to roll down the slope.

Go **O**nline
active art

For: Graphing Motion activity
Visit: PHSchool.com
Web Code: cgp-3011

Practicing Your Skills

5. OBSERVE: What was the average distance the marble rolled in 2 seconds?
6. CALCULATE: What was the average speed of the marble?

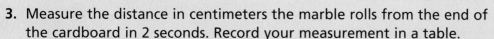

13-2 What are velocity and acceleration?

Objective

Differentiate between speed, velocity, and acceleration.

Key Terms

velocity (vuh-LAHS-uh-tee): speed and direction

acceleration (ak-sehl-uh-RAY-shuhn): rate of change in velocity over time

Speed, Velocity, and Direction When you move from place to place, you travel at different speeds. However, to describe your motion, you need to know more than just your average speed. You must also know the direction in which you are moving. Speed and direction describe **velocity.** An example of velocity is 90 km/h west. Your speed is 90 km/h and your direction is west. Together, these two values describe your velocity.

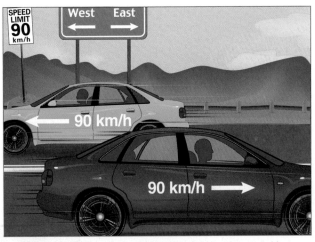

▲ **Figure 13-5** The cars are traveling at the same speed but their velocities are different.

▶ **INTERPRET:** In Figure 13-5, what is the velocity of the red car? The blue car?

Acceleration When a car changes speed or direction, it is accelerating. **Acceleration** is a change in velocity. When a car speeds up, its velocity is changing. The car is accelerating. When a car slows down, it is also changing velocity. It is

accelerating. When a car goes around a curve or turns a corner, it is changing direction. A change in direction is a change in velocity. The car is accelerating. The initial velocity of the runners in Figure 13-6 is 0. So, as soon as they move down the track, they are accelerating.

◀ **Figure 13-6** From the minute they leave the starting blocks, these runners are accelerating.

▶ **INFER:** Why is a car accelerating when it turns a corner?

Measuring Acceleration Acceleration describes how fast the velocity of a moving object is changing. To find average acceleration, you must know the change in velocity and the time it takes for the change to occur. The equation for finding acceleration in a straight line is shown here.

> acceleration = change in velocity ÷ time, or
> acceleration = (final velocity − initial velocity) ÷ time

Suppose a car is stopped at a red light. When the light turns green, the car accelerates to a speed of 150 m/sec. The car takes 10 seconds to reach this speed. What is its acceleration?

> acceleration = (150 m/s − 0 m/s) ÷ 10 s
> acceleration = 150 m/s ÷ 10 s
> acceleration = 15 m/s/s

The acceleration is 15 meters per second per second, or 15 m/s². This means that the car's velocity increases 15 m/s every second.

 3 ▶ INFER: What is the initial velocity of the car?

✓ CHECKING CONCEPTS

1. What is velocity?
2. What does velocity tell you about a moving object?
3. What is a change in velocity called?
4. What is the formula for finding acceleration?
5. How do you find a change in velocity?

💡 THINKING CRITICALLY

6. **CALCULATE:** A truck is traveling east on a highway at 80 km/h. What is its velocity?
7. **ANALYZE:** A highway speed limit is 90 km/h. Is this average speed or instantaneous speed? Explain.

BUILDING MATH SKILLS

Interpreting Tables When an object falls through the air, it accelerates as it falls. When it is released, its speed is zero. As it falls, its speed increases. Figure 13-7 shows how the speed of a falling object changes.

ACCELERATION OF A FALLING OBJECT	
Time (seconds)	Velocity (m/sec downward)
0	0
1	9.8
2	19.6
3	29.4
4	39.2
5	0

▲ Figure 13-7

What is the object's acceleration from 0 to 1 s? From 0 to 3 s? From 2 s to 4 s? Based on your calculations, what can you say about the acceleration of a falling object?

 ## Hands-On Activity

CHANGING ACCELERATION

You will need a large rubber band, a toy car, a metric ruler, a pencil, and paper.

1. Place the car on the floor. Hold one end of the rubber band on one side of the car while a partner holds the other end.
2. Pull the rubber band and the car a distance of 5 cm, as shown in the picture. Release the rubber band. Measure and record the distance the car travels.
3. Repeat Steps 1 and 2 two more times. The first time pull the rubber band and car back 10 cm. The second time pull them back 15 cm.

▲ STEP 2 Making the car accelerate

Practicing Your Skills

4. **ANALYZE:** What supplied the force to make the car accelerate?
5. **OBSERVE:** How did increasing the force affect the acceleration of the car?

13-3 What is momentum?

Objective

Define and describe how to calculate momentum.

Key Terms

momentum: a property of all moving objects

law of conservation of momentum: total momentum of any isolated system always remains the same

Momentum Picture a bowling ball with a mass of 5 kg rolling toward the pins at the end of the alley. In the next alley, a ball with a mass of 8 kg is rolling toward the pins with the same velocity. Which ball do you think is likely to knock over more pins? If you answered the ball with the greater mass, you are correct. As long as the two bowling balls are moving with the same velocity, the ball with the greater mass will strike the pins with greater energy. The combined effect of the mass and velocity of an object is momentum. **Momentum** is a property of all moving objects.

▲ **Figure 13-8** Momentum is transferred from the ball to the pins.

▶ **1** IDENTIFY: What two factors determine momentum?

Calculating Momentum The momentum of an object can be found by multiplying its mass by its velocity.

$$\text{momentum} = \text{mass} \times \text{velocity}$$

Let's look at the two bowling balls described earlier. Suppose the velocity of each ball is 20 m/s. Find the momentum of the 5-kg ball.

$$5 \text{ kg} \times 20 \text{ m/s} = 100 \text{ kg-m/s}$$

The 5-kg ball has a momentum of 100 kg-m/s. Now find the momentum of the 8-kg ball.

$$8 \text{ kg} \times 20 \text{ m/s} = 160 \text{ kg-m/s}$$

The 8-kg ball has a momentum of 160 kg-m/s. The ball with more momentum will knock over more pins.

▶ **2** CALCULATE: Find the momentum of a 10-kg object moving at a velocity of 20 m/s.

Conservation of Momentum When one moving object collides with another object, the motion of both objects changes. For example, when a bowling ball strikes the pins, the bowling ball slows down. It loses momentum. The pins move. The pins gain momentum. The important thing to remember is that the total momentum of the ball and the pins remains the same. In any isolated system, momentum can be transferred but cannot be lost. This is the **law of conservation of momentum.**

Figure 13-9 demonstrates this idea. If a sphere on the left is swung and strikes the row of spheres, a sphere on the other end will move. The momentum of the first sphere is transferred through the row of spheres to the sphere at the other end. No momentum is lost.

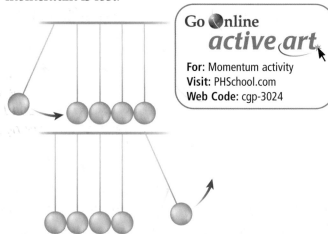

Go **O**nline
active art

For: Momentum activity
Visit: PHSchool.com
Web Code: cgp-3024

▲ **Figure 13-9** Momentum is conserved as it is transferred from sphere to sphere.

Now suppose two spheres are allowed to strike the remaining row of spheres. Figure 13-10 shows what would happen.

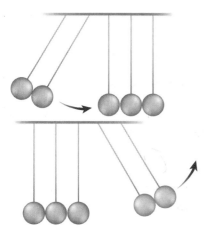

▲ **Figure 13-10** Momentum is still conserved.

 INFER: What will happen if three spheres are allowed to strike the row of spheres?

✓ CHECKING CONCEPTS

1. The momentum of an object depends on its _____ and its velocity.

2. When a bowling ball strikes the pins, the ball _____ momentum.

3. If the velocity of a car traveling at 50 km/h changes to 30 km/h, the momentum of the car will _____.

4. If several objects are traveling at the same velocity, the object with the greatest mass will have the greatest _____.

THINKING CRITICALLY

5. **DESCRIBE:** Describe the momentum changes that might occur when a large glass marble rolling across a smooth surface makes a direct hit on a smaller glass marble that is not moving.

6. **CALCULATE:** Find the momentum of a 25-kg mass moving with a velocity of 25 m/sec.

DESIGNING AN EXPERIMENT

Design an experiment to solve the following problem. Include a hypothesis, variables, a procedure, and a type of data to study.

PROBLEM: How can you show that the momentum of an object is related to its mass?

 Integrating Life Science

TOPICS: birds, bones

ANIMALS AND MOMENTUM

Most birds can fly. Their hollow bones make for a light body weight. The most difficult parts of a bird's flight are the takeoff and the landing. Both require a change in momentum.

▲ **Figure 13-11** Flamingos during takeoff

In order to take off, birds have to build up enough speed so the lift from their wings is greater than their body weight. Small birds can take off with a hop and a flap of their wings. Larger birds, like the flamingos in Figure 13-11, have more of a problem. Because they have more mass, they need more momentum to reach the speed needed to take off. They do this by running as fast as they can while they flap their wings.

For some birds, landing is even harder than taking off. Birds cannot just stop flapping their wings. They would drop like a stone. Instead, they twist and spread their wings so that they slow down gradually. In other words, they lose momentum slowly enough to allow them to make a safe landing.

Thinking Critically Why do large birds need more momentum than small birds do in order to take off?

THE Big IDEA

How does safety technology change momentum?

Momentum is a property of all moving objects. An object's momentum can be found by multiplying its mass by its velocity. Many safety devices, such as automobile airbags and protective helmets, are designed to decrease an object's momentum gradually. They do this by changing the velocity—and thus the momentum—of the moving object over as long a time as possible. Physicists use the term *impulse* to describe change in momentum over a given period of time.

Think about how an automobile airbag works. When a person moving at a high speed hits an inflated airbag, the person's momentum is transferred to the particles of air in the bag. The particles speed up. The person loses velocity and momentum, slowly and safely. If that person were to hit a hard object, such as the dashboard, that person's velocity and momentum would change all at once, perhaps resulting in serious injury.

Protective headgear, such as a bicycle helmet, has some sort of protective lining. When a hard object strikes the helmet, the lining absorbs much of the shock. The object loses momentum slowly, so the effect of its impact on your head is less severe.

Look at the photos and text that appear on these two pages. Then, follow the directions in the Science Log to find out more about "the big idea." ✦

Stuntperson's Fall Cushion

The trick to falling safely from a tall building is to land on something that moves with you when you hit it. The air-filled "pillow" at the base of the building acts like the airbag in a car. It allows the stuntperson to lose momentum slowly and safely.

Space Shuttle Parachute
The parachute increases air resistance. It helps decrease the momentum of the space shuttle slowly upon landing.

WRITING ACTIVITY

Science Log

Think of some safety devices that protect people in moving vehicles or in sports. Draw a picture of one piece of safety gear. Describe the forces involved and how the device gives protection. Start your search at www.conceptsandchallenges.com.

Highway Crash Barriers
These plastic containers are filled with sand. If a car hits such a container, much of the car's momentum is transferred to the sand. The car loses momentum much more slowly than it would if it ran directly into the concrete.

Car Airbags
Airbags give accident victims more time to slow down than they would have if they crashed into something hard, such as a steering wheel.

13-4 What is Newton's first law of motion?

INVESTIGATE

Observing Newton's First Law
HANDS-ON ACTIVITY

1. Lay a board about 2 m long on the floor. Place a toy car at one end of the board.
2. Slowly lift the end of the board with the toy car until the car starts to move. Hold the end of the board at that level. Have a partner measure the height to which the end of the board was raised. Record this measurement.
3. Press a piece of modeling clay on the top of the toy car to increase its mass. Repeat Steps 1 and 2.
4. Predict how adding a second piece of clay to the car will affect the height you will have to raise the board before the car moves. Record your prediction. Repeat Steps 1 and 2 to test your prediction.

THINK ABOUT IT: What keeps the car from moving along the board as it begins to rise? What outside force finally causes the car to move?

STEP 2

Objective
Describe Newton's first law of motion.

Key Term
inertia (ihn-UR-shuh)**:** tendency of an object to stay at rest or in motion

Inertia Place a book on your desk. Does the book move? Unless you push the book, it will remain where you put it without moving. Imagine a spacecraft moving through space. When the engines are turned off, the spacecraft will coast through space at the same speed and in the same direction. The book and the spacecraft have **inertia**. Because of inertia, an object at rest tends to stay at rest. An object in motion tends to keep moving at a constant speed in a straight line.

▶ 1 **IDENTIFY:** What causes a book on a table to remain at rest?

Newton's First Law Newton's first law of motion explains how inertia affects moving and nonmoving objects. Newton's first law states that an object will remain at rest or move at a constant speed in a straight line unless it is acted on by an unbalanced force.

According to Newton's first law, an unbalanced force is needed to move the book on your desk. You could supply the force by pushing the book. An unbalanced force is needed to change the speed or direction of the spacecraft. This force could be supplied by the spacecraft's engines.

▶ 2 **PREDICT:** According to Newton's first law of motion, what will happen to an object at rest if no unbalanced force acts on it?

Effects of Inertia You can see the effects of inertia everywhere. In baseball, for example, to overcome inertia a base runner has to "round" the bases instead of making sharp turns.

◀ **Figure 13-12** The base runner is fighting to overcome inertia as he rounds the bases.

280

As a more familiar example of inertia, think about riding in a car. You and the car have inertia. If the car comes to a sudden stop, your body tends to keep moving forward. When the car starts moving again, your body tends to stay at rest. You move forward because the car seat exerts an unbalanced force on your body.

 EXPLAIN: Why do you keep moving forward when the car in which you are riding stops?

✓ CHECKING CONCEPTS

1. In space, a spacecraft with its engines turned off will move with constant speed in the same _____.

2. A book will not move by itself because it has _____.

3. A book will remain at rest unless it is acted on by an _____ force.

4. When a car stops suddenly, your body tends to keep moving _____.

5. Newton's first law explains how inertia affects moving and _____ objects.

 ## THINKING CRITICALLY

6. **PREDICT:** Push a roller skate across a smooth surface. Will the skate keep moving when you stop pushing? Explain.

INTERPRETING VISUALS

Look at Figure 13-13 to answer the following question.

7. In terms of inertia, explain what happens to the coin when the card is flicked away.

▲ **Figure 13-13**

 Real-Life Science

SPORTS AND INERTIA

Inertia plays an important role in most sports. Look at the soccer ball in Figure 13-14. It's just sitting there. Because of inertia, it will stay there until some force causes it to move. As you can see, that force is on the way! Think of the goalkeeper waiting for a ball to be sent speeding toward the goal. If his reflexes are quick enough, he will be able to change the speed or direction of any ball coming his way.

A downhill skier deals with inertia throughout her run. At the top of the mountain, she has to push off to overcome her own inertia. Once she gets moving, inertia will tend to keep her moving down the slope in a straight line. But the course has a lot of curves! So she has to use all of her skill to twist and turn down the course. At the end, she must overcome inertia to bring herself to a safe stop.

Try to think of a sport or game that does not require a person to deal with inertia. Even a checker will stay on a square until someone moves it to another square!

Thinking Critically Who would have to overcome more inertia to move the ball, a golfer or a soccer player?

▲ **Figure 13-14** The inertia of the soccer ball is about to be changed by an unbalanced force.

13-5 What is Newton's second law of motion?

Objective
Describe Newton's second law of motion.

Key Term
newton: SI unit of force

Effects of Unbalanced Forces Unbalanced forces cause acceleration. When an unbalanced force acts on an object, the motion of the object is changed. If the object is at rest, the force makes it move. If the object is in motion, the force changes its velocity. Any change in velocity is an acceleration.

▶ **DESCRIBE:** What effect does an unbalanced force have on a moving object?

Force, Mass, and Acceleration The amount by which an object accelerates depends on three things. They are the size of the force, the direction in which the force acts, and the mass of the object. Look at Figure 13-15. If two forces act on the same object, the greater force will produce more acceleration than the smaller force.

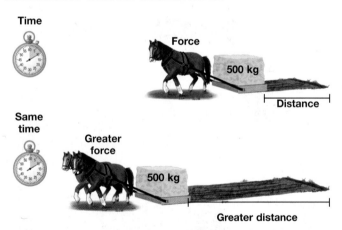

▲ **Figure 13-15** When acting on the same mass, a greater force moves the mass a greater distance over the same period of time.

Now look at Figure 13-16, which shows the same amount of force applied to two objects with different masses. The object with the smaller mass will be accelerated more than the object with the larger mass.

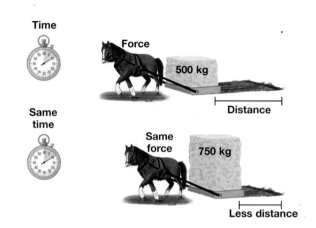

▲ **Figure 13-16** When acting on different masses, the same force will move the smaller mass a greater distance over the same period of time.

▶ **IDENTIFY:** What three factors affect the acceleration of an object?

Newton's Second Law Newton's second law describes the relationship among force, mass, and acceleration. Newton's second law states that the unbalanced force acting on an object is equal to the mass of the object times its acceleration. Newton's second law can be described by this equation.

$$F = m \times a$$

In this equation, F is the force, m is the mass, and a is the acceleration. When the mass is measured in kilograms and the acceleration is measured in meters per second per second, the force is measured in newtons (N). A **newton** is the SI unit of force. An unbalanced force of 1 N will accelerate a mass of 1 kg at 1 m/s². One newton of force is equal to one kilogram-meter per second per second (1 kg-m/s²).

▶ **DEFINE:** What is 1 N of force equal to?

Using Newton's Second Law If no friction is involved, how much force would you have to apply to a 10-kg object to make it accelerate at a rate of 45 m/s²? This may seem like a difficult problem at first. However, if you use the equation for Newton's second law, it becomes easy.

$$F = m \times a$$

$$F = 10 \text{ kg} \times 45 \text{ m/s}^2$$

$$F = 450 \text{ kg-m/s}^2$$

You would have to apply a force of 450 kg-m/s², or 450 N.

4 ► **CALCULATE:** How much force is needed to give a 5-kg mass an acceleration of 20 m/s²?

✓ CHECKING CONCEPTS

1. When it is acted on by an unbalanced force, an object will _____ .

2. When an unbalanced force acts on an object at rest, the object will _____ .

3. A change in velocity is called _____ .

4. A large force will cause _____ acceleration than a small force.

5. Newton's second law of motion states that force is equal to _____ times acceleration.

6. The _____ is a unit of force equal to 1 kg-m/s².

THINKING CRITICALLY

Use the equation F = m × a to answer the following questions. Show your calculations.

7. **CALCULATE:** What force is needed to accelerate a 2-kg mass at rest to a rate of 1 m/s²?

8. With what force would you have to push a 50-kg skater to increase the skater's speed by 2 m/s²?

INTERPRETING VISUALS

Look at Figure 13-17 to answer the question.

9. Will the acceleration of the piano be greater in A or in B? Use Newton's second law of motion to explain your answer.

▲ Figure 13-17

People in Science

SIR ISAAC NEWTON (1642–1727)

Isaac Newton was born in England on December 25, 1642. He was a physicist, an astronomer, and a mathematician. At the age of 45, Newton published his theories of motion and gravity. Newton's great book is usually called the *Principia*. It is considered one of the most important works in the history of science.

In the *Principia*, Newton explained his three laws of motion and his theory of gravitation. Newton also invented a branch of mathematics called calculus to help predict motion using his three laws. Newton also made many important discoveries about light and color.

Newton was a professor of mathematics at Cambridge University and a member of the Royal Society. He was knighted by Queen Anne in 1705. Newton once said about himself, "If I have seen further than others, it is because I have stood on the shoulders of giants."

▲ Figure 13-18 Sir Isaac Newton

Thinking Critically What do you think Newton meant by his statement?

13-6 What is Newton's third law of motion?

INVESTIGATE

Observing Newton's Third Law
HANDS-ON ACTIVITY

1. Blow up a balloon. Hold the neck of the balloon tightly to prevent air from escaping.

2. Hold the balloon at arm's length and observe which direction the neck of the balloon is facing.

3. Release the balloon and observe what happens.

THINK ABOUT IT: What happened when you released the balloon? What do you think caused this to happen? How was the behavior of the balloon related to the direction in which the neck of the balloon was facing?

STEP 3

Objective

Describe Newton's third law of motion.

Key Terms

action force: force acting in one direction

reaction force: force acting in the opposite direction

Action and Reaction Forces always act in pairs. The two forces act in opposite directions. When you push on an object, the object pushes back with an equal force. When the basketball player in Figure 13-19 shoots the ball, he pushes against it. This is the **action force.**

The ball pushes back against the player with a force of the same size. This **reaction force** will cause the wheelchair to move backward. Notice that the two forces act on different objects. The action force acts on the ball. The reaction force acts on the player.

▶ **1** CONTRAST: How are action and reaction forces different?

Newton's Third Law Newton's third law of motion describes action and reaction forces. The law states that for every action force, there is an equal and opposite reaction force. Imagine hitting a tennis ball. The racket exerts a force on the ball. This is the action force. The ball exerts an equal and opposite force on the racket. This is the reaction force.

▲ **Figure 13-19** When the player exerts a force on the ball, the ball exerts an equal force on him.

◀ **Figure 13-20** The tennis racket is about to exert an action force on the ball.

Newton's third law explains how many sports injuries are caused. The more force you use to hit a tennis ball, the more reaction force your arm receives from the racket. Every time your feet hit the ground when you are running, the ground hits your feet with an equal and opposite force.

▶ **2** **STATE:** What does Newton's third law of motion state?

Balloons and Rockets Newton's third law explains how balloons and rocket engines work. When the neck of an inflated balloon is released, the stretched rubber material pushes against the air in the balloon. The air rushes out of the neck of the balloon. The action of the air rushing from the balloon pushes against the balloon, moving it in the opposite direction.

When rocket fuel is burned, hot gases are produced. These gases expand rapidly and are forced out of the back of the rocket. This is the action force. The gases exert an equal and opposite force on the rocket itself. This is the reaction force. This force pushes the rocket upward.

▲ **Figure 13-21** Action and reaction forces during liftoff

▶ **3** **INFER:** What effect would blowing more air into a balloon have on the motion of the balloon when released?

✔ **CHECKING CONCEPTS**

1. Forces always act in _____.
2. A table exerts an upward _____ on objects resting on the table.
3. For every action force, there is an equal and _____ reaction force.
4. In a rocket engine, the _____ force pushes the rocket upward.
5. Action forces and reaction forces always act on _____ objects.

THINKING CRITICALLY

6. **INFER:** An object resting on a table weighs 100 N. With what force is the object pushing on the table? With what force is the table pushing on the object?
7. **CLASSIFY:** When you walk, your feet push against the ground. At the same time, the ground pushes against your feet. Which is the action force? Which is the reaction force?
8. **HYPOTHESIZE:** When you walk, you move forward. Does Earth move in the opposite direction? Explain your answer.

Web InfoSearch

VentureStar In 1996, NASA started plans to develop a replacement for the space shuttle. This replacement, called VentureStar, was to have many improvements over the present shuttle. At present, this project has been postponed. It may be revived in the future.

SEARCH: Use the Internet to find out what types of improvements NASA plans to incorporate in its next generation of space shuttles. What is the X-33? Why does NASA call the VentureStar a Reusable Launch Vehicle? Start your search at www.conceptsandchallenges.com. Some key search words are **X-33, Reusable Launch Vehicle, VentureStar,** and **Lockheed Martin VentureStar.**

LAB ACTIVITY
Investigating Newton's Second and Third Laws

Materials

Newton cart
Safety goggles
Plastic drinking straws
3 rubber bands
Film canister
Sand
Meter stick
String
Scissors

▲ **STEP 3** Use drinking straws to make a track.

▲ **STEP 4** Attach a string loop and rubber band to the Newton cart.

BACKGROUND

Newton's second law describes how force, mass, and acceleration are related. The ability of a rocket to take off from Earth's surface and climb into space depends on the generation of enough force. Newton's third law deals with the action-reaction forces at work when a rocket engine lifts the rocket and pushes it into space. Together, these two laws explain how a rocket is launched into space.

PURPOSE

In this activity, you will experiment with the relationship of mass, acceleration, and force.

PROCEDURE

1. On a separate sheet of paper, make a chart like the one shown in Figure 13-22.

2. Cut three 15-cm pieces of string. Tie the ends of each piece of string to form three loops. Make each loop the same size.

3. On a flat surface, make a track of 20 plastic drinking straws. Lay the straws parallel to each other 4 cm apart.

4. Slip a rubber band through one of the string loops. Slide the rubber band over the two end posts of a Newton cart. Stretch the rubber band until you can slide the string loop over the third post of the cart.

5. Fill a film canister with sand. Place the canister snugly inside the stretched rubber band on the cart.

6. Set the Newton cart on the straws near one end of the track. Point the end of the cart with the single post down the track.

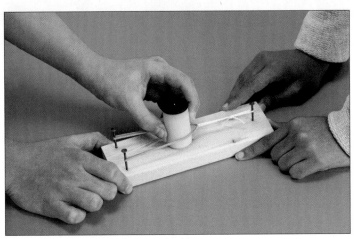

▲ **STEP 5** Place the canister on the Newton cart.

▲ **STEP 7** Launch the Newton cart down the track of straws.

7. Put on safety goggles. Then, carefully cut the string and quickly pull the scissors out of the way. Measure and record the distance that the cart travels.

8. Repeat the activity using two rubber bands and again using three rubber bands. Each additional rubber band increases the force.

Comparison of Acceleration and Distance for the Newton Cart		
Trial	Number of Rubber Bands	Distance Cart Traveled
1		
2		
3		

▲ **Figure 13-22** Copy this chart and use it to record your observations.

CONCLUSIONS

1. **OBSERVE:** What happened to the cart when you cut the string? What happened to the canister?

2. **ANALYZE:** What supplies the action force in this activity?

3. **ANALYZE:** What is the relationship between the amount of force applied and the distance the cart moved?

Chapter 13 Challenges

Chapter Summary

Lesson 13-1
- **Motion** is a change in position.
- **Average speed** is equal to the total distance traveled divided by the total time for the trip.

Lesson 13-2
- **Velocity** describes the speed and direction of a moving object.
- An object is accelerating when there is change in its velocity.
- To find **acceleration,** you must know the change in velocity and the time for the change to occur.

Lesson 13-3
- **Momentum** is a property of all moving objects.
- The momentum of an object is equal to its mass times its velocity.
- The **law of conservation of momentum** states that momentum may be transferred but cannot be lost.

Lesson 13-4
- **Inertia** is the tendency of an object to remain at rest or in motion.
- Newton's first law of motion states that an object will remain at rest or move at a constant speed in a straight line unless it is acted on by an unbalanced force.
- The effects of inertia can be felt every day.

Lesson 13-5
- Unbalanced forces cause objects to accelerate.
- The acceleration of an object depends on the mass of the object and the size and direction of the force acting on it.
- Newton's second law of motion describes the relationship among force, mass, and acceleration ($F = m \times a$).

Lesson 13-6
- Forces always act in pairs.
- Newton's third law of motion states that for every **action force,** there is an equal and opposite **reaction force.**
- Newton's third law explains how rocket engines work.

Key Term Challenges

acceleration (p. 274)
action force (p. 284)
average speed (p. 272)
inertia (p. 280)
law of conservation of momentum (p. 276)
momentum (p. 276)
motion (p. 272)
newton (p. 282)
reaction force (p. 284)
speed (p. 272)
velocity (p. 274)

MATCHING Write the Key Term from above that best matches each description.

1. speed and direction
2. change in velocity
3. mass × velocity
4. unit of force
5. change in position
6. tendency to remain at rest
7. distance traveled per unit of time

FILL IN Write the Key Term from above that best completes each statement.

8. An object's _____ does not include direction.
9. A property of all moving objects is _____.
10. The rush of gases from a rocket engine provides the _____.
11. Newton's first law deals with _____.
12. A change in position indicates that _____ has taken place.

Content Challenges TEST PREP

MULTIPLE CHOICE **Write the letter of the term or phrase that best completes each statement.**

1. When you move from place to place, you are changing your
   a. mass.
   b. inertia.
   c. position.
   d. speed.

2. An unbalanced force causes a moving object to change
   a. speed.
   b. direction.
   c. neither speed nor direction.
   d. either speed or direction.

3. A car's speedometer tells you
   a. average speed.
   b. instantaneous speed.
   c. acceleration.
   d. velocity.

4. Balanced forces are always opposite in
   a. direction.
   b. size.
   c. size and direction.
   d. size or direction.

5. Velocity includes speed and
   a. acceleration.
   b. inertia.
   c. direction.
   d. force.

6. Average speed is equal to total distance divided by
   a. average distance.
   b. average time.
   c. instantaneous speed.
   d. total time.

7. Action forces and reaction forces are described by Newton's
   a. first law of motion.
   b. second law of motion.
   c. third law of motion.
   d. law of gravitation.

8. According to Newton's second law of motion, force is equal to mass times
   a. acceleration.
   b. speed.
   c. velocity.
   d. inertia.

9. The newton is a unit of
   a. speed.
   b. force.
   c. velocity.
   d. acceleration.

10. Inertia is described by Newton's
    a. first law of motion.
    b. second law of motion.
    c. third law of motion.
    d. law of gravitation.

TRUE/FALSE **Write *true* if the statement is true. If the statement is false, change the underlined term to make the statement true.**

11. Speed is distance traveled in a given <u>direction</u>.

12. <u>Velocity</u> is found by multiplying mass by velocity.

13. <u>Momentum</u> can be transferred but cannot be lost.

14. Newton's <u>third</u> law of motion deals with inertia.

15. <u>Unbalanced</u> forces always result in motion.

Concept Challenges TEST PREP

WRITTEN RESPONSE Complete the exercises and answer each of the following questions in complete sentences.

1. **CONTRAST:** What is the difference between average speed and instantaneous speed?

2. **HYPOTHESIZE:** When does an object have zero acceleration? Explain.

3. **EXPLAIN:** Two cars are stopped at a red light. When the light turns green, both cars accelerate to a speed of 150 m/s. The first car takes 10 seconds to reach this speed. The second car takes 20 seconds. Which car has the greater acceleration?

4. **ANALYZE:** An unbalanced force acts on a moving object. The object slows down. In what direction is the unbalanced force acting? How do you know?

INTERPRETING A DIAGRAM Use Figure 13-23 to answer the following questions.

5. Does this diagram illustrate speed or velocity? Explain.

6. In what direction is the blue car traveling?

7. In what direction is the red car traveling?

8. What speed limit is shown in the diagram? Is this an average speed or an instantaneous speed?

9. If each car continues moving at an average speed of 90 km/h for 2 hours, how far will each car travel?

10. How much distance will separate the cars after 2 hours?

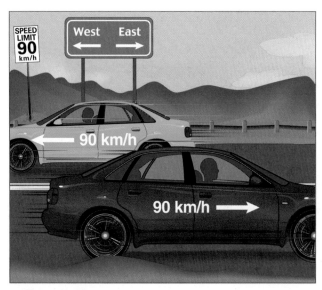

▲ Figure 13-23

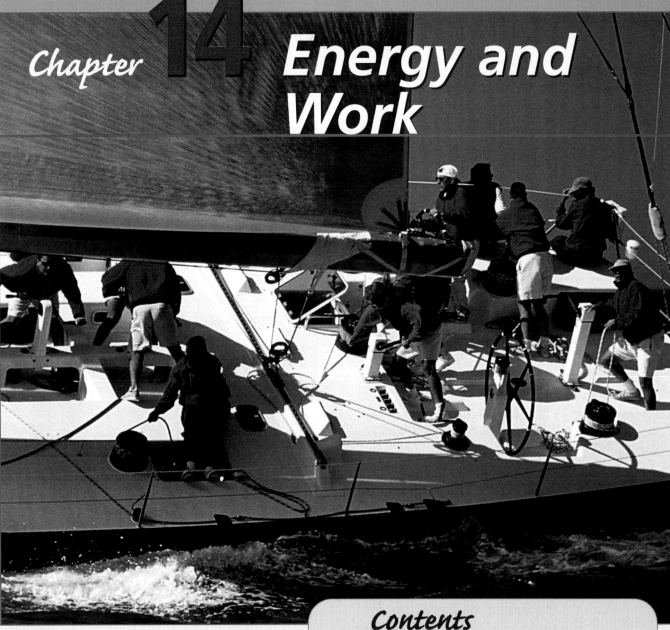

Chapter 14

Energy and Work

▲ **Figure 14-1** A sailboat race is hard work for everyone.

Say the word *sailing* and most people will think about a relaxed afternoon on the water. However, racing sailboats is a different story. This sport involves energy and work. From the minute the boat crosses the starting line until it crosses the finish line, nobody relaxes. The work involves turning cranks and pulling lines, raising and lowering sails. Crew members rush back and forth, straining to get every bit of speed possible from the boat.

▶ What outside force helps to move the sailboat?

Contents

14-1 What is energy?

Objective
Compare potential energy and kinetic energy.

Key Terms
energy: ability to make something happen

potential (poh-TEHN-shuhl) **energy:** stored energy

kinetic (kih-NEHT-ihk) **energy:** energy of motion

Energy Look at the picture of the dam in Figure 14-2. If you have ever taken a shower or stood out in the rain, you know that falling water has energy. The energy of the water falling through the spillways of a dam can be used to generate electricity. However, did you know that the quiet water in the lake behind the dam also has energy?

Energy is the ability to make something happen. There are two general kinds of energy. These are potential energy and kinetic energy.

▶ **1 DEFINE:** What is energy?

Potential Energy **Potential energy** is stored energy. The energy of the water in the lake behind the dam in Figure 14-2 is potential energy. The water has energy because of its position. Gravity can cause it to fall to the river below the dam. This kind of stored energy is called gravitational potential energy.

▲ **Figure 14-2** The water above this dam has gravitational potential energy.

The gravitational potential energy stored in a sample of matter depends on two factors. These factors are weight and height. The more weight an object has, the more potential energy it has. Potential energy also depends on height. The farther an object has to fall, the more potential energy it has.

The fireworks in Figure 14-3 have a different kind of potential energy called chemical potential energy. This potential energy is stored in the chemicals in the fireworks. When the fireworks are set off, the potential energy stored in the chemicals is released as heat, light, and sound.

▲ **Figure 14-3** Fireworks have chemical potential energy.

▶ **2 IDENTIFY:** What kind of energy is released when you strike a match?

Kinetic Energy **Kinetic energy** is energy of motion. Anything that is moving has kinetic energy. When you walk or run, you have kinetic energy. Like potential energy, kinetic energy also depends on two factors. With kinetic energy, the factors are mass and velocity. The faster you move, the more kinetic energy you have. The more mass a moving object has, the more kinetic energy it has.

Think about a car and a truck moving at 30 mph. The truck has the greater mass. So, even though both vehicles are traveling at the same speed, the truck will have more kinetic energy than the car.

◀ **Figure 14-4** Both runners are moving at the same speed. Because the runner on the left has more mass, he also has more kinetic energy than the runner on the right.

 LIST: What two factors determine how much kinetic energy a moving object has?

 CHECKING CONCEPTS

1. The ability to make something happen is _____.

2. Two kinds of energy are potential energy and _____ energy.

3. Stored energy is _____ energy.

4. Kinetic energy is energy of _____.

5. A diver on a diving board has _____ potential energy.

 THINKING CRITICALLY

6. **COMPARE:** What is the difference between potential energy and kinetic energy?

7. **ANALYZE:** A rock on the edge of a cliff has what kind of energy? When could the rock have both kinetic and potential energy? Explain.

BUILDING MATH SKILLS

If you know the weight of an object and know how high it is above the ground, you can use the formula shown here to find its gravitational potential energy (*PE*).

$$PE = \text{weight} \times \text{height}$$

Remember that weight is a measure of the pull of gravity on a mass. Weight is measured in newtons (N). Height is measured in meters (m). Therefore, potential energy is expressed in units called newton-meters, or N-m. Use the formula to find the gravitational potential energy of each of the following objects.

- a 50-N brick on top of a 4-m ladder

- a 780-N diver standing on a diving board 10 m above the water

◆ *Integrating Earth Science*

TOPIC: erosion

SCULPTING EARTH'S SURFACE

Forces can produce change. Over time, forces such as wind, moving water, and ice change the appearance of Earth's surface. The wearing away of Earth's surface in one place and building it up in another place is called erosion.

Moving water can pick up and carry sediments such as soil and gravel. When it is moving fast enough, water can even roll large rocks along the bed of a river. When these materials drag and bounce along a streambed, they carve new channels. Over millions of years, the Grand Canyon in Arizona was carved out by materials carried in the waters of the Colorado River.

Ocean waves carve the shoreline. They wear away rocks, making cliffs and terraces. Sediments carried by the water scrape against rocky shorelines. Sometimes this carves out caves and arches. Wind and moving ice, called glaciers, are other agents of erosion.

▲ **Figure 14-5** These canyons were carved by the moving water of a river.

Thinking Critically What part does kinetic energy play in sculpting Earth's surface?

What are different forms of energy?

14-2

Objectives

Identify and describe the different forms of energy.

Forms of Energy Your body gets energy from the food you eat. An automobile uses the energy in gasoline to make it move. A clock spring stores energy to turn the hands of the clock. These are some examples of different forms of energy. There are six main forms of energy. They are mechanical energy, electrical energy, electromagnetic energy, heat energy, chemical energy, and nuclear energy.

▶ **1 LIST:** What are six main forms of energy?

Using Forms of Energy You use the different forms of energy without ever noticing them. If energy came only in one form, the campers in Figure 14-6 might have light to see by but no heat for cooking. Each form of energy has its own characteristics and uses.

Mechanical Energy The energy in moving things is mechanical energy. This type of energy can occur as potential or kinetic energy, or both. For example, when you wind the spring on a toy car, you are storing mechanical energy in the spring. When the toy is turned on, the spring

unwinds and the mechanical energy of the spring is seen as the toy car moves. Until the spring winds down completely, it has both potential and kinetic energy.

Electrical Energy The energy that flows through wires and powers the lights and appliances in your house is electrical energy. This energy is in the form of moving electric charges.

Electromagnetic Energy Electromagnetic energy is a form of energy that can travel through a vacuum. Visible light, also called radiant energy, is the most familiar form of electromagnetic energy. Other forms of this energy include X rays, radio waves, and microwaves.

Heat Energy If you rub your hands together, they become warm. Heat energy, also called thermal energy, is the energy of the moving particles that make up matter. The faster the particles move, the more heat energy they have. All forms of matter contain some heat energy.

Chemical Energy The energy that holds particles of matter together is chemical energy. The energy stored in the head of a match is chemical energy. The energy stored in food and in fuels such as wood and coal is chemical energy.

▲ **Figure 14-6** Several forms of energy can be seen at this campsite.

Nuclear Energy Nuclear energy is the energy stored in the nucleus of an atom. Normally this energy is used to keep the protons and neutrons tightly bound together in the nucleus. However, when the nucleus of a large atom is split, as in a nuclear reactor, some of that energy is released as heat and light. Nuclear energy can also be released when nuclei of light atoms combine. The heat and light from the Sun are produced from this type of nuclear reaction.

 COMPARE: Choose two forms of energy. How are they alike? How are they different?

✔ CHECKING CONCEPTS

1. Where does your body get energy?
2. How many main forms of energy are there?
3. What is mechanical energy?
4. What is the most familiar form of electromagnetic energy?
5. What kind of energy is stored in wood?
6. What is nuclear energy?

THINKING CRITICALLY

7. **CLASSIFY:** Of the six main forms of energy, which forms are potential energy? Which are kinetic energy? Explain your answers.
8. **ANALYZE:** Identify each of the following objects as a source of mechanical, electromagnetic, heat, chemical, or nuclear energy. Some of the objects may be sources of more than one form of energy. Explain your answers.
   - **a.** gasoline
   - **b.** dynamite explosion
   - **c.** burning wood
   - **d.** river
   - **e.** lightning
   - **f.** the Sun

DESIGNING AN EXPERIMENT

Design an experiment to solve the following problem. Include a hypothesis, variables, a procedure, and a type of data to study.

PROBLEM: How can you show that sound is a form of mechanical energy?

Science and Technology
ENERGY IN MEDICINE

Throughout history, medicine has benefited greatly from advances in technology. Much of this technology uses energy. One of the most familiar medical devices is the X-ray machine. X rays are forms of electromagnetic energy. Like light, X rays can produce photographs, not of scenery but of bones inside the human body.

Computerized axial tomography is the tongue-twisting name for an advanced X-ray machine known as a CAT scanner. This device includes an X-ray tube. It rotates around a patient producing a three-dimensional image of the internal parts of the body on a computer screen.

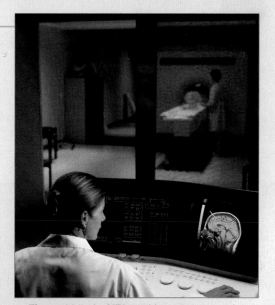
▲ **Figure 14-7** An MRI machine uses magnetic energy.

Magnetic energy and sound energy are also used in medicine. Magnetic resonance imaging (MRI) machines use magnetic energy to study soft tissues of the body. Ultrasound devices use the energy of sound waves to monitor the health of a developing fetus.

Thinking Critically Explain why energy is important to medical science.

14-3 How does energy change form?

INVESTIGATE

Observing Energy Change
HANDS-ON ACTIVITY

1. Place a windup toy on a flat surface.
2. Give the toy a little push and observe what happens.
3. Now, wind the spring of the toy. Pay attention to how the "feel" of the spring changes as you wind it.
4. Place the toy on a flat surface and release the spring.

THINK ABOUT IT: What kind of energy did the spring have after you wound it? How did this energy change?

STEP 3

Objective

Identify examples of energy changing form.

Key Terms

thermal (THUR-muhl) **pollution:** damage that occurs when waste heat enters the environment

law of conservation of energy: energy cannot be made or destroyed, but only changed in form

Changing Potential and Kinetic Energy
Energy can change from one form to another. Potential energy and kinetic energy often change form. Look at the bouncing ball in Figure 14-8. As the ball falls, potential energy is changed into kinetic energy and back into potential energy as it bounces to a higher position.

▲ **Figure 14-8** The energy of the bouncing ball is always changing form.

The ball in Figure 14-8 has the greatest amount of potential energy at its highest point. It has the greatest amount of kinetic energy just before it hits the ground.

1 ANALYZE: When does a bouncing ball have the least amount of kinetic energy?

Changing Forms of Energy You can observe many examples of changing forms of energy all around you. When you turn on an electric light, electrical energy is changed into light energy and heat energy. When you start an automobile, the engine changes the chemical energy in gasoline into mechanical energy. Nuclear reactors change nuclear energy into heat that is used to generate steam. Your muscles change the chemical energy in food into mechanical energy.

▲ **Figure 14-9** The light energy from the bulb is captured by the solar cells on the calculator. It is changed to electrical energy that powers the calculator.

Go Online
active art
For: Energy Transformations activity
Visit: PHSchool.com
Web Code: cgp-3053

2 IDENTIFY: What energy change takes place when you turn on an electric light?

Waste Heat When energy changes form, some of the energy is always changed into heat. Most of this heat energy is wasted. When waste heat energy escapes into the environment, it causes **thermal pollution.** For example, the water in lakes and rivers is used to remove waste heat from power plants. The waste heat makes the water warmer. The water may become too warm for living things. If the water gets too warm, fish in the lakes and rivers may die.

▶ **3 DEFINE:** What is thermal pollution?

Conservation of Energy You know that energy can change from one form to another. Energy also can move from place to place. However, energy can never be lost. Energy can never be created or destroyed. Energy can only be changed in form. This is the **law of conservation of energy.**

Before 1905, the law of conservation of energy did not seem to apply to nuclear energy. In the Sun, nuclear energy is changed into heat energy and light energy. The Sun seemed to be producing too much energy for its mass. In 1905, Albert Einstein showed that matter and energy are two forms of the same thing.

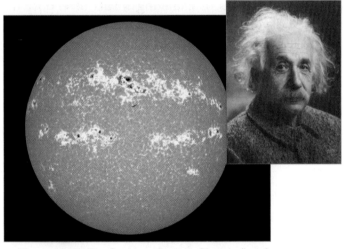

▲ **Figure 14-10** The Sun's energy gave Einstein (inset) the inspiration for his theory about matter and energy.

Einstein concluded that matter can be changed into energy, and energy can be changed into matter. The total amount of matter and energy in the universe does not change. Einstein stated this idea in the following equation.

$$E = mc^2$$

In this equation, E is energy, m is matter, or mass, and c is the speed of light. Einstein's equation showed that a small amount of matter could be changed into a huge amount of energy. This is what happens in the Sun.

▶ **4 DEFINE:** What is the law of conservation of energy?

✔ CHECKING CONCEPTS

1. A bouncing ball has the greatest amount of _____ energy at the top of its bounce.

2. When a bouncing ball is at the _____ of its bounce, it has the greatest amount of kinetic energy.

3. When you turn on a light, electrical energy is changed into light and _____.

4. An automobile engine changes _____ energy into mechanical energy.

5. The _____ energy in food is changed into mechanical energy by your muscles.

6. A nuclear reactor changes nuclear energy into _____ energy.

💡 THINKING CRITICALLY

7. **SYNTHESIZE:** Think of a thunderstorm. Describe the forms of energy that occur and the effects they have. Explain each time energy changes from one form to another.

INTERPRETING VISUALS

Study the drawings in Figure 14-11 and answer the following questions.

8. What two forms of energy make item A function?

9. How many forms of energy are shown in B? What are they?

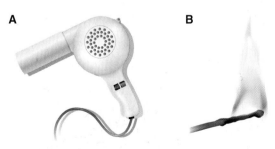

▲ **Figure 14-11**

THE Big IDEA

What are alternative sources of energy?

Think of the many ways people use energy every day. We use energy to heat and light our homes. Think of the hundreds of different ways we use electricity. Energy is also needed to run all forms of transportation.

Most of the energy people use today comes from burning fossil fuels—oil, coal, and natural gas. However, there are problems with this. Burning fossil fuels creates pollution and increases the greenhouse effect. Also, fossil fuels are not renewable. Once you burn a liter of fuel oil, it is gone forever. So someday, Earth's supply of fossil fuels will run out. It is time to develop some alternative sources of energy.

The Sun is a great energy source. Solar energy is free, and it will be available for billions of years. Drying clothes on a clothesline and using rooftop water heaters are simple ways to use solar energy. Solar panels can capture solar energy and convert it to heat, which can be used to heat our homes.

Wind is another form of "free" energy. This energy source has been used for thousands of years to sail ships, pump water, and grind grain in windmills. Wind can also be used to generate electricity.

The moving water in rivers and tidal basins and heat from below Earth's surface are other natural energy sources. In the future, each of these alternative energy sources may be developed to help replace the energy being produced from fossil fuels today. Look at the pictures on these pages. Then, follow the instructions in the Science Log to find out more about "the big idea."✦

Geothermal Power Generator

In places with lots of volcanic activity, heat energy inside Earth can be tapped to make electricity or heat buildings. Iceland plans to use geothermal and other energy sources to be free of fossil fuels by 2030.

Wind Farm

The energy of the wind can be used to spin an electric generator. In windy places, this is a great renewable energy source.

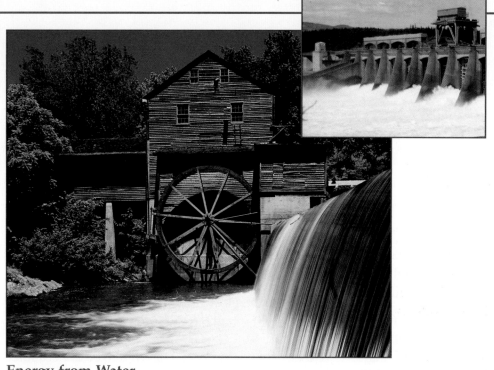

Energy from Water

For hundreds of years, moving water has turned water wheels to grind grain. Today, moving water is used in hydroelectric plants (above right) to generate electricity.

Solar-Powered Highway Emergency Phone

Some emergency phones on the highway are powered with photoelectric cells. In the daytime the Sun charges a battery so the phone can work at night.

SPEED LIMIT 15

Science Log

WRITING ACTIVITY

What alternative energy sources are available where you live? Find out about local renewable energy sources. Think about all the ways you use electricity and other forms of energy in your home. Then, design a house that uses renewable alternatives to fossil fuels to make its energy. Start your search at www.conceptsandchallenges.com.

14-4 What is work?

Objective
Relate work, force, and distance.

Key Term
work: force exerted through a distance

Work When are you doing work? **Work** is done when a force moves an object through a distance. This relationship can be shown in the following equation.

$$\text{work} = \text{force} \times \text{distance}$$

Suppose two boys push a car stuck in the mud. No matter how hard they push, they are not able to move the car. They are very tired afterward. Did the boys do any work?

The answer is no. For work to be done, something must be moved. The boys used a great deal of energy, but the car did not move. Work was not done.

▶ 1 **DESCRIBE:** What is the relationship between work, force, and distance?

Work and Energy Energy has been defined as the ability to make something happen. Energy is also often defined as the ability to do work. When a force moves an object, work is done.

Anything that can make something else move has energy. A moving bowling ball has energy. When the ball hits the pins, the pins move. The energy stored in gasoline can do work. It can make a car move. However, energy can be changed in form without any work being done. If you hold a heavy bag of groceries, your arms will get tired. Chemical energy in your muscles is changed to other forms of energy. However, because this energy is not being used to move the bag of groceries, you are not doing work.

▶ 2 **EXPLAIN:** How do you know a moving bowling ball has energy?

Direction of Motion For work to be done, a force must make an object move in the same direction as the force. Look at the three pictures in Figure 14-12. In the first picture, the girl is picking up a backpack. The backpack is moving in the direction of the force she used on it. She is doing work. In the middle picture, she is standing still with the pack on her back. She is using force, but no work is being done. In the third picture, she is moving the backpack as she begins to walk. Because she is causing the backpack to accelerate, she is doing work again.

▶ 3 **EXPLAIN:** Why is work done when you lift an object from the floor?

◀ **Figure 14-12** Work is being done in the first and last pictures but not the middle picture.

Natural Forces at Work Nature supplies the energy to do all kinds of work. Wind pushes sailboats across water and helps kites to fly. Wind energy turns windmills, which in turn generate electricity. The moving water of a river carries barges and pleasure boats. In the past, moving water turned water wheels that ran machinery in factories. Hurricanes, tornadoes, floods, and earthquakes provide the most dramatic examples of nature's ability to do work.

4 ▶ HYPOTHESIZE: What role does gravity play as a natural force doing work?

✔ CHECKING CONCEPTS

1. Work = force × _____.
2. Work is not done unless something is _____.
3. The ability to do work is _____.
4. For work to be done, the direction of the _____ must be the same as the direction of motion.

5. The stored _____ in gasoline can make a car move.

THINKING CRITICALLY

6. **ANALYZE:** Is work being done in each of the following examples? Explain your answers.
   a. Someone holds a heavy package for one hour.
   b. A football player kicks a field goal.
   c. A tennis player hits a tennis ball over the net.

HEALTH AND SAFETY TIP

Always be careful when picking up any heavy object from the floor. You should bend your knees and use your leg muscles, not your back muscles, to lift the object. Use library references to find out other ways to prevent back injuries.

Real-Life Science

SPORTS AND WORK

Athletes pride themselves on their ability to do work. Most sports involve forces that produce movement. Kicking a football is an example. The force applied to the ball causes it to move downfield in the direction of the force. A field-hockey ball is sent on its way when struck by a hockey stick. A push against a basketball sends the ball in the direction of the basket.

▲ **Figure 14-13** Work is done when the barbell is lifted.

Perhaps the most obvious work done in sports is carried out by weight lifters. The goal of weight lifters is to move heavy objects. Some events involve lifting a heavy barbell from the floor and raising it vertically above the head. Then, the barbell has to be slowly lowered back to the floor. The lowering of the barbell requires a great deal of energy, with the muscles acting against the force of gravity.

Thinking Critically Does the losing team in a tug-of-war contest do any useful work? Explain.

14-5 How can work be measured?

Objective

Use the proper units to measure and express work.

Key Term

joule (JOOL): SI unit of work; equal to 1 N-m (newton-meter)

Measuring Work To measure work, you must know two things. First, you must know the amount of force used to move an object. The SI unit of force is the newton (N). Second, you must know the distance that the object moves. Distance is usually measured in meters (m).

Work is measured in newton-meters (N-m). Work is equal to force times distance. This can be written as a formula.

$$W = F \times d$$

In this equation, W is work, F is force, and d is distance. Suppose you lift an object weighing 50 N. Remember that weight is a force. You move the object a distance of 2 m. To calculate the amount of work done, multiply the force times the distance.

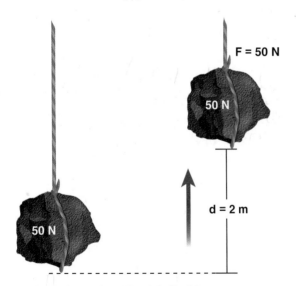

▲ **Figure 14-14** A 50-N rock is lifted 2m. The work done equals 100 N-m.

$$W = F \times d$$
$$W = 50 \text{ N} \times 2 \text{ m}$$
$$W = 100 \text{ N-m}$$

1 ▶ **LIST:** What two things must you know in order to measure work?

Unit of Work Scientists use a unit called a **joule** (J) to measure work. One joule of work is done when a force of 1 N moves an object a distance of 1 m. One joule is equal to 1 N-m of work.

2 ▶ **IDENTIFY:** What unit is used to measure work?

Direction of Force To measure work, you must measure the force applied in the direction of motion. This idea is illustrated in Figures 14-14 and 14-15. To lift a rock that weighs 50 N, you have to overcome gravity. You must apply a force of 50 N in an upward direction. Now, instead of lifting the rock, suppose you pulled the same 50-N rock a distance of 2 m along the ground. How much work have you done? Because you are overcoming friction instead of gravity, you will use less force— about 20 N. You must multiply this force times the distance moved. The work done equals 20 N × 2 m = 40 N-m, or 40 J.

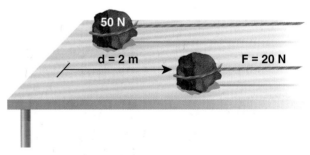

▲ **Figure 14-15** A 50-N rock is dragged 2 m using a force of 20 N. The work done equals 40 N-m or 40 J.

3 ▶ **CALCULATE:** How much work is done if you use 5 N of force to push a 20-N object 3 m across the floor?

✓ CHECKING CONCEPTS

1. The SI unit of force is the _____.

2. To measure work, you must know both force and _____.

3. Work can be measured in newton- _____.

4. The SI unit of work is the _____.

5. One joule is equal to 1 _____.

6. To measure work, you must know the amount of force applied in the direction of _____.

💡 THINKING CRITICALLY

7. **CALCULATE:** How much work is done in each of the following examples? Show all of your calculations.

   a. A child uses 4 N of force to pull a wagon a distance of 2 m along a sidewalk.

   b. A construction worker uses 30 N of force to drag a toolbox a distance of 3 m.

8. **COMPARE:** In which case is more work done? Explain your answer.

   a. You lift a 40-N object 2 m straight up.

   b. You use 10 N of force to pull the same 40-N object 2 m across the floor.

Web InfoSearch

James Prescott Joule The metric unit of work, the joule, is named after James Prescott Joule. Joule was a physicist. He was born in England in 1818. Joule was one of the four scientists who helped state the law of conservation of energy. Joule's law is also named after him.

SEARCH: Write a short biography about James Prescott Joule and the scientific Law named after him. Use the Internet to find out more. Start your search at www.conceptsandchallenges.com. Some key search words are **James Prescott Joule's Law.**

Hands-On Activity

MEASURING WORK

You will need a book, string, a spring scale, and a meter stick.

1. Tie a piece of string around a book.

2. Attach a spring scale to the book using the string.

3. Using the spring scale, lift the book a distance of 1 m. Record the amount of force shown on the spring scale. Calculate the amount of work done in joules.

▲ **STEP 4** Pull the book with the spring scale.

4. Using the spring scale, pull the book at a constant velocity for a distance of 1 m across your desk or tabletop. Record the amount of force shown on the spring scale. Calculate and record the amount of work done in joules.

Practicing Your Skills

5. **CALCULATE:** How much work did you do when you lifted the book?

6. **CALCULATE:** How much work did you do when you pulled the book across your desk?

7. **ANALYZE:** Based on your calculations, does it require more work to lift an object or to drag it?

14-6 What is power?

Objective
Explain how to measure power.

Key Terms
power: amount of work done per unit of time

watt: SI unit of power; equal to 1 J/s

Power The amount of work done per unit of time is called **power.** The term *power* describes the rate at which you do work. Suppose you took 30 minutes to shovel snow from a sidewalk. Your neighbor used a snowblower to clear a sidewalk of the same size in 10 minutes. If you both did the same amount of work, which one of you used more power? Your neighbor who did the work in less time used more power.

▲ **Figure 14-16** Shoveling snow is hard work and takes a long time.

▲ **Figure 14-17** The power of a snowblower helps a person do the same amount of work in less time.

▷ DEFINE: What is power?

Measuring Power To measure power, you must measure two things. First, you must measure the amount of work done. Second, you must measure the time needed to do the work. The formula used to measure power is as follows:

$$\text{power} = \text{work} \div \text{time}$$

Recall that work is equal to force times distance. The formula for power can also be written as

$$\text{power} = (\text{force} \times \text{distance}) \div \text{time}.$$

▷ **2** IDENTIFY: What is the formula used to measure power?

Unit of Power The SI unit of power is the **watt** (W). Power is equal to work divided by time. The unit of work is the newton-meter, or joule. The unit of time is the second. Therefore, one watt (1 W) is equal to 1 N-m/s, or 1 J/s. The watt is named after James Watt. Watt was a Scottish engineer who built the first useful steam engine.

Large amounts of power are measured in kilowatts (kW). One kilowatt (1 kW) is equal to 1,000 W. You are probably familiar with watts and kilowatts as units of electric power. For example, lightbulbs can be rated as 60 W, 100 W, or 250 W.

Electricity is not free. You have to pay for the electricity you use. How does the electric company know how much electricity your family uses? The electricity used in your house is measured by a meter like the one shown in Figure 14-18. The meter shows how many kilowatt-hours of electricity have been used.

▲ **Figure 14-18** An electric meter

▷ **3** HYPOTHESIZE: How does a 60-W lightbulb differ from a 100-W lightbulb?

CHECKING CONCEPTS

1. The rate at which work is done is

   _____.

2. Power is the amount of work done per unit of

   _____.

3. To measure power, you must find the amount of _____ and the time needed.

4. Power = (force × _____)/time.

5. The SI unit of power is the _____.

6. One _____ is equal to 1,000 W.

7. One watt is equal to 1 N-m/s, or

   1 _____ /s.

8. The unit of power is named after James

   _____.

THINKING CRITICALLY

9. **CALCULATE:** How much more power is used to move a weight of 500 N a distance of 20 m in 5 s than is used to move a weight of 1,000 N a distance of 30 m in 30 sec?

10. **CALCULATE:** Find the amount of power used in each of the following examples. Show your calculations.

   a. You use a force of 10 N to move a box 100 m in 10 seconds.

   b. An athlete lifting weights does 900 J of work in 1 second.

   c. A truck does 30,000 J of work in 15 seconds.

   d. A furniture mover uses a force of 150 N to push a large trunk 5 m across the floor in 5 seconds.

DESIGNING AN EXPERIMENT

Design an experiment to solve the following problem. Include a hypothesis, variables, a procedure, and a type of data to collect and study.

PROBLEM: How much power, in watts, do you use when you climb a flight of stairs?

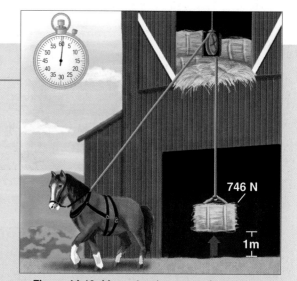

▲ **Figure 14-19** Measuring the power of one horse

How Do They Know That?

HORSEPOWER

You are probably familiar with the term *horsepower*. Engines and motors are commonly rated in horsepower. An automobile engine, for example, may have about 100 horsepower. Where does this unit of power come from?

James Watt was the first person to use the term *horsepower.* Watt was a Scottish engineer and inventor. In the 1760s, he built the first practical steam engine. Watt wanted to use a unit of power for his engine that would be familiar to most people. He decided to use the power of a horse as the standard unit of power for the steam engine. Watt found that a strong horse could lift a 746-N load a distance of 1 m in 1 second. In other words, a horse produced 746 J/s of power. Watt defined this amount of power as 1 horsepower (hp).

Today, the unit of power is the watt (W). It is named in honor of James Watt. One watt is equal to 1 J/s. Therefore, 1 hp is equal to 746 W. Real horses are no longer used as a standard of power.

Thinking Critically What types of machinery are still rated in horsepower?

CHAPTER 14: Energy and Work **305**

LAB ACTIVITY
Studying Energy Changes in a Roller Coaster

BACKGROUND

Have you ever ridden a roller coaster? If you have, you were probably more concerned with fun than the science behind its operation. Roller coasters are machines that use potential and kinetic energy.

PURPOSE

In this activity, you will experiment with how roller coasters change potential energy into kinetic energy and back again several times.

PROCEDURE

1. Raise one end of the plastic tubing about 1 1/2 m above the floor. Tape this end to a bookcase or some other object so it stays put. The tubing will serve as a roller-coaster track.

2. Use furniture, books, or other objects to make hills for your model roller coaster. Keep the track with its hills in a straight line. Do not include any turns. Tape the track securely so that it does not move.

Materials
Clear plastic tubing
Masking tape
Small ball bearing or glass bead
Meter stick
Pencil and paper

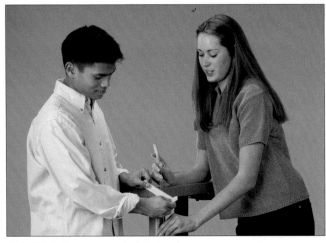

▲ **STEP 1** Tape one end of the track.

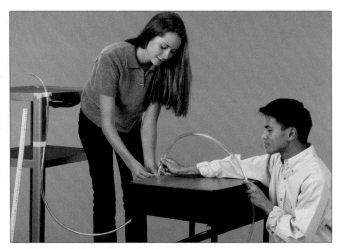

▲ **STEP 2** Create hills and valleys along one track.

3. Measure and record the height of the hills. Draw a sketch of your model roller coaster. Include your measurements.

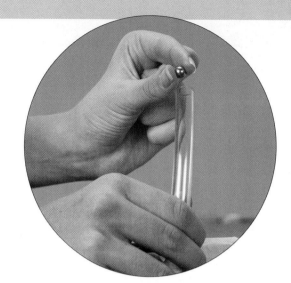

4. Insert a ball bearing into the tubing at the high end. Test your model. Does the ball bearing reach the end of the track? Explain why. If necessary, adjust your design so that the ball bearing travels the entire length of the track.

5. After testing your roller coaster, take it apart and make a new design for your track. You may wish to add curves or even some loops. Draw a sketch of your new design and test it. Record your observations.

▲ **STEP 4** Test your roller coaster.

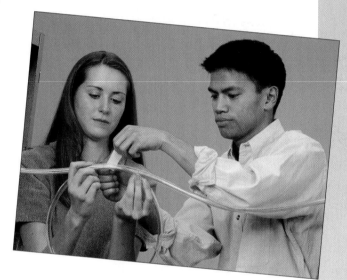

CONCLUSIONS

1. **OBSERVE AND DESCRIBE:** What happened to the ball bearing as you released it at the top of your roller-coaster track?

2. **ANALYZE:** Why does the first hill of a roller coaster have to be the highest hill?

3. **OBSERVE:** Compare the height of the hills as you move from the top to the bottom of the roller coaster.

4. **ANALYZE:** Why must the pattern of the hills be set up as it is?

5. **INFER:** Where on your roller coaster does the ball bearing have potential energy changing to kinetic energy? Where is kinetic energy changing to potential energy?

6. **INFER:** Where on your roller coaster does the ball bearing have the greatest potential energy? The least potential energy?

7. **INFER:** Where on your roller coaster does the ball bearing have the greatest kinetic energy? The least kinetic energy?

▲ **STEP 5** Make a new design for your track.

Chapter 14 Challenges

Chapter Summary

Lesson 14-1
- **Energy** is the ability to make something happen.
- There are two basic kinds of energy—potential energy and kinetic energy
- **Potential energy** is stored energy. **Kinetic energy** is energy of motion.

Lesson 14-2
- There are six main forms of energy: mechanical energy, electrical energy, electromagnetic energy, heat energy, chemical energy, and nuclear energy.

Lesson 14-3
- Energy can change from one form to another.
- When energy changes form, some of the energy is always changed into heat energy.
- The **law of conservation of energy** states that energy can never be created or destroyed but only changed in form.
- The total amount of matter and energy in the universe never changes.

Lesson 14-4
- **Work** is done when a force moves an object.
- For work to be done, the direction of the applied force must be the same as the direction of motion.

Lesson 14-5
- Work can be measured in newton-meters (N-m).
- The unit of work is the **joule** (J); 1 J = 1 N-m.
- When measuring work, you must measure the force applied in the direction of motion.

Lesson 14-6
- **Power** is the amount of work done per unit of time.
- Power = work/time, or (force × distance)/time.
- The SI unit of power is the **watt** (W).

Key Term Challenges

energy (p. 292)
joule (p. 302)
kinetic energy (p. 292)
law of conservation of energy (p. 296)

potential energy (p. 292)
power (p. 304)
thermal pollution (p. 296)
watt (p. 304)
work (p. 300)

MATCHING Write the Key Term from above that best matches each description.

1. stored energy
2. ability to make something happen
3. force times distance
4. energy of motion
5. metric unit of work
6. metric unit of power
7. work done per unit time

FILL IN Write the Key Term from above that best completes each statement.

8. The moving water in a waterfall has _____.
9. The _____ in a match is stored in the chemicals in the match head.
10. The faster you run, the more _____ you have.
11. Waste heat that escapes into the environment can cause _____.
12. The _____ states that energy cannot be made or destroyed but only changed in form.
13. When you use force to move an object, you are doing _____.
14. The _____ is the unit used to measure work.
15. The rate at which you do work is called _____.
16. The unit of power is the _____.

Content Challenges TEST PREP

MULTIPLE CHOICE **Write the letter of the term or phrase that best completes each statement.**

1. An object that is raised above the ground has
   a. heat energy.
   b. kinetic energy.
   c. potential energy.
   d. nuclear energy.

2. All moving objects have
   a. heat energy.
   b. kinetic energy.
   c. potential energy.
   d. nuclear energy.

3. Sound is a form of
   a. nuclear energy.
   b. electromagnetic energy.
   c. chemical energy.
   d. mechanical energy.

4. Electromagnetic energy includes X rays and
   a. light.
   b. sound.
   c. chemicals.
   d. atoms.

5. An automobile engine changes chemical energy into
   a. electricity.
   b. nuclear energy.
   c. mechanical energy.
   d. light.

6. In the Sun, nuclear energy is changed into light energy and
   a. sound energy.
   b. chemical energy.
   c. electrical energy.
   d. heat energy.

7. Work equals force times
   a. distance.
   b. mass.
   c. power.
   d. energy.

8. Work is measured in units called
   a. watts.
   b. meters.
   c. joules.
   d. newtons.

9. One watt is equal to
   a. 1 m/s.
   b. 1 J/s.
   c. 1 N/s.
   d. 1 kW/s.

TRUE/FALSE **Write *true* if the statement is true. If the statement is false, change the underlined term to make the statement true.**

10. Energy is the ability to do <u>work</u>.

11. Stored energy is <u>kinetic</u> energy.

12. <u>Potential</u> energy is energy of motion.

13. There are <u>six</u> main forms of energy.

14. The energy that holds atomic particles together is <u>nuclear</u> energy.

15. When energy changes form, some energy is always wasted as <u>sound</u>.

16. Energy <u>cannot</u> be made or destroyed.

17. Energy <u>cannot</u> be changed in form without work being done.

18. To measure work, you must know force and <u>time</u>.

19. For work to be done, an object must move in the <u>opposite</u> direction of the force applied to it.

20. In a light bulb, electrical energy is changed to light and <u>sound</u>.

Content Challenges TEST PREP

WRITTEN RESPONSE Complete the exercises and answer each of the following questions in complete sentences.

1. **COMPARE:** Explain the difference between potential energy and kinetic energy.

2. **ANALYZE:** Describe the changes in potential and kinetic energy that take place in a swinging pendulum.

3. **EXPLAIN:** How does Einstein's equation $E = mc^2$ support the law of conservation of energy?

4. **INFER:** How is it possible for energy to change form without any work being done?

5. **RELATE:** What is the relationship between work and power?

6. **INFER:** Why is gravitational potential energy called energy of position?

INTERPRETING A DIAGRAM Use Figures 14-20 and 14-21 to answer the following questions.

7. What is the weight of the object in Figure 14-20?

8. What distance is this object being lifted?

9. How much force is needed to lift this object?

10. How much work is being done to lift this object?

11. What is the weight of the object in Figure 14-21?

12. What distance is this object being pulled?

13. How much force is needed to pull this object?

14. How much work is being done to pull this object?

15. Is the amount of work being done in the two diagrams the same or different? Explain.

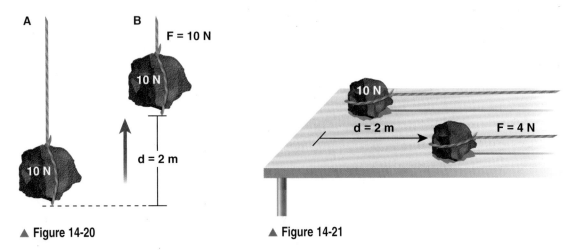

▲ Figure 14-20   ▲ Figure 14-21

Chapter 15 Machines

▲ **Figure 15-1** The Guggenheim Museum in New York City

The walkway around the inside walls of the Guggenheim Museum is one continuous ramp. The ramp is an inclined plane, a type of simple machine. You can walk along the ramp and view exhibits from the ground level to the top level without using stairs or an elevator.

►Is walking up a ramp easier than walking up a staircase? Explain.

Contents

15-1 What is a simple machine?

INVESTIGATE

Using Machines
HANDS-ON ACTIVITY

1. Create a chart that lists the items in the classroom and at home that you use daily.

2. Check off each item you believe to be a machine.

3. Choose an item from your list. Tell a partner how it works as a machine.

THINK ABOUT IT: What are the different parts of your machine? How does it make your life easier?

STEP 3

Objective

Describe how machines make work easier.

Key Terms

machine: device that makes work easier

wheel and axle: two different-sized wheels that turn together around the same point

effort force: force applied to a machine

resistance force: force that opposes the effort force

mechanical advantage: number of times a machine multiplies the effort force

ideal mechanical advantage: mechanical advantage a machine would have with no friction

Simple Machines People use machines to make work easier. Did you ever try to take the lid off a can of paint using only your hands? If the lid is on very tight, your fingers cannot supply enough force to remove the lid. However, you can use a screwdriver as a lever to help you pry off the lid. A lever is an example of a simple machine. A **machine** is a device that makes work easier. Machines make work easier by changing the size, direction, or speed of a force.

Most machines are made up of two or more of the six simple machines shown in Figure 15-2. They are the lever, the pulley, the inclined plane, the screw, the wheel and axle, and the wedge.

▶ **1** NAME: What are the six simple machines?

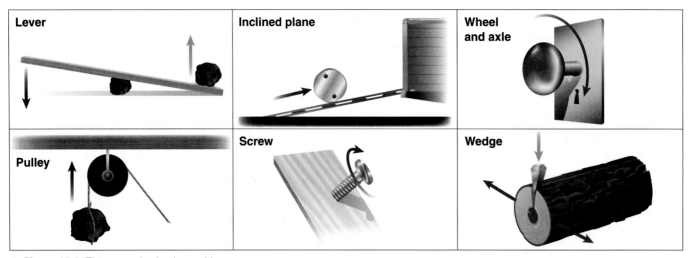

▲ **Figure 15-2** There are six simple machines.

Wheel and Axle The next time you open a door by turning a doorknob, stop for a minute and think. You have just used a simple machine called a wheel and axle. A **wheel and axle** is two different-sized wheels that turn together around the same point.

A wheel and axle is like a lever that moves in a circle. Many wheel-and-axle machines do not look like a wheel and axle. Figure 15-3 shows how a simple wrench can be a wheel and axle.

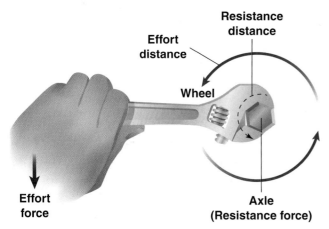

▲ **Figure 15-3** A wheel and axle machine

What makes a wheel and axle a simple machine? It makes work easier. It takes less force to turn the handle than it would to turn the axle by itself. You exert a small force on the handle, which exerts a larger force on the axle.

 EXPLAIN: What makes a wheel and axle a simple machine?

Effort Force and Resistance Force The force you apply to a machine is called the **effort force.** For example, the force you apply to a wrench is the effort force. The force that opposes the effort force is called the **resistance force.** The nut is the resistance force you are trying to overcome when you turn the handle. A machine like the wrench lets you use a small force to overcome a large force.

Machines make work easier but they do not change the *amount* of work you do. When you use a machine, you often sacrifice distance to multiply your effort force. Look again at the wrench in Figure 15-3. You can see that the effort force applied to the wrench has to move a greater distance then does the resistance force you overcome when you turn the nut.

 INFER: Does a wheel and axle change the size, direction, or speed of a force?

Mechanical Advantage Most machines help you do work by multiplying the effort force you apply to the machine. The number of times a machine multiplies the effort force is called the **mechanical advantage (MA)** of that machine. To find the mechanical advantage of a machine, divide the resistance force by the effort force. Use the example below to find the MA if you apply a force of 100 N to a machine to move a 1,500-N object.

$$MA = \text{resistance force} \div \text{effort force}$$
$$MA = 1{,}500 \text{ N} \div 100 \text{ N}$$
$$MA = 15$$

 DEFINE: What is mechanical advantage?

Ideal Mechanical Advantage The MA that a machine would have with no friction is known as the **ideal mechanical advantage (IMA)** of that machine. For example, the IMA of a single moveable pulley is 2. Such a pulley should multiply your effort force by 2. However, because of friction, and the weight of the pulley, the actual MA of the pulley will be less than 2.

 DESCRIBE: What is the IMA of a machine?

✓ CHECKING CONCEPTS

1. How can you find the IMA of a machine?
2. What is resistance force?
3. What is force effort?

💡 THINKING CRITICALLY

4. **INFER:** How does friction affect the IMA of a machine?
5. **ANALYZE:** Can the actual MA of a machine ever be greater than its IMA? Explain.

BUILDING MATH SKILLS

Calculating Use the data in Figure 15-4 to find the MA of simple machines *a* and *b*.

	Effort force	Resistance force
a.	300 N	3,000 N
b.	160 N	1,600 N

▲ **Figure 15-4**

15-2 What is efficiency?

Objective

Explain how to find the efficiency of a machine.

Key Terms

work output: work done by a machine

work input: work done on a machine

efficiency (eh-FIHSH-uhn-see): ratio of work output to work input

Work Input and Work Output The work done by a machine is **work output.** Work output is equal to the resistance force times the distance through which the resistance force moves.

work output = resistance force × resistance distance

The work done on a machine is **work input.** The work input equals the effort force times the effort distance. The effort distance is the distance through which the force moves.

work input = effort force × effort distance

Machines cannot increase the amount of work done. As a result, the work output of a machine is never greater than the work input.

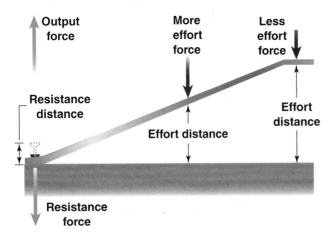

▲ **Figure 15-5** The longer the lever, the greater the effort distance. This reduces the needed effort force.

▶ **1** **NAME:** What is the work done by a machine called?

Efficiency Not all of the work put into a machine is changed into useful work. Some of the work input is used to overcome friction. This work is lost as heat energy. The **efficiency** of a machine is the ratio of work output to work input. It is usually expressed as a percentage.

You can find the percentage efficiency of a machine by dividing the work output by the work input and multiplying by 100.

percentage efficiency = work output ÷ work input × 100

Remember, the work done by a machine is always less than the work put into it. So, the efficiency of a machine is always less than 100 percent.

▶ **2** **INFER:** Why is the efficiency of a machine always less than 100 percent?

Increasing Efficiency The boat shown in Figure 15-6 is a racing shell. The oars used to move the shell through the water are levers. Each rower exerts an effort force on one end of an oar. As the oar moves through the water, it overcomes a resistance. The boat resists moving through the water because of the force of friction between the boat and the water.

Suppose some way could be found to reduce the force of friction between the boat and the water. This would decrease the resistance. Then, if each crew

▲ **Figure 15-6** Work is being done on the boat by eight simple machines.

member applies the same effort to the oars, the boat will move farther with each pull on the oars. In other words, the work input would remain the same, but the work output would be greater. This means that the efficiency has been increased.

3 ANALYZE: What is another way to increase efficiency besides decreasing the resistance force?

CHECKING CONCEPTS

1. The work put out by a machine is _____ than the work put into a machine.

2. The efficiency of a machine is usually expressed as a _____.

3. Some of the work you put into a machine is always used to overcome _____.

4. The work put into a machine is equal to the effort force multiplied by the effort _____.

5. The efficiency of a machine always is less than _____.

THINKING CRITICALLY

6. ANALYZE: Why can a machine not produce more work than is put into it?

7. HYPOTHESIZE: Why do you think many complex machines have very low efficiencies?

BUILDING MATH SKILLS

Calculating Complete the table in Figure 15-7 by calculating the missing value.

Work input	Work output	Efficiency
10 J	5 J	
20 J		40%
	30 J	60%
45 J	9 J	
	9 J	90%

▲ Figure 15-7

Real-Life Science

BICYCLING

The first successful bicycle was built by Baron Karl Von Drais de Sauerbrun in Karlsruhe, Germany, in 1817. This early bicycle had no pedals. Riders moved the bicycle forward by pushing backward against the ground with their feet. By 1839, a Scottish blacksmith, Kirkpatrick Macmillan, had added pedals. The modern bicycle began to be developed.

In Europe and Asia, bicycles are major means of transportation. In the United States, bicycles are used mainly for recreation and exercise. Streets in many cities and towns have specially marked bicycle lanes. Bike paths are set aside in parks and in rural areas. All cyclists should be aware of traffic and safety rules before riding their bicycles in any of these areas.

Special bicycles have been developed for racing. These bicycles are made of strong, lightweight materials, such as alloys of titanium and carbon. Racing tires are very narrow to reduce weight and frictional drag. To further reduce friction, cyclists wear tight, specially designed clothing and streamlined helmets. These people take their sport very seriously.

Thinking Critically What features might a bicycle designed for off-road trails have?

▲ Figure 15-8 Modern bicycles are made to be more efficient.

15-3 How does a lever work?

INVESTIGATE

Using a Lever
HANDS-ON ACTIVITY

1. Balance a meter stick on a wood block at the 50-cm mark.

2. Place a 5 N weight on one end of the meter stick. Attach a spring scale to the other end as shown in the picture.

3. Pull down on the spring scale. Record the effort force needed to lift the weight.

4. Repeat Step 3 with the wood block at the 45-cm mark and again with the block at the 55-cm mark.

THINK ABOUT IT: Is it easier to lift the weight when the wood block is closer to the weight or farther from it? In which case did the resistance move farthest?

STEP 3

Objectives
Explain how a lever makes work easier. Describe the three classes of levers.

Key Terms
lever (LEHV-uhr)**:** bar that is free to turn around a fixed point

fulcrum (FOOL-kruhm)**:** fixed point around which a lever pivots or turns

Levers Have you ever used a shovel or a crowbar? If so, then you have used a lever. A **lever** is a bar that is free to turn around a fixed point. The fixed point on which a lever turns is called the **fulcrum.** A lever can make work easier by increasing force. Levers also change the direction of a force and the distance over which a force acts.

A lever has two parts—an effort arm and a resistance arm. The effort arm is the distance from the effort force to the fulcrum. The resistance arm is the distance from the resistance force to the fulcrum.

You can find the IMA of a lever by dividing the length of the effort arm by the length of the resistance arm.

IMA = effort arm length ÷ resistance arm length

▶ **EXPLAIN:** How can you find the ideal mechanical advantage of a lever?

Classes of Levers There are three classes, or kinds, of levers. The classes of levers are based on the position of the resistance force, the effort force, and the fulcrum.

In a first-class lever, the fulcrum is between the effort force and the resistance force. These levers multiply force. The direction of the effort force is changed. Examples of first-class levers include crowbars, seesaws, and car jacks.

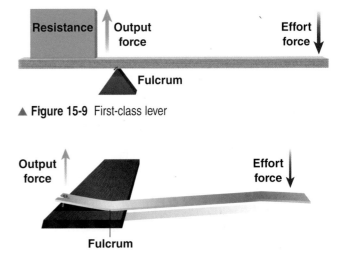

▲ **Figure 15-9** First-class lever

▲ **Figure 15-10** A crowbar is a first-class lever.

A second-class lever has the resistance between the effort force and the fulcrum. Second-class levers always multiply force. The direction of the effort force is not changed. Examples of second-class levers include wheelbarrows and nutcrackers.

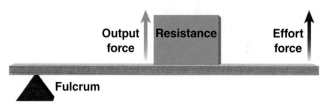

▲ **Figure 15-11** Second-class lever

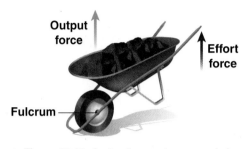

▲ **Figure 15-12** A wheelbarrow is a second-class lever.

In a third-class lever, the effort force is between the fulcrum and the resistance force. These levers multiply the distance the resistance force moves, but the direction of the effort force is not changed. In third-class levers, the effort arm is always shorter than the resistance arm. Examples of third-class levers include shovels, baseball bats, and brooms.

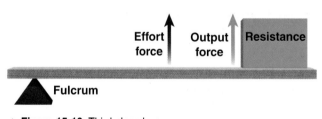

▲ **Figure 15-13** Third-class lever

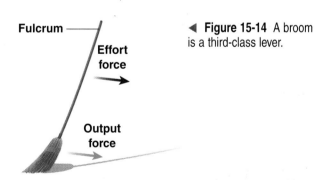

◄ **Figure 15-14** A broom is a third-class lever.

2 ▶ **IDENTIFY:** In what class of lever is the effort force between the fulcrum and the resistance force?

✓ CHECKING CONCEPTS

1. The fixed point around which a lever turns is called the _____.
2. There are _____ classes of levers.
3. The ideal mechanical advantage of a lever is equal to the length of the effort arm divided by the length of the _____ arm.
4. In a _____-class lever, the effort force is between the fulcrum and the resistance force.
5. The resistance arm is the distance from the resistance force to the _____.

💡 THINKING CRITICALLY

6. **CALCULATE:** What is the IMA of a lever with an effort arm 2 m long and a resistance arm 0.5 m long?
7. **HYPOTHESIZE:** How could you increase the IMA of a lever?
8. **CLASSIFY:** Classify each of the following as a first-, second-, or third-class lever: nutcracker, bottle opener, hammer, and hockey stick.

Web InfoSearch

Levers in Your Body Different parts of the human body act as levers. Your arm is a third-class lever. Suppose you hold a book in your hand. The book is the resistance. Your elbow is the fulcrum. The muscles in your forearms provide the effort force to lift the book.

SEARCH: Use the Internet to find what other parts of your body act as levers. Create a chart and draw a picture of the body part and an example of the lever action. Start your search at www.conceptsandchallenges.com. Some key search words are **human body levers** and **human body simple machine.**

Objectives

Explain how pulleys make work easier. Compare fixed and movable pulleys.

Key Term

pulley: rope wrapped around a wheel

Pulleys Look at Figure 15-15. A pulley is being used to raise a bucket. A **pulley** is a rope wrapped around a wheel. Pulleys can change the direction of a force, the size of a force, or both. The pulley in Figure 15-15 changes the direction of a force. When the rope is pulled down, the bucket moves up.

▶ **1** **DEFINE:** What is a pulley?

Fixed Pulleys A fixed pulley is attached to something that does not move. The pulley shown in Figure 15-15 is a fixed pulley. Fixed pulleys change the direction of the effort force. They do not increase the effort force. In a fixed pulley, the effort force is equal to the resistance force. As a result, the IMA of a fixed pulley is equal to 1.

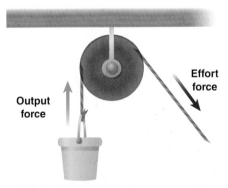

▲ **Figure 15-15** Fixed pulley

▶ **2** **EXPLAIN:** Why is the IMA of a fixed pulley equal to 1?

Movable Pulleys Unlike a fixed pulley, a movable pulley can move as the rope is pulled through it. Figure 15-16 shows a single movable pulley. As the free end of the rope is pulled up, the pulley and its load also move up. A movable pulley does not change the direction of the effort force. It does increase, or multiply, the size of the effort force. The IMA of a single movable pulley is equal to the number of supporting rope segments that lift the resistance. The IMA of a single movable pulley is 2. The effort distance is always twice the resistance distance.

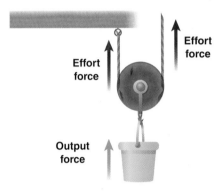

▲ **Figure 15-16** Movable pulley

▶ **3** **ANALYZE:** What is the IMA of the movable pulley in Figure 15-16? Why?

Pulley Systems A block and tackle is a pulley system. A pulley system is made up of both fixed and movable pulleys. The pulleys act together to increase the MA of the system. The IMA of a pulley system is equal to the number of supporting ropes. The rope attached to the fixed pulley is not counted. A block and tackle may have a large mechanical advantage, depending on the number of pulleys in the system.

▲ **Figure 15-17** Pulley system

Go **Online**
active art

For: Types of Pulleys activity
Visit: PHSchool.com
Web Code: cgp-3043

▶ **4** **INFER:** Why is the actual MA of a pulley system a lot smaller than its IMA?

1. A _____ pulley can increase the effort force.

2. The IMA of a fixed pulley is _____.

3. A _____ is an example of a pulley system.

4. The IMA of a pulley system with four supporting ropes is _____.

5. A _____ pulley can change only the direction of a force.

THINKING CRITICALLY

6. EXPLAIN: Why is the IMA of a single movable pulley greater than that of a single fixed pulley?

7. ANALYZE: What kind of pulley is used to raise a flag to the top of a flagpole?

8. INFER: What happens to the actual mechanical advantage of a pulley system as more pulleys are added?

INTERPRETING VISUALS

Figure 15-18 shows a block and tackle.

9. What is the IMA of the block and tackle?

◀ Figure 15-18

BUILDING SCIENCE SKILLS

Modeling Design a machine that uses at least two types of pulleys. Your machine should have a practical use. Draw a diagram or build a working model of your machine. Label each pulley type. Explain how your machine works.

Hands-On Activity

USING A MOVABLE PULLEY

You will need a spring scale, string, a movable pulley, a book, and tape.

1. Tie the string around the book. Attach the book to the spring scale.

2. Use the spring scale to lift the book. Record the effort force needed to lift the book.

3. Attach the movable pulley to the book and spring scale as shown.

4. Use the pulley to lift the book again. Record the effort force needed to lift the book.

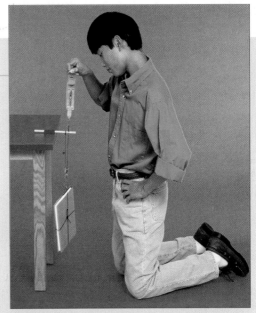

▲ STEP 3 Attach the pulley to the book and spring scale.

Practicing Your Skills

5. OBSERVE: How much force was needed to lift the book without the pulley?

6. OBSERVE: How much force was needed to lift the book with the pulley?

7. CALCULATE: What is the actual MA of the movable pulley?

LAB ACTIVITY
Pulley Advantage

Materials
Ring stand and ring
Pulleys
Cord
Lifting mass
Spring scale –
   250 g/5 N
Metric ruler
Calculator

BACKGROUND

Simple machines like levers, inclined planes, and pulleys make it seem like you get something for nothing. A difficult job becomes easier to do. What is really happening is a trade-off. The job is easier to do but it takes longer to do it. You can see this relationship with pulleys.

PURPOSE

In this activity, you will lift various masses with pulleys. You will then compare the effort forces and the distances the forces have to be exerted.

PROCEDURE

1. Copy the data table in Figure 15-19.

2. Make a single fixed pulley by attaching one pulley to the ring stand. Tie the cord to the mass and run the cord through the pulley. Tie a loop to the other end of the cord for hooking the spring scale.

3. Lift the weight off the tabletop slightly by pulling on the spring scale. Measure the force on the scale and record it in your data table.

4. Raise the weight 10 cm. Now, measure how far you had to pull the scale to raise the weight that distance. Record your answers in the data table.

5. Set up new pulley arrangements as shown in the picture labeled Step 5. Measure the forces and the distances as before.

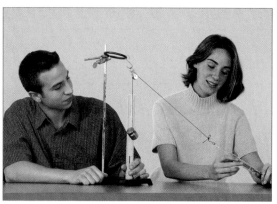

▲ **STEP 2** Set up the pulley.

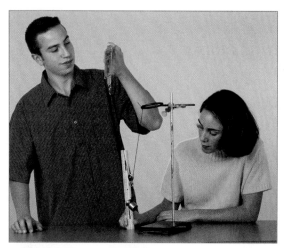

▲ **STEP 4** Measure the distances.

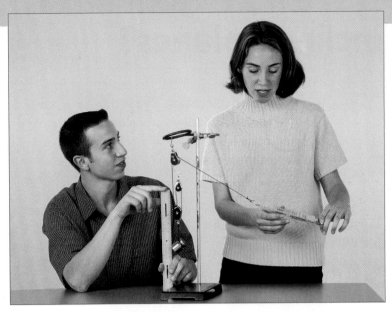

◀ **STEP 5**
Set up a pulley system.

Pulley Advantage

Setup	Number of Cords Holding Mass (mechanical advantage)	Lifting Mass	Lifting Force	Lifting Distance	Pulling Distance
1				10 cm	
2				10 cm	
3				10 cm	
4				10 cm	

▲ **Figure 15-19** Copy this chart and use it to record your observations.

CONCLUSIONS

1. **OBSERVE:** When you increased the number of supporting cords, what happened to the amount of force needed to lift the weight?

2. **OBSERVE:** When you increased the number of cords supporting the mass, what happened to the distance you had to exert the effort force?

3. **ANALYZE:** What is the relationship between force and distance when you increase the number of cords to two?

4. **INFER:** If you want to lift a very heavy mass with a pulley system, what should you do?

15-5 What are inclined planes?

Objective

Describe how an inclined plane makes work easier.

Key Term

inclined plane: slanted surface, or ramp

Inclined Planes A ramp is often used to help load barrels onto a truck. The barrels are rolled up the ramp onto the truck. The ramp is an inclined plane. The word *inclined* means "slanted." A plane is a flat surface. Therefore, an **inclined plane** is a slanted surface, or ramp. Inclined planes are simple machines that help make work easier.

▶ **DEFINE:** What is an inclined plane?

MA of an Inclined Plane An inclined plane makes work easier by changing the angle at which you have to exert force to lift resistance. Instead of lifting an object straight up against gravity, you push or pull the object up at an angle. Look at Figure 15-20 showing a man moving a box up an inclined plane. He is raising a 300-N box using only 100 N of effort force. In effect, the ramp has multiplied his effort force by 3. The MA of this ramp is 3.

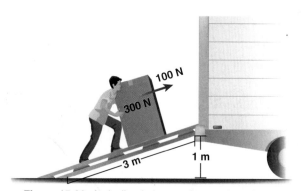

▲ **Figure 15-20** An inclined plane makes work easier.

You can find the IMA of an inclined plane by dividing its length by its height.

IMA = length ÷ height

IMA = 3 m ÷ 1 m

IMA = 3

▶ **EXPLAIN:** How can you find the approximate MA of an inclined plane?

Wedges and Screws A wedge is a kind of inclined plane. A wedge is most often made of two inclined planes back-to-back. A knife blade and an axe are examples of wedges.

◀ **Figure 15-21** A wedge is two inclined planes back-to-back.

A screw is an inclined plane wrapped around a cylinder. A screw is like the steps wrapped around the center of a spiral staircase. Bolts are examples of screws.

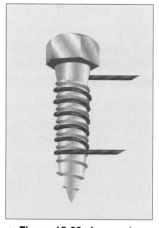

▲ **Figure 15-22** A screw is an inclined plane wrapped around a cylinder.

▲ **Figure 15-23** Screws are simple machines.

▶ **LIST:** What are two examples of wedges?

1. A _____ is an inclined plane wrapped around a cylinder.

2. The IMA of an inclined plane is equal to its length divided by its _____.

3. A plane is a _____ surface.

4. Bolts are examples of _____.

5. An inclined plane _____ the size of the effort force.

6. A wedge is made up of _____ inclined planes.

THINKING CRITICALLY

7. **HYPOTHESIZE:** How could you increase the IMA of an inclined plane?

8. **ANALYZE:** What happens to the IMA of an inclined plane if you increase the height?

INTERPRETING VISUALS

Figure 15-24 shows three ramps: A, B, and C.

9. Which ramp has the smallest IMA? Explain.

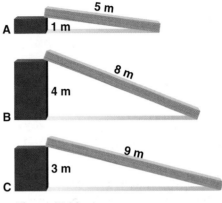

▲ Figure 15-24

Hands-On Activity

FINDING THE MA OF AN INCLINED PLANE

You will need a wooden board, a spring scale, string, a metric ruler, and three books.

1. Stack two books one on top of the other. Place one end of the wooden board on top of the books to make an inclined plane.

2. Use the metric ruler to measure the length and height of the inclined plane. Record your measurements.

3. Tie one end of the string around the third book. Tie the other end to the spring scale. Measure and record the weight of the book in newtons. The weight of the book is the resistance force, when no ramp is being used.

4. Use the spring scale to pull the book up the inclined plane. Record the effort force shown on the scale.

▲ **STEP 4** Use the spring scale to record the effort force.

Practicing Your Skills

5. **ANALYZE:** Find the IMA of the inclined plane using the formula IMA = length/height.

6. **CALCULATE:** Find the actual MA of the inclined plane using the formula IMA = resistance force/effort force.

7. **HYPOTHESIZE:** Why is the actual MA less than the IMA?

THE Big IDEA

How did the Egyptians build the Great Pyramid?

Is it possible to build something 480 ft tall using only simple machines? That is exactly what Khufu did, with a lot of help. The Egyptian Pharaoh Khufu had the Great Pyramid built at Giza 4,500 years ago. For most of recorded history, Khufu's pyramid was the world's largest building. It has a mass of almost 6 billion kilograms. It was originally 147 m tall; it covers an area of about ten football fields. Using only levers, wedges, inclined planes, muscle power, and engineering genius, Egyptian workers put more than 2 million huge blocks precisely in place to construct Khufu's monument.

Archaeologists do not agree on exactly how the Great Pyramid and the other pyramids of Giza were constructed. However, they do agree that these structures were built with the simplest of machines. The workers may not even have had the wheel.

Copper wedges were used to cut the huge stone blocks. The stones were probably dragged to the construction site on greased sleds. They were moved up the pyramid on inclined planes. Some historians believe a single ramp was used to move the stones to the top. Others suggest that spiral ramps were built around the sides of the pyramid.

Positioning the top stones and the huge stones that form the inside chambers of the pyramid must have been very tricky. Expert use of levers and wedges was needed to set these stones. Look at the illustrations and text on these two pages. Then, follow the directions in the Science Log to learn more about "the big idea."✦

Wheels and Levers
Did the Egyptians have the wheel? Did they use levers? An ancient painting shows soldiers climbing a ladder on wheels. Others are using levers to move the structure. This is the only known image of a wheel from those times.

Wedges
Stonecutters used chisels made of bronze and copper. These wedge-shaped tools were used to carve fine details in the stone.

Inclined Planes

Scientists agree that the inclined plane was an important machine used to build the pyramids. They do not agree how they were built. Some experts think the stones were dragged up spiral ramps such as these. Other scientists think that a single, straight ramp was built from the bottom up to the top. Either way, we know they used inclined planes.

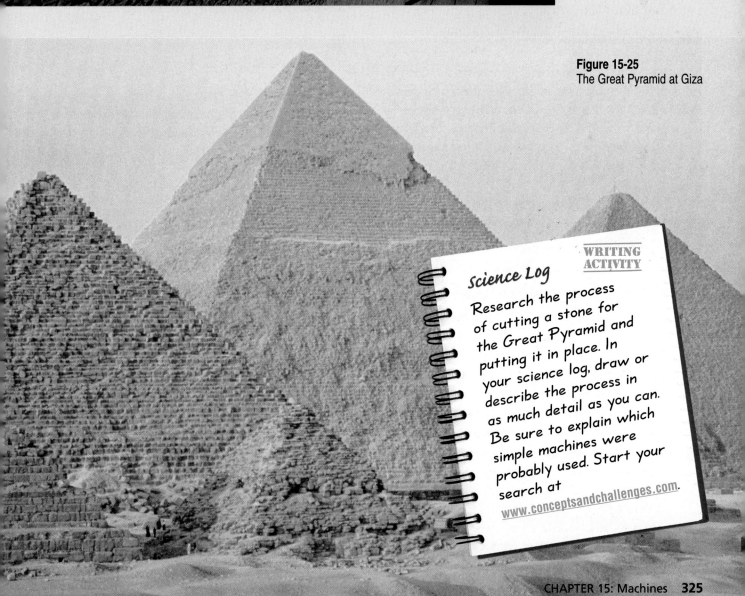

Figure 15-25
The Great Pyramid at Giza

Science Log

WRITING ACTIVITY

Research the process of cutting a stone for the Great Pyramid and putting it in place. In your science log, draw or describe the process in as much detail as you can. Be sure to explain which simple machines were probably used. Start your search at www.conceptsandchallenges.com.

What is a compound machine?

Objective
Name some compound machines.

Key Term
compound machine: machine that combines two simple machines or more

Compound Machines Most machines are made up of a combination of simple machines. Machines that combine two simple machines or more are called **compound machines.** Compound machines can do more complicated jobs than simple machines can. They also can have large MAs. The actual MA of a compound machine equals the product of the actual MAs of all of the simple machines that make it up.

▶ **1** DEFINE: What is a compound machine?

Examples of Compound Machines Most of the machines you use every day are compound machines. For example, a pair of scissors is a compound machine. A pair of scissors is made up of two levers joined by a screw. The screw is the fulcrum of the levers. Each blade of a pair of scissors is a wedge.

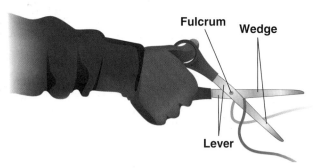

▲ **Figure 15-26** Scissors are compound machines.

A bicycle is another compound machine. What simple machines make up a bicycle? The wheels and pedals are wheels and axles. The pedals are attached to levers. The brakes, handlebars, and gearshift controls also are levers. The chains are pulleys. Screws are used in many places to hold parts of the bicycle together.

▲ **Figure 15-27** A bicycle is a compound machine.

▶ **2** IDENTIFY: What are some simple machines in a bicycle?

People and Machines Humans have been using machines for hundreds of thousands of years. Early humans made simple tools from stone. Centuries later, agricultural societies used machines to water their crops, crush grain into flour, and cut wood to build homes.

During the Industrial Revolution, steam began to replace animals as a source of energy for machines. Many inventions during those years, such as the telephone and the telegraph, helped improve communication. We also learned how to heat our homes and power our machinery.

Today, fossil fuels and nuclear energy are used to operate modern machines. Modern machines take us anyplace in the world and to the Moon. In the future, new technology may make even more complex machines possible.

▲ **Figure 15-28** The wheels of this train travel on a single track.

 NAME: What are two sources of energy for modern machines?

✓ CHECKING CONCEPTS

1. What are two simple machines that make up a pair of scissors?

2. What is a compound machine?

3. What type of simple machine are the wheels and handlebars of a bicycle?

4. On what does the MA of a compound machine depend?

💡 THINKING CRITICALLY

5. **COMPARE:** How does the MA of a compound machine compare with the MA of each of its simple machines?

6. **ANALYZE:** How does a bicycle make work easier?

7. **MODEL:** Draw a diagram of a pair of scissors. Label the simple machines that make up a pair of scissors on your diagram.

HEALTH AND SAFETY TIP

Machines are very helpful to people. However, if machines are not used properly, they can cause serious injury. It is important to use proper safety precautions when you use any kind of machine. Helmets, kneepads, and goggles are all safety items you might need. Different machines require different precautions. Choose a machine you are interested in and find out the safety precautions and safety equipment needed to use it. Make a poster that illustrates "Machine Safety."

 Science and Technology

ROBOTIC MACHINES

Robots are mechanical workers. Most robots are built to do special jobs. Using robots instead of human workers has some advantages. Robots can work 24 hours a day without resting. They can do the same job over and over without getting tired or bored.

More important, robots can work under conditions that would not be safe for humans. The Sewer Access Module robot, or SAM, was designed to do maintenance work in sewers. Today, it is also used to lay fiber-optic cable lines in the sewer.

Robots are used in a wide variety of places. Some surgeons use robots in the operating room to perform open-heart surgeries. The robot can grip, cut, and sew arteries and valves. Surgeons view the heart on a video monitor. They control the robot's movements with joysticks and foot pedals. Because robotic surgery requires a smaller incision, a patient's recovery time is faster.

▲ **Figure 15-29** This illustration shows a tiny robot used in open-heart surgery.

Thinking Critically For what other types of jobs could robots be used?

Chapter 15 Challenges

Chapter Summary

Lesson 15-1

- **Machines** make work easier by changing the size, direction, or speed of a force.
- The force you apply to a machine is the **effort force,** and the force that opposes the effort force is the **resistance force.**
- **Mechanical advantage** is the number of times a machine multiplies the effort force. It is equal to the resistance force divided by the effort force.
- There are six kinds of simple machines.

Lesson 15-2

- The work done by a machine is **work output.** The work done on a machine is **work input.** The **efficiency** of a machine is a ratio of work output to work input.

Lesson 15-3

- A **lever** is a bar that is free to turn around a fixed point. A lever has two parts called an effort arm and a resistance arm. The IMA of a lever is equal to the length of the effort arm divided by the length of the resistance arm.
- Levers are divided into three classes according to the position of the effort force, the resistance force, and the **fulcrum.**

Lesson 15-4

- A **pulley** is a rope wrapped around a wheel.
- Fixed pulleys change the direction of the effort force. Movable pulleys increase the size of the effort force. A pulley system is made up of fixed and movable pulleys.

Lesson 15-5

- An **inclined plane** is a slanted surface, or ramp.
- The IMA of an inclined plane is equal to its length divided by its height.
- A wedge is often two inclined planes back-to-back. A screw is an inclined plane wrapped around a cylinder.

Lesson 15-6

- A **compound machine** is composed of two or more simple machines.

Key Term Challenges

compound machine (p. 326)
efficiency (p. 314)
effort force (p. 312)
fulcrum (p. 316)
ideal mechanical advantage (p. 312)
inclined plane (p. 322)
lever (p. 316)
machine (p. 312)
mechanical advantage (p. 312)
pulley (p. 318)
resistance force (p. 312)
wheel and axle (p. 312)
work input (p. 314)
work output (p. 314)

MATCHING Write the Key Term from above that best matches each description.

1. force applied to a machine
2. rope wrapped around a wheel
3. slanted surface
4. work done by a machine
5. force that opposes the effort force
6. work done on a machine
7. point that a lever turns around

APPLYING DEFINITIONS Explain the difference between the words in each pair. Write your answers in complete sentences.

8. lever, fulcrum
9. simple machine, compound machine
10. mechanical advantage, efficiency
11. work input, work output
12. effort force, resistance force

Content Challenges TEST PREP

MULTIPLE CHOICE Write the letter of the term or phrase that best completes each statement.

1. Machines make work easier by changing a force's
   a. size.
   b. direction.
   c. speed.
   d. size, direction, or speed.

2. A machine with an actual MA of 10 multiplies the effort force
   a. 15 times.
   b. 10 times.
   c. 10%.
   d. 15%.

3. The efficiency of a machine is always less than
   a. 100%.
   b. the mechanical advantage.
   c. work output.
   d. work input.

4. If the percentage efficiency of a machine is 60% and the work input is 50 N-m, what will be the work output?
   a. 160 N-m.
   b. 60 N-m.
   c. 30 N-m.
   d. 100 N-m.

5. In a first-class lever, the fulcrum is between the effort force and
   a. the effort arm.
   b. the resistance arm.
   c. the resistance force.
   d. none of these

6. A wheelbarrow is an example of a
   a. first-class lever.
   b. second-class lever.
   c. third-class lever.
   d. wheel and axle.

7. A block and tackle is an example of a
   a. lever.
   b. pulley.
   c. pulley system.
   d. wheel and axle.

8. The IMA of a pulley system with six ropes supporting the load is
   a. 6.
   b. 3.
   c. 60%.
   d. 1.

9. An inclined plane makes work easier by increasing a force's
   a. direction.
   b. speed.
   c. MA.
   d. size.

10. If you use 50 N of force to push a box weighing 200 N up an inclined plane, the MA of the inclined plane is
    a. 50.
    b. 150.
    c. 4.
    d. 0.215.

FILL IN Write the term or phrase that best completes each statement.

11. People use _____ to make work easier.

12. The efficiency of a machine is equal to the _____ divided by the work input.

13. Some of the work put into a machine is used to overcome _____.

14. The _____ of a lever is the distance from the resistance force to the fulcrum.

15. A pulley can change either the size or the _____ of a force.

Concept Challenges TEST PREP

WRITTEN RESPONSE Complete the exercises and answer each of the following questions in complete sentences.

1. **RELATE:** Why is work input equal to the effort force times the effort distance?

2. **HYPOTHESIZE:** Why do you think compound machines are sometimes called complex machines?

3. **HYPOTHESIZE:** A perpetual motion machine would have more than 100 percent efficiency. Could such a machine ever be built? Explain your answer.

4. **EVALUATE:** Two piano movers want to raise a piano to the fifth floor of an apartment building. Should they use a fixed pulley, a movable pulley, or a block and tackle to make the work easier? Explain.

INTERPRETING A DIAGRAM Use Figure 15-30 to answer the following questions.

5. What is the length of the effort arm of this lever?

6. What is the length of the resistance arm?

7. What is the IMA of this lever?

8. What is the output force in this diagram?

9. How much effort force would be needed to produce the output force?

10. Is this lever a first-, second-, or third-class lever? Explain.

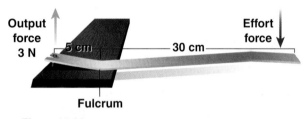

▲ Figure 15-30

Chapter 16 Heat

▲ **Figure 16-1** Because hot air rises, this balloon can fly.

Imagine floating high above Earth's surface in a hot-air balloon like the one in Figure 16-1. In order to keep the balloon high above the ground, air in the balloon must be heated. Heat energy from the flames causes the particles that make up air to gain energy. The particles move faster and spread farther apart. As a result, the balloon expands and rises high above Earth's surface.

►What do you think would happen if the air in the balloon were cooled?

Contents

16-1 What is heat?

INVESTIGATE

Observing Heat
HANDS-ON ACTIVITY

1. Hold a pinwheel over a light source that is not lit. Observe the action of the pinwheel for a full minute.
2. Turn on the light source and hold the pinwheel over it. Observe the action of the pinwheel for a full minute.

THINK ABOUT IT: Compare the action of the pinwheel in Steps 1 and 2. Did the light have any effect on the pinwheel? What type of energy is coming from the light?

STEP 2

Objective
Explain how heat is a form of energy.

Key Term
heat: energy of particles moving from warmer regions to cooler regions

Caloric Have you ever walked on a sandy beach on a hot, summer day? If you have, you probably know that the burning feeling in your feet was caused by the heat in the sand. At one time, people thought heat was a physical substance. They called this substance caloric (kuh-LAWR-ihk). Caloric was thought to flow like a liquid. Today, we know that heat is not a substance. It is a form of energy. The heat in the sand actually comes from energy absorbed from the Sun.

1 EXPLAIN: What is caloric?

Moving Particles You have learned that matter is made up of tiny particles called atoms and molecules. These tiny particles are always in motion. For example, a brick within a wall is motionless, but the tiny particles that make up the brick are constantly moving. The motion of these particles results in heat, or thermal energy.

◀ **Figure 16-2** The tiny particles that make up a brick are constantly moving.

Heat is the energy of particles moving in matter. It moves from a warmer region to a cooler region. All matter has heat. Even an ice cube contains heat, because the molecules of water that make up the ice are moving back and forth. If heat energy is added to the ice cube, the molecules move faster and farther apart. If enough heat energy is added to the ice, the molecules will gain enough energy to leave the solid state and become a liquid. With continued heating, the molecules will gain enough energy to break away from the liquid state and become a gas.

▲ **Figure 16-3** Adding heat energy to water makes the water molecules move faster and farther apart.

2 DEFINE: What is heat?

Movement of Heat What happens when you hold a glass of ice water in your hand? You may notice that after a few minutes, the ice in the water begins to melt. At the same time, your hand gets cold. This happens because heat energy moves from a warmer object to a cooler object. Your hand is warmer than the ice water. Heat from your hand moved into the glass. As heat entered the glass, the water and the ice absorbed the heat and became warmer. Your hand lost some heat energy so it began to feel cooler.

3 ▶ DESCRIBE: In what direction does heat move?

Heat and Work How do scientists know that heat is a form of energy? Energy can do work. Remember that something must be moved for work to be done. When you boil water, you can see the water bubbling and moving inside the container. Heat is doing work.

Heat does work when it causes a rocket to be lifted into the air. Heat causes the fuel in a rocket engine to explode, producing hot gases. These hot gases expand rapidly. The expanding gases rush out of the rocket engine. As they do, they push against the rocket, forcing it upward. The moving rocket shows that heat is a form of energy that can do work.

▲ **Figure 16-4** Expanding hot gases cause the rocket to move upward.

4 ▶ INFER: How do scientists know that heat is a form of energy?

 CHECKING CONCEPTS

1. At one time, people thought that heat was a substance called _____.

2. Moving particles have _____ energy.

3. The energy of particles moving from warmer regions to cooler regions is _____.

4. Adding heat energy makes particles of matter move _____.

5. For work to be done, something must be _____.

THINKING CRITICALLY

6. **INFER:** Explain how a piece of wood has kinetic energy.

7. **ANALYZE:** Suppose you hit a piece of metal several times with a hammer. When you touch the piece of metal, it feels hot. Explain why the metal gets hot after being hit with the hammer.

8. **HYPOTHESIZE:** Explain what will happen when you place an ice cube in a cup of hot coffee.

Web InfoSearch

Seeing Heat Because heat is energy, you usually cannot see it. Sometimes, however, you can see evidence of it. For example, when steam rises over a pot of boiling water, you can "see" the motion of the heat. Also, wavy air over a hot road is caused by heat. Scientists have invented a technology to see heat. Thermograms show the heat coming from a person or an object. This information is used in many ways.

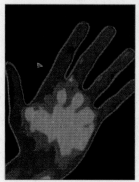

▲ **Figure 16-5** A thermogram shows the heat coming off a human hand.

SEARCH: Use the Internet to find out more about thermograms. What information might a thermogram of a house or office building tell you? Start your search at www.conceptsandchallenges.com. Some key search words are **thermogram heat loss, energy audit thermogram,** and **thermogram building envelope.**

16-2 What is temperature?

INVESTIGATE

Observing Temperature Differences
HANDS-ON ACTIVITY

1. Fill a pan with cold water. Fill a second pan with warm water. Fill a third pan with hot but not boiling water.
2. Put both of your hands in the warm water. Observe how your hands feel. Dry your hands. Put one hand into the cold water and the other hand into the hot water.
3. After 1 minute, put both of your hands into the warm water.

STEP 2

THINK ABOUT IT: Did the temperature of the warm water feel the same in both of your hands?

Objective

Differentiate between heat and temperature.

Key Terms

temperature: measure of the average kinetic energy of the particles in a sample of matter

calorie: unit of heat; amount of heat needed to raise the temperature of 1 g of water 1°C

Temperature The measure of the average kinetic energy of all the particles in a sample of matter is called **temperature.** If you compared a bowl of hot soup to a bowl of ice cream, you would find that the average kinetic energy of the soup's particles is greater than the average kinetic energy of the ice cream's particles. The temperature of the soup is higher than the temperature of the ice cream.

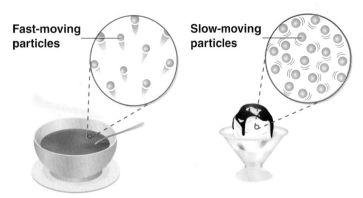

Fast-moving particles

Slow-moving particles

▲ **Figure 16-6** The average kinetic energy of the particles in the soup is greater than the average kinetic energy of the particles in the ice cream.

 DEFINE: What is temperature?

Heat and Temperature Heat is related to temperature, but they are not the same. Heat is the *total* kinetic energy of all the particles in a sample of matter. Temperature is the measure of the *average* kinetic energy of all the particles in a sample of matter.

Two samples of the same material may have the same temperature but not the same amount of heat. For example, a pail of ocean water may have a temperature of 27°C. The ocean water near the beach may also have a temperature of 27°C. However, because there are fewer particles of ocean water in the pail, the amount of heat in it is less than the amount of heat in the nearby ocean.

▲ **Figure 16-7** The pail of ocean water has fewer particles in it than the ocean does. So, at the same temperature, the pail of ocean water has less heat than the ocean.

COMPARE: At the same temperature, which has more heat, the water in a bucket or the water in an ocean?

Measuring Heat Heat is directly related to the temperature of a sample of matter. When heat is added to a sample of matter, the average kinetic energy of the particles of matter increases. So, the temperature of the sample goes up. The opposite is also true. When heat is removed from a sample of matter, the average kinetic energy of the particles of matter decreases. The temperature of the sample goes down.

The terms *hot* and *cold* are often used to describe how much heat energy a sample of matter contains. It is important to understand that these terms are not measures of heat energy. They are used to compare the temperature of one sample of matter to that of another.

Heat is measured by describing the temperature change it causes. Heat is measured in units called calories. A **calorie** is the amount of heat needed to raise the temperature of 1 gram of water 1°C. One gram of water is a small amount of water. So, a calorie is a small amount of heat.

 PREDICT: What happens when you add heat energy to a substance?

✔ CHECKING CONCEPTS

1. Two samples of the same substance may have the same temperature but not contain the same amount of _____.

2. When heat is removed from water, its temperature _____.

3. Heat affects the _____ of a substance.

4. A _____ is a unit of heat.

THINKING CRITICALLY

5. **COMPARE:** Compare the average kinetic energy of the particles in a cup of hot tea to the particles in a glass of iced tea.

DESIGNING AN EXPERIMENT

Design an experiment to solve the following problem. Include a hypothesis, variables, a procedure, and a type of data to study.

PROBLEM: Many people think that coldness can be added to a substance. How can you demonstrate that coldness is an absence of heat?

How Do They Know That?

HEAT IS A FORM OF ENERGY

Benjamin Thompson was born in Woburn, Massachusetts. During the Revolutionary War, Thompson remained loyal to Great Britain and acted as a spy for the British. During the war, Thompson fled the colonies to live in Great Britain. He was knighted by King George III in 1784. Seven years later, Thompson was made a count of the Holy Roman Empire.

▲ **Figure 16-8** Benjamin Thompson showed that heat is not a flow of caloric.

Thompson was also a scientist. Around 1798, Thompson was in charge of a factory that made cannons. The machines used to drill the cannons were turned by horses. Thompson observed that the cannons became very hot as they were drilled. He decided to try an experiment. He surrounded a cannon with a box filled with water. As the cannon was drilled, the water began to boil. The water continued boiling as long as the drilling went on. At that time, people believed that heat was a substance called caloric. Thompson concluded that the heat was produced by the motion of the drill, not a flow of caloric. This was the first step in showing that heat is a form of energy and not a substance.

Thinking Critically What do you think happened to the water once the drilling stopped?

Objective

Identify the freezing point and melting point of a substance.

Key Terms

freezing point: temperature at which a liquid changes to a solid

melting point: temperature at which a solid changes to a liquid

Freezing Water When water freezes, it changes to ice. Suppose you put a beaker of water into a freezer whose temperature is set at –10°C. As the water loses heat, its temperature will drop. When the temperature reaches 0°C, the water will begin to freeze. At this point, the temperature of the water stops going down. As the water changes to ice, more heat is lost. After a while, the water will completely change to ice.

The temperature at which a liquid turns to ice is called its **freezing point.** The freezing point of water is 0°C. Once the water has completely changed to ice, the temperature of the ice can drop below 0°C. Figure 16-9 shows how the temperature of water changes as it freezes.

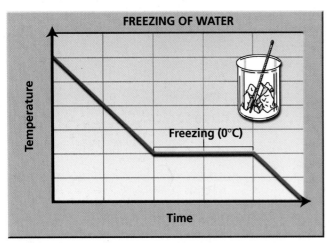

FREEZING OF WATER

Freezing (0°C)

Temperature

Time

▲ **Figure 16-9** When water reaches its freezing point, it stays at 0°C until it completely changes to ice. Its temperature can then fall below 0°C. The temperature will stop falling once it equals its surroundings.

▶ **DEFINE:** What is the freezing point of water?

Freezing Points of Other Liquids When heat is removed from a liquid, its temperature goes down. Removing heat from a liquid at its freezing point changes the liquid into a solid. Every liquid has its own freezing point. Figure 16-10 shows the freezing points of some liquids.

FREEZING POINTS OF SOME LIQUIDS	
Liquid	**Freezing point**
Acetic acid	17°C
Acetone	–95°C
Benzene	6°C
Ethyl alcohol	–117°C
Glycerine	17°C
Mercury	–39°C
Water	0°C

▲ **Figure 16-10**

▶ **STATE:** What is the freezing point of ethyl alcohol?

Absolute Zero As you remove heat from a sample of matter, the particles of the matter slow down. The temperature of the sample falls. If you continue to remove heat from the sample, you might expect to reach a point at which the particles of matter stop moving. At such a point, no more heat could be removed from the sample of matter. The temperature of the sample would be absolute zero.

Absolute zero is described as the coldest temperature possible. Its value is about –273°C! In order to lower the temperature of something, its heat must be transferred to something colder. Because absolute zero is the coldest possible temperature, it will never be reached.

▶ **DESCRIBE:** What happens to the particles of a substance as the temperature nears absolute zero?

Melting Point The temperature at which a solid changes to a liquid is called its **melting point.** The freezing point and the melting point of a substance can be the same. When heat is removed from a liquid, it changes to a solid. When heat is added to a solid, it changes back to a liquid. The melting point of ice is 0°C—the same as its freezing point.

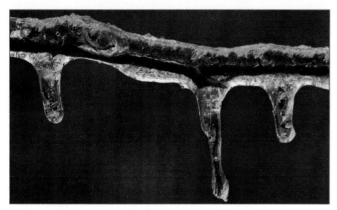

▲ **Figure 16-11** The freezing point and the melting point of water are the same, 0°C.

 STATE: What is the melting point of water?

✔ CHECKING CONCEPTS

1. What happens when water freezes?
2. At what temperature does water begin to freeze?

3. What is the temperature called at which all particle motion almost stops?
4. What is the melting point of ice?

💡 THINKING CRITICALLY

5. **HYPOTHESIZE:** The water in a lake has just reached 0°C. Explain why it may not be safe to go ice skating on the lake.
6. **COMPARE:** How are melting point and freezing point different? How are they alike?

INTERPRETING VISUALS

Look back at Figure 16-9 to answer the following questions.

7. **INFER:** What does the red part of the graph indicate?
8. **ANALYZE:** What happens to the temperature of water as time passes?
9. **STATE:** What happens to the temperature of water after it reaches the freezing point?

Science and Technology

CRYOGENICS

When heat energy is removed from a substance, the temperature of the substance goes down. When all of the available heat has been removed from a substance, its temperature cannot go down any further. At this temperature, all the particles of the substance almost stop moving. This is the lowest possible temperature that can be reached. It is called absolute zero. This temperature has never been reached. However, scientists have been able to cool substances to within 0.01°C of absolute zero. The study of such very low temperatures is called cryogenics (kreye-uh-JEH-nihks).

Cryogenics is important in the refrigeration of food, in space technology, and in medicine. In cryogenic surgery, a surgeon uses an extremely cold probe instead of a scalpel. Cryogenic surgery reduces bleeding. It can also reduce much of the pain felt after the surgery. Many cryogenic operations can be done in a doctor's office.

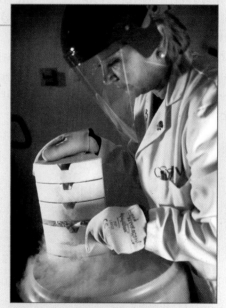

▲ **Figure 16-12** In a cryogenics laboratory, substances are cooled to very low temperatures.

Cryogenics may help the automobile industry. Hydrogen and oxygen are gases at normal temperatures. However, at very low temperatures, they become liquids. Liquid hydrogen and liquid oxygen are used as fuels in some rockets. In the future, liquid hydrogen may replace gasoline as a fuel for automobiles.

Thinking Critically How has cryogenics helped different industries?

16-4 What is boiling point?

Objectives

Identify the boiling point of a liquid. Differentiate between boiling and evaporation.

Key Terms

boiling point: temperature at which a liquid changes to a gas

evaporation (ee-vap-uh-RAY-shuhn)**:** change from a liquid to a gas at the surface of the liquid

Boiling Water When water boils, it changes to steam. Steam is water in the form of a gas. As you heat water, the temperature of the water rises. As the temperature of the water rises, small bubbles appear in the water. These bubbles show that a gas, steam, is being formed. As you continue to heat the water, more and more bubbles are formed. At 100°C, the bubbles start to leave the container. However, the temperature of the water stays at 100°C. The temperature remains at 100°C until all of the water has changed to steam.

The temperature at which a liquid changes to a gas is called its **boiling point.** The boiling point of water is 100°C. After all the water turns into steam, its temperature can then rise above 100°C. Figure 16-13 shows how the temperature of water changes as it boils.

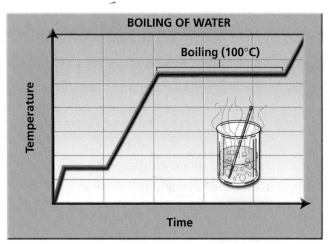

▲ **Figure 16-13** When water reaches its boiling point, it stays at 100°C until it completely changes to steam. The temperature of the steam can then rise above 100°C.

1 DEFINE: What is boiling point?

Boiling Points of Other Liquids When heat is added to a liquid, the temperature of the liquid rises. When the liquid reaches its boiling point, it begins to form a gas. Every liquid has its own boiling point. Figure 16-14 shows the boiling points of some liquids.

BOILING POINTS OF SOME LIQUIDS	
Liquid	**Boiling point**
Acetic acid	118°C
Acetone	57°C
Benzene	80°C
Ethyl alcohol	78°C
Glycerine	290°C
Mercury	357°C
Water	100°C

▲ **Figure 16-14**

2 ANALYZE: Which liquid listed in Figure 16-14 has the highest boiling point?

Evaporation When a liquid is allowed to stand uncovered at room temperature, it slowly changes to a gas. This change is called **evaporation.** Evaporation happens only at the surface of a liquid and can occur at temperatures below the boiling point. When a liquid evaporates, some particles at the surface of the liquid gain enough energy to escape into the air. This is different from when a liquid boils. When a liquid boils, bubbles form throughout the liquid and rise out of the liquid.

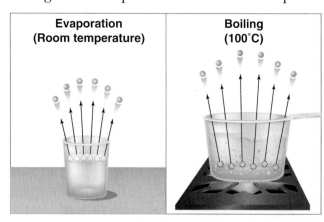

▲ **Figure 16-15** Evaporation occurs at the surface of a liquid (left). When a liquid boils, gas bubbles form throughout the liquid and then rise out of the liquid (right).

3 DEFINE: What is evaporation?

338

1. When water _____, it changes to steam.
2. The temperature at which water changes to steam is its _____.
3. The boiling point of water is _____ °C.
4. When a liquid reaches its boiling point, it begins to change to a _____.
5. An uncovered liquid changes to a gas at room temperature by the process of _____.
6. Evaporation occurs only at the _____ of a liquid.

THINKING CRITICALLY

7. COMPARE: In your own words, explain the difference between boiling and evaporation.
8. HYPOTHESIZE: Why is it possible to get a more serious burn from steam than from boiling water?

9. EXPLAIN: As water is heated, what evidence is there that a gas is forming?
10. INFER: When does the temperature of boiling water rise above 100°C?

Web InfoSearch

Boiling Point and Elevation The boiling point of liquids can change depending upon elevation above or below sea level. At elevations above sea level, the boiling point is lower. At elevations below sea level, the boiling point is higher.

SEARCH: Use the Internet to find the boiling point of water at different elevations above and below sea level. Why does elevation affect the boiling point of water? Start your search at www.conceptsandchallenges.com. Some key search words are **water boiling point altitude** and **water boiling point elevation.**

Hands-On Activity

CHANGING THE BOILING POINT OF WATER

You will need three beakers, water, a measuring cup, safety goggles, a balance, salt, a stirrer, a thermometer, and a hot plate.

1. Put on safety goggles and pour 100 mL of water into each beaker.
2. Add 10 g of salt to the first beaker. Add 20 g of salt to the second beaker. Do not add any salt to the third beaker. Stir the salt in the first and second beakers.
3. Heat the water in each beaker until it boils. Record the temperature of the water in each beaker as it boils.

▲ **STEP 3** Record the temperature of the water as it boils.

Practicing Your Skills

4. OBSERVE: What is the boiling point of the water in the first beaker? The second beaker? The third beaker?
5. INFER: How does adding 10 g of salt affect the boiling point of water?
6. INFER: How does adding 20 g of salt affect the boiling point of water?

16-5 What is conduction?

INVESTIGATE

Observing Heat Transfer
HANDS-ON ACTIVITY

1. Half-fill a jar with hot water. Place a wooden spoon, a metal spoon, and a plastic spoon into the jar. Do not allow the spoons to touch each other.
2. After a full minute, touch the handle of each spoon.

THINK ABOUT IT: Did the handles of all three spoons feel the same? If not, how can you explain the difference?

STEP 1

Objective
Describe how heat is transferred through solids.

Key Terms
conduction (kuhn-DUK-shuhn)**:** process of heat transfer in solids

conductor: material that conducts heat easily

insulator: material that does not conduct heat easily

Heat Transfer in Solids A blacksmith hammers a piece of iron to make horseshoes. When a blacksmith places a piece of iron into a flame, the iron gets very hot. The heat energy causes the particles in the iron to bump into each other. After a while, the iron gets hot enough so that it becomes soft. The piece of iron can then be hammered into shape.

▲ **Figure 16-16** As the iron gets hot, the particles within it bump into each other.

Heat is transferred through solids by **conduction.** You learned that heat moves from an object with a higher temperature to an object with a lower temperature. When fast-moving particles in a sample of matter bump into slow-moving particles, heat energy passes from the fast-moving particles to the slow-moving particles. As a piece of iron is heated, heat energy is transferred from the fast-moving particles to the slow-moving particles. The slow-moving particles gain energy and bump into other particles. In this way, heat energy is transferred throughout the sample of matter.

▶ **1** **DEFINE:** What is conduction?

Conductors of Heat All metals are good conductors of heat. A **conductor** is a material that allows heat to move through it easily. Copper, gold, silver, iron, aluminum, and steel are all good conductors of heat. Copper and silver are two of the best conductors of heat. Heat will travel faster through items made of copper and silver than it will through items made of iron or steel.

▶ **2** **IDENTIFY:** What substances are good conductors of heat?

Poor Conductors of Heat Many materials are poor conductors of heat. Materials that do not conduct heat easily are called **insulators.** Wood, paper, wax, and air are poor conductors of heat. These materials are insulators.

Insulators prevent heat from moving from place to place. Houses are insulated to keep them warm in winter and cool in summer. To insulate houses, spaces are left between the inside and outside walls of the house. The spaces are filled with an insulating material. During winter, this insulation helps keep heat from escaping to the outside. During the summer, insulation helps keep heat from getting into the house.

▲ **Figure 16-17** Pots made of copper are good conductors of heat. Handles made of plastic are good insulators.

 EXPLAIN: Why are insulators used in houses?

✓ **CHECKING CONCEPTS**

1. How does heat travel by conduction?
2. Name two materials that are good conductors of heat.
3. What is an insulator?
4. Name two materials that are good insulators.

THINKING CRITICALLY

5. INFER: Explain how food in a pot gets heated by conduction.
6. EXPLAIN: How is a blanket an insulator?

BUILDING SCIENCE SKILLS

Researching Insulators do not allow heat to move easily through them. Look throughout your home to find examples of insulators. Make a list of them and describe what kind of material they are made of. Explain how each one of them acts as an insulator.

 Real-Life Science

HOME INSULATION

In many parts of the United States, winters are cold and summers are hot. In these parts of the country, houses must be insulated. Home insulation keeps houses warm in winter and cool in summer. Home insulation can help reduce the amount of fuel needed to heat or cool a home. Good insulation can cut fuel use by as much as 50 percent.

▲ **Figure 16-18** Home insulation keeps houses warm in winter and cool in summer.

Insulation is needed in those parts of a house where the most heat is usually lost. In most homes, heat loss occurs through the attic floor, the ceiling of an unheated basement, and the side walls. Different types of insulation can be used in these places. For example, blankets of fiberglass can be inserted between beams in floors and ceilings. Liquid plastic foam can be sprayed into the spaces between the inside and outside walls.

A number called an R-value is used to grade insulating materials. An insulating material with a high R-value is best at preventing heat loss. Choosing insulation with the highest R-value can greatly reduce fuel costs.

Thinking Critically How does insulation keep a house cool in summer?

16-6 What is convection?

Objective
Describe how heat travels through gases and liquids.

Key Terms
convection (kuhn-VEHK-shuhn): transfer of heat in gases and liquids

convection current: movement of gases or liquids caused by differences in density

Heat Transfer in Gases and Liquids The transfer of heat in gases and liquids is called **convection.** When gases and liquids are heated, the particles gain energy and move faster and farther apart. Because these particles are farther apart, the heated gas or liquid becomes less dense than the cooler, surrounding gas or liquid. This makes the less-dense gas or liquid rise and the cooler, denser gas or liquid moves in to take its place. As it rises, the gas or liquid carries heat with it.

▶ **DEFINE:** What is convection?

Convection Currents Heat is carried in gases and liquids by means of convection currents. **Convection currents** are movements of gases or liquids caused by differences in density. Convection currents transfer heat. Air is a gas. Air at Earth's surface is warmed by the Sun and then rises. Cool air above the North Pole and the South Pole sinks. The rising of warm air and the sinking of cool air cause convection currents. Certain birds, such as eagles and hawks, use rising warm air in convection currents to soar above Earth's surface.

▲ **Figure 16-19** An eagle uses convection currents to soar.

Convection currents are found in liquids as well as in air. In bodies of water, warmer water rises to the surface and carries heat with it. Cooler water sinks to the bottom. Convection currents cause heat to be transferred through bodies of water. When water is heated in a pot, convection currents form. Figure 16-20 shows convection currents in a pot of boiling water.

◀ **Figure 16-20** Convection currents transfer heat in a liquid.

Just below Earth's crust is a layer of rock called the mantle. The mantle is heated from below by heat from Earth's core. Rock in the upper part of the mantle behaves like a very thick liquid. Scientists believe that convection currents traveling through the upper mantle are responsible for the very slow movement of large sections of Earth's crust. This concept is known as the theory of plate tectonics.

▶ **EXPLAIN:** How do convection currents transfer heat in liquids?

Uses of Convection Heat transfer by convection is used in some home heating systems. In a hot-water heating system, water is heated in a hot-water heater. The hot water is then pumped through pipes to each room in the house. The hot water flows through heaters near the floor of each room. The hot water warms the air near the floor by conduction. The warm air rises, carrying heat through each room by means of convection currents. Heat circulates through each room in this way. After the water loses some of its heat, it returns to the hot-water heater to repeat the process.

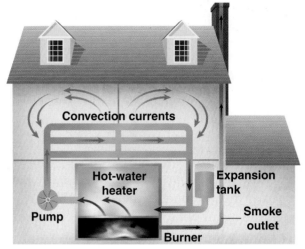

▲ **Figure 16-21** In a hot-water heating system, heated water travels through a system of pipes to heat a home.

 IDENTIFY: What method of heat transfer is used in a hot-water heating system?

 CHECKING CONCEPTS

1. Heat travels through gases by _____ .
2. Warm air is _____ dense than cold air.
3. Warm water rises and cool water_____ .
4. Convection takes place in gases and _____ .

☑ **THINKING CRITICALLY**

5. **ANALYZE:** To cool a room, should an air conditioner be placed at the bottom of a wall or at the top of a wall? Explain your answer.
6. **INFER:** Is heat transferred through solids by convection? Explain.

HEALTH AND SAFETY TIP

Smoke and gases from the burners of hot-water heaters contain pollutants. These pollutants are sent through an exhaust pipe that runs out through a chimney or vent in the roof. Hot air containing the pollutants rises up the chimney. Cool, clean air moves in from outside to take its place. Why do you think these pollutants need to be removed from a house?

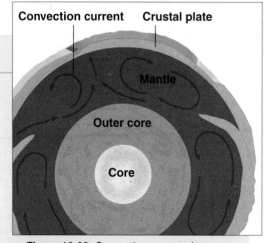

▲ **Figure 16-22** Convection currents in the mantle

Integrating Earth Science

TOPIC: plate tectonics

CONVECTION CURRENTS INSIDE THE MANTLE

Differences in density within a gas or liquid can cause convection currents within the gas or liquid. Under Earth's crust is a thick layer of rock called the mantle. The part of the mantle closest to Earth's core acts like a thick, hot liquid. The part of the mantle that is farthest from the core has the properties of a thick, cooler liquid. Scientists believe that the differences in the density in the mantle cause convection currents. The thick, hot liquid of the mantle rises and cools. The cooler liquid of the mantle sinks. As the cooler liquid gets closer to the core, it heats up and rises. The process repeats over and over again.

Scientists also believe that these convection currents cause the plates that make up the crust to continuously move. The crust floats on top of the mantle. The convection currents in the mantle carry the plates along so that the continents that sit on top of the plates slowly move, too. This concept supports the theory of plate tectonics. The theory of plate tectonics explains how Earth has changed over time.

Thinking Critically How do convection currents support the theory of plate tectonics?

LAB ACTIVITY
Creating Convection Currents

Materials

Safety goggles

Apron

Deep storage container

Small test tube

Warm water

Cold water

Food coloring (red, blue)

BACKGROUND

How does an entire pot of soup on a stove get hot when only the bottom of the pot touches the stove? Heat travels through the metal pot to the soup by conduction. Then another process takes over. In this activity, you will study heat transfer by convection currents.

PURPOSE

In this activity, you will create convection currents in liquids.

PROCEDURE

1. Copy the chart shown in Figure 16-23 onto a sheet of paper. Put on safety goggles and an apron.

2. Fill the storage container almost to the top with cold water. If you need to move the box to your table, snap the lid on before carrying it.

3. Fill the test tube with very warm water almost to the top. Add a few drops of red food coloring to the water. Gently shake the test tube from side to side to mix the food coloring and water together.

4. Place your thumb or pointer finger over the mouth of the test tube. Very gently, lower the test tube into the storage container until the test tube reaches the bottom and settles over on its side.

5. Remove your finger from the mouth of the test tube. Observe what happens to the colored water.

▲ **STEP 3** Add red food coloring to the warm water in the test tube.

▲ **STEP 4** Gently lower the test tube to the bottom of the container.

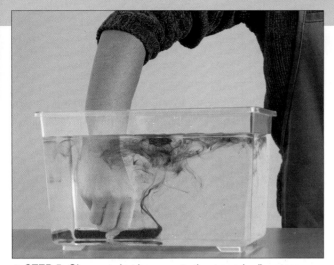

▲ **STEP 5** Observe what happens to the warm (red) water.

▲ **STEP 6** Remove your finger from the test tube near the surface of the water.

6. Repeat the experiment, this time using very warm water in the container and cold water, colored blue, in the test tube. Also, remove your finger from the test tube near the surface of the water. Observe what happens to the blue-colored water.

Creating Convection Currents

Observations of container with cold water and test tube with warm water	Observations of container with warm water and test tube with cold water

▲ **Figure 16-23** Copy this chart and use it to record your observations.

CONCLUSIONS

1. **OBSERVE:** What happened to the red, warm water in the test tube when you placed it in the cold water?

2. **OBSERVE:** What happened to the blue, cold water in the test tube when you placed it in the warm water?

3. **ANALYZE:** What caused the colored water to move in both experiments?

4. **INFER:** What would happen if, in the first experiment, you held the test tube at the surface of the cold water?

5. **INFER:** What would happen in the second experiment if you lowered the test tube to the bottom of the container?

Objective
Describe how heat travels through empty space.

Key Terms
vacuum: region where no matter exists

radiation (ray-dee-AY-shuhn)**:** transfer of energy through space

Heat from the Sun The Sun is about 150 million kilometers from Earth. Yet, Earth's surface is heated by energy from the Sun. In order for Earth to receive this energy, the energy must travel through the vacuum that exists in space between the Sun and Earth. You learned that a **vacuum** is a region where no matter exists. Because there are no particles of matter in a vacuum, the energy that reaches Earth cannot be transferred by conduction or convection.

▶ DEFINE: What is a vacuum?

Heat Transfer Through Space Energy from the Sun is transferred to Earth by radiation. **Radiation** is the transfer of energy through space. Particles of matter are not needed for the transfer of heat energy by radiation. The heat is in the form of electromagnetic waves.

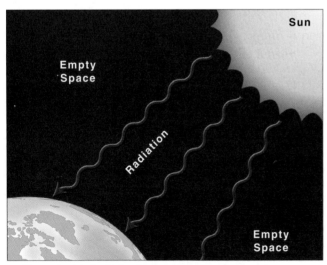

▲ **Figure 16-24** Radiation from the Sun travels through empty space.

▶ IDENTIFY: What is radiation?

Another Source of Radiation The Sun is not the only source of radiation on Earth. Hot objects also radiate heat. For example, food is kept warm under hot lights in some restaurants, and an electric heater can heat a room. Have you ever toasted a marshmallow over an open fire? You do not have to put the marshmallow directly into the fire. If the marshmallow is close enough to the flame, heat radiates from the fire to the marshmallow and melts it.

▲ **Figure 16-25** Radiation from the fire heats the marshmallow.

▶ IDENTIFY: List some sources of radiation.

Radiation in Home Heating Radiation from the Sun is used in some home heating systems. One type of heating system is called a passive solar-heating system. In this type of system, energy from the Sun heats a building directly. Large windows are usually placed where they will receive the maximum amount of sunlight. Energy from the Sun is absorbed by the walls and floors of the building and changed to heat. Shades covering the windows prevent heat loss at night.

Another type of heating system is an active solar-heating system. In an active solar-heating system, energy from the Sun is captured by solar collectors. Solar collectors are made of materials that absorb radiation from the Sun. They are usually installed on the roof or on the side of the house that faces the Sun. The energy captured by the solar collectors is used to heat water or air. The heated water or air is then circulated through the building. Because the amount of energy received from the Sun varies, backup heating systems are used in both passive and active solar-heating systems.

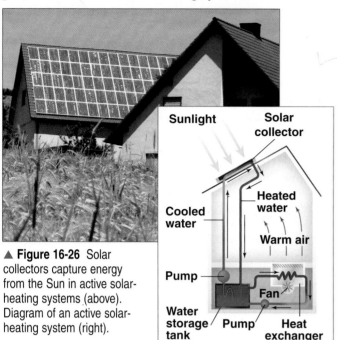

▲ **Figure 16-26** Solar collectors capture energy from the Sun in active solar-heating systems (above). Diagram of an active solar-heating system (right).

 NAME: What are two kinds of heating systems that use radiation?

 CHECKING CONCEPTS

1. Earth receives heat from the _____.
2. Space where no matter exists is called a _____.
3. Heat cannot travel from the Sun by _____ or convection.
4. The transfer of energy through empty space is called _____.
5. Two kinds of solar heating systems are active and _____ solar heating.

THINKING CRITICALLY

6. **INFER:** Why does your face get warm when you turn it toward the Sun?

INTERPRETING VISUALS

Use the diagram in Figure 16-26 to answer the question.

7. **EXPLAIN:** How does the heat exchanger help create convection currents in the house?

 Hands-On Activity

MEASURING THE EFFECT OF PASSIVE SOLAR HEATING

You will need two cardboard boxes, black construction paper, white paper, two thermometers, plastic wrap, scissors, and tape.

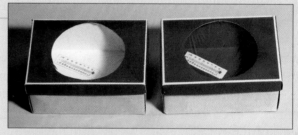

▲ **STEP 4** Place each box in direct sunlight.

1. Cut a large hole, or "window" in one side of each cardboard box. ⚠ CAUTION: Be careful when using scissors.
2. Completely line the inside of one box with black construction paper. Completely line the inside of the other box with white paper. Place a thermometer inside each box.
3. Cover each window with plastic wrap. Tape the plastic wrap tightly to the box.
4. Place each box in direct sunlight. Make sure that the window of each box fully faces the sunlight.
5. After about 20 minutes, open the boxes and read the temperature on each thermometer.

Practicing Your Skills

6. **MEASURE:** Which box got warmer?
7. **INFER:** Why did one box get warmer than the other?
8. **ANALYZE:** How does the box that got warmer model a passive solar heating system?

16-8 What is specific heat?

Objective

Describe the physical property of specific heat.

Key Term

specific heat: amount of heat needed to raise the temperature of 1 g of a substance 1°C.

Sand and Water Imagine a hot summer day at the beach. The sand is burning hot under your feet. You run into the water and it is "freezing" cold. How can the sand be so hot while the water is so cold? The answer is that different materials require a different amount of heat to raise their temperatures. Sand requires less heat to raise its temperature than water does. This is why the sand is so hot. However, water needs a much greater amount of heat to raise it to the same temperature as the sand. This is why the water is so much colder than the sand.

1 INFER: Which needs a greater amount of heat to raise its temperature, water or sand?

Specific Heat Adding heat to a substance increases its temperature. However, the rise in temperature for different types of substances is not the same, even if you have the same amount of each substance. For example, if you have equal amounts of sand and water, adding the same amount of heat to both samples will not give you the same temperature in both samples. The temperature of the sand will always be higher than the temperature of the water. The amount of heat needed to raise the temperature of any substance depends on the chemical makeup of the substance.

▲ **Figure 16-27** When heat is added to equal samples of sand and water, the temperature of the sand will always be higher than the temperature of the water.

The ability of a substance to absorb heat is called its specific heat. **Specific heat** is the amount of heat needed to raise the temperature of 1 g of a substance 1°C. For example, it takes 0.09 calories of heat to raise the temperature of 1 g of copper 1°C. Specific heat is a physical property. Every pure substance has its own specific heat. Figure 16-28 shows the specific heats of some substances.

SPECIFIC HEATS OF SOME SUBSTANCES	
Substance	**Specific heat (cal/g°C)**
Aluminum	0.22
Copper	0.09
Gold	0.03
Iron	0.11
Lead	0.03
Water	1.00

▲ **Figure 16-28**

2 INFER: If the same amount of heat is added to equal samples of gold and aluminum, which sample will have a higher temperature?

Applications of Low Specific Heat A substance with a low specific heat gets hot easily. Not only are metals such as copper and aluminum good conductors of heat, they also have low specific heats. This means that it does not take much heat energy to raise these metals to high temperatures.

3 PREDICT: Do substances with high specific heats get hot quickly or slowly?

Water Is Unique Water can take in or give off a lot of heat energy without a large change in temperature. Its specific heat is much higher than other earth materials, such as those that make up air and soil. That is why in winter, the air temperature around a lake can be as low as −20°C, but the water temperature may be 20°C. In summer, the air near the same lake can warm up to 25°C, whereas the water temperature remains a comfortable 12°C.

Water has an unusually high specific heat. One calorie of heat energy only raises the temperature of 1 g of water 1°C. Water's specific heat is about ten times greater than that of iron. This means that one calorie of heat raises the temperature of 1 g of iron about 10°C.

 HYPOTHESIZE: On a very cold day, which is apt to be warmer, water in a lake or the air around the lake?

✓ CHECKING CONCEPTS

1. Specific heat is the amount of heat needed to increase the temperature of _____ of a substance 1°C.

2. If a material has a _____ specific heat, it gets hot easily.

3. Iron gets _____ times hotter than water does when the same amount of heat is applied to both.

4. Specific heat is a _____ property.

💡 THINKING CRITICALLY

5. **PREDICT:** Which would you expect to be hotter in the summer, a city near a large lake or a city that is far from any body of water? Explain your answer.

6. **ANALYZE:** A silver spoon and a stainless steel spoon are both placed in a cup of hot tea. The silver spoon becomes too hot to handle within minutes. The stainless steel spoon is warm. Explain the difference in the two substances.

DESIGNING AN EXPERIMENT

Design an experiment to solve the following problem. Include a hypothesis, variables, a procedure, and a type of data to study.

PROBLEM: Does ocean water have the same specific heat as pure water? If not, which has the higher specific heat?

 Hands-On Activity

COMPARING THE SPECIFIC HEATS OF TWO METALS

You will need safety goggles, plastic gloves, an apron, two blocks of paraffin wax, a strip of copper, a strip of aluminum, a pencil, a beaker, water, a hot plate, tongs, and a timer.

1. Put on safety goggles, an apron, and plastic gloves.

2. Half-fill the beaker with water. Heat the beaker on a hot plate. ⚠ CAUTION: Hot plates and hot water can cause burns.

3. When the water boils, drop both metal strips into the beaker. Boil gently for 5 minutes.

4. Using the tongs, remove the copper strip from the beaker. Place it on top of one paraffin block.

5. Using the tongs, remove the aluminum strip from the beaker. Place it on top of the other paraffin block.

6. Observe the blocks of paraffin for 5 minutes.

▲ **STEP 6** Place the heated metal strips on blocks of paraffin wax. Observe for 5 minutes.

Practicing Your Skills

7. **IDENTIFY:** Which metal strip melted the most wax?

8. **INFER:** Which metal has the lower specific heat?

What is thermal expansion?

Objective

Describe what happens to solids, liquids, and gases when they are heated.

Key Term

thermal expansion: expansion of matter caused by heating

Heat and Expansion The expansion of matter caused by heating is called **thermal expansion.** Most materials expand, or get larger, when they are heated. You have learned that when heat energy is applied to a material, the particles of matter gain kinetic energy. The particles move faster and spread farther apart. As a result, the material expands. This happens even when the material does not change its state of matter.

What happens to a material as it cools? The particles move closer together. The material contracts, or gets smaller. Most solids contract when they are cooled.

▶ **DEFINE:** What is thermal expansion?

Expansion in Solids Have you ever seen the spaces between the joints on a bridge? The spaces are there because they allow the metals in the bridge to expand. Metals, like most solids, expand when the weather gets hot. Without the spaces, the bridge could be badly damaged.

▲ **Figure 16-29** Spaces between the joints allow the metals in the bridge to expand.

Spaces are built into concrete sidewalks, railroad tracks, and other structures for the same reason. You may be familiar with expansion in solids, too. If you have ever placed the lid of a jar under hot water, you know that the heat from the water can make the lid expand enough to loosen it.

▶ **EXPLAIN:** What happens to most solids when they are heated?

Expansion in Liquids Most liquids expand when they are heated. The particles of the liquid move farther apart as the liquid is heated. The opposite is usually true, too. When a liquid is cooled, the particles move closer together. The substance contracts, or gets smaller. However, water is an exception. Water contracts until it reaches a temperature of 4°C. Then it expands instead of contracting. The freezing point of water is 0°C. When water is cooled from 4°C to 0°C, it expands and its volume increases. As the volume of water increases, the density decreases. As a result, ice is less dense than water. This is why ice floats.

▲ **Figure 16-30** Ice floats because it is less dense than water.

▶ **STATE:** What happens to water as it is cooled from 4°C to 0°C?

Expansion in Gases Gases also expand when they are heated and contract when they are cooled. Hot-air balloons rise because of the expansion of heated air.

Thermal expansion of a gas within a container can be dramatic. The particles in a gas are farther apart and move faster than the particles in a solid or a liquid. Adding heat to a gas will cause its particles to collide with one another and the sides of their container. If a gas in a container becomes too hot, the increased pressure can cause the container to burst. This is the reason why food should not be heated in a tightly sealed container.

 EXPLAIN: How does the expansion of gas cause a hot-air balloon to rise?

✔ CHECKING CONCEPTS

1. What is the expansion of materials caused by heating called?
2. What happens to most solids when they are cooled?
3. What happens to most liquids when they are heated?
4. What can happen if a gas in a container is heated?
5. What happens to gases when they are cooled?

💡 THINKING CRITICALLY

6. **COMPARE:** What happens to the particles of most solids when they are heated? What happens to the particles in most solids when they are cooled?
7. **HYPOTHESIZE:** What would happen to a sidewalk on a hot day if there were no cracks between the squares in the sidewalk?

INTERPRETING VISUALS

Look at Figure 16-31 to answer the following question.

8. **ANALYZE:** Explain how the drawings illustrate thermal expansion.

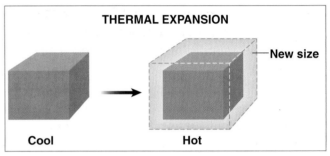

THERMAL EXPANSION

New size

Cool   Hot

▲ **Figure 16-31** Thermal expansion

 ## *Science and Technology*

BIMETALLIC THERMOSTATS

Thermal expansion can be used to help control how a home is heated and cooled. A device called a thermostat regulates the temperature in most homes. Inside the thermostat is a strip made of two metals. The device is called a bimetallic thermostat. The prefix *bi-* means "two."

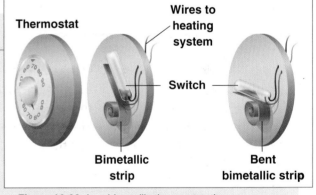

Thermostat

Wires to heating system

Switch

Bimetallic strip

Bent bimetallic strip

▲ **Figure 16-32** In a bimetallic thermostat, the bending and unbending of the bimetallic strip controls a switch.

The two metals in the thermostat expand when they are heated. However, they expand at different rates. One of the metals will expand faster than the other. It will also contract faster when cooled. As a result, the bimetallic strip bends when it is heated. It straightens out when it is cooled. This bending and unbending controls a switch.

The switch controls an electric circuit, which turns the home heating system on and off. For example, when the temperature in a room gets too high, the thermostat switches off the electric current. The heating system goes off, and the temperature drops. When the temperature gets too low, the thermostat switches the current back on. The heating system goes on, and the temperature rises.

Thinking Critically Why do you think the metal strip needs to be made of two different metals?

THE Big IDEA

How do animals control their body temperatures?

Many animals are able to live in areas where the climate is extremely hot or extremely cold. The abilities of these animals to regulate their body temperatures and to behave in certain ways help them to live under extreme weather conditions.

Animals are classified into two groups—warm-blooded animals and cold-blooded animals. These terms are a bit confusing because both kinds of animals can be warm. Therefore, many scientists call warm-blooded animals endotherms (EHN-doh-thurms) and cold-blooded animals ectotherms (EHK-toh-thurms).

An endotherm regulates its body temperature to maintain a constant internal temperature. The endotherm has no control over this process. For example, when an endotherm is in cold surroundings, its body shivers to keep warm. When it is in hot surroundings, its body perspires or "sweats" to cool off.

The body temperature of an ectotherm can adjust to the temperature of the environment outside of its body. For example, the body temperature of an ectotherm that lives in water can decrease to better adapt to the temperature of the water. An ectotherm can also increase its body temperature by lying in the Sun. An ectotherm has some control over its body temperature because it can move from colder environments to warmer environments and vice versa.

Read about the endotherms and ectotherms that appear on these two pages. Then, follow the directions in the Science Log to find out more about "the big idea."◆

Walruses
Endotherms that live in cold environments have adaptations that help them to keep from losing heat. Sea mammals, such as these walruses, have a thick layer of insulating fat called blubber that retains body heat.

Lizards
A lizard is an ectotherm. It lies out in the Sun to absorb heat. Absorbing heat increases its body temperature.

Figure 16-33 Endotherms and ectotherms are found around the world.

Polar Bears

Polar bears are endotherms that maintain the same body temperature even when swimming in freezing water.

WRITING ACTIVITY

Science Log

On a map, look at the regions that are very cold or very hot. Pick a region and research what kinds of animals can be found there. In your science log, list the animals and classify them as either endotherms or ectotherms. Describe the behaviors that the animals have that help them live in their environments. Start your search at www.conceptsandchallenges.com.

Elephants

Some endotherms have to work to keep cool. Elephants enjoy baths to keep cool. Also, their large ears increase the surface area to radiate more heat out of their bodies.

Fishes

Ocean water can drop below freezing. The Arctic cod is an ectotherm that has a special protein in its blood that keeps its tissues from freezing.

Chapter 16 Challenges

Chapter Summary

Lesson 16-1
- **Heat** is energy of particles moving from warmer to cooler regions.
- All matter has heat.
- Heat energy moves from a warmer object to a cooler object.

Lesson 16-2
- **Temperature** is a measure of the average kinetic energy of the particles of a substance.
- Heat affects the temperature of a substance.

Lesson 16-3
- The temperature at which a liquid changes to a solid is its **freezing point.**
- The temperature at which a solid changes to a liquid is its **melting point.**

Lesson 16-4
- The temperature at which a liquid changes to a gas is its **boiling point.**

Lesson 16-5
- Heat moves through solids by **conduction.**
- Heat travels by conduction when moving particles of matter bump into one another.

Lesson 16-6
- Heat is transferred in gases and liquids by **convection.**
- **Convection currents** are found in liquids and gases.

Lesson 16-7
- Energy from the Sun travels through empty space.
- Transfer of energy through space is called **radiation.**

Lesson 16-8
- **Specific heat** is the amount of heat needed to raise the temperature of 1 g of a substance 1°C.

Lesson 16-9
- **Thermal expansion** is the expansion of a material caused by heating.

Key Term Challenges

boiling point (p. 338)
calorie (p. 334)
conduction (p. 340)
conductor (p. 340)
convection (p. 342)
convection
  current (p. 342)
evaporation (p. 338)
freezing point (p. 336)

heat (p. 332)
insulator (p. 340)
melting point (p. 336)
radiation (p. 346)
specific heat (p. 348)
temperature (p. 334)
thermal
  expansion (p. 350)
vacuum (p. 346)

MATCHING Write the Key Term from above that best matches each description.

1. change from a liquid to a gas at the surface of the liquid

2. total kinetic energy of all the particles in a sample of matter

3. region where no matter exists

4. transfer of heat through space

5. temperature at which a solid changes to a liquid

6. transfer of heat through a gas or liquid

7. measure of the average kinetic energy of the particles in a sample of matter

8. expansion of a material caused by heating

FILL IN Write the Key Term from above that best completes each statement.

9. The temperature at which a liquid changes to a solid is called the _____.

10. The heat transfer in solids is called _____.

11. Materials that do not conduct heat easily are called _____.

12. The up-and-down movements of gases or liquids that cause heat to be transferred is called _____.

13. A _____ is a unit of heat.

14. Substances with low _____ get hot easily.

Content Challenges TEST PREP

MULTIPLE CHOICE Write the letter of the term or phrase that best completes each statement.

1. Before Benjamin Thompson's experiment, people thought that heat was a
   a. force.
   b. gas.
   c. form of energy.
   d. substance.

2. A unit used to measure heat is the
   a. calorie.
   b. gram.
   c. degree Celsius.
   d. liter.

3. When water freezes, it changes to
   a. heat.
   b. ice.
   c. caloric.
   d. absolute zero.

4. Scientists now know that heat is a
   a. force.
   b. liquid.
   c. form of energy.
   d. substance.

5. When you add or remove heat from a material, you change its
   a. mass.
   b. weight.
   c. potential energy.
   d. temperature.

6. When water boils, it changes to
   a. ice.
   b. small particles.
   c. a solid.
   d. steam.

7. Water changes to ice at
   a. 0°C.
   b. 22°C.
   c. 100°C.
   d. 212°F.

8. Warm air
   a. floats.
   b. sinks.
   c. rises.
   d. turns into steam.

9. The freezing point of a substance is the same as its
   a. boiling point.
   b. elevation point.
   c. dew point.
   d. melting point.

10. Energy moves through a vacuum by
    a. conduction.
    b. convection.
    c. radiation.
    d. evaporation.

TRUE/FALSE Write *true* if the statement is true. If the statement is false, change the underlined term to make the statement true.

11. Adding heat energy makes particles of matter move <u>slower</u>.

12. Most solids <u>expand</u> as they freeze.

13. Absolute zero is about <u>–273°C</u>.

14. Particles of matter are always <u>moving</u>.

Concept Challenges ~~TEST PREP~~

WRITTEN RESPONSE **Complete the exercises and answer each of the following questions in complete sentences.**

1. **COMPARE:** What is the difference between temperature and heat?

2. **EXPLAIN:** How is thermal expansion applied in a thermometer?

3. **HYPOTHESIZE:** Do you think it is possible to reach absolute zero in a laboratory? Why or why not?

4. **COMPARE:** Describe the differences between the transfer of heat by conduction, convection, and radiation.

5. **EXPLAIN:** How did Benjamin Thompson's experiment disprove the caloric theory?

INTERPRETING A TABLE **Use Figure 16-34 to answer the following questions.**

6. Which substance has the highest specific heat?

7. Which substance has the lowest specific heat?

8. Which substance has a specific heat of 0.22 cal/g °C?

9. Which substance heats up faster, copper or iron?

10. Which substance heats up slower, gold or aluminum?

SPECIFIC HEATS OF SOME SUBSTANCES	
Substance	Specific heat (cal/g°C)
Aluminum	0.22
Copper	0.09
Gold	0.03
Iron	0.11
Lead	0.03
Water	1.00

▲ Figure 16-34

Chapter 17 Waves

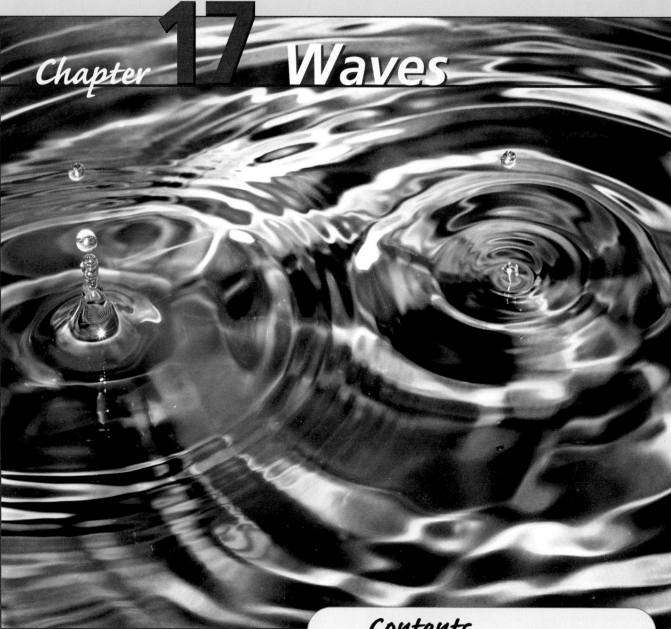

▲ **Figure 17-1** Pebbles dropped in a pond create waves in circular patterns.

A pebble falls and disturbs the smooth, calm surface of a pond. The energy of the falling pebble is transferred to the water. Small waves called ripples move out in all directions from the place where the pebble entered the water. These waves carry the energy to the edges of the pond.

▶ What will happen when the water drops from the splash fall back to the pond's surface?

Contents

Objective

Identify a wave as energy traveling through a medium.

Key Terms

wave: disturbance that transfers energy from place to place

mechanical wave: wave that transfers energy through matter

electromagnetic (ee-lehk-troh-mag-NEHT-ihk) **wave:** wave that transfers energy through empty space

medium: material through which mechanical waves can travel

Waves and Energy If you have ever stood in heavy surf, like that shown in Figure 17-2, you know that water waves have a lot of energy. **Waves** are disturbances that transfer energy from place to place.

▼ Figure 17-2 There is a great amount of energy in heavy surf.

Mechanical waves transfer energy through some form of matter. **Electromagnetic waves,** such as light and radio waves, do not need matter. They can transfer energy through empty space. You will learn more about this type of wave in a later chapter.

▲ Figure 17-3 The swimmer and his feathered friends create V-shaped waves as they move through the water. These waves transfer energy supplied by the swimmers.

1 DEFINE: What are waves?

Mechanical Waves Mechanical waves can travel only through some kinds of matter. Any material through which mechanical waves travel is called a **medium.** The picture in Figure 17-3 shows how water can serve as a medium. Air serves as a medium for sound waves.

When a wave travels through a medium, only energy moves from place to place. The particles of the medium do not move forward with the wave. Think of a bottle floating on water as shown in Figure 17-4. What happens as a wave moves past the bottle? The bottle moves up and down. It does not move forward in the same direction as the wave. The wave moves through the water.

2 ▶ **STATE:** Do all mechanical waves need a medium?

Particle Motion in a Medium When a wave travels through a medium such as water, the particles of the medium do not move forward with the wave. Figure 17-4 shows a wave moving through water. As described earlier, the bottle does not travel with the wave. It bobs up and down. This up-and-down motion of the bottle is caused by the motion of the water particles.

As a wave moves through the water, each water particle follows a circular path. The size of the circles is greatest at the surface of the water and decreases with depth. The water does not move forward with the wave. The energy of the wave is transferred forward to the next group of water particles, which also move in circles.

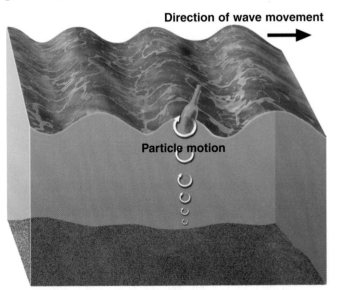

▲ **Figure 17-4** As a wave passes, a bottle will bob up and down but will not move forward.

3 ▶ **DESCRIBE:** What happens to water particles as a wave moves through the water?

✓ CHECKING CONCEPTS

1. Water waves carry _____.
2. Water is a _____ for waves.
3. Particles move in _____ as wave energy moves forward.
4. Some waves, such as _____ waves, do not require a medium.
5. Light waves can travel through _____.
6. When a wave moves through a medium, only _____ moves from place to place.

💡 THINKING CRITICALLY

7. **EXPLAIN:** You are sitting in a rowboat in the middle of a lake when a motorboat passes by, making waves that hit your boat. Describe what happens to your boat.
8. **ANALYZE:** Does the engine of a space shuttle produce sound as it orbits Earth?

HEALTH AND SAFETY TIP

During a hurricane or other large storm, a great deal of energy is carried by ocean waves. Storm waves can cause serious damage when they hit the shore. You should stay away from the shore during a hurricane. Look at Figure 17-5 for a safety checklist. Check with your local Red Cross for anything specific in your area.

HURRICANE SAFETY TIPS	
What You Need	**What You Have to Do**
☐ A full gas tank in your car	☐ Cover windows with plywood
☐ Necessary medications	☐ Close shutters
☐ First-aid kit	☐ Stay inside or evacuate
☐ Canned goods	☐ Fill tub with water
☐ Fresh batteries	☐ Tie down movable items outside
☐ Flashlight	☐ Stay on the side of the house away from the wind
☐ Portable radio	☐ Beware of downed power lines and broken gas mains

▲ **Figure 17-5**

17-2 How do waves travel through matter?

Observing Waves in a Rope
HANDS-ON ACTIVITY

1. Tie a colored ribbon to the middle of a 3-m length of rope.
2. Tie one end of the rope to a doorknob. Hold the other end of the rope and stand opposite the door.
3. Quickly move your end of the rope up and down. Observe the ribbon's motion.
4. Increase the speed at which you move the end of the rope up and down. Observe the resulting waves.

THINK ABOUT IT: a. What happened to the ribbon when you moved the rope?
b. What happened when you increased the speed of your movements? **c.** What happened to the wavelength?

STEP 3

Objective
Classify waves as transverse or longitudinal.

Key Terms
transverse (trans-VUHRS) **wave:** wave in which the particles of the medium move up and down at right angles to the direction of the wave motion

crest: high point of a transverse wave

trough (TRAWF): low point of a transverse wave

longitudinal (lahn-juh-TOOD-uhn-uhl) **wave:** wave in which the particles of the medium move back and forth in the direction of the wave motion

compression (kuhm-PRESH-uhn): part of a medium where the particles are close together

rarefaction (rer-uh-FAK-shuhn): part of a medium where the particles are far apart

Transverse Waves There are two types of mechanical waves, transverse and longitudinal. The difference between the two kinds of waves is the way the particles of the medium move. In a **transverse wave,** the particles of the medium move at right angles, or perpendicular, to the direction of the wave motion. Water waves are transverse waves.

There are two parts to a transverse wave. The **crest** is the high point of a transverse wave. The **trough** is the low point of the wave.

You can demonstrate a transverse wave by tying one end of a rope to a doorknob and jerking the other end with a sharp up-and-down motion as shown in Figure 17-6.

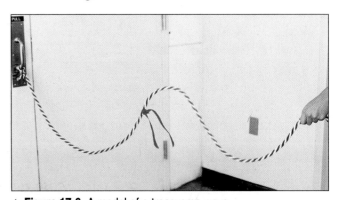

▲ **Figure 17-6** A model of a transverse wave

1 LIST: What are the two parts of a transverse wave?

Longitudinal Waves The sound of thunder moves in a series of longitudinal waves. A **longitudinal wave** is a wave in which particles of the medium move back and forth, parallel to the direction of the wave motion. The air is the medium that carries the energy of the thunderclap.

A longitudinal wave has two parts. A clap of thunder pushes the particles of air close together. This part of the wave is called a **compression.** The compressed particles move forward in the direction of the wave motion. As the particles move forward, they leave behind part of the wave where the particles are far apart. This part of the wave is called a **rarefaction.** The rarefaction also moves forward.

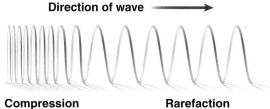

Direction of wave ⟶

Compression   Rarefaction

▲ **Figure 17-7** A model of a longitudinal wave

 DEFINE: What are rarefactions?

✓ CHECKING CONCEPTS

1. All waves carry _____.
2. The difference between waves depends on how the _____ of the medium move.
3. The particles of the medium move up and down in a _____ wave.
4. The particles of the medium move back and forth in a _____ wave.
5. The parts of a transverse wave are the crest and the _____.

💡 THINKING CRITICALLY

6. **INFER:** Are ocean waves transverse waves or longitudinal waves? How do you know?
7. **CLASSIFY:** Clap your hands together. What kind of wave did you make?
8. **INFER:** Have you ever seen fans do "the wave" at a baseball or football game? What kind of wave did they make?

Integrating Earth Science

TOPICS: earthquakes, seismic waves

EARTHQUAKE WAVES

In October 1989, a large earthquake struck San Francisco and Oakland, California. The earthquake registered 7.1 on the Richter scale. The Richter scale is a measure of how much energy an earthquake releases. The California earthquake of 1989 was very powerful.

The energy of an earthquake produces waves that travel through the Earth. All earthquakes produce three main types of waves. These waves are called primary waves (P-waves), secondary waves (S-waves), and long waves (L-waves). L-waves are also called surface waves. They cause the surface of the Earth to rise and fall. L-waves cause the greatest damage during an earthquake.

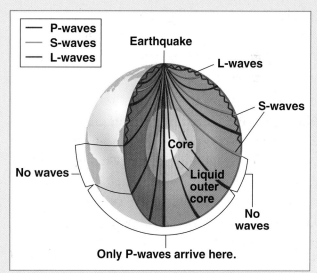

▲ **Figure 17-8** A diagram of three kinds of seismic waves

Scientists record earthquake waves on an instrument called a seismograph. P-waves, S-waves, and L-waves travel at different speeds. Scientists calculate the difference in arrival times of the three waves. They use this information to locate the area of Earth's surface directly above the earthquake's origin.

Thinking Critically Which waves cause the most damage? Explain your answer.

17-3 What are the features of a wave

Objectives

Describe the features of a wave. Relate wave speed, frequency, and wavelength.

Key Terms

wavelength: distance between two neighboring crests or troughs

frequency (FREE-kwuhn-see)**:** number of complete waves passing a point in a given time

amplitude (AM-pluh-tood)**:** height of a transverse wave

speed: distance a wave travels in one unit of time

hertz (HURTS)**:** unit used to measure the frequency of a wave

Features of Transverse Waves All waves have some basic features. These features are wavelength, frequency, and amplitude. Figure 17-9 shows these features in a transverse wave.

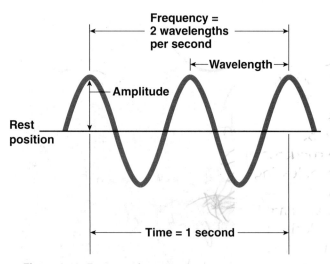

▲ Figure 17-9 Features of a transverse wave

All waves have a certain length. The distance from the crest or trough of one wave to the crest or trough of the next wave is the **wavelength.** Wavelength can be measured in meters or centimeters.

A certain number of waves pass a point in a given amount of time. The number of complete waves per unit of time is called **frequency.** Frequency is expressed in waves per second.

When a wave moves through a medium, the particles of the medium are moved from their rest position. The height the particles are moved is called the **amplitude** of the wave.

1 ▶ LIST: What are some basic features of a wave?

Features of Longitudinal Waves Longitudinal waves have the same features as transverse waves. The distance from one compression to another or from one rarefaction to another is the wavelength. The number of waves that pass a certain point each second is the frequency. The amplitude of a longitudinal wave depends on the amount of energy in the wave. This is shown by how tightly or loosely compressed the particles are.

2 ▶ DEFINE: What is the amplitude of a longitudinal wave?

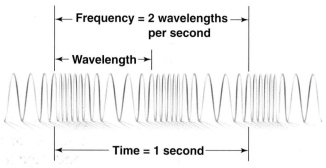

▲ Figure 17-10 Features of a longitudinal wave

Speed of a Wave All waves move. Their speed of movement is related to their frequency and wavelength. **Speed** is the distance a wave travels in one unit of time. Wave speed is equal to frequency times wavelength.

speed = frequency × wavelength

Scientists use a unit called a **hertz** to measure frequency. One hertz (Hz) is equal to one wave per second. When frequency is measured in hertz and wavelength is measured in meters, speed is measured in meters per second (m/s).

3 ▶ IDENTIFY: What is the equation used to find the speed of a wave?

✓ CHECKING CONCEPTS

1. All waves have amplitude, _____, and frequency.

2. Amplitude is the _____ of a transverse wave.

3. Wavelength can be measured in _____ or centimeters.

4. The number of _____ passing a point in a given time is called frequency.

5. The speed of a wave is equal to _____ multiplied by wavelength.

6. The _____ is the unit used to measure frequency.

7. One hertz is equal to one _____ per second.

💡 THINKING CRITICALLY

8. **LIST:** Name the parts of a transverse wave and the corresponding parts of a longitudinal wave.

9. **COMPARE:** What is the difference between amplitude in a transverse wave and amplitude in a longitudinal wave?

BUILDING MATHEMATICS SKILLS

Use the equation to complete the following questions:

$$\text{speed} = \text{frequency} \times \text{wavelength}$$

a. A wave has a frequency of 50 Hz and a wavelength of 10 m. What is the speed of the wave?

b. The speed of a wave is 5 m/s. Its wavelength is 2 m. What is the frequency of the wave?

c. The frequency of a wave is 20 Hz. Its speed is 100 m/s. What is the wavelength of the wave?

How Do They Know That?

HEINRICH HERTZ

During the 1800s, the physicist James Clerk Maxwell developed a theory of electromagnetism. Using Maxwell's findings, Heinrich Hertz, a physics professor, sought to perfect Maxwell's theory. Hertz conducted a series of experiments in which he proved that electricity can be transmitted in electromagnetic waves. He set up a condenser using two metal rods. He placed the rods end to end, leaving space between them small enough for a spark. When charged, the rods produced a spark that traveled back and forth between them. Thus, Hertz proved that the velocity of radio waves can be timed. Their velocity is the same as that of light. He was also able to solve the problem of how to free the waves from electric and magnetic fields.

A young inventor used Hertz's findings to develop both the telegraph and the radio. Radar is also based on Hertz's work.

The unit used to measure frequency of waves, Hertz (Hz), is named after this great physicist.

Thinking Critically What important discovery concerning electricity was made by Hertz?

▲ **Figure 17-11** Heinrich Hertz

Go **O**nline
active art

For: Modulating Electromagnetic Waves activity
Visit: PHSchool.com
Web Code: cgp-4042

LAB ACTIVITY
Making Waves

Materials
Safety goggles
Coil spring
Meter stick
Clock with second
  hand
Stopwatch

BACKGROUND

One of the ways energy is transmitted is through waves. Water waves carry kinetic energy across oceans to pound on distant shorelines. Sound is carried in waves that cause the eardrums in our ears to vibrate. How do waves carry energy?

PURPOSE

You will create waves in a spring and observe their properties.

PROCEDURE

1. Select an area in which to conduct your experiment. The test area should be 3 to 4 meters long.

2. Copy the chart in Figure 17-12 onto a sheet of paper. Put on safety goggles.

3. Select two members of your group to operate the springs for the first tests.

4. Stretch the spring the length of the test area.

5. Begin making waves in the spring by moving just one end of the spring side to side. The movement should be slow and easy.

6. Measure the length of the waves produced. Then, use the stopwatch to count how many waves arrive at the other end of the spring each second (frequency). Record your observations.

7. Increase the number of waves by moving one end of the spring faster. Again, measure the wavelength and the number of waves arriving at the other end each second.

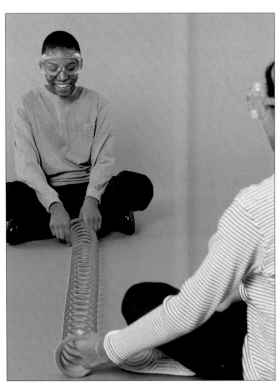

▲ **STEP 4** Stretch the spring.

▲ **STEP 5** Move one end side to side to make waves.

▲ **STEP 7** Move the spring faster to increase the wave frequency.

8. Increase the number of waves again and make the same observations as before.

9. Switch jobs in your group and repeat the tests.

Wavelengths, Frequency, and Energy			
	Wavelength (length between crests)	Frequency (waves per second)	Energy Needed (small, medium, or large)
Test 1			
Test 2			
Test 3			

▲ **Figure 17-12** Copy this chart and use it to record your observations.

CONCLUSIONS

1. **OBSERVE:** When the wavelengths are long, is the frequency low or high?

2. **OBSERVE:** When the wavelengths are short, is the frequency low or high?

3. **ANALYZE:** Which waves are easier to make, short waves or long waves?

4. **INFER:** If you hear a low sound, what can you infer about its frequency?

5. **INFER:** If you hear a high sound, does it have a low frequency or a high frequency?

17-4   How are waves reflected?

Objectives

Describe what happens when a wave strikes a barrier. State the law of reflection.

Key Terms

reflection: bouncing of a wave after striking a barrier

incident wave: wave that strikes a barrier

reflected wave: wave that bounces off a barrier

normal: line at right angles to a barrier

Waves and Barriers   What happens when a wave hits a barrier like the rocks in Figure 17-13? Remember that all waves carry energy. Some of the wave's energy may be absorbed by the barrier. If the barrier does not absorb the wave's energy, the wave bounces off the barrier. This bouncing of a wave from a barrier is called **reflection.**

▲ **Figure 17-13** An incident wave strikes a barrier and is reflected.

▶ **DESCRIBE:** What happens when a wave strikes a barrier that does not absorb all of its energy?

Reflection   Some familiar examples of reflections include a ball bouncing off a wall, your image coming from a mirror, and an echo in an empty room. Figure 17-14 shows what happens when a wave strikes a barrier. The red arrows show the direction of the wave. The wave that strikes the barrier is called the **incident wave.** The wave that bounces off the barrier is called the **reflected wave.**

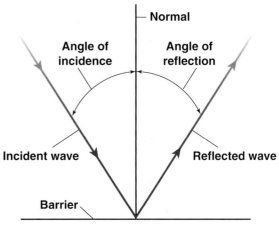

▲ **Figure 17-14** The angle of incidence equals the angle of reflection.

▶ **DEFINE:** What is a reflected wave?

Law of Reflection   The law of reflection describes what happens when a wave is reflected from a barrier. The angle at which an incident wave strikes a barrier is called the angle of incidence, or i. The angle at which the wave is reflected is called the angle of reflection, or r. These angles are measured from a line called the normal. The **normal** is a line at a right angle to the barrier. A right angle is equal to 90°. The law of reflection states that the angle of incidence is equal to the angle of reflection. Suppose a wave strikes a barrier at a 45° angle. The reflected wave will bounce off the barrier at a 45° angle.

▶ **STATE:** What is the law of reflection?

CHECKING CONCEPTS

1. What happens when a wave strikes a barrier?
2. What is reflection?
3 What is a wave that strikes a barrier called?
4. What is a wave that bounces back from a barrier called?
5. What is the normal?
6. What is the angle formed by the normal and the barrier?

Web InfoSearch

Standing Waves Use the Internet to find out what standing waves are and how they are formed. Write a report of your findings. Include a diagram of standing waves in a rope. Start your search at www.conceptsandchallenges.com. Some key search words are **standing waves** and **reflected waves**.

THINKING CRITICALLY

Use Figure 17-15 to answer the following questions.

7. **CONTRAST:** What is the difference between the angle of incidence and the angle of reflection?
8. **ANALYZE:** Which arrow represents the incident wave?
9. **ANALYZE:** Which arrow represents the reflected wave?
10. **ANALYZE:** Which angle is the angle of incidence?
11. **ANALYZE:** Which angle is the angle of reflection?

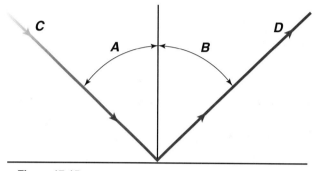

▲ Figure 17-15

 Hands-On Activity

MEASURING THE ANGLE OF INCIDENCE AND THE ANGLE OF REFLECTION

You will need a small rubber ball, dark construction paper, a protractor, ruler, a small amount of talcum powder, safety goggles, apron, and a marking pen.

1. Fold the construction paper in half lengthwise. Open the paper and lay it on the floor with the short side against the wall. The line of the fold represents the normal.
2. Measure an angle of 45° between the wall and the normal and mark it. Put on safety goggles and apron. Spread a small amount of talcum powder on this side of the normal.
3. Lay a ruler along the marked angle as shown. Slowly roll the ball along the edge of the ruler.
4. Observe the ball as it bounces off the wall. It should leave a light path of powder. Mark the angle of this path from the wall and measure it.
5. Label the angles of incidence and reflection.

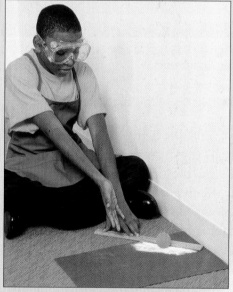

▲ **STEP 3** Using the ruler as a guide, roll the ball toward the wall.

Practicing Your Skills

6. **MEASURE:** What is the size of the angle of incidence?
7. **MEASURE:** What is the size of the angle of reflection?

17-5 How are waves refracted?

Objective

Describe what happens to a wave when it moves from one medium to another.

Key Term

refraction: bending of a wave as it moves from one medium to another

Changing the Medium Waves travel in straight lines through a medium. What happens to a wave when it moves from one medium to another? Suppose a wave moves from air into water. If the wave enters the water at an angle other than 90°, the wave bends. This bending of a wave as it moves from one medium to another is called **refraction.**

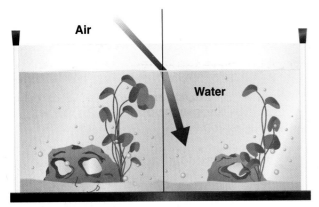

▲ **Figure 17-16** As the wave leaves the air and enters the water, it is refracted.

 DEFINE: What is refraction?

Refraction and Wave Speed Waves bend when they go from one medium to another because they change speed. Water is denser than air. When a light wave moves from air into water, it slows down. When a light wave moves from water into air, it speeds up. This change in speed causes the wave to be refracted, or bent.

You can see the results of refraction by performing a simple experiment. Place a pencil into a glass of water at an angle. The pencil appears to be broken where it enters the water. As light waves move from air into water, they slow down. This change in speed causes the light waves to be refracted. As a result, the pencil appears broken.

◀ **Figure 17-17** A pencil placed in water at an angle appears broken.

 EXPLAIN: What causes refraction as waves move from one medium to another?

Laws of Refraction The three laws of refraction describe how waves are refracted when they move from one medium to another.

- When a wave moves at an angle from a less dense medium to a more dense medium, it is bent toward the normal.

- When a wave moves at an angle from a more dense medium to a less dense medium, it is bent away from the normal.

- When a wave moves from one medium to another along the normal, it is not bent.

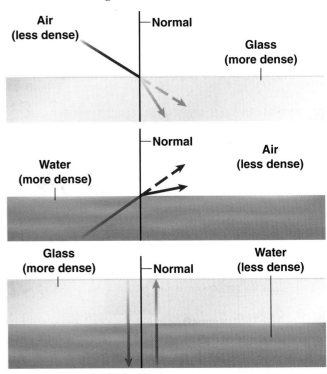

▲ **Figure 17-18** These diagrams illustrate the three laws of refraction.

 DESCRIBE: In what direction is a wave bent when it moves at an angle from a more dense medium to a less dense medium?

1. Waves travel through a medium in _____ lines.

2. When a wave moves at an angle from one medium to another, it _____.

3. The bending of a wave is called _____.

4. Refraction is caused by a change in _____.

5. The speed of a light wave _____ when it moves from water into air.

6. When a wave moves at an angle from a less dense medium to a more dense medium, it is bent _____ the normal.

💡 THINKING CRITICALLY

Use Figure 17-19 to answer question 7.

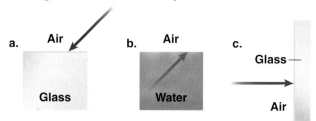

a. Air / Glass b. Air / Water c. Glass — Air

▲ Figure 17-19

7. ANALYZE: Copy the diagrams onto a separate sheet of paper. Draw arrows to show how the light waves will be refracted in each example.

8. HYPOTHESIZE: Have you ever tried to pick up an object underwater? Why do you think the object appeared closer to the surface of the water than it really was?

Web InfoSearch

Ocean Waves Ocean waves change direction as they come close to a shoreline. Waves almost always approach the shore at an angle. However, they usually hit the shore straight on. As waves approach the shallow water near shore, they slow down. This change in speed causes the waves to change direction.

SEARCH: Use the Internet to find out more about the direction of ocean waves. Start your search at www.conceptsandchallenges.com. Some key search words are **ocean waves, wave,** and **ocean wave refraction.**

Hands-On Activity

OBSERVING THE EFFECTS OF REFRACTION

You will need safety goggles, a small bowl, water, and a penny.

1. Put on safety goggles and then place a penny into a small bowl.

2. Move away from the bowl until you can no longer see the penny.

3. Without changing your position, have a partner add water to the bowl until you can see the penny again.

Practicing Your Skills

4. ANALYZE: Why could you not see the penny when you moved away from the bowl?

5. HYPOTHESIZE: Why could you see the penny again after water was added to the bowl?

6. MODEL: Draw a diagram showing how light waves reflected from the penny were refracted as they moved from the water into the air.

▲ **STEP 3** Add water until your partner can see the penny.

Integrating Earth Science

THE Big IDEA

Tsunami: How big can a wave get?

How big can an ocean wave get? Think about a 100-foot-tall wave that is traveling at 800 km/h (480 mph). Does it sound like a horror movie? Such waves actually exist. They are called seismic sea waves or *tsunamis*, a Japanese word meaning "harbor wave." They occur most commonly in the Pacific.

Tsunamis are fast, high-energy waves related to earthquakes or volcanic eruptions on the seafloor. Sometimes people call them tidal waves. However, they are not caused by tides. A tsunami is caused by seismic activity, which is the movement of the Earth's crust. Energy from violent seismic movement on the ocean floor is transmitted into the water as a waveform. The high-energy wave can travel thousands of kilometers from its source.

In the deep open ocean, a tsunami might be only 1 m high, but when it reaches shore, watch out. The wave crest might be 18 m higher than normal waves.

In 2004, the second-strongest earthquake ever recorded caused a tsunami in the Indian Ocean. Waves 100 meters high crashed over South Asian shores. It killed nearly 230,000 people.

Most countries have a tsunami warning system to protect people. When seismographs (earthquake detectors) detect a seafloor earthquake starting a tsunami, loud alarms go off along the coast warning people to head for the hills. Surprisingly, it is also safe to be out at sea. In the open ocean, a passing tsunami would just feel like a large wave. Its awesome power is only revealed when the tsunami moves into the shallow water near the shore.

Look at the illustrations and photos that appear on these two pages. Then, follow the directions in the Science Log to find out more about "the big idea."✦

Figure 17-20 Woodcut by Japanese artist Hokusai

Tsunami Damage

Out at sea a tsunami doesn't appear much larger than other waves. However, when the high energy of the tsunami hits the shore, it can be very destructive. In 2004, South Asian shores suffered great damage.

Science Log

Find out how the tsunami warning system in Hawaii works. Your job is running part of the warning system. What data do you need to collect? How will you analyze the data? What do you think are the best ways to warn people? How will you make sure the people of your island are prepared to respond to a potential tsunami? To research a warning system, visit www.conceptsandchallenges.com.

Warning Signal

Although tsunamis move very fast, warning sirens like this give people time to get to the safety of higher ground.

Evacuation Map

This map can be found in local Hawaiian phone books. It shows which areas must be evacuated when a tsunami is detected.

EVACUATE ALL SHADED AREAS

Seismograph

Seismographs detect the seafloor earthquakes that start a tsunami. That is the key to the early warning system.

Chapter Summary

Lesson 17-1

- **Waves** are disturbances that transfer energy from place to place.
- Any substance through which waves can travel is called a **medium.**
- The particles of a medium do not move in the same direction as a wave but in small circles.

Lesson 17-2

- In a **transverse wave,** the particles of the medium move up and down at right angles to the direction of the wave motion. Its parts are the **crest** and the **trough.**
- In a **longitudinal wave,** the particles of the medium move back and forth in the same direction as the wave motion. Its parts are the **compression** and the **rarefaction.**

Lesson 17-3

- **Wavelength** is the distance from crest to crest or from trough to trough.
- **Frequency** is the number of complete waves passing a point in a given amount of time.
- **Amplitude** is the height of a wave.
- The **speed** of a wave is equal to the frequency multiplied by the wavelength.

Lesson 17-4

- A wave that strikes a barrier is called the **incident wave.**
- A wave that bounces off a barrier is called the **reflected wave.**
- The law of **reflection** states that the angle of incidence is equal to the angle of reflection.

Lesson 17-5

- The laws of **refraction** describe how waves are refracted, or bent, when they move from one medium to another.

Key Term Challenges

amplitude (p. 362)
compression (p. 360)
crest (p. 360)
electromagnetic wave (p. 358)
frequency (p. 362)
hertz (p. 362)
incident wave (p. 366)
longitudinal wave (p. 360)
mechanical wave (p. 358)
medium (p. 358)
normal (p. 366)
rarefaction (p. 360)
reflected wave (p. 366)
reflection (p. 366)
refraction (p. 368)
speed (p. 362)
transverse wave (p. 360)
trough (p. 360)
wavelength (p. 362)
wave (p. 358)

MATCHING Write the Key Term from above that best matches each description.

1. substance through which waves can travel
2. high point of a wave
3. height of a wave
4. unit used to measure frequency
5. wave that strikes a barrier
6. line at 90° to a barrier
7. disturbances in a medium

FILL IN Write the Key Term from above that best completes each statement.

8. In a _____, the particles of the medium move up and down at right angles to the direction of the wave motion.

9. In a _____, the particles of the medium move back and forth in the direction of the wave motion.

10. The two parts of a longitudinal wave are the _____ and the rarefaction.

11. The basic features of all waves are amplitude, _____, and frequency.

12. _____ occurs when a barrier does not absorb all of a wave's energy.

Content Challenges

MULTIPLE CHOICE **Write the letter of the term or phrase that best completes each statement.**

1. Waves are caused by
   a. potential energy.
   b. kinetic energy.
   c. heat energy.
   d. nuclear energy.

2. Mechanical waves cannot travel through
   a. air.
   b. water.
   c. metal.
   d. empty space.

3. When a longitudinal wave moves through a medium, the particles of the medium move
   a. in circles.
   b. up and down.
   c. back and forth.
   d. in the direction of the wave motion.

4. The two kinds of waves are transverse and
   a. circular.
   b. normal.
   c. longitudinal.
   d. compression.

5. The crest of a wave is the wave's
   a. low point.
   b. length.
   c. speed.
   d. high point.

6. In a transverse wave, the particles of the medium move
   a. at right angles to the direction of wave motion.
   b. back and forth to the direction of wave motion.
   c. at opposite angles to the wave motion.
   d. backward against the wave motion.

7. In a rarefaction, the particles are
   a. squeezed together.
   b. lined up.
   c. spread apart.
   d. not moving.

8. Wavelength can be measured in
   a. meters.
   b. hertz.
   c. angles.
   d. number of waves.

9. The wave's speed is equal to the frequency of the wave multiplied by the
   a. amplitude.
   b. wavelength.
   c. height.
   d. medium.

10. The angle between the normal and a barrier is equal to
    a. 45°.
    b. 90°.
    c. 180°.
    d. 360°.

TRUE/FALSE **Write *true* if the statement is true. If the statement is false, change the underlined term to make the statement true.**

11. The angle of incidence is equal to the angle of <u>refraction</u>.

12. When a wave is refracted, it is <u>bent</u>.

13. In a rarefaction, the particles are <u>spread apart</u>.

14. <u>Mechanical</u> waves do not need a medium to transfer energy.

Concept Challenges TEST PREP

WRITTEN RESPONSE Answer each of the following questions in complete sentences.

1. **HYPOTHESIZE:** You can make transverse waves in a rope tied to a doorknob. What happens to the waves when they reach the door?

2. **COMPARE:** How are the crests and troughs of a transverse wave like the compressions and rarefactions of a longitudinal wave?

3. **HYPOTHESIZE:** Suppose that light waves needed a medium through which to travel. How do you think the world would be different?

INTERPRETING A DIAGRAM Use Figure 17-21 to answer the following questions.

4. Which letter represents the wavelength of the wave?

5. Which letter represents the amplitude?

6. Which letter represents the frequency?

7. What is the relationship between speed, wavelength, and frequency?

8. If the frequency of a wave increases and the speed stays the same, what happens to the wavelength?

9. If the speed of a wave does not change but the wavelength increases, what happens to the frequency?

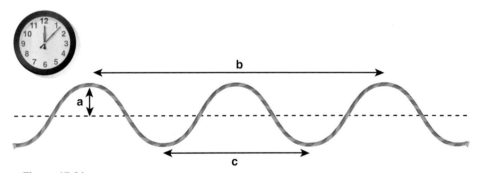

▲ **Figure 17-21**

Chapter 18 Sound

▲ **Figure 18-1** The instruments in this band make very recognizable sounds.

Sounds are all around you. When you hear a sound, most of the time you will recognize its source. For example, you would be able to tell the difference between the sound made by a bagpipe and one made by a bass drum. Although sounds are different, they all have something in common. All sounds are produced by objects that are moving back and forth rapidly.

►How does striking a drum produce a sound?

Contents

18-1 What is sound?

Objective
Identify sound as a form of energy caused by vibrations.

Key Terms
sound: form of energy that travels as waves
vibration: rapid back-and-forth movement

Sound and Energy There are sounds all around you. Some sounds are loud and others are very faint. Walking in a park, you may hear the sounds of birds singing and dogs barking. In a quiet room, you may hear the sound of an alarm clock ticking. Sound is a form of energy. **Sound** energy travels in the form of waves.

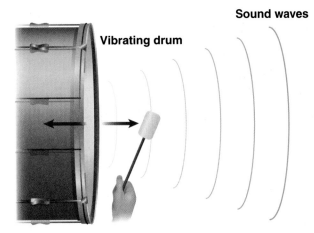

▲ **Figure 18-2** When a drum is struck, it vibrates and causes the air around it to vibrate.

1 DEFINE: What is sound?

Vibrations All sounds are caused by vibrations. A **vibration** is a rapid back-and-forth movement. Suppose you are listening to the sound from a stereo speaker. If you place your hand on the speaker, you will feel a vibration.

Objects that vibrate produce sound. Place your fingers on the front of your throat. When you speak, you can feel something vibrate. That something is your vocal cords (see Figure 18-3). The sound of your voice is produced when your vocal cords cause the air around them to vibrate.

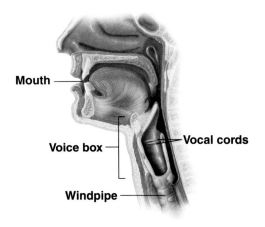

▲ **Figure 18-3** The sound of your voice is caused by the vibrations of your vocal cords.

2 DEFINE: What is a vibration?

Forming Sound For every sound that you hear, some object is vibrating. Strum a guitar. The guitar strings vibrate. When a string vibrates in one direction, it pushes on the air on that side of it. Air particles are squeezed together. The squeezed-together particles form a compression. When the string moves back, those air particles spread apart. The spread-out particles form a rarefaction. As the string continues to vibrate, compressions and rarefactions move away from the string. They form a sound wave.

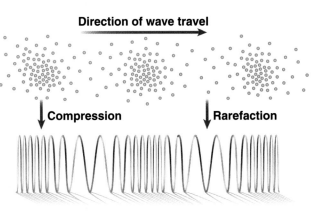

▲ **Figure 18-4** Sound waves are made up of a series of compressions and rarefactions.

3 DESCRIBE: What forms a sound wave?

Sources of Sounds You now know that when you hear a sound, something is vibrating to produce it. Different sounds can come from different sources. Figure 18-5 shows sources of a few of the sounds you might hear every day.

SOURCES OF SOUNDS	
Sound	**Vibration Source**
Violin	Strings
Drum beat	Drum skin and sticks
Human voice	Vocal cords
Knocking door	Door
Car revving	Engine
Pencil scratching	Lead and paper

▲ **Figure 18-5**

 DESCRIBE: How many other sounds and sources can you add to the list in Figure 18-5?

 CHECKING CONCEPTS

1. A sound is caused by a _____.
2. Sound is a form of _____ that travels as waves.

3. A _____ is a rapid back-and-forth movement.
4. All vibrating objects produce _____.
5. Sound waves are formed by compressions and _____.
6. If you place your fingers on your windpipe while you are speaking, you will feel a _____.
7. When you strum a guitar, the _____ vibrate.

THINKING CRITICALLY

8. **PREDICT:** What will happen if you place a glass of water on a stereo speaker?
9. **HYPOTHESIZE:** Is it possible to make a sound without causing a vibration? Why or why not?
10. **OBSERVE:** Sit by an open window. What sounds do you hear? What is causing each sound?

DESIGNING AN EXPERIMENT

Design an experiment to solve the following problem. Include a hypothesis, variables, a procedure, and a type of data to study.

PROBLEM: Can sound travel through solid objects?

Hands-On Activity

OBSERVING VIBRATIONS IN A TUNING FORK

You will need a tuning fork, safety goggles, and a glass of water.

1. Put on safety goggles. Place the glass of water on a flat surface. Let the glass sit for a few seconds until the water is still.
2. Gently strike the tuning fork against the edge of a table. Observe what happens.
3. Strike the edge of the table again with the tuning fork. Touch the ends of the tuning fork onto the surface of the water. Observe what happens to the water in the glass.

Practicing Your Skills

4. **OBSERVE:** What happened to the tuning fork when you struck it against the table? Did you hear a sound?
5. **OBSERVE:** What happened when you put the tuning fork into the glass of water?

▲ **STEP 3** Put the ends of the vibrating tuning fork in the water.

LAB ACTIVITY
Experimenting With Vibrations

Materials
Plastic metric ruler
(15-cm)
Pencil and paper

BACKGROUND

Sound is created when an object vibrates. The vibrations are converted to waves that travel through the air. Different speeds of vibration produce different sounds. What is the relationship between the rate of vibration and the highness or lowness of the sound you hear?

PURPOSE

You will experiment with vibrations and sound and create a simple musical instrument.

PROCEDURE

1. Copy the chart in Figure 18-6 on a separate sheet of paper.

2. Place a plastic ruler on a table so that the end of the ruler extends 5 cm past the edge of the table. Hold the ruler on the table with one finger at the 10-cm mark.

3. With your other hand pull up on the end of the ruler and release it. This action will cause the ruler to vibrate. Listen to the sound it produces. Record your observations in the chart.

4. Press down on the ruler at the 9-cm mark with a second finger. Again, pull up and release the end of the ruler and listen to the sound. Watch how fast the ruler vibrates.

5. Move the second finger to the 8-cm mark and again pull up and release the ruler. Repeat with your finger on the 7-cm and the 6-cm marks.

▲ **STEP 2** Hold a ruler near the edge of a table.

▲ **STEP 3** Make the ruler vibrate.

6. Try other positions with the ruler to make different sounds. Extend the ruler out farther over the edge or bring it closer.

7. Use the data in your chart to write the "finger positions" as your "musical notes." Have a partner try to play your "song" from your written notes. See if you can play someone else's "song."

▲ **STEP 7** Play someone else's song.

Changing Sound			
Trial	Finger Position in Centimeters	Speed of Vibration (very slow, medium, very fast, etc.)	Highness or Lowness of Sound (lowest, medium, highest, etc.)
1	10		
2	9		
3	8		
4	7		
5	6		
6			
7			
8			

▲ **Figure 18-6** Copy this chart and use it to record your observations.

CONCLUSIONS

1. **OBSERVE:** When the part of the ruler that vibrates is long, are the vibrations slow or fast?

2. **OBSERVE:** When the part of the ruler that vibrates is short, are the vibrations slow or fast?

3. **INFER:** If you hear a low sound, such as the sound produced by a foghorn, is it caused by slow vibrations or fast vibrations?

4. **INFER:** What kind of sound is produced by an object that vibrates fast?

18-2 How do sound waves travel?

INVESTIGATE

Observing Sound in a String Phone
HANDS-ON ACTIVITY

1. Make a small hole in the bottom of each of two paper cups.

2. Insert one end of a 10-m piece of string through the hole in each cup and tie a large knot at each end of the string.

3. Take one of the cups and give your partner the other. Move apart until the string is tight.

4. Have your partner speak into one cup while you hold the other cup to your ear. Take turns speaking into the cups.

THINK ABOUT IT: How does the sound travel from one cup to the other?

STEP 4

Objective

Describe how sound waves travel.

Key Terms

longitudinal (lahn-juh-TOOD-uhn-uhl) **wave:** wave in which the particles of the medium move back and forth in the direction of the wave motion

medium: material through which mechanical waves can travel

echo: reflected sound waves

Sound Waves Sound waves are longitudinal waves. In a **longitudinal wave,** the particles of the medium move back and forth in the direction of the wave motion. Figure 18-7 shows how a sound wave moves through the air. Compressions and rarefactions of air particles move in the same direction as the sound waves.

1 **DESCRIBE:** Why are sound waves longitudinal waves?

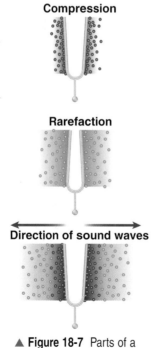

Compression

Rarefaction

Direction of sound waves

▲ **Figure 18-7** Parts of a sound wave.

Medium for Sound A **medium** is a material through which mechanical waves can travel. Air is a medium for sound waves. All sound waves need a medium through which they can travel. Sound waves can travel through gases, liquids, and solids. In each medium, the sound waves are made up of compressions and rarefactions of the particles that make up the medium.

Dolphins and whales use sound to communicate with each other. They can do this because sounds travel faster through water. Sounds also travel faster through solids. If you put your ear against a wall, you may hear sounds in the next room.

2 **EXPLAIN:** Why is water a good medium for communication between dolphins?

No Sound in a Vacuum On the Moon, astronauts cannot use sound to communicate. There is no air on the Moon. In a vacuum, there are no particles of a medium to compress. This means sound waves cannot be produced.

3 **INFER:** Would astronauts on the Moon be able to hear a rocket engine?

▲ **Figure 18-8** There is no sound on the Moon.

Reflected Waves Reflection is the bouncing back of a wave from a barrier that does not absorb its energy. If you clap your hands in a carpeted room, the sound will be absorbed by the carpeting. Suppose you clap your hands in an empty room with a wooden floor. You will hear the sound of the clap reflected from the floor and the walls. When a sound wave is reflected, the reflected sound wave is called an **echo**.

 IDENTIFY: What is a reflected sound wave called?

✓ CHECKING CONCEPTS

1. In a _____ wave, the particles of the medium move in the same direction as the wave motion.

2. A sound wave needs a _____ in which to travel.

3. Sound waves are made up of moving compressions and _____.

4. Whales can use sounds to communicate, because sound waves can travel through _____.

5. Sound cannot be heard in a vacuum, because there is no _____ for the sound waves.

6. Sound can travel through liquids such as water, gases such as air, and _____ such as walls.

7. Sound waves that are reflected from a surface are called _____.

8. When a sound wave is not reflected, the energy of the sound has been _____ by the surroundings.

 THINKING CRITICALLY

9. **INFER:** If you clapped your hands on the Moon, would you hear the sound? Explain.

Web InfoSearch

Echolocation The biggest difference between bats and other animals is the way that they see. Most animals see by using their eyes. However, most bats "see" by using a system called echolocation.

SEARCH: Use the Internet to find out more about echolocation. Then, create a poster showing how echolocation in animals works. Start your search at www.conceptsandchallenges.com. Some key search words are **echolocation, bat sonar,** and **bat sight.**

 Science and Technology
SONAR

Echoes can be used to measure distances under water. This method of using echoes is called sonar. The word *sonar* stands for **so**und **n**avigation **a**nd **r**anging. Sound waves are sent from a transmitter on a ship to the bottom of the ocean. The time it takes for the sound wave to reach the bottom and bounce back as an echo is measured. This time is then divided in half to find out how long the sound took to go one way. Suppose sound waves were sent out and returned in 4 seconds. The time for the sound waves to go one way is 2 seconds. The speed of sound in water is about 1,500 m/s. Therefore, the water is about 3,000 m deep. Sonar can be used to make maps of the ocean floor. It is also used to locate objects, such as boats and fish.

Thinking Critically How do you think sonar can be used to find schools of fish?

▲ **Figure 18-9** A sonar screen shows the locations of echoes.

18-3 What is the speed of sound?

Objective

Describe how the speed of sound changes in different materials.

Key Terms

supersonic: faster than the speed of sound for that medium

sonic boom: loud noise caused by breaking the sound barrier

Speed of Sound The speed of sound in air is about 340 m/s. This speed is much slower than the speed of light. In a thunderstorm, a flash of lightning is seen before the sound of thunder is heard. The light from the lightning flash travels much faster than the sound of the thunder produced by the lightning.

▲ **Figure 18-10** Lightning causes thunder.

You can use the speed of sound to estimate how far away a lightning flash is from your location. Start counting the seconds as soon as you see a flash of lightning. Stop counting when you hear the thunder. Sound travels about 1 km in 3 seconds. If it takes 3 seconds for the sound of the thunder to reach you, the lightning is about 1 km away.

 STATE: What is the speed of sound in air?

Speed of Sound in Different Materials Sound travels at different speeds in different materials and at different temperatures. In water, sound travels at about 1,500 m/s. Figure 18-11 lists the approximate speeds of sound in some different materials.

SPEEDS OF SOUNDS AT 25°C	
Material	**Speed (m/sec)**
Air	346
Cork	500
Freshwater	1,493
Steel	5,200
Rubber	60
Glass	5,400
Wood (oak)	1,850

▲ **Figure 18-11**

 ANALYZE: In which of the materials listed in Figure 18-11 does sound travel fastest?

Faster than Sound Many jet airplanes can travel faster than the speed of sound. Some airplanes can travel two or three times the speed of sound. Any speed faster than the speed of sound is said to be **supersonic.** When an airplane travels at supersonic speeds, it moves faster than the sound produced by its engines. When a plane traveling at supersonic speed passes overhead, it will be some distance away before you hear the sound of its engines. Figure 18-12 shows the first airplane, the Glamorous Glennis, to travel faster than the speed of sound. When something moves through air at speeds faster than the speed of sound, a loud noise is created. This noise is called a **sonic boom.**

▲ **Figure 18-12** Chuck Yeager piloted the first plane to travel at supersonic speeds.

In 1997, Andy Green broke the sound barrier on land with his car named Thrust. He did so exactly fifty years after the sound barrier was broken by Captain Chuck Yeager. Figure 18-13 shows the supersonic car that Green used to accomplish this feat.

▲ **Figure 18-13** Andy Green's supersonic car

3 DEFINE: What is supersonic speed?

✔ CHECKING CONCEPTS

1. The speed of sound in air is about _____.

2. You can see a _____ airplane before you hear it because it is moving faster than sound.

3. Light travels _____ than sound.

4. A flash of lightning can be seen _____ the sound of thunder it produces can be heard.

💡 THINKING CRITICALLY

Use the information in Figure 18-11 to answer the following questions.

5. **COMPARE:** Would the sound of an approaching train travel faster through the metal railroad tracks or through the air? Explain.

6. **HYPOTHESIZE: a.** Why do you think rubber is sometimes used for soundproofing a room? **b.** What other materials in the table would be good for soundproofing? Explain.

BUILDING MATH SKILLS

Calculating Find out how long it would take sound to travel through 2 m of the following materials.

a.	air	**e.**	glass
b.	water	**f.**	wood
c.	steel	**g.**	cork
d.	rubber		

Science and Technology

SUPERSONIC AIRPLANES

The speed of sound in air is called Mach 1. Before October 14, 1947, no airplane had ever reached the speed of Mach 1. On that day, Chuck Yeager became the first person to fly faster than the speed of sound. He had broken the sound barrier.

Today, supersonic planes can fly at speeds of Mach 2 or even Mach 3. For example, the supersonic *Concorde* can cross the Atlantic Ocean in much less time than other passenger airplanes.

▲ **Figure 18-14** The *Concorde* is an airliner that can travel at supersonic speeds.

One disadvantage of planes that travel at supersonic speeds is that they produce loud noises called sonic booms. A sonic boom is caused when a plane breaks the sound barrier. Sonic booms can be so loud that they break windows and knock pictures off walls. To avoid the problem of sonic booms, supersonic planes are not allowed to fly over heavily populated areas.

Thinking Critically The *Concorde* can only travel at supersonic speeds over the ocean. Why do you think this is so?

18-4 What is intensity?

Objective

Explain the relationship between the intensity and the loudness of a sound.

Key Terms

intensity: amount of energy in a sound wave

decibel: unit used to measure the intensity or loudness of a sound

Intensity Sound energy travels in the form of waves. Some sounds are loud. Others are soft. Figures 18-15 and 18-16 show wave patterns for a soft sound and a loud sound.

▲ **Figure 18-15** Wave pattern of soft sound

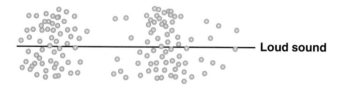

▲ **Figure 18-16** Wave pattern of loud sound

The amount of energy a sound has is called the **intensity** of the sound. As Figures 18-15 and 18-16 show, a wave carrying a loud sound has a greater amplitude than that of a wave carrying a soft sound. So, molecules in a wave carrying a loud sound travel farther than do the molecules in a wave carrying a soft sound. The molecules in the loud wave have more energy.

▲ **Figure 18-17** Which instrument will produce sounds of greater intensity?

 DEFINE: What is intensity?

Measuring Intensity Intensity is measured in units called **decibels** (dB). The sound of people talking has an intensity of about 65 decibels. The softest sound a human can hear is about 20 decibels. The sound of a train going by may have an intensity of 95 decibels. Sounds louder than 120 decibels can be dangerous. They can damage your ears. Figure 18-18 shows the intensity of different sounds measured in decibels.

INTENSITY OF SOUND	
Sound	**Intensity (dB)**
Cat purring	10–20
Soft music	30
Average home	40–50
Conversation	60–70
Heavy traffic	70–80
Loud music	80–100
Thunder	110
Rock concert	115–120
Jet engine	170
Rocket engine	180

▲ **Figure 18-18**

 ANALYZE: What is the intensity of the sound at a rock concert?

1. When you raise the volume on a radio, you are increasing the _____ of the sound waves.

2. The _____ in a sound wave determines the amplitude of the wave.

3. The _____ of a sound wave is the amount of energy it has.

4. The unit used to measure intensity is the _____.

5. The more intensity a sound wave has the _____ the sound.

THINKING CRITICALLY

6. **INFER:** Which is more dangerous to your ears, heavy traffic noise or a rock concert? Explain.

7. **HYPOTHESIZE:** Two people hear a loud sound. One person is 10 m from the source of the sound. The other person is 50 m from the source. The sound does not seem as loud to the person 50 m from the source as it does to the person standing closer. What does this tell you about the intensity of a sound wave?

HEALTH AND SAFETY TIP

Your ears are very sensitive to sound. Loud sounds can damage your hearing. An intensity of 120 dB is called the threshold of pain. This means that a sound louder than 120 dB is so loud that it will hurt your ears. You should keep this in mind when listening to live music or when using earphones to listen to a recording. Use library references to find out how to protect yourself from dangerously loud sounds. Write a short report on your findings.

Integrating Environmental Science

TOPIC: noise pollution

TOO MUCH SOUND

The world is full of sounds. There are many sources of sound. Some of the loudest sounds come from machines. These loud machine sounds may cause noise pollution. Any loud, unwanted sound is called noise. In cities, the sounds of street traffic, of machines at construction sites, and of airplanes all combine to cause noise pollution.

Noise pollution is a nuisance and it can also be a hazard. Too much noise can damage the ears by destroying the delicate hairs and tiny muscles in the ears. Noise can also cause stress. People who live or work around too much noise may develop high blood pressure or a stress-related illness.

There are ways to decrease noise pollution. People are encouraged to use mass transit to decrease the amount of traffic on city streets. Laws have been passed to keep people from playing radios too loudly in public places. You are encouraged to use ear protection when exposed to loud noises over an extended period of time.

▲ **Figure 18-19** Construction work contributes to noise pollution.

Thinking Critically What can you do to help prevent noise pollution?

What are frequency and pitch?

Objective
Explain how frequency and pitch are related.

Key Terms
pitch: how high or low a sound is

ultrasonic (uhl-truh-SAHN-ihk)**:** sound above 20,000 Hz frequency

infrasonic: sound below 20 Hz frequency

Frequency of a Sound Different sounds have different frequencies. The frequency of a wave is the number of complete waves that pass a point each second. Each pair of compressions and rarefactions is a complete sound wave. The frequency of a sound wave is the number of compressions and rarefactions produced per second. Frequency is measured in hertz (Hz). One hertz is equal to one wave per second.

▶ **IDENTIFY:** What is frequency?

Frequency and Pitch Frequency and pitch are related. A sound's **pitch** tells how high or low a sound is. A high-frequency sound has a high pitch. A low-frequency sound has a low pitch. A toy whistle has a frequency of about 1,000 Hz. This is a high-pitched sound. Thunder, a low-pitched sound, has a frequency of about 100 Hz.

▲ **Figure 18-20** These instruments can make both high- and low-pitched sounds.

▶ **DESCRIBE:** How are the frequency and the pitch of a sound related?

Changing Pitch A guitar can make sounds of many different pitches. If you look at the strings of the guitar in Figure 18-21, you will see that some are thick and some are thin. The thick strings make low-pitched sounds. The thin strings make high-pitched sounds. A guitar has tuning pegs that tighten or loosen the strings. Changing the tightness of the strings also changes the pitch. Placing your fingers on the frets across the neck of the guitar changes the length of the string. This action changes the pitch of the sound produced.

▲ **Figure 18-21** The different strings on a guitar make sounds of different pitch.

▶ **HYPOTHESIZE:** How does changing the tightness of a string affect the sound it produces?

Range of Hearing Humans can hear sounds with frequencies between 20 Hz and 20,000 Hz. This is called the range of human hearing. Sounds that have frequencies higher than 20,000 Hz are called **ultrasonic.** The prefix *ultra-* means "above." Ultrasonic sounds have too high a pitch to be heard by humans. The range of human hearing decreases as a person gets older. Children can hear higher-frequency sounds better than adults can.

Some animals can hear ultrasonic sounds. Dogs can hear sounds with frequencies up to about 50,000 Hz. Often, dogs are trained using ultrasonic whistles. The dogs hear it but people do not.

▶ **DEFINE:** What is an ultrasonic sound?

Infrasonic Sound Sound that is too low for humans to hear is called **infrasonic.** The prefix *infra-* means "below." Infrasonic is any sound below 20 Hz.

Elephants communicate distress with infrasonic sound at about 6 Hz. They stamp on the ground with their feet. The sound produces waves that travel many miles to other elephants.

◀ Figure 18-22 Elephants communicate with infrasonic sounds.

 DEFINE: What is an infrasonic sound?

✓ CHECKING CONCEPTS

1. The unit used to measure frequency is the _____.

2. Sounds that humans can hear are between 20 and _____ Hz.

3. Even if two sounds have the same intensity, they can have different _____.

4. One hertz is equal to one _____ per second.

💡 THINKING CRITICALLY

5. COMPARE: Which sound has a lower pitch, a sound with a frequency of 20 Hz or one with a frequency of 20,000 Hz? How do you know?

6. HYPOTHESIZE: The sound of a siren coming toward you has a higher pitch than the sound of a siren that is standing still. What does this tell you about the frequency of a sound that is moving toward you?

Web InfoSearch

Ultrasound A technique called ultrasound can be used to see inside solid objects. Ultrasound uses very high-pitched sounds. Most of the sound waves pass through the object, but some are reflected. The reflected waves produce an image on a screen. Ultrasound images are similar to X rays.

SEARCH: Use the Internet to find out how ultrasound is used in the fields of medicine, engineering, and construction. Start your search at www.conceptsandchallenges.com. Some key search words are **ultrasound, medicine, engineering,** and **construction.**

🧪 *Hands-On Activity*

OBSERVING CHANGES IN PITCH

You will need 5 test tubes, a test-tube rack, a metric ruler, and a container of water.

1. Place the test tubes in the test-tube rack.

2. Pour different amounts of water into each test tube. Use the metric ruler to measure the height of the column of air above the water in each test tube. The heights should be as follows: 2 cm, 4 cm, 6 cm, 8 cm, and 10 cm.

3. Blow across the top of each test tube. Observe the pitch of the sound you hear from each tube.

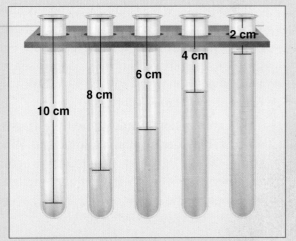

▲ **STEP 2** Set up the test tubes so each has a different amount of air above the water.

Practicing Your Skills

4. INFER: How does the height of the column of air affect the pitch of the sound?

5. OBSERVE: Which test tube produced the highest pitch?

6. OBSERVE: Which test tube produced the lowest pitch?

THE Big IDEA

How do animals use sound?

Listen to the world around you. Vibrations in the air make your eardrum move. Tiny bones in your middle ear amplify the vibrations. Then, your inner ear changes the vibrations into messages for your brain. Human ears work in the range of about 20 to 20,000 vibrations per second, or hertz.

Some animals make sounds that are too high- or too low-pitched for our ears to detect. Sounds above the range of human hearing are called ultrasonic and sounds below the range of human hearing are called infrasonic.

Bats make ultrasonic chirps with a wide range of frequencies. They use the echoes of their chirps to locate food with sonar. Dolphins and other sea mammals also use ultrasonic sounds for communication and sonar.

Humpback whales are amazing vocalists. They sing mostly in the autumn before migrating to tropical feeding grounds. Each group's song changes from season to season. Humpback songs can last for 30 minutes and range from 30 to 8,000 Hz.

Elephants communicate with infrasonic sounds that travel many kilometers. When some family groups of elephants come together, they flap their ears and exchange greetings in the range of 5 to 24 Hz, a very low-pitched way of saying hello.

Look at the illustrations that appear on these two pages. Then, follow the directions in the Science Log to find out more about "the big idea." ✦

Elephants
When elephants greet each other, they stand side by side and exchange rumbling infrasonic hellos that vary from 5 to 24 Hz.

Whales
Humpback whales sing complex, eerie-sounding songs that range from 30 to 8,000 Hz. Long ago sailors believed the songs were the cries of sailors' ghosts.

Bats

Bats are so good at using ultrasound to locate that they can catch moths and mosquitoes even when they are flying at full speed. Bat chirps have a frequency from 30,000 to more than 120,000 Hz.

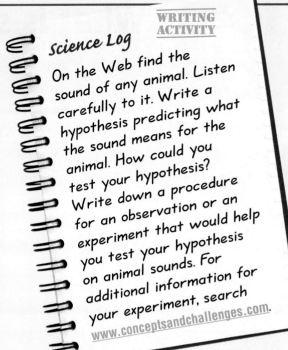

WRITING ACTIVITY

Science Log

On the Web find the sound of any animal. Listen carefully to it. Write a hypothesis predicting what the sound means for the animal. How could you test your hypothesis? Write down a procedure for an observation or an experiment that would help you test your hypothesis on animal sounds. For additional information for your experiment, search www.conceptsandchallenges.com.

Dolphins

Bottlenose dolphins make sounds for echolocation and communication. Each task has a different range of sound, varying from about 1 Hz to 150,000 Hz. The frequency during echolocation is about 100,000 Hz. Many people wonder if they have languages like humans.

Wolves

Some researchers believe that wolves can hear sounds all the way up to 80,000 Hz. Wolves have many calls. The wolf's "lonesome" call ranges from 200 to 2,200 Hz.

18-6 What is sound quality?

INVESTIGATE

Listening to a String Instrument
HANDS-ON ACTIVITY

1. Pluck the lowest-pitched string of a violin or guitar.

2. Lightly touch the string in the center to change its vibrations. Listen for the higher note.

3. Pluck the same string again. Touch it one-third of the way along its length to get the next highest note.

STEP 3

THINK ABOUT IT: How do the pitch and loudness of these sounds affect the quality of the sound heard?

Objective
Explain how overtones affect sound quality.

Key Terms
timbre (TAM-buhr)**:** sound quality

fundamental tone: lowest-pitched sound produced when an object vibrates

overtones: sounds that have a higher pitch than the fundamental tone

music: a pleasing combination of sounds

noise: unpleasant combination of sounds with irregular patterns of vibration

Sound Quality Suppose a trumpet player and a clarinet player play the same note. The sounds they make have the same frequency and the same intensity. Can you hear a difference between the two sounds? The sounds are different even though the frequency and the intensity are the same. The sounds differ because of their **timbre,** or sound quality. The sounds of a trumpet and a clarinet have different timbres.

▶ **DEFINE:** What is timbre?

Fundamental Tone When an object vibrates, it produces a sound with a certain frequency. Figure 18-23 shows a vibrating string. Notice that the whole string is vibrating. When the whole string vibrates, it produces the lowest possible frequency

and pitch. The lowest-pitched sound produced is called the **fundamental tone.**

▲ **Figure 18-23** Fundamental tone

▶ **DEFINE:** What is a fundamental tone?

Overtones Parts of the string shown in Figure 18-24 can vibrate faster than the whole string. When parts of the string are vibrating, the string produces sounds with a higher pitch than the fundamental tone. The high-pitched sounds produced when different parts of a string vibrate are called **overtones.**

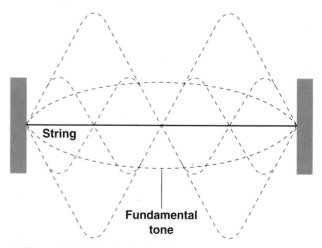

▲ **Figure 18-24** The dashed red lines are overtones.

390

The sounds produced by a musical instrument or a human voice also have overtones. The quality of a sound is a result of these overtones. Without overtones, all vibrations of the same frequency would have the same quality.

 DEFINE: What are overtones?

Music Different musical instruments have different sound qualities. How do the different instruments in an orchestra combine to make music? **Music** is a pleasing combination of sounds. Some elements of music are rhythm, melody, and harmony.

- **Rhythm** The basic beat in music is known as the rhythm. When you listen to music, the rhythm you hear might come from drums or a bass guitar. If you clap your hands to the beat of the music, you are adding rhythm.

- **Melody** The combination of musical notes is called the tune or the melody. If you hum or sing a song, you are repeating the melody.

- **Harmony** In an orchestra or chorus, different instruments or voices perform together. Many different notes are heard at the same time. Combining the different notes is called harmony. Good harmony makes music sound better.

 IDENTIFY: What are three elements of music?

Musical Instruments Musical instruments can be divided into three main groups.

- **Percussion Instruments** These instruments include drums, pianos, and any instrument that is played by being tapped or hit.

- **String Instruments** These instruments make music from the sound of vibrating strings. Examples include guitars, violins, and cellos.

- **Wind Instruments** These instruments make music when air is blown through them. Examples include trumpets, clarinets, and flutes.

 NAME: What are the three main groups of musical instruments?

Noise **Noise** is an unpleasant combination of sounds with irregular patterns of vibration. Unlike music, noise has no agreeable quality.

 DEFINE: What is noise?

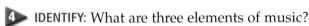

✔ CHECKING CONCEPTS

1. The quality of a sound is its _____.

2. When a whole string vibrates, it produces a _____.

3. All sounds are a combination of fundamental tones and_____.

4. Two sounds can have the same _____ and intensity but still sound different.

5. Higher-pitched sounds produced when parts of a string vibrate are called _____.

6. Unpleasant sounds are _____.

7. Rhythm, melody, and harmony combine to make _____.

 THINKING CRITICALLY

8. **INFER:** What would human voices sound like without overtones?

9. **INFER:** A violin and a piano are playing the same musical note with the same frequency and the same intensity. Why do they sound different?

10. **CLASSIFY:** Identify each of the following instruments as percussion, string, or wind instruments.
    a. tuba   c. harp
    b. kettle drum d. trumpet

Web InfoSearch

The Musical Scale Our musical scale is made up of eight notes. Each musical note has its own pitch. Each note is represented by a letter of the alphabet. A set of eight notes is called an octave. The last note in an octave has twice the frequency of the first note. The human ear can hear a total of about 10 octaves.

SEARCH: Use the Internet to find out what a musical scale looks like. Draw a scale with all the notes placed properly. Start your search at www.conceptsandchallenges.com. Some key search words are **music** and **musical scale.**

Go Online
active art

For: Musical Instruments activity
Visit: PHSchool.com
Web Code: cgp-5023

18-7 What is the Doppler effect?

Objective

Explain what is meant by the Doppler effect.

Key Term

Doppler effect: apparent change in the frequency of waves

Changing Frequency The frequency of a wave sometimes changes. Remember that frequency is the number of complete waves that pass a point in a given time. Frequency seems to change when a wave source moves toward you or away from you. Imagine you are sitting on a dock. You can count the number of waves hitting the dock. As a motorboat passes you, many waves hit the dock. The frequency of the waves is high. As the boat continues on, fewer waves hit the dock. The frequency returns to what it was before the boat passed.

▲ **Figure 18-25** The frequency of waves changes as a boat passes.

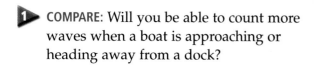 **COMPARE:** Will you be able to count more waves when a boat is approaching or heading away from a dock?

Doppler Effect An apparent change in the frequency of waves is called the **Doppler effect.** The Doppler effect occurs when there is relative motion between the source of the waves and an observer. The frequency of waves appears to change when the observer is moving toward or away from the source of the waves. The frequency also seems to change when the source of the waves is moving and the observer is standing still. For the Doppler effect to take place, either the source or the observer must be moving.

 DEFINE: What is the Doppler effect?

Doppler Effect and Sound You are probably most familiar with the Doppler effect in sound waves. The frequency of sound waves seems to change as the source of the waves moves toward or away from you. Suppose you are waiting for a train to pass a crossing. You can hear the train whistle as the train approaches the crossing. The waves are pushed closer together by the motion of the train. The pitch of the sound seems to get higher as more and more waves per second reach your ears. As the train passes you, the sound waves spread out. Fewer waves reach your ear every second. The pitch of one sound seems to get lower.

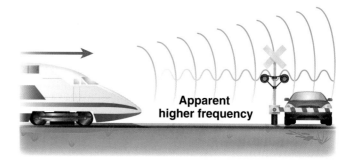

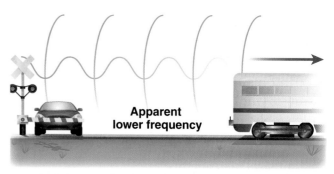

▲ **Figure 18-26** The Doppler effect causes the sound of a train whistle to change as it passes.

 COMPARE: Does the frequency of sound waves from a train whistle become higher or lower as the train comes toward you?

1. The apparent change in the frequency of waves is called the _____.

2. Waves hit a dock more often when a boat is moving _____ the dock.

3. The Doppler effect is caused by _____.

4. The frequency of waves appears to change when either the source of the waves or the _____ is moving.

5. The frequency of sound waves is _____ when the source of the waves is moving away from you.

6. As a boat moves toward you, the frequency of the water waves appears _____ than if the boat were moving away from you.

THINKING CRITICALLY

7. EXPLAIN: Describe how the sound of a car horn changes as the car approaches you and then passes you.

Use Figure 18-27 to answer question 8.

8. PREDICT: Will the pitch of the sound of the fire engine's siren seem higher to a person standing at point A or point B? Explain.

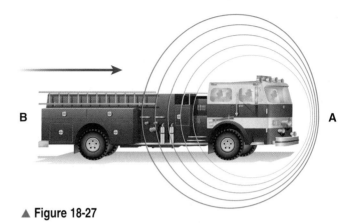

▲ Figure 18-27

BUILDING SCIENCE SKILLS

Researching Visit your local police station. Many police forces use Doppler radar to measure the speed of passing cars. Find out how Doppler radar works. How do radar detectors in cars work? How is Doppler radar used to track the path of fast-moving storms? What are other uses of Doppler radar? Describe your findings to the class.

Integrating Earth Science

TOPICS: stars, universe

REDSHIFT

Astronomers study the wavelength of light from the stars to find out about the universe. The wavelength of light determines the color of the light. Red light has a long wavelength. Blue light has a short wavelength.

▲ Figure 18-28 Galaxies are moving apart.

The Doppler effect causes an apparent change in the frequency of a wave. It also causes an apparent change in wavelength. If a light source is moving away from an observer, the wavelength of the light appears to change. The light appears redder than it would if the source were not moving. This change in wavelength is called the redshift.

Astronomers have studied the redshifts of many different galaxies. They found that all of the galaxies are moving away from Earth. Each galaxy is also moving away from every other galaxy. This suggests that the universe is expanding, or getting bigger.

Thinking Critically What would astronomers see if the universe were shrinking?

18-8 How do you hear?

Objective
Trace the path of sound waves through the ear to the brain.

Key Terms
hearing: one of the five human senses

ear: sense organ that detects sound

eardrum: thin sheet of tissue that vibrates when sound waves strike it

cochlea (KOHK-lee-uh)**:** organ that changes sound vibrations into nerve signals

Hearing Sounds One of the five human senses is **hearing.** What happens when you hear a sound? For a sound to be heard, three things are needed: a source of the sound, a medium to transmit the sound, and a sense organ to detect the sound.

In humans, the sense organ that detects sound is the **ear.** Look at the diagram of the human ear in Figure 18-29. There are three main parts to the ear: the outer ear, the middle ear, and the inner ear.

1▶ NAME: What are the three main parts of the human ear?

How the Ear Hears A sound wave first enters the outer ear. The outer ear funnels the sound wave into the ear. The sound wave moves through the ear canal to the eardrum. The **eardrum** is a thin sheet of tissue that vibrates when sound waves strike it. The vibrating air particles in the sound wave make the eardrum vibrate.

The vibrations from the eardrum are transferred to the middle ear. There are three small bones in the middle ear. They are the hammer, the anvil, and the stirrup. The vibrations are transferred from the hammer, to the anvil, and then to the stirrup.

The vibrations are then transmitted to the inner ear. In the inner ear, the vibrations are transferred to the cochlea. The **cochlea** is the organ that changes sound vibrations into nerve impulses. The cochlea is filled with liquid and is attached to nerve fibers. The nerve fibers join to form one nerve. The nerve transmits the impulses to the brain. In the brain, the nerve impulses are interpreted as sound.

2▶ NAME: Which parts of the ear vibrate when a sound is heard?

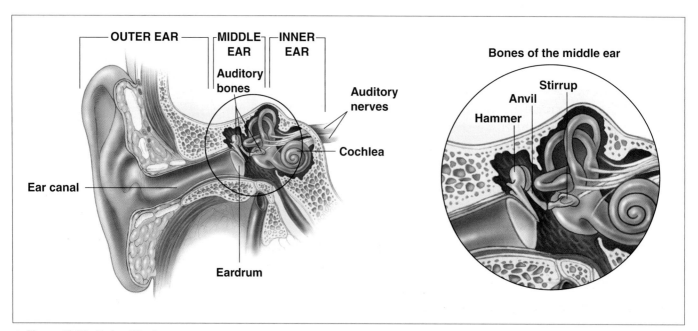

▲ **Figure 18-29** Parts of the human ear

Dizziness The inner ear has another important role that has nothing to do with hearing. The inner ear maintains balance. After you ride a roller coaster, you may feel dizzy. Dizziness is a temporary loss of balance. It is often caused by an ear infection. The infection irritates the tiny hair cells that project into fluid-filled canals in the inner ear's balance center. When irritated, these hair cells send mixed-up messages to the brain, tricking the brain into thinking you are spinning.

 INFER: Why is it important to maintain balance?

 ## ✔ CHECKING CONCEPTS

1. The _____ is the organ that detects sound.
2. Of the five senses, the one that is involved with sound is _____.
3. Sound waves travel from the outer ear, to the _____, and then to the inner ear.
4. The part of the ear that vibrates first is the _____.
5. The _____ converts the sound vibrations into nerve impulses.

 ## THINKING CRITICALLY

6. **SEQUENCE:** Arrange the following steps in the correct order.
   a. The vibrations are transferred to the hammer, anvil, and stirrup. **b.** The vibrations of air particles in the sound wave cause the eardrum to vibrate. **c.** The vibrations are transferred to the cochlea. **d.** The brain interprets the electrical impulses as sounds. **e.** A sound wave is transmitted by the source. **f.** The vibrations are converted to electrical impulses along a nerve that goes to the brain. **g.** The sound waves travel through the medium. **h.** The sound waves enter the outer ear and go into the ear canal.

INTERPRETING VISUALS

Look at Figure 18-29 to help you answer the following questions.

7. Where is the liquid that helps you maintain balance located?
8. Which parts of the ear have a liquid medium for sound to travel?
9. Which parts of the ear have a solid medium?
10. Which parts of the ear have a gaseous medium?

Real-Life Science

THE CHANGING TELEPHONE

In 1876, Alexander Graham Bell received a patent for the first working telephone. Two years later, telephone service began in the United States. Since that time, the telephone has undergone many changes and improvements.

In 1977, communications companies began testing mobile, or cellular, telephones. By 1987, more than one million people had subscribed to cellular phone systems. Today, personal computers can be used to connect to regular telephones and can be used to make video phone calls.

The next dramatic change in the telephone will likely be disposable cellular telephones. Prototypes of these telephones have already been produced. They are as thin as a credit card and can be recycled.

▲ **Figure 18-30** Alexander Graham Bell testing his phone

THINKING CRITICALLY: What are some advantages of disposable phones?

Chapter Summary

Lesson 18-1
- **Sound** is a form of energy that travels as waves. All sounds are caused by **vibrations.**

Lesson 18-2
- Sound waves are **longitudinal waves.** All sound waves need a **medium** through which to travel. A reflected sound wave is called an **echo.**

Lesson 18-3
- The speed of sound is much slower than the speed of light. Sound travels at different speeds in different materials. Jet airplanes can reach supersonic speeds.

Lesson 18-4
- Loud sounds have more energy than soft sounds do. The **intensity** of a sound wave determines the loudness of the sound. Intensity is measured in **decibels** (dB).

Lesson 18-5
- Different sounds have different frequencies. A high-frequency sound has a high pitch. A low-frequency sound has a low pitch.
- Some animals can hear **ultrasonic** or **infrasonic** sounds.

Lesson 18-6
- The sounds of a trumpet and a clarinet differ because of their sound quality, or **timbre.**
- When a string vibrates as a whole, it produces a **fundamental tone.**
- When different parts of a string vibrate, they produce **overtones.**
- **Music** is a pleasing combination of rhythm, melody, and harmony. **Noise** is an unpleasant combination of sounds with no regular pattern of vibrations.

Lesson 18-7
- The **Doppler effect** is caused by motion of the observer or of the source of the waves.

Lesson 18-8
- The **ear** is the human sense organ that detects sound.

Key Term Challenges

cochlea (p. 394)
decibel (p. 384)
Doppler effect (p. 392)
ear (p. 394)
eardrum (p. 394)
echo (p. 380)
fundamental tone (p. 390)
hearing (p. 394)
infrasonic (p. 386)
intensity (p. 384)
longitudinal wave (p. 380)
medium (p. 380)
music (p. 390)
noise (p. 390)
overtone (p. 390)
pitch (p. 386)
sonic boom (p. 382)
sound (p. 376)
supersonic (p. 382)
timbre (p. 390)
ultrasonic (p. 386)
vibration (p. 376)

MATCHING Write the Key Term from above that best matches each description.

1. how high or low a sound is
2. speed faster than sound
3. rapid back-and-forth movement
4. frequency above the fundamental tone
5. sound quality
6. sense organ that detects sound
7. includes rhythm, melody, and harmony
8. one of the human senses
9. form of energy that travels as waves
10. unit of intensity

FILL IN Write the Key Term from above that best completes each statement.

11. A sound wave needs a _____ in which to travel.
12. A reflected sound wave is an _____.
13. The amount of energy in a sound wave is the _____ of the wave.
14. Sound with a frequency greater than 20,000 Hz is _____.
15. The _____ is the lowest-pitched sound produced when a whole string vibrates.

Content Challenges TEST PREP

MULTIPLE CHOICE **Write the letter of the term or phrase that best completes each statement.**

1. To find their way in the dark, bats use
   a. overtones.
   b. ultrasound.
   c. echolocation.
   d. timbre.

2. A high-pitched sound has a
   a. low frequency.
   b. fundamental tone.
   c. high frequency.
   d. low intensity.

3. Two sounds with the same frequency and intensity will sound different because of
   a. timbre.
   b. pitch.
   c. vibrations.
   d. wavelength.

4. The speed of sound in air is
   a. 125 m/s.
   b. 340 m/s.
   c. 430 m/s.
   d. 540 m/s.

5. The unit of frequency is the
   a. hertz.
   b. decibel.
   c. m/s.
   d. pitch.

6. Sound travels fastest in
   a. liquids.
   b. solids.
   c. gases.
   d. a vacuum.

7. Dolphins communicate by making
   a. low-frequency sounds.
   b. high-intensity sounds.
   c. high-frequency sounds.
   d. low-intensity sounds.

8. Music consists of rhythm, melody, and
   a. intensity.
   b. harmony.
   c. percussion.
   d. frequency.

9. Before your eardrum vibrates, the sound wave has to travel through the
   a. anvil.
   b. ear canal.
   c. inner ear.
   d. cochlea.

10. A sound wave consists of compressions and
    a. overtones.
    b. fundamental tones.
    c. rarefactions.
    d. frequencies.

TRUE/FALSE **Write *true* if the statement is true. If the statement is false, change the underlined term to make the statement true.**

11. Sound cannot travel through a <u>vacuum</u>.

12. A high-intensity sound wave has a lot of <u>energy</u>.

13. Sound waves cause the <u>ear canal</u> to vibrate.

14. An echo is a sound wave that has been <u>made louder</u>.

15. One hertz is equal to one <u>compression</u> per second.

16. A drum is an example of a <u>percussion</u> instrument.

17. The beat of the music is the <u>melody</u>.

18. There are <u>three</u> main types of musical instruments.

19. Vibrations from the eardrum enter the <u>outer</u> ear.

20. Humans can hear sounds between <u>20 Hz</u> and 20,000 Hz.

Content Challenges TEST PREP

WRITTEN RESPONSE Answer each of the following questions in complete sentences.

1. **HYPOTHESIZE:** Why does sound travel faster in a solid than in a gas?

2. **PREDICT:** What happens after a sound wave makes the eardrum vibrate?

3. **INFER:** What does a vibrating guitar string do to the air around it?

4. **EXPLAIN:** Which sound wave has a larger amplitude, a 20-dB sound or a 50-dB sound? How do you know?

5. **PREDICT:** What might happen to your sense of hearing if you were exposed to loud noises over a long period of time?

INTERPRETING VISUALS Use Figure 18-31 to answer the following questions.

6. When a sound is heard, what part of the ear vibrates first?

7. Which parts make up the inner ear?

8. Where is the energy of a sound wave converted to electrical impulses?

9. Why do you think the bones in the middle ear are called the hammer, the anvil, and the stirrup?

10. Cupping your hand to your ear helps you to hear sounds more clearly. Why?

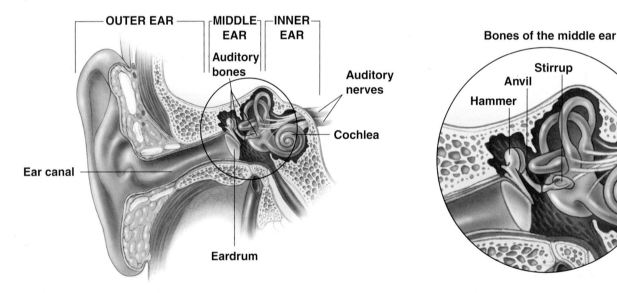

▲ **Figure 18-31** The human ear

Chapter 19 Light

▲ **Figure 19-1** A bundle of optical fibers

Light is a form of energy. Much of our information comes to us in the form of light images. Light can travel through empty space. It can also travel through other materials, such as glass, water, and air. Many technologies that use light, such as fiber optics, have been developed. In fiber optics, light is carried through thin cables of a glasslike material. Fiber optics are used in many areas of life, particularly communications.

►Name something you use daily that works by fiber optics.

Contents

19-1 What is the electromagnetic spectrum?

Objective

Identify the parts of the electromagnetic spectrum.

Key Terms

electromagnetic (ih-lehk-troh-mag-NEH-tihk) **spectrum:** range of electromagnetic waves

visible spectrum: seven colors that make up white light

Electromagnetic Waves Light is a form of energy. Sometimes light behaves as if it is made up of tiny particles of energy called photons. Unless disturbed, photons travel in straight lines. Other times, light behaves as an electromagnetic wave. Unlike mechanical waves, electromagnetic waves can travel through empty space.

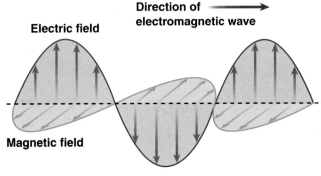

▲ **Figure 19-2** Electromagnetic waves are made up of two transverse waves.

Electromagnetic waves have both electrical properties and magnetic properties. These waves are made up of two transverse waves that vibrate at right angles to each other.

1▶ COMPARE: How are electromagnetic waves different from mechanical waves?

The Electromagnetic Spectrum Light that you can see is called visible light, or white light. Visible light waves make up a small part of a much larger band of waves called the **electromagnetic spectrum**. Figure 19-3 shows the different types of waves that make up the electromagnetic spectrum. As the figure shows, the energy of a wave is related to its wavelength and its frequency.

- Radio waves Radio waves have the longest wavelength and the lowest frequency. They are used for radio, television, and radar signals.

- Microwaves Microwaves are used for wireless communications and microwave ovens.

- Infrared rays All objects give off infrared rays. You cannot see infrared rays, but you can feel them as heat.

- Visible spectrum The only part of the electromagnetic spectrum that can be seen by the human eye is the **visible spectrum**. It is made up of the colors red, orange, yellow, green, blue, indigo, and violet.

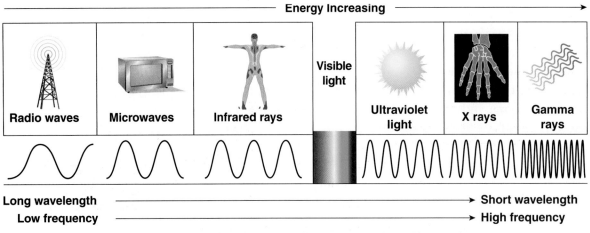

▲ **Figure 19-3** The electromagnetic spectrum is made up of different wavelengths and frequencies.

- **Ultraviolet rays** Ultraviolet rays can cause sunburn. Ultraviolet light is used to kill bacteria.

- **X rays** X rays have a very short wavelength and a high frequency. X rays are used in medicine to form images of bones and internal organs.

- **Gamma rays** Gamma rays have a shorter wavelength and a higher frequency than X rays do. They are given off during nuclear reactions.

2 LIST: What are the electromagnetic waves that make up the electromagnetic spectrum?

✓ CHECKING CONCEPTS

1. Waves with the longest wavelength and the lowest frequency are _____.
2. Waves usually given off during nuclear reactions are _____.
3. Only those waves in the _____ can be seen by the human eye.

4. Waves with wavelengths slightly longer than visible light are _____.
5. Rays usually felt as heat are _____.

THINKING CRITICALLY

6. **HYPOTHESIZE:** Microwaves are high-frequency radio waves. Microwave ovens can be used to cook food quickly. The microwaves are absorbed by the food. Why do you think that food in a microwave oven gets hot, but a glass dish does not?

HEALTH AND SAFETY TIP

High-frequency electromagnetic waves are dangerous. Too much exposure to X rays is harmful. Find out why X-ray technicians wear lead aprons or stand behind a lead screen when taking X-ray pictures. Why are pregnant women advised not to have X-rays taken?

Science and Technology
CELL PHONES

Cellular, or cell, phones have helped change the way we communicate. These phones are small radio transmitters and receivers. One of hundreds of antennae receives radio signals when you make a call. These radio signals are transmitted on a radio frequency to a local cell site. A mobile telephone switching office (MTSO) picks up the signals and sends them through regular wired phones. The MTSO tracks and transfers your calls as you move from area to area. It reverses when you get a call.

Two kinds of wireless phone networks are analog and digital. In analog, voices are carried on radio waves with limitations. This service is easy to steal, and busy signals and static are common. Conversations can be picked up on radio scanners.

Digital service is newer. Voices convert to computer language and then change back to voices on the receiving end. Busy signals and static are less common. Your conversation cannot be heard on a scanner. This service is hard to steal. The newest technology is PCS (personal communication service). Computer language is transmitted on a range of frequencies that are always changing. This technology allows you to access the Internet and have paging and text messaging capabilities.

▲ **Figure 19-4** Cell phones receive and transmit radio waves.

Go **O**nline
active art

For: Electromagnetic Waves activity
Visit: PHSchool.com
Web Code: cgp-5032

Thinking Critically How have cell phones changed the way we communicate?

19-2 What is light?

Objective
Describe light as a form of electromagnetic energy.

Key Terms
light: form of electromagnetic energy made up of streams of photons

photon (FOH-tahn): tiny bundle of energy

ray: straight line that shows the direction of light

Light Energy When you sit in bright sunlight, you can feel your skin get warm. Objects warm up in sunlight. **Light** is a form of electromagnetic energy. Light energy can be changed into heat, electricity, and other forms of energy.

▶ **1 CLASSIFY:** What is light?

Particles of Light Light sometimes behaves as if it is made up of small bundles of energy called **photons**. Photons are such small particles that a single photon cannot be seen. A beam of light is made up of a stream of many photons. Each photon carries a certain amount of energy. Some photons have more energy than others.

▶ **2 DESCRIBE:** Of what is a light beam made?

Rays of Light When you turn on a flashlight, you see a beam of light. The beam of light from the flashlight looks like a straight line. Light travels in straight lines. A **ray** of light is a straight line that shows the direction of a light beam. A ray of light will continue to travel in a straight line unless its direction is changed. There are many ways to model light. Scientists model light in different ways, depending on the question they want to answer.

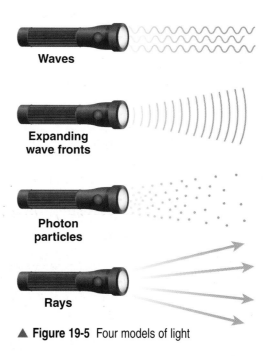

Waves

Expanding wave fronts

Photon particles

Rays

▲ Figure 19-5 Four models of light

▶ **3 DESCRIBE:** What does a ray of light look like?

☑ CHECKING CONCEPTS

1. You cannot see individual _____ of light because they are very small.

2. Light travels in _____ lines.

3. A stream of photons makes up a _____ beam.

4. Light is a form of _____ energy.

5. A _____ of light shows the direction of a light beam.

THINKING CRITICALLY

6. **INFER:** Turn on a lamp and hold your hand near the light bulb. Do you feel heat? What is the source of the heat?

7. **EXPLAIN:** Give two common examples to show that light travels in straight lines.

Web InfoSearch

Light Years: Speed of Light The speed of light is 300,000 km/s. Light takes about two seconds to reach Earth from the Moon. The distance light travels in one year is called a light-year. The nearest star is 4.2 light-years away from Earth. Light from this star takes 4.2 years to reach Earth.

SEARCH: Use the Internet to find out more about light-years. How are light-years used? What is another measurement of distance in space? Start your search at www.conceptsandchallenges.com. Some key search words are **light-years, measuring distance stars,** and **stellar distances.**

How Do They Know That?

PHOTONS AND THE THEORY OF LIGHT

Research for hundreds of years supports the idea that light is made up of particles of energy called photons.

In the late 1600s, Sir Isaac Newton studied how light acts as it meets objects in its path. Newton noticed that light could not travel around objects as other waves could. For example, sound can travel around a corner, but light cannot. He suggested that light was made up of tiny streams of energy particles.

In 1887, Heinrich Hertz found that some frequencies of light, such as violet, would cause metals to give off their electrons. When he used red light, no matter how strong, nothing happened. This experiment showed that the particles in violet light were more energetic than those in red light. This is called the photoelectric effect.

In 1900, Max Planck published a theory on electromagnetic radiation. Albert Einstein used this theory to help explain his theory on photons. He said that a photon's energy depends on the frequency of the light. This theory won Einstein the Nobel Prize in physics.

The photoelectric effect has many everyday uses. Light meters in cameras, soundtracks in films, and automatic street lights all work because of the photoelectric effect. The photons in a light source make an electric current that controls these light-sensitive machines.

Thinking Critically Why do you think it is important to understand the nature of light?

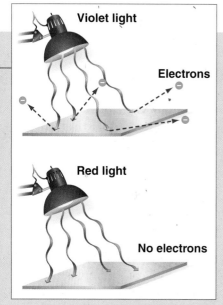

▲ **Figure 19-6** Hertz's experiment

19-3 How do light waves travel?

Objective
Describe how light travels as transverse waves.

Key Term
transverse (trans-VURS) **wave:** wave in which the particles of the medium move up and down at right angles to the direction of the wave motion

Light Waves Light is made up of streams of photons. However, light also behaves like a wave. Light is a type of electromagnetic wave. Electromagnetic waves are different from sound waves. Sound is a longitudinal wave. A sound wave needs a medium in which to travel. Sound cannot be heard in a vacuum, or empty space.

Light waves are different from sound waves in two ways. Light travels in transverse waves. In **transverse waves**, the particles move up and down at right angles to the direction of wave motions. Also, light waves do not need a medium in which to travel. Light can travel through a vacuum.

▶ 1 CONTRAST: How do light waves differ from sound waves?

Photons and Light Waves Some experiments with light show that it is made up of photons. Other experiments show that light acts as a wave. Scientists have learned that some waves act as if they are made up of particles.

▶ 2 DESCRIBE: How do light waves act?

Properties of Light Waves Like all waves, light waves have four properties. They are speed, wavelength, frequency, and amplitude.

- The speed of light is 300,000 km/s in a vacuum. Light and all other electromagnetic waves travel at this speed. The speed of light in a vacuum is the fastest possible speed.

- The wavelength of light is the distance from the crest or trough of one wave to the crest or trough of the next wave.

- The number of light waves that pass by a point each second is the frequency.

- The amplitude is the height of a wave. A bright light has a greater amplitude than a dim light does.

▶ 3 LIST: What are the four properties of a light wave?

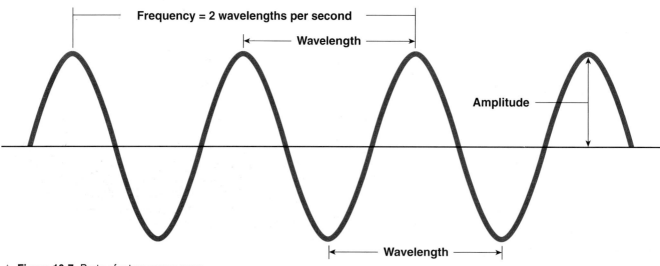

▲ **Figure 19-7** Parts of a transverse wave

1. In a _____ wave, the particles of the medium move at right angles to the direction of the wave motion.

2. A light wave is a moving stream of _____.

3. The properties of light waves include speed, _____, frequency, and amplitude.

4. Light waves travel fastest in a _____.

5. Light waves do not need a _____ in which to travel.

💡 THINKING CRITICALLY

6. CLASSIFY: Identify each of the following as a sound wave or a light wave.

   a. longitudinal wave

   b. does not travel through a vacuum

   c. waves seem to be made up of particles

   d. transverse waves

   e. can travel in a vacuum

7. RELATE: Light waves with very high frequencies are called ultraviolet light. Ultraviolet light cannot be seen by the human eye. How is ultraviolet light similar to ultrasonic sound?

INTERPRETING VISUALS

Look at Figure 19-8. Compare the two waves by discussing wavelength, frequency, amplitude, and speed.

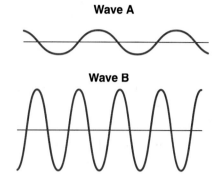

▲ Figure 19-8 Compare the waves.

 Real-Life Science

FILM AND DIGITAL PHOTOGRAPHY

Photography is a popular activity that can teach you a lot about light. The word *photography* means "writing with light." To take a photograph, you need a camera, a place to store the image, and a good source of light.

A camera has a lens and an opening for light to enter. This opening is called an aperture. When you take a picture, the aperture is open for only a short period of time. In a film camera, the light goes through the lens and onto the film. Film is very sensitive to light. In a digital camera, light is converted into electrical charges. These charges create the image on the memory card. Too much light will cause the photograph to be too bright, or overexposed. If there is not enough light, the photograph will be too dark, or underexposed.

▲ Figure 19-9 The varied light made parts of this photo brighter and darker.

Many schools have amateur photography clubs. Joining a photography club is a good way to learn more about taking photographs.

Thinking Critically How is film underexposed or overexposed?

19-4 What are sources of light?

Objectives

Differentiate between luminous and illuminated objects. Describe what happens when light strikes different materials.

Key Terms

luminous (LOO-muh-nuhs) **object:** object that gives off its own light

illuminated (ih-LOO-muh-nayt-uhd) **object:** object that reflects light

opaque (oh-PAYK): a property that does not transmit light

transparent (trans-PEHR-uhnt): a property that transmits light and preserves an image

translucent (trans-LOO-suhnt): a property that transmits some light and blurs an image

Luminous Objects A flashlight, a candle, and a lightbulb are sources of light. Objects that give off their own light are called **luminous objects**. The Sun is a luminous object. It is the source of light for Earth and other planets in the solar system.

▶ **DEFINE:** What is a luminous object?

Illuminated Objects What happens when the light from a luminous object strikes another object?

The light may be reflected. An object that reflects light is called an **illuminated object**.

The Moon is an illuminated object. The Moon is not the source of its own light. Sunlight strikes the Moon and is reflected from its surface. You see the Moon by reflected sunlight.

 IDENTIFY: What is an object that reflects light called?

Opaque, Transparent, and Translucent Materials When light shines on a material, one of three things can happen. The material may block the light and form a shadow. Material that blocks light is called an **opaque** object. When you place your hand in front of a light source, you will see a shadow. Your hand is opaque.

A material may allow light to pass through unchanged. This kind of material is called **transparent**. A sheet of clear glass allows light and images to pass through. The glass is transparent.

A material may allow some of the light to pass through. This kind of material is called **translucent**. A stained-glass window will allow some light to pass through, but no details of images are visible. The stained-glass is translucent.

▶ **NAME:** What are three types of materials that affect light differently?

An opaque vase

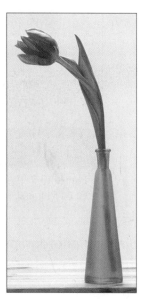

A translucent vase

A transparent vase

◀ **Figure 19-10** You cannot see the stem of the flower through the opaque vase. A blurry view of the stem is seen through the translucent vase. The entire stem can clearly be seen through the transparent vase.

1. When you shine a flashlight on objects in a dark room, the objects that you see are _____ objects.

2. An object that blocks light and casts a shadow is an _____ object.

3. The Moon is an _____ object.

4. A sheet of clear glass is _____ because it allows light to pass through easily.

5. A sheet of stained glass is _____ because it only allows some light to pass through.

6. An illuminated object _____ the light from another source.

7. The Sun is a _____ because it gives off light.

8. **INFER:** You cannot see the Sun on a cloudy day even though sunlight can still illuminate objects. Are clouds transparent or translucent?

9. **CLASSIFY:** Which of the following objects are luminous and which are illuminated?
   a. the flame of a candle
   b. Earth
   c. a star
   d. a campfire
   e. a sheet of paper

DESIGNING AN EXPERIMENT

Design an experiment to solve the following problem. Include a hypothesis, variables, a procedure, and a type of data to study.

PROBLEM: Do transparent objects allow more light to pass through than translucent objects do?

Integrating Earth Science

Topic: lunar eclipse

ASTRONOMICAL SHADOWS

Opaque objects cast shadows by blocking the light shining on them. Your body is opaque. It blocks the Sun's light. You have probably seen your shadow on a sunny afternoon.

During a lunar eclipse, Earth blocks the light from the Sun. The Moon passes through Earth's shadow. Like most shadows, Earth's shadow consists of both an umbra (UM-bruh) and a penumbra (pih-NUM-bruh). The umbra is a sharp, black inner part of a shadow. The penumbra is the gray outer part of the shadow.

When a point source shines directly on an object, the shadow will only have an umbra. A spotlight is an example of a point source of light. Most light comes from sources of light that spread out. A fluorescent light is an example of a source of light that spreads out.

Thinking Critically Why do most shadows have penumbras?

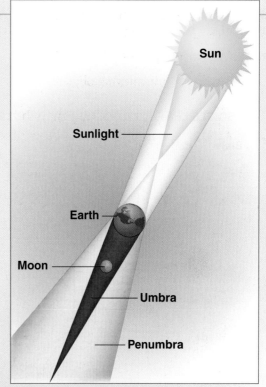

▲ **Figure 19-11** During a lunar eclipse, Earth hides the Moon from the Sun.

19-5 What is photosynthesis?

Objective

Explain how plants use the energy of the Sun to make food.

Key Terms

photosynthesis (foht-oh-SIHN-thuh-suhs): process by which plants use energy from the Sun to make food

chlorophyll (KLAWR-uh-fihl): substance in plants that absorbs the Sun's light and gives plants their green color

chloroplast: part of green plant cells where photosynthesis takes place

Light and Energy Any form of energy can be converted to another form of energy. Light energy can be changed into heat energy, electrical energy, chemical energy, or other forms of energy. Plants convert the electromagnetic energy of sunlight into the chemical energy stored in food. The plants use the chemical energy to make their own food.

▶ **1** INFER: Why do plants need sunlight?

Photosynthesis The process by which a plant uses sunlight to make food is called **photosynthesis**. The leaves of a plant absorb the most sunlight. The flat part of a leaf always tries to face the Sun. As the Sun moves across the sky, the leaves respond by moving to continue facing the Sun. The food that plants make is sugar. Plants can change this sugar into starch, fats, and proteins. These nutrients are stored in the plants as chemical energy. This energy can be used at a later time.

Photosynthesis is a chemical process. During this process, water, carbon dioxide, and energy from the Sun are used to make the sugar. Roots absorb the needed water from the soil. Veins carry the water up the stem and into the leaves. Carbon dioxide enters the plant through openings called stomata. Sunlight supplies the energy the plant needs to make the sugar. During photosynthesis, oxygen is given off as a by-product. The formula for photosynthesis is shown below.

$$CO_2 + H_2O \xrightarrow[\text{Grow Plants}]{\text{Light}} (CH_2O) + O_2 + H_2O$$

Carbon dioxide   Water   Sugar   Oxygen   Water

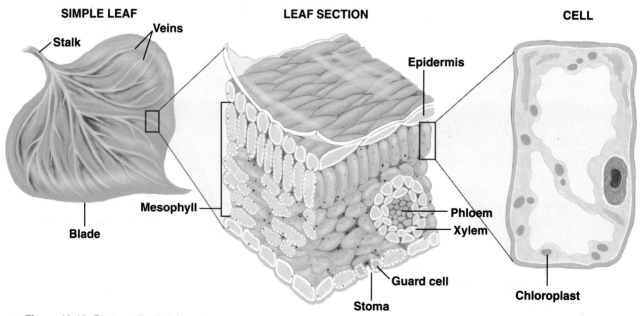

SIMPLE LEAF   LEAF SECTION   CELL

Stalk — Veins — Epidermis — Blade — Mesophyll — Phloem — Xylem — Guard cell — Stoma — Chloroplast

▲ **Figure 19-12** Photosynthesis takes place in the chloroplasts of a leaf cell.

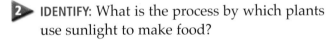
▲ **Figure 19-13** A rain forest ecosystem

Most organisms depend on plants and photosynthesis for survival. When animals eat plants, they take in food that has stored chemical energy. Animals that only eat other animals still depend on plants because the animals that they eat, eat plants. Plants are an important part of most ecosystems, such as the rain forest shown in Figure 19-13.

2 IDENTIFY: What is the process by which plants use sunlight to make food?

Chlorophyll The substance in a leaf that absorbs sunlight is called **chlorophyll**. Chlorophyll is a chemical pigment, or coloring, needed for photosynthesis. It absorbs all the colors of the visible spectrum except green, which it reflects. As a result, leaves look green. Without chlorophyll, photosynthesis could not take place. Wherever there is chlorophyll, photosynthesis can occur.

The chlorophyll is located inside special parts of plant cells. The cell parts that contain chlorophyll are called **chloroplasts**. The cells in the upper layer of the leaf contain many chloroplasts. Therefore, most photosynthesis takes place in this layer.

3 PREDICT: What color would leaves appear if chlorophyll reflected only blue light?

✔ CHECKING CONCEPTS

1. In photosynthesis, electromagnetic energy is turned into _____ energy.
2. The food that a plant makes is _____.
3. Food is a form of _____ energy.
4. The substance that gives plants their green color is _____.
5. A plant's _____ always face the Sun in order to get the most amount of sunlight.
6. Chlorophyll absorbs all the Sun's light except _____ light.

THINKING CRITICALLY

7. **INFER:** Plants always make more food than they need. The extra food is stored in the plant. What happens when an animal eats a plant?
8. **HYPOTHESIZE:** What happens to the energy that plants do not store as food?

Web InfoSearch

Photoelectric Cells A process that can be compared to photosynthesis is used to produce electricity from solar energy. Sunlight is absorbed by photoelectric cells. Photoelectric cells convert sunlight into electrical energy. The electrical energy is stored in batteries. This process is similar to what a plant does, except that the plant stores the energy as food. Many photoelectric cells are put together to make solar panels. Solar panels are used on homes, office buildings, and satellites.

SEARCH: Use the Internet to write a report on how a solar panel works. Start your search at www.conceptsandchallenges.com. Some key search words are **solar panels, photoelectric cells, photovoltaic panels,** and **solar power.**

19-6 How do lenses refract light?

Objective
Compare and contrast how light rays are bent by a concave lens and a convex lens.

Key Terms
lens: transparent material that bends light

real image: image that can be projected onto a screen

virtual image: image that cannot be projected onto a screen

convex lens: lens that curves outward

concave lens: lens that curves inward

Refraction of Light Light rays travel in straight lines. When light moves from one medium into another at an angle other than 90°, the direction of the light changes. Suppose a beam of light passes from air into another material, such as glass. The path of light will be bent, or refracted. Light rays passing through the lenses in Figures 19-14 and 19-15 are refracted.

1 ▶ PREDICT: What happens to a beam of light when it passes from air into water?

Lenses A **lens** is a transparent material that bends, or refracts, light. All lenses have either one or two curved surfaces. There are two main types of lenses. They are convex and concave lenses.

2 ▶ HYPOTHESIZE: Why is a lens made of a transparent material?

Real and Virtual Images A lens can form a real image. A **real image** is an image that can be projected onto a screen.

The image you see when you look into a mirror is a **virtual image**. It is always right-side up. This image is called virtual because the image does not really exist, even though you see it. A virtual image cannot be projected onto a screen.

3 ▶ DEFINE: What is a real image?

Convex Lenses A **convex lens** curves outward. Figure 19-14 shows a convex lens. Light that passes through a convex lens is bent inward. When a convex lens refracts light, the light rays are brought together at a point called the focal point. The distance between the lens and the focal point is the focal length.

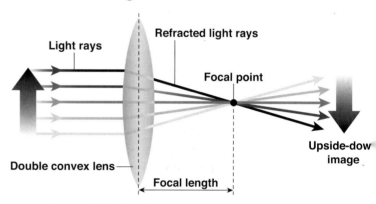

▲ **Figure 19-14** A double convex lens forms a real upside-down image.

Light is refracted as it enters the lens. It also is refracted as it leaves the lens. The amount of refraction depends on how curved the lens is.

4 ▶ IDENTIFY: What is the focal length of a convex lens?

Concave Lenses A **concave lens** curves inward. Light that passes through a concave lens is bent away from the lens. The light rays are spread apart. Figure 19-15 shows a concave lens.

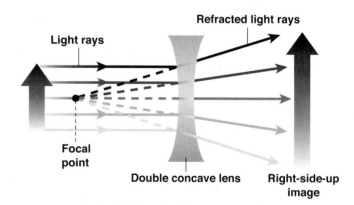

▲ **Figure 19-15** A double concave lens forms a virtual image.

5 ▶ DESCRIBE: What happens to light rays as they pass through a concave lens?

CHECKING CONCEPTS

1. A _____ image cannot be projected onto a screen.

2. A _____ lens curves inward.

3. A _____ can be projected onto a screen.

4. A _____ lens curves outward.

5. The _____ is where rays of light are brought together by a convex lens.

6. The _____ is the distance from the focal point to the lens.

7. A _____ image will be right-side up.

THINKING CRITICALLY

8. **COMPARE:** Explain the difference between a real image and a virtual image.

9. **ANALYZE:** How are light rays brought together after passing through a convex lens?

Web InfoSearch

Telescopes A telescope is a device that allows you to see objects at great distances. From the giant Hubble Space Telescope, which orbits Earth, to the personal telescope used at home or at school, telescopes come in many sizes and strengths.

SEARCH: Use the Internet to find out more about telescopes. How do they work? Why do some telescopes show an upside-down image? Start your search at www.conceptsandchallenges.com. Some key search words are **refractor telescopes**, **how telescopes work**, and **telescopes' refractor lenses**.

People in Science

ASTRONOMERS

Astronomy is the study of stars, planets, and the solar system. Astronomers are the scientists who study how these objects originated, what they are made of, and how and where they move. Astronomers may choose from many different jobs. Some study the formation of galaxies, solar astronomy, the origins of stars, or planetary science. Some astronomers design programs to observe the universe; others observe just our solar system.

Astronomers have a very hard job because they cannot see, touch, smell, weigh, or perform experiments on the objects they are studying. Instead they need to observe the light given off or reflected by objects. The motion of objects is also measured. In order to become an astronomer, a solid background in physics is necessary. You also need to know how to work a computer. Good math, observation, reasoning, and communication skills are necessary.

Astronomers do not spend all day looking through a telescope. They study the data recorded by a telescope and sent to a computer. Then, they have to put that information into readable form. Astronomers also give lectures, teach, and write articles.

Thinking Critically Why is an astronomer's job difficult?

▲ **Figure 19-16** This is the telescope and data recording area of the Lowell Telescope at Perth Observatory in Australia.

INVESTIGATE

How Does the Eye React to Light?
HANDS-ON ACTIVITY

1. Work with a partner. You need a penlight, a sheet of paper, and a pencil.

2. Stand face-to-face.

3. Darken the room. Record what you observe about each other's eyes.

4. Now, shine the penlight into the eye of your partner. Record what you observe in your partner's eye.

5. Alternate roles so you each get a chance to observe what happens.

THINK ABOUT IT: In dim light, your iris contracts and the pupil gets bigger. What happens in bright light?

STEP 4

Objectives
Identify the parts of the eye. Describe how the eye senses light.

Key Terms
eye: sense organ that detects light
sight: one of the five human senses
image: picture formed by the eye

Observing Light You see an object when light from the object enters your eye. The **eye** is the human organ that detects light. **Sight** is one of the five human senses.

▶ **RELATE:** How is the eye related to sight?

Parts of the Eye The eye is made up of parts that work together to help you see. Look at Figure 19-17. The front of the eye is covered with a clear layer called the cornea. The cornea is a protective layer that keeps dirt and bacteria from damaging the inner eye. The cornea covers the pupil. The pupil is the opening through which light enters the eye.

The amount of light that enters the eye is controlled by the iris. The iris is a muscle that contracts or expands, depending on the amount of light available. When there is too much light, the iris contracts. When there is not enough light, the iris expands.

After light enters the eye, it is focused by the lens. It is the clear part behind the pupil. The lens can change shape so that the eye can concentrate on an object. The lens works like the autofocus on a camera.

▶ **NAME:** What are the parts of the eye involved in sight?

The Retina Light entering the eye is focused by the lens onto the retina. The lens, a convex lens, focuses light on the retina, producing an upside-down image. An **image** is a picture that is formed by the eye.

The retina converts the image into electrical impulses. The impulses travel along the optic nerve to the brain. The brain changes the electrical impulses to the right-side-up image.

▶ **RELATE:** How do the lens and the retina work together?

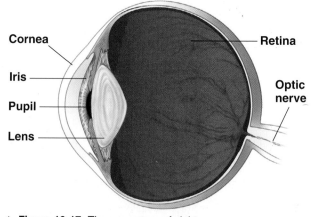

Cornea — Retina
Iris —
Pupil — Optic nerve
Lens —

▲ **Figure 19-17** The eye, organ of sight

✓ CHECKING CONCEPTS

1. Electrical impulses travel along the _____ to the brain.
2. The _____ is the opening that lets light into the eye.
3. The _____ controls the amount of light that can enter the eye.
4. The _____ is a clear protective layer over the eye.
5. The eye is a sense organ that detects _____.
6. An image formed on the _____ is upside down.

💡 THINKING CRITICALLY

7. **INFER:** What energy changes take place when you see an image?
8. **SYNTHESIZE:** Suppose you walk into a dark room after being out in bright sunlight. Several minutes pass before you can see objects in the room clearly. What happened to your eyes during that time?

INTERPRETING VISUALS

Use Figure 19-18 to answer the following questions.

9. What type of corrective lens is used to correct nearsightedness?
10. What type of corrective lens is used to correct farsightedness?

Nearsightedness (eyeball too long)

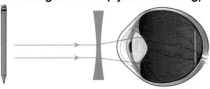

Farsightedness (eyeball too short)

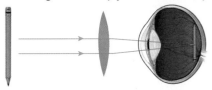

▲ **Figure 19-18** Identify the lenses.

Science and Technology

LASIK EYE SURGERY

Laser is an acronym for light amplification by the stimulated emission of radiation. Lasik (LAY-sik) is an acronym for laser in situ keratomileusis. Lasik eye surgery corrects some vision problems using lasers.

Lasik has been practiced in the United States since 1996. It was invented in Colombia by Drs. Virgilio Galvis and Luis Ruiz. The laser used and approved in the United States is called the VISX. It can correct nearsightedness and some other eye problems. During lasik eye surgery, a flap of the cornea is cut and folded over. A laser beam then takes away some of the tissue from the inside of the cornea. A metal ring is used with an infrared tracking device to make sure that the laser points to the right spot. The laser reshapes that part of the cornea. Then, the flap is put back.

▲ **Figure 19-19** Laser surgery corrects vision by reshaping the cornea.

There are benefits if you can have the surgery. It is same-day surgery. You have it done in the doctor's office and can leave after a short stay. However, not everyone with poor vision can be helped by this surgery. Also, like any surgery, lasik surgery does have some risk involved, such as infection. It is very important to seek medical advice before allowing any surgery to be done.

Thinking Critically Why do you think recovery from lasik surgery is so quick?

LAB ACTIVITY
Comparing Convex and Concave Lenses

Materials

Convex lens
(10-cm focal length),
Concave lens
(10-cm focal length),
Flashlight,
Metric ruler,
Dark construction paper
or cardboard,
1 Sheet of white paper,
Notebook paper,
Tape, scissors, pencil,
Hardcover book

BACKGROUND

A lens is an object that bends, or refracts, light. When light passes through a lens, an image is created. Images can be real or virtual. A real image will be inverted, or upside down. A virtual image will be right-side up. Real images can be projected; virtual ones cannot. There are two types of lenses, convex and concave. Convex lenses curve outward in the center. Concave lenses curve inward in the center.

PURPOSE

In this activity, you will compare the images formed by convex and concave lenses.

PROCEDURE

1. Copy the chart shown in Figure 19-21 onto a sheet of paper.

2. Write your name on a sheet of notebook paper. Write it as you normally write it—not too big and not too small.

3. Hold the convex lens over your name and look through it. Slowly lift the lens toward your eye. Observe your name through the lens. You may have to move the lens back and forth to focus the image of your name. Record your observations on your chart.

4. Repeat Step 3 using the concave lens.

5. Create a "projection screen" as shown in the Step 5 photo. Tape a sheet of white paper onto a large hardcover book. Then, stand the book upright so that the "screen" is at one end of your desk or table.

6. Now, make a "projector." Lay the construction paper flat on a table. Place the head of the flashlight onto the paper and trace it to make a circle. Cut out the circle. Fold the circle in half. In the center, draw

▲ **STEP 3** Hold the lens over your name.

▲ **STEP 5** Set up a projection screen.

a triangle connected to a rectangle along the folded edge of the paper, as shown in Figure 19-20. Now, cut out the shape and unfold the paper. You should have an arrow-shaped hole in the middle of the circle. Tape the circle over the head of the flashlight. Be careful not to put tape over the cutout arrow.

◀ **Figure 19-20** Draw and cut out this shape.

7. Hold the flashlight about 50 cm from the "screen." Turn on the flashlight and point it at the screen. Hold the convex lens in front of the lighted flashlight. Move the lens back and forth to focus the image of the arrow on the screen. You may have a partner hold the light steady while you focus. You also may need to turn the lens slightly until you see the arrow clearly. Record your observations.

8. Now, repeat Step 7 using the concave lens. Record your observations. Remember, only real images can be projected.

▲ **STEP 7** Focus the lens so you see an image on the screen.

Comparison of Convex and Concave Lenses

	Eye	Flashlight
Convex		
Concave		

▲ **Figure 19-21** Copy this chart and use it to record your observations.

CONCLUSIONS

1. **OBSERVE:** What did the convex lens do to your name?

2. **OBSERVE:** What did the concave lens do to your name?

3. **ANALYZE:** Which lens allowed you to see real images? How do you know?

4. **INFER:** Which type of lens do you think would be used in a magnifying glass?

5. **SYNTHESIZE:** How are different lenses used to correct people's vision?

Objective

Describe how mirrors form clear images.

Key Terms

regular reflection: reflection that forms a clear image

diffuse reflection: reflection that forms a fuzzy image

plane mirror: smooth surface that reflects light and forms images

Reflected Light Light not completely absorbed or transmitted by an object will be reflected. The type of surface affects the type of reflection. There are two types of reflection. They are regular reflection and diffuse reflection.

When a beam of light strikes a smooth surface, the light is reflected from that surface at the same angle. A **regular reflection** forms a clear image. For example, the light reflected from the surface of a still pond will form clear images of the objects around the pond. A regular reflection only occurs when a surface is completely smooth and even, as shown in Figure 19-22.

When light strikes a rough surface, it will be reflected at different angles. The reflected light from a **diffuse reflection** forms a fuzzy image because light is scattered in many directions. On a windy day, the surface of a pond is not smooth. The light reflected from the surface of the pond will form fuzzy images as shown in Figure 19-23. It is by diffuse reflection that we are able to see nonluminous objects.

1 IDENTIFY: What are the two types of reflection called?

Plane Mirrors Mirrors form regular reflections. A **plane mirror** is a smooth surface that reflects light and forms images. The light from an object striking a mirror at an angle will be reflected from the mirror at the same angle. Figure 19-24 shows a baseball reflected in a mirror at a 45° angle. This is the angle of incidence. The reflected beam bounces off the mirror at a 45° angle. This is the angle of reflection. According to the law of reflection, the angle of incidence is equal to the angle of reflection. The image formed by the mirror is the same distance behind the reflecting surface as the object is in front of it. Figure 19-24 shows that distances *A* and *B* are equal.

▲ **Figure 19-22**
Regular reflection

▲ **Figure 19-23**
Diffuse reflection

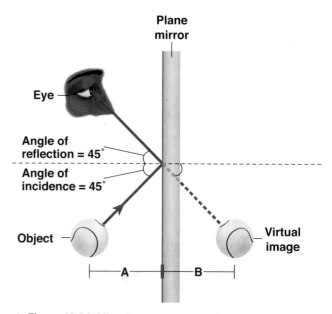

▲ **Figure 19-24** Mirror image

2 INFER: Why does a mirror form a clear image?

Convex and Concave Mirrors Not all mirrors are flat, or plane. Some have curved surfaces. A mirror with a surface that curves outward is called a convex mirror. The images reflected in a convex mirror appear to be smaller and farther away. These images are always virtual. Convex mirrors are used in car side-view mirrors and for security in stores.

A mirror with a surface that curves inward is called a concave mirror. Images can be real or virtual, depending on the position of the object. Sometimes images reflected in a concave mirror will appear magnified. Concave mirrors are used in makeup mirrors and as headlight reflectors.

 APPLY: Why do you think a car's side-view mirror would be convex?

✓ CHECKING CONCEPTS

1. On a windy day, the surface of a pond will form a _____ reflection.
2. A plane mirror forms _____ images.
3. The angle of incidence is equal to the angle of _____.

4. If an incident ray is at a 45° angle, the _____ ray will also be at a 45° angle.
5. A _____ is a smooth surface that reflects light and forms images.
6. A _____ mirror has a surface that curves inward.

💡 THINKING CRITICALLY

7. **INFER:** How does reflection help us see nonluminous objects?
8. **PREDICT:** A bathroom mirror is covered with steam. Will the mirror produce a diffuse reflection or a regular reflection? Explain.

BUILDING MATH SKILLS

Measuring the Difference Look at Figure 19-24. Measure the distance from the object to the mirror. Compare this distance with the distance from the image to the mirror. Now, compare the height of the object and the height of the image. What does this tell you about the image formed by a flat mirror?

 Hands-On Activity

HOW TO MAKE A PERISCOPE

You will need scissors, heavy oak tag, rubber cement, and two round pocket mirrors.

1. Draw solid lines on your oak tag like the lines in Figure 19-25.
2. Cut along the solid lines to make the frame and slits for the mirrors. ⚠ CAUTION: Be careful when using scissors.
3. Fold the oak tag by following the dotted lines in the pattern. Glue or tape the long edges together.
4. Place mirrors at opposite ends of this box. One mirror should be angled toward the middle of the box; the other should be angled toward its nearest end opening. Glue the mirrors in place. Then, glue the top and bottom.
5. Now, test your periscope.

Practicing Your Skills

6. **IDENTIFY:** What parts in the periscope help you see around corners?
7. **EXPLAIN:** How is this possible?

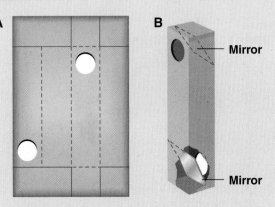

▲ Figure 19-25

Go Online
active art

For: Mirrors activity
Visit: PHSchool.com
Web Code: cgp-5042

19-9 What is color?

Objectives

Describe how a prism forms a visible spectrum.

Explain why different objects have different colors.

Key Terms

prism (PRIZ-uhm): triangular piece of transparent glass that separates white light into a band of colors

dispersion (di-SPUR-shuhn): separation of white light into its component colors

Visible Spectrum Visible light, or white light, is made up of seven different colors. These colors, which combine to make up the visible spectrum, are red, orange, yellow, green, blue, indigo, and violet. Each of these colors of light has its own wavelength. Red light has the longest wavelength. Violet light has the shortest wavelength.

DISPERSION OF WHITE LIGHT

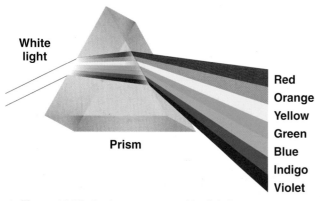

White light

Prism

Red
Orange
Yellow
Green
Blue
Indigo
Violet

▲ **Figure 19-26** A prism separates white light into the colors of the visible spectrum.

A triangular piece of clear glass called a **prism** can be used to separate white light into its colored spectrum. Light is bent, or refracted, as it enters the prism and again as it leaves the prism. Each color of light is refracted by a slightly different amount, causing the white light to break up into its individual colors. This process of separating white light into its individual colors is called **dispersion.**

▶ **DESCRIBE:** How does wavelength affect the color of light?

Color of Objects When white light reflects from an object, the object may appear to have a color. The object absorbs all the colors of the spectrum except the color it reflects. When white light shines on a red object, all colors except red are absorbed. The red light is reflected, and the object appears red.

White light

▲ **Figure 19-27** An object appears red because it absorbs all colors except red.

Some objects absorb all of the light and do not reflect any color. These objects appear black. Other objects reflect all of the light. They do not absorb any of the colors. These objects appear white. Others absorb all colors but one. The color you see is the color reflected by the object.

White light

▲ **Figure 19-28** A black object absorbs all light. None is reflected.

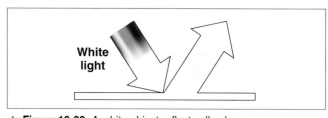

White light

▲ **Figure 19-29** A white object reflects all colors.

▶ **PREDICT:** What color will an object appear if it reflects only green light?

✓ CHECKING CONCEPTS

1. A blue object absorbs all the colors of the visible spectrum except _____.

2. A _____ separates white light into the colors of the visible spectrum.

3. Red has the _____ wavelength of all the colors of the visible spectrum.

4. An object appears _____ because it absorbs all the colors of the visible spectrum.

💡 THINKING CRITICALLY

5. **INFER:** The frequency of a wave increases as its wavelength decreases. Which color of light has the highest frequency? Which has the lowest?

6. **COMPARE:** How is a rainbow like a visible spectrum?

Web InfoSearch

Color blindness The inability to see the colors red, green, or blue is called color blindness. A color-blind person sees these colors as gray. Color blindness is a genetic disorder. It is inherited from a person's parents. Men are color-blind more often than are women.

SEARCH: Use the Internet to find out more about color blindness. Explain why men have this disorder more often than women do. Start your search at www.conceptsandchallenges.com. Some key search words are **color blindness, color receptors,** and **color-blind genes.**

 Integrating Life Science

TOPICS: animals, ecology, adaptations, camouflage

COLOR IN ANIMALS

A pigment is a substance found in living things that absorbs light. Different pigments absorb different wavelengths of light and reflect others.

Animals contain pigments in their skin that cause them to be a certain color. These pigments are contained in special cells called chromatophores. Many animals have colors that help them blend into their surroundings. This is called camouflage. Camouflage is an adaptation that allows the animal to hide itself from predators. For example, the flounder has coloring that closely matches the color of the seafloor.

▲ **Figure 19-30** A green tree frog is well hidden in the leaves.

Not all animals try to blend in. Sometimes organisms do just the opposite. Some animals, especially those that are poisonous, have very bright colors. These colors are called warning colors. Poison dart frogs from the South American rain forest have been found in a wide array of colors and patterns. These frogs can be found in blue, yellow, orange, and even purple. These colors warn predators, "Don't eat me. I'm poisonous!"

Thinking Critically Some frogs of the rain forest are brightly colored but are not poisonous. What do you think is the reason for this?

19-10 How can light be used?

Objective
Identify uses of light in different areas of life.

Key Terms
laser: device that produces a powerful beam of light

total internal reflection: occurs when light is repeatedly reflected within a given material

fiber optics: use of optical fibers

Lasers Have you ever heard of a powerful beam of light that can cut through a steel plate? This kind of light is different from white light. This light comes from a laser. A **laser** is a device that produces a very powerful beam of light.

The difference between white light and laser light is their wavelengths and energy content. White light is made up of many different wavelengths. It includes all the visible colors. Laser light is made up of only one wavelength. As a result, laser light is only one color. Unlike the light waves in white light, the waves in laser light are all in step. A beam of laser light can travel long distances in a straight line. It does not spread out as a beam of white light does.

▶ **DEFINE:** How is laser light different from normal white light?

Uses of Lasers Lasers have many uses. In medicine, lasers can be used to repair a detached retina and prevent blindness. A detached retina results when the retina comes loose from the back of the eye. The heat of a laser beam can attach the retina back into place. Lasers are also used to treat skin tumors, birthmarks, and some cancers.

▲ Figure 19-31 A laser beam cutting metal

In industry, lasers can be used for cutting, welding, and drilling. For example, a laser beam can make a clean cut through thick layers of cloth. You maybe familiar with the use of lasers in Compact disc (CD) and digital versatile disc (DVD) players. Lasers are also used in supermarkets to read the bar codes on many different products.

▶ **EXPLAIN:** How can a laser repair a detached retina?

Optical Fibers Glasslike fibers that can transmit information in the form of light pulses are called optical fibers. These fibers are able to send information much more quickly and clearly than copper wire or radio waves can.

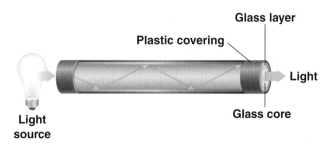

Glass layer
Plastic covering
Light
Light source
Glass core

▲ Figure 19-32 Total internal reflection

The reason light travels through optical fibers so quickly is because it reflects within the glass. If light is reflected at a great enough angle, the light does not refract through the glass. Instead, it reflects repeatedly within the optical fiber. This is called **total internal reflection**.

▶ **DESCRIBE:** How does light travel so quickly through an optical fiber?

Uses of Fiber Optics The use of optical fibers is called **fiber optics**. Fiber optics is used in many industries. One industry using fiber optics more and more is the communications industry.

Phone companies use fiber optics in most of their new wiring. They also are replacing their remaining copper wiring with fiber optics. Cable television (TV) companies have also begun to use fiber optics. TV signals are sent to entire communities, using optical fibers. Then, the signal is split into regular cable wiring, which is sent to each home.

The computer industry is also using fiber optics. Many universities and businesses use fiber optics in their local area networks. A local area network, or LAN, is a group of connected computers that share data, software, and hardware.

Fiber optics is used in medicine. Doctors can attach cameras to optical fibers. The optical fibers are then inserted into the body through a small incision, such as in the knee. This allows doctors to see within the body so they can operate making small incisions. This allows patients to recover more quickly from surgery.

 EXPLAIN: How do fiber optics help patients and doctors?

✓ CHECKING CONCEPTS

1. What is a laser?

2. What can lasers be used for in industry?

3. In what form do optical fibers transmit information?

4. What is fiber optics?

 THINKING CRITICALLY

5. **CONCLUDE:** How does total internal reflection help make optical fibers work so well?

6. **INFER:** Why can the light from a laser travel a greater distance than light from a normal source of white light?

BUILDING SCIENCE SKILLS

Inferring One major difference between optical fibers and copper wiring is the way that they send and receive information. Optical fibers transmit information using pulses of light. Copper wiring uses pulses of electricity. This difference makes optical fibers less sensitive to power surges and electrical interference. Why do you think this makes optical fibers more useful in computers and computer networks?

 Science and Technology

HOLOGRAMS

There is a special kind of photography that uses laser light. This process is known as holography (hah-LAHG-ruh-fee). Laser light is used to produce a three-dimensional image. The image is known as a hologram (HAHL-uh-gram).

With the invention of the laser in 1960, Dennis Gabor, the hologram inventor, was finally able to produce crisp holographic images. He was awarded the Nobel Prize in Physics in 1971 for his work.

▲ **Figure 19-33** Holograms use laser light to create a three-dimensional effect.

To make a hologram, two pictures of an object are taken. Each picture is taken from a slightly different angle. Then, the two pictures are combined into one hologram.

When you look at a hologram, you can view the original object from different angles. It is as if the object were in front of you, even though you are seeing only an image of the object.

There are several practical uses for holograms. Architects can use holograms to show three-dimensional views of buildings. Structural engineers can use holograms to test the sturdiness of a solid object.

Thinking Critically How did the invention of the laser help Gabor complete his design of the hologram?

THE Big IDEA

How is light used in the home?

Technology is the practical application of knowledge. Beginning with the first stone tools, people have used technology to accomplish tasks. A new technology often improves on older methods. It may be faster, save energy, and produce better results. Society must always weigh the risks of new technologies against their benefits. They must always be environmentally friendly.

Advances in technology have expanded our choices at home. We can chop with a knife or a food processor. We can cook with fire, electricity, or microwaves. Newer "flash bake" ovens use light to cook foods rapidly.

We also have more forms of entertainment and communication. Music on CDs sounds clearer than music on records or tapes. Besides broadcast TV, choices today include cable, satellites, videotapes, and DVDs. Fiber-optic cable makes long-distance phone calls clearer. The Internet has created another way to communicate with friends and family far away.

Like lamps and mirrors, many types of technology at home use light. Look at the boxes of text that appear on this page and the next. They point out devices that are typical in homes today and some that may become common in the future. Then, follow the directions in the Science Log to learn more about "the big idea."✦

Grow Lights
Fluorescent grow lights mix blue and red wavelengths. Blue light promotes leaf growth. A combination of red and blue lights encourages flowering.

Speed Cook Oven
A combination of intense visible light and infrared energy cooks food in one-fourth the time of conventional ovens. First used in restaurants, these ovens are now sold for homes.

▲ **Figure 19-34** Inside a house

Fiber-Optic Phone Lines

In the future, most communications will use fiber-optic cables because they can transmit so much information so clearly. Laser light carries sound or other data through glass strands in the cables.

Solar Heating Panels

Large, flat-plate collectors capture sunlight and convert it into thermal energy. The energy heats air and water in the house.

Motion Detector Lighting

When motion sensors detect infrared waves that radiate from moving objects, they electronically turn on the outdoor lights.

Television

A light-sensitive device in a TV camera converts light into electrical impulses. These impulses make up the video signal. The TV receiver changes it back into a picture.

CD Player

A laser beam follows the spiral track of tiny "bumps" that hold data on the compact disc. A sensor detects changes in how the bumps reflect the laser light.

WRITING ACTIVITY

Science Log

Look at the house. Which kind of technology do you or would you like to use in your home? In your science log, research and write about how light is used in this technology and why you would like to use it. Include a model of its being used in your home. Start your search at www.conceptsandchallenges.com.

Chapter Summary

Lesson 19-1

• The **electromagnetic spectrum** includes radio waves, microwaves, infrared waves, visible light, ultraviolet rays, X rays, and gamma rays.

Lesson 19-2

• **Light** is a form of electromagnetic energy.

Lesson 19-3

• Light travels in **transverse waves**. Light does not need a medium in which to travel.

Lesson 19-4

• **Luminous objects** give off their own light. **Illuminated objects** reflect light.

• **Opaque, transparent,** and **translucent** are three types of objects that affect light differently.

Lesson 19-5

• **Chlorophyll** is a substance in plants that absorbs the Sun's light and allows **photosynthesis** to occur.

Lesson 19-6

• A **convex lens** curves outward. A **concave lens** curves inward.

• A convex lens is used to form **real images.** A concave lens can form **virtual images.**

Lesson 19-7

• The parts of the **eye** are the cornea, pupil, iris, lens, retina, and optic nerve.

• Light is focused onto the retina by the lens. The brain interprets the **image** on the retina to make it look right-side up.

Lesson 19-8

• A **plane mirror** is a smooth surface that reflects light and forms images.

• **Regular reflection** produces a clear image. **Diffuse reflection** produces a fuzzy image.

Lesson 19-9

• A **prism** can separate white light into the colors of the spectrum.

• The color of an object depends on what part of the spectrum it reflects or absorbs.

Lesson 19-10

• A **laser** produces a powerful beam of light.

• Optical fibers are glass fibers that can quickly transmit information in the form of light pulses.

Key Term Challenges

chlorophyll (p. 408)
chloroplast (p. 408)
concave lens (p. 410)
convex lens (p. 410)
diffuse reflection (p. 416)
dispersion (p. 418)
electromagnetic spectrum (p. 400)
eye (p. 412)
fiber optics (p. 420)
illuminated object (p. 406)
image (p. 412)
laser (p. 420)
lens (p. 410)
light (p. 402)
luminous object (p. 406)
opaque (p. 406)
photon (p. 402)
photosynthesis (p. 408)
plane mirror (p. 416)
prism (p. 418)
ray (p. 402)
real image (p. 410)
regular reflection (p. 416)
sight (p. 412)
total internal reflection (p. 420)
translucent (p. 406)
transparent (p. 406)
transverse wave (p. 404)
virtual image (p. 410)
visible spectrum (p. 400)

MATCHING Write the Key Term from above that best matches each description.

1. organ used for sight

2. straight line that shows the direction of light travel

3. image that can be projected

4. seven colors that make up white light

5. small bundle of energy

6. material that allows light to pass through easily

7. device that produces a powerful beam of light

8. range of electromagnetic waves

9. reflection that forms a fuzzy image

FILL IN Write the Key Term from above that best completes each statement.

10. By the process of _____, a plant makes its own food from the Sun's light.

11. When you shine a light in a dark room, the objects that you see are _____.

12. An _____ forms on the retina.

13. Lamps are _____ because they give off their own light.

14. A _____ is a smooth surface that reflects and refracts images.

Content Challenges TEST PREP

MULTIPLE CHOICE **Write the letter of the term or phrase that best completes each statement.**

1. Chlorophyll absorbs all the colors of the visible spectrum except
   a. red.
   b. green.
   c. blue.
   d. violet.

2. The refracted image from a convex lens is
   a. right-side up.
   b. reversed.
   c. upside down.
   d. none of the above.

3. The color that is not one of the seven colors of the visible spectrum is
   a. red.
   b. blue.
   c. indigo.
   d. brown.

4. The type of electromagnetic wave that can be felt as heat is
   a. gamma rays.
   b. infrared rays.
   c. X rays.
   d. ultraviolet rays.

5. The part of the eye that controls the amount of light entering the eye is the
   a. pupil.
   b. cornea.
   c. iris.
   d. retina.

6. In photosynthesis, electromagnetic energy is converted to
   a. electrical energy.
   b. nuclear energy.
   c. chemical energy.
   d. mechanical energy.

7. Unlike a beam of white light, a laser beam has
   a. no color.
   b. one wavelength.
   c. two colors.
   d. no wavelength.

8. The point where the light that passes through a lens is brought together is called the
   a. focal length.
   b. refraction point.
   c. focal point.
   d. retina.

9. Light reflects completely within a fiber-optic cable because of
   a. gravity.
   b. total internal reflection.
   c. photosynthesis.
   d. regular reflection.

10. An object that absorbs all colors of light and does not reflect any appears
    a. green.
    b. white.
    c. black.
    d. blue.

TRUE/FALSE **Write *true* if the statement is true. If the statement is false, change the underlined term to make the statement true.**

11. According to the law of <u>refraction</u>, the angle of incidence is equal to the angle of reflection.

12. Illuminated objects, such as the <u>Sun</u>, reflect light.

13. The reason light travels through optical fibers so quickly is because it <u>refracts</u> within the glass.

14. The parts of a cell where photosynthesis takes place are called <u>chloroplasts</u>.

15. All electromagnetic waves are streams of <u>photons</u>.

Concept Challenges TEST PREP

WRITTEN RESPONSE Answer each of the following questions in complete sentences.

1. **COMPARE:** What are two ways that a photon is similar to a particle?
2. **EXPLAIN:** How does a prism separate white light into a spectrum?
3. **INFER:** Why do electromagnetic waves travel best in a vacuum?
4. **EXPLAIN:** Why does a laser beam not spread out over long distances?
5. **HYPOTHESIZE:** Some animals can hear ultrasonic sounds, even though humans cannot. Do you think that some animals can see ultraviolet light, even though humans cannot? Why or why not?
6. **MODEL:** Think of your eye as a camera. A camera has an opening for light to enter called an aperture. Which part of the eye is similar to the camera's aperture? Which part is similar to the film or the memory card in the camera? Which part is similar to the camera lens?

INTERPRETING A DIAGRAM Use Figure 19-35 to answer the following questions and to complete the exercise.

7. What type of lens is shown?
8. Which letter on the diagram represents the focal length of the lens?
9. Which letter represents the focal point?
10. Copy the diagram on a sheet of paper. Show the path of light rays passing through the lens.
11. Are the light rays brought together or spread apart by the lens?
12. What kind of image would be formed at point C?

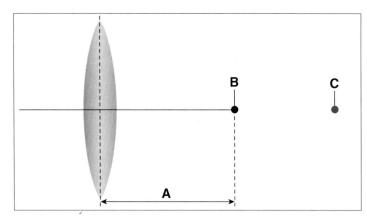

▲ Figure 19-35

426

Chapter 20 Electricity

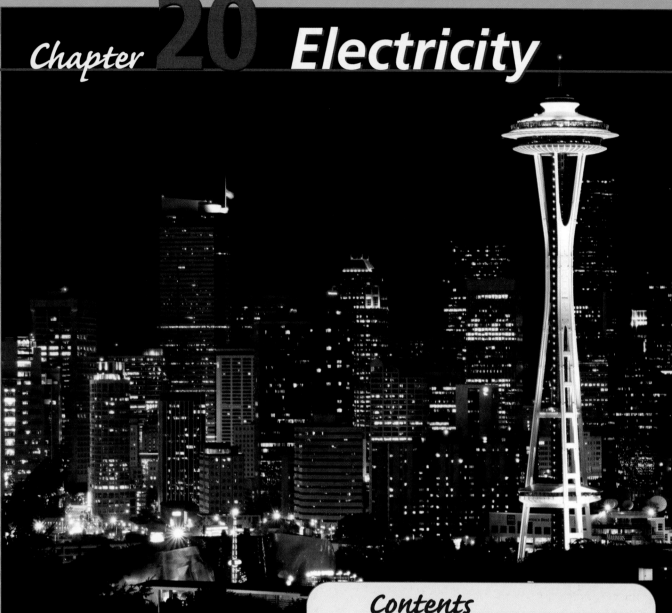

▲ **Figure 20-1** The skyline at night in Seattle, Washington

Electricity provides the energy that lights up the skyline of the city in Figure 20-1. Electricity can make a city look beautiful at night, but it also plays a very important role in your life. From providing power to the appliances in your home to helping your body function properly, you rely on electricity. Although it is a very useful source of energy, electricity can be dangerous. Safety rules must be followed when using electricity.

► Can you name some safety rules to follow when using electricity?

Contents

20-1 What is electric charge?

INVESTIGATE

Observing Electric Charges
HANDS-ON ACTIVITY

STEP 3

1. Blow up a rubber balloon. Tie the end into a knot.

2. Rub the balloon with a piece of wool or nylon.

3. Dim the lights in your classroom. Bring your finger near the balloon. Observe what happens between the balloon and your finger.

THINK ABOUT IT: What did you observe between your finger and the balloon? Has something like this ever happened to you before?

Objective
Explain how objects become electrically charged.

Key Terms
proton: atomic particle with a positive electric charge

electron: atomic particle with a negative electric charge

neutron: atomic particle with neither a negative nor a positive electric charge

static electricity: buildup of electric charges in an object

Atoms You have learned that all matter is made up of atoms. The three basic parts of an atom are protons, neutrons, and electrons. Protons and neutrons are found in the nucleus of an atom, and electrons are found in the electron cloud that surrounds the nucleus.

1▶ NAME: What are the three main parts of an atom?

Electric Charge Protons and electrons have a property called electric charge. **Protons** have positive electric charge (+). **Electrons** have negative electric charge (−). The strength of the positive electric charge on a proton is the same as the strength of the negative electric charge on an electron. **Neutrons** do not have charge. They are neutral.

Electric charge is not a physical property that can be seen or touched. However, electric charge exerts a force that affects the behavior of matter. Matter that is electrically charged follows these rules:

- Objects with like charges repel, or push away, from each other.

- Objects with unlike charges attract each other.

Because they have opposite charges, protons and electrons attract each other. However, because they have the same electric charge, protons do not attract each other. They repel, or push away, from each other. Electrons also repel each other.

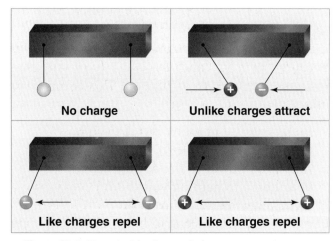

No charge	Unlike charges attract
Like charges repel	Like charges repel

▲ **Figure 20-2** How electric charges behave

2▶ EXPLAIN: How do protons and electrons affect each other?

Neutral Objects Although an atom is made up of electrically charged particles, the atom as a whole has no electric charge. The number of protons and the number of electrons in an atom is always the same. Therefore, the electric charges cancel each other. The atom is neutral.

Most matter is electrically neutral. However, neutral objects can become electrically charged. An object becomes electrically charged when its atoms lose or gain electrons. The electrons in the atoms of some matter are held loosely to the atoms. If these electrons are separated from their atoms, the atoms become electrically charged. For example, when you walk across a carpet, your feet can rub off and pick up electrons from the carpet. Your body then gets a small electric charge. If you then touch a metal doorknob, electrons can jump from your hand to the doorknob. You can see a spark.

3▶ DESCRIBE: Why are atoms always neutral?

Static Electricity Protons are held tightly in the nucleus of all atoms. However, electrons are free to move from a region of negative electric charge to a region of positive electric charge. The buildup of electric charges on an object is called **static electricity**. The word *static* means "not moving." In static electricity, electrons do not flow. They remain at rest for a time but will eventually leave the object.

Static electricity can be produced when different materials rub against each other. For example, if a sock and a shirt rub against each other in a clothes dryer, electrons may be transferred between both items. The sock may lose some of its electrons to the shirt and become positively charged. The shirt gains these electrons and becomes negatively charged. Because the sock and the shirt have opposite charges, they stick to each other. This attraction is called static cling.

4▶ INFER: Why can a sock stick to a shirt after coming out of a clothes dryer?

Static Discharge Objects that have static electricity will eventually lose their charge. The extra electrons will move onto other objects, and the original object will return to its neutral condition. The loss of static electricity is called static discharge.

A dramatic example of static discharge is lightning. During a storm, water particles in clouds swirl around and rub against each other. This friction produces electric charges in different areas of the clouds. The negative area of the cloud repels the negatively charged electrons on the surface of the ground below. The surface of the ground then becomes positively charged. An attraction develops between the negatively charged area of the cloud and the positively charged ground. If the force of attraction becomes great enough, electrons from the cloud will jump to the ground. When this happens, a spark of lightning is produced.

▲ **Figure 20-3** The force of attraction between charges in clouds and the ground can produce lightning.

5▶ EXPLAIN: How does lightning occur?

✔ CHECKING CONCEPTS

1. An electron has a _____ charge.
2. A _____ object has neither a positive nor a negative charge.
3. Static electricity is the buildup of _____ on an object.
4. Two electrons will _____ each other.

💡 THINKING CRITICALLY

5. **EXPLAIN:** What can happen if you walk across a carpet and then touch a metal doorknob?
6. **INFER:** Why is the buildup of electric charge on an object called static electricity?

INTERPRETING VISUALS

Use Figure 20-2 to answer the following questions.

7. **INFER:** How do like charges behave?
8. **EXPLAIN:** How do objects without a charge behave?

LAB ACTIVITY
Observing Static Electricity

Materials
Sheet of tracing paper
Compass
Ruler
Scissors
Plastic pen
Metal pie plate
Piece of silk

BACKGROUND

Static electricity is produced when different materials rub against each other. Electrons from one object may be gained by another object. The object that loses electrons becomes positively charged. The object that gains electrons becomes negatively charged. The opposite charges cause the two objects to stick to each other.

PURPOSE

In this activity, you will observe how static electricity can attract an object.

PROCEDURE

1. Copy the chart in Figure 20-4 onto a sheet of paper.

2. Use a compass to lightly draw a large circle on a sheet of tracing paper. The circle should be about 20 cm in diameter. Be careful not to tear the tracing paper.

3. Use scissors to cut the circle out of the tracing paper. Place the tip of a pen in the center of the circle. Draw a spiral that goes all the way to the very edge of the circle. Again, draw carefully so that you do not tear the tracing paper.

4. Carefully cut along the spiral line that you drew. When you are finished, you should have one long continuous piece of tracing paper. Lay the spiral in a metal pie plate.

5. Place the end of your pen above the center of the spiral without touching the tracing paper. Observe what happens. Record your observations on the chart.

6. Rub your pen with a piece of silk a few times. Again, place the end of the pen slightly above the center of the spiral. Do not touch the tracing paper. Slowly lift your pen up. Observe what happens. Record your observations.

▲ **STEP 2** Draw a 20-cm-wide circle on tracing paper.

▲ **STEP 4** Cut along the spiral line.

▲ **STEP 5** Place your pen above the center of the spiral.

▲ **STEP 6** Rub your pen with a piece of silk.

Observing Static Electricity

Experiment	Observations
Pen above spiral	
Pen above spiral after rubbing with a piece of silk	

▲ **Figure 20-4** Copy this chart and use it to record your observations.

CONCLUSIONS

1. **OBSERVE:** What happened the first time you placed your pen above the spiral tracing paper? What happened after you rubbed the pen with the piece of silk?

2. **ANALYZE:** Why was there a different result?

3. **INFER:** What was the purpose of rubbing the pen with the piece of silk?

4. **INFER:** Why did you use tracing paper instead of regular paper?

5. **HYPOTHESIZE:** After Step 6, what eventually happened to the spiral tracing paper?

20-2 What is a battery?

INVESTIGATE

Making a Lemon Wet Cell
HANDS-ON ACTIVITY

1. Wrap several turns of wire around a magnetic compass.

2. Wrap one end of the wire around the end of a strip of copper. Wrap the other end of the wire around the end of a strip of zinc.

3. Insert the free end of the copper strip into the side of a lemon. Insert the free end of the zinc strip next to the copper strip. Make sure that the strips do not touch each other.

THINK ABOUT IT: What happens to the needle of the compass? What do you think takes place?

STEP 3

Objectives

Identify a battery as a series of electrochemical cells that are connected together. Compare a wet cell and a dry cell.

Key Terms

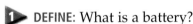

electrochemical cell: device that changes chemical energy to electrical energy

battery: a series of electrochemical cells that are connected to each other

electrolyte: substance that forms ions when melted or dissolved in water

Electrochemical Cell Under certain conditions, chemical energy can be converted to electrical energy. A device that changes chemical energy to electrical energy is called an **electrochemical cell**. A series of two or more electrochemical cells that are connected to each other is called a **battery**.

▶ **DEFINE:** What is a battery?

Wet Cell The simplest type of electrochemical cell is called a wet cell. A wet cell is made up of a negative pole, a positive pole, and an electrolyte. An **electrolyte** is a substance that forms ions when melted or dissolved in water. The electrolyte in most wet cells is an acid or a base. The negative and positive poles of a wet cell are called electrodes. The ions transfer the negative charge between the electrodes in a cell. Zinc can be used

as a negative electrode. Copper can be used as a positive electrode.

A chemical reaction in a wet cell causes electrons to move from the copper electrode to the zinc electrode. As Figure 20-5 shows, when the two electrodes are connected to each other by a metal wire, electrons flow from the zinc electrode through the wire to the copper electrode.

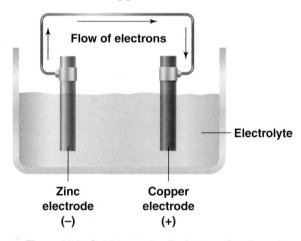

Flow of electrons

Electrolyte

Zinc electrode (−)

Copper electrode (+)

▲ **Figure 20-5** Outside a wet cell, electrons flow through a wire from the negative electrode to the positive electrode.

▶ **IDENTIFY:** What are the three parts of a wet cell?

Dry Cell A dry cell is used as a source of electrical energy in flashlights and portable electronic devices. A dry cell works in the same way that a wet cell does. The electrolyte is a moist paste inside the cell. The zinc casing of the cell is the negative electrode. The positive electrode runs down the center of the battery and is usually made of carbon.

When the two electrodes are connected by a conductor, electrons flow through the conductor from the carbon to the zinc.

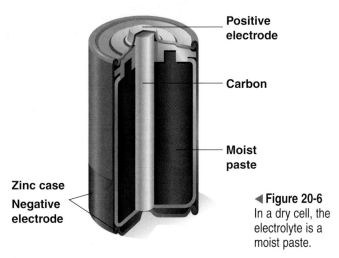

Positive electrode

Carbon

Moist paste

Zinc case
Negative electrode

◄ **Figure 20-6** In a dry cell, the electrolyte is a moist paste.

 CONTRAST: How is the electrolyte in a dry cell different from that in a wet cell?

✓ CHECKING CONCEPTS

1. A series of electrochemical cells that are connected to each other makes up a _____.

2. A _____ cell is used in a flashlight.

3. An electrochemical cell converts chemical energy into _____ energy.

4. The negative electrode of a wet cell is usually made of _____.

 ## THINKING CRITICALLY

5. **ANALYZE:** In a wet cell, the electrons flow from the zinc electrode to the copper electrode. Why do they not flow from the copper to the zinc?

Web InfoSearch

Rechargeable Batteries Batteries that can be used over and over again are called rechargeable batteries. Two types of rechargeable batteries are lithium batteries and nickel-cadmium batteries. These types of batteries can be used in cellular phones, laptop computers, and digital cameras.

SEARCH: Use the Internet to find out how they work. Start your search at www.conceptsandchallenges.com. Some key search words are **batteries** and **rechargeable**.

 Real-Life Science

DISPOSAL OF BATTERIES

Every year, Americans use billions of batteries. When used up, most of these batteries are thrown into the trash. These batteries are then buried in landfills or they are burned in incinerators. However, some batteries contain poisonous metals that can leak into the groundwater through landfills. They can also be released into the air when batteries are incinerated, or burned. Two of these metals, mercury and cadmium, are very dangerous. Mercury can cause harm to the nervous systems in humans and in fish. Cadmium can cause cancer.

Batteries should be separated from ordinary trash and disposed of in special hazardous-waste landfills. Such landfills are built on top of clay to stop poisons from leaking into groundwater. Many cities now have special sites for the collection of batteries. To prevent the release of dangerous materials into the environment, we must dispose of batteries safely.

▲ **Figure 20-7** The proper disposal of batteries is an important environmental concern.

Thinking Critically Why is the proper disposal of batteries so important?

20-3 What are insulators and conductors?

Objective

List some examples of conductors and insulators.

Key Terms

conductor: material through which electric charge can flow easily

insulator: material through which electric charge does not flow easily

Conductors A material through which electric charge can flow easily is called a **conductor**. Most metals are good conductors of electricity.

If a metal wire is placed between the positive and negative poles of a battery, a path is created so that electrons can flow. Suppose metal wires are used to attach a light source to the positive and negative poles of a battery. Electrons will flow through the wire and the lightbulb will light up. If a piece of rubber is used instead of metal wires, electrons will not flow. The lightbulb will not light up.

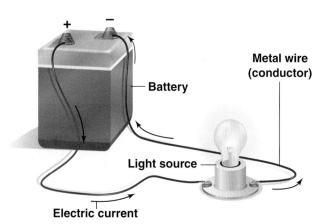

▲ **Figure 20-8** Electrons will flow if a metal wire is attached to both poles of a battery.

Some conductors are better than others. Wire made of copper is one of the best conductors of electricity. Wire made of aluminum is lighter and is less expensive than wire made of copper. However, aluminum is not as good a conductor of electricity.

▶ **DEFINE:** What is a conductor?

Insulators A material through which electric charge does not flow easily is called an **insulator**. Rubber is an insulator. When a piece of rubber is placed between two oppositely charged objects, charges will not flow. Electrons in the atoms of rubber are held tightly together so that they cannot move freely throughout the material. Other insulators are cork, wood, cloth, plastic, and air.

 INFER: What happens when a piece of rubber is placed between two oppositely charged objects?

Insulated Wires Electrical cords use both insulators and conductors. The conductor is usually made of copper. The copper wire is covered with an insulator, such as rubber. The rubber prevents electric charges from leaving the bare wire.

The rubber insulation of electric cords may become cracked or worn. Such electric cords are dangerous because they can cause a short circuit. A short circuit results when two uninsulated wires touch, allowing a large amount of electric charge to jump between them. Wires carrying too much charge can become very hot, perhaps causing a fire.

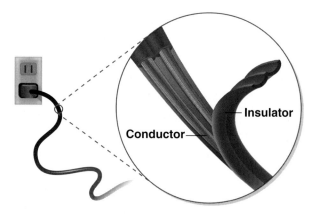

▲ **Figure 20-9** Most household cords have two wires covered with rubber insulation to prevent electric charges from leaving the wire.

 EXPLAIN: Why are electric cords often covered with rubber?

1. A _____ allows current to flow easily through it.
2. Rubber is an _____ because it does not allow an electric charge to flow easily through it.
3. In an insulated electrical wire, the conductor is often _____.
4. An electric cord is safe to touch because it is covered with _____.
5. If two conducting wires in an electric cord touch, a _____ will result.
6. Cork is a good _____.
7. A copper wire is one of the best _____.
8. A short circuit results when two _____ wires touch, allowing an electric charge to jump between them.

THINKING CRITICALLY

9. **INFER:** A lightning rod is supposed to keep a bolt of lightning from damaging a house. The rod is placed at the top of the house and is connected to the ground. What material would make a good lightning rod? Explain.
10. **COMPARE:** How is a conductor different from an insulator? Give an example of each.
11. **APPLY:** Why is it safe to use an insulated wire but not safe to use an uninsulated wire?

HEALTH AND SAFETY TIP

You should not try to repair or rewire electric appliances yourself. They use large amounts of electricity and can be quite dangerous. Frayed or worn electric wires can cause a bad electric shock. What should you do if wires or appliances in your home need repair?

People in Science

BENJAMIN FRANKLIN (1706–1790)

Benjamin Franklin was a politician, a writer, a businessman, and an inventor. He is probably most famous for an experiment that he performed in the summer of 1752. One night, Franklin tied a key to the string of a kite. He then flew the kite during an electrical storm. He was hoping to collect an electric charge from lightning directly onto the key. He wanted to prove that lightning is really an electric charge sent through the air. During the experiment, Franklin was successful in conducting the charge from nearby lightning to the key.

▲ **Figure 20-10** Benjamin Franklin conducted lightning to the ground by using a kite and a key.

Franklin performed many experiments with lightning during the course of his life. Because he understood the danger of electricity, Franklin invented the lightning rod to protect ships and buildings. He realized that lightning is attracted to tall, pointed objects. So, he invented a pointed metal object that could be mounted on the roof of tall structures. When lightning occurred, lightning bolts would be attracted to the metal rod rather than to the ship or the building.

In addition to being the first person to understand that lightning is a huge electric discharge, Franklin also gave the names *positive* and *negative* to opposite electric charges.

Thinking Critically Why is Benjamin Franklin's experiment with the kite considered dangerous?

20-4 What are two kinds of electric current?

Objective

Differentiate between direct current and alternating current.

Key Terms

electric current: flow of electric charge through a conductor

direct current: current in which electrons always flow in the same direction

alternating current: current in which electrons constantly change direction at a regular rate

Useful Electricity You have learned that the electric charges that build up on objects with static electricity do not flow. Instead, these negative charges can jump between objects. Static electricity cannot be used to run the electrical appliances in your home. In order for electricity to be useful, the electric charges must flow steadily.

When a conductor is connected to an appliance and to the opposite poles of a battery, electrons will flow steadily through the conductor. The flow of electric charge through a conductor is called an **electric current**. An electric current is like a stream of water. However, instead of a flow of water, it is a continuous flow of electrons.

▶ **EXPLAIN:** Why can static electricity not be used to run electrical appliances?

Direct Current An electric current in which charges flow in one direction only is called **direct current (DC).** The current produced by electrochemical cells, including dry cells, is direct current. Figure 20-11 shows two dry cells in a flashlight. When the flashlight is turned on, the electric current produced by the dry cells keeps the bulb lit. Notice that the current flows in one direction.

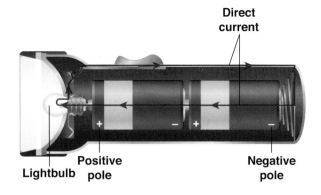

▲ **Figure 20-11** The arrows show the path followed by direct current in a flashlight.

 DEFINE: What is direct current?

Alternating Current A second type of electric current does not flow in one direction only. An **alternating current (AC)** constantly changes direction at a regular rate. Most of the electricity found in homes, schools, and businesses is alternating current.

The main advantage of alternating current over direct current is that alternating current can be transported more easily over long distances. Another advantage is that the voltage of an alternating current can be increased or decreased.

▲ **Figure 20-12** Electricity from power plants travels as alternating current to homes.

Alternating current can be changed to direct current. In the home, many electronic devices such as computers, television sets, and CD players use direct current. Converters built into these devices are designed to change the alternating current from the household outlet to direct current.

 DEFINE: What is alternating current?

CHECKING CONCEPTS

1. The flow of electric charge through a conductor is called _____.

2. Current that reverses direction at a regular rate is called _____ current.

3. A battery is a source of _____ current.

4. Most of the electricity that is used in everyday life comes from _____ current.

5. The type of electric current supplied by power plants is _____ current.

THINKING CRITICALLY

6. **COMPARE:** How is alternating current different from direct current?

7. **ANALYZE:** A toy manufacturer is making an electric toy that plugs into a wall outlet. The toy needs direct current in order to operate. How should the toy be made?

DESIGNING AN EXPERIMENT

Design an experiment to solve the following problem. Include a hypothesis, variables, a procedure, and a type of data to study.

PROBLEM: Will a battery last longer if it is kept in a freezer before it is used?

▲ **Figure 20-13** An electric eel (top) and a platypus (bottom) both use electricity to survive.

Integrating Life Science

TOPICS: nervous system, adaptation, predator, prey

ANIMALS THAT USE ELECTRICITY

Electric currents, or impulses, are also found in living things. The nervous system of most organisms uses electric charges. Some organisms, however, have more specialized uses of electricity.

An electric eel can stun or kill its prey with a strong electric charge. The electric eel has special musclelike cells that generate electricity. Eels also use their electric ability for self-defense against predators.

The duck-billed platypus uses electricity to find its food, even in total darkness. Duck-billed platypuses live in streams in Australia. With a special sense that detects electricity, they can find tasty crayfish and other prey, even at night in muddy water. The platypus has a special organ on the end of its soft bill that picks up faint electric signals coming from the muscles of animals swimming nearby.

Animals that produce and use electricity are usually found in water habitats. They are not found on land because water can conduct electricity, whereas air is a good insulator.

Thinking Critically Do you think that an electric eel can produce electricity outside of water as well as it does in water? Explain your answer.

20-5 What is a series circuit?

INVESTIGATE

Making an Electric Circuit
HANDS-ON ACTIVITY

STEP 1

1. Obtain a dry-cell (size D) battery, two insulated wires, and one lightbulb in a holder from your teacher.
2. Connect the lightbulb holder to the battery by using the wires. You will know if you have connected everything properly when the lightbulb lights up.

THINK ABOUT IT: What purpose do the wires serve? What are the three main parts to this setup?

Objectives
Explain how electricity flows through a closed circuit. Describe a series circuit.

Key Terms
electric circuit: path that an electric current follows

series circuit: circuit in which electric current follows only one path

Circuits An **electric circuit** is the path that an electric current follows. All electric circuits have three parts: a source of electric energy, a load or device that uses the electric energy, and wires. The source of the electric energy can be a battery or a wall outlet. The load can be a lightbulb, an appliance, or some other electric device. Wires connect the source to the load.

▲ **Figure 20-14** An electric circuit has three parts: a source, wires, and a load.

▶ DEFINE: What is an electric circuit?

Open and Closed Circuits What would happen if the only bridge over a river was closed for repair? Vehicles using that bridge would not be able to cross the river. The path that connects both sides of the river would no longer be complete. The same situation occurs in an electric circuit. If the electric circuit is not complete, then the electric charges cannot flow. An electric circuit that is incomplete or has a break in the pathway is called an open circuit. Electric charges cannot flow through an open circuit. Electric charges can flow only through a complete or closed circuit. In a closed circuit, there are no breaks in the path.

A switch is used to control (open and close) an electric circuit. When a switch is in the "off" position, the circuit is open. Electric charges will not flow when a switch is in the off position. When the switch is in the "on" position, the circuit is closed. Electric charges will flow when the switch is in the on position.

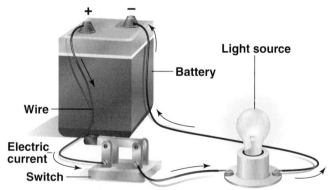

▲ **Figure 20-15** Electric charges flow when a switch is in the closed, or on, position.

▶ EXPLAIN: Why is a switch used in an electric circuit?

Series Circuit The simplest type of electric circuit is called a **series circuit**. In a series circuit, the electric charges follow only one path through all elements of the circuit. Figure 20-16 shows a series circuit. In this circuit, a battery is connected to two light sources. The current goes through the first light, then through the second light, and then back to the battery.

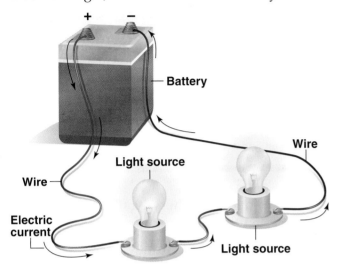

▲ **Figure 20-16** In a series circuit, electric current follows one path.

3 DEFINE: What is a series circuit?

☑ CHECKING CONCEPTS

1. What is the path that an electric current follows called?
2. What are the three parts of an electric circuit?
3. In what kind of electric circuit does electric current follow only one path?
4. In which position will a switch allow electric charges to flow?

THINKING CRITICALLY

5. **HYPOTHESIZE:** In a series circuit with two lamps, what do you think would happen if one of the lamps was not working? Explain your answer.

INTERPRETING VISUALS

Use Figure 20-15 to answer the following questions.

6. **IDENTIFY:** Which object is the load?
7. **HYPOTHESIZE:** What would happen if the switch was in the off position? Explain your answer.

Science and Technology

COMPUTER CHIPS—INTEGRATED CIRCUITS

Computers are all around us. Some computers are used on a desktop, and others are used to operate microwave ovens. The main functions of a computer are to store, process, and retrieve information.

Computers process information using computer chips. Computer chips are very small pieces of a semiconductor that contain many integrated circuits. They are like miniature electric mazes with many pathways. They can perform millions of different functions. A computer's central processing unit, or CPU, may have 10 million electronic parts all packed into a 3-cm^2 silicon wafer. Electroni signals flow through integrated circuits on a computer chip at very high speeds.

▲ **Figure 20-17** A computer chip contains many integrated circuits.

Pretty

Computer chips are extremely useful, inexpensive, and small. You can find powerful chips in computers and simpler ones in everything from key chains and electronic greeting cards to cars and stereos.

Thinking Critically Why do you think computer chips are used in so many different kinds of devices?

20-6 What is a parallel circuit?

Making Another Kind of Electric Circuit
HANDS-ON ACTIVITY

1. Obtain a dry-cell (size D) battery, four insulated wires, and two lightbulbs in holders from your teacher.

2. Connect the lightbulbs to the battery using the wires. Do not make a series circuit. Make sure that you use all four wires to create separate paths. You will know that you have correctly connected the wires when you remove one of the lightbulbs and the other stays lit.

THINK ABOUT IT: What is the difference between this type of electric circuit and a series circuit?

STEP 2

Objectives

Describe a parallel circuit. Compare a parallel circuit and a series circuit.

Key Term

parallel circuit: circuit in which an electric current can follow more than one path

Parallel Circuit In a series circuit, there is only one path that an electric current can follow. In a **parallel circuit** an electric current can follow more than one path. The illustration on the right in Figure 20-18 shows a parallel circuit. Two lamps

are connected to one battery. Notice how the wires are connected to each lamp. If one lamp goes out, charges can still flow through the other path. The other lamp will remain lit.

 DEFINE: What is a parallel circuit?

Series Circuits Versus Parallel Circuits In a series circuit with two lamps, what would happen if one of the lamps went out? The charges flowing to that lamp would stop. Because there is a break in the path, neither lamp would light. This is a great disadvantage in using a series circuit.

However, if the two lamps were set up in a parallel circuit, this problem could be avoided. In a

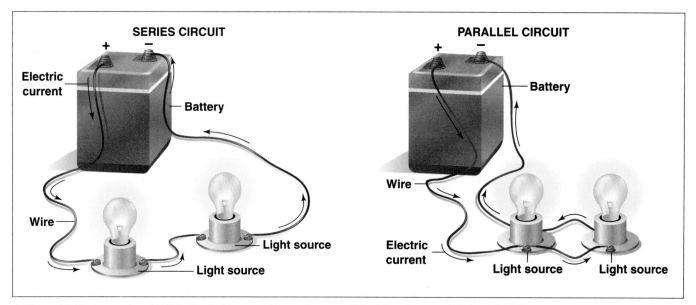

▲ **Figure 20-18** In a series circuit (left), electric current has only one path to follow. In a parallel circuit (right), electric current can follow more than one path.

parallel circuit, the current can follow more than one path. If the lamps were connected in different paths, one lamp would not stop working if the other lamp went out. Because the charges could follow different paths, electric current could still reach the other lamp. This is the reason why electric circuits in homes and businesses are parallel circuits.

2 DESCRIBE: What happens to the current in a series circuit when a lamp goes out?

✓ CHECKING CONCEPTS

1. In a _____ circuit, the current follows only one path.
2. In a _____ circuit, the current can follow more than one path.
3. Homes, offices, and schools use _____ electric circuits.

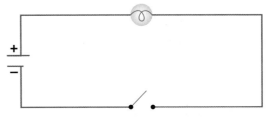

💡 THINKING CRITICALLY

4. HYPOTHESIZE: How could you change a series circuit into a parallel circuit?

BUILDING SCIENCE SKILLS

Labeling a Diagram Figure 20-19 shows an open series circuit with one lamp connected to the current source. Copy the diagram into your notebook. Identify and label each of the following parts in the diagram: the source of the electric energy, the lamp, the wire, and the switch.

▲ **Figure 20-19** Open series circuit

 ## *People in Science*

ELECTRICIAN

An electrician is a person who is trained to install and repair electric equipment. An electrician must know how much electricity a building needs. A house with basic appliances such as a refrigerator and a television needs a certain amount of electricity. A high-rise apartment building needs much more electricity.

Most homes have wall outlets that supply a certain amount of electricity. However, different kinds of appliances may need a different amount of electricity. An electrician has to make sure that the correct amount is being used. An electrician must also be familiar with different types of wires. Most houses use copper wiring, but some use aluminum. Older homes may need to have all the wiring replaced. An electrician needs to make sure that the correct type of wiring is used.

Anyone interested in a career as an electrician should take courses in mathematics, physics, and chemistry in high school. They can also participate in apprenticeship programs that take four to five years to complete.

Thinking Critically What are some of the things an electrician must know when installing wiring in a home?

▲ **Figure 20-20** An electrician needs to know how much electricity a building needs.

Go **Online**
active art

For: Series and Parallel Circuits activity
Visit: PHSchool.com
Web Code: cgp-4023

20-7 How is electricity measured?

Objective

Use the correct units to measure voltage, current, and resistance.

Key Terms

voltage: energy available to move charges through a circuit

volt: unit used to measure voltage

ampere: unit used to measure electric current

resistance: opposition to the flow of electric current

ohm: unit used to measure resistance

Voltage Energy is needed to make something move, even something as tiny as an electron. The energy available to move charges through a circuit is called **voltage**. Voltage is measured in units called **volts** and is measured with an instrument called a voltmeter.

 EXPLAIN: What is voltage?

Current The amount of electric current depends on the number of charges flowing through a wire. The unit for measuring electric current is the **ampere**, or amp. An ampere is a measure of the number of charges flowing past a point in a circuit in one second. A device used to measure the amount of electric current is called an ammeter.

 IDENTIFY: What is an ampere a measure of?

Resistance **Resistance** is the tendency for materials to oppose the flow of electric charges. Some insulating materials, such as rubber and plastic, have very high resistance. Other materials that are good conductors, especially metals, have lower resistance. The unit for measuring resistance is the **ohm.**

Four things affect the resistance of a wire.

- **Length** The longer a wire is, the more resistance it has.

- **Diameter** The thinner a wire is, the more resistance it has.

- **Material** Wires made of poor conductors have more resistance than wires made of good conductors.

- **Temperature** As a wire gets hotter, its resistance increases.

The resistance of a material to the flow of electricity can be useful. For example, a lightbulb lights up because of the resistance of the wire inside the bulb. As electric current passes through a lightbulb, the wire inside the bulb resists the electric current. Its resistance to the electric current heats up the wire so that it glows.

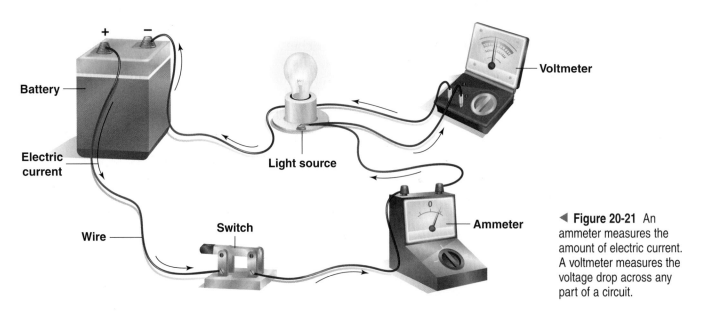

◄ **Figure 20-21** An ammeter measures the amount of electric current. A voltmeter measures the voltage drop across any part of a circuit.

◀ Figure 20-22 Resistance to electric current causes the wire in the lightbulb to glow.

 3 DEFINE: What is resistance?

✓ CHECKING CONCEPTS

1. Energy available to move charges through a circuit is called _____.

2. Current is measured in _____.

3. The unit for resistance is the _____.

4. A long wire has _____ resistance than a short wire.

 THINKING CRITICALLY

5. **HYPOTHESIZE:** Which has more resistance, a conductor or an insulator? Explain.

6 **EXPLAIN:** How is resistance useful in a toaster?

7. **EXPLAIN:** How could you measure the amount of electric current running through a circuit?

Web InfoSearch

Volts, Amps, Ohms Volt, ampere, and ohm are units of measurements taken from the names of famous scientists.

SEARCH: Use the Internet to find out about each scientist for whom each unit of measurement is named. Start your search at www.conceptsandchallenges.com. Some key search words are **volt, ampere,** and **ohm.**

 ## Science and Technology

SUPERCONDUCTORS

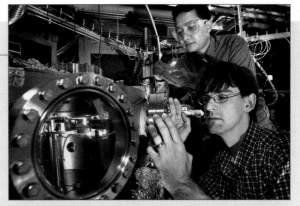

▲ Figure 20-23 Scientists working with superconductors

When a conductor such as a wire carries an electric current, the conductor becomes hot. This causes the resistance of the conductor to increase. However, there are materials that show no resistance to the flow of electrons at temperatures close to absolute zero. Absolute zero is –273°C. Scientists are working to develop materials that have near-zero resistance at temperatures well above absolute zero. Such materials are called superconductors.

Some materials become superconductors at temperatures below –250°C. Liquid helium has been used to cool materials to this temperature. However, liquid helium is very expensive. Scientists have found that some materials become superconductors when cooled with liquid nitrogen. So, researchers are looking to use liquid nitrogen as a coolant. Liquid nitrogen does not reach temperatures as low as liquid helium, but it is much less expensive. However, much research is needed before such "warm" superconductors become part of our daily lives.

Thinking Critically Why do you think finding materials that are superconductors at room temperature can be useful?

20-8 What is Ohm's law?

Objective
Explain the relationships between electric current, voltage, and resistance.

Key Term
Ohm's law: current in a wire is equal to the voltage divided by the resistance

I, V, and R Every closed circuit has an electric current (I), voltage (V), and resistance (R). Current, voltage, and resistance vary from circuit to circuit. Different power sources have different amounts of voltage. For example, a D-cell battery has 1.5 volts, while the standard amount of voltage used in our homes is at 120 volts.

◀ **Figure 20-24** Different power sources have different amounts of voltage.

Resistance in a circuit depends on the kind of wires used and the kind of load through which the current moves. A wire made of copper has less resistance than one made of tin. A toaster will offer more resistance than a mixer. The amount of current in a circuit depends on the voltage and on the total resistance offered by the load.

 NAME: What do I, V, and R stand for?

Ohm's Law Even though the current, voltage, and resistance vary from circuit to circuit, there is often a simple relationship among them. This relationship is called Ohm's law. **Ohm's law** states that the current (I) in a wire is equal to the voltage (V) divided by the resistance (R).

$$\text{Current} = \text{Voltage} \div \text{Resistance}$$
$$\text{or}$$
$$I = V \div R$$

The units of measurements used would be amperes, which is shown by the following formula.

$$\text{Amperes} = \text{Volts} \div \text{Ohms}$$

 DESCRIBE: What does Ohm's law state?

Using Ohm's Law Suppose a 6-volt battery is connected to a circuit with a resistance of 3 ohms. What is the current?

$$I = V \div R$$
$$I = 6 \text{ volts} \div 3 \text{ ohms}$$
$$I = 2 \text{ amps}$$

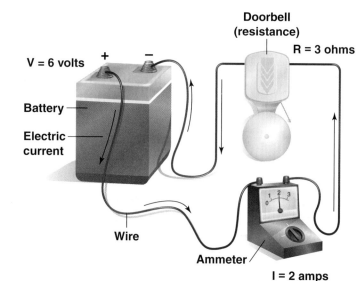

▲ **Figure 20-25** Applying Ohm's law

You can rearrange the formula so that you can find resistance or voltage. To find the voltage (V), multiply the current (I) by the resistance (R). To find the resistance, divide the voltage by the current. As long as you know any two values, you can use Ohm's law to find the remaining value.

Voltage	Resistance
$V = I \times R$	$R = V \div I$

▲ **Figure 20-26**

444

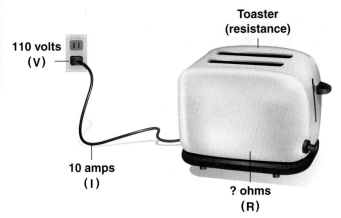

110 volts
(V)

Toaster
(resistance)

10 amps
(I)

? ohms
(R)

▲ **Figure 20-27** Find the resistance at the moment when I = 10 amps and V = 110 volts.

3 ▶ CALCULATE: What is the resistance of the toaster in Figure 20-27?

 CHECKING CONCEPTS

1. Every closed circuit has an electric current, voltage, and _____.
2. According to Ohm's law, I = _____ ÷ R.

3. Resistance is measured in _____.
4. Electric current is measured in _____.

THINKING CRITICALLY

5. INFER: How is electric current related to resistance and voltage?

BUILDING MATH SKILLS

Calculating Copy the table in Figure 20-28 on a sheet of paper. Use Ohm's law (I = V ÷ R) to complete the chart. Express your answer in whole numbers or decimals.

I (amps)	V (volts)	R (ohms)
?	10	70
15	250	?
5	?	25
5	110	?

▲ **Figure 20-28** Find the missing values.

Science and Technology

ELECTRIC CARS

Today's gasoline-powered cars use up much of America's oil supply. The gases that they give off account for almost half the amount of pollution in the air. However, the supply of oil and other resources are limited, and the increasing pollution in the air is a health concern. As a result, some automakers are looking to make electric cars an alternative to gasoline-powered cars.

Electric cars would reduce the use of gasoline and oil. Because electric cars do not rely on the burning of fuels, they also would create less pollution. Electric cars are also more efficient than gas-powered cars. An electric car does not waste as much of the power it produces as a gas-powered car does.

▲ **Figure 20-29** An electric car

The electric cars available today use lead-acid batteries. These batteries can be charged using household current from a wall plug. However, these batteries are expensive, and they limit the distance that the car can travel. Instead of relying on batteries, some cars are being built with parts that store large amounts of electricity. Manufacturers are also looking to develop fuel cells that use hydrogen to generate electricity.

Thinking Critically Why are electric cars better for the environment than gas-powered cars?

How can you use electricity safely?

Objective
Describe ways to use electricity safely.

Key Terms
fuse: thin piece of metal that melts and breaks a circuit if too much current is flowing

circuit breaker: switch that opens a circuit if too much current is flowing

Overloaded Circuits Electricity is a wonderful source of energy, but it can also be dangerous. Too many appliances connected to one outlet may cause an overloaded circuit. In an overloaded circuit, too much current flows through a wire. The wire may overheat. It can then melt its insulation and cause a short circuit. Heat and sparks could result in a fire. A frayed wire can also cause a fire.

▲ **Figure 20-30** An overloaded circuit or a frayed wire can cause a fire.

 IDENTIFY: What happens in an overloaded circuit?

Fuses The electricity that comes into your home travels through power lines. The power lines lead to a distribution center. From this center, separate wires go to different circuits in the house or building. These wires are connected to the wall outlets that provide the local power.

Some distribution centers, especially in older homes, have fuses. A **fuse** is a thin piece of metal that melts or "blows" when too much current flows through it. By melting, the fuse stops current from flowing and prevents an overloaded circuit. When you replace the fuse, the current begins moving again. The electrical system in cars and many appliances have fuses to prevent overloaded circuits.

 DEFINE: What is a fuse?

Circuit Breakers Once a fuse blows, it has to be replaced in order for the current to flow again. In order to avoid having to replace fuses, most newer homes use circuit breakers. A **circuit breaker** is a switch that turns off when there is too much current flowing. A circuit breaker is another way of preventing an overloaded circuit. To start the current flowing again, the breaker must be turned back on.

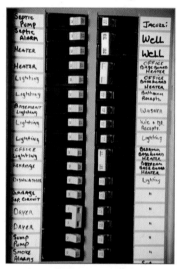

▲ **Figure 20-31** Circuit breakers prevent overloaded circuits.

 DESCRIBE: How does a circuit breaker prevent an overloaded circuit?

Electricity in Humans Cells in your body use electricity to carry out very important life processes. For example, the rate at which your heart beats is controlled by electrical signals sent out by certain cells in your body. The muscles that control the movement of your body and your nerves work in a similar manner. This small amount of electricity is produced within your body. It is very dangerous if your body receives an electric current from an outside source. Normal processes within your body can be disrupted by such an electric shock.

 INFER: List ways in which your body uses electricity.

Electrical Safety Rules Electricity can be dangerous if it is not used carefully. Here are some safety rules to follow when using electricity.

- Do not plug too many appliances into one outlet.
- Do not allow electric cords to become worn.
- Do not run electric cords under carpets.

5 ▶ **STATE:** State an electrical safety rule.

✓ CHECKING CONCEPTS

1. Too many appliances connected to one outlet may cause an _____ circuit.
2. Heat and sparks from a frayed wire may cause a _____.
3. Power lines that come into your home lead to a _____.
4. A _____ is a thin piece of metal that melts when too much current moves through it.

💡 THINKING CRITICALLY

5. **HYPOTHESIZE:** Resistance in a wire increases with the length of the wire. Do you think it is a good idea to connect several extension cords to a single outlet? Explain.
6. **ANALYZE:** What can happen if too many appliances are connected to one wall outlet?

HEALTH AND SAFETY TIP

A bolt of lightning can heat the air around it to a temperature hotter than the surface of the Sun! During a lightning storm, if you cannot go indoors, make sure that you stay away from tall buildings and trees. Avoid metal objects, such as baseball bats and even metal umbrellas. Do not go swimming or play in an open field. Why should you not stand under a tree during a lightning storm?

Science and Technology
PACEMAKERS

Heart muscle responds to electrical signals. These signals are used to control the rate of the heart's rhythm. The natural pacemaker of the heart is a small amount of tissue that generates electric charge. This charge spreads through the chambers of the heart to keep them pumping or beating in a repeated rhythm. If this natural pacemaker stops working properly, the normal functions of the body are interrupted. A surgeon may have to insert an artificial pacemaker to keep the heart pumping normally.

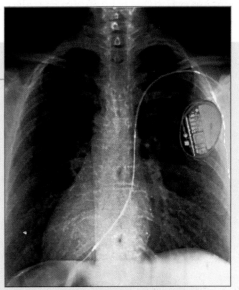

▲ **Figure 20-32** An artificial pacemaker is inserted near the heart.

Artificial pacemakers contain a battery. The battery sends electric charges through a wire inserted into a vein that leads to the heart. The heart muscle responds to these weak electrical charges in the same way that it would to a natural pacemaker. Without electric charges to regulate its pumping rhythm, the heart may beat irregularly. An irregular heartbeat can lead to a heart attack.

Thinking Critically How does an artificial pacemaker work?

Integrating History

THE Big IDEA

How have electrical inventions changed history?

If you have ever switched on a lightbulb, listened to recorded music, or watched a movie, you have used a device that runs on electricity. Benjamin Franklin first investigated electricity in the mid 1700s. Now, electricity is a very important source of energy.

The use of electricity has changed history throughout the world. Homes, businesses, and schools all depend on appliances that are powered by electricity. Many of the inventions that use electricity are the products of a famous inventor, Thomas Alva Edison.

Thomas Edison received more than 1,000 patents. Some of these patents were for his own inventions, such as the phonograph, the first practical electric lightbulb, motion picture technology, and the alkaline storage battery. The other patents were for devices that he improved upon, such as the telephone, the typewriter, the stock ticker, and the printing telegraph.

These inventions, and many others, have had a lasting influence on the world. Because of these many devices that run on electricity, our lives are made easier and more enjoyable. We are able to communicate faster and more easily. We can do more work and perform it faster. We can enjoy music and movies. We can travel safer and faster, and our homes are also filled with electrical devices that make our lives more comfortable.

Learn about some of Thomas Edison's inventions that appear on these two pages. Then follow the directions in the Science Log

Figure 20-33 ▶
Thomas Alva Edison (1847–1931) This American inventor applied for a patent every two weeks during his working career.

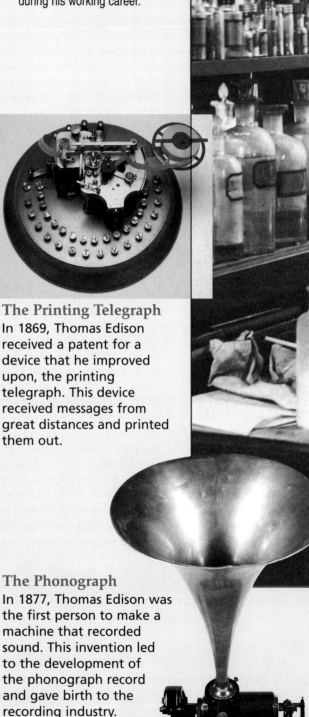

The Printing Telegraph
In 1869, Thomas Edison received a patent for a device that he improved upon, the printing telegraph. This device received messages from great distances and printed them out.

The Phonograph
In 1877, Thomas Edison was the first person to make a machine that recorded sound. This invention led to the development of the phonograph record and gave birth to the recording industry.

Science Log

Thomas Edison invented devices that he thought were needed by people. Brainstorm about devices that you think people have a need for. In your science log, design one of these devices. Describe it and make labeled drawings. Research how you would have this device patented. Start your search at www.conceptsandchallenges.com.

The First Practical Lightbulb

In 1879, with the help of skilled assistants, he tested hundreds of materials to create the first practical lightbulb. This lightbulb used a filament made of carbon.

The Kinetoscope

In 1892, Edison and his staff completed work on a device that showed moving pictures. The moving pictures were seen through a wooden box called a kinetoscope.

Chapter Summary

Lesson 20-1
• Atoms have three basic parts: **protons, electrons,** and **neutrons.**

Lesson 20-2
• The two types of **electrochemical cells** are a wet cell and a dry cell.

Lesson 20-3
• A **conductor** allows electric charges to flow easily.
• An **insulator** prevents electric charges from flowing through it easily.

Lesson 20-4
• The flow of charges through a conductor is called **electric current**.
• The two types of electric current are **direct current** (DC) and **alternating current** (AC).

Lesson 20-5
• In a **series circuit,** electric current follows only one path.

Lesson 20-6
• In a **parallel circuit,** the electric current can follow more than one path.

Lesson 20-7
• **Volts, amperes,** and **ohms** are the units used to measure **voltage,** current, and **resistance.**

Lesson 20-8
• **Ohm's law** states that current in a wire is equal to the voltage divided by the resistance.

Lesson 20-9
• Electricity must be used safely.

Key Term Challenges

alternating current (p. 436)
ampere (p. 442)
battery (p. 432)
circuit breaker (p. 446)
conductor (p. 434)
direct current (p. 436)
electric circuit (p. 438)
electric current (p. 436)
electrochemical cell (p. 432)
electrolyte (p. 432)
electron (p. 428)
fuse (p. 446)
insulator (p. 434)
neutron (p. 428)
ohm (p. 442)
Ohm's law (p. 444)
parallel circuit (p. 440)
proton (p. 428)
resistance (p. 442)
series circuit (p. 438)
static electricity (p. 428)
volt (p. 442)
voltage (p. 442)

MATCHING Write the Key Term from above that best matches each description.

1. unit for measuring resistance

2. series of electrochemical cells

3. circuit in which the current follows one path

4. electric current that changes direction at a regular rate

5. unit for measuring electric current

6. emergency switch that opens a circuit if too much current is flowing

7. circuit in which electric current can follow more than one path

FILL IN Write the Key Term from above that best completes each statement.

8. A metal is a good _____ of electricity.

9. Current that flows in the same direction is called _____.

10. According to _____, the current in a closed circuit is equal to the voltage divided by the resistance.

11. The buildup of electrons on an object is called _____.

12. The energy available to move charges through a circuit is called _____.

Content Challenges TEST PREP

MULTIPLE CHOICE Write the letter of the term or phrase that best completes each statement.

1. A battery in a flashlight is an example of
   a. a wet cell.
   b. a dry cell.
   c. alternating current.
   d. a parallel circuit.

2. According to Ohm's law, current is equal to
   a. resistance.
   b. voltage divided by resistance.
   c. resistance multiplied by voltage.
   d. voltage plus resistance.

3. One of the best conductors of electric current is a wire made of
   a. brass.
   b. magnesium.
   c. copper.
   d. rubber.

4. Electric current can follow more than one path in
   a. a series circuit.
   b. an alternating circuit.
   c. a direct circuit.
   d. a parallel circuit.

5. The most common type of current used in homes, offices, and schools is
   a. direct current.
   b. alternating current.
   c. both alternating and direct current.
   d. neither alternating nor direct current.

6. The resistance in a wire will increase if
   a. the thickness of the wire is decreased.
   b. the temperature of the wire is increased.
   c. the length of the wire is increased.
   d. all of the above.

7. If several appliances are connected in series circuit and one of the appliances stops working
   a. none of the appliances will work.
   b. the rest of the appliances will continue to work.
   c. there may be a short circuit.
   d. the current needs to be increased.

8. A circuit breaker is useful in case there is
   a. an overloaded circuit.
   b. not enough current.
   c. not enough voltage.
   d. too much static electricity.

9. Electric current is measured in
   a. volts.
   b. ohms.
   c. amps.
   d. electrons.

10. Most of the circuits in the home are
    a. series circuits.
    b. parallel circuits.
    c. electronic circuits.
    d. short circuits.

TRUE/FALSE Write *true* if the statement is true. If the statement is false, change the underlined term to make the statement true.

11. In a dry cell battery, the electrolyte is a <u>dry</u> paste.

12. Current can flow only in a <u>closed</u> circuit.

13. A <u>circuit breaker</u> is used to turn a circuit on or off.

14. In a <u>parallel</u> circuit, the current follows only one path.

Concept Challenges TEST PREP

WRITTEN RESPONSE Answer each of the following questions in complete sentences.

1. **HYPOTHESIZE:** During a storm, a power line falls from its pole. Is it safe to touch the wires? Explain.

2. **ANALYZE:** A string of decorative lights goes out when one bulb stops working. Are the lights connected in a series circuit or a parallel circuit? How do you know?

3. **CALCULATE:** Which circuit has more current? **a.** voltage = 12 volts, resistance = 2 ohms **b.** voltage = 32 volts, resistance = 6 ohms **c.** voltage = 24 volts, resistance = 8 ohms

4. **ANALYZE:** How is lightning an example of static discharge?

INTERPRETING VISUALS Use Figure 20-34 to answer the following questions.

5. What kind of circuit is shown in the diagram?

6. What are the four parts of this circuit?

7. If you were to connect a lightbulb in the circuit, what would happen to the resistance of the circuit?

8. If the voltage was increased to 18 volts, what would be the new value for I?

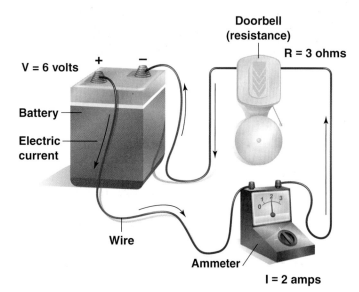

▲ **Figure 20-34** A circuit diagram

Chapter 21 Magnetism

▲ **Figure 21-1** The aurora over the North Pole

The beautiful glow in the sky in Figure 21-1 is not an unusual sight near the North and South poles. The glowing lights are called an aurora. They are caused by particles from the Sun colliding with atoms in Earth's upper atmosphere. Like all objects that have the property of magnetism, Earth has magnetic poles. These magnetic poles produce a magnetic field around Earth. Earth's magnetic field prevents many of the particles from the Sun from entering Earth's atmosphere.

►How does the magnetic field around Earth protect it?

Contents

21-1 What is a magnet?

Objective
Describe the properties of a magnet.

Key Terms
magnetism: force of attraction or repulsion
pole: end of a magnet

Magnetism When you hold a magnet close to certain types of metals, the metals move toward the magnet. The metals are pulled toward the magnet by a force called magnetism. **Magnetism** is a force of attraction or repulsion by magnetic materials.

Not all matter is attracted to a magnet. For example, if you hold a magnet near a piece of wood, the wood will not be attracted to the magnet. Copper, aluminum, plastics, and glass are other materials that are not attracted to a magnet. Elements that are attracted to a magnet include iron, nickel, and cobalt. Objects made of steel, which is mostly iron, are also attracted to magnets.

◀ **Figure 21-2**
Materials such as iron and steel are attracted to magnets.

 DEFINE: What is magnetism?

Magnetic Poles Each end of a magnet is called a magnetic **pole.** The magnetic forces of a magnet are strongest at its poles. Every magnet has two poles—a north pole (N) and a south pole (S). If you hang a magnet by a string, it will turn until its north pole points north and its south pole points south. Thus, the north pole of a magnet is sometimes called the north-seeking pole and the south pole of a magnet

is sometimes called the south-seeking pole. Magnets always have two poles. Even if a magnet were broken up into tiny pieces, each tiny piece would still have a north pole and a south pole.

 DEFINE: What is a pole?

Properties of a Magnet Magnetic poles behave in the same way that electric charges do when like and unlike charges are brought together. If a north pole of one magnet and a south pole of another magnet are brought together, they will attract each other. The unlike poles of any two magnets always attract each other in the same way that unlike electric charges attract each other.

If the north pole of one magnet is brought near the north pole of another magnet, they will repel, or push away from, each other. Two magnetic south poles will also repel each other. The like poles of any two magnets always repel each other in the same way that like electric charges repel each other.

Unlike poles attract

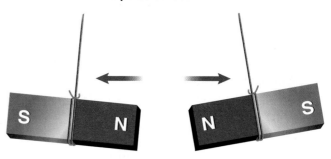

Like poles repel
▲ **Figure 21-3** How magnets behave

DESCRIBE: How do the poles of a magnet affect each other?

Uses of Magnets You may not realize it, but magnets play a very important role in your life. They are used in electric can openers, telephones, doorbells, stereo speakers, electric motors, and alarm systems. Magnets are also used in high-energy particle research and to run special high-speed trains.

 LIST: Name some ways in which magnets are used.

✓ CHECKING CONCEPTS

1. Magnetism is a force of _____ or repulsion by magnetic materials.

2. When hung from a string, the north pole of a magnet points _____.

3. The south pole of a magnet is sometimes called the _____.

4. The north pole of one magnet will _____ the south pole of another magnet.

5. Elements attracted to a magnet are iron, _____, and cobalt.

6. If you cut a magnet in half, each half will have a north pole and a _____.

💡 THINKING CRITICALLY

7. **INFER:** Why could the north pole of a magnet be called the north-seeking pole?

8. **DESCRIBE:** Describe what will happen if you bring the north pole of one magnet near the north pole of another magnet.

9. **ANALYZE:** How are magnets similar to electric charges?

10. **INFER:** How do you think a magnet is used in an electric can opener?

DESIGNING AN EXPERIMENT

Design an experiment to solve the following problem. Include a hypothesis, variables, a procedure, and a type of data to study.

PROBLEM: A homeowner has a door that she wants to keep slightly open. How can magnets be used to keep the door from shutting?

 How Do They Know That?

MAGNETIC COMPASS

Magnets can be found in nature. Naturally occurring substances with magnetic properties are called natural magnets. The ancient Greeks found natural deposits of magnetic iron ore. They discovered this ore in a region of Turkey known as Magnesia. The ore is called magnetite (MAG-nuh-tyt). Magnetite can also be found in many other parts of the world.

▲ **Figure 21-4** Sailors once used magnetic compasses.

Magnetite was used by sailors and navigators to find directions at sea. Pieces of magnetite were called lodestone, because sailors found that a piece of magnetite always pointed toward the North Star. The North Star was called the lodestar, or leading star. Sailors made magnetic compasses with a pointer made of lodestone.

Today, magnetic compasses are often used by hikers and backpackers. The pointer of a magnetic compass always points north. Once you know where north is, you can easily locate the other three directions, or compass points.

Thinking Critically If a hiker is trying to hike in an easterly direction, would a compass be of any help to the hiker? Explain your answer.

21-2 What causes magnetism?

INVESTIGATE

Finding the Pole of a Magnet
HANDS-ON ACTIVITY

1. Cover the pole markings of a bar magnet with masking tape. Tie one end of a piece of string around the center of the magnet. Tape the other end of the string to the edge of your desk or table. Allow the magnet to hang from your desk or table.

2. Use another bar magnet to determine the poles of the hanging magnet.

THINK ABOUT IT: How did you determine the poles of the hanging magnet?

STEP 1

Objective
Demonstrate the shape of a magnetic field.

Key Terms
magnetic field: describes the region of magnetic force around a magnet

magnetic lines of force: lines that show the shape of a magnetic field

magnetic domain: groups of atoms whose magnetic poles are all lined up in the same direction

Magnetic Field If you bring a magnet close to an iron object, the magnetic force will attract the object. The magnet does not need to touch the object in order for the magnetic force to attract it. This attraction happens because every magnet has a magnetic field around it. The **magnetic field** describes the region of magnetic force around a magnet.

The magnetic fields around different magnets are not the same. Some magnets may have a stronger magnetic field than others do. Figure 21-5 shows the magnetic field around a bar magnet. Iron filings have been sprinkled over the bar magnet. The iron filings line up around the magnet showing the shape of the magnet's magnetic field.

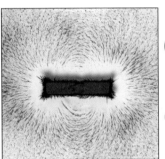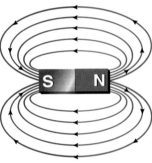

▲ **Figure 21-5** Iron filings sprinkled on plastic covering a bar magnet line up along the magnetic lines of force around the magnet.

 DEFINE: What is a magnetic field?

Magnetic Lines of Force A magnetic field is made up of **magnetic lines of force.** When iron filings are sprinkled around a magnet, they will line up along the magnetic lines of force. Magnetic lines of force always begin at one pole and end at the opposite pole. They are also closest together at the poles because the magnetic field is strongest at the poles.

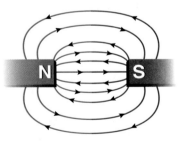

▲ **Figure 21-6** Magnetic lines of force show that unlike poles attract.

The magnetic lines of force between two like poles can be seen in Figure 21-7. The lines of force show that two like poles repel each other. The lines of force from the north pole of each magnet are bent away from the north pole of the other magnet.

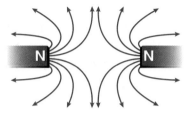

▲ **Figure 21-7** Magnetic lines of force show that like poles repel.

Two unlike poles attract each other. The lines of force from the north pole of one magnet bend toward the south pole of the other magnet.

 DESCRIBE: What do the magnetic lines of force show?

Magnetic Domains All matter is made up of atoms. The motion of electrons causes all atoms to have magnetic properties. In magnetic materials such as iron, groups of atoms can join together so that the magnetic fields of each atom point in the same direction. The north poles of all atoms point in the same direction. The south poles of all atoms point in the opposite direction. Groups of atoms whose magnetic poles are all lined up in the same direction are called **magnetic domains.**

Most of the magnetic domains of magnetic materials point in the same direction. However, the domains of unmagnetized materials point in different directions. Because the domains point in different directions, their magnetic fields cancel each other.

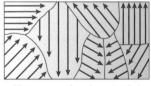

Unmagnetized material

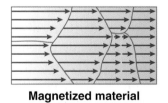

Magnetized material

▲ **Figure 21-8** The domains of unmagnetized materials point in different directions. The domains of magnetized materials point in the same direction.

DEFINE: What is a magnetic domain?

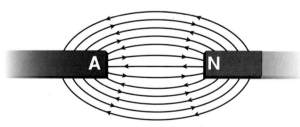

▲ **Figure 21-9** Magnetic lines of force around two magnets

Go **O**nline
active art

For: Magnetic Field Lines activity
Visit: PHSchool.com
Web Code: cgp-4011

21-3 How can you make a magnet?

Objectives
Explain how materials can be magnetized. Compare permanent magnets and temporary magnets.

Key Term
magnetic induction: process by which a material can be made into a magnet

Natural Magnets Some magnets occur in nature. These magnets are called natural magnets. Magnetite, or lodestone, is an example of a natural magnet. Certain materials that are not natural magnets can be made into magnets, or magnetized (MAG-nuh-tyzd). For example, rubbing an iron nail with a magnet in one direction will magnetize the nail. The magnetized nail will have the same properties as a natural magnet.

▲ **Figure 21-10** Magnetite, or lodestone, is a natural magnet.

▶ 1 NAME: What is an example of a natural magnet?

Magnetic Induction The process by which a material is magnetized, or made into a magnet, is called **magnetic induction.** In magnetic induction, the domains of certain materials are made to point in the same direction. They become magnetized. Some materials are easier to magnetize than others. Alloys of iron, nickel, and cobalt are easy to magnetize. Rubbing objects made of these materials with a magnet can cause the domains within the

objects to point in the same direction. When this happens, these materials become magnetized. Other materials show weak magnetic properties. For example, if an aluminum object is placed in the magnetic field of a strong magnet, the atoms of the metal may be weakly affected by the magnetism. However, when the object is removed from the magnetic field, the domains will go back to pointing in different directions.

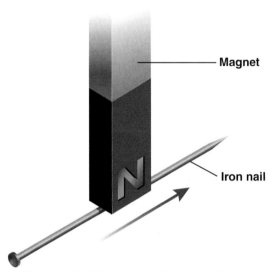

Magnet

Iron nail

▲ **Figure 21-11** Magnetic induction causes the iron nail to become magnetized.

▶ 2 DEFINE: What is magnetic induction?

Temporary and Permanent Magnets Once a material is magnetized, it may or may not remain magnetized. Iron is easily magnetized, but the iron loses its magnetism quickly. A material that is easily magnetized tends to lose its magnetism quickly. A magnet made of this kind of material is called a temporary magnet.

Materials that are hard to magnetize can stay magnetized for a long time. A piece of steel is harder to magnetize than a piece of iron. However, the steel will keep its magnetic properties much longer than will a piece of iron. A magnet that is hard to magnetize but tends to keep its magnetism is called a permanent magnet.

▶ 3 CLASSIFY: Is an iron magnet a temporary magnet or a permanent magnet?

Losing Magnetism All magnets, even permanent magnets, can lose their magnetism. If you drop a magnet, you can cause the magnetic domains inside of it to stop pointing in the same direction. When the magnetic domains point in different directions, the magnet loses some or all of its magnetic properties. Heating a magnet can also cause it to become demagnetized. The energy from the heat can cause the atoms to move faster and farther apart. When this happens, the magnetic domains are no longer aligned.

 EXPLAIN: What are two ways in which a magnet can become demagnetized?

 CHECKING CONCEPTS

1. An example of a natural magnet is _____.

2. Rubbing an iron nail in the same direction with a magnet will _____ the nail.

3. When a piece of iron becomes magnetized, the magnetic _____ point in the same direction.

4. A _____ magnet is hard to magnetize.

5. A _____ magnet will not keep its magnetic properties for a long time.

6. All magnets can lose their _____.

7. Dropping a magnet can cause its _____ to point in different directions.

THINKING CRITICALLY

8. **INFER:** An iron nail has been magnetized. Does the magnetized nail have a north pole and a south pole? Explain.

9. **CONTRAST:** What is the difference between a temporary magnet and a permanent magnet?

10. **PREDICT:** Soft iron is very easy to magnetize. Will soft iron make a good permanent magnet? Why or why not?

11. **EXPLAIN:** How does dropping a magnet affect the magnetic domains within the magnet?

BUILDING SOCIAL STUDIES SKILLS

Researching The properties of the ore magnetite have been known for more than 2,000 years. The ancient Chinese may have discovered the properties of magnetite as early as 2600 B.C. Use library references, encyclopedias, and the Internet to find out how the ancient Chinese used magnetite and how they explained its properties in stories and myths.

Hands-On Activity

MAKING A MAGNETIC COMPASS

▲ **STEP 4** Observe in which direction the needle points.

You will need a sewing needle, a bar magnet, a pushpin, a cork, a small plastic container of water, and a magnetic compass.

1. Insert the pushpin into the bottom of the cork.

2. Float the cork, with the pushpin pointing down, in a container of water.

3. Rub the magnet against the needle about 20 times. Rub in one direction only.

4. Lay the needle on top of the cork. Observe in which directions the needle points when it stops turning. Using a magnetic compass away from your setup, compare the direction of the needle with the direction of the compass pointer.

Practicing Your Skills

5. **DESCRIBE:** What effect does rubbing with a magnet have on the needle?

6. **OBSERVE:** In which directions does the floating needle point?

21-4 How is Earth like a magnet?

Objective

Explain how Earth acts like a magnet.

Key Term

magnetosphere (mag-NEET-uh-sfeer)**:** region of Earth's magnetic field

William Gilbert In the early 1600s, British scientist William Gilbert made several observations about magnetism. Gilbert observed that if you hang a bar magnet from a string, one pole of the magnet always points north and the other pole always points south. William Gilbert was the first person to suggest an explanation for this observation. He proposed that Earth itself is a magnet, and just like any magnet, Earth has a north pole and a south pole.

▶ **1** **STATE:** How did Gilbert's proposal compare Earth to a magnet?

Earth's Magnetic Poles Scientists have discovered that William Gilbert's proposal was correct. Earth does act as if a huge bar magnet were buried deep inside it. This causes Earth to have two magnetic poles. One of Earth's magnetic poles is near the geographic North Pole in Canada. The other magnetic pole is near the geographic South Pole in Antarctica. The magnetic poles of Earth are not exactly at Earth's geographic poles. In fact, the magnetic pole near Earth's geographic North Pole is about 1,300 kilometers away from it.

▶ **2** **EXPLAIN:** Where are Earth's magnetic poles in relation to Earth's geographic poles?

Earth's Magnetic Poles Are Not Earth's Geographic Poles You have learned that the north pole of a magnet always points north. However, like magnetic poles repel each other. This means that when a magnet points to the geographic North Pole, the North Pole is near Earth's magnetic south pole. It also means that when the south pole of a magnet faces Earth's

geographic South Pole, the South Pole must be Earth's magnetic north pole. Figure 21-12 shows Earth's magnetic poles and geographic poles.

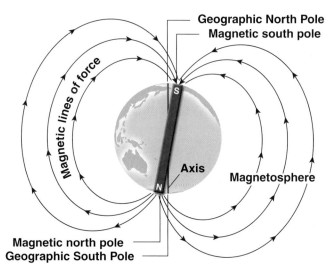

Geographic North Pole
Magnetic south pole
Magnetic lines of force
Axis
Magnetosphere
Magnetic north pole
Geographic South Pole

▲ **Figure 21-12** Earth's magnetic poles are not the same as Earth's geographic poles.

▶ **3** **INFER:** Why is Earth's geographic North Pole called the magnetic south pole?

The Magnetosphere Like any magnet, Earth is surrounded by a magnetic field. The magnetic field is strongest near the north and south magnetic poles. Earth's magnetic field extends far into space. The magnetic field around Earth is called the **magnetosphere.**

The magnetosphere traps charged particles released by the Sun. Most of these particles are deflected by the magnetosphere. However, some particles do get through it. When these charged particles hit Earth's atmosphere, they interact with other particles, causing the air above Earth's surface to glow. This glowing area is called an aurora (uh-RAWR-uh).

Auroras seen in the Northern Hemisphere near the North Pole are also called the northern lights or aurora borealis. Auroras seen in the Southern Hemisphere near the South Pole are called the southern lights, or aurora australis.

▲ **Figure 21-13** The southern lights are caused by particles from the Sun interacting with particles in Earth's atmosphere.

 DEFINE: What is the magnetosphere?

 CHECKING CONCEPTS

1. When a compass points north, it is pointing to Earth's magnetic _____ pole.
2. Earth's magnetic south pole attracts the _____ pole of a magnet.

3. Earth's geographic North Pole is near Earth's magnetic _____ pole.
4. Earth is surrounded by a magnetic field called the _____.

 THINKING CRITICALLY

5. **CLASSIFY:** Is Earth a permanent magnet or a temporary magnet? How do you know?
6. **INFER:** Explain why auroras occur in both the Northern Hemisphere and the Southern Hemisphere.

BUILDING SCIENCE SKILLS

Making a Model The Sun produces a stream of high-energy particles called solar wind. Solar wind causes the magnetosphere to form into a special shape. Find out the shape of the magnetosphere. Then, use markers and poster board to make a model of it. Share your illustration with your class.

How Do They Know That?

THE HISTORY OF EARTH'S MAGNETISM IN ROCKS

Scientists have found that Earth acts like a giant magnet. The magnetism comes from deep within the planet. Earth's center, or core, is surrounded by hot liquid metal. As the liquid metal flows, it produces a magnetic field. The flowing liquid metal around the core changes over time. These changes cause Earth's magnetic field to change with it. In fact, every few thousand years, the magnetic field of the Earth reverses itself. Geologists discovered this fact by studying the magnetic fields in certain rocks.

▲ **Figure 21-14** Volcanic rock contains magnetic stripes that can be detected by special instruments.

Rocks containing the metal iron can become permanent magnets when they form. These magnetic rocks can form inside volcanoes. As lava from the volcano cools, Earth's magnetic field pulls on the magnetic materials in the rock. The magnetic materials in the rock line up to match the magnetic field of Earth at the time the rock formed.

Geologists study the magnetic patterns inside these rocks. Special instruments are used to study these rocks because the magnetic patterns cannot be seen with the unaided eye. From the magnetic patterns in many of the rocks, scientists have learned about the reversals of Earth's magnetic field. A reversal of Earth's magnetic field occurs every few thousand years.

Thinking Critically How can magnetic rocks reveal that Earth's magnetic field reverses itself?

21-5 How are electricity and magnetism related?

INVESTIGATE

Observing Magnetism and Electricity
HANDS-ON ACTIVITY

1. Note in what direction the pointer of a magnetic compass points.
2. Connect two insulated wires to a dry cell (size D) battery and a lightbulb in a holder.
3. When the lightbulb lights up, carefully bring the compass near the wires. Observe the pointer of the compass.

THINK ABOUT IT: What happens to the pointer of the compass?

STEP 3

Objective

Explain the relationship between electricity and magnetism.

Key Terms

electromagnetism: relationship between electricity and magnetism

electromagnetic induction: process by which an electric current is produced by moving a wire in a magnetic field

Oersted's Discovery Have you ever used a magnetic compass around an electrical device? If you have, you may have noticed that the pointer of the compass gets "confused." The pointer may no longer point north. This happens because of the relationship between electricity and magnetism. This relationship is called **electromagnetism.** The Danish scientist Hans Christian Oersted (UR-sted) was the first person to show that this relationship does exist.

More than 150 years ago, Oersted discovered an important property of electric current. Oersted connected a simple series circuit made up of a battery and a wire. As charges flowed through the wire, Oersted noticed that a nearby compass pointer moved. When the circuit was disconnected, the compass pointer returned to its original position. He also noticed that when the direction of the current was reversed, the pointer moved in the opposite

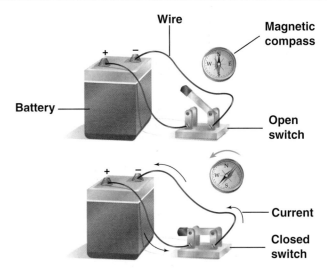

▲ Figure 21-15 When electric current flows through a circuit, a magnetic field is produced.

direction. Hans Christian Oersted discovered that an electric current produces a magnetic field.

▶ **DESCRIBE:** What did Hans Christian Oersted discover?

Electromagnetic Induction An electric current produces a magnetic field. Does a magnetic field produce an electric current? A British scientist named Michael Faraday tried to answer this question. He hung a wire that remained still. Then he moved a strong magnet around it. He found that when the magnet was held still, no electric current moved through the wire. However, when he moved the magnet toward and away from the wire continuously, electric charges flowed through the wire. He also noticed that the direction of the current depended upon the direction of the movement of the magnet.

Faraday also tried moving a wire coil around a stationary magnet and got the same results. Thus, Faraday found that electric current will be produced in a wire that is exposed to a changing magnetic field. The process by which an electric current is produced when a wire is exposed to a changing magnetic field is called **electromagnetic induction.** The current is induced, or caused to flow, in a wire when the wire cuts across magnetic lines of force.

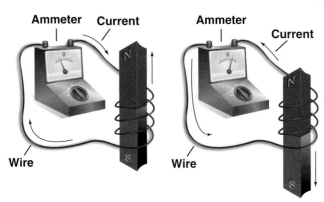

▲ **Figure 21-16** In electromagnetic induction, electric current is produced in a wire by a changing magnetic field.

 DEFINE: What is electromagnetic induction?

1. Oersted discovered that an _____ caused a magnetic field.

2. An electric current is produced when a wire is exposed to a _____ magnetic field.

3. Faraday discovered electromagnetic _____.

4. Electromagnetism is the relationship between _____ and magnetism.

THINKING CRITICALLY

5. **DESCRIBE:** What determines the direction of electric current in a wire when a magnet is moved around the wire?

6. **EXPLAIN:** What happens to a nearby compass when you disconnect a circuit?

7. **EXPLAIN:** Why will an electric current not be produced in a wire that is exposed to a stationary magnetic field?

 People in Science

JOSEPH HENRY (1797–1878)

Joseph Henry was an American scientist. He studied electricity and magnetism. He and the British scientist Michael Faraday made similar discoveries at about the same time. Henry discovered that a changing magnetic field will induce a current in a conductor. However, Faraday is given credit for making the same discovery.

Henry was born in Albany, New York, on December 17, 1797. He helped Samuel Morse develop the telegraph. In 1831, Henry built a telegraph of his own. He also built one of the most powerful devices known at the time. Henry's device used electromagnetism to lift more than a ton of weight.

▲ **Figure 21-17** Joseph Henry

In 1846, Henry was appointed to head the Smithsonian Institution in Washington, D.C. He was also the main organizer of the National Academy of Science and started the U.S. Weather Service. In honor of Henry, the unit for electromagnetic induction is called the henry.

Thinking Critically Why is the unit for electromagnetism called the henry?

21-6 What is an electromagnet?

Objective

Describe how to make an electromagnet.

Key Term

electromagnet: temporary magnet made by wrapping a current-carrying wire around a metal core

---

Magnetic Field Strength A wire carrying an electric current always has a magnetic field around it. The magnetic field around a straight wire is not very strong. If the wire is wound into a coil, the magnetic field becomes much stronger. The magnetic fields around each coil of wire add together. The more turns you add to the coil, the stronger the magnetic field will become. Increasing the amount of current running through the wire will also increase the magnetic field around the wire.

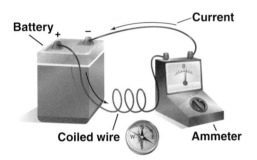

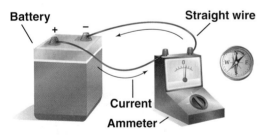

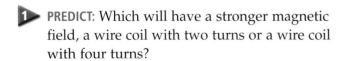

▲ **Figure 21-18** The compasses show that strength of the magnetic field around a coiled wire is stronger than the strength of the magnetic field around a straight wire.

1 ▶ PREDICT: Which will have a stronger magnetic field, a wire coil with two turns or a wire coil with four turns?

Electromagnets The strength of the magnetic field around a wire can be increased by adding turns to the wire coil and by increasing the amount of current flowing through the wire. However, wrapping coils of wire around a piece of metal, such as iron, will produce the greatest strength in the magnetic field around the wire. The magnetic field around the wire aligns the magnetic domains within the piece of iron. The strength of the magnetic field around the coiled wire and the strength of the magnetic field around the iron add together.

When electric current flows through a coil of wire that is wrapped around an iron core, a strong magnet is produced. This type of magnet is called an **electromagnet.** The magnetic material in the center of an electromagnet is called a core. An electromagnet is a temporary magnet. As long as current is flowing through the wire, the electromagnet has a strong magnetic field. When the current is turned off, there is no longer a magnetic field.

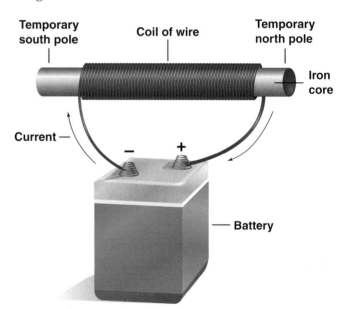

▲ **Figure 21-19** An electromagnet is made up of an energy source, a wire coil, and a metal core.

The strength of an electromagnet can be increased in two ways. Adding more turns to the wire coil around the magnetic core makes an electromagnet stronger. Increasing the current through the wire also makes an electromagnet stronger.

2 ▶ INFER: What are two ways to make an electromagnet stronger?

Uses of Electromagnets Electromagnets have many important uses. They are used in devices, such as radios, telephones, and computers. Large electromagnets are used to lift heavy pieces of metal. Electromagnets are very useful because they can be turned on and off.

▲ **Figure 21-20** Electromagnets can be used to lift heavy objects.

 EXPLAIN: Why are electromagnets so useful?

 CHECKING CONCEPTS

1. What is an electromagnet?
2. Why is an electromagnet considered to be a temporary magnet?
3. What are two ways to increase the strength of the magnetic field around a wire?
4. Name three devices that use electromagnets.

THINKING CRITICALLY

5. **CONTRAST:** How is an electromagnet different from a permanent magnet?
6. **LIST:** What are the materials needed to make an electromagnet?

INTERPRETING VISUALS

Look at Figure 21-19 of an electromagnet to answer the following questions.

7. **PREDICT:** What would happen if you were to disconnect the wires from the dry cell?
8. **ANALYZE:** What would happen if there were fewer coils wrapped around the metal core?

 Hands-On Activity

MAKING AN ELECTROMAGNET

You will need paper clips, a D-cell battery, a 6-volt battery, insulated wire, and an ungalvanized nail.

1. Wrap 20 turns of wire around an ungalvanized nail. Connect the ends of the wire to the terminals of the D-cell battery.
2. Try to pick up some paper clips.
3. Now, wrap 40 turns of wire around the nail. Connect the ends of the wire to the same battery. See how many paper clips you can pick up.
4. Connect the electromagnet with 40 turns of wire to the 6-volt battery. See how many paper clips you can pick up.

▲ **STEP 4** Pick up paper clips with your electromagnet.

Practicing Your Skills

5. **OBSERVE:** How many paper clips did the electromagnet with 20 turns of wire connected to the D-cell battery pick up? With 40 turns?
6. **COMPARE:** Were you able to pick up more paper clips when the electromagnet was connected to the D-cell battery or to the 6-volt battery? Explain.

21-7 What is a transformer?

Objectives

Explain how a transformer works. Compare a step-up and a step-down transformer.

Key Term

transformer: device in which alternating current in one coil of wire induces a current in a second coil of wire

Transformers Suppose you wrap two coils of wire around a nail. You attach one of the coils to a dry cell and a switch. This coil is called the primary coil. You connect the other coil to an ammeter. This is the secondary coil. When you close the switch in the primary coil, the ammeter shows that a current flows in the secondary coil. This current quickly dies out. When you open the switch, current again flows in the secondary coil. Again, it quickly dies out. To keep current flowing to the secondary coil, you must keep opening and closing the switch.

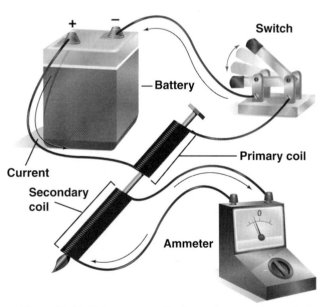

▲ **Figure 21-21** To keep current flowing to the secondary coil, the switch has to be opened and closed over and over again.

A **transformer** is a device that uses alternating current in the primary coil to induce a current in the secondary coil. The primary coil is connected to a source of alternating current.

▶ **DEFINE:** What is a transformer?

Step-Up Transformers A transformer can be used to increase the voltage of alternating current. This kind of transformer is called a step-up transformer. A step-up transformer has more turns of wire in the secondary coil than in the primary coil. The more turns of wire there are in the secondary coil, the higher the voltage will be. Power companies use step-up transformers to produce high-voltage electricity to send over long distances.

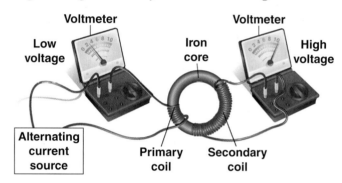

▲ **Figure 21-22** A step-up transformer has fewer coils in the primary coil than in the secondary coil.

▶ **DESCRIBE:** What does a step-up transformer do?

Step-Down Transformers A transformer can also decrease the voltage of alternating current. A transformer that decreases voltage is called a step-down transformer. A step-down transformer has fewer turns of wire in the secondary coil than in the primary coil. The fewer the turns of wire in the secondary coil, the lower the voltage will be. Step-down transformers lower the high voltage carried by power lines.

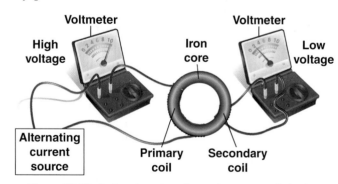

▲ **Figure 21-23** A step-down transformer has more coils in the primary coil than in the secondary coil.

▶ **EXPLAIN:** What does a step-down transformer do?

Transmission of Electricity Power plants use transformers to send electricity to homes, businesses, and schools. Very often, power plants are located in areas far away from where electricity is needed. Electricity has to travel long distances to reach these areas. At power plants, electricity is produced at low voltage. However, when electricity travels long distances, there is a loss of energy. By using a step-up transformer, power companies are able to send high-voltage electricity over long distances without too much loss of energy. Because electricity is usually used at a lower voltage, step-down transformers lower the voltage before the electricity is sent into homes, businesses, and schools.

 INFER: When is a step-down transformer used?

 CHECKING CONCEPTS

1. What is a transformer?
2. Which coil of a transformer is attached to a source of current?

3. What kind of transformer can be used to increase voltage?
4. What kind of transformer can be used to decrease voltage?

 THINKING CRITICALLY

5. CONTRAST: What is the difference between a step-up transformer and a step-down transformer?

BUILDING SCIENCE SKILLS

Investigating The voltage from a wall outlet in your home is 120 volts. Unplug and look at several appliances around your home. How much voltage do they need to operate? The voltage is usually given on the appliance or in the owner's manual. Which appliances need less than 120 volts? Which need more than 120 volts? Do the appliances use step-down or step-up transformers?

Real-Life Science

BIRDS ON A WIRE

High-voltage electricity is transmitted through electric power lines. The voltage can range from about 7,200 to 800,000 volts. Electricity that escapes from these lines can do great damage. Sparks from fallen lines can cause fires.

You should never go near power lines. You can be seriously injured if enough electricity passes through your body. Power workers who repair power lines have to wear protective clothing when they work on the lines.

▲ **Figure 21-24** Birds do not form a circuit with the electricity in a power line.

Yet, birds can sit on power lines all day long without getting hurt. Why are birds not in danger when they sit on electric power lines?

The answer is that birds do not form a circuit with the electricity in the power lines. Because they are not connected to the ground or another wire, current never flows through their bodies. Electric current stays in the wire. As long as a bird's body is only in contact with a line at the same voltage, it is safe. However, if a bird extends its wing and touches another wire at a different voltage, it would get a shock. Also, if a bird's wing touched a tree while it was sitting on a power line, it would get a shock.

Thinking Critically Why would a bird get shocked if its wing touched another wire at a different voltage?

21-8 What is an electric motor?

Objective

Explain how an electric motor works.

Key Term

electric motor: device that changes electrical energy into mechanical energy

Reversing Magnetic Poles By changing the direction of an electric current running through an electromagnet, you can reverse the poles of the electromagnet. Suppose that you connect an electromagnet to a dry cell. As the current flows, one end of the electromagnet becomes a north pole. The other end becomes a south pole. You can use a compass to identify the poles. What will happen if you switch the connections to the dry cell? The direction of the current will be reversed. The magnetic poles of the electromagnet will also be reversed. The compass will indicate the new magnetic poles.

1 ▶ PREDICT: What will happen to the poles of an electromagnet if you change the direction of the electric current?

Electric Motor The ability to reverse the poles of an electromagnet explains how an electric motor works. An **electric motor** changes electrical energy into mechanical energy. You learned earlier that mechanical energy is the energy of motion.

An electric motor is a device made up of an electromagnet, a permanent magnet, and a source of alternating current. The electromagnet is free to rotate. It is attached to a source of alternating current. When current flows, the poles of the electromagnet are attracted to the opposite poles of the permanent magnet. As the direction of the current changes, the poles of the electromagnet are reversed. The poles of the electromagnet are now repelled by the like poles of the permanent magnet. This repulsion causes the electromagnet to rotate.

Attraction and repulsion between the electromagnet and the permanent magnet cause the electromagnet to rotate. As long as alternating current is supplied, the electromagnet rotates continuously. The mechanical energy of the rotating magnet enables the motor to do work. The rotating magnet can be connected to a device such as a fan or a wheel.

2 ▶ INFER: How does an electric motor change electrical energy into mechanical energy?

Reversing Direct Current If direct current were used to run an electric motor, the electromagnet would not rotate continuously. Because the direction of the current would not change, the poles of the electromagnet would not reverse.

However, direct current can be used to run an electric motor if a special switch is used. This switch, called a commutator, reverses the direction of the current. Constantly reversing the direction of the current will cause the electromagnet to rotate.

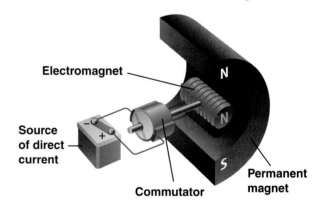

Electromagnet — N
Source of direct current
Commutator
Permanent magnet

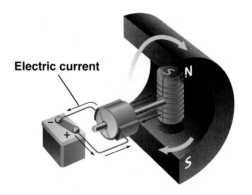

Electric current

▲ **Figure 21-25** An electric motor at rest (top). When current flows (bottom), attraction and repulsion between the permanent magnet and the electromagnet cause the electromagnet to rotate. A commutator reverses the direct current to keep the electromagnet rotating.

3 ▶ INFER: What is the purpose of a commutator?

Uses of Electric Motors Many electrical appliances have electric motors. Electric fans, food processors, and refrigerators all use electric motors. There are many kinds of electric motors that are designed for specific uses. All electric motors have one thing in common. They all use the force of magnetism to change electrical energy into useful mechanical energy.

▲ **Figure 21-26** Electric toys use electric motors to run.

 EXPLAIN: Why does an electrical appliance need a motor?

 CHECKING CONCEPTS

1. The poles of an electromagnet are reversed when the _____ of an electric current is changed.

2. An electric motor changes electrical energy into _____ energy.

3. An electric motor contains an electromagnet and a _____ magnet.

4. The _____ in an electric motor is free to rotate.

THINKING CRITICALLY

5. **EXPLAIN:** Explain how an electric motor uses magnetism.

DESIGNING AN EXPERIMENT

Design an experiment to solve the following problem. Include a hypothesis, variables, a procedure, and a type of data to study.

PROBLEM: How can you design a toy or tool that uses an electric motor to run?

 People in Science

AUTOMOBILE MECHANIC

An automobile engine is a complex machine. It is made up of a motor, a battery, a generator, and many other electrical parts. Many jobs for automobile mechanics are available in automobile service stations, government installations, or in the service departments of automobile dealerships.

▲ **Figure 21-27** An automobile mechanic maintains and repairs different parts of a car.

Automobile mechanics are trained to inspect, maintain, and repair the mechanical and electrical parts in different types of automobiles. They install and replace parts, adjust brakes, and use computers to check different parts of a car. Beginning mechanics get on-the-job training. Some receive classroom instruction together with hands-on practice. They may also work with an experienced mechanic. Specialty mechanics may work on only one part of a car's engine.

To be an automobile mechanic, you should graduate from high school and then complete a formal training program in automotive repair. Good reading, mathematics, and computer skills are usually required.

Thinking Critically Why do you think an automobile mechanic should have computer skills?

LAB ACTIVITY
Making an Electric Motor

BACKGROUND

Magnetism and electricity are closely related. Many devices you use every day, such as radios, CD players, and vacuum cleaners, depend on this relationship. How can this relationship be demonstrated?

PURPOSE

You will construct a simple electric motor.

PROCEDURE

1. Copy the chart shown in Figure 21-28. Put on goggles and an apron.

2. Starting about 8 cm from one end of a piece of magnet wire, wrap the wire around a film canister seven times. Cut the long end of the wire, leaving an 8-cm end free.

3. Slide the coiled wire off the film canister and wrap the two free ends around the coil two or three times to keep the coil from unwinding.

4. Use fine sandpaper to remove all of the insulation from about 3 cm of one end of the wire. Then place the other end of the wire flat on your work surface and sand off the insulation from *half* of the wire for a length of about 3 cm.

5. Using needle-nose pliers, bend two large paper clips to make supports for the coil. First, bend open the paperclip. Then, bend the smaller end down to form a loop. Use electrical tape to attach the paper clips to the ends of a D-cell battery.

6. Place the battery setup on a piece of clay to hold it steady.

Materials

Safety goggles and apron
D-cell battery
Magnet wire, 1 meter
Small film canister
Fine sandpaper
2 large metal paper clips
Ceramic magnet
Wire cutters
Needle-nose pliers
Electrical tape
Modeling clay
Pencil and paper

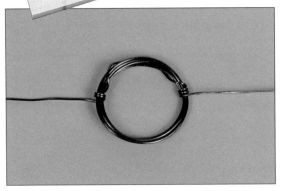

▲ STEP 3 Wrap the coil to keep it from unwinding.

▲ STEP 4 Sand off insulation from half of the wire.

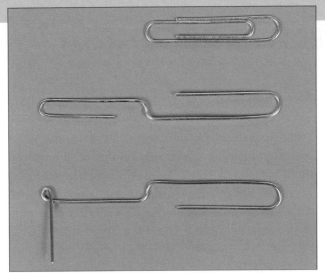

▲ **STEP 5** Bend the paper clip as shown above.

▲ **STEP 8** Your motor should look like this.

7. Place the coil in the cradle formed by the ends of the paper clip.

8. Put the magnet on the table under but not touching the coil.

9. Turn the coil slowly with your hand. Give the coil a gentle push to spin it. Record your observations.

Making an Electric Motor

Experiment	Observations
Turning the coil by hand	
Spinning the coil	

▲ **Figure 21-28** Copy this chart and use it to record your observations.

CONCLUSIONS

1. **INFER:** What is the purpose of the battery and the magnet?

2. **OBSERVE:** What did you feel and observe as you moved the coil by hand?

3. **INFER:** What causes the coil to keep spinning after your initial push?

4. **ANALYZE:** What would happen if you were to increase the number of turns of wire?

5. **HYPOTHESIZE:** Is a circle the best shape? Do you think that an oval or square would be better? Give reasons for your answers.

21-9 What is an electric generator?

Objective

Explain how an electric generator works.

Key Term

electric generator: device that changes mechanical energy into electrical energy

Induced Current A current can be induced in a loop of wire by spinning the loop inside a magnetic field. Remember that an electric current is induced when a wire cuts across magnetic lines of force. Figure 21-29 shows a loop of wire in a magnetic field. The loop is spinning clockwise. As the wire moves across the magnetic field, it cuts the magnetic lines of force. As a result, current flows through the wire. When the wire moves down through the magnetic field, the current flows in one direction. When the wire moves up, the current flows in the opposite direction. The change in current direction produces an alternating current in the wire.

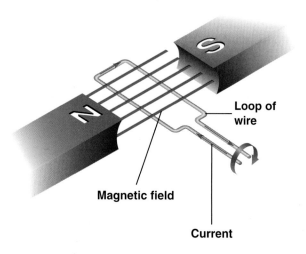

▲ **Figure 21-29** As the loop of wire spins inside the magnetic field of the magnets, alternating current is produced in the wire.

▶ IDENTIFY: What kind of current is induced when a loop of wire spins in a magnetic field?

Electric Generators An **electric generator** is a device that changes mechanical energy into electrical energy. It is the opposite of an electric motor, which changes electrical energy to mechanical energy. An electric generator is made up of an insulated coil of wire and a magnet. The coil of wire is attached to a power source that causes the coil to spin. Spinning the coil of wire in the magnetic field of the magnet exposes the wire to a changing magnetic field. When this happens, electric current is produced in the coil of wire. The mechanical energy used to spin the coil of wire is changed into electrical energy. The ends of the coil of wire can be connected to a load, such as a lightbulb. When electricity runs through the wires, the bulb will light.

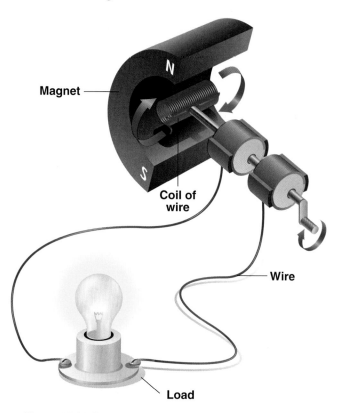

▲ **Figure 21-30** Turning the handle of this generator will cause the coil of wire to spin in the magnetic field of the magnet. An alternating electric current will be produced in the wires. As the current flows through the wires, the lightbulb will light up.

▶ DEFINE: What is an electric generator?

Uses of Generators Most of the electricity you use every day comes from generators. Power plants use large generators to supply electricity to homes, offices, schools, and other buildings. These large generators use very strong magnets and many coils of wire to produce a great amount of energy. The mechanical energy for these generators is supplied by turbines (TUR-bihnz). A turbine is a large wheel that is turned by steam or moving water. The water used to turn a turbine may come from a dam or river. Steam is produced by burning fuels, such as coal or oil, or from nuclear energy.

 NAME: What are two fuels that are burned to make steam for turbines in generators?

✓ CHECKING CONCEPTS

1. What happens when a loop of wire cuts magnetic lines of force?

2. What kind of electric current is induced when a loop of wire turns in a magnetic field?

3. What is a generator?

4. What supplies the mechanical energy in a generator?

5. What is a turbine?

6. Name two sources of energy that are used to make steam for turbines.

💡 THINKING CRITICALLY

7. **CONTRAST:** Explain how a generator is the opposite of an electric motor.

8. **INFER:** What would happen if the coil of wire in a generator stopped spinning?

9. **HYPOTHESIZE:** The mechanical energy used to spin the coil of wire in a generator comes from a turbine. Think of ways in which you could supply the mechanical energy to run a turbine.

Web InfoSearch

Geothermal Energy In some parts of the world, heat inside Earth produces steam and boiling water. This heat is called geothermal (jee-oh-THUR-muhl) energy.

SEARCH: Use the Internet to find out how geothermal power plants use steam and boiling water to spin turbines and generate electricity. Start your search at www.conceptsandchallenges.com. Some key search words are **geothermal energy** and **generators.**

 Science and Technology

ELECTRIC POWER PLANTS

Electric power plants provide electricity for large numbers of people. Electric power plants use generators to produce electricity. Instead of a simple loop of wire spinning in the magnetic field of a magnet, these generators use many coils of wire and strong electromagnets. The spinning wires are connected to a turbine. The energy to spin the turbine comes from steam or moving water.

Some generators use the energy from waterfalls to spin the turbine. These generators are known as hydroelectric (hy-droh-ih-LEHK-trihk) plants. Hydroelectric plants are usually built near dams and reservoirs. Hydroelectric plants provide only a limited amount of power in the United States. The high cost to build them and the damage to the environment that they cause are some reasons why hydroelectric power plants are not a major source of electricity.

Thinking Critically Why are hydroelectric power plants usually built near dams and reservoirs?

▲ Figure 21-31 Moving water spins turbines in this hydroelectric power plant.

Go Online
active art
For: Motors and Generators activity
Visit: PHSchool.com
Web Code: cgp-4033

THE Big IDEA

How does a maglev train work?

Imagine using the power of magnets to make a train float above its tracks. It sounds a lot like science fiction, but it is real. Trains that use electromagnets are called magnetic levitation trains, maglevs for short.

Currently, maglevs are an experimental form of transportation. These trains use the properties of magnets to float above their tracks. In some maglevs, electromagnets generate magnetic forces that cause the train and the track to repel each other. These magnetic forces are similar to the forces that cause the like poles of two magnets to repel each other. In other types of maglevs, a force of attraction is generated by electromagnets that lift up the train. This force of attraction is similar to the attraction between the unlike poles of two magnets. In both types of maglevs, the trains run on a cushion of air a few centimeters above their tracks.

There seem to be many advantages to maglev trains compared to conventional trains. Maglevs do not have many moving parts and could, therefore, require less maintenance. Because maglevs float above their tracks, there is no friction between the train and the track. Without friction, maglevs produce less noise than conventional trains. Maglevs are also expected to be much faster than conventional trains. They can travel up to 500 km/h.

In Germany, engineers have designed a maglev train that uses attractive magnetic forces to lift up the train. Read about the German maglev train, the Transrapid, that appears on these two pages. Find out how this type of train operates. Then, follow the Science Log to learn more about "the big idea." ✦

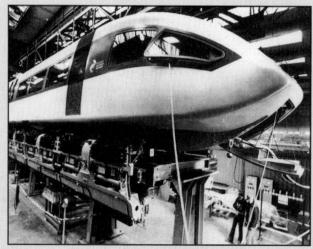

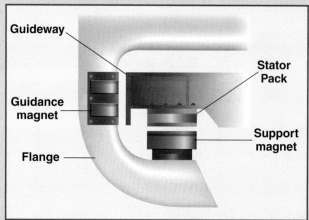

The Flanges

The bottom of the German Transrapid has extensions on both sides. These extensions, called flanges (FLAN-jez), wrap around a special track, called a guideway. The inside of a flange can be seen in the top photo. The diagram below it shows how magnets are used to lift the train. Magnetic attraction between the support magnet and the stator (STAT-uhr) pack, a highly magnetic material, causes the train to float about 10 mm above the guideway. Guidance magnets keep the train on the track.

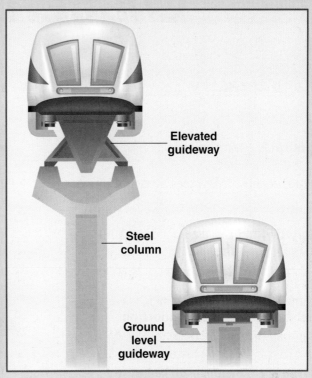

Elevated guideway

Steel column

Ground level guideway

The Guideway

The guideway can be mounted on an elevated steel column (left illustration) or it can be mounted at ground level (right illustration).

WRITING ACTIVITY

Science Log

Maglev trains are expensive to build, but they may provide a very fast way to travel between cities. Find out more about maglevs. In your science log, describe the advantages and disadvantages of this form of transportation. Compare maglev technology to cars, planes, and ordinary trains. Start your search at www.conceptsandchallenges.com.

The Transrapid

The German Transrapid maglev train can reach a maximum speed of about 500 km/h. The shape of its front portion helps it to travel fast by allowing it to move efficiently through air. It also cuts down on the amount of noise that the train makes.

Chapter 21 Challenges

Chapter Summary

Lesson 21-1
- **Magnetism** is a force of attraction or repulsion by magnetic materials.
- Like **poles** repel. Unlike poles attract.

Lesson 21-2
- A **magnetic field** is the area around a magnet where magnetic forces act.

Lesson 21-3
- The process by which a material is made into a magnet is called **magnetic induction.**
- A temporary magnet tends to lose its magnetism quickly.
- A permanent magnet tends to keep its magnetism.

Lesson 21-4
- Earth has a magnetic north pole and a magnetic south pole.
- The magnetic field around Earth is called the **magnetosphere.**

Lesson 21-5
- The relationship between electricity and magnetism is called **electromagnetism.**

Lesson 21-6
- An **electromagnet** is made by wrapping current-carrying coils of wire around a metal core.

Lesson 21-7
- A **transformer** uses alternating current in the primary coil to induce a current in the secondary coil.
- A step-up transformer increases the voltage of alternating current.
- A step-down transformer decreases the voltage of alternating current.

Lesson 21-8
- An **electric motor** is a device that changes electrical energy into mechanical energy.

Lesson 21-9
- An **electric generator** is a device that uses magnets to change mechanical energy into electrical energy.

Key Term Challenges

electric generator (p. 472)
electric motor (p. 468)
electromagnet (p. 464)
electromagnetic induction (p. 462)
electromagnetism (p. 462)
magnetic domain (p. 456)
magnetic field (p. 456)
magnetic induction (p. 458)
magnetic lines of force (p. 456)
magnetism (p. 454)
magnetosphere (p. 460)
pole (p. 454)
transformer (p. 466)

MATCHING **Write the Key Term from above that best matches each description.**

1. force of attraction or repulsion by magnetic materials

2. end of a magnet

3. temporary magnet formed by wrapping a current-carrying coil of wire around a metal core

4. process of making an object into a magnet

FILL IN **Write the Key Term from above that best completes each statement.**

5. Because of _____, a current will flow in a wire moving across a magnetic field.

6. A _____ converts mechanical energy into electrical energy.

7. The magnetic field around Earth is also called the _____.

8. The area around a magnet is called the _____.

9. The relationship between electricity and magnetism is called _____.

10. An _____ converts electrical energy into mechanical energy.

Content Challenges

MULTIPLE CHOICE Write the letter of the term or phrase that best completes each statement.

1. In a step-down transformer,
   a. the secondary coil has more turns.
   b. the primary coil has fewer turns.
   c. the secondary coil has fewer turns.
   d. the primary and secondary coils have the same number of turns.

2. Oersted discovered
   a. that an electric current flows through a compass.
   b. magnetic induction.
   c. the magnetosphere.
   d. that an electric current produces a magnetic field.

3. A temporary magnet
   a. keeps its magnetic properties for a long time.
   b. is hard to magnetize.
   c. loses its magnetic properties quickly.
   d. is a natural magnet.

4. When the north and south poles of two magnets are facing each other, they
   a. attract each other.
   b. repel each other.
   c. have no effect on each other.
   d. magnetize each other.

5. One way to increase the strength of an electromagnet is to
   a. increase the resistance in the wire.
   b. decrease the voltage in the wire.
   c. decrease the current in the wire.
   d. increase the current in the wire.

6. In order for a 9-volt appliance to use the 120 volts from a wall outlet, it needs
   a. a step-up transformer.
   b. a step-down transformer.
   c. a coil.
   d. an electric motor.

7. William Gilbert was one of the first scientists to study
   a. electric motors.
   b. generators.
   c. electromagnetism.
   d. magnetism.

8. Earth's magnetic north pole is located
   a. near the geographic North Pole.
   b. near the geographic South Pole.
   c. at the geographic North Pole.
   d. at the geographic South Pole.

9. An iron bar becoming magnetized is an example of
   a. magnetic induction.
   b. electromagnetic induction.
   c. a transformer.
   d. an electric motor.

10. Electromagnetic induction was studied by
    a. Tesla.
    b. Oersted.
    c. Faraday.
    d. the Ancient Greeks.

TRUE/FALSE Write *true* if the statement is true. If the statement is false, change the underlined term to make the statement true.

11. In a step-up transformer, the <u>primary</u> coil has fewer turns of wire.

12. An electric <u>motor</u> converts electrical energy into mechanical energy.

13. To increase the strength of an electromagnet, <u>decrease</u> the number of turns of wire around the metal core.

14. Earth's magnetic south pole is the same as the <u>south</u> pole of a bar magnet.

Concept Challenges TEST PREP

WRITTEN RESPONSE Answer each of the following questions in complete sentences.

1. **COMPARE:** Explain the difference between magnetic induction and electromagnetic induction.

2. **CONTRAST:** Describe the energy changes that take place in an electric motor and in an electric generator.

3. **DESCRIBE:** How could you use a compass to identify the north and south poles of a magnet?

4. **ANALYZE:** Why does a spinning loop of wire in a magnetic field produce alternating current instead of direct current?

5. **HYPOTHESIZE:** In most transformers, some energy is lost between the primary coil and the secondary coil. What do you think might cause this loss of energy?

INTERPRETING VISUALS Use Figures 21-32 and 21-33 to answer each of the following questions.

6. In Diagram *A*, which coil has more turns of wire?

7. In Diagram *B*, which coil has more turns of wire?

8. Which diagram shows a step-up transformer? Which shows a step-down transformer?

9. Which kind of transformer would you use to change the voltage from 10 volts to 50 volts? Explain.

10. Which kind of transformer would you use to change the voltage from 50 volts to 10 volts? Explain.

11. Which kind of transformer must be used before the electricity from power lines can be used in your home? Explain.

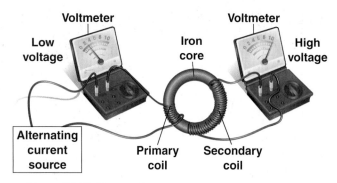

▲ **Figure 21-32** Diagram A

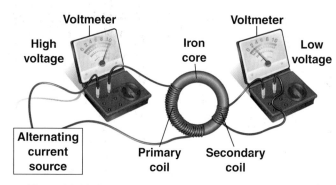

▲ **Figure 21-33** Diagram B

Appendix A Metric System

The Metric System and SI Units

The metric system is an international system of measurement based on units of ten. More than 90 percent of the nations of the world use the metric system. In the United States, both the English system and the metric system are used.

The *Système International*, or SI, has been used as the international measurement system since 1960. The SI is a modernized version of the metric system. Like the metric system, the SI is a decimal system based on units of ten. When you want to change from one unit in the metric system to another unit, you multiply or divide by a multiple of ten.

- When you change from a smaller unit to a larger unit, you divide.

- When you change from a larger unit to a smaller unit, you multiply.

COMMON METRIC PREFIXES			
micro-	0.000001 or 1/1,000,000	deka-	10
milli-	0.001 or 1/1,000	hecto-	100
centi-	0.01 or 1/100	kilo-	1,000
deci-	0.1 or 1/10	mega-	1,000,000

▲ Figure 2

METRIC UNITS		
LENGTH	SYMBOL	RELATIONSHIP
kilometer	km	1 km = 1,000 m
meter	m	1 m = 100 cm
centimeter	cm	1 cm = 10 mm
millimeter	mm	1 mm = 0.1 cm
AREA	SYMBOL	RELATIONSHIP
square kilometer	km^2	$1 km^2 = 1,000,000 m^2$
square meter	m^2	$1 m^2 = 1,000,000 mm^2$
square centimeter	cm^2	$1 cm^2 = 0.0001 m^2$
square millimeter	mm^2	$1 mm^2 = 0.000001 m^2$
VOLUME	SYMBOL	RELATIONSHIP
cubic meter	m^3	$1 m^3 = 1,000,000 cm^3$
cubic centimeter	cm^3	$1 cm^3 = 0.000001 m^3$
liter	L	1 L = 1,000 mL
milliliter	mL	1 mL = 0.001 L
MASS	SYMBOL	RELATIONSHIP
metric ton	t	1 t = 1,000 kg
kilogram	kg	1 kg = 1,000 g
gram	g	1 g = 1,000 mg
centigram	cg	1 cg = 10 mg
milligram	mg	1 mg = 0.001 g
TEMPERATURE	SYMBOL	
Kelvin	K	
degree Celsius	°C	

▲ Figure 1

METRIC-STANDARD EQUIVALENTS	
SI to English	English to SI
LENGTH	
1 kilometer = 0.621 mile (mi)	1 mi = 1.61 km
1 meter = 1.094 yards (yd)	1 yd = 0.914 m
1 meter = 3.28 feet (ft)	1 ft = 0.305 m
1 centimeter = 0.394 inch (in.)	1 in. = 2.54 cm
1 millimeter = 0.039 inch	1 in. = 25.4 mm
AREA	
1 square kilometer = 0.3861 square mile	$1 mi^2 = 2.590 km^2$
1 square meter = 1.1960 square yards	$1 yd^2 = 0.8361 m^2$
1 square meter = 10.763 square feet	$1 ft^2 = 0.0929 m^2$
1 square centimeter = 0.155 square inch	$1 in.^2 = 6.452 cm^2$
VOLUME	
1 cubic meter = 1.3080 cubic yards	$1 yd^3 = 0.7646 m^3$
1 cubic meter = 35.315 cubic feet	$1 ft^3 = 0.0283 m^3$
1 cubic centimeter = 0.0610 cubic inch	$1 in.^3 = 16.39 cm^3$
1 liter = 0.2642 gallon (gal)	1 gal = 3.79 L
1 liter = 1.06 quarts (qt)	1 qt = 0.946 L
1 liter = 2.11 pints (pt)	1 pt = 0.47 L
1 milliliter = 0.034 fluid ounce (fl oz)	1 fl oz = 29.57 mL
MASS	
1 metric ton = 0.984 ton	1 ton = 1.016 t
1 kilogram = 2.205 pounds (lb)	1 lb = 0.4536 kg
1 gram = 0.0353 ounce (oz)	1 oz = 28.35 g
TEMPERATURE	
Celsius = 5/9(°F − 32)	Fahrenheit = 9/5°C + 32
0°C = 32°F (Freezing point of water)	72°F = 22°C (Room temperature)
100°C = 212°F (Boiling point of water)	98.6°F = 37°C (Human body temperature)
Kelvin = (°F + 459.67)/1.8	Fahrenheit = (K × 1.8) − 459.67

▲ Figure 3

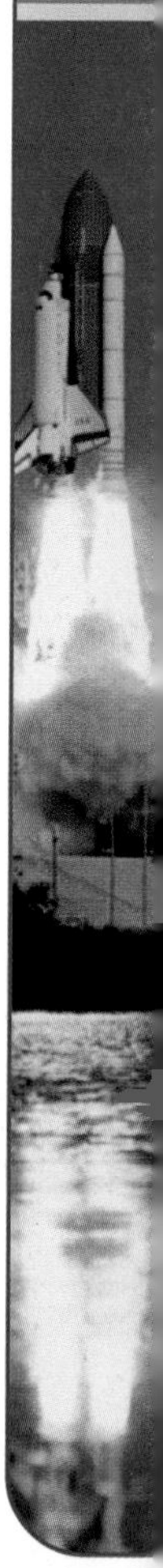

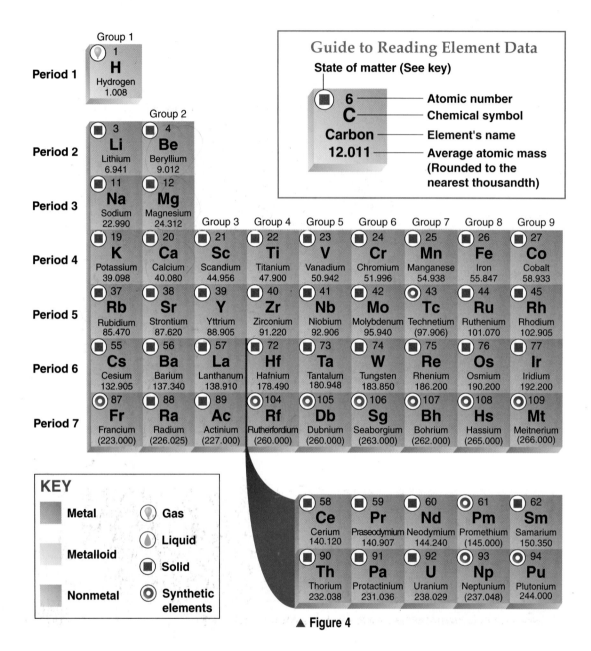

▲ Figure 4

						Group 18
						2 **He** Helium 4.003

Group 13	Group 14	Group 15	Group 16	Group 17	
5 **B** Boron 10.811	6 **C** Carbon 12.011	7 **N** Nitrogen 14.007	8 **O** Oxygen 15.999	9 **F** Fluorine 18.998	10 **Ne** Neon 20.183
13 **Al** Aluminum 26.982	14 **Si** Silicon 28.086	15 **P** Phosphorus 30.974	16 **S** Sulfur 32.066	17 **Cl** Chlorine 35.453	18 **Ar** Argon 39.948

Group 10	Group 11	Group 12					
28 **Ni** Nickel 58.690	29 **Cu** Copper 63.546	30 **Zn** Zinc 65.370	31 **Ga** Gallium 69.720	32 **Ge** Germanium 72.590	33 **As** Arsenic 74.922	34 **Se** Selenium 78.960	35 **Br** Bromine 79.909	36 **Kr** Krypton 83.800
46 **Pd** Palladium 106.400	47 **Ag** Silver 107.870	48 **Cd** Cadmium 112.400	49 **In** Indium 114.820	50 **Sn** Tin 118.690	51 **Sb** Antimony 121.750	52 **Te** Tellurium 127.600	53 **I** Iodine 126.904	54 **Xe** Xenon 131.300
78 **Pt** Platinum 195.090	79 **Au** Gold 196.967	80 **Hg** Mercury 200.590	81 **Tl** Thallium 204.370	82 **Pb** Lead 207.200	83 **Bi** Bismuth 208.980	84 **Po** Polonium (209.000)	85 **At** Astatine (210.000)	86 **Rn** Radon (222.000)
110 **Ds** Ununnilium (269)	111 **Rg** Unununium (272)	112 **Uub** Ununbium (277)	113 **Uut** (284)	114 **Uuq** Ununquadium (296)	115 **Uup** (288)	116 **Uuh** (298)	117 **Uus** (Not yet recognized) (?)	118 **Uuo** (294)

63 **Eu** Europium 151.960	64 **Gd** Gadolinium 157.250	65 **Tb** Terbium 158.924	66 **Dy** Dysprosium 162.500	67 **Ho** Holmium 164.930	68 **Er** Erbium 167.260	69 **Tm** Thulium 168.934	70 **Yb** Ytterbium 173.040	71 **Lu** Lutetium 174.970
95 **Am** Americium (243.000)	96 **Cm** Curium (247.000)	97 **Bk** Berkelium (247.000)	98 **Cf** Californium (251.000)	99 **Es** Einsteinium (254.000)	100 **Fm** Fermium (257.000)	101 **Md** Mendelevium (258.000)	102 **No** Nobelium (259.000)	103 **Lr** Lawrencium (262.000)

*Atomic masses in parentheses are of the most common form of the atom.

Appendix C   Chemical Elements

LIST OF CHEMICAL ELEMENTS		
Element	Atomic Symbol	Atomic Number

LIST OF CHEMICAL ELEMENTS		
Element	Atomic Symbol	Atomic Number
Actinium	Ac	89
Aluminum	Al	13
Americium	Am	95
Antimony	Sb	51
Argon	Ar	18
Arsenic	As	33
Astatine	At	85
Barium	Ba	56
Berkelium	Bk	97
Beryllium	Be	4
Bismuth	Bi	83
Bohrium	Bh	107
Boron	B	5
Bromine	Br	35
Cadmium	Cd	48
Calcium	Ca	20
Californium	Cf	98
Carbon	C	6
Cerium	Ce	58
Cesium	Cs	55
Chlorine	Cl	17
Chromium	Cr	24
Cobalt	Co	27
Copper	Cu	29
Curium	Cm	96
Dubnium	Db	105
Dysprosium	Dy	66
Einsteinium	Es	99
Erbium	Er	68
Europium	Eu	63
Fermium	Fm	100
Fluorine	F	9
Francium	Fr	87
Gadolinium	Gd	64
Gallium	Ga	31
Germanium	Ge	32
Gold	Au	79

▲ Figure 5

LIST OF CHEMICAL ELEMENTS		
Element	Atomic Symbol	Atomic Number
Hafnium	Hf	72
Hassium	Hs	108
Helium	He	2
Holmium	Ho	67
Hydrogen	H	1
Indium	In	49
Iodine	I	53
Iridium	Ir	77
Iron	Fe	26
Krypton	Kr	36
Lanthanum	La	57
Lawrencium	Lr	103
Lead	Pb	82
Lithium	Li	3
Lutetium	Lu	71
Magnesium	Mg	12
Manganese	Mn	25
Meitnerium	Mt	109
Mendelevium	Md	101
Mercury	Hg	80
Molybdenum	Mo	42
Neodymium	Nd	60
Neon	Ne	10
Neptunium	Np	93
Nickel	Ni	28
Niobium	Nb	41
Nitrogen	N	7
Nobelium	No	102
Osmium	Os	76
Oxygen	O	8
Palladium	Pd	46
Phosphorus	P	15
Platinum	Pt	78
Plutonium	Pu	94
Polonium	Po	84
Potassium	K	19
Praseodymium	Pr	59
Promethium	Pm	61

LIST OF CHEMICAL ELEMENTS		
Element	Atomic Symbol	Atomic Number
Protactinium	Pa	91
Radium	Ra	88
Radon	Rn	86
Rhenium	Re	75
Rhodium	Rh	45
Rubidium	Rb	37
Ruthenium	Ru	44
Rutherfordium	Rf	104
Samarium	Sm	62
Scandium	Sc	21
Seaborgium	Sg	106
Selenium	Se	34
Silicon	Si	14
Silver	Ag	47
Sodium	Na	11
Strontium	Sr	38
Sulfur	S	16
Tantalum	Ta	73
Technetium	Tc	43
Tellurium	Te	52
Terbium	Tb	65
Thallium	Tl	81
Thorium	Th	90
Thulium	Tm	69
Tin	Sn	50
Titanium	Ti	22
Tungsten	W	74
Ununnilium	Uun	110
Unununium	Uuu	111
Ununbium	Uub	112
Ununquadium	Uuq	114
Uranium	U	92
Vanadium	V	23
Xenon	Xe	54
Ytterbium	Yb	70
Yttrium	Y	39
Zinc	Zn	30
Zirconium	Zr	40

Appendix **D**   Science Terms

Analyzing Science Terms

You can often unlock the meaning of an unfamiliar science term by analyzing its word parts. Prefixes and suffixes, for example, each carry a meaning that comes from a word root. This word root usually comes from the Latin or Greek language. The following list of prefixes, suffixes, and combined forms of words provides clues to the meaning of many science terms.

WORD PART	MEANING	EXAMPLE
-ate	salt of an acid	nitrate
bar-, baro-	weight, pressure	barometer
bi-	two	binary
carbo-	containing carbon	carbonate
co-	with, together	coagulation
de-	remove from	decomposition
electro-	electricity	electrolyte
-graph	write	thermograph
hydro-	water, containing hydrogen	hydrometer, hydrocarbon
-ide	binary compound	sulfide
in-	not	insoluble
-logy	study of	cosmology
-lysis	decomposition	electrolysis
magneto-	magnetism	magnetosphere
-meter	measuring device	manometer
non-	not	nonmetal
photo-	light	photoelectric
poly-	many	polyatomic
re-	again, back	reflection
-sonic	sound	supersonic
-sphere	ball, globe	magnetosphere
sub-	under, beneath	subscript
super-	above, more than	supersonic
therm-, thermo-	heat	thermometer
trans-	across, beyond	transparent
ultra-	beyond	ultrasound
un-	not	unsaturated

▲ Figure 6

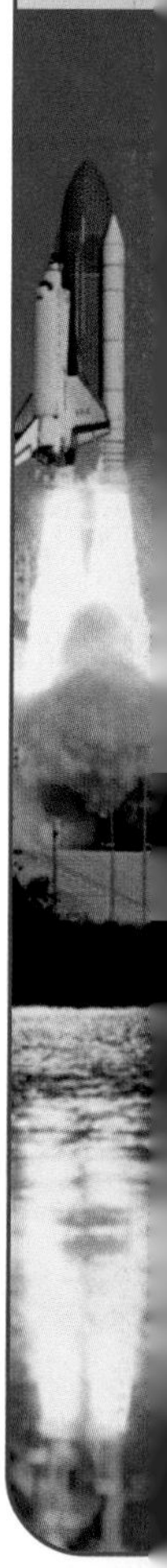

Appendix **E**   Mathematics Review

Adding Integers

You can add integers with unlike signs on a number line.

Add $^-5 + {}^+7$

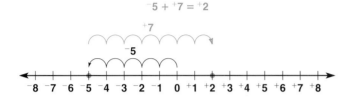

Subtracting Integers

To subtract an integer, add its opposite.

Subtract $^-6 - {}^+2$

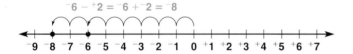

Multiplying Integers

When you multiply integers, you must decide if the answer is positive or negative.

If the signs of the integers are the same, the product is positive.

$$^+5 \times {}^+4 = {}^+20$$
$$^-5 \times {}^-4 = {}^+20$$

If the signs of the integers are different, the product is negative.

$$^+5 \times {}^-4 = {}^-20$$
$$^-5 \times {}^+4 = {}^-20$$

Dividing Integers

The rules for dividing integers are the same as the rules for multiplying integers.

If the signs of the integers are the same, the quotient is positive.

$$^-36 \div {}^-9 = {}^+4$$
$$^+36 \div {}^+9 = {}^+4$$

If the signs of the integers are different, the quotient is negative.

$$^-36 \div {}^+9 = {}^-4$$
$$^+36 \div {}^-9 = {}^-4$$

Solving an Equation

To solve an equation, find the value of the variable that makes the equation true.

Is $b = 3$ the solution to the equation?
$$4b = 12$$
Replace b with 3 in the equation.
$$4 \times 3 = 12$$
$$12 = 12$$
Yes, $b = 3$ is the solution to the equation.

Adding and Subtracting Decimals

When adding or subtracting decimals, always be sure to line up the decimal points correctly.

Add 3.4 km, 20.95 km, and 153.6 km.

$$
\begin{array}{r}
3.4 \\
20.95 \\
+\ 153.6 \\
\hline
177.95 \text{ km}
\end{array}
$$

Subtract 13.5 mL from 35.75 mL.

$$
\begin{array}{r}
35.75 \\
-\ 13.5 \\
\hline
22.25 \text{ mL}
\end{array}
$$

Multiplying and Dividing Decimals

When multiplying or dividing decimals, it is not necessary to line up the decimal points.

Multiply 0.5 N by 11.25 m to find the amount of work done in joules.

W = F × d

W = 0.5 N × 11.25 m

W = 5.625 J

Notice that the number of places to the right of the decimal point in the answer is equal to the sum of the places to the right of the decimal point in the numbers being multiplied.

Divide 4.05 m by 0.5 m to find the mechanical advantage of a lever.

MA = effort arm length/resistance arm length

MA = 4.05 m/0.5 m

MA = 8.1

When dividing a decimal by another decimal, you must first change the divisor to a whole number. For example, change 0.5 to 5 by moving the decimal point one place to the right. You must also change the dividend by moving the decimal point one place to the right. The result is $40.5 \div 5 = 8.1$.

Changing a Decimal to a Percent

To change a decimal to a percent, multiply the decimal by 100 percent.

Find the efficiency of a machine if the work output is 5 J and the work input is 10 J.

Efficiency = work output ÷ work input × 100%

Efficiency = 5 J ÷ 10 J × 100%

Efficiency = 0.5 × 100%

Efficiency = 50%

Notice that when you multiply 0.5 by 100 percent, the decimal point moves two places to the right.

Measuring Angles

Use a protractor to measure an angle. Place the center of the protractor's straight edge on the vertex. One ray must pass through 0°.

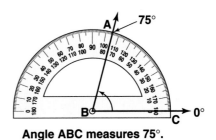

Angle ABC measures 75°.

Solving Word Problems

To solve distance problems, you can use $d = r \times t$ or $d = rt$.

The Smiths drove 220 miles at an average speed of 55 miles per hour. How long did the trip take?

PLAN
Substitute the values you know into the equation $d = r \times t$.
Then solve.

DO

$$220 = 55t$$

$$220 \div 55 = 55t \div 55$$

$$4 = t$$

SOLUTION
The trip took 4 hours.

Appendix F   Formulas for Physical Science

MATTER

Density

Density is measured in grams per cubic centimeter (g/cm^3).

Density = mass ÷ volume

or

$D = m ÷ v$

or

$D = \dfrac{m}{v}$

Specific Gravity

Specific gravity has no units of measure.

To find the specific gravity of a sample of matter, divide the density of the sample by the density of water ($1.0\ g/cm^3$).

Specific gravity = $x\ g/cm^3 ÷ 1.0\ g/cm^3$

Area

1. The area of a rectangle is found by multiplying the length (*l*) by the width (*w*). Answers are given in square units (cm^2).

   $A = l \times w$

2. The area of a square is found by squaring the side.

   $A = s^2$

3. The area of a circle is found by multiplying pi by the radius squared (r^2).

   $(\pi \approx 3.14) \times r^2$
   $A = \pi r^2$

Volume of a Solid Shape

1. The volume of a cylinder is found by multiplying pi by the radius squared (r^2) by the height (*h*).

   $V = \pi \times r^2 \times h$

2. To find the volume of a rectangular prism or cube, multiply the length by the width by the height.

   $V = l \times w \times h$

3. The volume of a sphere is found by multiplying 4/3 by pi by the radius cubed (r^3).

   $V = 4/3 \times \pi \times r^3$

WORK

Mechanical Advantage

1. Mechanical Advantage = resistance force ÷ effort force

   or

   $MA = \dfrac{\text{resistance force}}{\text{effort force}} = \dfrac{F_r}{F_e}$

   or

   $MA = F_r ÷ F_e$

2. MA (of an inclined plane) = length × height

   $MA = l \times h$

   $MA = lh$

Efficiency

Efficiency is expressed as a percentage.

Efficiency = Work output ÷ Work input × 100%

or

$E = \dfrac{W_{out}}{W_{in}} \times 100\%$

or

$E = W_{out} ÷ W_{in} \times 100\%$

Work

Work is measured in joules (J). One joule equals one newton-meter (N-m).

W = force × distance

or

$W = F \times d$

Power

Power is measured in watts (W).

One watt is equal to one joule per second (J/s).

Power = Work ÷ time

or

$P = \dfrac{W}{t}$

or

$P = W ÷ t$

FORCE AND MOTION

Speed

Velocity is speed and direction.

1. Speed = distance ÷ time

or

$$v = \frac{d}{t}$$

or

$$v = d \div t$$

2. Change in velocity = final velocity − initial velocity

3. Acceleration = change in velocity ÷ time

Distance

Distance traveled is measured in miles or kilometers per hour (mph or km/h).

Distance = rate × time

or

$$d = r \times t$$

or

$$d = rt$$

Momentum

Momentum = mass × velocity

Force

Force = mass × acceleration

Force = pressure × area

Pressure

Pressure is expressed in pascals.

$$1 \text{ Pa} = 1 \frac{N}{m^2}$$

Pressure = force ÷ area

or

$$P = \frac{F}{a}$$

or

$$P = F \div a$$

ENERGY

Energy

Energy = mass × speed of light^2

or

$$E = m \times c^2$$

or

$$E = mc^2$$

Ohm's Law

Current is measured in amperes, or amps.

Current = voltage ÷ resistance

or

$$I = \frac{V}{R}$$

or

$$I = V \div R$$

Gravitational Potential Energy

PE = weight × height

PE (N-m) = N × m

Speed of a Wave

Velocity = frequency × wavelength

$$v = f \times D$$

Glossary

Pronunciation and syllabication have been derived from *Webster's New World Dictionary, Second College Edition, Revised School Printing* (Prentice Hall, 1985). Syllables printed in capital letters are given primary stress. (Numbers in parentheses indicate the page number, or page numbers, on which the term is defined.)

PRONUNCIATION KEY					
Symbol	Example	Respelling	Symbol	Example	Respelling
a	transverse	(trans-VURS)	oh	coagulation	(koh-ag-yoo-LAY-shuhn)
ah	velocity	(vuh-LAHS-uh-tee)	oo	amplitude	(AM-pluh-tood)
aw	trough	(TRAWF)	oi	colloid	(KAHL-oid)
ay	radiation	(ray-dee-AY-shuhn)	s	solute	(SAHL-yoot)
eh	convection	(kuhn-VEHK-shuhn)	sh	suspension	(suh-SPEHN-shuhn)
ee	decomposition	(dee-kahm-puh-ZIH-shuhn)	u	fulcrum	(FUL-kruhm)
f	coefficient	(koh-uh-FIHSH-uhnt)	uh	barometer	(buh-RAHM-uht-uhr)
ih	specialization	(spehsh-uhl-ih-ZAY-shuhn)	y, eye	binary, ion	(BY-nuh-ree), (EYE-uhn)
j	homogenization	(huh-mahj-uh-nih-ZAY-shuhn)	yoo	insoluble	(ihn-SAHL-yoo-buhl)
k	calorie	(KAL-uh-ree)	z	ionization	(eye-uh-nih-ZAY-shuhn)

absolute zero: lowest possible temperature; temperature at which particles of matter almost stop moving (p. 7)

acceleration (ak-sehl-uh-RAY-shuhn): rate of change in velocity over time (p. 274)

acid: substance that releases hydrogen ions (H^+) when dissolved in water (p. 190)

action force: force acting in one direction (p. 284)

air pressure: pressure caused by the force exerted by Earth's atmosphere (p. 262)

air resistance: force that opposes the movement of an object in air (p. 258)

alkali metals: metals in Group 1 of the periodic table (p. 218)

alkaline earth metals: metals in Group 2 of the periodic table (p. 218)

alloy: substance made of a mixture of two or more metals (p. 214)

alternating current: current in which electrons constantly change direction at a regular rate (p. 436)

amino acids: building blocks of proteins (p. 96)

ampere: unit used to measure electric current (p. 442)

amplitude (AM-pluh-tood): height of a transverse wave (p. 362)

Archemedes' (ar-kuh-MEE-deez) **principle:** the buoyant force on an object in a fluid equals the weight of the fluid that the object displaces (p. 44)

atom: smallest part of an element that can be identified as that element (p. 54)

atomic mass: total mass of the protons and neutrons in an atom, measured in atomic mass units (amu) (p. 60)

atomic number: number of protons in the nucleus of an atom (p. 58)

average speed: total distance traveled divided by the time it takes to travel that distance (p. 272)

balanced forces: forces that are equal in size but opposite in direction (p. 246)

barometer (buh-RAHM-uh-tuhr): instrument used to measure air pressure (p. 262)

base: substance that releases hydroxyl ions (OH⁻) when dissolved in water (p. 192)

battery: a series of electrochemical cells that are connected to each other (p. 432)

Bernoulli's principle: as the speed of a fluid increases, its pressure decreases (p. 262)

binary (BY-nuh-ree) **compound:** compound containing two elements (p. 152)

boiling point: temperature at which a liquid changes to a gas (pp. 116, 338)

boiling point elevation: increase in the boiling point of a liquid solvent because of the addition of a solute (p. 116)

buoyant (BOI-uhnt) **force:** the upward force that a fluid (liquid or gas) exerts on an object (p. 44)

calorie (KAL-uh-ree): unit of heat; amount of heat needed to raise the temperature of 1 g of water 1°C (p. 334)

carbohydrates (kahr-boh-HY-drayts): sugars and starches (p. 96)

chain reaction: uncontrolled series of fission reactions (p. 238)

chemical bond: force of attraction that holds atoms together (p. 82)

chemical change: change that produces new substances (p. 26)

chemical equation: statement in which chemical formulas are used to describe a chemical reaction (p. 172)

chemical formula: way of writing the name of a compound using chemical symbols (p. 148)

chemical reaction: process in which new substances with new chemical and physical properties are formed (p. 168)

chemical symbol: shortened way of writing the name of an element (p. 64)

chemistry (KEHM-ihs-tree): branch of science that deals with the interaction of atoms and molecules (p. 16)

chlorophyll (KLAWR-uh-fihl): substance in plants that absorbs the Sun's light and gives plants their green color (p. 408)

chloroplast: part of green plant cells where photosynthesis takes place (p. 408)

circuit breaker: switch that opens a circuit if too much current is flowing (p. 446)

coagulation (koh-ag-yoo-LAY-shuhn): use of chemicals to make the particles in a suspension clump together (p. 132)

cochlea (KOHK-lee-uh): organ that changes sound vibrations into nerve signals (p. 394)

coefficient (koh-uh-FIHSH-uhnt): number that shows how many molecules of a substance are involved in a chemical reaction (p. 172)

colloid (KAHL-oid): suspension in which the particles are permanently suspended (p. 136)

communication: sharing information (p. 8)

compound: substance made up of two or more elements that are chemically combined (p. 80)

compound machine: machine that combines two simple machines or more (p. 326)

compression (kuhm-PREHSH-uhn): part of a medium where the particles are close together (p. 360)

concave lens: lens that curves inward (p. 410)

concentrated solution: solution containing a large amount of solute compared with the amount of solvent present (p. 112)

condensation (kahn-duhn-SAY-shuhn): change from a gas to a liquid (pp. 22, 118)

conduction (kuhn-DUK-shuhn): process of heat transfer in solids (p. 340)

conductor: material that conducts heat easily (p. 340); material through which an electric charge can flow easily (p. 434)

constant: something that does not change (p. 11)

controlled experiment: experiment in which all of the conditions except one are kept constant (p. 11)

convection (kuhn-VEHK-shuhn): transfer of heat in gases and liquids (p. 342)

convection current: movement of gases or liquids caused by differences in density (p. 342)

convex lens: lens that curves outward (p. 410)

corrosion: chemical change in a metal (p. 220)

covalent bond: bond formed when atoms share electrons (p. 92)

crest: high point of a transverse wave (p. 360)

data (DAYT-uh): information (p. 3)

decibel: unit used to measure the intensity or loudness of a sound (p. 384)

decomposition (dee-kahm-puh-ZISH-uhn) **reaction:** reaction in which a complex substance is broken down into two or more simpler substances (p. 178)

degree Celsius (SEL-see-uhs): metric unit of temperature (p. 6)

density (DEHN-suh-tee): mass per unit volume (p. 34)

diatomic molecule: molecule made up of only two atoms (p. 158)

diffuse reflection: reflection that forms a fuzzy image (p. 416)

dilute solution: solution containing a small amount of solute compared with the amount of solvent present (p. 112)

direct current: current in which electrons always flow in the same direction (p. 436)

dispersion (dih-SPUR-shuhn): separation of light into its component colors (p. 418)

displacement (dihs-PLAYS-muhnt): the replacement, or pushing aside, of a volume of water, or any fluid, by an object (p. 40)

dissolve (dih-ZAHLV): go into solution (p. 104)

distillation (dihs-tuh-LAY-shuhn): process of evaporating a liquid and then condensing the gas back into a liquid (p. 118)

Doppler effect: apparent change in the frequency of waves (p. 392)

double-replacement reaction: reaction in which elements from two different compounds replace each other, forming two new compounds (p. 182)

ductile (DUK-tuhl): able to be drawn into thin wires (p. 68)

E

ear: sense organ that detects sound (p. 394)

eardrum: thin sheet of tissue that vibrates when sound waves strike it (p. 394)

echo: reflected sound waves (p. 380)

efficiency (eh-FIHSH-uhn-see): ratio of work output to work input (p. 314)

effort force: force applied to a machine (p. 312)

electric circuit: path that an electric current follows (p. 438)

electric current: flow of electric charge through a conductor (p. 436)

electric generator: device that changes mechanical energy into electrical energy (p. 472)

electric motor: device that changes electrical energy into mechanical energy (p. 468)

electrochemical cell: device that changes chemical energy into electrical energy (p. 432)

electrode: negative or positive pole of an electrochemical cell (p. 432)

electrolysis (ih-lehk-TRAH-luh-suhs): process by which a substance is decomposed using an electric current (p. 178)

electrolyte (ee-LEHK-troh-lyt): substance that conducts an electric current when it is dissolved in water; substance that forms ions when melted or dissolved in water (pp. 204, 432)

electromagnet: temporary magnet made by wrapping a current-carrying wire around a metal core (p. 464)

electromagnetic induction: process by which an electric current is produced by moving a wire in a magnetic field (p. 462)

electromagnetic (ih-lehk-troh-mag-NEH-tihk) **spectrum:** range of electromagnetic waves (p. 400)

electromagnetic wave: wave that transfers energy through empty space (p. 358)

electromagnetism: relationship between electricity and magnetism (p. 462)

electron: particle that has a negative charge (p. 56); atomic particle with a negative electrical charge (p. 428)

electroplating (ee-LEHK-troh-playt-ing): use of an electric current to plate one metal with another metal (p. 224)

element (EHL-uh-muhnt): substance that cannot be chemically broken down into simpler substances (pp. 52, 80)

emulsion (ee-MUL-shuhn): suspension of two liquids (p. 134)

energy: ability to make something happen (p. 292)

energy level: place in an electron cloud where an electron is most likely to be found (p. 62)

evaporation (ee-vap-uh-RAY-shuhn): change from a liquid to a gas at the surface of the liquid (pp. 22, 118, 338)

eye: sense organ that detects light (p. 412)

F

fiber optics: use of optical fibers (p. 420)

filtration: separation of particles in a suspension by passing the suspension through filter paper or some other porous material (p. 132)

force: a push or a pull (p. 246)

formula mass: sum of the mass numbers of all the atoms in a molecule or ions in an ionic compound (p. 160)

freezing: change from a liquid to a solid (p. 22)

freezing point: temperature at which a liquid changes to a solid (pp. 114, 336)

freezing point depression: decrease in the freezing point of a liquid solvent because of the addition of a solute (p. 114)

frequency (FREE-kwuhn-see): number of complete waves passing a point in a given time (p. 362)

friction: force that opposes the motion of an object (p. 254)

fulcrum (FUL-kruhm): fixed point around which a lever pivots or turns (p. 316)

fundamental (fun-duh-MEHN-tuhl) **tone:** lowest-pitched sound produced when an object vibrates (p. 390)

fuse: thin piece of metal that melts and breaks a circuit if too much current is flowing (p. 446)

gas: state of matter that has no definite shape or volume (p. 20)

gram: basic unit of mass (p. 4)

gravity: force of attraction between all objects in the universe (p. 248)

group: vertical column of elements in the periodic table (p. 64)

halogens: elements that make up Group 17 in the periodic table (p. 70)

hearing: one of the five human senses (p. 394)

heat: energy of particles moving from warmer to cooler regions (p. 332)

hertz (HURTS): unit used to measure the frequency of a wave (p. 362)

homogenization (huh-mahj-uh-nih-ZAY-shuhn): formation of a permanent emulsion (p. 134)

hydrometer (hy-DRAHM-uh-tuhr): device used to measure specific gravity (p. 38)

hydroxyl (hy-DRAHK-sihl) **ion:** negative ion made up of one atom of hydrogen and one atom of oxygen (p. 192)

hypothesis (hy-PAHTH-uh-sis): suggested solution to a problem (p. 10)

ideal mechanical advantage: mechanical advantage a machine would have with no friction (p. 312)

illuminated (ih-LOO-muh-nayt-uhd) **object:** object that reflects light (p. 406)

image: picture formed by the eye (p. 412)

incident wave: wave that strikes a barrier (p. 366)

inclined plane: slanted surface, or ramp (p. 322)

indicator (IHN-dih-kay-tuhr): substance that changes color in an acid or a base (p. 194)

inertia (ihn-UR-shuh): tendency of an object to stay at rest or in motion (p. 280)

infer: to form a conclusion (p. 8)

infrasonic (ihn-fruh-SAHN-ihk): sound below 20 Hz frequency (p. 386)

insoluble (ihn-SAHL-yoo-buhl): not able to dissolve (p. 106)

insulator: material that does not conduct heat easily (p. 340); material through which electric charge does not flow easily (p. 434)

intensity: amount of energy in a sound wave (p. 384)

ion (EYE-uhn): atom with an electrical charge (p. 90)

ionic bond: bond formed between atoms that have gained or lost electrons (p. 90)

ionization (eye-uh-nih-ZAY-shuhn): formation of ions (p. 204)

isotope (EYE-suh-tohp): atom of an element with the same number of protons as the other atoms but a different number of neutrons (p. 72)

joule (JOOL): SI unit of work; equal to 1 N-m (newton-meter) (p. 302)

kinetic (kih-NEHT-ihk) **energy:** energy of motion (p. 292)

laser: device that produces a powerful beam of light (p. 420)

law of conservation of energy: energy cannot be made or destroyed but only changed in form (p. 296)

law of conservation of matter: matter cannot be created or destroyed by a chemical change (p. 168)

law of conservation of momentum: total momentum of any isolated system always remains the same (p. 276)

lens: transparent material that bends light (p. 410)

lever (LEHV-uhr): bar that is free to turn around a fixed point (p. 316)

light: form of electromagnetic energy made up of streams of photons (p. 402)

lipids: fats and oils (p. 96)

liquid: state of matter with a definite volume but no definite shape (p. 20)

liter (LEE-tuhr): basic metric unit of volume (p. 4)

longitudinal (lahn-juh-TOOD-uhn-uhl) **wave:** wave in which the particles of the medium move back and forth in the direction of the wave motion (pp. 360, 380)

lubricants (LOO-brih-kuhnts): substances that reduce friction (p. 256)

luminous (LOO-muh-nuhs) **object:** object that gives off its own light (p. 406)

luster (LUHS-tuhr): the way a material reflects light (pp. 68, 230)

machine: device that makes work easier (p. 312)

magnetic domain: groups of atoms whose magnetic poles are all lined up in the same direction (p. 456)

magnetic field: describes the region of magnetic force around a magnet (p. 456)

magnetic induction: process by which a material can be made into a magnet (p. 458)

magnetic lines of force: lines that show the shape of a magnetic field (p. 456)

magnetism: force of attraction or repulsion (p. 454)

magnetosphere (mag-NEET-oh-sfeer): region of Earth's magnetic field (p. 460)

malleable (MAL-ee-uh-buhl): able to be hammered into different shapes (p. 68)

mass: amount of matter in an object (p. 4)

mass number: number of protons and neutrons in the nucleus of an atom (p. 60)

matter: anything that has mass and takes up space (p. 18)

mechanical advantage: number of times a machine multiplies the effort force (p. 312)

mechanical wave: wave that transfers energy through matter (p. 358)

medium: material through which mechanical waves can travel (pp. 358, 380)

melting: change from a solid to a liquid (p. 22)

melting point: temperature at which a solid changes to a liquid (p. 336)

meniscus (muh-NIHS-kuhs): curved surface of a liquid in a graduated cylinder (p. 4)

metal: element that has the property of shiny luster, ductility, and malleability (p. 68)

metalloid: element that has properties of both metals and nonmetals (p. 232)

meter (MEET-uhr): basic SI and metric unit of length (p. 4)

mixture: two or more substances that have been physically combined (p. 80)

model: tool scientists use to represent an object or a process (p. 3)

molecule: smallest part of a substance that has all the properties of that substance (p. 82)

momentum: property of all moving objects (p. 276)

motion: change in position relative to some fixed object or place (p. 272)

music: a pleasing combination of sounds (p. 390)

N

neutral: neither acidic nor basic (p. 196)

neutralization (noo-truh-lih-ZAY-shuhn): reaction between an acid and a base to produce a salt and water (p. 202)

neutron: atomic particle with neither a negative nor positive charge (pp. 56, 428)

newton: SI unit of force (pp. 44, 252, 282)

noble gases: elements that make up Group 18 in the periodic table (p. 70)

noise: unpleasant combination of sounds with irregular patterns of vibration (p. 390)

nonelectrolyte: substance that will not conduct an electric current when it is dissolved in water (p. 204)

nonmetal: element that has the property of dull luster and is not ductile and not malleable; element that has different properties from metals (pp. 68, 230)

normal: line at right angles to a barrier (p. 366)

nuclear energy: energy stored in the nucleus of the atom and released during a nuclear reaction (p. 238)

nuclear fission: reaction in which a large nucleus is split into smaller nuclei and energy is released (p. 238)

nuclear fusion: reaction in which two smaller nuclei are joined to form a larger nucleus (p. 238)

nucleic acids: compounds made up of carbon, oxygen, hydrogen, nitrogen, and phosphorus (p. 96)

nucleus: center, or core, of an atom (p. 56)

ohm: unit used to measure resistance (p. 442)

Ohm's law: current in a wire is equal to the voltage divided by the resistance (p. 444)

opaque (oh-PAYK): a property that does not transmit light (p. 406)

ore: rock or mineral from which a useful metal or element can be removed economically (p. 210)

organic chemistry: study of organic compounds (p. 94)

organic compound: compound containing carbon (p. 94)

overtones: sounds that have a higher pitch than the fundamental tone (p. 390)

oxidation (ahk-sih-DAY-shuhn): chemical change in which electrons are lost (p. 174)

oxidation number: number of electrons an atom gains, loses, or shares when it forms a chemical bond (p. 150)

parallel circuit: circuit in which electric current can follow more than one path (p. 440)

period: horizontal row of elements in the periodic table (p. 64)

periodic (pihr-ee-AHD-ihk): repeating pattern (p. 64)

pH scale: measure of the concentration of hydrogen ions in a solution (p. 196)

photon (FOH-tahn): tiny bundle of energy (p. 402)

photosynthesis (foht-oh-SIHN-thuh-suhs): process by which plants use energy from the Sun to make food (p. 408)

physical change: change that does not produce new substances (p. 26)

physics: branch of science that deals with the interactions of energy, matter, space, and time (p. 16)

pitch: how high or low a sound is (p. 386)

plane mirror: smooth surface that reflects light and forms images (p. 416)

plasma (PLAZ-muh): state of matter made up of electrically charged particles (p. 20)

plating: coating one metal with another metal (p. 224)

polar molecule: molecule in which one end has a positive charged and the other end has a negative charge (p. 108)

pole: end of a magnet (p. 454)

pollution (puh-LOO-shuhn): release of harmful substances into the environment (p. 140)

polyatomic (pahl-ee-uh-TAHM-ihk) **ion:** group of atoms that acts as a charged atom, or ion, when combining with other atoms (p. 154)

polymers: large molecules that are formed by many smaller, simpler molecules (p. 94)

potable (POHT-uh-buhl) **water:** water that is safe to drink (p. 140)

potential (puh-TEHN-shuhl) **energy:** stored energy (p. 292)

power: amount of work done per unit of time (p. 304)

precipitate (pree-SIHP-uh-tayt): solid that settles to the bottom of a mixture (p. 182)

predict: to state ahead of time what you think is going to happen (p. 8)

pressure: force per unit of area (p. 260)

prism (PRIZ-uhm): triangular piece of transparent glass that separates white light into a band of colors (p. 418)

product: substance that is formed in a chemical reaction (p. 168)

properties (PRAHP-uhr-teez): characteristics used to describe an object (p. 18)

proteins: compounds used to build and repair body tissues (p. 96)

proton: particle that has a positive charge; atomic particle with a positive electric charge (pp. 56, 428)

pulley: rope wrapped around a wheel (p. 318)

R

radiation (ray-dee-AY-shuhn): energy and particles released from the nucleus of a radioactive element (p. 234); transfer of energy through space (p. 346)

radioactive element: unstable element whose nucleus breaks down (p. 234)

radioisotope: isotope that releases radiation (p. 234)

rarefaction (rer-uh-FAK-shuhn): part of a medium where the particles are far apart (p. 360)

ray: straight line that shows the direction of light (p. 402)

reactant: substance that is changed in a chemical reaction (p. 168)

reaction force: force acting in the opposite direction (p. 284)

real image: image that can be projected onto a screen (p. 410)

reduction (rih-DUK-shuhn): chemical change in which electrons are gained (p. 174); process of removing oxygen from an ore (p. 212)

reflected wave: wave that bounces off a barrier (p. 366)

reflection: bouncing back of a wave after striking a barrier (p. 366)

refraction: bending of a wave as it moves from one medium to another (p. 368)

regular reflection: reflection that forms a clear image (p. 416)

resistance: opposition to the flow of electric charges (p. 442)

resistance force: force that opposes the effort force (p. 312)

roasting: process in which an ore is heated in air to produce an oxide (p. 212)

S

salt: substance formed from the negative ion of an acid and the positive ion of a base (p. 202)

saturated solution: solution containing all the solute it can hold at a given temperature (p. 112)

scientific method: series of steps that can serve as a guide to solving problems or answering questions (p. 9)

series circuit: circuit in which electric current follows only one path (p. 438)

sight: one of the five human senses (p. 412)

simulation: computer model that usually shows a process (p. 3)

single-replacement reaction: reaction in which one element replaces another element in a compound (p. 180)

solid: state of matter with a definite shape and volume (p. 20)

solubility: maximum amount of a substance that will dissolve in a given quantity of a solvent at a given temperature (p. 106)

soluble (SAHL-yoo-buhl): able to dissolve (p. 106)

solute (SAHL-yoot): substance that is dissolved in a solvent (p. 106)

solution: mixture in which the particles of one substance are evenly mixed with the particles of another substance (p. 104)

solvent: substance in which a solute dissolves (p. 106)

sonic boom: loud noise caused by breaking the sound barrier (p. 382)

sound: form of energy that travels as waves (p. 376)

specialization (spehsh-uh-lih-ZAY-shuhn): studying or working in one area of a subject (p. 16)

specific (spuh-SIF-ik) **gravity:** density of a substance compared with the density of water (p. 38)

specific heat: amount of heat needed to raise the temperature of 1 g of a substance 1°C (p. 348)

speed: distance traveled per unit of time (p. 272); distance a wave travels in one unit of time (p. 362)

state of matter: any of the four physical forms of matter (p. 20)

static electricity: buildup of electric charges in an object (p. 428)

structural formula: molecular model that uses straight lines to indicate bonds (p. 94)

sublimation: change from a solid directly to a gas (p. 22)

subscript: number written to the lower right of a chemical symbol in a chemical formula (p. 148)

substance: any element or compound (p. 80)

supersaturated solution: solution containing more solute than it can normally hold at a given temperature (p. 112)

supersonic: faster than the speed of sound for that medium (p. 382)

suspension (suh-SPEHN-shuhn): mixture of two or more materials that separate on standing (p. 130)

synthesis (SIHN-thuh-sihs) **reaction:** reaction in which substances combine to form a more complex substance (p. 176)

temperature: measure of the amount of heat energy something contains (p. 4); measure of the average kinetic energy of the particles in a sample of matter (p. 334)

terminal velocity: speed at which air resistance and gravity acting on a falling object are equal (p. 258)

theory: set of hypotheses that have been supported by testing over and over again (p. 10)

thermal (THUR-muhl) **expansion:** expansion of matter caused by heating (p. 350)

thermal pollution: damage that occurs when waste heat enters the environment (p. 296)

timbre (TAM-buhr): sound quality (p. 390)

total internal reflection: occurs when light is repeatedly reflected within a given material (p. 420)

transformer: device in which alternating current in one coil of wire induces a current in a second coil of wire (p. 466)

translucent (trans-LOO-suhnt): a property that transmits some light and blurs an image (p. 406)

transparent (trans-PEHR-uhnt): a property that transmits light and preserves an image (p. 406)

transverse (trans-VURS) **wave:** wave in which the particles of the medium move up and down at right angles to the direction of the wave motion (pp. 360, 404)

trough (TRAWF): low point of a transverse wave (p. 360)

ultrasonic (uhl-truh-SAHN-ihk): sound above 20,000 Hz frequency (p. 386)

unbalanced forces: forces that cause a change in the motion of an object (p. 246)

unit (YOO-nit): amount used to measure something (p. 4)

unsaturated solution: solution containing less solute than it can hold at a given temperature (p. 112)

vacuum: empty space; region where no matter exists (pp. 258, 346)

valence electron: electron in the outermost energy level of an atom (pp. 90, 150)

variable: anything that can affect the outcome of an experiment (p. 11)

velocity (vuh-LAHS-uh-tee): speed and direction (p. 274)

vibration: rapid back-and-forth movement (p. 376)

virtual image: image that cannot be projected onto a screen (p. 410)

visible spectrum: seven colors that make up white light (p. 400)

volt: unit used to measure voltage (p. 442)

voltage: energy available to move charges through a circuit (p. 442)

volume: amount of space an object takes up (p. 4)

watt: SI unit of power; equal to 1 J/s (p. 304)

wave: disturbance that transfers energy from place to place (p. 358)

wavelength: distance between two neighboring crests or troughs (p. 362)

weight: measure of the pull of gravity on a sample of matter (p. 5)

wheel and axle: two different-sized wheels that turn together around the same point (p. 312)

work: force exerted through a distance (p. 300)

work input: work done on a machine (p. 314)

work output: work done by a machine (p. 314)

Index

Photo Credits

Chapter 9: P189 Photos.com/Jupiter Images; P190 Jodi Jacobson/ Peter Arnold, Inc.; P192 Corbis; P195 Joe Gough/Shutterstock; P200 Professors P.M. Motta & S. Correr/Science Photo Library/Photo Researchers, Inc.; P203 Paul A. Souders/Corbis; P206 Photos.com/ Jupiter Images; P207 Photos.com/Jupiter Images; P208 Photos.com/ Jupiter Images.

Chapter 10: P209 Mark & Audrey Gibson/Stock Connection/Jupiter Images; P210 col. 1 t E. R. Degginger/Animals Animals/Earth Scenes P210 col. 1 b Jodi Jacobson/Peter Arnold, Inc.; P210 col. 2 t Breck P. Kent/Animals Animals/Earth Scenes P210 col. 2 b Colin Keates/Dorling Kindersley Limited; P210 col. 3 t Harry Taylor/Dorling Kindersley Limited; P210 col. 3 b Harry Taylor/Dorling Kindersley Limited; P211 Richard A. Cooke/Corbis; P212 GS International/Greenshoots Communications/Alamy; P213 Jim Wark/Peter Arnold, Inc.; P215 t Jenny Solomon/Shutterstock; P215 b Fritz Prenzel/Animals Animals/ Earth Scenes; P215 inset Christopher Cormack/Corbis; P216-217 Jodi Jacobson/Peter Arnold, Inc.; P219 Milepost 92 1/2/Corbis; P219 l Casey K. Bishop/Shutterstock; P220 r Galen Rowell/Corbis; P224 tl Jozsef Szasz-Fabian/Shutterstock; P224 tr Dorling Kindersley Limited; P224 br Tom Hollyman/Shutterstock; P226 Mark & Audrey Gibson/ Stock Connection/Jupiter Images; P227 Mark & Audrey Gibson/Stock Connection/Jupiter Images; P228 t Mark & Audrey Gibson/Stock Connection/Jupiter Images; P228 b Dorling Kindersley Limited.

Chapter 11: P229 NASA; P233 Tan Kian Khoon/Shutterstock; P235 Corbis/Jupiter Images; P236 Bob Ainsworth/Shutterstock; P237 tl Reuters NewMedia, Inc./Corbis P237 tr Kenneth Garrett/Getty Images; P237 bl Renee Lynn/Photo Researchers, Inc.; P237 bl inset Mark Stouffer/Animals Animals/Earth Scenes; P242 NASA; P243 NASA; P244 NASA.

Chapter 12: P245 Wally Bauman/Alamy; P248 Bridgeman Art Library; P249 Stocktrek Images/Getty Images; P252 Larry Lefever/Grant Heilman Photography, Inc.; P254 Patrick Behar/Photo Researchers, Inc.; P257 t L T O'Reilly/Shutterstock; P257 b Tomas Kopecny/Alamy; P259 Clara Natoli/Shutterstock; P264 Graca Victoria/Shutterstock; P268 Wally Bauman/Alamy; P269 Wally Bauman/Alamy; P270 Wally Bauman/Alamy.

Chapter 13: P271 Xavier Pironet/Shutterstock; P272 Leonard Lessin/Peter Arnold, Inc.; P274 Fotopic/Omni-Photo Communications; P276 Oleksii/Shutterstock; P277 Sebastien Burel/Shutterstock; P278 t Lucas Jackson/Reuters/Landov P278 b Lucas Jackson/Reuters/Landov P279 t PhotoDisc/Getty Images; P279 b Insurance Institute for Highway Safety; P279 b David Woods/Corbis; P280 b Bettmann/Corbis; P281 George & Judy Manna/Photo Researchers, Inc.; P283 Bridgeman Art Library; P284 l Matthew Totton/Alamy; P284 r Jim Boorman/Pixland/ Jupiter Images; P285 Brand X/Space Exploration/Jupiter Images; P288 Xavier Pironet/Shutterstock; P289 Xavier Pironet/Shutterstock; P290 Xavier Pironet/Shutterstock.

Chapter 14: P291 Melba Photo Agency/Alamy; P292 l Walter H. Hodge/Peter Arnold, Inc.; P292 r Galyna Andrushko/Shutterstock; P292 inset Michael Matisse/PhotoDisc/Getty Images; P293 t AP Wide World Photos; P293 b C. C. Lockwood/Animals Animals/Earth Scenes; P294 Johnny Johnson/Animals Animals/Earth Scenes; P295 Will & Deni McIntyre/Photo Researchers, Inc.; P296 Gary S. Settles/Photo Researchers, Inc.; P297 NASA; P297 inset Library of Congress; P298 t Simon Fraser/Science Photo Library/Photo Researchers, Inc.; P298-299 b Amos Zezmer/Omni-Photo Communications; P299 tl Adam Jones/Photo Researchers, Inc.; P299 inset Billie Johnson/United States Corps. of Engineers, Washington; P299 tr David R. Frazier Photolibrary/Photo Researchers, Inc.; P301 Armando Franca/AP Wide World Photos; P304 tl Michael Habicht/Animals Animals/Earth Scenes; P304 bl Richard Kolar/Animals Animals/Earth Scenes; P304 br Zina Seletskaya/Shutterstock; P308 Melba Photo Agency/Alamy; P309 Melba Photo Agency/Alamy; P310 Melba Photo Agency/Alamy.

Chapter 15: P311 ExaMedia Photography/Shutterstock; P312 Geostock/PhotoDisc/Getty Images P314 Pixel/Alamy; P315 NizamD/ Shutterstock; P322 t Michael Thompson/Animals Animals/Earth Scenes; P322 b Esbin/Anderson/Omni-Photo Communications; P324 t British Museum/Dorling Kindersley Limited; P324 m Peter Hayman/ British Museum/Dorling Kindersley Limited; P324 b Dorling Kindersley Limited; P325 t Dassault Systemes Handout/epa/Corbis; P324-325 bkgd Geoff Brightling/Dorling Kindersley Limited; P326 t Jodi Jacobson/ Peter Arnold, Inc.; P327 t Robin Smith/Getty Images; P001 b Geoff Brighting/Dorling Kindersley Limited; P328 ExaMedia Photography/ Shutterstock; P329 ExaMedia Photography/Shutterstock; P330 ExaMedia Photography/Shutterstock.

Chapter 16: P331 Oryx Digital/Alamy; P333 l Brand X/Jupiter Images; P333 r Alfred Pasieka/Photo Researchers, Inc.; P334 Nic Miller/ Organics Image Library/Alamy; P335 The Granger Collection, New York; P337 t Dean Pennala/Shutterstock; P337 b Colin Cuthbert/Photo Researchers Inc.; P340 Robert Cook/PicturesByRob/Alamy; P341 t Grantly Lynch/UK Stock Images Ltd/Alamy; P341 b Carlos Davila/Alamy; P342 FloridaStock/Shutterstock; P346 Sumos/Alamy; P347 AllrightImages/Face to Face Bildagentur GmbH/Alamy; P350 l Richard Choy/Peter Arnold, Inc.; P352 t Doug Allen/Oxford Scientific/Jupiter Images; P352 b Rod Planck/Photo Researchers, Inc.; P353 t PhotoDisc/Getty Images; P353 bl Regien Paassen/Shutterstock; P353 br Wolfgang Polzer/Alamy; P354 Oryx Digital/Alamy; P355 Oryx Digital/Alamy; P356 Oryx Digital/Alamy.

Chapter 17: P357 Kevin Atiyeh/Shutterstock; P358 l Eduardo Gonzalez del a Pena/Shutterstock; P358 r Nina Leen/Stringer/Time & Life Pictures/Getty Images; P363 Hulton-Deutsch Collection/Corbis; P366 Gail Johnson/Shutterstock; P370-371 bkgd Burstein Collection/ Corbis; P370 inset India Images/Dinodia Images/Alamy; P371 l inset Ken M. Johns/Photo Researchers, Inc.; P371 m inset Courtesy Pacific Tsunami Museum; P371 r inset State of Hawaii, Department of Defense, Civil Defense Division; P372 Kevin Atiyeh/Shutterstock; P373 Kevin Atiyeh/Shutterstock; P374 Kevin Atiyeh/Shutterstock.

Chapter 18: P375 Mary A. Lupo/Shutterstock; P380 NASA; P381 Robert Marien/Index Stock Imagery/Photolibrary; P382 l Murk/Shutterstock; P382 r Robert A. Hoover/NASA/Dryden Flight Center; P383 t Eric Risberg/AP Wide World Photos; P383 b AP Wide World Photos; P385 Robert Brenner/Photo Edit; P386 b Jack Parsons/ Omni-Photo Communications; P386 t Miodrag Gajic/Shutterstock; P387 Mark Newman/Photo Researchers, Inc.; P388 t E. R. Degginger/ Animals Animals/Earth Scenes; P388 b Francois Gohier/Photo Researchers, Inc.; P389 t S. Dalton, OSF/Animals Animals/Earth Scenes; P389 bl Vasily Smirnov/Shutterstock; P389 br Henry William Fu/Shutterstock; P393 National Optical Astronomy Observatories/ Coloured by Science Photo Library/Photo Researchers, Inc.; P395 Pictorial Press Ltd/Alamy; P396 Mary A. Lupo/Shutterstock; P397 Mary A. Lupo/Shutterstock; P398 Mary A. Lupo/Shutterstock.

Chapter 19: P399 SuperStock/Alamy; P401 Susan Wides/UpperCut Images/Alamy; P405 Janis Christie/PhotoDisc/Getty Images; P409 John Anderson/Alamy; P409 David Julian/Phototake; P411 Robert Garvey/Corbis; P413 Alexander Tsiaras/Science Course/Photo Researchers, Inc.; P416 l Mike Norton/Shutterstock; P416 r Jeremy Woodhouse/PhotoDisc/Getty Images; P419 David M. Schleser/Nature's Images/Photo Researchers, Inc.; P420 Maximilian Stock LTD/Phototake Inc./Alamy; P421 Philippe Plail/Photo Researchers, Inc.; P424 SuperStock/Alamy; P425 SuperStock/Alamy; P426 SuperStock/Alamy.